Advancing Accessibility Through Software Development for Disability and Neurodivergence

Teresita de Jesús Álvarez Robles
https://orcid.org/0000-0002-3545-5668
Universidad Veracruzana, Mexico

Mónica Adriana Carreño León
Universidad Autónoma de Baja California Sur, Mexico

Samuel Montané Baños
https://orcid.org/0009-0000-8153-8088
Universidad Autonoma de Baja California Sur, Mexico

Francisco Javier Álvarez Rodríguez
https://orcid.org/0000-0001-6608-046X
Universidad Autonoma de Aguascalientes, Mexico

Jesús Andrés Sandoval Bringas
Universidad Autonoma de Baja California Sur, Mexico

IGI Global
Scientific Publishing
Publishing Tomorrow's Research Today

Published in the United States of America by
IGI Global Scientific Publishing
701 East Chocolate Avenue
Hershey, PA, 17033, USA
Tel: 717-533-8845 | Fax: 717-533-7115
Website: https://www.igi-global.com E-mail: cust@igi-global.com

Library of Congress Cataloging-in-Publication Data

Names: Álvarez Robles, Teresita de Jesús, 1988- editor | Carreño León, Mónica Adriana, 1972- editor | Montané Baños, Samuel, 1990- editor | Álvarez Rodríguez, Francisco Javier editor | Sandoval Bringas, Jesús Andrés, 1972- editor

Title: Advancing accessibility through software development for disability and neurodivergence / edited by: Teresita Álvarez Robles, Mónica Adriana Carreño León, Samuel Montané Baños, Francisco Javier Álvarez Rodríguez, Jesús Andrés Sandoval Bringas.

Description: Hershey PA : IGI Global Scientific Publishing, [2026] | Includes bibliographical references. | Summary: "This book examines how software development can move beyond compliance to embrace accessibility as a core design principle. Through research, case studies, and participatory approaches, it highlights strategies to create inclusive digital systems that empower individuals with disabilities and neurodivergent conditions, fostering equity and meaningful participation"-- Provided by publisher.

Identifiers: LCCN 2025045738 (print) | LCCN 2025045739 (ebook) | ISBN 9798337360331 hardcover | ISBN 9798337360348 paperback | ISBN 9798337360355 ebook

Subjects: LCSH: Assistive computer technology | People with disabilities--Services for

Classification: LCC HV1569.5 .A385 2026 (print) | LCC HV1569.5 (ebook)

LC record available at https://lccn.loc.gov/2025045738

LC ebook record available at https://lccn.loc.gov/2025045739

British Cataloguing in Publication Data
A Cataloguing in Publication record for this book is available from the British Library.

Table of Contents

Detailed Table of Contents

In a progressively digitized environment, the demand for inclusive, accessible, and universally designed digital infrastructures has escalated considerably. Nevertheless, inequalities in accessibility and usability remain evident, particularly for individuals with disabilities and neurodivergent populations. This chapter examines the core principles and optimal practices of universal and inclusive design as they are applied across web, mobile, desktop, and embedded platforms. Drawing from a multitude of interdisciplinary perspectives—including human-computer interaction (HCI), assistive technology, disability studies, and inclusive pedagogy—the chapter provides a critical examination of the shortcomings inherent in platform-centric development paradigms and advocates for a transition towards user-centered, ability-diverse design. It introduces frameworks, tools, and standards that promote inclusive design, such as WCAG 3.0, ISO 9241-210, and inclusive UX guidelines, while demonstrating their practical application through case studies from the realms of education, healthcare, and social services. The chapter additionally emphasizes the intersectionality of disability with various social identities, highlighting the necessity of designing with equity in mind. Ultimately, this scholarly contribution aspires to reconcile technical advancement with humanistic principles, presenting a comprehensive roadmap for developers, educators, and policy-makers to create systems that genuinely accommodate all users.

The profile of children with ASD have difficulty interacting with conventional HCI methods. This work proposes to evaluate through eye-tracking the use of a UX focused on this profile through the design and development of mechanisms that use augmented reality and tangible interfaces. After an experimental deployment with a population of 7 children with different levels of support needs, it was possible to detect patterns among the children who had problems solving the activities. It is expected that these findings will allow a more schematic design using new technologies that will open the range of interaction methods.

Preface

Over the last few decades, digital technologies have become deeply woven into almost every aspect of our personal, educational, and professional lives. We use digital tools to communicate, to learn, to shop, to work, and to navigate a world that is increasingly mediated by screens and platforms. Yet, even as technology continues to advance at an extraordinary pace, many people remain excluded from fully participating in digital environments. Accessibility—although frequently discussed—still does not occupy the place it deserves in mainstream technological development. Far too often, individuals with disabilities, or with linguistic or cultural differences, find themselves navigating systems that were simply not designed with them in mind.

This book was created with the intention of addressing these persistent gaps. Technologies for Inclusive and Accessible Digital Environments bring together researchers, designers, educators, and innovators from different countries who share a common goal: to build technologies that do not leave people behind. The chapters assembled here present diverse approaches to accessible digital design, from conceptual frameworks and participatory methodologies to tangible case studies that show what is possible when inclusion becomes a core design principle instead of an afterthought.

In today's world, accessibility is not a luxury; it is a necessity. Digital participation has become synonymous with social participation. Students attend classes online, employees join hybrid meetings, and public services—from government paperwork to healthcare appointments—are increasingly delivered through digital channels. At the same time, international organizations emphasize the importance of digital inclusion as part of broader human rights efforts. Given this global shift, the need for thoughtful, well-designed accessible technologies has never been more urgent.

The chapters included in this book extend beyond disability in the traditional sense. They speak to cultural and linguistic barriers, neurodiversity, sensory differences, and the need to involve users directly in the design process. They remind us that accessibility is not a single fixed standard, but a constantly evolving effort to understand the full range of human experience.

Although the topics explored here are broad, the book is especially valuable for:

- Researchers in computer science, HCI, educational technology, disability studies, and related fields.
- Designers and developers who are actively building digital systems and want to integrate accessibility more intentionally.
- Teachers, instructional designers, and educational leaders who depend on digital tools to support diverse learners.
- Professionals in psychology, special education, speech therapy, or social sciences who work with individuals requiring specialized accommodations.
- Graduate students seeking real-world cases of inclusive design.
- Policymakers and program coordinators responsible for implementing accessibility guidelines at institutional or governmental levels.

The interdisciplinary nature of the contributions ensures that readers from different backgrounds will find both theoretical depth and practical ideas they can apply immediately.

Below is an overview of the chapters that make up this volume, written to show not only what each chapter covers but also why each one matters in the broader conversation about digital accessibility.

CHAPTER 1: UNIVERSAL AND INCLUSIVE PRINCIPLES IN CROSS-PLATFORM DIGITAL SYSTEMS: DESIGNING FOR ALL

The opening chapter lays essential groundwork by explaining key universal design principles and how they apply to digital systems that operate across platforms. It provides a clear, conceptual starting point for readers who may be new to accessibility, while also offering experienced practitioners a structured way of thinking about inclusivity from the earliest stages of development.

CHAPTER 2: FROM BARRIERS TO BRIDGE – INCLUSIVE DIGITAL DESIGN FOR NEURODIVERGENT AND DISABLED USERS

Here, the focus shifts to neurodivergence and cognitive accessibility. The authors discuss how digital interfaces can inadvertently overwhelm, distract, or confuse users with certain cognitive profiles. Their proposals illustrate how subtle design choices—visual contrast, information structure, interaction patterns—can make the difference between exclusion and meaningful participation.

CHAPTER 3: ACTIVE MODEL FOR CO-BUILDING APPS WITH DEAF USERS THROUGH WORKSHOPS

This chapter presents a hands-on, participatory model where deaf users actively co-design applications alongside developers. The workshop approach described here emphasizes collaboration and shared decision-making. It demonstrates why involving users with lived experience is not just beneficial but essential if we truly want solutions that reflect their needs.

CHAPTER 4: PROTECTIC: DESIGN OF AN INCLUSIVE UX/UI APPLICATION FOR CYBER FRAUD PREVENTION

In an increasingly connected world, cybersecurity is a universal concern. However, some users are more vulnerable than others. This chapter introduces an inclusive UX/UI application that helps protect users from cyber fraud. It stands out because it brings together two areas—security and accessibility—that are rarely discussed together but are deeply interconnected.

CHAPTER 5: DESIGN OF INTERACTION MECHANISMS USING TANGIBLE INTERFACES, AUGMENTED REALITY AND EYE-TRACKING FOR UX FOCUSED ON CHILDREN WITH ASD: A CASE STUDY

The authors present an innovative combination of technologies—tangible interfaces, AR, and eye-tracking—to support children with autism spectrum disorder. The case study shows how these tools can improve engagement and interaction, offering a powerful example of how emerging technologies can be adapted to meet very specific needs.

CHAPTER 6: CUSTOMIZABLE SERIOUS GAMES TO SUPPORT SOCIAL INTEGRATION IN CHILDREN WITH AUTISM SPECTRUM DISORDER: A MODULAR AND ACCESSIBLE SOFTWARE ARCHITECTURE

Building on the previous chapter's focus on ASD, this contribution looks at serious games designed to help children develop social skills. Its modular architecture allows for customization, acknowledging that individuals with ASD have diverse needs and levels of sensitivity. This chapter merges technical innovation with educational value.

CHAPTER 7: TEA-MARK: GAMIFIED VIRTUAL REALITY PLATFORM FOR LEARNING SHOPPING SKILLS IN CHILDREN WITH ASD

This chapter presents a VR platform that teaches practical, real-life skills—specifically, shopping skills—to children with ASD. By simulating real-world environments, the system provides a safe and engaging way for children to learn and practice tasks that may otherwise be overwhelming. It highlights the transformative potential of virtual reality when applied thoughtfully.

CHAPTER 8: TECHNOLOGICAL INNOVATION FOR INCLUSIVE EDUCATION: A DIGITAL VOICE ASSISTANT AS SUPPORT FOR NAVIGATION IN VIRTUAL LEARNING ENVIRONMENTS

Virtual learning has become a core component of modern education, but it is not always designed with accessibility in mind. This chapter describes a digital voice assistant that helps students navigate online learning platforms more easily, particularly those who struggle with visual or cognitive tasks. It emphasizes the importance of accessible learning during a time when online education continues to expand.

CHAPTER 9: DEVELOPMENT OF AN ENGLISH LEARNING APPLICATION FOR BLIND USERS: HAPPYBLINDGLISH

This chapter introduces a tool that enables blind users to learn English through an application built specifically for them. The design considers auditory interactions, navigation patterns, and usability elements that are often overlooked in mainstream apps. It serves as a reminder that educational technology must be adapted—not simply repurposed—for learners with disabilities.

CHAPTER 10: TOOL FOR TEACHING MEXICAN STATES AND CAPITALS IN LSM

Here, the authors present a digital tool that teaches geography using Mexican Sign Language (LSM). This contribution is important because it respects linguistic identity while promoting inclusive education. It highlights how technology can honor cultural and linguistic communities by designing with, rather than for, them.

CHAPTER 11: DIGITAL APPLICATION TO ENCOURAGE READING FOR CHILDREN WITH PHONOLOGICAL DYSLEXIA

The final chapter addresses one of the most common learning challenges: dyslexia. The authors describe a reading-support application that integrates exercises aimed at strengthening phonological awareness. This chapter closes the book with a practical and urgently needed tool, reinforcing that accessibility in education must support all types of learners.

Taken together, the chapters in this book provide a wide-ranging and multidimensional view of digital accessibility. They demonstrate that accessibility is not a box to be checked, but a mindset that influences every decision in the design process. By bringing forward both conceptual insights and real-world technologies, this volume offers readers a glimpse of what inclusive digital environments can look like when empathy, research, and innovation come together.

More importantly, the book underscores a simple but powerful truth: accessible technologies make digital spaces richer, fairer, and more humane—not only for people with disabilities, but for everyone. If this collection succeeds in encouraging researchers, designers, or educators to rethink how they approach digital inclusion, then it will have achieved its purpose.

Acknowledgment

We would like to express our deepest gratitude to the entire team at IGI Global for their unwavering support throughout the development of this book. Their professionalism, prompt attention to our questions, and constant guidance made this process both efficient and enriching. We are sincerely thankful for their commitment to maintaining high standards at every stage of publication.

Our heartfelt appreciation also goes to the authors who contributed their knowledge, experience, and time to this project. Their chapters reflect a remarkable level of dedication and expertise, and without their valuable participation, this book simply would not have been possible. Each contribution has added depth and diversity to the discussion, strengthening the collective understanding of the topics addressed.

We additionally acknowledge the reviewers, whose thoughtful feedback and rigorous evaluations helped refine the quality of each chapter. Their insights played a crucial role in shaping the final version of this work.

Finally, we extend our thanks to all individuals and institutions that, directly or indirectly, supported this endeavor. Their collaboration and encouragement have been fundamental to bringing this project to completion.

Section 1
Conceptual Foundations and General Principles of Accessibility

Chapter 1
Universal and Inclusive Principles in Cross-Platform Digital Systems:
Designing for All

Ratan Sarkar
https://orcid.org/0009-0008-5480-0165
Tezpur University, India

ABSTRACT

In a progressively digitized environment, the demand for inclusive, accessible, and universally designed digital infrastructures has escalated considerably. Nevertheless, inequalities in accessibility and usability remain evident, particularly for individuals with disabilities and neurodivergent populations. This chapter examines the core principles and optimal practices of universal and inclusive design as they are applied across web, mobile, desktop, and embedded platforms. Drawing from a multitude of interdisciplinary perspectives—including human-computer interaction (HCI), assistive technology, disability studies, and inclusive pedagogy—the chapter provides a critical examination of the shortcomings inherent in platform-centric development paradigms and advocates for a transition towards user-centered, ability-diverse design. It introduces frameworks, tools, and standards that promote inclusive design, such as WCAG 3.0, ISO 9241-210, and inclusive UX guidelines, while demonstrating their practical application through case studies from the realms of education, healthcare, and social services. The chapter additionally emphasizes the intersectionality of disability with various social identities, highlighting the necessity of designing with equity in mind. Ultimately, this scholarly contribution

DOI: 10.4018/979-8-3373-6033-1.ch001

aspires to reconcile technical advancement with humanistic principles, presenting a comprehensive roadmap for developers, educators, and policy-makers to create systems that genuinely accommodate all users.

1. INTRODUCTION

The twenty-first century is increasingly characterized as the digital epoch, a historical period defined by the omnipresence of information and communication technologies (ICTs) across all dimensions of human life (Kamalipour & Friedrichsen, 2017). From smartphones and laptops to artificial intelligence (AI), the Internet of Things (IoT), and immersive environments such as virtual or augmented reality, digital technologies no longer serve as supplementary tools; they function as foundational infrastructures mediating how individuals and societies live, learn, work, and participate in governance (Gangneux, 2019).

The transformative impact of digital systems on communication is perhaps the most visible. Where communication was once constrained by geography and time, digital technologies have enabled instantaneous and borderless interaction (de Kare-Silver, 2011). Social networking platforms, email, and messaging applications have not only altered interpersonal relationships but also reshaped the nature of communities and political mobilization (Koc-Michalska & Lilleker, 2016). Events such as the Arab Spring or #MeToo demonstrate the political power of digitally mediated networks. At the same time, however, these platforms reproduce inequities, as inaccessible design features often exclude users with visual, auditory, or cognitive impairments from full participation.

In education, digital transformation has redefined pedagogical paradigms. Learning Management Systems (LMS), Massive Open Online Courses (MOOCs), digital libraries, and blended learning models have expanded access to learning opportunities. Students can engage with instructors asynchronously across time zones, access vast open educational resources, and collaborate in virtual classrooms (Monisha & Valanteena, 2022). Yet, for learners with disabilities, this digital promise often becomes a barrier (Sciarretta, 2025). Videos without captions, documents incompatible with screen readers, and interfaces cluttered with unnecessary animations create obstacles to equitable participation. The COVID-19 pandemic, which accelerated global reliance on online education, also highlighted the exclusionary effects of inaccessible design.

Employment landscapes are equally transformed. The digital economy has created new forms of work, from platform-based gig labor to remote, flexible arrangements facilitated by collaborative software ecosystems (Sadia et al., 2023). Online recruitment systems, algorithmic screening tools, and digital productivity platforms dominate the employment sector. While these systems expand opportunities for many, they also risk excluding individuals with disabilities when job portals, assessment systems, or workplace applications are not designed inclusively (Nacheva, 2024). Accessibility barriers can effectively deny equal opportunity, reinforcing structural inequities within labor markets.

Healthcare has embraced digitalization through telemedicine, electronic health records, wearable health monitoring devices, and AI-assisted diagnostic systems. Digital platforms enable remote consultations, improve record-keeping, and enhance preventive care through data-driven insights (Attar, 2024). Nevertheless, inaccessible telemedicine platforms—those lacking captioning for consultations, failing to provide voice-based navigation, or designed without consideration for cognitive diversity—deny equitable healthcare access (Keptner & Heath, 2023). Such exclusions are particularly troubling given that persons with disabilities are often among those with the greatest need for healthcare innovation.

Civic participation has also been restructured by digital technologies. Governments increasingly deliver services through e-portals, while e-voting systems, digital petitions, and civic apps expand opportunities for citizen engagement. Yet inaccessible design limits participation (Veit & Huntgeburth, 2013). An e-voting system without screen reader compatibility or an e-governance portal with poor contrast ratios can marginalize voters with disabilities, effectively disenfranchising them in democratic processes. Thus, the digitalization of civic participation, though promising inclusivity, can paradoxically perpetuate exclusion.

In sum, the digital epoch is characterized by both extraordinary promise and significant peril. It democratizes opportunities for communication, education, healthcare, employment, and civic life, yet simultaneously reproduces and amplifies inequalities when inclusivity is neglected.

1.1 Problem Statement

The rapid expansion of digital technologies has often been celebrated as a great equalizer, a force capable of transcending barriers of geography, mobility, and identity (Holley & Oliver, 2011). Yet the reality for millions of people with disabilities and neurodivergent conditions tells a different story- one in which technology too often reinforces exclusion rather than dismantling it (Watling, 2011). Despite decades of international advocacy, carefully crafted policy frameworks, and advances in assistive technologies, digital inaccessibility continues to be widespread and deeply entrenched (Dobransky & Hargittai, 2016).

Recent evidence underscores this troubling persistence. The WebAIM Million 2024 Report revealed that more than ninety-six percent of the world's most visited websites contain detectable accessibility errors (Abuaddous et al., 2016). Missing alternative text, insufficient colour contrast, and poorly structured headings are not minor oversights but critical failures that make digital content effectively unusable for people who rely on screen readers or other assistive technologies (McCall & Chagnon, 2022). For such users, the digital sphere- often described as commons open to all- becomes fragmented, unreliable, and frequently hostile.

These problems are not confined to websites. Mobile applications, which now mediate much of daily life, are frequently designed around gesture-heavy interactions (Chen, 2008). Such designs implicitly assume a user with fine motor control and full dexterity, thereby excluding those with physical impairments. In the domain of education, platforms that could potentially level the playing field often create new inequities (Luke, 2001). Cluttered interfaces, overstimulating visuals, or illogical navigation systems overwhelm learners with dyslexia, ADHD, or autism, transforming a tool of empowerment into a source of frustration and fatigue (Fryia et al., 2009). Even in public spaces, digital infrastructures such as kiosks and ATMs-technologies that promise independence and efficiency- often lack tactile buttons, audio guidance, or haptic feedback (Omari, 2013). Instead of providing autonomy, these systems reproduce dependency by forcing users to seek assistance for tasks that should be simple and private.

The persistence of these barriers points not to isolated mistakes but to structural patterns. The culture of digital design and development continues to privilege speed, scalability, and market efficiency over inclusivity (Abascal et al., 2016). In the fast-paced environments of Agile or DevOps workflows, accessibility is too often treated as a late-stage fix- something to be patched after the "real" design is complete- rather than as a principle guiding every decision (Christopherson, 2022). Compounding this is the dominance of a compliance mentality. Organizations may strive to "check the box" of legal obligations by conforming to accessibility guidelines, but such compliance is frequently superficial. A website that passes automated audits can still feel unintuitive, overwhelming, or exhausting for real users navigating it with assistive technologies (Kirkpatrick, 2007).

Another dimension of the problem lies in platform fragmentation. Web, mobile, desktop, and embedded systems each operate with different assumptions and affordances, and accessibility practices often fail to travel seamlessly between them (Keates, 2020). What is accessible on a desktop environment may be inaccessible on mobile, while features implemented in one country's ATMs may be absent in another's. For individuals with disabilities, this inconsistency creates a constant negotiation of unfamiliar and uneven accessibility landscapes (Setianti et al., 2020).

Perhaps most overlooked of all is the neglect of neurodiversity. While accessibility discourse has historically centered visual, auditory, or motor impairments, it has been less attentive to cognitive diversity (Deetjen-Ruiz et al., 2024). For neurodivergent individuals, such as those with autism or ADHD, inaccessibility is experienced not in the absence of ramps or captions but in the presence of overwhelming sensory environments: flashing animations, persistent notifications, or cluttered page layouts (Hortizuela, 2022). For learners with dyslexia, inconsistent font usage or confusing page hierarchies can transform even simple tasks into exhausting cognitive labor. These less visible but equally profound barriers reveal the narrow scope through which accessibility has often been imagined.

What emerges from this landscape is a striking paradox. Digital technologies are routinely presented as vehicles of democracy and inclusion, promising to bring marginalized voices into the fold of education, employment, healthcare, and civic participation (McCarthy, 2016). Yet by failing to account for the diversity of human ability, they frequently end up reconstituting the very exclusions they are meant to overcome. The dream of the digital age as a space of universal participation cannot be realized if accessibility continues to be treated as peripheral. Unless inclusivity is woven into the very fabric of design and development- rather than added as an afterthought- the digital epoch risks becoming not a story of empowerment but one of replicated inequities.

1.2 Theoretical Framework

1.2.1 Accessibility

Accessibility forms the foundational layer of all efforts toward inclusive digital design. It refers to the practice of creating products, services, devices, and environments that can be used effectively by the broadest possible range of people, regardless of disability or functional limitation (Buß, 2020). Within digital environments, accessibility is most comprehensively defined by the World Wide Web Consortium (W3C, 2018), whose Web Content Accessibility Guidelines (WCAG) articulate the POUR principles: systems must be *Perceivable, Operable, Understandable*, and *Robust*. These principles serve as universal criteria for ensuring that digital interfaces do not systematically exclude users across sensory, motor, cognitive, and technological variations (Henry et al., 2014).

Practically, accessibility requires removing barriers that impede engagement—for example, alternative text enables visually impaired users to interpret images through screen readers; captions and transcripts support deaf and hard-of-hearing individuals; adaptable interfaces assist users with cognitive differences; and keyboard navigation enables access for those with mobility limitations (Chadli et al., 2021; Lazar, Goldstein, & Taylor, 2015). However, despite clear evidence of the effectiveness of such measures, accessibility practices are often inconsistently implemented or addressed late in the development cycle.

A central critique in accessibility research concerns its reduction to checklist-based compliance. Lewthwaite (2014) argues that accessibility is frequently approached as a technical obligation rather than a lived experience, leading to systems that satisfy guidelines yet remain confusing, overwhelming, or cognitively demanding. Lazar and colleagues (2015) similarly highlight that accessibility compliance audits cannot capture the complexity of real user experiences. This disconnect reveals that accessibility is not purely a design issue but a socio-technical one that intersects with broader economic, cultural, and infrastructural barriers.

Globally, accessibility is unevenly implemented due to economic constraints, infrastructural disparities, and systemic inequalities. Research on the digital disability divide shows that the cost of assistive technologies, limited broadband coverage, outdated devices, and inadequate institutional funding disproportionately affect disabled users, particularly in low-income and rural contexts (Dobransky & Hargittai, 2016; Goggin & Ellis, 2020). Organizational studies further indicate that many institutions view accessibility as an expense rather than an investment, leading to insufficient budgets, lack of trained personnel, and minimal organizational accountability (Kelly et al., 2019; Abascal, Arrue, Fajardo, & Tomás, 2015).

Social barriers compound these issues. Ableism and stigma surrounding disability influence design priorities, resulting in technologies that normalize "ideal users" while sidelining those who deviate from normative assumptions (Ellcessor, 2016; Ellis & Kent, 2017). Awareness gaps among developers, educators, and policymakers also undermine adoption of accessible practices (Shinohara & Wobbrock, 2011). These social dynamics produce environments where accessibility is perceived as a niche concern rather than a universal right.

Theoretically, accessibility has expanded from a narrow, compliance-oriented framework toward a rights-based, justice-oriented approach grounded in disability studies and human-centered computing. The UNCRPD (2006) positions accessibility not merely as a technical feature but as a precondition for full citizenship, participation, and equality. Scholars in critical disability studies argue that accessibility must consider intersectionality, cognitive load, cultural difference, and emotional experience, rather than focusing solely on functional accommodation (Hamraie, 2017; Bennett & Rosner, 2019). This view reframes accessibility as a dynamic, relational process requiring ongoing refinement, user engagement, and structural transformation.

In summary, accessibility provides the essential baseline for inclusive digital systems. Yet for accessibility to be effective, it must be understood as an evolving commitment to equity, usability, and dignity—one that addresses not only technical guidelines but also the economic, social, and political realities shaping users' experiences.

1.2.2 Universal Design (UD)

The concept of Universal Design (UD), pioneered by architect Ronald Mace (1998), significantly broadened earlier understandings of accessibility. Mace argued that instead of modifying environments after the fact to accommodate disabled individuals, design should be universal from the outset—anticipating human diversity and creating environments that support people of all abilities, ages, and circumstances. This shift from reactive retrofitting to proactive planning has since become a foundational paradigm in accessibility discourse. Building on Mace's vision, the Center for Universal Design (1997) articulated seven core principles that continue to guide both physical and digital design practices:

1. **Equitable Use** – Designs should be equally useful and accessible to people with diverse abilities.
2. **Flexibility in Use** – Designs should accommodate a wide spectrum of preferences, abilities, and ways of interacting.
3. **Simple and Intuitive Use** – Interfaces should be easy to understand, regardless of users' experience, language proficiency, or cognitive abilities.
4. **Perceptible Information** – Information must be communicated effectively, regardless of sensory abilities or environmental conditions.
5. **Tolerance for Error** – Designs should minimize hazards and reduce negative consequences of accidental actions.
6. **Low Physical Effort** – Systems should be operable efficiently and comfortably with minimal fatigue.
7. **Size and Space for Approach and Use** – Adequate space should be provided for interaction, regardless of body size, posture, mobility, or assistive device use.

Figure 1. Seven Principles of Inclusive Design

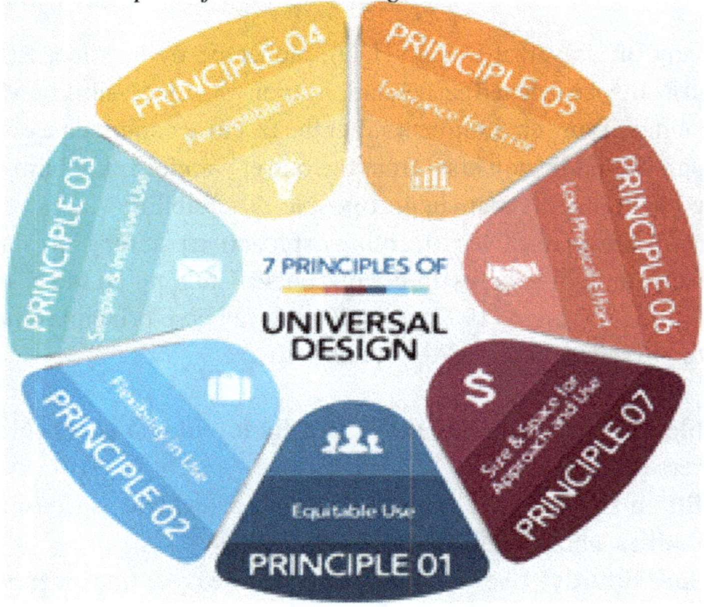

These principles have had a far-reaching impact—first in architecture and product design, and increasingly in digital technologies. A frequently cited example is the "curb cut effect": ramps initially installed for wheelchair users also benefit parents pushing strollers, travellers with rolling luggage, delivery workers, and older adults. In digital contexts, captioning offers similar benefits: while critical for people who are deaf or hard of hearing, captions are also widely used by viewers in noisy public spaces, language learners, and users multitasking during media consumption. Such examples demonstrate UD's potential to create environments that support everyone, not only disabled users.

However, scholars and practitioners caution against interpreting UD as a literal "one size fits all" solution. Human diversity is multidimensional, shaped by intersecting factors such as disability, age, culture, neurodivergence, language background, and technological context. A single universal design may not fully meet the needs of all individuals—particularly those with complex or multiple disabilities. Critics therefore argue that UD, while visionary, must not be treated as a static or totalizing blueprint. Instead, it should be seen as a foundational starting point: a commitment to anticipate diversity while recognizing that continuous adaptation, customization, and user involvement remain essential.

In this sense, UD remains invaluable for shifting design culture from afterthought to foresight—but its principles must be complemented by more participatory and adaptive approaches, such as Inclusive Design, to address the nuances and specificities of lived experiences across diverse user groups.

1.2.3 Inclusive Design (ID)

Inclusive Design (ID) builds upon and diverges from Universal Design (UD) by explicitly emphasizing diversity, adaptability, and user participation. While UD aspires to create solutions that can be used by the widest possible population without modification, ID challenges the assumption that any design can fully serve everyone equally in all contexts (Keates & Clarkson, 2004). Instead of striving for universality in a static sense, ID embraces human variation as the norm rather than the exception. It prioritizes flexibility, personalization, and iterative improvement, acknowledging that accessibility needs evolve across different abilities, cultures, technologies, and environments. In this approach, systems are not expected to be universally perfect from inception; rather, they are expected to grow and adapt through continuous engagement with diverse users.

Figure 2. Inclusive Design Dimensions

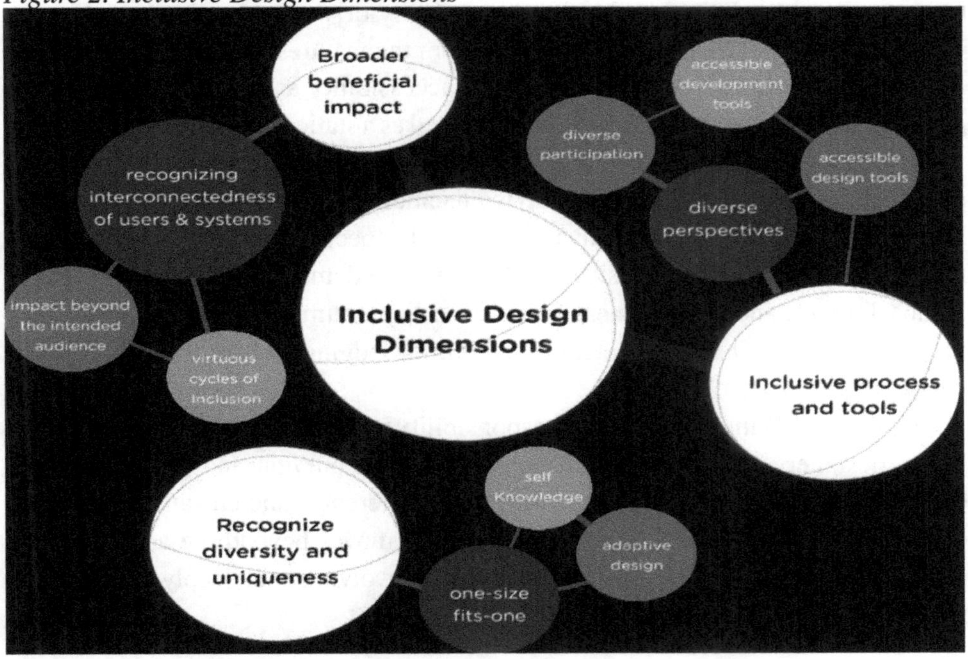

A defining principle of Inclusive Design is its commitment to *co-design*. Traditional design paradigms often position people with disabilities as passive beneficiaries or "end-users." In contrast, ID reframes them as active partners, collaborators, and knowledge producers. By insisting on designing *with* people with disabilities—rather than *for* them—ID validates the epistemic authority of lived experience. Bennett and Rosner (2019) argue that disabled and neurodivergent individuals possess forms of embodied knowledge that designers or engineers cannot replicate, no matter how empathetic or technically skilled they may be. Co-design therefore not only enriches the design process but also challenges power hierarchies that privilege technical expertise over experiential insight. This democratizing impulse aligns ID with broader movements in participatory design, disability justice, and community-centered innovation.

Another hallmark of Inclusive Design is its intentional focus on *edge cases*—users who have been historically marginalized or excluded by mainstream design norms. Whereas conventional design often optimizes for the mythical "average" user, ID recognizes that designing around the needs of the most excluded leads to more robust, flexible, and widely beneficial solutions. The "curb cut effect" illustrates this principle: innovations originally intended for disabled users frequently become mainstream conveniences. Speech-to-text tools, for instance, were developed to support individuals with hearing impairments but are now widely used for dictation, real-time meeting captioning, and language learning. This cascading effect underscores ID's premise that accessibility-driven innovation enriches the entire user population, not just those for whom the features were initially created.

Importantly, Inclusive Design reframes accessibility as a dynamic, relational, and ongoing practice. Accessibility is not treated as a static compliance milestone—something achieved once and assumed complete. Instead, ID understands accessibility as a dialogue between designers, evolving technologies, and diverse communities. Needs change as technologies advance, societal expectations shift, and new forms of participation emerge. Inclusive Design therefore demands continuous iteration, feedback loops, and a willingness to revise earlier assumptions. It promotes a culture of learning, reflexivity, and humility, acknowledging that inclusivity is always a work in progress.

In this way, ID integrates ethical responsibility with practical innovation. It challenges designers to rethink not only *what* they create but *how* and *with whom* they create it. By centering multiplicity, embracing difference, and elevating the voices of those historically excluded, Inclusive Design moves beyond the aspirations of UD to cultivate technologies that are responsive, evolving, and deeply rooted in the lived realities of diverse users.

Figure 3. Equity by Design

1.2.4 Human-Centered Design (HCD)

Human-Centered Design (HCD), codified in ISO 9241-210, is a methodological framework that ensures design processes are grounded in the needs, contexts, and goals of actual users (Miki, 2013). HCD emphasizes iterative development cycles, participatory engagement, and real-world usability testing. Its strength lies in shifting focus from the capabilities of technology to the experiences of users (Hirasawa et al., 2010). In practice, HCD involves stages of understanding user contexts, specifying requirements, producing prototypes, and evaluating designs through feedback (Susanto et al., 2021). This iterative loop allows systems to evolve in alignment with human needs rather than technological imperatives. However, HCD is not without critique.

In industry, it is often applied in ways that prioritize the "average" or "typical" user, sidelining those with atypical needs. Without an explicit orientation toward marginalized populations, HCD risks reproducing exclusion under the guise of user-centeredness (Friedland & Yamauchi, 2011). For example, usability testing conducted primarily with non-disabled participants may produce designs that function well for the majority while ignoring accessibility barriers experienced by others. When combined with UD and ID, however, HCD becomes a powerful framework (Sears & Hanson, 2012). It ensures that inclusivity is not abstract but anchored in concrete, real-world user contexts. Together, these approaches expand the scope of design beyond compliance or universality toward participatory, justice-oriented practices (Reed & Monk, 2010).

Figure 4. Human Centered Design

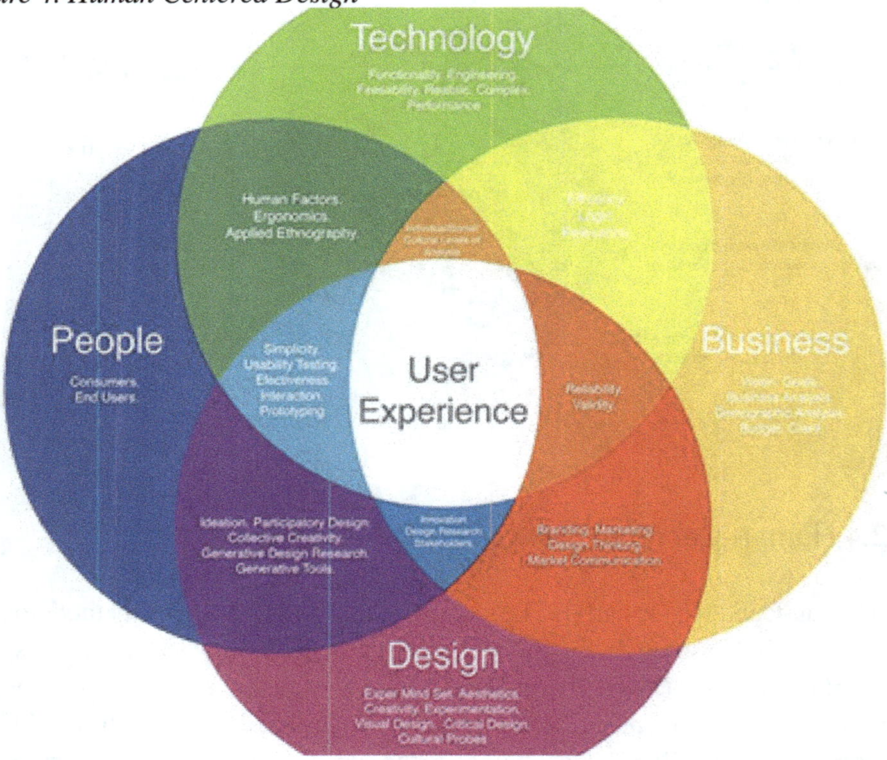

1.3 Synthesizing the Frameworks

When viewed in isolation, accessibility, universal design, inclusive design, and human-centered design each appear as distinct approaches to the problem of exclusion in digital systems. Yet, when brought together, they form a richer and more comprehensive framework for inclusive practice. Accessibility establishes the minimum threshold of usability through compliance with technical standards, ensuring that no user is outright excluded by preventable barriers. Universal Design extends this foundation by urging designers to think proactively, embedding inclusivity into the design process from the very beginning rather than retrofitting solutions after problems emerge. Inclusive Design adds another dimension by foregrounding diversity and participation. It challenges the assumption that a single universal solution can meet the needs of all, instead emphasizing the value of co-design with people whose experiences are often overlooked.

By centering "edge cases," inclusive design ensures that those most at risk of exclusion are placed at the heart of innovation, which often results in solutions that benefit everyone. Human-Centered Design, in turn, situates these principles in real-world contexts. It reminds us that design is not an abstract exercise but a continuous, iterative process of testing, feedback, and refinement that must remain responsive to the lived realities of users. Taken together, these approaches should not be seen as competing paradigms but as complementary layers of an inclusive ecosystem. Accessibility sets the floor by removing the most immediate barriers; Universal Design raises the baseline by embedding inclusivity as a design philosophy; Inclusive Design ensures that diversity and lived experience shape innovation; and Human-Centered Design grounds all of these ideals in the practical contexts of everyday life. The strength of this synthesis lies in its ability to move digital design away from reactive retrofits and toward a more holistic vision—one that aspires not only to compliance but to equity, dignity, and meaningful participation for all.

1.4 Significance

Inclusive design in digital technologies is not only a technical upgrade or a competitive feature but an ethical, legal, and social responsibility essential for justice, dignity, and equity in the digital age (Keates & Clarkson, 2004). Ethically, exclusionary technologies limit autonomy and participation, reinforcing dependency and marginalization, whereas inclusive systems empower individuals to act independently, as emphasized by Ladner (2015). However, many design cultures still prioritize efficiency, speed, and cost, treating accessibility as optional and revealing a moral gap where profit outweighs equity. Ensuring inclusivity is therefore not the sole duty of designers but also of corporations, governments, and institutions that shape digital infrastructures; without shared ethical commitment, technology continues to privilege already advantaged groups while excluding those most vulnerable (Gill, 2007).

Legally, international and national frameworks—including the United Nations Convention on the Rights of Persons with Disabilities (UNCRPD, 2006), the Americans with Disabilities Act (ADA) and Section 508 in the U.S., EN 301 549 in Europe, and India's Guidelines for Government Websites (GIGW)—recognize accessibility as a right, framing digital access as essential for citizenship and social participation. Yet their effectiveness is often limited by weak enforcement, minimal penalties, and compliance-oriented audits that reduce accessibility to a checklist. Many legal measures intervene only after exclusion has already occurred, resulting in gaps between legal ideals and practical implementation (Jordanoski & Nielsen, 2023; Yu, 2003). Stronger accountability systems, adequate funding, and integrating accessibility into procurement and policy processes are necessary to move legal commitments from symbolic to substantive (Reid, 2022).

Socially, inclusive design contributes to equity and social cohesion, directly supporting global development agendas. SDG 4 (Quality Education) requires accessible digital learning; SDG 8 (Decent Work) depends on inclusive workplace technologies; and SDG 10 (Reduced Inequalities) demands digital access across abilities, geographies, and socio-economic contexts (Huffaker, 2015). The "curb cut effect" further shows that accessibility features often benefit all users: voice recognition, originally created for people with physical disabilities, now supports mainstream AI assistants, while closed captioning, developed for deaf and hard-of-hearing communities, is widely used in multilingual communication and media (Aycinena, 2008). Despite these universal benefits, accessibility features still suffer from uneven investment and lack of prioritization when users are perceived as too few or unprofitable—reflecting broader economic and political barriers that continue to marginalize vulnerable groups (Abascal et al., 2015).

Taken together, the ethical, legal, and social dimensions create a strong case for inclusive digital design. However, each dimension has limitations: ethics motivate but lack enforcement, laws mandate but often fail to transform culture, and social benefits can be overshadowed by market logic (Andrade & Techatassanasoontorn, 2020). Achieving meaningful change requires an integrated approach—one where ethical values support respect and dignity, legal frameworks ensure accountability and proactive action, and social imperatives emphasize collective benefit (Jaeger, 2015). Only through such integration can inclusive design move beyond compliance to advance digital justice, treating accessibility not as an optional add-on but as a fundamental requirement for dignity, equity, and meaningful participation in a digital world (Jaeger, 2015).

1.5 Positionality of the Chapter

This chapter situates itself at the intersection of theory, policy, and practice, addressing the gap between rhetorical commitments to accessibility and the persistent reality of digital exclusion. Rather than offering technical prescriptions, it critiques dominant efficiency-driven design cultures that reduce accessibility to compliance with standards like WCAG, arguing instead for a justice-oriented approach that foregrounds dignity, agency, and participation. It advances the integration of key frameworks-*Accessibility, Universal Design, Inclusive Design, and Human-Centered Design*- demonstrating that they are complementary rather than competing, and essential for building cross-platform systems that empower rather than marginalize. Central to its stance is a participatory ethos that repositions people with disabilities as co-designers and epistemic agents, challenging paternalistic models that sideline lived expertise. Drawing on interdisciplinary insights and case studies from education, healthcare, and civic participation, the chapter highlights both achievements and enduring shortcomings, framing inclusivity as a collective, structural responsibility. Ultimately, it offers a critical roadmap for reimagining design beyond fragmented or compliance-driven practices toward participatory, justice-oriented, and genuinely inclusive digital futures.

2. METHODOLOGY

This chapter employs a qualitative, conceptual, and integrative methodological approach that synthesizes interdisciplinary scholarship, global standards, legal frameworks, and sectoral case evidence to develop a comprehensive understanding of inclusive, cross-platform digital design. Secondary sources—including peer-reviewed literature in human–computer interaction, disability studies, accessibility engineering, and inclusive pedagogy—were systematically reviewed alongside key international guidelines such as WCAG, ISO 9241-210, ISO/IEC 29138, EN 301 549, the UNCRPD, ADA, RPwD Act, and GIGW. A thematic document analysis was undertaken to identify recurring patterns, platform-specific barriers, and emerging design opportunities across web, mobile, desktop, and embedded systems. This was complemented by comparative analysis of global policy–practice gaps and case studies from education, healthcare, public services, and industry to highlight both persistent exclusion and successful inclusive design practices. Although no primary empirical data were collected, the methodology is grounded in participatory and disability-justice perspectives by drawing on studies, reports, and lived-experience narratives authored by persons with disabilities. Together, this integrative methodological strategy enables a critical, justice-oriented exploration of how universal, inclusive, and human-centered frameworks can be operationalized to create equitable digital ecosystems.

3. THEORETICAL AND CONCEPTUAL FOUNDATIONS

3.1 Defining Core Concepts

Accessibility represents the baseline principle of ensuring that digital systems are usable by people with diverse abilities, including those with sensory, motor, cognitive, and neurological differences. The World Wide Web Consortium (W3C, 2018) defines accessibility as the capacity for people with disabilities to "perceive, understand, navigate, and interact with the Web, and they can contribute to the Web," a vision formalized through the POUR framework—Perceivable, Operable, Understandable, and Robust. This framework guides developers to embed accessibility into usability: perceivable systems provide alternatives such as captions or alt-text; operable systems allow keyboard navigation; understandable systems present information consistently and logically; and robust systems ensure compatibility with assistive technologies. However, accessibility risks becoming reductive when framed narrowly as compliance with technical standards such as WCAG 2.1/2.2. While such compliance is necessary, it is insufficient without addressing the experiential realities of disabled and neurodivergent users (Kelly, Phipps, & Swift, 2005). Moving beyond compliance, Universal Design (UD), a term coined by Ronald Mace, is defined as "the design of products and environments to be usable by all people, to the greatest extent possible, without the need for adaptation or specialized design" (Mace, 1998).

The Center for Universal Design (1997) articulated seven principles- equitable use, flexibility in use, simple and intuitive use, perceptible information, tolerance for error, low physical effort, and size and space for approach and use—that have influenced fields from architecture to ICT. For instance, video captioning benefits not only those with hearing impairments but also language learners and viewers in noisy settings, an example of the curb cut effect (Blackwell, 2017). Yet, UD has been critiqued for its tendency to assume universal solutions can serve everyone equally; disability scholars caution against "flattening diversity" under the guise of universality, emphasizing the importance of attending to difference and specificity (Imrie, 2012). In contrast, Inclusive Design (ID), popularized by the Inclusive Design Research Centre at OCAD University (Treviranus, 2018), emphasizes diversity and participation. Unlike UD's attempt at universality, ID foregrounds difference and insists on co-design with marginalized users. It stresses designing with, rather than for, people with disabilities, positioning lived experience as a form of essential expertise (Pullin, 2009).

Further, ID acknowledges "edge cases"—users most often excluded- and highlights that designing for them frequently generates innovations beneficial to all (Clarkson, Coleman, Keates, & Lebbon, 2013). While UD risks a one-size-fits-all orientation, ID embraces pluralism and flexibility, yet both share a rejection of retrofitted accommodations and a commitment to proactive inclusivity. Complementing these approaches, Human-Centered Design (HCD), codified in ISO 9241-210 (2019), places the needs, contexts, and goals of end-users at the center of iterative processes of understanding users, specifying requirements, prototyping, and evaluation. HCD's strength lies in grounding technology in real-world contexts; however, critical scholars argue it often defaults to designing for the "average" user, thereby reinforcing exclusion (Bannon, 2011). Unless explicitly oriented toward marginalized groups, HCD risks reproducing structural inequalities. When integrated with UD and ID, however, HCD provides the methodological backbone for operationalizing inclusive principles through participatory processes and continuous feedback.

3.2 Historical Evolution

The historical evolution of inclusive design can be traced to the mid-20th-century architectural accessibility movements, where disability activism in the United States during the 1960s and 1970s led to concepts such as curb cuts and barrier-free design (Steinfeld & Maisel, 2012). These initiatives not only reshaped physical environments but also laid the foundation for Universal Design principles. Simultaneously, product design began to integrate ergonomic considerations, reflecting an emerging recognition that human diversity in age, ability, and context must be accommodated (Story, Mueller, & Mace, 1998). As societies entered the digital era, these principles migrated into technological domains, marking both a natural and necessary extension.

By the 1990s, with the rise of the Internet, accessibility debates expanded into digital spaces, and the establishment of the Web Accessibility Initiative (WAI) by W3C in 1997 signaled institutional recognition of digital accessibility (Henry, 2007). The Web Content Accessibility Guidelines (WCAG), published in successive versions in 1999, 2008, and 2018 and now evolving into WCAG 3.0, provided structured criteria for accessible websites and digital systems. However, the rapid expansion of mobile devices, embedded systems, and AI-driven platforms has complicated the accessibility landscape: digital inclusion now extends beyond static websites to encompass dynamic, cross-platform ecosystems such as mobile applications and Internet of Things (IoT) devices. This shift underscores the need to approach accessibility as a systemic and integrated concern rather than as a checklist applied to isolated platforms.

Crucially, the rise of disability rights movements reframed design discourse, as the social model of disability articulated by Oliver (1990) emphasized that disability arises from social barriers rather than individual impairments, directly influencing accessibility and inclusive design by centering the removal of such barriers in technology, education, and employment. At the policy level, the United Nations Convention on the Rights of Persons with Disabilities (CRPD, 2006) codified access to ICTs as a human right, reinforcing the global imperative for digital inclusion. Parallel to this, inclusive pedagogy movements highlighted the necessity for educational technologies to serve learners with diverse needs, integrating assistive technologies and flexible environments to promote equity in learning (Florian & Beaton, 2018). Taken together, this historical trajectory demonstrates how architectural accessibility, disability activism, and ICT development converged to shape contemporary understandings of inclusive digital design.

Table 1. Historical Evolution of Accessibility & Inclusive Design

Period	Key Milestones	Frameworks / Standards	Significance
1960s–70s	Disability rights activism, curb cuts	Barrier-free design	Shift from charity to rights
1990s	ADA, WAI (W3C), CRPD drafting	WCAG 1.0 (1999)	Institutionalizing accessibility
2000s	Rise of e-learning & mobile apps	WCAG 2.0 (2008), Section 508	Broadening to ICT
2010s	Global South adoption, UDL frameworks	WCAG 2.1, EN 301 549, RPwD Act 2016	Universalization attempts
2020s	AI/ML, XR/VR integration	WCAG 3.0 (draft), ISO 9241-210	Toward dynamic, participatory inclusion

3.3 Ethical and Philosophical Principles

Accessibility in digital systems is not merely a technical or economic concern but a question of empowerment and justice (Jaeger, 2015). As Ladner (2015) emphasizes, the central goal of inclusive technologies must be "design for user empowerment," ensuring that systems expand autonomy rather than foster dependency. Assistive technologies such as screen readers and speech recognition function not simply as tools but as enablers of independence, education, and participation (Tang et al., 2004).

Yet genuine empowerment requires more than functional provision; it demands agency in design processes. When technologies are created without the input of disabled communities, they risk paternalism, reinforcing dependency instead of enabling self-determination (Cook, 2010). Building on this, the notion of digital justice reframes accessibility as a broader issue of equity in the digital age. Costanza-Chock (2020) articulates design justice as a framework that prioritizes marginalized voices, redistributes power, and interrogates structural inequalities embedded in design cultures. Central to this vision is participatory inclusion, which insists that disabled and neurodivergent individuals be engaged as co-designers and epistemic agents, recognizing the authority of lived experience as irreplaceable by technical expertise alone (Laitano, 2017).

At its foundation, inclusive design is rooted in equity and dignity: equity demands that systems acknowledge difference and provide fair opportunities for participation, while dignity underscores respect, autonomy, and recognition of disabled individuals as full participants in digital life (Clarkson et al., 2003). These principles are enshrined globally in the United Nations Convention on the Rights of Persons with Disabilities (CRPD, 2006) and reinforced by the Sustainable Development Goals, which link accessibility to equitable education (SDG 4), decent work (SDG 8), and reduced inequalities (SDG 10) (Tebbutt et al., 2016). Thus, the ethical and philosophical grounding of inclusive design transcends narrow compliance with technical standards, anchoring accessibility within a justice-oriented vision that seeks to transform digital environments into spaces of equity, dignity, and human rights.

4. POLICY AND STANDARDS LANDSCAPE

4.1 Global Legal Frameworks

The policy and standards landscape for accessibility reflects the growing recognition that access to digital technologies is not a matter of convenience but of human rights and social justice. As the digital ecosystem expands into education, employment, healthcare, and civic participation, international and national frameworks have sought to codify accessibility as both a legal obligation and a social necessity. This section examines key global and regional frameworks, highlighting their scope, significance, and limitations.

4.1.1 The UN Convention on the Rights of Persons with Disabilities (CRPD, 2006)

The CRPD represents the most comprehensive global commitment to disability rights. Article 9 mandates that States Parties take appropriate measures to ensure access "to information and communications, including information and communications technologies and systems" (United Nations, 2006). By elevating ICT accessibility to the level of a human right, the CRPD reframes it as a matter of dignity, equality, and participation. The CRPD also emphasizes participatory governance: Article 4.3 requires governments to consult with persons with disabilities in policy-making. This principle aligns legal accessibility with democratic inclusion. However, the CRPD's strength—its universal ratification—also reveals its weakness. Implementation depends heavily on national legislation, and monitoring relies largely on self-reporting. Many countries sign and ratify but fail to create strong enforcement structures, resulting in uneven global progress (Degener, 2016).

4.1.2 The Americans with Disabilities Act (ADA, 1990) and Section 508

In the United States, the ADA has been a cornerstone of disability rights. Title III prohibits discrimination in "places of public accommodation," and U.S. courts increasingly interpret this to include websites and digital platforms (Robles v. Domino's Pizza, LLC, 2019). This case law affirms that inaccessible websites violate civil rights, thereby extending accessibility mandates into the digital domain.

Complementing this, Section 508 of the Rehabilitation Act (1973, amended in 1998 and refreshed in 2017) specifically requires federal agencies to procure, develop, and maintain accessible ICT. The 2017 "Section 508 Refresh" harmonized requirements with the Web Content Accessibility Guidelines (WCAG) 2.0 (U.S. Access Board, 2017). This alignment has provided global influence, setting benchmarks for accessibility in government procurement and technology design. Yet challenges persist. ADA enforcement depends on litigation, often placing burdens on individuals to sue. Section 508 applies mainly to federal agencies, leaving much of the private sector unregulated. Despite this, U.S. policy has shaped global accessibility debates, especially through its legal interpretations and harmonization with WCAG.

4.1.3 EN 301 549 and the European Accessibility Act

In Europe, accessibility is structured by the European Accessibility Act (EAA, 2019) and the technical standard EN 301 549. EN 301 549 specifies accessibility requirements for ICT, covering hardware, software, mobile apps, and electronic documents (ETSI, 2021). It is directly tied to public procurement, meaning that products and services must meet accessibility standards to be sold to EU institutions. The EAA obliges Member States to adopt accessibility measures for key services (banking, e-commerce, transport, etc.) by 2025. This regional harmonization prevents fragmentation and ensures cross-border consistency in accessibility requirements. Critically, the EU approach links accessibility to the single market: non-compliant companies risk exclusion from procurement opportunities and market access. This creates strong economic incentives. However, scholars caution that enforcement and monitoring remain uncertain, and without robust penalties, compliance risks being superficial (European Commission, 2022).

4.1.4 Indian Frameworks: RPwD Act and GIGW

India's Rights of Persons with Disabilities (RPwD) Act, 2016 aligns national law with the CRPD. Section 42 mandates that government ensure "all contents available in audio, print and electronic media are in accessible format" (Government of India, 2016). This represents a clear recognition that digital accessibility is a matter of rights. Supporting this, the Guidelines for Indian Government Websites (GIGW) set standards for accessible design of e-government platforms, aligning with WCAG 2.0/2.1. The GIGW is particularly important in India's multilingual and socioeconomically diverse context, where digital inclusion initiatives like Digital India intersect with accessibility policy. Despite this strong legal framework, implementation remains weak. Studies of government websites reveal persistent WCAG violations, poor use of alt-text, and lack of accessibility in regional languages (Yesodharan &

Saumya, 2020; Raj & Singh, 2021; Singh & Ghai, 2022). Moreover, enforcement in the private sector (e-commerce, online banking, edtech) is minimal. Thus, while India's laws are progressive on paper, they have yet to translate fully into practice.

4.1.5 Mexico and Regional Standards in Latin America

Latin American countries have taken varied approaches to digital accessibility. In Mexico, Normas Oficiales Mexicanas (NOMs) include standards for electronic records, digital signatures, and accessibility requirements in ICT (Toudert, 2019). These frameworks align with WCAG principles while responding to regional priorities such as mobile-first access and linguistic diversity. Other countries—such as Brazil (Decree No. 5.296/2004) and Chile (Law 20.422/2010)—mandate accessibility in digital systems. Brazil's framework explicitly includes ICT accessibility, while Chile requires accessible government websites. However, enforcement is inconsistent, and regional approaches often lack the centralized harmonization seen in the EU. Civil society advocacy has played a critical role in advancing ICT accessibility in Latin America. Organizations of persons with disabilities have pressured governments to incorporate CRPD principles into law. Nevertheless, the region continues to face challenges of economic inequality, infrastructure deficits, and linguistic diversity that complicate implementation.

A critical comparison of existing frameworks reveals both significant advances and enduring shortcomings. While the CRPD establishes universal standards for accessibility, its normative strength is undermined by practical weakness: enforcement depends on domestic translation into law, and without robust accountability mechanisms, ratification risks becoming largely symbolic. Similarly, many frameworks reduce accessibility to technical conformity—such as WCAG compliance—while neglecting the experiential dimensions of usability, leaving many digital environments formally compliant yet functionally exclusionary. Enforcement gaps further weaken impact, as illustrated by the reactive nature of ADA lawsuits in the United States, weak monitoring structures in India, and the still untested provisions of the European Accessibility Act (EAA).

Moreover, many legal frameworks disproportionately regulate government ICT systems while granting exemptions to vast segments of the private digital economy, including social media, e-commerce, and gig platforms, which remain central to everyday participation. These limitations underscore that legal framework, though indispensable, provide only the necessary conditions for accessibility and not the sufficient conditions for genuine inclusion. Moving beyond compliance requires cultural transformation, participatory design practices that center disabled voices, and institutional accountability that together advance a justice-oriented vision of digital accessibility.

4.2 International Accessibility Guidelines

While legal frameworks establish the normative basis for digital accessibility, technical guidelines and standards translate these principles into actionable design practices. These guidelines provide developers, designers, and policymakers with benchmarks for inclusive systems, but they also encode broader philosophical orientations toward inclusivity. This section examines four influential frameworks: the Web Content Accessibility Guidelines (WCAG), ISO/IEC 29138, ISO 9241-210, and industry-specific inclusive design guidelines.

4.2.1 WCAG 2.1 and the Emerging WCAG 3.0

The Web Content Accessibility Guidelines (WCAG), developed by the W3C's Web Accessibility Initiative (WAI), remain the most widely adopted accessibility standards. Since WCAG 1.0 (1999), revisions have produced WCAG 2.0 (2008), 2.1 (2018), and 2.2 (2023), with WCAG 3.0 under development (W3C, 2018; 2021). WCAG 2.1 is structured around the POUR principles—Perceivable, Operable, Understandable, and Robust—operationalized through success criteria at three conformance levels (A, AA, AAA). Examples include alt-text for images, sufficient color contrast, keyboard operability, and consistent navigation. WCAG 2.1 advanced accessibility for mobile devices, low vision, and cognitive disabilities through criteria on text spacing, orientation, and alternative input modalities. WCAG 3.0 aims to replace rigid pass/fail models with a flexible, outcome-based scoring system, extending beyond the web to immersive environments such as VR and IoT (W3C, 2021). Despite their global adoption and influence on legislation (e.g., EU's EN 301 549, India's GIGW, and U.S. Section 508), WCAG is often criticized for fostering checklist compliance at the expense of user experience (Kelly et al., 2005) and for insufficiently addressing cultural and linguistic diversity.

Figure 5. WCAG Compliance: Principles & Requirements

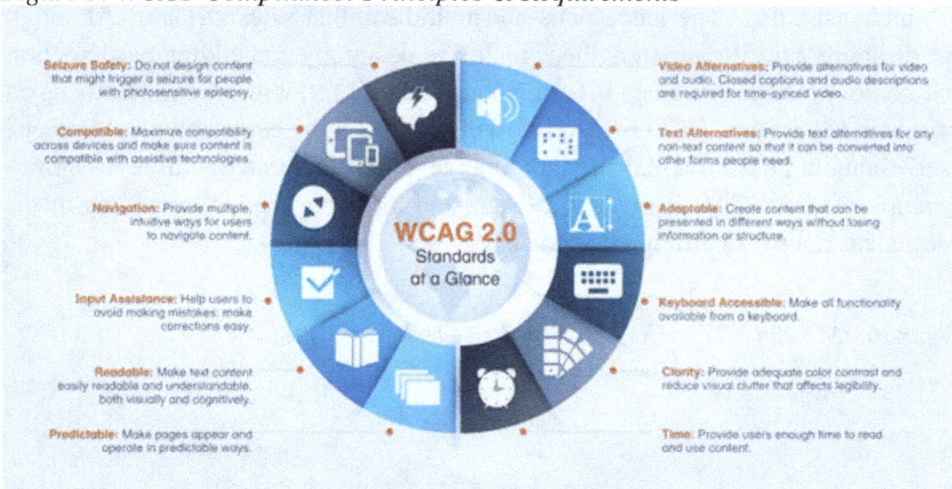

4.2.2 ISO/IEC 29138: User Accessibility Needs

The ISO/IEC 29138 series (2009) provides a broader, user-centered orientation to accessibility (ISO, 2009).

- **Part 1** summarizes user needs across sensory, cognitive, and motor domains.
- **Part 2** guides standards developers in embedding accessibility into ICT specifications.
- **Part 3** outlines an accessibility resource center for developers and policymakers.

Rather than prescribing technical fixes, ISO/IEC 29138 emphasizes human diversity, shifting focus from an "average user" paradigm to recognition of varied capabilities and contexts. However, it is less widely implemented than WCAG due to its complexity and orientation toward standards development. Its greatest value lies in reinforcing that accessibility begins with user needs, positioning it as a meta-framework shaping instruments like EN 301 549.

4.2.3 ISO 9241-210: Human-Centered Design

ISO 9241-210:2019, part of the ergonomics family of standards, codifies Human-Centered Design (HCD) as an iterative, participatory approach to systems development (ISO, 2019). It is guided by six principles: explicit understanding of users and environments, user involvement throughout development, iterative evaluation, comprehensive user experience focus, and multidisciplinary design teams. Although not disability-specific, it strengthens inclusive design by embedding participation and iteration, challenging one-off compliance audits. Yet, without explicit focus on marginalized groups, HCD risks reinforcing exclusion by centering the "average" user (Bannon, 2011). Its real strength emerges when integrated with accessibility principles from WCAG, Universal Design, and Inclusive Design, providing methodological rigor for participatory practice.

Figure 6. ISO 9241-210: Human-Centered Design

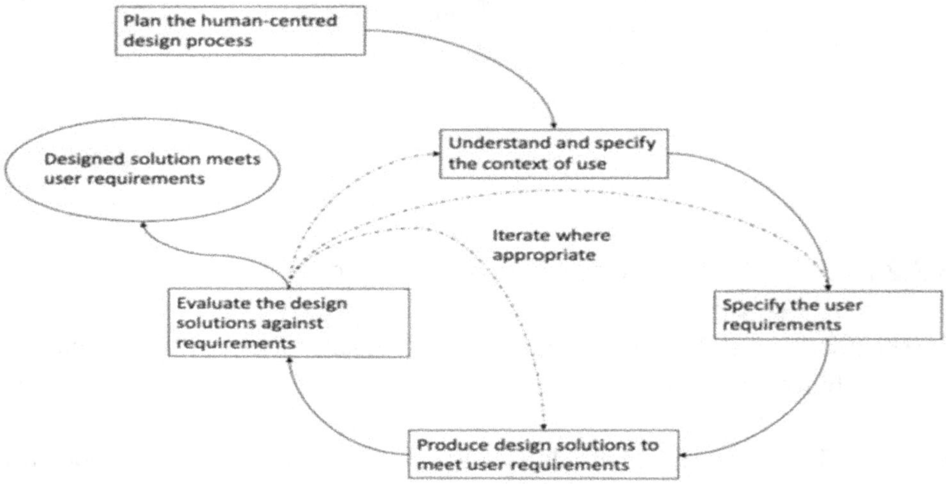

4.2.4 Industry Inclusive UX Guidelines

Major technology companies have expanded accessibility through proprietary guidelines that influence global practice.

- ***Apple*** integrates accessibility into its Human Interface Guidelines (Apple, 2023), embedding VoiceOver, Switch Control, Dynamic Type, and Live Captions into iOS and macOS. These features illustrate the "curb-cut effect," benefiting both disabled and nondisabled users.
- ***Google*** advances accessibility through Material Design Accessibility Guidelines and the Android Accessibility Suite (Google, 2022), emphasizing scalable practices such as color contrast, touch target sizes, and compatibility with assistive tools.

- ***Microsoft*** promotes its Inclusive Design Toolkit (Microsoft, 2016), grounded in three principles: recognize exclusion, learn from diversity, and solve for one, extend to many. Co-design with people with disabilities and innovations such as Immersive Reader and Seeing AI reflect its emphasis on participation and productivity.

These industry frameworks push accessibility beyond legal minimums and often frame inclusivity as both innovation and brand identity. However, their proprietary nature and uneven implementation, particularly outside flagship platforms, highlight the risks of accessibility being shaped by market incentives rather than collective justice.

The landscape of international accessibility guidelines demonstrates both meaningful progress and persistent limitations. The Web Content Accessibility Guidelines (WCAG) remain the most widely operationalized framework, yet their binary compliance model risks reducing accessibility to a checklist, often overlooking the lived experiences of disabled users. ISO/IEC 29138 offers greater philosophical depth by foregrounding user needs and diversity, but its potential remains underutilized in practice. ISO 9241-210 adds methodological value by embedding participation and iteration, though its effectiveness depends on a deliberate orientation toward marginalized groups, without which it may replicate exclusion. Meanwhile, industry leaders such as Apple, Google, and Microsoft have advanced accessibility within mainstream user experience, but their innovations remain tied to proprietary ecosystems and market incentives rather than collective justice. A critical synthesis suggests that no single framework is sufficient: WCAG secures minimum compliance, ISO standards provide user-centered and methodological depth, and industry guidelines demonstrate innovation. Taken together, they form a layered ecosystem of accessibility guidance that spans legal compliance, design methodology, and participatory justice.

4.3 Beyond Compliance: Critique of "Checklist Culture"

A persistent challenge in digital accessibility is the dominance of "checklist culture," where accessibility is treated as a set of technical requirements—most often WCAG criteria—rather than as an ongoing, user-centered process. While checklists provide measurable benchmarks and legal protection under frameworks such as Section 508 (U.S.) or EN 301 549 (EU), they risk reducing accessibility to compliance rather than meaningful usability (Kelly, Phipps, & Howell, 2005). Automated testing tools exacerbate this, flagging only 30–40% of issues (Vigo,

Brown, & Conway, 2013), while critical barriers—confusing navigation for screen reader users or cognitive overload for neurodivergent learners—remain unaddressed.

The result is "formal accessibility" that satisfies audits but fails to deliver substantive accessibility, as seen in e-learning platforms that pass WCAG checks yet remain exhausting for students with dyslexia, ADHD, or autism (Seale, 2014). Checklist culture also fosters a deficit view, framing accessibility as remediation rather than as an opportunity for innovation and equity (Ellis & Goggin, 2017).

Moving beyond compliance requires holistic integration of accessibility across design and development.

- First, accessibility must be a cultural value, embedded in organizational missions and strategies, as exemplified by Microsoft's positioning of accessibility as core to innovation (Microsoft, 2016).
- Second, accessibility by design—modeled after "privacy by design" (Cavoukian, 2010)—ensures inclusivity from requirements gathering through release, avoiding costly retrofits.
- Third, participatory co-design must replace paternalistic models by involving disabled people as knowledge producers, as championed by the Inclusive Design Research Centre (Treviranus, 2018).
- Fourth, cross-platform integration is essential, since fragmented practices—accessible websites but inaccessible apps—still exclude users; harmonized standards such as EN 301 549 and WCAG 3.0 aim to bridge these gaps.

Finally, accessibility must extend to usability and UX, recognizing that technically conformant systems may still be overwhelming; here, outcome-based evaluation (WCAG 3.0) and Human-Centered Design principles (ISO 9241-210) are crucial.

Ultimately, the shift from checklist culture to holistic integration reflects a philosophical transition from accessibility as compliance to accessibility as justice. Standards like WCAG and ISO provide necessary baselines, but genuine inclusion demands cultural change, participatory design, and continuous evaluation grounded in lived experience. Only then can digital systems evolve into equitable, empowering ecosystems.

5. CHALLENGES IN CROSS-PLATFORM ACCESSIBILITY

5.1 Platform-Specific Barriers

Accessibility guidelines such as WCAG, ISO standards, and national policies establish general principles, yet implementation varies across platforms—web, mobile, desktop, and embedded systems—each with distinct barriers. On the web, lack of semantic markup, misuse of ARIA roles, and inconsistent navigation remain common obstacles; WebAIM (2024) reported 67% of screen reader users cite complex menus as a top barrier (Baldwin & Ching, 2021; Lomellini et al., 2025; Leporini & Paterno, 2008). Despite WCAG, design trends like parallax scrolling and autoplay media continue to undermine usability. On mobile, problems include unlabeled buttons, inaccessible custom widgets, and reliance on gestures that exclude motor-impaired users; sensory overload from animations and notifications disproportionately affects neurodivergent users (Fan et al., 2020).

Localization issues further marginalize users in regions such as India and Africa. In desktop environments, barriers include poor keyboard navigation, inaccessible enterprise software, and incompatibility with assistive technologies like JAWS or NVDA; magnification tools are often unsupported due to fixed pixel-based layouts (Calvo et al., 2016). Accessibility regressions following software updates highlight the need for continuous testing. For embedded systems such as ATMs, kiosks, and IoT devices, the absence of tactile or speech interfaces and reliance on touchscreens exclude blind and low-vision users, while speech-based smart devices marginalize those with speech impairments (Manduchi & Kurniawan, 2017). Fragmentation across industries and manufacturers exacerbates inconsistencies. Collectively, these barriers reveal systemic neglect, with accessibility treated as a retrofit rather than integrated design.

5.2 Development Culture

Technical barriers are reinforced by development cultures prioritizing speed and efficiency. Agile and DevOps encourage rapid iteration but often sideline accessibility, as tasks perceived to delay release cycles are deprioritized (Sverdrup, 2018; Tasneem et al., 2025). Automated tools dominate CI/CD pipelines but detect only 30–40% of issues (Vigo, Brown, & Conway, 2013). User stories rarely include disabled perspectives, and MVPs risk embedding inaccessible designs (Stephens et al., 2020). Treating accessibility as late-stage QA makes it reactive and costlier, while accessibility-first design—proactive, iterative, and participatory—aligns with UD and ID principles (Clarkson et al., 2013).

Microsoft's Inclusive Design Toolkit exemplifies this by innovating through edge-case design (Microsoft, 2016). Training gaps compound the problem: most professionals lack formal instruction, with only 24% reporting accessibility training (WebAIM, 2021). Designers often overlook neurodiversity and cognitive load (Seale, 2014), while engineers underuse assistive technologies. Addressing this requires embedding accessibility in curricula, professional certifications (Ellis & Kent, 2017), and distributed team literacy. Cultural transformation thus demands shifts from speed vs. accessibility to speed with accessibility, from remediation to design-first, and from siloed expertise to collective fluency (Lazar et al., 2015).

5.3 Social and Neurodiverse Barriers

Beyond technical and organizational issues, accessibility must address cognitive ergonomics, neurodivergence, and intersectionality. Inaccessible environments impose high cognitive load, especially for individuals with autism (sensory overload from flashing content), ADHD (distractibility from pop-ups), or dyslexia (inconsistent fonts, spacing, and contrast) (Seale, 2014; Al-Azawei, Serenelli, & Lundqvist, 2016). Intersectional barriers compound exclusion: women with disabilities face "double exclusion" including higher risks of online harassment (UN Women, 2020); older adults encounter age-related decline exacerbated by poor design (Czaja & Lee, 2007); low-income users lack access to updated devices and bandwidth (Robinson et al., 2015); and Global South contexts highlight gaps in localization and linguistic accessibility (Ellis & Goggin, 2017). As Crenshaw (1989) argues, these intersecting inequities reveal that accessibility cannot be reduced to visible impairments or checklist compliance. Instead, justice-oriented accessibility requires cognitive ergonomic design (Hollnagel, 1997), intersectional approaches, and participatory inclusion (Treviranus, 2018). Without this shift, accessibility risks reinforcing rather than dismantling inequity (Ladner, 2015; Couldry & Mejias, 2019).

6. FRAMEWORKS AND METHODOLOGIES FOR INCLUSIVE DESIGN

Inclusive digital systems need robust, practiced frameworks that move accessibility from compliance to a proactive philosophy of equity and participation. Universal Design (UD) and Inclusive Design (ID) provide that backbone: UD offers baseline, anticipatory inclusivity (Center for Universal Design, 1997; Story, Mueller, & Mace, 1998), while ID centers co-creation with marginalized users and responsiveness to neurodivergence (Sanders & Stappers, 2008; Seale, 2014; Al-Azawei, Serenelli, & Lundqvist, 2016).

6.1 Universal Design Principles (Center for Universal Design, 1997)

UD dissolves the "mainstream/special" divide by embedding inclusion from the outset. Its seven principles translate cleanly to digital systems: Equitable Use (same core functionality without stigma; captions exemplify curb-cut benefits) (Story,

Mueller, & Mace, 1998); Flexibility in Use (multiple input/output pathways, e.g., voice and text); Simple & Intuitive Use (predictable flows that lower cognitive load) (Hollnagel, 1997); Perceptible Information (multimodal cues; contrast/legibility) (WebAIM, 2024); Tolerance for Error (undo, confirmations, recoverability); Low Physical Effort (efficient navigation, optimized tab order); Size & Space for Approach & Use (responsive layouts, large touch targets). UD is foundational but not exhaustive: universality can "flatten difference," so UD should be complemented by ID to address specificity and lived experience (Center for Universal Design, 1997; Story, Mueller, & Mace, 1998).

6.2 Inclusive Design Practices

ID extends UD by designing with, not for. Participatory workshops, journey mapping, and iterative prototyping position disabled and neurodivergent people as knowledge producers, yielding solutions that improve both assistive-tech compatibility and overall IA/UX (Sanders & Stappers, 2008; Seale, 2014). Edge-in design treats "edge cases" as primary, seeding mainstream innovations (e.g., voice recognition, captioning) and countering exclusionary "average user" assumptions (Kat Holmes, 2018; Seale, 2014). Neurodiversity-centered approaches provide sensory-friendly modes, controllable notifications, chunked content, and customizable typography/spacing, aligning with evidence on dyslexia-supportive interfaces (Al-Azawei, Serenelli, & Lundqvist, 2016) and with cognitive ergonomics (Hollnagel, 1997). Together, UD (baseline) + ID (participatory specificity) operationalize dignity and equity in cross-platform ecosystems (Seale, 2014; Sanders & Stappers, 2008).

6.3 Embedding Accessibility into Lifecycles

Accessibility must be integral across the SDLC. Scoping/Requirements: declare accessibility as non-negotiable (e.g., WCAG 2.2 AA text alternatives; full keyboard operability; AT support) and include disabled/neurodivergent personas to de-normalize able-bodied defaults (Microsoft, 2016; Lazar et al., 2015). Prototyping & Iteration: test early/often with disabled users; catch ARIA misuse, sensory overload, and cognitive load before hardening designs (Ellcessor, 2016; Seale, 2014). DevOps/CI-CD: embed automated checks (axe-core, WAVE, Lighthouse) while recognizing automation finds only ~30–40% of issues; pair with expert audits and user testing; add acceptance criteria, linting, and regression gates so features cannot ship without accessibility sign-off (Vigo, Brown, & Conway, 2013; Microsoft, 2016; Lazar et al., 2015; Clarkson et al., 2013). The shift is epistemic: accessibility as design infrastructure, not post-hoc QA (Lazar et al., 2015; Clarkson et al., 2013).

6.4 Emerging Technologies

AI/ML personalization can auto-adapt fonts, contrast, and input modes and power tools like real-time captioning and scene description (Shinohara & Wobbrock, 2016), e.g., Lookout and Seeing AI, but biased datasets misidentify disabled users and non-normative expressions, and personalization raises privacy/surveillance risks (Buolamwini & Gebru, 2018). NLP/voice expands hands-free access and multilingual inclusion yet struggles with atypical speech, accents, and noise, necessitating multimodal alternatives (Aziz et al. 2021). AR/VR can support social-skills rehearsal, inline captions/signing, and rehab (Laver et al., 2017) but often assumes complex gestures, stereoscopic vision, and high sensory load; inclusive XR needs standards and multimodal inputs per XR Access guidance (Azenkot, 2024). Across AI, NLP, and XR, the ethical imperative remains empowerment over dependency (Ladner, 2015): integrate accessibility at concept stage, co-design with disabled users, and govern data/models to avoid amplifying inequity (Shinohara & Wobbrock, 2016; Buolamwini & Gebru, 2018; Azenkot, 2024).

7. CASE STUDIES AND BEST PRACTICES

7.1 Education

Education is among the most critical arenas for digital accessibility, since inequities here directly shape learners' access to future opportunities in work and civic life. With higher education and schools increasingly dependent on Learning Management Systems (LMS) such as Moodle, Canvas, Blackboard, and Google Classroom, inclusive design has become imperative. Yet accessibility varies widely, reflecting both institutional implementation and faculty practices.

Key Barriers in LMSs

Persistent obstacles include complex navigation structures that overwhelm screen reader or cognitively disabled users; multimedia without captions, transcripts, or OCR; inaccessible assessments like timed quizzes and drag-and-drop tasks; and inconsistent adherence to standards across modules (Moodle, 2023).

Best Practices in LMS Accessibility

1. Standards Compliance: Platforms must align with WCAG 2.2 AA and Section 508. Moodle, for instance, offers WCAG-compliant themes.

2. Semantic Structure: Proper headings, ARIA roles, and consistent navigation improve usability for blind and low-vision learners.
3. Multimodal Content: Captions, transcripts, and alt-text should be universal to serve deaf, blind, and neurodivergent students.
4. Customizability: Interfaces must allow control of font size, contrast, and text-to-speech.
5. Inclusive Assessment: Alternatives to timed tasks, accessible equation editors, and varied input modalities (keyboard, voice, switch devices) enhance equity.

Examples include Canvas LMS, which integrates an Accessibility Checker that prompts for alt-text and table headers, and Blackboard Ally, which audits uploaded materials and generates alternative formats (audio, ePub, Braille-ready).

Inclusive E-Learning Initiatives

- Microsoft Immersive Reader: Offers text-to-speech, line focus, spacing, picture dictionaries, and translation, aiding dyslexic, ADHD, and multilingual learners (Al-Azawei et al., 2016).
- Moodle Plugins: The Brickfield Accessibility Toolkit automates audits, while Accessibility Block gives learners control over fonts, contrast, and TTS.
- Accessible OER: Bookshare and the Accessible Textbook Network provide materials in DAISY, Braille, and audio formats.
- Universal Design for Learning (UDL): CAST (2018) emphasizes multiple means of representation, engagement, and expression, e.g., captioned lectures, flexible engagement channels, and multimodal assignments. Universities embedding UDL (e.g., Minnesota) report wider engagement across student groups.

Accessibility can be technically codified into platforms, as with Canvas or Blackboard Ally, but without faculty commitment—captioning videos, diversifying assessments, and adopting flexible pedagogy—exclusion persists. Tools like Immersive Reader or UDL-aligned practices show that designing for marginalized learners benefits all (the curb-cut effect). However, challenges in the global South—bandwidth, limited training, and weak localization—limit adoption. Achieving universal accessibility in education thus requires not only technical tools but also supportive policy, funding, and sustained institutional capacity building.

7.2 Healthcare

Healthcare has rapidly digitalized through telemedicine, electronic health records (EHRs), and mHealth applications, yet accessibility remains uneven. For disabled persons, inclusive healthcare platforms are not conveniences but matters of life and dignity.

Accessible Telemedicine

The pandemic-driven surge in telemedicine exposed key gaps: lack of real-time captioning for deaf patients, poor contrast and small fonts for low-vision users, CAPTCHAs blocking screen readers, and non-compatible video platforms (Amwell in the U.S. addressed these by integrating screen reader compatibility; India's *e-Sanjeevani* has added multilingual and audio navigation; Horizon 2020 projects in Europe embedded sign language relay). Best practice demands WCAG 2.1/3.0 compliance, multimodal input (voice, tactile, simplified layouts), and participatory co-design with disabled patients.

Assistive mHealth Apps

Inclusive apps illustrate accessibility's potential: *Be My Eyes* connects blind users to volunteers; Microsoft's *Seeing AI* narrates environments; *Proloquo2Go* enables non-verbal communication; AI-driven *Moodpath* and *Woebot* provide simplified mental health support. Yet many mHealth apps remain inaccessible—complex navigation, poor AT integration, and weak privacy protections exclude users, particularly in low- and middle-income countries where affordability and connectivity barriers persist. Developers must adopt UD principles (high-contrast modes, scalable text, multimodal interaction) and align with health standards like HL7 FHIR accessibility, while engaging disabled persons' organizations (DPOs).

Digital healthcare demonstrates both empowerment and exclusion. Features like speech-to-text or captioning, initially designed for accessibility, benefit mainstream users (the curb-cut effect). Still, accessibility is often treated as an afterthought. To fulfill healthcare's emancipatory promise, inclusivity must be framed as a rights-based obligation under the CRPD (2006) and SDGs 3 and 10.

7.3 Public Services

Digital public services—e-governance portals, ATMs, kiosks, ticketing systems—are central to civic participation. Yet inaccessibility often denies equal citizenship.

E-Governance Portals

Despite global commitments, many government portals remain inaccessible: screen-reader-incompatible forms, heavy text, and inaccessible PDFs persist (W3C, 2018). Best practices include India's *GIGW* (mandating WCAG and multilingual access), Estonia's fully digitized accessible system, and Canada's *GCWeb Accessibility Framework*. Beyond compliance, plain language, captioned video, multilingual support, and cognitive-friendly design (Seale, 2014) are essential, reinforced through continuous testing with disabled users.

ATMs, Kiosks, and Ticketing

Exclusion persists when ATMs lack tactile/audio features, kiosks rely solely on touch, or ticketing systems omit captions (Ladner, 2015). Progress includes India's rollout of talking ATMs (Reserve Bank of India, 2014), Japan's multisensory kiosks (Ishihara et al., 2019), and Transport for London's tactile, audio, and NFC-enabled systems (TfL, 2021). Best practice requires multimodal interaction (touch, voice, tactile, visual), adherence to UD principles (Center for Universal Design, 1997), and reliable maintenance of accessibility features.

Public Services Highlight the Paradox of Digitalization

designed for efficiency yet often perpetuating exclusion. Accessibility here is not optional but a state obligation under the CRPD (2006) and SDG 10. Inclusive services—when designed with participatory input—function as democratic infrastructures, extending equal rights to all citizens.

7.4 Industry Examples

Industry leaders shape accessibility culture by embedding inclusivity into mainstream products. Case studies of Apple, Microsoft, and Google reveal distinct strategies.

Apple VoiceOver

Launched in 2009, VoiceOver is a pre-installed iOS screen reader that normalizes accessibility as default, benefiting blind and low-vision users while also aiding sighted users in low-visibility contexts (Marr, 2019). Yet affordability of Apple devices limits global reach.

Microsoft Inclusive Toolkit

First introduced in 2015, the Toolkit reframes disability as a mismatch between users and environments, embedding inclusivity into design culture (Microsoft, 2016). It influenced innovations like the *Xbox Adaptive Controller* (Yuan et al., 2021). However, critics caution that without organizational accountability, such frameworks risk symbolic adoption (Shinohara & Wobbrock, 2019).

Google Accessibility Scanner

Launched in 2016, this Android tool democratizes accessibility audits by flagging issues like low contrast or missing descriptions (Google, 2020). It integrates into Agile/DevOps workflows but, like all automated tools, detects only a fraction of issues and cannot replace participatory testing (Ellcessor, 2016).

Comparative Lessons

- Apple shows the power of integration (default accessibility).
- Microsoft highlights culture change (developer education).
- Google demonstrates democratization (tools for scale).

Collectively, they illustrate that inclusive industry practice succeeds when accessibility is embedded as default, reinforced by culture, and validated through participatory testing. Economic barriers, uneven implementation, and overreliance on automation remain unresolved challenges.

Table 2. Cross-Sector Application of Inclusive Design

Sector	Barriers	Inclusive Practices	Example(s)
Education	Videos w/o captions, timed quizzes	UDL, multimodal assessments	Canvas Accessibility Checker
Healthcare	Inaccessible telemedicine	Multimodal interfaces, participatory design	e-Sanjeevani (India)
Public Services	ATMs without tactile/audio	Talking ATMs, multisensory kiosks	Japan's multisensory kiosks
Industry	Cost-driven neglect	Edge-case design, inclusive toolkits	Microsoft's Inclusive Toolkit

7.5 Critical Reflections

The case studies across education, healthcare, public services, and industry reveal a dual narrative: digital accessibility is increasingly codified into systems and tools, yet persistent barriers continue to expose the limits of compliance-driven approaches. In education, for instance, Learning Management Systems (LMS) such as Canvas, Blackboard Ally, and Moodle plugins demonstrate how technical compliance with standards like WCAG can embed accessibility directly into platforms. However, these tools alone cannot dismantle exclusion. Without cultural change among educators—through practices such as consistent captioning, multimodal assessments, and UDL-informed pedagogy—students with disabilities remain disadvantaged. The curb-cut effect, where features designed for marginalized learners benefit all, is evident, but structural constraints in the Global South—including bandwidth limitations, lack of localization, and insufficient faculty training—significantly curtail adoption (CAST, 2018; Al-Azawei et al., 2016).

Healthcare underscores even more starkly how accessibility failures can jeopardize life and dignity. Telemedicine platforms such as Amwell in the U.S. and India's e-Sanjeevani, alongside assistive apps like Be My Eyes and Microsoft's Seeing AI, illustrate the emancipatory potential of inclusive technologies. Yet this potential coexists with risks of exclusion through inaccessible interface design, poor integration with assistive technologies, and inequitable data practices. Here, accessibility is not an optional enhancement but a rights-based obligation, firmly anchored in the CRPD (2006) and aligned with Sustainable Development Goals 3 and 10. Failures in this sector translate not only into diminished usability but also into direct threats to health, privacy, and autonomy.

Public services similarly highlight how accessibility defines the contours of citizenship. E-governance portals and embedded systems such as ATMs and kiosks become mechanisms of exclusion when they fail to meet accessibility standards. Screen-reader-incompatible forms, inaccessible PDFs, or touch-only kiosks effectively deny disabled citizens fundamental rights such as voting, mobility, and financial independence (Ladner, 2015). Best practices—such as India's Guidelines for Indian Government Websites (GIGW), Estonia's fully digitized system, Canada's GCWeb Accessibility Framework, and Japan's multisensory kiosks—demonstrate progress. Yet uneven implementation continues to undermine equity, particularly in low-resource contexts where accessibility is dismissed as secondary to efficiency (Guidelines for Indian Government Websites [GIGW], 2018; e-Estonia, 2025; Accessibility Standards Canada, 2024; Li et al., 2023). Accessibility in this domain is not merely a technical add-on but a civic infrastructure; its neglect reproduces systemic exclusion.

Industry-led initiatives provide another perspective, showcasing both innovation and inequality. Apple's VoiceOver exemplifies the power of integrating accessibility as a default feature, normalizing inclusive practices across mainstream devices (Marr, 2019). Microsoft's Inclusive Toolkit emphasizes culture change, reframing disability as a mismatch between users and environments and inspiring innovations such as the Xbox Adaptive Controller (Microsoft, 2016; Yuan et al., 2021). Google's Accessibility Scanner, meanwhile, democratizes accessibility audits by equipping developers to identify barriers during design (Google, 2020). Yet these corporate approaches also reveal systemic limitations: Apple's innovations are restricted by affordability barriers, Microsoft's commitments risk symbolic adoption without accountability, and Google's reliance on automated audits can reinforce a compliance culture that prioritizes metrics over lived experience (Shinohara & Wobbrock, 2019; Ellcessor, 2016; Ellis & Goggin, 2017). Industry thus illustrates both the promise of inclusivity and the persistence of inequities when accessibility is mediated by market logics.

Taken together, these cases highlight a broader synthesis: compliance is necessary but insufficient. WCAG and ISO standards provide essential baselines, yet without participatory design, accessibility risks becoming symbolic. Accessibility must also be systemic—embedded across lifecycles, platforms, and sectors, rather than treated as an add-on or afterthought. Ultimately, digital justice should be the guiding principle, ensuring equity, dignity, and participation by centering the lived experiences of disabled and neurodivergent communities (Ladner, 2015; Ellis & Goggin, 2017). Inclusive design, therefore, succeeds not when accessibility is framed as charity, market advantage, or box-ticking, but when it is recognized as a justice-oriented obligation that underpins pedagogy, healthcare, governance, and industry. Only then can digital systems transcend the limits of compliance to become instruments of empowerment, equity, and universal participation.

8. FUTURE DIRECTIONS

The future of inclusive digital systems requires a fundamental shift from static, compliance-driven models toward dynamic, anticipatory, and justice-oriented approaches. As digital technologies continue to permeate every sphere of social, educational, and economic life, accessibility can no longer function as an afterthought or a corrective mechanism. Instead, it must become a guiding principle embedded at the earliest stages of technological design and policy development. This future will be shaped by multiple overlapping forces—advances in artificial intelligence, evolving governance structures, new models of collaboration, and global development priorities. Understanding how these forces converge provides a roadmap for constructing digital ecosystems that are genuinely inclusive, equitable, and sustainable.

8.1 AI and Smart Accessibility

Artificial intelligence stands at the forefront of the next generation of accessibility innovation. Unlike traditional standards, which tend to be static and universalized, AI has the capacity to recognize and respond to the unique needs of individual users. This creates the possibility of **responsive and adaptive accessibility**, where systems evolve alongside users' behaviors, preferences, and abilities.

One of the most promising developments is predictive personalization. In such systems, algorithms observe patterns in user interaction—such as scrolling difficulty, response times, navigation choices, or sensory overload triggers—and adjust interfaces accordingly. For example, a neurodivergent user who becomes overwhelmed by excessive visual content may be offered a simplified interface, while a person with low vision may automatically receive optimized contrast, enlarged fonts, or voice-first interaction options. This adaptive capability transforms accessibility from a reactive process into one that anticipates barriers before they arise.

AI is also reshaping the landscape of accessibility auditing. Historically, audits depended on human experts, specialized tools, and time-intensive manual testing. These barriers often placed accessibility out of reach for smaller organizations. AI-driven auditing tools can now scan websites and platforms in real time, identifying missing alt text, improper heading structures, insufficient contrast ratios, or inaccessible navigation pathways. However, these tools cannot yet interpret nuanced barriers—like cognitive load, emotional triggers, or cultural misalignment—that require lived experience and expert judgment. Thus, while AI can significantly enhance the efficiency of accessibility work, it must remain grounded in human-centered and participatory testing. The future lies in *hybrid accessibility systems*, where automated precision is balanced with empathetic, experiential knowledge.

8.2 Policy and Governance

The next stage of inclusive digital development will depend heavily on the strength of policy and governance ecosystems. Although international agreements and national guidelines—such as the CRPD (2006), ADA, EN 301 549, and India's GIGW—provide foundational commitments, compliance remains uneven and often symbolic. Many organizations still treat accessibility as a recommendation rather than a responsibility.

In the future, accessibility will need to be supported by robust enforcement mechanisms that ensure accountability. Governments must move toward systematic monitoring, mandatory reporting, and meaningful consequences for non-compliance. Such measures will help prevent accessibility from being reduced to a mere performative gesture.

At the same time, policy frameworks should shift from punitive models to incentive-driven approaches that encourage innovation. Governments could recognize accessible design as an indicator of technological leadership and reward organizations that integrate accessibility into their core processes. This may involve providing grants, tax benefits, or competitive advantages in procurement processes to companies that demonstrate accessibility excellence. When inclusivity becomes synonymous with quality, creativity, and global competitiveness, designers and technologists will perceive accessibility not as an obligation but as an opportunity. In this way, governance can help reshape the culture of design from compliance to commitment.

8.3 Collaboration Models

The future of accessibility will rely on collaborative practices that bridge the traditional divides between academia, industry, government, and civil society. Each of these sectors brings unique expertise that, when combined, can generate comprehensive and sustainable solutions.

Academic institutions contribute theoretical depth, critical analysis, and empirical research that can inform the ethical and social dimensions of accessibility. Industry partners bring technological capacity, innovation networks, and the ability to scale solutions efficiently. Governments offer regulatory authority, funding, and mechanisms of public accountability. Disabled People's Organizations (DPOs) provide lived experience, community knowledge, and grounded insights that are indispensable for meaningful inclusion.

Collaboration enables co-creation, where users are not merely consulted but actively involved as partners in the design process. This participatory model challenges paternalistic assumptions and ensures that technologies respond to actual lived realities. Moreover, the growth of *open-source accessibility ecosystems* demonstrates the power of collective collaboration. Tools such as NVDA, WAI-ARIA frameworks, and community-developed assistive technologies are testament to the potential of distributed, community-led innovation. Strengthening these ecosystems through cross-sectoral partnerships can reduce fragmentation, encourage global knowledge exchange, and make accessibility tools more widely available, especially in low-resource contexts.

8.4 Aligning with Global Goals

The work of accessibility does not occur in isolation; it is deeply connected to global movements for sustainability, equity, and justice. The United Nations Sustainable Development Goals (SDGs) provide a powerful framework for understanding accessibility as a global responsibility. SDG 4 emphasizes the need for inclusive and equitable education, an objective increasingly dependent on accessible digital learning and assessment systems, especially in the era of hybrid and remote learning. SDG 8 underscores the importance of accessible workplaces and technologies that support meaningful employment for people with disabilities. Most critically, SDG 10 identifies the reduction of inequality as a central humanitarian goal, directly linking digital accessibility to social justice.

Embedding accessibility within SDG reporting frameworks ensures that digital inclusion is not marginalized but integrated into broader developmental priorities. Governments, corporations, and institutions can adopt accessibility indicators as part of their sustainability and equity commitments, thereby institutionalizing accessibility within global progress metrics.

8.5 Future Directions and Practical Implications

Looking ahead, inclusive digital ecosystems will flourish only when visionary innovation is paired with concrete, actionable strategies. Designers, policymakers, and practitioners all play essential roles in this transformation.

For designers and technologists, the future demands a commitment to embedding accessibility from the earliest design stages. Rather than retrofitting accessible features at the end of development cycles, designers must adopt flexible and modular frameworks that allow for personalized interfaces and multimodal interaction. Inclusive personas, participatory testing, and scenario-based evaluations can ensure that systems anticipate the diversity of real-world users. Cognitive accessibility—often neglected—must become a priority, guiding the creation of interfaces that reduce informational overload, simplify navigation pathways, and provide multiple means of engagement.

Policymakers must cultivate environments that support sustained accessibility improvements. This involves systematic audits, strong enforcement systems, and alignment with global frameworks such as the CRPD and SDGs. Policies should also expand supportive infrastructure by funding accessibility research hubs, training programs, and inclusive innovation incubators. Procurement policies represent a powerful mechanism: when governments require accessibility as a condition for digital contracts, they set industry-wide expectations.

For practitioners—educators, administrators, service providers, and organizational leaders—accessibility must be embedded within everyday operations. This means adopting accessible platforms, creating inclusive communication materials, building institutional cultures of accessibility, and maintaining continuous user-feedback loops. Training programs and capacity-building efforts will be essential in ensuring that accessibility becomes a common practice rather than specialized knowledge.

Ultimately, the future of inclusive digital design lies in the convergence of these forces. As AI-driven innovation, effective governance, collaborative ecosystems, and global development frameworks intersect, accessibility can evolve into a foundational principle of digital life. By embracing this future, societies can build digital environments that honor dignity, expand opportunity, and support meaningful participation for all.

9. CONCLUSION

Inclusive design in the digital age must be recognized as more than a technical refinement or an optional add-on; it is an ethical, legal, and social necessity. Ethically, it affirms the dignity and agency of all individuals, rejecting the marginalization of persons with disabilities and neurodivergent populations. Legally, it is mandated by global and national frameworks such as the UN Convention on the Rights of Persons with Disabilities (CRPD, 2006), the Americans with Disabilities Act (ADA), and the Guidelines for Indian Government Websites (GIGW), which affirm accessibility as a fundamental right rather than a negotiable feature. Socially, inclusive design ensures that education, healthcare, employment, and civic participation remain open and equitable, thereby strengthening the very fabric of democratic societies.

This chapter has emphasized that accessibility must be reframed as empowerment, not charity. When technologies are designed as charitable accommodations, they reinforce a deficit model that portrays disabled users as dependent recipients of benevolence. By contrast, reframing accessibility as empowerment positions disabled individuals as co-creators and innovators, whose lived experiences contribute essential expertise to the design process. In this framing, inclusive systems are not acts of generosity but of justice, ensuring equal opportunities to participate fully in digital life.

The way forward requires a universal, participatory, and sustainable approach to digital inclusivity. Universal design principles must ensure that accessibility is embedded into every digital system from its inception. Participatory practices must involve persons with disabilities directly in co-design, challenging traditional hierarchies that exclude their voices. Finally, sustainability must guide future strategies, ensuring that inclusive technologies evolve alongside emerging innovations such as artificial intelligence, extended reality, and smart infrastructures.

Inclusive design is not merely about compliance with standards but about building digital ecosystems that reflect humanity's diversity and uphold equity as a non-negotiable value. To achieve this, developers, policymakers, educators, and industry leaders must work collaboratively, guided by the recognition that accessibility is a shared responsibility. Only through such collective commitment can digital technologies transcend exclusionary legacies and become instruments of empowerment, justice, and universal participation.

DECLARATIONS

- **Ethical Compliance:** The chapter follows established academic and ethical standards. No human or animal participants were involved.
- **Consent to Participate / Publish:** Not applicable.
- **Conflict of Interest:** The author declares no competing financial, non-financial, or personal interests.
- **Funding:** No external funding was received.
- **Data Availability:** Not applicable, as no datasets were generated or analyzed.
- **Use of AI Tools:** Grammarly and Paperpal (Premium) were used solely for language refinement and readability. No generative or content-producing AI tools were used in the conceptualization, analysis, or writing of the chapter.

ACKNOWLEDGEMENTS

The author expresses sincere gratitude to all scholars, practitioners, and accessibility advocates whose work continues to inspire advancements in inclusive digital design. Appreciation is also extended to colleagues and reviewers whose insightful feedback helped refine and strengthen the arguments presented in this chapter.

REFERENCES

Abascal, J., Arrue, M., Fajardo, I., & Tomás, J. (2015). Inclusive design and the future of accessibility. *Universal Access in the Information Society*, *14*(4), 445–455.

Abascal, J., Barbosa, S. D. J., Nicolle, C., & Zaphiris, P. (2015). Rethinking universal accessibility: A broader approach considering the digital gap. *Universal Access in the Information Society*, *15*(2), 179–182. DOI: 10.1007/s10209-015-0416-1

Abuaddous, H., Zalisham, M., & Basir, N. (2016). Web accessibility challenges. *International Journal of Advanced Computer Science and Applications*, *7*(10). Advance online publication. DOI: 10.14569/IJACSA.2016.071023

Accessibility Standards Canada. (2024). *Accessibility requirements for ICT products and services*. Retrieved from https://accessible.canada.ca/sites/default/files/2024-06/can-asc-en301549-20240226-v02-en-aoda.pdf. Accessed on 26.07.2025.

Al-Azawei, A., Serenelli, F., & Lundqvist, K. (2016). Universal Design for Learning (UDL): A content analysis of peer-reviewed journal papers from 2012 to 2015. *The Journal of Scholarship of Teaching and Learning*, *16*(3), 39–56. DOI: 10.14434/josotl.v16i3.19295

Andrade, A. D., & Techatassanasoontorn, A. A. (2020). Digital enforcement: Rethinking the pursuit of a digitally-enabled society. *Information Systems Journal*, *31*(1), 184–197. DOI: 10.1111/isj.12306

Apple. (2023). *Human Interface Guidelines: Accessibility*. Apple Developer. Retrieved from: https://developer.apple.com/design/human-interface-guidelines/accessibility/. Accessed on 12.11.2025.

Attar, N. M. (2024). *Digitized health care*. DOI: 10.58532/V3BFMS7P1CH10

Aycinena, P. (2008). Access for all. *Communications of the ACM*, *51*(8), 12–14. DOI: 10.1145/1378704.1378709

Azenkot, S. (2024). XR access: Making virtual and augmented reality accessible to people with disabilities. *2024 IEEE Conference on Virtual Reality and 3D User Interfaces (VR)*, xxvi. IEEE. DOI: 10.1109/VR58804.2024.00014

Aziz, F.. (2021). *Inclusive voice interaction techniques for creative object manipulation.* In *Proceedings of the International Conference on Multimodal Interaction.* DOI: 10.1145/3462244.3479937

Baldwin, S. J., & Ching, Y. H. (2021). Accessibility in online courses: A review of national and statewide evaluation instruments. *TechTrends, 65*(6), 731–742. DOI: 10.1007/s11528-021-00624-6

Bannon, L. J. (2011). Reimagining HCI: Toward a more human-centered perspective. *Interactions (New York, N.Y.), 18*(4), 50–57. DOI: 10.1145/1978822.1978833

Bennett, C. L., & Rosner, D. (2019). The promise of user empowerment: Participatory design and disability. *ACM Transactions on Computer-Human Interaction, 26*(6), 1–30.

Bennett, C. L., & Rosner, D. K. (2019, May 2). The promise of empathy: Design, disability, and knowing the "Other." *Human Factors in Computing Systems*. DOI: 10.1145/3290605.3300528

Blackwell, A. (2017). The curb-cut effect. *Stanford Social Innovation Review, 15*(1), 28–33.

Buolamwini, J., & Gebru, T. (2018). Gender shades: Intersectional accuracy disparities in commercial gender classification. *Proceedings of Machine Learning Research, 81*, 1–15.

Buß, J. (2020). Digital accessibility: A systematic review. *International Journal of Human-Computer Studies, 143*, 102488.

Buß, R. (2020). Inclusive Design – Go beyond accessibility. In *Lecture notes in computer science* (pp. 400–407). DOI: 10.1007/978-3-030-49065-2_28

Calvo, R., Seyedarabi, F., & Savva, A. (2016). Beyond web content accessibility guidelines: Expert accessibility reviews. In *Proceedings of the 7th International Conference on Software Development and Technologies for Enhancing Accessibility and Fighting Info-exclusion (DSAI '16)* (pp. 77–84). ACM. https://doi.org/DOI: 10.1145/3019943.3019955

CAST. (2018). *Universal Design for Learning guidelines version 2.2*. CAST. Retrieved from: http://udlguidelines.cast.org. Accessed on 23.08.2025.

Cavoukian, A. (2010). *Privacy by design: The 7 foundational principles*. Information and Privacy Commissioner of Ontario. Retrieved from: https://www.ipc.on.ca/wp-content/uploads/resources/7foundationalprinciples.pdf. Accessed on 23.08.2025.

Center for Universal Design. (1997). *The principles of universal design*. North Carolina State University. Retrieved from: https://projects.ncsu.edu/design/cud/about_ud/udprinciplestext.htm. Accessed on 23.08.2025.

Chadli, A.. (2021). Assessing accessibility in digital environments. *Journal of Accessibility and Design for All, 11*(1), 1–20.

Chadli, F. E., Gretete, D., & Moumen, A. (2021). Digital accessibility: A systematic Literature Review. *SHS Web of Conferences, 119*, 06005. DOI: 10.1051/shsconf/202111906005

Chen, T. (2008). *Input to the mobile web is situationally-impaired.* In *Assets '08: Proceedings of the 10th International ACM SIGACCESS Conference on Computers and Accessibility* (pp. 303–304). ACM. https://doi.org/DOI: 10.1145/1414471.1414550

Christopherson, R. (2022, April 25). Out with accessibility - in with inclusive design. *International Cross-Disciplinary Conference on Web Accessibility*. DOI: 10.1145/3493612.3520444

Clarkson, J., Coleman, R., Keates, S., & Lebbon, C. (Eds.). (2013). *Inclusive design: Design for the whole population*. Springer.

Costanza-Chock, S. (2020). *Design justice: Community-led practices to build the worlds we need*. MIT Press. DOI: 10.7551/mitpress/12255.001.0001

Couldry, N., & Mejias, U. (2019). *The costs of connection: How data is colonizing human life and appropriating it for capitalism*. Stanford University Press.

Crenshaw, K. (1989). Demarginalizing the intersection of race and sex: A Black feminist critique of antidiscrimination doctrine. *University of Chicago Legal Forum, 1989*(1), 139–167.

Czaja, S. J., & Lee, C. C. (2007). The impact of aging on access to technology. *Universal Access in the Information Society*, *5*(4), 341–349. DOI: 10.1007/s10209-006-0060-x

De Kare-Silver, M. (2011). The technology revolution. In *Palgrave Macmillan UK eBooks* (pp. 1–5). DOI: 10.1057/9780230343368_1

Deetjen-Ruiz, R., Daniel, M. P., Telus, J., & Deetjen, L. (2024). Advancing cognitive accessibility: The role of artificial intelligence in enhancing inclusivity. *Mini-Review, 4*(2). Advance online publication. DOI: 10.56831/PSEN-04-108

Degener, T. (2016). Disability in a human rights context. *Laws*, *5*(3), 35. DOI: 10.3390/laws5030035

Dobransky, K., & Hargittai, E. (2016). Unrealized potential: Exploring the digital disability divide. *Poetics*, *58*, 18–28. DOI: 10.1016/j.poetic.2016.08.003

e-Estonia. (2025). *E-Estonia: We have built a digital society*. Retrieved from: https:// e-estonia.com/. Accessed on 26.07.2025.

Ellcessor, E. (2016). *Restricted Access: Media, Disability, and the Politics of Participation*. NYU Press. DOI: 10.18574/nyu/9781479867431.001.0001

Ellis, K., & Goggin, G. (2017). *Disability and the Media*. Bloomsbury Publishing.

Ellis, K., & Kent, M. (2017). *Disability and digital television cultures*. Routledge.

European Commission. (2022). *Union of equality: Strategy for the rights of persons with disabilities 2021–2030*. Publications Office of the European Union., DOI: 10.2775/52556

European Telecommunications Standards Institute (ETSI). (2021). *EN 301 549 V3.2.1: Accessibility requirements for ICT products and services*. ETSI. Retrieved from: https://www.etsi.org/. Accessed on 12.11.2025.

Fan, M., Li, Z., & Li, F. M. (2020). Eyelid gestures on mobile devices for people with motor impairments. In *Proceedings of the 22nd International ACM SIGACCESS Conference on Computers and Accessibility (ASSETS '20)*. DOI: 10.1145/3373625.3416987

Florian, L., & Beaton, M. (2018). Inclusive pedagogy in action: Getting it right for every child. *International Journal of Inclusive Education*, *22*(8), 870–884. DOI: 10.1080/13603116.2017.1412513

Fryia, G. D., Wachowiak-Smolikova, R., & Wachowiak, M. P. (2009, December 18). Human-computer interface design in an e-Learning system for individuals with cognitive and learning disabilities. *International Conference on Digital Information Management*. DOI: 10.1109/ICDIM.2009.5356784

Gangneux, J. (2019). Digital citizenship in a datafied society. *Information Communication and Society*, *22*(14), 2211–2213. DOI: 10.1080/1369118X.2019.1635186

Gill, S. P. (2007). Designing for inclusivity. In *Lecture notes in computer science* (pp. 98–106). https://doi.org/DOI: 10.1007/978-3-540-73279-2_12

Goggin, G., & Ellis, K. (2020). *Disability and digital inequalities*. Springer.

Google. (2020). *Accessibility Scanner*. Retrieved from: https://support.google.com/accessibility/android/answer/6376570. Accessed on 02.07.2025.

Google. (2022). *Material Design Accessibility Guidelines*. Google Design. Retrieved from: https://m3.material.io/foundations/accessibility/overview. Accessed on 02.07.2025.

Government of Canada. (2022). *GCWeb accessibility framework*. Retrieved from: https://www.canada.ca/en/government/system/digital-government/web-accessibility.html. Accessed on 02.07.2025.

Government of India. (2016). *The Rights of Persons with Disabilities Act, 2016*. Ministry of Law and Justice. Retrieved from: https://legislative.gov.in/. Accessed on 02.07.2025.

Guidelines for Indian Government Websites (GIGW). (2018). *DarPG manual: Guidelines for Indian Government Websites (Revised)*. Government of India. Retrieved from: https://darpg.gov.in/sites/default/files/gigw-manual_Revised2018.pdf? Accessed on 26.07.2025.

Hamraie, A. (2017). *Building Access: Universal Design and the Politics of Disability*. University of Minnesota Press.

Henry, S. L. (2007). *Just ask: Integrating accessibility throughout design*. W3C.

Henry, S. L., Abou-Zahra, S., & Brewer, J. (2014). The role of accessibility guidelines. W3C WAI.

Holley, D., & Oliver, M. (2011). Negotiating the digital divide. In *SensePublishers eBooks* (pp. 101–113). https://doi.org/DOI: 10.1007/978-94-6091-580-2_8

Hollnagel, E. (1997). Cognitive ergonomics: It's all in the mind. *Ergonomics*, *40*(10), 1170–1182. DOI: 10.1080/001401397187685

Holmes, K. (2018). *Mismatch: How inclusion shapes design*. MIT Press. DOI: 10.7551/mitpress/11647.001.0001

Hortizuela, R. D. (2022). Towards Web Equality: Efforts on Web Accessibility for Persons with Cognitive Disability. *Deleted Journal*, *23*, 1–16. DOI: 10.55529/ijrise23.1.16

Huffaker, R. (2015). Enforcing eAccessibility: Is the current legal framework adequate? *International Review of Law Computers & Technology*, *29*(2–3), 207–225. DOI: 10.1080/13600869.2015.1055663

Imrie, R. (2012). Universalism, universal design and equitable access to the built environment. *Disability and Rehabilitation, 34*(10), 873–882. DOI: 10.3109/09638288.2011.624250

International Organization for Standardization (ISO). (2009). *ISO/IEC 29138-1: Information technology – User accessibility needs – Summary*. ISO.

International Organization for Standardization (ISO). (2019). *ISO 9241-210: Ergonomics of human-system interaction – Human-centered design for interactive systems*. ISO.

Ishihara, K., Takagi, H., & Asakawa, C. (2019). Designing multimodal kiosks for universal access in Japan. *International Journal of Human-Computer Interaction, 35*(9), 768–782. DOI: 10.1080/10447318.2018.1543087

Jaeger, P. T. (2015). Disability, human rights, and social justice: The ongoing struggle for online accessibility and equality. *First Monday*. Advance online publication. DOI: 10.5210/fm.v20i9.6164

Jordanoski, Z., & Nielsen, M. M. (2023). The challenge of web accessibility: An evaluation of selected government websites and service portals of high-, middle-, and low-income countries. In *ICEGOV '23: Proceedings of the 16th International Conference on Theory and Practice of Electronic Governance* (pp. 101–110). ACM. https://doi.org/DOI: 10.1145/3614321.3614343

Kamalipour, Y. R., & Friedrichsen, M. (2017). Introduction: Digital Transformation in a Global world. In *Springer eBooks* (pp. 1–4). DOI: 10.1007/978-3-319-27786-8_1

Keates, S., & Clarkson, J. (2004). Understanding inclusive design. In *Springer eBooks* (pp. 50–64). https://doi.org/DOI: 10.1007/978-1-4471-0013-3_4

Keates, S., & Clarkson, J. (2004). Why the interest in inclusive design? In *Countering design exclusion*. Springer., DOI: 10.1007/978-1-4471-0013-3_2

Kelly, B.. (2019). Institutional accessibility challenges. *Journal of Web Engineering, 17*(2), 97–118.

Kelly, B., Phipps, L., & Howell, C. (2005). Implementing a holistic approach to e-learning accessibility. *ALT-J. Research in Learning Technology, 13*(1), 69–78. DOI: 10.1080/0968776042000339777

Kelly, B., Phipps, L., & Swift, E. (2005). Developing a holistic approach for e-learning accessibility. *Canadian Journal of Learning and Technology, 31*(3). Advance online publication. DOI: 10.21432/T2D60S

Keptner, K. M., & Heath, M. (2023). The impact of resistance on telemedicine uses for people with disabilities. *Journal of Telemedicine and Telecare*. Advance online publication. DOI: 10.1177/1357633X231213412

Kirkpatrick, A. (2007). Overview of accessible technologies. In *Apress eBooks* (pp. 85–100). DOI: 10.1007/978-1-4302-0188-5_4

Koc-Michalska, K., & Lilleker, D. (2016). Digital Politics: Mobilization, engagement, and participation. *Political Communication*, *34*(1), 1–5. DOI: 10.1080/10584609.2016.1243178

Ladner, R. E. (2015). Design for user empowerment. *interactions, 22*(2), 24–29. https://doi.org/DOI: 10.1145/2723869

Laver, K., Lange, B., George, S., Deutsch, J. E., Saposnik, G., & Crotty, M. (2017). Virtual reality for stroke rehabilitation. *The Cochrane Library*, *11*(1), CD008349. Advance online publication. DOI: 10.1002/14651858.CD008349.pub4

Lazar, J., Goldstein, D. F., & Taylor, A. (2015). *Ensuring digital accessibility through process and policy*. Morgan & Claypool Publishers., DOI: 10.1016/C2013-0-19101-7

Leporini, B., & Paternò, F. (2008). Applying web usability criteria for vision-impaired users: Does it really improve task performance? *International Journal of Human-Computer Interaction*, *24*(1), 17–47. DOI: 10.1080/10447310701771472

Lewthwaite, S. (2014). Digital accessibility and lived experience. *Disability & Society*, *29*(7), 1185–1198.

Lewthwaite, S. (2014). Web accessibility standards and disability: Developing critical perspectives on accessibility. *Disability and Rehabilitation*, *36*(16), 1375–1383. DOI: 10.3109/09638288.2014.938178

Li, J., Yan, Z., Shah, A., Lazar, J., & Peng, H. (2023). *Touchal1y: Making inaccessible public touchscreens accessible*. arXiv.

Lomellini, A., Lowenthal, P. R., Snelson, C., & Trespalacios, J. H. (2025). Accessible and inclusive online learning in higher education: A review of the literature. *Journal of Computing in Higher Education*, *37*(3), 1306–1329. DOI: 10.1007/s12528-024-09424-2

Luke, R. (2001, August 6). Courseware accessibility: recommendations for inclusive design. *International Conference on Advanced Learning Technologies*. DOI: 10.1109/ICALT.2001.943951

Mace, R. L. (1998). Universal design in housing. *Assistive Technology*, *10*(1), 21–28. DOI: 10.1080/10400435.1998.10131957

Manduchi, R., & Kurniawan, S. (2017). *Assistive technology for blindness and low vision*. CRC Press., DOI: 10.1201/9781315216935

Marr, B. (2019). How Apple became the most inclusive tech company with Voice-Over. *Forbes*. Retrieved from: https://www.forbes.com. Accessed on 26.07.2025.

McCall, K., & Chagnon, B. (2022). Rethinking alt text to improve its effectiveness. In *Lecture notes in computer science* (pp. 26-33). https://doi.org/DOI: 10.1007/978-3-031-08645-8_4

McCarthy, M. T. (2016). The big data divide and its consequences. *Sociology Compass*, *10*(12), 1131–1140. DOI: 10.1111/soc4.12436

Microsoft. (2016). *Inclusive Design Toolkit*. Microsoft Design. Retrieved from: https://inclusive.microsoft.design. Accessed on 26.07.2025.

Microsoft. (2020). *Immersive Reader: Tools to support reading and learning*. Microsoft Education. Retrieved from: https://education.microsoft.com/en-us/resource/immersive-reader. Accessed on 26.07.2025.

Miki, H. (2013). Reconsidering the notion of user experience for Human-Centered design. In *Lecture notes in computer science* (pp. 329–337). DOI: 10.1007/978-3-642-39209-2_38

Monisha, M., & Valanteena, D. (2022). Digital transformation in education. EPRA *International Journal of Economic and Business Review*, 58–64. https://doi.org/DOI: 10.36713/epra11864

Moodle. (2023). *Accessibility in Moodle*. Retrieved from: https://docs.moodle.org/403/en/Accessibility. Accessed on 26.07.2025.

Nacheva, R. (2024). Hired by Artificial Intelligence: Digital Inclusion Practices for People with Disabilities. *Journal of Underrepresented & Minority Progress*, *8*(2). Advance online publication. DOI: 10.32674/66c03968

Oliver, M. (1990). *The Politics of Disablement*. Palgrave Macmillan. DOI: 10.1007/978-1-349-20895-1

Omari, O. J. (2013). Investigating ATM System Accessibility for People with Visual Impairments. *IOSR Journal of Computer Engineering*, *15*(5), 13–18. DOI: 10.9790/0661-1551318

Pullin, G. (2009). *Design Meets Disability*. MIT Press.

Raj, S., & Singh, A. (2021). An evaluation of Indian government websites for web accessibility compliance. *International Journal of Human-Computer Interaction, 37*(12), 1121–1134. DOI: 10.1080/10447318.2021.1888487

Reid, B. (2022). Two paths for digital disability law. *Communications of the ACM, 65*(5), 36–38. DOI: 10.1145/3527201

Reserve Bank of India. (2014). *Circular on talking ATMs and accessibility for persons with disabilities.* Retrieved from: https://rbidocs.rbi.org.in. Accessed on 12.11.2025.

Robinson, L., Cotten, S. R., Ono, H., Quan-Haase, A., Mesch, G., Chen, W., Schulz, J., Hale, T. M., & Stern, M. J. (2015). Digital inequalities and why they matter. *Information Communication and Society, 18*(5), 569–582. DOI: 10.1080/1369118X.2015.1012532

Sadia, R., Tuli, F. A., & Lal, K. (2023). Digitization History and its Impact on the Economy, Employment, and Society. *Global Disclosure of Economics and Business, 12*(1), 15–24. DOI: 10.18034/gdeb.v12i1.707

Sanders, E. B. N., & Stappers, P. J. (2008). Co-creation and the new landscapes of design. *CoDesign, 4*(1), 5–18. DOI: 10.1080/15710880701875068

Sciarretta, E. (2025). Inclusive education: Is applying web Content Accessibility guidelines to digital learning materials enough? *European Journal of Education, 60*(2), e70104. Advance online publication. DOI: 10.1111/ejed.70104

Seale, J. (2014). *E-learning and disability in higher education: Accessibility research and practice* (2nd ed.). Routledge.

Setianti, Y., Hafiar, H., Subekti, P., & Priyatna, C. C. (2020, November 18). Social conditions and expectations of customers with disabilities regarding policies and provision of accessible banking technology. DOI: 10.4108/eai.11-12-2019.2302150

Shinohara, K., & Wobbrock, J. O. (2011). In the shadow of misperception: Designing for people with disabilities. *CHI Conference Proceedings*, 705–714.

Shinohara, K., & Wobbrock, J. O. (2016). Self-conscious or self-confident? A diary study conceptualizing the social accessibility of assistive technology. *ACM Transactions on Accessible Computing, 8*(2). *ACM Transactions on Accessible Computing, 5*(2), 1–31. DOI: 10.1145/2827857

Singh, R., & Ghai, S. (2022). Web accessibility of e-governance portals in multilingual India: A study of regional inclusivity. *Universal Access in the Information Society, 21*(3), 559–571. DOI: 10.1007/s10209-021-00788-9

Steinfeld, E., & Maisel, J. (2012). *Universal Design: Creating Inclusive Environments*. Wiley.

Stephens, K., Butler, M., Holloway, L. M., Goncu, C., & Marriott, K. (2020). Smooth sailing? Autoethnography of recreational travel by a blind person. In *Proceedings of the 22nd International ACM SIGACCESS Conference on Computers and Accessibility (ASSETS '20)* (Article 26, pp. 1-12). ACM. https://doi.org/DOI: 10.1145/3373625.3417011

Story, M. F., Mueller, J. L., & Mace, R. L. (1998). *The Universal design file: Designing for people of all ages and abilities.* NC State University, Center for Universal Design.

Susanto, H., Ibrahim, F., Nazmudeen, S. H., Mohiddin, F., & Setiana, D. (2020). Human-Centered design to enhance the usability, human factors, and user experience within digital destructive ecosystems. In *Advances in business strategy and competitive advantage book series* (pp. 76–94). DOI: 10.4018/978-1-7998-4787-8.ch005

Sverdrup, N. (2018). *Accessibility testing in agile software development: Empowering agile developers with accessibility methods* (Master's thesis, University of Oslo). Faculty of Mathematics and Natural Sciences, Department of Informatics.

Tasneem, N., Zulzalil, H. B., & Hassan, S. (2025). Enhancing agile software development: A systematic literature review of requirement prioritization and reprioritization techniques. *IEEE Access : Practical Innovations, Open Solutions, 13*, 32993–33034. DOI: 10.1109/ACCESS.2025.3539357

Tebbutt, E., Brodmann, R., Borg, J., MacLachlan, M., Khasnabis, C., & Horvath, R. (2016). Assistive products and the sustainable development goals (SDGs). *Globalization and Health, 12*(1), 79. DOI: 10.1186/s12992-016-0220-6

Toudert, D. (2019). Digital divide, frequent use and use of the Internet in Mexico. *Convergencia, 26*(79), 1–26. DOI: 10.29101/crcs.v0i79.10332

Transport for London. (2021). *Accessibility at stations and ticket machines.* https://tfl.gov.uk

Transport for London. (2021). *Accessibility at stations and ticket machines.* Retrieved on December 15, 2025, from https://tfl.gov.uk

Treviranus, J. (2018). *The three dimensions of inclusive design.* Inclusive Design Research Centre. Retrieved on December 15, 2025, from https://idrc.ocadu.ca/resources/idrc-online/the-three-dimensions-of-inclusive-design

UNCRPD. (2006). *Convention on the Rights of Persons with Disabilities.* United Nations.

United Nations. (2006). *Convention on the Rights of Persons with Disabilities*. Retrieved December 15, 2025, from https://www.un.org/disabilities/documents/convention/convoptprot-e.pdf

United Nations. (2006). *Convention on the Rights of Persons with Disabilities (CRPD)*. UN General Assembly. Retrieved on December 15, 2025, from https://www.un.org/disabilities/

U.S. Access Board. (2017). *Revised 508 Standards and 255 Guidelines: Information and communication technology*. Retrieved on December 15, 2025, from https://www.access-board.gov/ict/

Veit, D., & Huntgeburth, J. (2013). Impact of digital governments. In *Springer texts in business and economics* (pp. 19–32). DOI: 10.1007/978-3-642-38511-7_2

Vigo, M., Brown, J., & Conway, V. (2013). Benchmarking web accessibility evaluation tools: Measuring the harm of sole reliance on automated tests. *Proceedings of the 10th International Cross-Disciplinary Conference on Web Accessibility*, 1–10. DOI: 10.1145/2461121.2461124

W3C. (2018). *Web Content Accessibility Guidelines (WCAG) 2.1*. W3C Recommendation.

Watling, S. (2011). Digital exclusion: Coming out from behind closed doors. *Disability & Society*, *26*(4), 491–495. DOI: 10.1080/09687599.2011.567802

WebAIM. (2021). *WebAIM Million – Accessibility of the top 1,000,000 home pages*. WebAIM. Retrieved on December 15, 2025, from https://webaim.org/projects/million/

WebAIM. (2024). *WebAIM Million – 2024 report*. Retrieved on December 15, 2025, from https://webaim.org/projects/million/

WebAIM. (2024). *WebAIM Screen Reader User Survey #10 results*. WebAIM. Retrieved on December 15, 2025, from https://webaim.org/projects/screenreadersurvey10/

Women, U. N. (2020). *The digital divide: Gender gaps in access to ICTs*. United Nations. Retrieved on December 15, 2025, from https://www.unwomen.org/en/digital-library/publications/2020/09/the-digital-divide

World Wide Web Consortium. (W3C). (2018). *Web Content Accessibility Guidelines (WCAG) 2.1*. Retrieved on December 15, 2025, from https://www.w3.org/TR/WCAG21/

World Wide Web Consortium. (W3C). (2021). *W3C Accessibility Guidelines (WCAG) 3.0 – Working Draft*. Retrieved on December 15, 2025, from https://www.w3.org/TR/wcag-3.0/

Yesodharan, D., & Saumya, S. (2020). Accessibility evaluation of Indian government portals: Issues and challenges. *Journal of Information and Knowledge Management, 19*(4), 2050046. DOI: 10.1142/S0219649220500460

Yu, H. (2003). Web accessibility and the law. In *IGI Global eBooks* (pp. 1–24). https://doi.org/DOI: 10.4018/978-1-59140-107-0.ch001

Yuan, B., Folmer, E., & Harris, F. C. (2021). Game accessibility: A survey. *Universal Access in the Information Society, 20*(4), 713–733. DOI: 10.1007/s10209-020-00746-9

Chapter 2

From Barriers to Bridge: Inclusive Digital Design for Neurodivergent and Disabled Users

Shivnath Ghosh
https://orcid.org/0000-0001-7368-7139
Brainware University, India

Olivia Jana
https://orcid.org/0009-0009-2101-9513
Brainware University, India

ABSTRACT

Access to software systems is now a fundamental necessity for engagement in contemporary education, work, communication, healthcare, and civic life in a society that is becoming more and more digitalized. However, digital access continues to be a major obstacle for people with disabilities and those who are neurodivergent. A large portion of the digital ecosystem still excludes or fails to adequately serve people with a variety of cognitive, sensory, and physical needs, despite advancements in web and software standards and the global push for adherence to accessibility laws. The need for a paradigm change toward inclusive, human-centered software development practices is highlighted by the shortcomings of compliance-focused frameworks.

1 INTRODUCTION

Access to technology is now necessary for meaningful engagement in civic life, work, education, and healthcare in an increasingly digital world. Digital en-

DOI: 10.4018/979-8-3373-6033-1.ch002

vironments, however, can pose serious challenges for people with neurodivergent conditions and disabilities. This chapter examines the complex issues surrounding digital exclusion, especially for populations with cognitive diversity, and makes a technical, ethical, and social case for software systems to become truly inclusive rather than merely compliant.

1.1 The Digital Divide and Cognitive Exclusion

The gap between those who have and do not have access to digital technologies, including computing devices, internet connectivity, and digital literacy, is commonly referred to as the "digital divide." But in recent years, scholars and activists have stressed that this gap encompasses more than just economic and infrastructure barriers; it also includes cognitive exclusion, a less obvious but no less significant obstacle. The inability of digital systems to support people who process information, perceive stimuli, or engage with technology in non-normative ways is known as cognitive exclusion. Many digital environments are still inaccessible to those who think and learn differently, even though internet connectivity and device availability have improved globally due to increased affordability and expanded infrastructure.

Conventional user interfaces may be challenging for people with neurodivergent conditions like dyslexia, attention-deficit/hyperactivity disorder (ADHD), autism spectrum disorder (ASD), and others. These systems frequently make assumptions about linear thinking, long attention spans, short-term memory, and the capacity to interpret complex or dense language and visual data. Long text passages, for instance, may be difficult for someone with dyslexia, but a visually cluttered interface with flashing elements or unclear icons may be too much for someone with ASD to handle (Seeman et al., 2017).

Digital products that employ technical jargon, don't provide user instructions, or don't allow for layout, color contrast, or reading mode customization are the ones that exhibit cognitive exclusion the most. These obstacles can keep users from accessing vital services like job portals, educational materials, and healthcare information in addition to being inconvenient. As a result, cognitive exclusion disproportionately impacts individuals who are already marginalized and exacerbates already-existing social and economic disparities.

Furthermore, digital disenfranchisement—a state in which people feel excluded, irritated, or stigmatized due to their incapacity to use digital tools efficiently—can result from cognitive exclusion. This affects their autonomy as well as their involvement in professional, educational, and democratic processes. A paradigm change in the way digital equity is conceived is necessary to address this problem. Access to devices and connectivity alone is insufficient for true digital inclusion; usability, adaptability, and the variety of human thought processes must all be taken into account. Therefore, a critical first step in creating inclusive technologies that leave no one behind is acknowledging cognitive accessibility as a fundamental component of digital equity.

Websites with a lot of jargon, apps with cluttered interfaces, and systems that don't allow for customization are examples of cognitive exclusion. These obstacles may limit access to necessary information and services, exacerbating broader social injustices. An essential first step toward inclusive technology is acknowledging cognitive accessibility as a fundamental element of digital equity.

1.2 Beyond Compliance: A Call for Inclusive Innovation

Digital accessibility has advanced thanks in large part to legal and policy frameworks like the European Accessibility Act, the Americans with Disabilities Act (ADA), and the Web Content Accessibility Guidelines (WCAG), which were created by the W3C. These tools have set minimum requirements to guarantee that people with disabilities can use websites, apps, and other digital interfaces. Despite their importance and necessity, these regulatory frameworks are largely concerned with compliance—the bare minimum needed to show due diligence and stay out of trouble with the law. Accessible technology must go beyond what the law requires, though, as compliance is not the same as inclusion (Henry et al., 2014).

Accessibility is frequently viewed by organizations as a checkbox exercise, a last-minute addition to the development process that is only addressed after the primary engineering and design work is finished. This reactive strategy frequently leads to "retrofitting," or superficial fixes, which may technically satisfy legal requirements but have little impact on improving usability for a variety of users in the real world. Even worse, it can perpetuate a mentality that views accessibility as a liability rather than a chance for creativity, innovation, and user empowerment (Abascal & Nicolle, 2005).

A paradigm shift is necessary to genuinely promote inclusive innovation, one that reframes users as unique people with a range of skills, backgrounds, and life experiences rather than as abstract averages. Developers and designers are urged by inclusive innovation to embrace human diversity as a source of inspiration and insight rather than creating for the fabled "average user." This entails taking into account user interaction's cognitive, sensory, physical, and emotional aspects right from the start of the design process.

It is imperative that technologies become intuitive, adaptable, and collaboratively developed with the communities they are intended to serve. Iterative feedback loops, user-led prototyping, and participatory design are crucial techniques for integrating accessibility into the core of innovation.

Additionally, inclusive innovation supports market expansion and corporate objectives. Research indicates that accessible goods and services frequently result in better usability for everyone, not just people with disabilities. This is referred to as the curb-cut effect (Blackburn, 2016). Additionally, there is a growing need for easily accessible digital solutions due to aging populations and increased awareness of neurodivergence. Businesses that put an emphasis on inclusivity can stand out in increasingly cutthroat markets and connect with underrepresented clientele.

In the end, going beyond compliance means more than simply surpassing expectations; it means redefining what success in the digital age means. A dedication to fairness, dignity, and the fundamental human right to access and engage with the digital world is embodied by inclusive innovation. Future technology will be richer, more compassionate, and more inclusive when accessibility is viewed as a design imperative rather than a requirement.

1.3 Neurodivergence and Disability: A Spectrum of Needs

Natural variances in human brain function and cognitive processing that deviate from what is conventionally referred to as "neurotypical" are referred to as neurodivergence. The term, which was first used by the autistic community to counter medicalized narratives of cognitive disability, was coined by sociologist Judy Singer in 1998. Since then, it has expanded into a larger neurodiversity movement that encompasses disorders like Tourette syndrome, dyslexia, dyspraxia, attention deficit hyperactivity disorder (ADHD), and autism spectrum disorder (ASD).

The neurodiversity paradigm stresses that these conditions reflect alternative, equally valid ways of thinking, sensing, learning, and interacting with the world, rather than only seeing them through a deficit-based lens (Walker, 2021). Because their surroundings don't meet their needs, neurodivergent people frequently have special talents like creativity, pattern recognition, or hyperfocus that go unrealized. A growing number of neurodivergent individuals view this aspect of their thinking as a fundamental component of who they are, rejecting attempts at "normalization" or "cure" in favor of acceptance, empowerment, and recognition.

Digital systems often fail to meet the varied needs of neurodivergent users, despite increased societal awareness. Access can be severely hampered by the one-size-fits-all interaction model, which is typified by static layouts, inflexible workflows, and overstimulating visuals. For example, traditional navigation structures may be overwhelming to people with executive function differences, particularly when they are presented with a large number of options, non-linear paths, or no context cues. Similar to this, users with sensory sensitivity—which is prevalent among people on the autism spectrum—may become distressed by animated transitions, loud notifications, or flashing content.

Another serious issue is cognitive overload. High working memory and sustained attention are required for many websites and apps because of their dense text blocks, unclear instructions, or irregular user flows. Such interfaces may make it more difficult for people with learning disabilities or ADHD to complete tasks or understand them. Digital exclusion is often exacerbated for neurodivergent users who are unable to modify content layout, timing, and stimulus exposure (Seeman et al., 2017).

Accessibility solutions need to be adaptable, modular, and user-configurable in light of these difficulties. For neurodivergent users, personalization features like user-controlled animation, reading modes, simplified layouts, and adjustable text size and spacing can significantly increase usability. Broader inclusion is also guaranteed by accommodating different interaction preferences, such as voice input, predictive text, or visual task breakdowns. Additionally, using clear visuals, consistent feedback systems, and simple language can all help to lessen cognitive load and confusion.

Crucially, neurodivergent people must participate in co-creation processes for the design of these systems rather than relying only on presumptions or heuristics. User-led evaluation and participatory design can help identify neglected issues and showcase innovations that are more in line with the real-world experiences of neurodivergent communities (Brown et al., 2021). In the end, considering neurodiversity as a range of needs and abilities pushes us to think beyond constrained notions of normalcy. By doing this, we advance toward a digital environment that respects cognitive diversity, is equitable, empowering, and complies with accessibility standards.

1.4 The Ethical Imperative for Inclusive Technology

Digital technologies are not optional tools in today's world; rather, they are vital infrastructures that influence social participation, public services, work, healthcare, and educational opportunities. Who is included—and who is excluded—by the design of these systems assumes significant ethical significance as they become more and more woven into the fabric of daily life. Digital systems' exclusion of neurodivergent and disabled users is not just a technical error; it is also an ethical transgression that perpetuates systemic discrimination and historical patterns of inequality.

In this case, inclusive design goes beyond legal compliance or usability issues. It manifests as a moral duty based on the values of justice, autonomy, and dignity. Affirming everyone's right to fully engage in digital society, irrespective of cognitive, sensory, or physical differences, is the essence of inclusive design. This acknowledgement forces designers, technologists, and legislators to prioritize the lived experiences of people with disabilities and neurodivergence—not as exceptions, but as essential components of the design process. The ethical underpinnings of inclusive technology are derived from a number of important human rights and philosophical frameworks. First, it is consistent with the capabilities approach put forth by Amartya Sen and Martha Nussbaum, which contends that justice necessitates allowing people to operate in ways that they have good reason to value. Technology, when designed inclusively, acts as a capability amplifier—unlocking opportunities for communication, learning, and autonomy that might otherwise remain inaccessible (Nussbaum, 2006).

Second, the social model of disability, which places the blame for disability on societal barriers like inaccessible technology rather than the individual, is in line with inclusive design. Developers can contribute to the dismantling of the systemic exclusion that prevents disabled and neurodivergent people from participating equally in digital life by removing these barriers through careful design (Oliver, 1990).

Third, a growing trend in responsible innovation and value-sensitive design urges technologists to consider the wider effects of their work. Identifying and addressing algorithmic bias, avoiding paternalism, protecting privacy and consent, and enabling users—particularly those from historically underrepresented groups—to influence their technological environments are all part of this (Friedman & Hendry, 2019). According to this perspective, inclusive technology is a way to redistribute power by providing those who are frequently left behind with agency, visibility, and a voice.

Furthermore, there are quantifiable real-world repercussions for being excluded from digital systems. People experience increased marginalization when they are unable to use digital government services, apply for jobs online, engage in remote learning, or manage their healthcare online. For neurodivergent users, this could entail systems that disregard sensory sensitivity, are unpredictable, or use language that is inaccessible, thereby excluding a segment of the population from important facets of contemporary life.

On the other hand, inclusive technology fosters psychological health, economic independence, and social cohesiveness. It establishes areas where people can interact with others without worrying about being misinterpreted or left out, express themselves honestly, and pursue their objectives on their own terms. Additionally, inclusive systems are advantageous to society as a whole because they produce innovations that enhance usability for all, lower social costs, and represent common ethical values of empathy and justice.

Accordingly, inclusive design needs to be viewed as a type of digital justice—a proactive approach to equity that rejects the normalization of exclusion under the pretense of technical neutrality. Digital architects must take into account the cognitive and sensory accessibility of their designs, just as architects and city planners are now required by ethics to take physical accessibility into account. Failing to do so perpetuates inequality in the digital age and is more than just a lost opportunity.

In the end, inclusive technology's ethical imperative goes beyond functionality to consider who matters, whose needs are taken into consideration, and the type of digital world we are creating. Technologists must commit to long-term, inclusive engagement with the communities they serve in order to fulfill this imperative.Only then can we realize a truly equitable and humane digital future—one where everyone, regardless of neurocognitive profile, has the opportunity to thrive.

2 FOUNDATIONS OF INCLUSIVE SOFTWARE DESIGN

It is more important than ever to create digital environments that can serve a wide variety of users, as software systems are becoming more and more integrated into every aspect of contemporary life. Enhancing accessibility for people with disabilities is only one aspect of inclusive software design; another is developing systems that are functional and useful for all users, irrespective of their situational, cognitive, sensory, or physical limitations. The theoretical and practical underpinnings of inclusive design are examined in this chapter, along with how it differs from related paradigms, cognitive and sensory factors, and important heuristics and ethical frameworks that influence the creation of equitable technology.

2.1 Universal Design vs. Inclusive Design

Although the terms universal design and inclusive design are frequently used interchangeably, they come from different fields and have different goals. The goal of universal design, which has its roots in architecture and product design, is to make environments and products as naturally accessible as possible to everyone without the need for special design or adaptation. This method places a strong emphasis on "one-size-fits-all" solutions that can serve the widest range of users. For instance, a ramp that takes the place of a staircase is advantageous to delivery workers, parents pushing strollers, and people in wheelchairs (Mace, 1985).

On the other hand, the fields of interaction design and digital technologies gave rise to inclusive design. It acknowledges that universally applicable solutions might not fully cater to the complex requirements of every user. In order to guarantee that the finished product takes into account the various ways that people view and use technology, inclusive design promotes flexibility and adaptability and places a strong emphasis on co-designing with marginalized users. By providing a variety of input modalities (voice, keyboard, and gesture) and adjustable font sizes, Inclusive Design encourages multiple pathways to access and engagement rather than focusing on a single solution.

The philosophical stance taken by each method is a crucial difference. By optimizing for the general population, Universal Design assumes that edge cases will be included by accident. However, Inclusive Design begins with edge cases, or people on the edge of usability, and works its way out. This leads to systems that prioritize real-world variability in ability, language, culture, and environment, and are not only accessible but also context-aware and user-centered. Consequently, Inclusive Design is more sensitive to changing and intersecting user needs in digital ecosystems, even though Universal Design and Inclusive Design both aim to increase access. It is especially well-suited to the intricacies of contemporary software systems since it necessitates constant engagement, contextual awareness, and ethical responsibility.

Figure 1. Comparative infographic

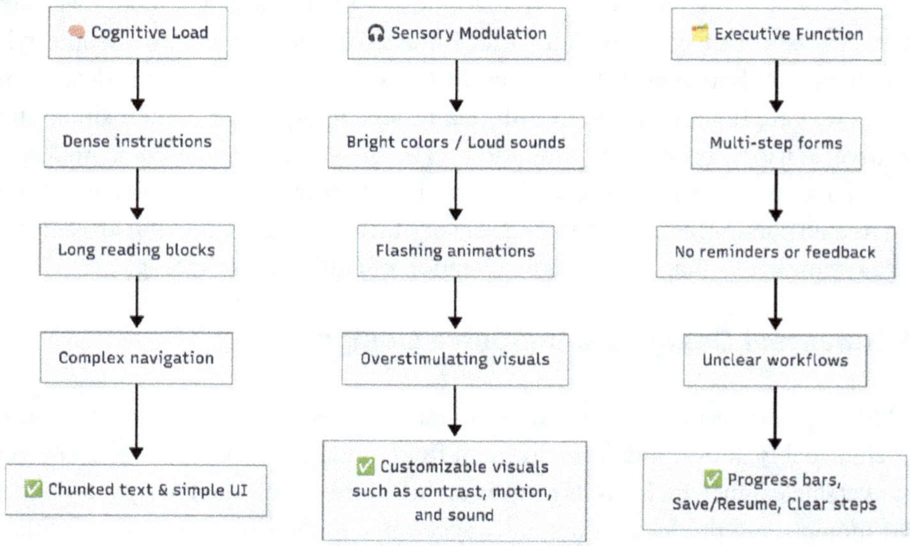

2.2 Cognitive Load, Sensory Modulation, and Executive Functioning

The cognitive and sensory diversity of users is a fundamental factor in inclusive software design. The amount of mental energy expended in working memory is referred to as cognitive load. Understanding, making decisions, and finishing tasks can all be hampered by a high cognitive load, particularly for users who suffer from anxiety, learning disabilities, ADHD, or autism spectrum disorders. Therefore, designers should work to minimize unnecessary distractions, use clear and consistent language, and simplify interfaces in order to reduce extraneous cognitive load (Sweller et al., 2011).

The way people control their senses—such as sight, sound, and touch—is known as sensory modulation. Bright colors, flashing animations, or loud audio may be upsetting to sensory-sensitive users, while other users may need or want more sensory input to stay interested. By offering customizable sensory settings, such as the ability to mute sounds, reduce motion, enable high contrast views, or modify tactile feedback, inclusive design must take these differences into consideration.

Additionally, executive functioning—which controls memory, planning, goal-setting, and impulse control—is essential to inclusive software. Multi-step procedures, poorly designed navigation, or unclear feedback mechanisms can be difficult for users with executive functioning impairments. To encourage sustained attention and self-regulation, inclusive interfaces should provide chunked information, reminders, progress indicators, and clear task flows. For instance, simplifying complicated forms into digestible chunks with feedback and autosave can greatly improve usability for these users. Designers can go beyond superficial accessibility and create environments that are truly cognitively inclusive by taking these cognitive and sensory factors into account. These systems enable users with a variety of neurological profiles to succeed in digital environments by accommodating and empowering them.

2.3 Designing for Flexibility and Customization

The idea of flexibility, or a system's ability to be tailored to suit different needs, preferences, and situations, is fundamental to inclusive design. Multiple entry points, interaction modes, and presentation styles are provided by flexible design, as opposed to rigid interfaces that dictate a single method of interacting with content. Because of this, users can customize their digital experiences to fit their learning styles, languages, abilities, and environmental contexts. Adjustable font sizes, color schemes (like dark mode or dyslexia-friendly fonts), input modalities (voice, keyboard, and eye-tracking), and adaptive content layouts are examples of customization features. For instance, more equitable learning environments are offered by learning management systems (LMS) that let students select text, audio, or video formats for lessons.

Furthermore, flexibility should be extended to context-aware design, in which the system dynamically adjusts to the needs of the situation or user behavior. A smartphone app might, for example, recognize low light levels and automatically transition to voice-guided or high contrast modes. Contextual flexibility accommodates both temporary and permanent impairments and enables users to interact with systems more naturally in real-world situations. In the end, designing for adaptability and personalization improves accessibility as well as general usability and user satisfaction. Software systems can achieve increased resilience, equity, and engagement by implementing a user-centered design approach that anticipates and supports variability.

2.4 Inclusive Design Heuristics and Design Justice Principles

Practitioners must embrace strict heuristics and ethical frameworks in order to operationalize inclusive design in actual development cycles. Nielsen (1994) and other traditional usability heuristics offer a helpful starting point, but inclusive design heuristics expand on this framework by taking into account underrepresented user experiences. Heuristics such as "Provide alternative ways to access content," "Support user autonomy and control," and "Minimize assumptions about cultural or physical norms" are among them.

The Design Justice framework, which specifically challenges the power dynamics present in design processes, is a useful addition to these heuristics. The Design Justice Network developed this framework, which prioritizes intersectionality, community-led design, and redistributing design power to people who have historically been shut out of technological innovation (Costanza-Chock, 2020).

In actuality, this entails including users from underrepresented groups as co-creators and decision-makers during the design process, in addition to serving as testers. It also entails challenging prevailing design logics, such as giving priority to innovation over equity or speed over clarity. Automated decision-making systems, for instance, need to be assessed for possible biases, transparency, and effects on vulnerable groups.

Software design moves beyond the technical realm and into the ethical realm, where inclusivity is a core value rather than a feature, by combining inclusive heuristics with Design Justice principles. This method pushes designers to view accessibility as a fundamental duty toward social justice and technological democracy rather than as an afterthought.

3 NEURODIVERGENCE-CENTERED UX PRACTICES

A sophisticated grasp of neurodivergence—differences in the human brain associated with sociability, learning, attention, mood, and other cognitive processes—is necessary when creating inclusive digital experiences. People with autism, ADHD, dyslexia, and sensory processing disorders are examples of neurodivergent users who frequently face particular challenges when using traditional user interfaces (UIs). By adapting design procedures, tools, and interactions to account for cognitive diversity rather than treating it as an exception, neurodivergence-centered UX practices aim to highlight the experiences of these users. This chapter outlines fundamental tactics that improve neurodivergent inclusion through adaptive technologies, sensory modulation, interface design, and user research.

3.1 Personas and Journey Mapping for Neurodivergent Users

Although journey mapping and personas are fundamental tools in user experience design, they require reconfiguration when viewed through a neurodivergence-centered lens. Neurodivergent viewpoints may be marginalized by traditional personas, which frequently generalize user needs and behaviors based on normative or average assumptions. UX professionals need to create inclusive personas that take into account neurodivergent communication preferences, cognitive styles, and sensory sensitivity in order to more accurately represent this diversity. These personas ought to be based on qualitative observations made by neurodivergent people during participatory design sessions, diary studies, or interviews.

The emotional, sensory, and cognitive aspects of user interaction over time should also be captured by journey mapping. A neurodivergent user's experience with an online registration process, for instance, may reveal confusion from inconsistent labeling, cognitive overload from lengthy forms, or anxiety brought on by countdown timers. Teams can find friction points that might not show up in standard usability testing by mapping such challenges. Additionally, it promotes a change from purely functional objectives (like finishing a task) to sympathetic objectives like lowering stress or fostering autonomy.

Additionally, adding neurodivergent experiences to journey maps guarantees that all user interaction is taken into account, including elements such as executive dysfunction, routine disruption, and reliance on assistive technology. With these insights, designers can create UX flows that provide flexibility, predictability, and scaffolding. For users with working memory issues, for instance, implementing a "save progress" feature or visually decomposing difficult tasks can significantly enhance task retention.

Teams can create more resilient and equitable systems that represent diversity in the real world by incorporating neurodivergent-informed personas and journeys early in the design process. In addition to helping neurodivergent people, this produces stronger design results for the general user base.

3.2 Interface Simplicity and Sensory Considerations

Interfaces that are straightforward, dependable, and consistent are frequently advantageous to neurodivergent users. Cognitive overload and heightened frustration can result from abrupt layout changes, inconsistent navigation, or excessive visual clutter. Clarity, structure, and information hierarchy are given priority in a simple interface, not a lack of functionality. Effective use of whitespace, cutting back on superfluous animations, and keeping button placements consistent throughout pages can greatly enhance comprehension and lessen anxiety in users with autism or ADHD.

Equally significant are sensory factors. A large number of neurodivergent people exhibit either hypersensitivity or hyposensitivity to sensory stimuli. For some users, loud notification sounds, autoplay videos, flashing banners, and bright colors can be annoying or even overwhelming. Others, on the other hand, might require more sensory input to remain interested. Inclusive interfaces should provide customizable sensory settings, like the ability to switch between motion effects, muffle sounds, or select different visual themes, in order to accommodate this spectrum.

Additionally, users who benefit from visual continuity or have slower cognitive processing speeds can be supported by the use of soft animations and transitions (when needed). In a similar vein, the use of semantic HTML and ARIA roles guarantees that information is accurately conveyed to users with visual or auditory processing differences by screen readers and assistive technology.

Users view technology through a variety of perceptual lenses, which is acknowledged by a thoughtful sensory design. Designers can create spaces that allow neurodivergent users to interact on their own terms by minimizing unnecessary stimulation and allowing for personalized controls. This fosters comfort, trust, and agency.

3.3 Distraction Reduction and Attention-Supportive Features

People who are neurodivergent, especially those who suffer from attention deficit disorders, frequently find it difficult to stay focused in digital settings. Task completion may be hampered by websites and applications with pop-ups, auto-refreshing content, persistent notifications, or multiple focal points because these features can cause frequent attentional shifts. Therefore, reducing distractions is an important design factor. Focused layouts, distraction-free modes, and interface decluttering can help achieve this.

Focused layouts reduce visual competition and give priority to a single task per screen. Offering a "reader mode" that eliminates unnecessary navigation and ads, for example, can assist users in focusing on the content. Progressive disclosure is another tool that designers can use to only reveal complex functionality when necessary. This keeps advanced features available while lowering the immediate cognitive load.

Users can maintain their orientation with the aid of attention-supporting features like ambient progress indicators, visual timers, step-by-step instructions, and task reminders. Users who struggle with executive functioning and may lose track of time or forget the next step will find these tools especially helpful. Additionally, using positive reinforcement techniques, like straightforward badges or affirmations, can inspire users and lessen performance-related anxiety.

It's also critical to be able to pause, resume, and save tasks without incurring penalties. Numerous neurodivergent users might require non-linear task revisits or breaks. Enabling temporal flexibility in digital systems promotes more independent and self-assured engagement while acknowledging the variety of users' cognitive rhythms.

3.4 Multimodal Interactions and Accessibility Layers

By enabling users to engage with software via a variety of channels, including text, voice, gesture, and visual symbols, multimodal interaction design improves inclusivity. Because neurodivergent users have a wide range of communication and perception preferences and skills, this flexibility is crucial. Some users with dyslexia might find visual icons or audio cues more useful than reading dense text, while some autistic users might prefer text over voice because of auditory sensitivity.

By enabling multimodal access, users can select the option that best suits their preferences and innate strengths. Alternative means of communication include gesture controls, voice assistants, and keyboards that can be customized. Redundancy should be considered in the design of these; only one input mode should be required. For example, a speech-enabled feature should also offer a keyboard fallback to ensure usability for individuals with speech anxiety or mutism.

Furthermore, software overlays and adaptive modules, also known as accessibility layers, can aid in bridging the gap between a generic interface and customized requirements. Screen readers, live captioning, AI-powered personalization, and streamlined user interface toggles are a few examples of these layers. These tools allow for real-time flexibility without necessitating a thorough system redesign. When properly applied, accessibility layers serve as cognitive ramps that let users alter and move through digital spaces in ways that increase comfort and autonomy.

Crucially, rather than being imposed, these multimodal and layered approaches need to be user-configurable. Users who are neurodivergent should continue to have control over which aids and modalities are used. This upholds the idea of user sovereignty in interaction and guarantees that assistive features are empowering rather than stigmatizing.

4 AI AND PERSONALIZATION FOR ACCESSIBILITY

Digital systems' accessibility is changing due to artificial intelligence (AI), which is changing the paradigm from static, one-size-fits-all interfaces to dynamic, customized experiences. Real-time system adaptation to user behaviors, preferences, and needs is made possible by AI-driven personalization, which is especially advantageous for people with neurodivergent conditions or disabilities. This chapter examines how predictive accessibility tools, adaptive interfaces, and customized input/output modalities can be used to leverage AI technologies to build more inclusive environments. Designers and developers must also manage ethical issues pertaining to data privacy, transparency, and user agency as personalization grows more sophisticated and automated.

4.1 Adaptive Interfaces and Context-Aware AI

Systems that modify their behavior, structure, or presentation in response to user-specific data—such as interaction patterns, environmental cues, and assistive needs—are referred to as adaptive interfaces. These interfaces can provide context-aware responsiveness when AI is used, which is a significant step in the direction of inclusive design. According to real-time performance metrics, an AI-enabled educational platform, for instance, can identify when a student is having trouble understanding the material and either simplify it or switch to a different modality (such as from text to video) (Chen et al., 2021).

To maximize accessibility features, context-aware AI systems use situational and environmental information, such as device type, location, time of day, and background noise. When a user is in a public place, a voice assistant may turn on captions or turn down the volume in noisy environments.

Similarly, to help users with photosensitivity or visual impairments, a mobile app may automatically switch to a high contrast theme when the user is outside in direct sunlight. By eliminating the need for manual adjustments, these AI-driven solutions provide seamless accessibility.

Crucially, transparent and user-consent-driven adaptive systems are required. In addition to having the ability to override or opt out of specific adaptations, users should be aware of when and why changes are made. AI personalization runs the risk of becoming dehumanizing or even exclusive in the absence of these safeguards. Designers also need to make sure that adaptive behavior doesn't unintentionally reinforce biases, like oversimplifying content based on erroneous user capacity interpretations.

Developers can create software that proactively supports a wide range of users in different real-world contexts by utilizing adaptive and context-aware AI.These systems foster greater digital independence and participation for individuals whose abilities fluctuate or who experience dynamic accessibility needs.

4.2 Personalizing Input/Output Based on Cognitive Needs

Customizing input and output modalities to fit unique cognitive profiles is one of AI's most promising uses in accessibility. Users with learning disabilities, attention disorders, memory impairments, and autism spectrum conditions are all included in cognitive accessibility; each of these groups may need different interface modifications. AI systems can adjust feedback techniques, interface pacing, interaction cues, and communication formats based on user behavior and interaction history.

A user with ADHD might benefit from a more straightforward layout with visual timers and sequential task guidance, whereas a user with dyslexia might prefer text-to-speech output with natural intonation and adjustable reading speeds. In order to prevent users from having to repeatedly configure the same settings, AI can gradually recognize these preferences and adjust the experience. For users with physical or motor disabilities, machine learning models can also customize gesture recognition, eye-tracking sensitivity, and keyboard shortcuts (Brumberg et al., 2020).

AI can offer intelligent prediction and error correction on the input side, which is particularly helpful for users who struggle with fine motor skills or have cognitive processing delays. AI-enhanced image selection tools, voice recognition optimized for unusual speech patterns, or predictive typing can all greatly lower interaction barriers. Cognitive chunking, in which information is presented in digestible, scaffolded chunks, and visual cues, such as progress indicators or text with symbols, are further examples of output personalization.

Most importantly, personalization needs to be user-configurable and non-intrusive. Because cognitive preferences change over time, systems should allow users to customize or turn off AI support. What a user finds effective one day might not be the same the next. Experiences become more respectful and equitable when users are given the ability to co-author their digital environments with the help of AI.

4.3 Predictive Accessibility Features and Learning Algorithms

Predictive systems—interfaces that foresee user needs before they are articulated—are the next step up from responsive systems in AI-driven accessibility. In order to anticipate accessibility issues, predictive accessibility tools use contextual patterns, biometric signals, and information from previous interactions. An AI system might, for instance, discover that a user usually enlarges text at particular times of day and proactively apply those settings. Or, depending on previous user behavior, it might recommend turning on focus mode during a planned work session.

Such intelligent anticipation is made possible in large part by learning algorithms, especially those employed in supervised machine learning and reinforcement learning. By examining user engagement, drop-off points, interaction delays, or error patterns, these systems are constantly improving. They can eventually offer alternate media formats, suggest more effective routes for navigation, or implement accessibility features that adapt to changing requirements. These features are particularly helpful for people with episodic or fluctuating disabilities, whose abilities can change over time and in different contexts.

Predictive AI can also improve communication tools. Apps for augmentative and alternative communication (AAC), for example, can learn from a user's vocabulary usage and provide quicker predictive phrase suggestions, greatly lowering the effort required of non-verbal people. Likewise, AI-powered sign-language avatars or predictive captioning can guarantee real-time accessibility in multimedia content without requiring user intervention.

To prevent overfitting or overreach, where systems make erroneous assumptions and restrict user freedom, predictive systems must be closely watched. To preserve inclusivity and trust, AI decision-making processes must be transparent (e.g., by providing an explanation for a particular modification) and have user feedback and correction mechanisms. The objective is to enhance the user experience in a deliberate, moral manner rather than automate tasks for their own sake.Bottom of Form

5 INCLUSIVE IMMERSIVE AND GAMING TECHNOLOGIES

Through the simulation of real-world environments or the addition of virtual elements, immersive technologies like Virtual Reality (VR), Augmented Reality (AR), and Mixed Reality (MR) are transforming digital interaction. These technologies present important chances to improve inclusion and accessibility, especially for people with disabilities and those who are neurodivergent. Traditional barriers of motor function, cognition, and communication can be overcome by games and immersive experiences. Designers must, however, approach these tools with an inclusive mindset—incorporating accessibility principles from the outset rather than treating them as afterthoughts—if they are to fulfill this potential. The connections between immersive technology, neurodivergent-inclusive design, and innovative gaming are examined in this chapter.

5.1 Accessible Design in XR/VR/AR

Intentionally rethinking spatial interaction, visual processing, and input mechanisms is necessary when designing accessible experiences in Extended Reality (XR) environments, such as VR, AR, and MR. Users with restricted mobility, difficulties with sensory processing, or cognitive differences are frequently left out by traditional design assumptions. Many VR systems, for example, rely on hand tracking, quick reaction times, or 360-degree awareness, which could be too much for or difficult for people with motor impairments or sensory sensitivity.

Universal design principles are embraced by accessible XR design, which includes providing customizable interface layouts, permitting alternate control schemes (like voice commands or gaze tracking), and minimizing motion sickness with movable motion settings. Designing for neurodivergent users also entails giving users clear, consistent cues for interaction and navigation, as well as minimizing overstimulation by allowing them to filter visual or auditory information.

By highlighting the need for adaptable environments that let people adjust the degree of realism, complexity, and feedback to suit their comfort level and cognitive style, groups like AbleGamers and the XR Access Initiative have started to promote accessibility in immersive technologies. XR affordances like spatial audio guidance, sensory attenuation, and interaction pacing are also highlighted in Microsoft's Inclusive Design Toolkit as essential components of more accessible experiences (XR Access Initiative, 2021).

5.2 Neurodivergent-Friendly Game Mechanics

The way users navigate, learn, compete, and cooperate in gaming environments is largely determined by game mechanics. Mainstream game designs that presume consistent sensory processing, executive functioning, or social cognition frequently present difficulties for neurodivergent players, such as those with autism spectrum disorder (ASD), ADHD, dyslexia, or dyspraxia.

Clarity, predictability, and flexibility are the cornerstones of neurodivergent-friendly game mechanics. These could include turn-based pacing, visual task schedules, text-to-speech or speech-to-text capabilities, varying degrees of difficulty, and less dependence on quick multitasking. Furthermore, gameplay can be made more approachable and pleasurable by implementing affordances like colorblind-friendly palettes, customizable interfaces, and simplified goal structures.

Some developers use neurodivergence as a creative force rather than as a limitation. First-person depictions of sensory overload or psychosis are found in games like Auti-Sim and Senua's Hellblade: Sacrifice, which encourage empathy while providing players with a safe environment in which to explore neurodivergent experiences. Similarly, open-ended, stress-free interaction is possible in sandbox games like Animal Crossing and Minecraft, which suits the needs of many neurodivergent players who prefer independence and less stress (Cermak-Sassenrath, D. 2020) (Zolyomi, A., & Schmalz, M. 2017).

5.3 Case Study: Educational Games for Cognitive Inclusion

The use of educational games that are adapted to cognitive diversity is one compelling example of inclusive design. Through gamified motivation, repetition, and multisensory reinforcement, educational games can offer dynamic, captivating environments that enhance learning. These inclusively created games assist neurodivergent students in meeting learning objectives that may be challenging to accomplish with traditional teaching methods.

One notable example is the early literacy development game Endless Reader. It helps kids, including those with dyslexia or ASD, connect phonics to meaning through animated characters, vibrant graphics, and auditory feedback. Another example is Mindset Works' Brainology, which uses gaming to improve emotional control and executive functioning. Virtual reality-based simulations, such as Project VOISS (Virtual Reality Opportunities to Implement Social Skills), have demonstrated promise in higher education by providing autistic students with a safe, non-threatening environment in which to practice social scripts, workplace interactions, and emotional recognition. Allowing users to control their sensory input, move at their own pace, and get constant positive reinforcement are all essential components of successful use of these educational tools (Mindset Works, 2020) (Smith, M. J., et al. 2020).

5.4 Haptic Feedback and Multisensory Design Considerations

In inclusive immersive systems, multisensory design—the use of multiple senses in digital environments—is essential. Particularly important is haptic feedback, which provides tactile signals that supplement or substitute visual and auditory cues. Haptics can assist users with visual impairments in navigating virtual environments. Vibrotactile cues can be used to enhance in-game alerts or communication for people who are deaf or hard of hearing or who have auditory processing disorders.

But designers also need to exercise caution. Strong or unexpected haptic feedback can be upsetting or distressing for certain neurodivergent people, particularly those who are sensitive to sensory processing. Therefore, it is essential to have user-adjustable vibration intensity, duration, and frequency settings. Similarly, multisensory design should balance stimulation without being overpowering. Gentle haptics, subdued color schemes, and subdued audio can all be combined to create a soothing, accessible environment.

More subtle feedback is made possible by developments in wearable haptics, such as armbands, gloves, or suits, which enhances interaction and immersion for people with impaired motor function. The advantages of combining temperature and aroma in therapeutic virtual reality settings intended to control anxiety or emotions have also been demonstrated by research. To make sure they meet a variety of user needs, these new modalities need to be critically evaluated through inclusive trials (Schneider, O., et al. 2017) (Maes, P., & Chang, A. 2021).

6 TESTING, METRICS, AND CONTINUOUS ACCESSIBILITY

Maintaining accessibility throughout the software lifecycle is just as important as designing inclusive digital systems. In addition to following standards like the Web Content Accessibility Guidelines (WCAG), accessibility needs to be verified through practical testing with a range of users. Traditional checklists may not be sufficient, particularly when dealing with neurodivergent users and those who have invisible or cognitive disabilities. This chapter looks at new accessibility testing tools, goes beyond compliance metrics, and explains how accessibility can be incorporated into contemporary development processes such as Continuous Integration and Continuous Deployment (CI/CD).

6.1 Beyond WCAG: Measuring Cognitive Accessibility

Measuring cognitive accessibility also involves analyzing emotional engagement, distraction potential, and adaptability. For example, neurodivergent users may benefit from personalized interfaces, fewer distractions, and progressive disclosure of information. These considerations require qualitative feedback from user testing as well as quantitative metrics that reflect ease of use, trust, and cognitive effort. Metrics like the System Usability Scale (SUS), NASA Task Load Index (NASA-TLX), and the Cognitive Walkthrough method are also helpful in assessing user task comprehension, usability, and mental effort.

Assessing cognitive accessibility also entails examining adaptability, emotional engagement, and distraction potential. For instance, progressive information disclosure, reduced distractions, and customized interfaces may be advantageous for neurodivergent users. These factors necessitate quantitative measures that represent usability, trust, and cognitive effort in addition to qualitative input from user testing.

6.2 Tools for Manual and Automated Accessibility Testing

Both automated and manual methods are included in accessibility testing. Automated tools are good at finding problems like color contrast failures, incorrect heading structures, and missing alt text. In order to enforce baseline accessibility, tools such as axe-core, Lighthouse, WAVE, and Pa11y are frequently used during the development process. These tools provide developers with real-time feedback and can be incorporated into browser extensions or development environments.

However, only roughly 30 to 50 percent of accessibility issues are usually detected by automated tools. Manual testing is crucial, particularly when it comes to problems with focus states, keyboard navigation, error recovery, and screen reader compatibility. Manual testing becomes even more important for cognitive accessibility. Methods like user interviews, heuristic evaluation, guided walkthroughs, and participatory design sessions with neurodivergent people can reveal obstacles that scripts might miss.

It is essential to include actual users in testing, particularly those with a range of cognitive profiles. Deeper understanding of a design's inclusivity can be gained by using personas based on neurodivergent traits, modeling cognitive load scenarios, or utilizing tools like Accessibility Insights for both automated and assisted manual review. Broader usability is ensured by testing on a variety of devices, input modalities (such as speech, touch, and keyboard-only), and cognitive states.

6.3 Integrating Accessibility into CI/CD Workflows

Agile and DevOps-based software development now relies heavily on continuous integration and deployment, or CI/CD. It is crucial to incorporate accessibility practices throughout these workflows since they place a high priority on automated testing, frequent code integration, and quick deployment. Retrofitting compliance can be expensive and inefficient if accessibility is only taken into account at the end of the cycle. Automated accessibility tests must be incorporated into build pipelines in order to integrate accessibility into CI/CD. To run tools like axe-core CLI, Tenon, or Lighthouse CI with each commit, developers can set up continuous integration (CI) tools like GitHub Actions, Jenkins, or GitLab CI. Accountability is enforced early in development when builds fail because of accessibility regressions.

Code review checklists, adding accessibility acceptance criteria to user stories, and matching developers with accessibility experts are ways to improve accessibility gates beyond automation. To keep track of unresolved issues, progressive organizations use "accessibility sprints" and accessibility debt logs. Whether through frequent usability reviews or bug triage, involving neurodivergent stakeholders in feedback loops guarantees that accessibility develops alongside the product. Teams can track accessibility over time by using tools like Siteimprove or Deque's axe Monitor to continuously monitor accessibility performance. This method reinforces that accessibility is a continuous process rather than a one-time accomplishment, which is consistent with the DevOps philosophy of observability and feedback.

7 PARTICIPATORY DESIGN AND CO-CREATION

Designing with people is more important than designing for them when it comes to creating inclusive digital experiences. The inclusion of disabled and neurodivergent people as equal partners in creating digital environments, rather than just as testers or consultees, is emphasized by participatory design and co-creation. These methods aim to rebalance the conventional power dynamics between designers and users and have their roots in democratic, human-centered design. Participatory practices utilize the lived expertise of those most affected by inaccessibility, rather than relying on generalized personas or assumptions. This chapter examines how more efficient and moral digital design can be achieved by eschewing token consultation, adopting open-source collaboration, emphasizing equity, and creating long-term feedback mechanisms.

7.1 Moving from Consultation to Collaboration

Disabled and neurodivergent people are frequently restricted to feedback roles in traditional accessibility approaches, where they are consulted at the end of the design process or serve as validation points for solutions that have already been established. Despite its good intentions, this method may perpetuate ableist presumptions and ignore the complex requirements of a wide range of users. By involving users as co-creators from the beginning and allowing their viewpoints to influence problem definitions, ideation, prototyping, and testing, participatory design, on the other hand, changes this paradigm.

The origins of this model can be found in the cooperative design traditions of Scandinavia, where workers shaped the technologies that impacted their work (Bødker & Kyng, 1994). This idea is applied to digital accessibility through inclusive co-design meetings, where developers and designers collaborate with disabled people to generate ideas, evaluate designs, and influence results. In digital projects, researchers like Elizabeth Goodman (2011) emphasize shared authorship and mutual respect, arguing that the design process should "create with" rather than just "design for."

Participatory collaboration creates room for a variety of communication and cognitive styles, especially for neurodivergent users. It respects sensory preferences, encourages nonlinear thinking, and permits multimodal feedback (such as voice notes and visual sketches)—all of which allow for various forms of participation rather than imposing strict structures. This method creates innovative ideas, builds trust, and produces solutions that are intentionally more inclusive.

7.2 Community-Led Innovation and Open-Source Practices

Strong models for decentralizing authority and empowering marginalized groups can be found in open-source design and community-led innovation. Software that is highly customized, context-aware, and morally consistent with user values is produced when disabled or neurodivergent communities take the initiative to develop their own tools—often out of need and annoyance with mainstream exclusion.

Open-source philosophies of transparency, remixability, and shared ownership naturally align with the disability justice movement's long-standing emphasis on "nothing about us without us" (Benjamin, 2019). Examples of community-initiated tools that have grown through open collaboration include AbleGamers' APX design patterns and Funkify, a browser extension made to simulate disabilities for developers. Neurodivergent contributors can engage asynchronously in settings that encourage independence and low-pressure participation on GitHub and other open platforms.

What Sasha Costanza-Chock calls "design justice," which prioritizes underrepresented voices in both the process and the final product, includes such practices as well. Open-source initiatives can foster innovation and inclusivity when they are regulated by inclusive codes of conduct and give priority to accessibility in contribution workflows (Costanza-Chock, 2020). Furthermore, by fostering skill-sharing and cross-pollination, these ecosystems enable disabled users to become innovators and changemakers in addition to consumers.

7.3 Equity-Centered Design Workshops

Workshops on equity-centered design provide a methodical approach to bringing to light lived experiences, exposing prejudice, and collaboratively creating inclusive solutions. By specifically addressing privilege, power, and systemic injustice, these workshops go beyond typical user testing or brainstorming sessions. The Equity-Centered Community Design (ECCD) model, which was developed by organizations such as Creative Reaction Lab, encourages facilitators to identify historical marginalization and use process design to actively disrupt it.

Equity workshops may incorporate activities like privilege mapping, disability storytelling, and empathy interviews in accessibility contexts. These techniques give participants a forum to discuss how digital tools have benefited or hurt them and to jointly envision more equitable options. Facilitators must guarantee both cognitive and physical access, for instance by providing breaks, speaking in simple terms, and offering a variety of expression options, such as writing, drawing, or verbal discussion.

Designers and developers must critically examine themselves when using equity-centered approaches. Exclusion is frequently inadvertent, but inclusion is also unintentional unless it is purposefully planned, as Kat Holmes contends in Mismatch: How Inclusion Shapes Design (Holmes, 2018). As a result, these workshops are a development resource as well as a teaching tool that help teams integrate inclusion into their corporate culture rather than just their output.

7.4 Sustained Engagement and Inclusive Feedback Loops

Inclusive design is a continuous effort rather than a one-time occurrence. Establishing trust, fostering long-term relationships with neurodivergent and disabled communities, and putting in place mechanisms for ongoing feedback and adaptation are all necessary for sustained engagement. These might be user advocacy panels, advisory councils, or seasoned beta testing teams that are valued for their contributions and paid for their work.

Additionally, these feedback loops need to be accessible on their own. Not every user will benefit from traditional feedback methods like surveys or official usability reports. Richer, more genuine answers can be obtained using alternate formats like voice memos, screen recordings, or visual storytelling. Not just through static checklists or recurring audits, inclusive digital products develop via discussion, iteration, and responsiveness to real-world use.

Importantly, feedback should influence strategic choices, such as branding and feature prioritization, in addition to bug fixes. According to Anne-Marie Imafidon, 2022 "Diversity without power is decoration." Transparency and accountability must therefore be incorporated into the design lifecycle, and sustained engagement must entail both hearing and acting upon marginalized voices.

8 LEGAL, ETHICAL, AND POLICY FRAMEWORKS

Building truly inclusive digital environments necessitates a thorough understanding of legal requirements, ethical responsibilities, and sociocultural dynamics in addition to technological solutions and design heuristics. The rights of people with disabilities to access digital services are safeguarded by legally binding standards. But inclusion is not the same as compliance. Beyond the bare minimum, ethical development recognizes the complex identities and global diversity of people with disabilities and neurodivergent people, while also acknowledging power, privacy, and participation. This chapter examines the ways in which intersectional thinking, responsible software development, and accessibility laws combine to create more equitable digital futures.

8.1 Global Accessibility Standards (WCAG, ADA, EN 301 549)

Technical standards and legal requirements serve as the cornerstones of accessibility compliance. The Web Content Accessibility Guidelines (WCAG), created by the World Wide Web Consortium (W3C), are the most extensively used framework. These guidelines specify how to make digital content robust, comprehensible, operable, and perceptible for users with a range of disabilities. Although WCAG is not a law in and of itself, it is incorporated into numerous national regulations, such as Section 508 in the United States, and is essential to both public and private sector legal obligations.

Despite being passed in 1990, the Americans with Disabilities Act (ADA) has been interpreted by the Department of Justice and courts to apply to digital spaces, particularly under Titles II and III. As a result, businesses have been held responsible for their failure to make their websites and mobile apps accessible in a number of historic cases (such as Robles v. Domino's Pizza). Courts frequently use WCAG guidelines for adjudication because the ADA lacks a specific technical standard for web accessibility.

With EN 301 549, the European accessibility standard mandated for all websites and mobile applications in the public sector under the EU Web Accessibility Directive, Europe has adopted a more standardized approach. WCAG 2.1 is incorporated into EN 301 549, but it is expanded to include ICT products such as hardware, software, and documentation. Although many nations in Asia, Latin America, and Africa have begun implementing or citing WCAG-based policies, regional differences in awareness and enforcement practices are significant.

Even with these standards in place, usability is not always guaranteed by compliance, particularly for users who are neurodivergent. For example, a website may be cognitively overwhelming even though it complies with WCAG color contrast guidelines. In order to provide functional accessibility that satisfies actual user needs, designers must exercise critical and creative thinking, even though legal standards set a minimum threshold.

8.2 Ethical Software Development and Data Governance

Although following the law is crucial, developing software that is ethical requires a deeper moral commitment to user autonomy, justice, and well-being. When designing for neurodivergent and disabled users, whose needs might not be adequately met by current regulations, this is especially important. Informed consent, openness, privacy by design, and human supervision are all emphasized in ethical frameworks; these are particularly important in AI-driven systems and adaptive interfaces.

Data governance is one of the main issues in ethical development. Personalization engines, predictive text, and emotion recognition tools are just a few of the accessibility features that depend on gathering and evaluating private user data. Such information may disclose facets of cognitive or psychological identity that users would rather not be seen when working with neurodivergent populations. According to ethical standards, data collection must be reasonable, purpose-specific, and expressly consented to, with risks and benefits clearly explained.

European frameworks such as the General Data Protection Regulation (GDPR) provide a model for responsible data governance by enforcing stringent user rights regarding data portability, erasure, and consent. Algorithmic bias can arise when systems are trained on normative datasets that disregard disability variance, which is another requirement for ethical development. In addition to inviting disabled stakeholders to participate in every stage of development—not just for feedback, but also for shared authorship—developers must test for unintentional exclusion.

Furthermore, accountability is necessary for ethical development. This entails setting up grievance procedures for users to report harms, publishing accessibility impact assessments, and putting ethics review boards into place. Ethical design must confront the systems that make marginalized groups seem like afterthoughts in the first place, as scholars like Ruha Benjamin contend in Race After Technology. Developing technology that actively empowers neurodivergent and disabled users is more important than simply "doing no harm."

8.3 Intersectionality and Cross-Cultural Accessibility

Disability is not a single entity. It shapes wildly disparate experiences of access and exclusion by intersecting with language, geography, class, gender, and race. We can better comprehend how overlapping identities create compound barriers to digital access by using the term "intersectionality," which was first used by Kimberlé Crenshaw. For instance, a low-income neurodivergent woman of color may experience infrastructural limitations, cultural stigma, and financial constraints—all of which exacerbate digital exclusion.

Intersectionality in accessibility design necessitates context-sensitive methods. A blind user who speaks an indigenous language without digital text-to-speech support might not benefit from an English-language screen reader. Similarly, autistic users from collectivist cultures might interact with social or educational technologies differently than those from individualistic societies due to their different experiences and expressions of neurodivergence. These observations cast doubt on the applicability of one-size-fits-all criteria.

Digital literacy, technological infrastructure, and sensitivity to local values are also necessary for cross-cultural accessibility. For example, cognitive aids might need to be localized to take into consideration regional metaphors or culturally specific learning styles, while tactile interfaces might be more appropriate in low-bandwidth areas. Furthermore, there is a great deal of social stigma associated with disabilities in some nations, which deters people from expressing their needs or asking for accommodations. Designers need to make inclusive spaces that are easily adjustable, respectful of cultural differences, and anonymous when needed.

Using intersectional and cross-cultural frameworks improves the robustness and relevance of design while also increasing inclusivity. Instead of being a static checklist, it reframes accessibility as a dynamic and changing practice. The most marginalized people must be at the center of inclusive design, as Sasha Costanza-Chock highlights in Design Justice, and they must be held accountable for both the design process and its results. Accessibility needs to be as varied as the users it seeks to serve in today's globally interconnected world.

9 SECTORAL CASE STUDIES

Across industries that have a direct impact on people's daily lives, inclusive digital design takes the form of real-world applications. In the fields of public infrastructure, health care, education, and finance, either deliberate inclusion can significantly empower people or bad design can make exclusion worse. The application of universal and neurodivergent-inclusive principles in complex systems is demonstrated through sector-specific case studies. These studies also highlight areas that urgently require more innovation and policy changes. Designers, technologists, and legislators can create more accessible, human-centered solutions by examining what works (and what doesn't) in each of these fields.

9.1 Inclusive Health Tech Interfaces

With the growing use of digital tools in the healthcare industry, such as electronic health records (EHRs) and telehealth platforms, accessible interface design is crucial to providing equitable care. Inadequately designed health technology can lead to missed diagnoses, misinterpreted medical instructions, or increased anxiety in neurodivergent and disabled users. People with autism, ADHD, or cognitive impairments find it especially difficult to use interfaces that are overflowing with modal popups, jargon, or visually overwhelming information. Customizability, simplicity, and clarity are given top priority in inclusive health tech interfaces. During medical interactions, features like visual scheduling tools, simplified layouts, and adjustable font sizes can lessen cognitive load. Though they also raise issues with data privacy and clinical oversight, mental health apps like Woebot and Wysa, which use AI-driven chatbots, show how conversational user interfaces with sympathetic language can support neurodivergent users.

Accessibility features like screen reader compatibility, real-time captioning, and pre-visit questionnaires with instructions in plain language are now being included in telehealth platforms. Role-based access is being investigated by systems such as MyChart and Teladoc Health, which allow support staff or caregivers to help without sacrificing user autonomy. Widespread adoption is still uneven, though, especially among low-income and underserved communities, where infrastructure and digital literacy are further obstacles.

9.2 Neurodivergent-Aware Educational Platforms

Neurodivergent students can benefit greatly from educational technologies, but many mainstream platforms are built on the neurotypical presumptions of linear progression, focus, and memorization. Because of their inconsistent user interface patterns, subpar navigation hierarchies, and lack of support for multimodal learning, platforms like Google Classroom and Blackboard can be cognitively overwhelming. Disengagement or even withdrawal from formal education settings may result from this.

Individualized learning pathways, sensory modulation, and executive functioning are all supported by neurodivergent-aware platforms. To help with understanding and memory, Glean (formerly Sonocent) enables students to record lectures while adding voice cues and color-coded notes. In a similar vein, ModMath uses a structured, touch-based interface that eliminates the need for handwritten input to assist students with dyslexia and dysgraphia in solving math problems.

To encourage visual thinking and task organization, other platforms, such as MindMeister or Trello, are being modified for use in inclusive classrooms. More sophisticated programs, such as CogBooks, use adaptive learning algorithms that modify the pace and level of difficulty in response to student performance. This method is especially helpful for autistic students who might need constant reinforcement. To prevent ableist bias in digital pedagogy, inclusive design in education must also encompass classroom management tools, communication channels, and content moderation.

9.3 Simplified Interfaces in Financial and Public Services

Government services and financial systems are notoriously hard to use, with complicated authentication procedures, a lot of text, ambiguous form fields, and strict deadlines. Such complexity makes it extremely difficult for neurodivergent users to participate in basic life activities like banking, tax filing, and social benefit applications, particularly for those who suffer from cognitive fatigue, anxiety, or low literacy.

Fintech apps like Cleo, Monzo, and Cash App are increasingly using chat-based interactions, emoji-labeled buttons, and AI-powered budgeting tools to make user interaction easier. All users gain from these features, but those who are intimidated or confused by traditional interfaces will find them especially useful. For example, Cleo provides real-time budgeting advice in natural language when users ask questions like "Can I afford pizza tonight?"

Services like GOV.UK and MyGov India are leading the way in the public sector in terms of simplifying user interfaces. To guarantee that vital government services are accessible to people of all abilities, features like accessible iconography, plain-language content, and progressive disclosure are being implemented. These initiatives must, however, extend beyond desktop access and guarantee inclusivity on mobile devices, as many users of digital services come from low-income or rural backgrounds.

9.4 Smart Cities and Public Infrastructure Technologies

Ensuring accessibility in smart city infrastructure is a crucial equity issue as cities incorporate digital systems into urban planning, safety, transportation, and utilities. Wayfinding technologies, sensor-enabled street crossings, public kiosks, and transit apps are frequently created without enough input from stakeholders who are disabled or neurodivergent, which results in features that are hazardous or challenging to use.

Curb-level digital signage with programmable brightness, real-time navigation apps with text-to-speech and haptic cues, and smart ticketing systems with cognitively friendly workflows are all examples of smart cities that incorporate inclusive principles. Blind and low-vision people can navigate more easily thanks to the Navilens system, which is used in places like Barcelona and New York and offers visual markers that smartphones can read from a distance.

Furthermore, inclusive urban technology incorporates participatory governance in addition to assistive features. Users can tag and evaluate public spaces' accessibility using tools like AccessNow and Mapathon projects (like Wheelmap), which provide information for local decision-making. With the use of disabled citizens' real-world context, these feedback loops assist city planners in identifying gaps and making improvements.

The flexibility of smart cities holds promise, but if they are not planned with inclusivity in mind from the beginning, these infrastructures run the risk of automating exclusion. Public-private partnerships must include disability advocacy organizations, implement digital access guidelines, and make a commitment to ongoing accessibility audits of urban technologies in order to stop this.

10 CONCLUSION

10.1 Reframing Accessibility as Innovation

Accessibility has traditionally been viewed as an afterthought, something that is added after the fact to satisfy public relations or legal requirements. However, as this book's chapters have shown, accessibility is about maximizing human diversity, not just about addressing edge cases. More user-friendly, effective, and broadly applicable technologies become possible when accessibility is viewed as a catalyst for innovation rather than a list of requirements. We are forced by inclusive design to rethink what digital systems can be—not just more equitable, but also more innovative, flexible, and future-ready.

The philosophical underpinnings of this concept were established in Chapter 1, which demonstrated how designing with users—particularly those who are neurodivergent and disabled—reveals gaps in traditional thinking. For example, text-to-speech and predictive text—features created for individuals with disabilities—have become commonplace technologies that are utilized by all. Design that integrates emotional intelligence, sensory adaptation, and cognitive flexibility benefits all users, not just those who are marginalized. Digital experiences can become more responsive and human-centric by dynamically adapting to user needs through AI-driven personalization and context-aware interfaces, as demonstrated in later Chapter.

We saw how rethinking accessibility as a catalyst for better design benefits inclusive health tech, education, finance, and smart cities throughout the sectoral case studies (Chapter 9). Public services employing streamlined digital workflows, financial platforms like Cleo, and educational tools like Glean or ModMath show that what benefits neurodivergent users also benefits aging populations, busy professionals, and non-native speakers. Innovation driven by accessibility is a competitive advantage, not a concession. In a similar vein, smart cities that incorporate participatory accessibility mapping or haptic wayfinding become more responsive and livable for all residents, not just a select few.

Changes in ethics, policy, and procedure are also necessary to reframe accessibility as innovation. As explained in Chapter 8, justice cannot be guaranteed by merely following the law; in order to create systems that change with users, ethical design, collaborative co-creation (Chapter 7), and ongoing community involvement (Chapter 6) are required. Intersectionality must be taken into consideration when governing accessibility, and accessibility must be integrated into CI/CD processes and continuously monitored. This entails accepting diversity as a model for more resilient, inclusive technology ecosystems rather than as a hurdle to be surmounted. In the end, accessibility is an invitation to create better systems, cultivate greater empathy, and create a more inclusive digital future rather than a limitation.

11 REFERENCES

Abascal, J., & Nicolle, C. A. (2005). Moving towards inclusive design guidelines for socially and ethically aware HCI. *Interacting with Computers*, *17*(5), 484–505. DOI: 10.1016/j.intcom.2005.03.002

Benjamin, R. (2019). *Race After Technology: Abolitionist Tools for the New Jim Code*. Polity Press.

Blackburn, D. (2016). The Curb-Cut Effect: How making public spaces accessible helps everyone. *Stanford Social Innovation Review*.

Bødker, S., & Kyng, M. (1994). Participatory Design that Matters—Facing the Big Issues. *Communications of the ACM*.

Brown, L., Eynon, R., & Johnson, H. (2021). Cognitive accessibility: The overlooked dimension of digital inclusion. *Disability & Society*, *36*(5), 789–808.

Brumberg, J. S., Pitt, K. M., & Burnison, J. D. (2020). Adaptive interfaces for AAC: The role of machine learning. *Disability and Rehabilitation. Assistive Technology*, *15*(4), 397–404.

. Cermak-Sassenrath, D. (2020). *Designing Games for Diverse Players: A Framework for Including Neurodivergent Gamers*. Journal of Game Design & Development Education.

Chen, G., Davis, K., & Li, Y. (2021). Context-aware adaptive learning environments: A review of research and practice. *Computers & Education*, *163*, 104114.

Costanza-Chock, S. (2020). *Design Justice: Community-Led Practices to Build the Worlds We Need*. MIT Press. DOI: 10.7551/mitpress/12255.001.0001

. Creative Reaction Lab. (2021). *Equity-Centered Community Design Field Guide*.

Crenshaw, K. (1991). Mapping the Margins: Intersectionality, Identity Politics, and Violence Against Women of Color. *Stanford Law Review*, *43*(6), 1241. DOI: 10.2307/1229039

. Deque Systems. (2023). *axe Accessibility Engine*. Retrieved from

Design Justice Network. (2018). *Design Justice Principles*. Retrieved from.

. European Union. (2016). *General Data Protection Regulation (GDPR)*. Official Journal of the EU.

Friedman, B., & Hendry, D. G. (2019). *Value Sensitive Design: Shaping Technology with Moral Imagination*. MIT Press. DOI: 10.7551/mitpress/7585.001.0001

GitLab Docs. (2023). Accessibility [*CD*. Retrieved from]. *Test*, •••, CI.

Goodman, E. (2011). Three Questions About Design and Ethics. *Interaction*.

Henry, S. L., Abou-Zahra, S., & Brewer, J. (2014). The role of accessibility in a universal web. *Journal of Web Engineering*, *13*(1–2), 1–18.

Holmes, K. (2018). *Mismatch: How Inclusion Shapes Design*. MIT Press. DOI: 10.7551/mitpress/11647.001.0001

Imafidon, A. (2022). *She's in CTRL: How Women Can Take Back Tech*. Transworld.

Mace, R. (1985). *Universal Design: Barrier-Free Environments for Everyone*. North Carolina State University, The Center for Universal Design.

Maes, P., & Chang, A. (2021). *Multisensory Virtual Reality for Neurodivergent Audiences. Proceedings of the IEEE International Symposium on Mixed and Augmented Reality*.

. Microsoft Inclusive Design Toolkit. (2020). *Designing for Cognitive Diversity*.

. Microsoft Inclusive Design Toolkit. (2020). *Designing for Neurodiversity*.

Microsoft Inclusive Design Toolkit. (2023).

. Mindset Works. (2020). *Brainology: Growth Mindset Curriculum*.

Nielsen, J. (1994). *Heuristic Evaluation*. In *Usability Inspection Methods*.

. Nussbaum, M. (2006). *Frontiers of Justice: Disability, Nationality, Species Membership*. Harvard University Press.

Oliver, M. (1990). *The Politics of Disablement*. Palgrave Macmillan. DOI: 10.1007/978-1-349-20895-1

Schneider, O.. (2017). Haptic Feedback in Virtual Reality: The Importance of User Preferences. *IEEE Transactions on Haptics*.

. Seeman, L., et al. (2017). *Making content usable for people with cognitive and learning disabilities*. W3C Working Group Note.

Singer, J. (1998). *Odd People In: The Birth of Community Amongst People on the Autistic Spectrum*. PhD thesis, University of Technology, Sydney.

Smith, M. J.. (2020). Project VOISS: Virtual Reality to Promote Employment Skills in Adolescents with Autism. *Journal of Autism and Developmental Disorders*.

Sweller, J., Ayres, P., & Kalyuga, S. (2011). *Cognitive Load Theory*. Springer. DOI: 10.1007/978-1-4419-8126-4

. U.S. Department of Justice. (2022). *Guidance on Web Accessibility and the ADA*.

Walker, N. (2021). *Neuroqueer Heresies: Notes on the Neurodiversity Paradigm, Autistic Empowerment, and Postnormal Possibilities*. Autonomous Press.

. XR Access Initiative. (2021). *Making XR Accessible*.

Zolyomi, A., & Schmalz, M. (2017). Developing Inclusive Games for Children with Autism Spectrum Disorder. *ACM Transactions on Accessible Computing*, *10*(4), 54.

Section 2
Methodologies and Inclusive Design Models

Chapter 3
Active Model for Co-Building Apps With Deaf Users Through Workshop

Andrés Eduardo Fuentes-Cortázar
Universidad Veracruzana, Mexico

José Rafael Rojano-Cáceres
https://orcid.org/0000-0002-3878-4571
Universidad Veracruzana, Mexico

ABSTRACT

The inclusion of Deaf communities in technology development is essential for creating accessible and culturally sensitive solutions; however, challenges remain in ensuring their active participation. This study proposes and validates an Active Model for Co-Building Apps with Deaf Users to facilitate their involvement in the design, development, and adoption of tailored technological solutions through user workshops. A participatory virtual workshop was conducted in four phases—Preparation, Implementation, Development, and Results—which incorporated visual communication methods, sign language interpreters, accessible resources, and hands-on activities. Participants developed, installed, and shared functional mobile application prototypes, demonstrating the model's effectiveness in fostering technical skills, creativity, and autonomy. The Active Model proves to be an effective strategy for co-creating inclusive technologies with Deaf users, ensuring culturally appropriate solutions and contributing to the digital and social inclusion of the community.

DOI: 10.4018/979-8-3373-6033-1.ch003

INTRODUCTION

Contemporary software development demands going beyond the fulfillment of strictly functional criteria. It is no longer sufficient for an application to operate correctly from a technical standpoint; it has become essential to integrate a deep and nuanced understanding of users' expectations, perceptions, and needs (Allam & Dahlan, 2013; Norman, 2013; Orero, 2022). This perspective is critical not only for ensuring the operational efficiency of digital products, but also for creating user experiences that are meaningful, satisfying, and emotionally resonant.

Inclusive technology design requires genuine collaboration with end users, particularly those belonging to communities that are often overlooked in traditional development processes (Harrison et al., 2015; Santoso & Schrepp, 2019). In this context, the *Active Model for Co-Constructing Applications with Deaf Users* addresses this need by providing a structured and participatory framework tailored to the unique cultural, linguistic, and accessibility characteristics of Deaf individuals.

This model is organized into four distinct yet interconnected phases: (1) Preparation Phase; (2) User Workshop Execution Phase; (3) Development, Documentation, and Analysis Phase; and (4) Implementation of Results Phase. Each phase encompasses specific components that foster effective communication, cultural sensitivity, and iterative co-creation. Through this approach, the model supports the creation of accessible technological solutions that authentically reflect the needs and preferences of Deaf users.

By following the Active Model, developers and researchers can systematically engage Deaf communities, ensuring that their perspectives and lived experiences are integrated throughout the design process. The model also emphasizes ethical considerations—such as informed consent and participant validation—thereby fostering trust, respect, and accountability. The sections that follow describe each phase in detail, providing a comprehensive roadmap for replicating and adapting this methodology across diverse educational and research contexts.

This study presents a methodological framework grounded in a participatory and culturally sensitive approach for the co-construction of mobile applications with Deaf users. The key findings are based on an evaluation of the framework's effectiveness through the participation of Deaf users during a user workshop and the final prototypes generated by the participants. The results demonstrate that, by actively involving Deaf users in design decisions, it is possible to develop technological solutions that are more inclusive and better aligned with their actual needs.

It is worth noting that the development process proposed in this paper follows an iterative approach, in which users themselves participate in decision-making at multiple stages, rather than adhering to a single, linear product development cycle. This strategy promotes not only the creation of functional prototypes but also the strengthening of technical competencies and the empowerment of the Deaf community through ownership of the process, thereby ensuring effective and authentic participation throughout all phases of development.

DEAFNESS

The term deafness is used to describe a significant or total hearing loss that affects an individual's ability to communicate and engage socially. According to the definition provided by the World Health Organization (WHO), hearing loss is considered disabling when an individual has hearing difficulties greater than 40 decibels in the better-hearing ear for adults, or greater than 30 decibels for children. This level of hearing impairment presents a substantial barrier to perceiving and understanding environmental sounds and everyday speech (Sheffield & Smith, 2019). The term "Deaf" with a capital "D" is used to describe a cultural group that identifies through the use of sign language as their primary means of communication (Leigh et al., 2020). This community, known as the Deaf Community, shares not only a hearing condition but also a distinct cultural and linguistic identity.

Factors Associated with Hearing Loss

Hearing loss can occur at various stages throughout life, depending on a wide range of biological, environmental, and social factors. Although it may develop at any age, there are particularly critical periods during which susceptibility to auditory impairments is heightened, whether due to congenital, acquired, or degenerative conditions. Below is an overview of the main stages of human development and the factors associated with the onset of hearing loss in each of them (Ensing, et al., 2025).

Prenatal Period

During the prenatal stage, hearing loss is often associated with genetic or hereditary causes, which may include specific mutations responsible for congenital hearing impairments. Additionally, acquired factors such as intrauterine infections can affect the development of the fetal auditory system, leading to structural or functional damage that may become evident at birth or later in life.

Perinatal Period

During the perinatal period, which includes birth and the immediate postnatal phase, various events can compromise the integrity of the auditory system. Among the most significant risk factors are perinatal asphyxia, hyperbilirubinemia, prematurity, and other morbidities associated with childbirth. These conditions can cause sensorineural damage to the auditory pathway or affect the inner ear, resulting in varying degrees of hearing loss.

Childhood and Adolescence

During childhood and adolescence, hearing loss may result from infectious and/or inflammatory factors. Chronic or recurrent otitis media, as well as serious infectious diseases such as meningitis, can lead to temporary or permanent hearing impairment. Additionally, limited access to adequate healthcare services during these stages can contribute to delayed diagnosis, which in turn may negatively affect language development, learning, and socialization.

Adulthood and Old Age

In adulthood—and more frequently in old age—hearing loss is often linked to degenerative processes and chronic illnesses. Presbycusis, or age-related progressive hearing loss, is one of the most common causes. Other contributing conditions include otosclerosis, sudden sensorineural hearing loss, and cardiovascular or metabolic diseases that impair blood flow and the functioning of the inner ear.

Lifelong Factors

There are also factors that can occur at any stage of life and pose ongoing risks to hearing. These include traumatic brain injuries or direct damage to the ear, prolonged or repeated exposure to high-intensity noise, the use of ototoxic substances, and certain viral infections acquired at different points throughout the lifespan. All these factors can have a cumulative—and often irreversible—impact on auditory function.

Understanding Deaf Culture

The study of the cultural context of Deaf individuals is fundamental for understanding the particularities, challenges, and strengths that characterize this community. Deafness not only entails a physiological condition or a disability but also constitutes a cultural and linguistic dimension that profoundly influences identity, social practices, and forms of interaction among its members (Hidden reference).

The Deaf community (or Deaf communities, in plural) shares a set of values, norms, traditions, and modes of communication that form the foundation of their collective identity. Deaf culture is not limited to the presence of a hearing impairment, but also encompasses linguistic, social, and cultural aspects that are transmitted from generation to generation.

It is essential to recognize that within the Deaf community, sign language is not merely a communication tool but a fundamental pillar of cultural identity. There are various sign languages around the world—such as Mexican Sign Language (LSM), American Sign Language (ASL), or Brazilian Sign Language (LIBRAS)—each with its own grammar, vocabulary, and expressiveness, reflecting unique ways of understanding and interacting with reality. Valuing sign language not only acknowledges the specificity of the Deaf experience but also challenges hegemonic notions of communication, expanding our understanding of what it means to exist and engage within a community (Lillo-Martin & Henner, 2021).

The cultural identity of Deaf individuals is deeply rooted in their language and social practices. Many Deaf people view their condition not as a limitation but as a dimension of their cultural identity, one with which they feel pride and empowerment. However, they also face challenges arising from social marginalization, discrimination, and communication barriers that limit their full inclusion in various social, economic, and educational spheres.

Understanding these dynamics is essential for designing inclusive technologies. Recognizing the linguistic, social, and cultural particularities of Deaf users enables the creation of solutions that are both accessible and culturally relevant, while supporting the community's ability to make independent decisions and fully participate in the use and development of these technologies.

INTERNATIONAL FRAMEWORKS AND CONSORTIA ON TECHNOLOGICAL ACCESSIBILITY

Several international consortia and organizations have established frameworks, guidelines, and standards to promote accessibility in digital technologies, thereby facilitating the inclusion of individuals with diverse abilities. The *World Wide Web Consortium (W3C)* stands out for its leadership in this field, having developed the *Web Content Accessibility Guidelines (WCAG)*, which provide concrete recommendations to ensure that digital content is *perceivable, operable, understandable,* and *robust* for all users, including those with disabilities such as the Deaf community (World Wide Web Consortium, 2024).

Similarly, the *Google Material Design* consortium has incorporated accessibility principles into its design guidelines to ensure inclusive digital environments, encouraging features such as screen reader compatibility, adequate color contrast, and accessible interactive elements (Google Design Team, 2025).

In addition, institutions such as the *National Institute of Standards and Technology (NIST)* in the United States and the *European Union Agency for Cybersecurity (ENISA)* provide specific guidance for integrating accessibility into emerging technologies such as artificial intelligence and augmented reality (Bostelman, 2010).

These international frameworks reflect a global commitment to inclusive digital transformation. Adopting these standards in research and technological development projects ensures that products are universal and adaptable to the needs of diverse communities, including Deaf individuals. Integrating these guidelines into the design process fosters the creation of truly accessible and responsible solutions, contributing to the reduction of digital divides and the promotion of full and equitable participation.

MODELS AND ACCESSIBILITY

The literature presents a range of proposals focused on the development of models aimed at enhancing accessibility to various technological solutions. These models are designed to ensure that technological systems are not only functional but also inclusive, addressing the diverse needs of users, particularly those with disabilities, and facilitating their access to technology in an equitable manner.

Accessibility Models

Some proposals criticize traditional approaches, such as the waterfall model or the spiral model, noting that, although they meet the needs of people without disabilities, they often overlook those of people with disabilities. To address this limitation, a Process Model was developed that integrates accessibility and usability, promoting more inclusive systems tailored to a greater diversity of users (Nganji & Nggada, 2011).

Another relevant proposal is the Conceptual Model for Accessible Software Development, which emphasizes the integration of electronic accessibility as a core aspect of the development process. This model treats accessibility not as an isolated stage, but as a cross-cutting feature that should be present throughout the entire software development lifecycle (Silva & Branco, 2019).

One of these models is the Usability and Accessibility Engineering Process Model (MPIu+a), which proposes a user-centered approach to the development of interactive systems. Its main objective is to maximize usability and the user experience in the final system, while consistently maintaining an accessibility-focused perspective (Pascual Almenara & Granollers, 2024).

The lack of accessibility in software products presents a complex challenge, largely due to the absence of accessible support tools and the limited training of software professionals in accessibility-related matters. In response to this issue, the model-driven development approach has gained the interest of the accessible software community, thanks to its potential to automatically generate code from models. In this context, research has emerged that, through systematic reviews, compiles studies related to model-driven accessible software development (Ordoñez et al., 2022).

DESIGNING TOGETHER: AN ACTIVE MODEL FOR CO-BUILDING APPS WITH DEAF USERS

This section presents the Active Model for Co-Building Apps with Deaf Users, which has been designed based on a structure composed of various interrelated components that enable its systematic implementation and adaptation to the specific needs of deaf individuals.

Throughout the following subsections, the model's key components, internal structure, and guiding principles will be detailed, with the aim of providing a comprehensive understanding that facilitates its replicability and adjustment across different intervention contexts.

1. **Phase 1: Preparation Phase**
   a. Components:
      i. Definition of the Workshop Objectives
      ii. Planning of the Workshop Sessions
      iii. Selection of the Profile of Deaf Users
      iv. Inclusion of Sign Language Interpreters
      v. Adapting the Physical or Virtual Environment
      vi. Design Accessible Materials
      vii. Sensitization of the Organizing Team
2. **Phase 2: User Workshop Execution Phase**
   a. Components:
      i. Participant Introduction Activities
      ii. Use of Sign Language as the Primary Channel of Communication
      iii. Culturally Sensitive Moderation
      iv. Data Collection During the Workshop
3. **Phase 3: Development, Documentation and Analysis Phase**
   a. Components:
      i. Workshop Recordings
      ii. Visual-Linguistic Transcription and Translation

iii. Deaf Users Validation

4. **Phase 4: Implementation of Results Phase**
   a. Components:
      i. Translating Needs into Requirements
      ii. Iterative Participatory Design
      iii. Accessible Communication and Feedback to the Community
      iv. Delivering the Final Technological Solution to the Deaf Community

Phase 1: Preparation Phase

Set the necessary conditions for the development of the accessible user workshop, ensuring that all communicative, logistical, and inclusive aspects are considered from the outset. This phase is critical to guarantee the effective participation of Deaf individuals, who face cognitive and communicative barriers in conventional research or technological development contexts. Proper preparation promotes not only formal inclusion but also meaningful participation.

Definition of the Workshop Objectives

One of the fundamental initial steps in organizing an accessible workshop for deaf participants is the clear and precise definition of its objectives. Establishing in advance what is expected to be achieved through this activity allows for a coherent direction in both its methodological design and practical implementation. These objectives should align with the overall goals of the technological development project within which the workshop is framed, ensuring they contribute meaningfully to its progress.

In this regard, it is essential to consider a series of key questions: What type of information is intended to be gathered from the participating deaf individuals? What will be the scope of the workshop in terms of content and expected outcomes? Is the primary purpose to identify needs, validate existing prototypes, or generate ideas during the early stages of the design process?

Formulating these objectives not only defines the workshop's purpose but also enables the selection of the most appropriate participatory techniques, the identification of user profiles to be invited, and the establishment of criteria for evaluating the results obtained. A rigorous definition of the objectives thus serves as the central pillar around which the comprehensive planning of the workshop is structured.

Planning of the Workshop Sessions

The planning of the workshop sessions constitutes a fundamental component to ensure effectiveness and coherence in the development of the activity. This stage involves structuring each meeting by defining both the content to be covered and the participatory dynamics that facilitate interaction and meaningful learning for Deaf participants. It is equally important to list the materials required for the workshop.

To develop an appropriate plan, it is necessary to consider the specific objectives of the workshop and the profile of the participants, adapting the content and methodologies to respond to their communicative and cognitive characteristics. Each session should be designed with an inclusive approach, incorporating accessible visual and technological resources, as well as the continuous presence of Sign Language interpreters to ensure effective communication.

Furthermore, a clear schedule should be established to distribute topics and activities evenly, avoiding cognitive overload and allowing sufficient time for reflection, exchange of ideas, and feedback. Additionally, the planning must include the necessary flexibility to address unforeseen circumstances and adapt to group dynamics, fostering a collaborative and trusting environment.

Selection of the Profile of Deaf Users

A crucial aspect in organizing accessible workshops for deaf individuals is the clear definition and selection of a representative participant profile. This selection should take into account various factors that capture the diversity inherent within the deaf community. Relevant variables include age, educational background, literacy level, technology usage, Sign Language proficiency, as well as the type and degree of hearing loss.

The selection process should aim to reflect the diversity present within the community—considering not only audiological differences but also sociocultural, linguistic, and regional factors. A well-defined and inclusive participant profile is a foundational element for any participatory design initiative, as it ensures that it represents the multiplicity of experiences and needs within the Deaf community.

Inclusion of Sign Language Interpreters

The presence of professional Sign Language interpreters is an essential requirement for conducting truly accessible workshops aimed at deaf participants. It is crucial to plan in advance for the availability of qualified interpreters, ideally with experience in technical or academic settings, where the accuracy and fidelity of interpretation are critical to ensuring the correct transmission of information. Additionally, it is recommended to have more than one interpreter present during activities to ensure continuous coverage and to prevent physical and mental fatigue, which can impact the quality of interpretation.

In certain contexts, the inclusion of deaf mediators—deaf individuals who serve as cultural bridges between hearing and Deaf communities—can also be highly beneficial. These mediators help facilitate intercultural communication and contribute to creating a more inclusive environment that is sensitive to the cultural specificities of the Deaf community.

Adapting the Physical or Virtual Environment

The setting in which the workshop takes place must be appropriately adapted to ensure optimal conditions that support visual communication—the primary channel used by deaf individuals. In physical spaces, this includes ensuring proper lighting, arranging participants in a circular or semicircular layout to allow direct visual contact, eliminating visual obstructions between users and interpreters, and providing accessible visual resources for everyone.

In the case of virtual workshops, it is essential to ensure that Deaf participants have prior knowledge of how to use videoconferencing platforms. This involves not only becoming familiar with the general interface, but also mastering basic functions necessary for active and seamless participation, such as turning the camera on and off, muting and unmuting the microphone, and using the chat function. Moreover, the chosen platform must allow for the simultaneous visibility of interpreters, facilitators, and shared materials, thereby ensuring a fully accessible and integrated communication experience.

Designing Accessible Materials

All visual or textual content used during the workshop must be carefully adapted to the specific needs of Deaf participants. To achieve this, it is recommended to use:

- Videos with subtitles or Sign Language interpretation.
- Slide presentations with minimal text, supported by icons, pictograms, or infographics to aid comprehension.
- Clear and plain language, avoiding unnecessary technical jargon.
- Questionnaires or interactive activities that do not rely exclusively on written text.

The design of these materials should be carried out in collaboration with accessibility experts or, ideally, with Deaf persons themselves to ensure both cultural and functional appropriateness.

Sensitization of the Organizing Team

Before the workshop begins, it is essential that all members of the organizing team—facilitators, technicians, designers, and researchers—receive basic training on Deaf culture, Deaf identity, and inclusive communication practices. This training not only improves interaction with participants but also promotes an attitude of respect, empathy, and openness toward diverse forms of communication.

It is especially important to understand that Sign Language is not a literal translation of spoken or written Spanish, but a fully developed language with its own grammar and structure. This awareness helps prevent misunderstandings and unethical practices during the workshop.

Phase 2: User Workshop Execution Phase

Set the necessary conditions for the development of the accessible user workshop, ensuring that all communicative, logistical, and inclusion aspects are considered from the outset. This phase is critical to guarantee the effective participation of Deaf individuals, who face cognitive and communicative barriers in conventional research or technological development contexts. Proper preparation promotes not only formal inclusion but also meaningful participation.

Participant Introduction Activities

Before beginning the specific workshop activities, it is essential to create an environment of trust, closeness, and familiarity among participants. Introduction dynamics are designed to facilitate mutual recognition, encourage spontaneous interaction, and establish a solid foundation for inclusive communication throughout the entire process.

In the context of Deaf participants, these activities should be designed with a highly visual approach, featuring a clear structure and adapted to Sign Language as the primary means of interaction. Recommended strategies include:

- Introduction rounds where each participant shares their name sign along with a few personal interests or hobbies.
- Physical activities based on the use of classifiers that promote relaxation and trust-building.

These initial dynamics not only help reduce social anxiety but also foster group cohesion and lay the groundwork for active, meaningful, and barrier-free participation throughout the workshop.

Use of Sign Language as the Primary Channel of Communication

Throughout the workshop, Sign Language should be established as the central and prioritized channel of communication. Promoting its use as the natural means of expression for Deaf participants not only ensures their full inclusion but also honors their linguistic and cultural identity. To support this approach, the following strategies are recommended:

- Encourage Deaf participants to communicate directly in their natural language. However, in virtual settings, written language may be used as an alternative means of communication when necessary.
- The facilitators must speak slowly and clearly to ensure accurate interpretation by sign language interpreters.
- Use of whiteboards or digital tablets during explanations to draw or visually represent core ideas, in parallel with spoken or signed communication. In virtual settings, software that allows for live annotations and drawings should be used.

Whenever possible, include at least one Deaf individual as an assistant facilitator in the workshop. This role not only reinforces the peer-to-peer approach but also helps balance the communicative dynamic and provides positive role models within the group.

Culturally Sensitive Moderation

The facilitation of the workshop must be carried out with deep respect for the identity, culture, and unique forms of interaction of the Deaf community. Deaf individuals share distinct values, practices, and communicative modes; therefore, moderation should be inclusive and attentive to these specificities, ensuring a barrier-free and discrimination-free environment. Key aspects of culturally sensitive moderation include:

- Adjusting the pace of communication, recognizing that Sign Language operates under different temporal dynamics than spoken language. Incorporating planned pauses allows all participants to properly process information, formulate questions, and gives interpreters the time they need to work without overload.

- Ensuring equitable and non-paternalistic treatment of participants, avoiding unfounded assumptions about their ability to understand or their need for constant assistance.
- Maintaining fair and balanced moderation, ensuring all opinions are valued. To support this, clear rules of interaction—such as raising a hand to request a turn—can be established.
- Adapting timing to the actual needs of the group, understanding that each person processes visual information at a different pace. Repeating information, clarifying concepts, and adjusting activities are essential practices to sustain effective inclusion throughout the session.

Data Collection During the Workshop

Data collection during the workshop implementation is an essential process for accurately and systematically documenting the findings, behaviors, and contributions of the participants. To ensure the effectiveness of this task, it is crucial to establish a clear distribution of roles among the organizing team members, assigning specific responsibilities related to the observation and recording of relevant information in real time.

One team member should be dedicated to taking detailed notes, focusing on capturing both verbal and non-verbal interactions, participants' reactions, and any observations that may contribute to a thorough subsequent analysis. This record is complemented by the use of auxiliary resources, such as notebooks and audiovisual recordings, which help preserve a faithful record of the sessions and facilitate comprehensive review of the collected information.

Moreover, direct and continuous observation throughout the workshop is positioned as a central method to understand group dynamics, identify communication barriers, and recognize participation patterns. This observation must be conducted discreetly and respectfully, ensuring that it does not interfere with the natural flow of activities or cause discomfort among participants.

Phase 3: Development, Documentation and Analysis Phase

The main objective of this phase is to systematically record all the information gathered during the workshop, process it with methodological rigor and cultural sensitivity, and extract findings that guide the design of inclusive solutions. This stage is crucial not only to ensure the traceability and reproducibility of the process, but also to guarantee that the voices of deaf individuals are represented faithfully and respectfully throughout the technology development cycle.

Workshop Recordings

Whenever possible, and after obtaining the informed consent of participants, it is recommended to make audiovisual recordings of the workshop sessions. This practice allows for detailed documentation of fundamental aspects of the participatory process, such as:

- The visual and gestural expressions used by participants.
- Contributions made in Sign Language, which might otherwise be lost or distorted in conventional written transcriptions.
- Group interaction dynamics and the level of user engagement with the proposed activities.

These recordings serve as a primary and valuable source of information for subsequent analysis and must be managed in accordance with ethical principles and current data protection regulations. It is essential to establish protocols for confidentiality, secure storage, restricted access, and limited use exclusively for research or participatory design purposes, always respecting the privacy and rights of the individuals involved.

Visual-Linguistic Transcription and Translation

Contributions made in Sign Language should be transcribed and, when necessary, translated into written language with the support of professional interpreters or deaf mediators experienced in research or co-design processes. This work must be carried out with great care to avoid subjective interpretations, potential biases, or the loss of significant nuances conveyed through visual expression.

Beyond conventional textual transcription, it is also possible—and advisable—to produce visual translations that graphically represent emerging ideas and concepts. This may include the creation of diagrams, concept maps, infographics, or visual schemes that faithfully reflect the participants' logic of thought and the relationships between the elements they proposed.

This multidimensional approach to information processing not only preserves the expressive richness inherent in Sign Language, but also facilitates subsequent analysis from an inclusive and accessible perspective.

Deaf Users Validation

One of the fundamental pillars of designing workshops centered on Deaf persons is the participatory validation of the findings obtained. This stage aims to verify that the interpretations made by the organizing team accurately reflect the ideas, needs, priorities, and proposals expressed by participants during the workshop.

Validation serves multiple purposes: on the one hand, it ensures fidelity in data processing; on the other, it strengthens the bond of trust between facilitators and users by acknowledging their active and central role in the process. Moreover, it creates a space for deaf participants to correct or expand upon what was previously expressed, engaging in an ongoing exercise of co-constructing knowledge.

For this stage to be effective, it must take place under fully accessible conditions, with the support of Sign Language interpreters and adapted visual resources. This inclusive methodology not only enhances the quality and relevance of the results, but also reinforces an ethical approach based on mutual respect, active listening, and shared responsibility in the creation of technological solutions that are truly centered on the Deaf community.

Phase 4: Results Implementation Phase

The purpose of this phase is to apply the knowledge gathered throughout the research and participatory process to guide the development of technological solutions that specifically address the communicative, cognitive, and cultural needs of deaf individuals. This involves translating the workshop findings into concrete actions for design and implementation, ensuring that the resulting products authentically reflect the users' experiences and expectations.

Translating Needs into Requirements

This stage involves a systematic exercise of organizing, analyzing, and reinterpreting the findings—both qualitative and quantitative—gathered during the previous phases of the workshop. The main objective is to transform this information into technical guidelines or clear requirements that inform the design, development, and evaluation of accessible technological products or systems.

The needs expressed by deaf individuals must be translated into concrete technical specifications, universal design principles, and operational criteria that ensure an inclusive user experience. This translation must be carried out with methodological rigor and cultural sensitivity, ensuring that design decisions faithfully reflect the needs, communication modes, interaction preferences, and everyday challenges expressed by Deaf users in technological contexts.

It is essential that this conversion is not based solely on abstract technical criteria, but also incorporates the subjective, social, and cultural dimensions that emerged during the participatory process—thus ensuring the development of solutions that are truly centered on Deaf individuals.

Iterative Participatory Design

The development of accessible solutions should not be conceived as a linear process or limited to a one-time user consultation, but rather as an iterative cycle of participatory design that remains active throughout the various phases of the project. In this regard, the continuous involvement of deaf individuals—either those who participated in the initial workshops or others with similar profiles—is encouraged during later stages such as prototype design, functional validation, and usability testing.

This collaborative approach allows for the adjustment and refinement of technological solutions based on the direct experience of those who will ultimately use them. As a result, the final products are more likely not only to meet technical accessibility standards, but also to meaningfully respond to the expectations, preferences, and real-life usage contexts of deaf individuals.

Moreover, this sustained participation strengthens the relationship between designers and users, fosters a sense of ownership of the developed technologies within the community, and supports the consolidation of an inclusive, ethical, and user-centered innovation model.

Accessible Communication and Feedback to the Community

A fundamental ethical and methodological dimension of the process is ensuring that the results are shared not only with the individuals who participated in the workshops, but also with the broader Deaf community. This feedback must be delivered through accessible formats that are both culturally and linguistically appropriate, acknowledging the communicative diversity within the community. To achieve this, a variety of formats can be used, such as:

- Informative videos in Sign Language.
- In-person or virtual presentations with simultaneous interpretation.
- Printed materials with clear, understandable visual design, adapted to different levels of literacy.

This action is not only a form of community validation for the work carried out, but also serves to strengthen ties with the community, foster mutual trust, and encourage a culture of sustained participation. Furthermore, it enables the results to be discussed, adopted, and utilized by other social, educational, or institutional entities working in the field of accessibility and inclusion for deaf individuals.

Delivering the Final Technological Solution to the Deaf Community

An essential step in the process of inclusive and participatory design is ensuring that the final technological solution is effectively delivered to the Deaf community. At the end of the entire development cycle, the product is ultimately intended for this community—therefore, it is both ethically and practically important that they have direct access to the outcome.

Providing the final product is not merely a matter of dissemination; it is an act of recognition, accountability, and respect. It affirms the value of the contributions made by Deaf individuals throughout the participatory process and ensures that the benefits of innovation return to the very community that shaped its development.

This delivery should be carried out through accessible channels and accompanied by appropriate guidance and support to facilitate adoption and use. When possible, this stage can also serve as a space for continued dialogue, allowing users to explore the functionalities of the solution, provide feedback for future improvements, and share the tool within their networks.

Applicability of the Framework in Different Contexts

The Active Framework for the Co-Construction of Apps with Deaf Users is designed to be implemented both in educational settings and in research activities. In education, the framework seeks to facilitate the active participation of Deaf students in the design of accessible digital resources, promoting cultural and linguistic inclusion while fostering the development of technical skills and autonomy in technological creation processes.

In the research context, the framework enables the exploration of participatory and culturally sensitive methodologies for the co-construction of technological solutions, strengthening knowledge in inclusive design and in the generation of knowledge emerging from Deaf communities. The modular and adaptable structure of the model supports validation and replication across different studies and academic environments, fostering innovation in socially responsible technology. Furthermore, through research initiatives, the framework aims to contribute to the development of new accessible solutions for the Deaf community.

Development of the Workshop through Model

To validate and refine the Active Model for Co-Building Apps with Deaf Users, a virtual co-design workshop was conducted with a group of five Deaf users from different regions of Mexico. Participants were selected to ensure diversity in communication profiles and levels of technological experience.

Phase 1: Preparation Phase

Definition of the Workshop Objectives:

The main objective of the workshop was to provide Deaf users with a theoretical and practical introduction to mobile application development, thereby facilitating their engagement with basic software development tools and concepts. The specific objectives that Deaf participants were expected to achieve by the end of the workshop were as follows:

- Identify a relevant issue affecting the Deaf community.
- Design a solution by creating paper prototypes.
- Develop a mobile application using the *MIT App Inventor* platform.
- Install the application on their own mobile devices.
- Share the application with others, both within and outside the community.

Planning of the Workshop Sessions:

The workshop sessions were carefully planned to ensure a balanced combination of theoretical learning, practical activities, and open interaction, all within an accessible and culturally sensitive framework. The planning process considered the linguistic and cognitive preferences of Deaf users, integrating visual communication strategies and flexible pacing to support participant engagement and comprehension. The workshop was structured into four main sessions, each with a specific focus:

- **Session 1:** Course introduction and participant engagement. Activities included presenting objectives, duration, and schedule; participant introductions; trigger questions to foster interaction; an explanation of problem formulation and computational solutions; and the initial design of a paper prototype.
- **Session 2:** Presentation of paper prototypes. Participants shared their designs and explained the motivations behind their proposals.
- **Session 3:** Introduction to *MIT App Inventor*. The session covered platform configuration, installation of the AI2 Companion app, creating a simple proj-

ect with a text button, and replicating the exercise independently for the following session.

- **Session 4:** Review and reinforcement of prior knowledge. Participants revisited the previous activity, received feedback as needed, explored new GUI components, and learned how to compile and build projects for smartphone deployment.
- **Session 5:** Exploration of advanced components. The relevance of containers for grouping elements was explained, along with demonstrations on embedding videos and using the vibration feature.
- **Session 6:** Prototype implementation and presentations. Participants developed their paper prototypes in *MIT App Inventor* and concluded with a presentation round to share and discuss their applications.

Each session was designed to last approximately 90 minutes, including scheduled pauses to ensure effective interpretation and prevent cognitive fatigue. The structure remained flexible to accommodate the pacing needs of the group and ensure full participation. For the course development, it was necessary for participants to have specific tools to facilitate their learning. These included a computer with either *Windows* or *Mac OS* operating system, as well as a mobile phone with an *Android* or *iOS* platform. Additionally, a USB cable was required to connect the phone to the computer for testing the prototypes. Finally, paper and pencils were used to support note-taking and prototyping activities during the workshop.

Selection of the Profile of Deaf Users:

For the development of the user workshop, five Deaf individuals with diverse profiles and characteristics were selected to ensure a representative range within the participant group. Prior to the start of the sessions, a diagnostic questionnaire was administered to gain a deeper understanding of the users' characteristics and skills, allowing for the appropriate adaptation of the workshop content and activities.

Table 1. Deaf participants characteristics

No. of participants	Gender	Age	Education	Sign Language Level	Degree of hearing loss
4	Male	20-25	Undergraduate	Intermediate	Deep – only very loud noises.
1	Female	30-35	Graduate	Advanced	Moderate – doesn't not hear speech

Inclusion of Sign Language Interpreters:

During the user workshop, a Mexican Sign Language (LSM) interpreter participated, bringing over ten years of experience in interpretation within educational and governmental institutions. Her strong professional background, along with her close and active involvement in the Deaf community, contributed significantly to facilitating communication and fostering an atmosphere of trust and inclusion throughout the sessions.

Adapting the Physical or Virtual Environment:

The user workshop was conducted virtually, which required careful planning to ensure both accessibility and effective communication. The hearing instructor and the Mexican Sign Language (LSM) interpreter were assigned as moderators of the video call, allowing their videos to be pinned and remain constantly visible to all participants.

Basic interaction rules were also established to maintain an orderly and respectful environment during the sessions: (a) Use the "raise hand" function on the platform; (b) When a participant is signing or communicating, wait until they have finished before responding; and (c) Keep attention focused on the moderators to minimize distractions. The Deaf users' prior familiarity with videoconferencing platforms significantly contributed to the successful development of the workshop in this format.

Designing Accessible Materials:

The workshop design prioritized visual strategies to support comprehension among Deaf users. Activities focused on the use of predominantly visual resources, including slide presentations with explanatory images and minimal text written in clear and simple language. In addition, subtitled videos were used as educational support materials. The instructor's discourse was also carefully adapted, employing straightforward and accessible language to ensure effective communication for all participants.

Sensitization of the Organizing Team:

The workshop organizing team was composed of three key roles: a lead instructor with experience in software development, a LSM interpreter, and an internal moderator responsible for providing technical support during the video call. Both the instructor and the moderator had prior experience in research related to accessibility for Deaf individuals, which gave them deep insight and a particular sensitivity to the needs, dynamics, and identity of this community. This team structure ensured an inclusive, accessible, and technically smooth learning experience.

Phase 2: User Workshop Execution Phase

Participant Introduction Activities:

During the initial session of the user workshop, the instructor, the interpreter, and the moderator introduced themselves to the Deaf participants, sharing relevant information about their roles and interests. This was followed by a group introduction round, in which each participant stated their name and corresponding sign name. Notably, during this activity, some participants asked questions to get to know their peers better. Integration activities were also carried out, including group dynamics using classifiers related to software development.

Use of Sign Language as the primary channel of communication:

The entire workshop was conducted entirely in Sign Language, which was established as the primary means of communication for delivering all content. This approach ensured an accessible and direct experience for Deaf participants. Nevertheless, a written channel was also made available through the chat interface, allowing attendees to ask questions, express concerns, or request clarifications via that medium. Throughout the workshop, the lead instructor made strategic pauses to allow the interpreter to translate and sign the information to participants, thereby ensuring clear and effective communication for everyone involved.

Culturally Sensitive Moderation:

The workshop was moderated with a strong emphasis on cultural sensitivity towards the Deaf community. Both the instructor and the interpreter maintained an awareness of Deaf culture, norms, and values throughout the sessions, fostering an environment of respect and inclusion. Communication etiquette specific to Deaf participants was observed, such as allowing uninterrupted signing, avoiding speaking over participants, and encouraging turn-taking in discussions. This culturally informed approach helped build trust among participants, facilitating more open and meaningful interactions during the workshop.

Data Collection During the Workshop:

A designated member of the research team was responsible for taking detailed observational notes during each session, capturing interactions in Sign Language, gestures, facial expressions, and the level of participant engagement. These notes were complemented by video recordings of the virtual meetings, providing a reliable and detailed record for subsequent review.

Additionally, participants were encouraged to share their feedback and reflections verbally during the sessions. These dynamics aimed to capture their personal experiences, perceptions of the methodology, and suggestions for improvement. Attention was also given to monitoring the participants' learning progress in developing their functional prototypes, with the goal of adapting different teaching strategies accordingly.

Phase 3: Development, Documentation and Analysis Phase

Workshop Recordings (with Informed Consent):

To ensure accurate documentation and facilitate post-workshop analysis, the entire virtual workshop sessions were recorded. Prior to the start of the workshop, all participants were fully informed about the recording process, its purpose, and how the recordings would be used and stored. Explicit informed consent was obtained from each participant, guaranteeing their voluntary agreement to be recorded. The recordings were reviewed by the entire organizing team in order to deepen the findings of each Deaf user.

Visual-Linguistic Transcription and Translation:

This involved video recordings and annotations being carefully reviewed by the LSM interpreter, who produced detailed transcriptions and translations into written Spanish. These transcriptions not only captured the linguistic content but also considered non-manual markers, facial expressions, and body language critical for meaning in sign language. The translation process was conducted with cultural sensitivity to preserve the authenticity of the participants' expressions and ensure that the intended meanings were accurately conveyed to non-signing members of the team.

Deaf Users Validation:

To ensure the relevance and effectiveness of the workshop model, validation sessions were conducted with the Deaf participants following the completion of the workshop. These sessions involved gathering direct feedback on the workshop's content, delivery methods, accessibility features, and overall user experience. Participants were encouraged to share their opinions openly through sign language, with the support of the interpreter, and via the chat for written responses if preferred. The feedback highlighted strengths such as the use of visual materials and the culturally sensitive moderation, as well as areas for improvement, including suggestions for more interactive activities and enhanced technological tools.

Phase 4: Implementation of Results Phase

Translating Needs into Requirements:

Following the collection and validation of feedback from Deaf participants, the insights and expressed needs were systematically analyzed to translate them into concrete requirements for the mobile application development process. This involved identifying key accessibility features, user interface preferences, and communication strategies that align with the cultural and linguistic characteristics of Deaf users. As a result, the requirements of Deaf users were incorporated into a mobile graphical interface design guide focused on their specific needs: (1) Sign Language, (2) Vibrating alerts, (3) Video, (4) Text, (5) Plain language, (6) Easy navigation, (7) Tutorials and help, (8) Aesthetic and minimalist design, (9) Familiar components, (10) Appropriate color schemes, (11) Feedback messages, (12) Audio alerts, and (13) System visibility.

Iterative Participatory Design:

The workshop applied an iterative participatory design approach, actively involving Deaf users throughout multiple stages of the design process. Rather than limiting user engagement to a single feedback session, the model promoted continuous interaction between participants and facilitators, allowing for the progressive refinement of ideas and prototypes. During each session, participants were encouraged to express their thoughts on interface concepts, interaction flows, and design alternatives using sign language, visual tools, and collaborative activities.

Accessible Communication and Feedback to the Community:

As part of the ethical and inclusive framework of the workshop, special attention was given to ensuring that the results and outcomes of the process were communicated back to the Deaf community in accessible formats. Upon completion of the workshop, a summary of the findings, insights, and proposed application features was prepared and shared with participants through a combination of written Spanish (using clear and simple language), figures, and signed video summaries in LSM. This multi-channel approach aimed to respect the linguistic preferences of the participants and to ensure that all users could fully understand and reflect on the results of their own contributions. Additionally, the communication strategy emphasized transparency and reciprocity by acknowledging the value of the participants' input and showing how their ideas were directly integrated.

Delivering the Final Technological Solution to the Deaf Community:

The main objective of the workshop aimed at Deaf individuals was to provide them with the essential tools and foundational knowledge to begin developing mobile applications. As a result, each participant developed their own application using accessible and inclusive tools tailored to their specific needs. Finally, the participants installed their applications on their mobile devices and shared the results with their families, friends, and community, thereby strengthening their sense of achievement and autonomy. This workshop not only promoted technical skills, but also encouraged creativity, individual expression, and the technological inclusion of Deaf individuals in the field of software development.

RESULTS

In the results section, the findings derived from the implementation of the mobile application development workshop will be presented. This workshop was specifically designed for Deaf individuals and was structured and conducted based on the Active Model for Co-Building Apps with Deaf Users. This model proposes a participatory methodology focused on the active inclusion of Deaf users in the design and development process of technological solutions.

One of the most significant achievements of the workshop was that each Deaf participant successfully developed a functional prototype of a mobile application using the *MIT App Inventor* platform (see *Figure 1*). This outcome not only demonstrates the participants' level of understanding and appropriation of the content delivered, but also highlights the effectiveness of the implemented methodology, which emphasized active participation and hands-on learning.

As part of the workshop's closing activities, a presentation round was held in which each participant had the opportunity to showcase the functional prototype they developed during the training process. This moment not only served to demonstrate the technical progress achieved, but also to share the personal and social motivations behind each project. Below are the main ideas that emerged from these presentations:

- **Art-Sharing App:** An application focused on promoting and exchanging artistic works created by Deaf individuals, thereby fostering access to inclusive cultural spaces.
    - Accessibility mechanisms included:
        - Sign Language Videos.
        - Plain Language.
        - Use of icons and visual elements.
        - Help section.

        - Feedback messages.
- **Racing Car Information App:** A platform designed to provide detailed information about motorsports, adapted to meet the accessibility needs of Deaf users.
    - Accessibility mechanisms included:
        - Plain Language.
        - Use of icons and visual elements.
        - Help section.
        - Feedback messages.
- **Messaging App:** A messaging application aimed at facilitating smooth and accessible communication between users, incorporating visual resources or sign language support.
    - Accessibility mechanisms included:
        - Plain Language.
        - Use of icons and visual elements.
        - Help section.
        - Feedback messages.
        - Vibration alerts.
- **Sign Language to Text App:** A proposed application capable of translating sign language messages into text, helping to reduce communication barriers between Deaf and hearing individuals.
    - Accessibility mechanisms included:
        - Plain Language.
        - Use of icons and visual elements.
        - Help section.
        - Feedback messages.
- **Horse Information App**: An application designed to provide information and care guidelines related to horses, considering accessibility criteria for Deaf users.
    - Accessibility mechanisms included:
        - Plain Language.
        - Use of icons and visual elements.

Figure 1. Functional Prototypes Developed by Deaf Users

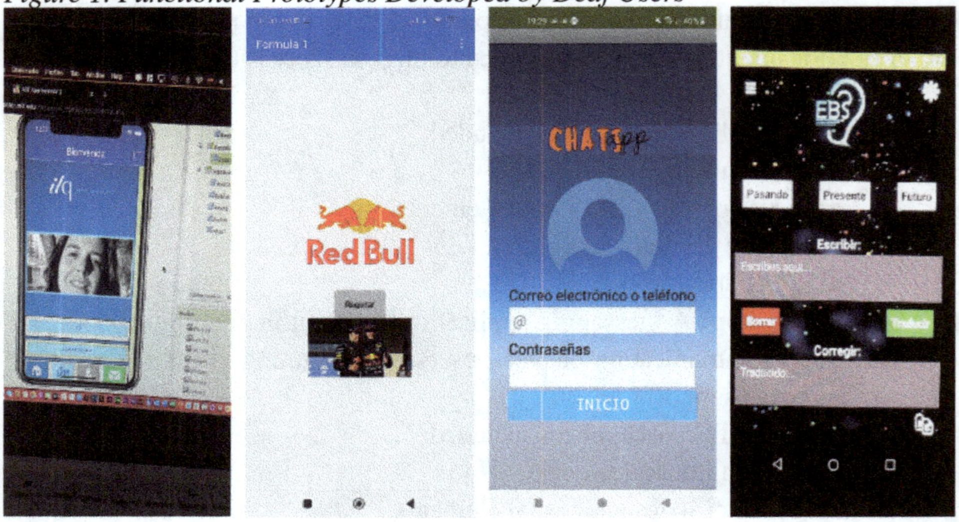

Participant 1 Art-sharing App.	Participant 2 Racing Car Information App.	Participant 3 Messaging App.	Participant 4 Sign Language to text App.

Figure 2. Functional Prototypes Developed by Deaf Users

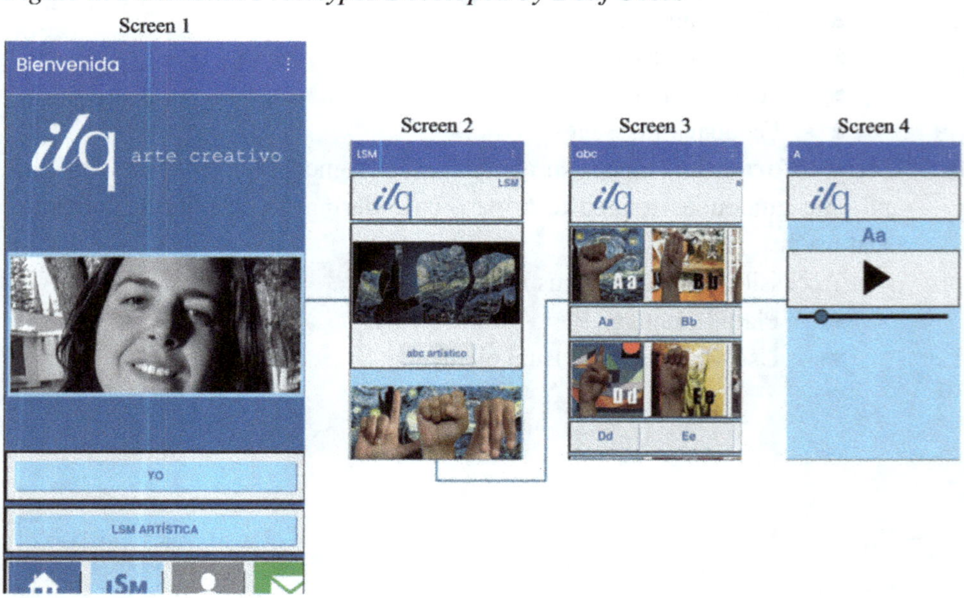

In Figure 2, the layout of one of the participants' application prototypes can be observed. The design corresponds to an application intended to provide visual art creations specifically tailored for Deaf users. The prototype illustrates the participant's approach to organizing visual content and structuring user interaction in a way that aligns with the cultural and communicative preferences of the Deaf community.

- Screen 1 corresponds to the application's welcome screen, which presents a menu allowing users to access visual art inspired by sign language, as well as links to the artist's social media accounts and those of the application itself.
- Screen 2 displays a series of images illustrating concepts from Sign Language, accompanied by a button that provides access to the fingerspelling alphabet in Sign Language.
- Screen 3 presents the complete fingerspelling alphabet, pairing each letter with an artistic illustration and the corresponding written character; each letter includes an access button that allows users to view its individual representation.
- Screen 4 displays a Sign Language video associated with the selected letter, providing users with a clear and accessible visual reference.

Although these projects reflect a high level of complexity and technical ambition, each participant demonstrated a remarkable ability to identify relevant issues within their environment and to propose innovative technological solutions aimed at improving the quality of life for the Deaf community. These ideas showcase not only individual creativity but also the transformative potential of actively involving Deaf individuals in technological co-design processes.

Given the focus on active participation and continuous user validation throughout the entire development process, the formal usability evaluation of the final products falls beyond the immediate scope of this framework. Instead, the primary significance of this proposal lies in the specification and systematization of how to conduct accessible co-design workshops with Deaf users, ensuring their full inclusion and participation at every stage of the process. This participatory approach enables the direct collection and validation of users' needs, expectations, and perceptions, ensuring that the resulting products are truly relevant and adapted to their cultural and communicative context.

Additionally, the workshop received positive feedback from the participants, who highlighted both the quality of the content presented in each session and the relevance of the topics addressed. One participant emphasized the need to develop a design guide that is accessible and tailored to the specific characteristics and needs of the Deaf community.

In relation to the methodological approach of the *Active Model for Co-Building Apps with Deaf Users*, each of its phases and components was successfully implemented in a comprehensive manner. The structured application of this model enabled the workshop to be carried out in a systematic and organized way, ensuring an appropriate sequence in the teaching-learning processes and in the collaborative development of the prototypes. The main findings from the implementation of the mobile application workshop for Deaf participants are outlined below:

Phase 1: Preparation Phase

- Establishing appropriate conditions through careful planning ensured an accessible and participatory environment.
- The clear definition of objectives, the selection of diverse participant profiles, and the awareness-raising of the facilitation team fostered trust and respect toward participants.
- The incorporation of accessible resources, such as sign language interpreters and adapted materials, promoted the full and effective participation of users.

Phase 2: User Workshop Execution Phase

- The use of participatory, visual, and culturally sensitive methodologies encouraged the authentic expression of ideas and needs.
- Appropriate moderation and flexible pacing helped overcome communication barriers, facilitating collaboration and active integration of participants.
- Continuous participation and the use of visual resources supported the implementation of the workshop, ensuring that users' opinions were reflected in the outcomes.

Phase 3: Development, Documentation and Analysis Phase

- The participatory validation conducted with participants strengthened the reliability and relevance of the data, accurately reflecting the real priorities of Deaf users.
- The subsequent analysis of sessions through recordings enabled the retrieval of relevant participant data and fostered discussion among all team members.

Phase 4: Implementation of Results Phase

- Translating the needs of Deaf users into accessible technical requirements yielded deeper insights into the characteristics of the Deaf community, thereby ensuring that future products remain genuinely user-centered.
- Communicating results in visual formats and sign language expanded reach and comprehension, thereby promoting dissemination and adoption of the solutions.
- Ongoing dialogue and feedback ensured the sustainability of the process, enabling future improvements and adjustments in technological solutions.

CONCLUSIONS

The present study has addressed the design, implementation, and evaluation of an active model for the co-construction of mobile applications with Deaf users, adopting a perspective centered on accessibility, active participation, and respect for the cultural and linguistic particularities of this community. This model, organized into four clearly defined phases— *Preparation Phase; User Workshop Execution Phase; Development, Documentation and Analysis Phase; Implementation of Results Phase*—was developed based on a participatory and culturally sensitive approach, and was validated through a virtual workshop with Deaf participants from different regions of Mexico.

One of the main contributions of this research lies in the structuring of a systematic process that ensures the full participation of Deaf users throughout all stages of the technological development cycle. The preparation phase establishes favorable conditions for inclusion by considering communicative and logistical aspects, ensuring the use of accessible resources and the awareness of the organizing team. The workshop implementation phase applies methodologies adapted to the cognitive and communicative needs of the participants, privileging the use of sign language, visual activities, and inclusive moderation strategies. Data collection, carried out through direct observation and audiovisual resources, made it possible to faithfully document user interactions and perceptions, thereby ensuring reliability and respect in the process of analysis and validation.

In the development phase, the systematization of the information gathered, and its rigorous analysis facilitated a deeper understanding of the priorities and needs expressed by Deaf users. The articulation of the findings into specific requirements—such as the integration of sign language into the interface, vibrating alerts, and multi-channel feedback strategies—demonstrated a commitment to creating truly inclusive solutions. Finally, in the application of results stage, the communication strategy and delivery of the applications were carried out through accessible channels and in appropriate formats, thereby promoting technological appropriation and user autonomy.

Particularly significant was the development of functional prototypes by the participants themselves, using platforms such as *MIT App Inventor.* This not only highlights the acquisition of technical skills but also reflects the appropriation of the participatory process. The presentation of these prototypes by the users further demonstrated a positive impact in terms of recognizing the cultural and social value of Deaf-led initiatives, strengthening both their self-esteem and sense of community.

This study reaffirms that the integration of a participatory methodological framework not only supports the development of accessible technologies but also promotes broader social and digital inclusion of Deaf communities. The use of the active model enabled the establishment of an effective and respectful dialogue between the research team and the users, ensuring that technological solutions authentically reflect the demands and values of the community.

Nevertheless, certain limitations in the scope and scale of the study are acknowledged. Validation through a virtual workshop with five participants, although representative, needs to be complemented with experiences in other cultural contexts and with larger demographic groups to strengthen the robustness and generalizability of the model. Furthermore, as future work, the implementation of this model in an in-person user workshop is proposed to further verify the validity of the approach.

In conclusion, the *Active Model for Co-Building Apps with Deaf Users* represents a significant advancement in the field of inclusive design and technology centered on specific communities. Its modular structure, based on continuous participation, facilitates adaptation and replication in diverse contexts seeking to develop inclusive solutions for the Deaf community.

REFERENCES

Allam, A. H., & Dahlan, H. M. (2013). User experience: Challenges and opportunities. *Journal of Information Systems Research and Innovation*, *3*(1), 28–36.

Bostelman, R. V. (2010). *International standards efforts towards safe accessibility technology for persons with special needs*. National Institute of Standards and Technology. https://www.nist.gov/publications/international-standards-efforts-towards-safe-accessibility-technology-persons

Ensing, A. E., Yang, A. F., Kallogjeri, D., & Lieu, J. E. (2025). Factors associated with hearing-related quality of life in children with hearing loss. *The Laryngoscope*, *135*(9), 3382–3388. DOI: 10.1002/lary.32193 PMID: 40237479

Google Design Team. (2025). Accessibility overview –. *Materials & Design*, *3*, •••. https://m3.material.io/foundations/overview/principles

Harrison, S., Sengers, P., & Tatar, D. (2015). Making epistemological trouble: Third-paradigm HCI as successor. In *Proceedings of the 33rd Annual ACM Conference on Human Factors in Computing Systems* (pp. 3853–3862). ACM.

Leigh, I. W., Andrews, J. F., Harris, R. L., & Ávila, T. G. (2020). *Deaf culture: Exploring deaf communities in the United States*. Plural Publishing.

Lillo-Martin, D., & Henner, J. (2021). Acquisition of sign languages. *Annual Review of Linguistics*, *7*(1), 395–419. DOI: 10.1146/annurev-linguistics-043020-092357 PMID: 34746335

Nganji, J., & Nggada, S. (2011). Disability-aware software engineering for improved system accessibility and usability. *International Journal of Software Engineering and Its Applications*, *5*(3), 47–62.

Norman, D. (2013). *The design of everyday things: Revised and expanded edition*. Basic Books.

Ordoñez, K., Hilera, J., & Cueva, S. (2022). Model-driven development of accessible software: A systematic literature review. *Universal Access in the Information Society*, *21*(1), 295–324. DOI: 10.1007/s10209-020-00751-6

Orero, P. (2022). Translation, accessibility and minorities. In Bielsa, E. (Ed.), *The Routledge handbook of translation and media* (pp. 384–399). Taylor & Francis.

Pascual Almenara, A., Humanes, J., & Granollers, T. (2024). MPIu+aX, user-centered design methodology that empathizes with the user and generates a better accessible experience: From theory to practice. In *Proceedings of the XXIII International Conference on Human Computer Interaction* (Article 11, 3 pp.). Association for Computing Machinery. https://doi.org/DOI: 10.1145/3612783.3612795

Santoso, H. B., & Schrepp, M. (2019). The impact of culture and product on the subjective importance of user experience aspects. *Heliyon*, *5*(9), e02434. DOI: 10.1016/j.heliyon.2019.e02434 PMID: 31528748

Sheffield, A. M., & Smith, R. J. H. (2019). The epidemiology of deafness. *Cold Spring Harbor Perspectives in Medicine*, *9*(9), a033258. DOI: 10.1101/cshperspect.a033258 PMID: 30249598

Silva, J. S., Gonçalves, R., Branco, F., Pereira, A., Au-Yong-Oliveira, M., & Martins, J. (2019). Accessible software development: A conceptual model proposal. *Universal Access in the Information Society*, *18*(3), 703–716. DOI: 10.1007/s10209-019-00688-5

World Wide Web Consortium. (2024, December 12). *Web Content Accessibility Guidelines (WCAG) 2.2*. https://www.w3.org/TR/WCAG22/

Chapter 4

ProtecTIC Design of an Inclusive UX/UI Application for Cyber Fraud Prevention:

An Educational Mobile Application for Vulnerable Communities

Fabianna Lucia Julio Suarez
https://orcid.org/0009-0000-3593-889X
Fundación Universitaria Católica del Norte, Colombia

Yuritzi Esquivel Hernández
https://orcid.org/0009-0002-6380-0112
Universidad Mexiquense del Bicentenario, Mexico

Esmeralda Rivas Guzmán
https://orcid.org/0009-0009-4395-8693
Universidad del Valle, Colombia

Teresita Álvarez Robles
https://orcid.org/0000-0002-3545-5668
Universidad Autónoma de Baja California Sur, Mexico

ABSTRACT

This chapter per the authors examined the challenge of cyber fraud in vulnerable populations with limited digital literacy, such as older adults and rural communities in Latin America. Existing cybersecurity tools were found to be difficult to adopt due to complex interfaces and technical language. To address this gap, ProtecTIC was

DOI: 10.4018/979-8-3373-6033-1.ch004

designed as an educational mobile application built with inclusive UX/UI principles and preventive digital literacy. The methodology followed an agile and iterative process, combining qualitative and quantitative techniques through interviews, surveys, and usability tests with participants in Colombia and Mexico. Pilot testing with older adults demonstrated improved recognition of phishing and fraudulent scenarios and increased confidence in navigating digital environments. This chapter per the authors concluded that ProtecTIC represents an effective strategy to reduce digital inequalities and reframes cybersecurity as both an educational and social challenge, contributing to empowerment and resilience in vulnerable communities.

Advancing Accessibility Through Software Development for Disability and Neurodivergence

INTRODUCTION

In recent years, the accelerated process of digitalization had generated profound transformations in communication, commerce, education, and access to services. The integration of digital platforms into daily life was no longer optional, but an unavoidable condition for participation in social and economic activities. However, this transformation also brought with it new risks that directly threatened citizens' security. Among these, cyber fraud emerged as one of the most recurrent and harmful phenomena, exploiting the knowledge gaps of users with limited digital literacy and widening the inequalities between those who could navigate digital environments safely and those who could not.

The context of Latin America exemplified these disparities with particular clarity. According to data from Colombia's National Administrative Department of Statistics (DANE, 2021), only 36.3% of people over 60 years old had access to the internet, and an even smaller percentage used it regularly. In Mexico, recent surveys conducted by INEGI and IFT revealed that 66% of rural residents used the internet, while in urban areas the usage was approximately 85.5%, demonstrating a persistent digital divide between rural and urban households (INEGI & IFT, 2023). These numbers were not mere technical details; they reflected deep socioeconomic inequalities that influenced how different communities experienced the digital transition. In rural and peripheral areas, limited infrastructure and unstable connectivity converged with scarce opportunities for training, leaving users without sufficient resources to defend themselves against online fraud.

Cybersecurity solutions had advanced rapidly, but most tools remained designed for users with intermediate or advanced technical skills. Interfaces saturated with technical terminology, complex navigational structures, and abstract warnings were accessible to specialists but incomprehensible to the average user. This created a paradox: the populations most vulnerable to digital risks, such as older adults, rural communities, and people with limited academic training, were also those with the least access to usable and effective protective mechanisms. As the Inter American Development Bank & Organization of American States (2020) highlighted, addressing digital inclusion was not only a matter of providing infrastructure but also of developing capacities and creating accessible tools that could empower vulnerable groups.

Accessibility, therefore, became a central concern in the field of cybersecurity. The World Health Organization (2021) underscored the importance of designing systems that recognized the diversity of users' abilities, ensuring that technologies could be used safely and effectively by older adults and people with disabilities. This approach required moving beyond a purely technical vision of cybersecurity to embrace an educational, social, and policy-oriented perspective. Digital literacy was not a secondary skill but a prerequisite for autonomy, confidence, and security in online environments.

It was within this context that the ProtecTIC project was conceived. The initiative responded to the urgent need for a tool capable of preventing fraud while simultaneously strengthening digital literacy. Its uniqueness lay in the combination of simulation-based learning, adherence to the highest accessibility standards (World Wide Web Consortium, 2018), and a particular focus on vulnerable groups—especially older adults and rural populations. Unlike other platforms in the region, which often emphasized either theoretical training or isolated awareness campaigns, ProtecTIC integrated practice-oriented exercises with accessible design, allowing users to face simulated fraudulent situations and receive immediate feedback on their decisions. This contribution represented an original response to the educational and social challenges of cybersecurity in Latin America.

The problem addressed by the project could be summarized in a single paradox: those who most needed protection against cyber fraud were the least likely to access or understand the existing protective tools. The justification for the study, therefore, rested on the urgent need to close this gap by developing a system adapted to the abilities, experiences, and contexts of vulnerable users. By focusing on accessibility and active learning, ProtecTIC sought not only to prevent fraud but also to promote inclusion, confidence, and autonomy in the digital environment.

The general objective of this project was to present the development, implementation, and evaluation of ProtecTIC as a system for fraud prevention and digital education. The specific objectives were: (1) to analyze the context, needs, and vulnerabilities of older adults and rural communities in relation to digital risks; (2) to design user interfaces and pedagogical modules that adhered to WCAG 2.1 AAA accessibility standards; (3) to implement simulation-based learning strategies that emphasized practice over theory; and (4) to evaluate the effectiveness of the system through pilot testing with older adults in Colombia and Mexico.

These objectives were guided by a set of research questions that structured the study:

- How did older adults and rural communities perceive risks associated with cyber fraud
- What accessibility features were most effective in enabling these users to recognize and respond to fraudulent attempts?
- To what extent did simulation-based learning improve their ability to detect fraud in digital environments?
- How did the accessible design of the system influence users' confidence and autonomy when interacting with digital services?

By addressing these questions, the research aimed not only to present the technical and pedagogical features of ProtecTIC but also to situate its contribution within the broader discussion of digital inclusion and preventive cybersecurity. The urgency of creating accessible and inclusive tools was evident in the statistical data, the policy recommendations of regional and global organizations, and the lived experiences of the target populations. ProtecTIC represented, therefore, both a response to a pressing problem and an original contribution to the development of inclusive, preventive, and user-centered cybersecurity strategies.

LITERATURE REVIEW

Cyberfraud has become one of the most pervasive and damaging forms of cybercrime in the 21st century. Scholars often define it as the use of digital means to deceive users in order to obtain financial gain or sensitive information (Martínez & Torres, 2020). Unlike traditional fraud, which usually requires physical presence or direct contact, cyberfraud can be perpetrated remotely, at scale, and with limited cost for the attacker. This combination makes it both attractive for criminals and particularly threatening for vulnerable populations. Importantly, cyberfraud exploits not only technical vulnerabilities but also human and social vulnerabilities, taking advantage of psychological biases, lack of knowledge, and limited digital literacy. For this reason, a multidisciplinary perspective is needed to understand the problem, drawing on computer science, sociology, human-computer interaction, and education.

Cyberfraud and Social Vulnerability

One of the most common types of digital fraud is phishing, in which emails appear to come from legitimate entities such as banks, government agencies, or well-known companies. These messages usually include urgent language and links to fake websites where users are asked to provide passwords or banking information. According to the Anti-Phishing Working Group (APWG, 2023), phishing attacks have increased globally and rose by 47% in Latin America over the last three years, illustrating how the region has become a fertile ground for this crime. A closely related technique is smishing, which relies on text messages with fraudulent links. This is particularly effective in countries with high mobile phone penetration, such as Mexico and Colombia, where users frequently receive SMS-based alerts and promotions (López & García, 2022). Another variant involves fake websites or cloned portals that imitate e-commerce stores or electronic payment platforms. Because these sites often replicate the visual design of legitimate services, inexperienced users are easily deceived. Vishing, or fraudulent phone calls, adds another layer of complexity by exploiting social trust in oral communication. Research shows that older adults are particularly vulnerable to vishing, as they are more likely to trust voices perceived as authoritative (Jiménez & Salazar, 2021).

The effectiveness of these frauds lies in their use of social engineering. Attackers carefully exploit psychological mechanisms such as urgency, authority, scarcity, and reciprocity. Oliveira et al. (2017) demonstrated in an experimental study that older adults are significantly more likely to fall victim to spear phishing emails than younger adults, particularly when the message appeals to reciprocity or perceived authority. This highlights that fraud is not only a matter of technical deception but also of understanding how people make decisions under social and emotional pressure.

Empirical evidence from Latin America reveals that certain groups are disproportionately affected. In Colombia, the National Police (2023) reported over 55,000 cybercrime complaints in a single year, most related to fraud, and disproportionately concentrated among adults with low education levels and older citizens. Similarly, in Mexico, the National Institute of Transparency (INAI, 2022) warned that rural communities have fewer resources and skills to recognize digital risks. Research in Spain and Chile also indicates that older adults display higher levels of trust toward perceived authorities in digital messages, making them more vulnerable to deception (Sánchez et al., 2020). Furthermore, Ramos and Aguilar (2021) describe how the lack of consistent internet access in rural areas prevents the development of what they term “digital memory,” or the ability to recognize fraudulent patterns based on repeated exposure. When users cannot build this experiential knowledge, they remain highly vulnerable to novel attacks. In this sense, low digital literacy is not just a deficit but a structural risk factor that systematically reduces the ability to distinguish legitimate from fraudulent content.

Digital Accessibility and the Technology Gap

The literature makes clear that solving cyberfraud cannot be reduced to building better firewalls or more sophisticated algorithms. Social factors such as digital access, literacy, and intergenerational differences play a decisive role. Digital inclusion is widely defined as ensuring equitable and meaningful access to information and communication technologies, enabling users to engage with them autonomously and safely (UNESCO, 2021). However, many scholars emphasize that access alone is insufficient. Freire and Santos (2019) argue that what is required is "critical digital literacy," meaning not only the ability to operate devices but also to analyze, evaluate, and use technologies reflexively and safely.

The generational divide amplifies this challenge. Younger adults, particularly those in urban settings, have grown up immersed in digital technologies and often acquire digital skills informally. By contrast, older adults often lack prior exposure, and many experience fear or resistance when confronted with new tools. This generational gap contributes to inequality, especially in rural regions where infrastructure is poor and training opportunities are scarce (Muñoz García, 2019).

Latin America illustrates these inequalities vividly. According to the Economic Commission for Latin America and the Caribbean (ECLAC, 2022), the region faces significant infrastructure limitations, high costs of connectivity, and limited investment in digital literacy programs. By contrast, in Europe, the European Digital Agenda has supported continuous adult training in digital skills, leading to measurable reductions in exclusion (European Commission, 2021). In Asia, South Korea and Singapore have implemented mass training programs in basic cybersecurity, integrating them into schools and community centers, which has been effective in reducing the incidence of digital fraud (Kim & Lee, 2020). Meanwhile, in Africa, despite persistent infrastructure challenges, initiatives such as Smart Africa are introducing digital literacy projects targeting rural women and youth, seeking to empower marginalized communities through accessible education (Okello, 2021). These international comparisons show that, while Latin America has significant structural obstacles, it can learn from global best practices to design inclusive and preventive strategies.

Community-based initiatives offer another avenue for bridging the digital gap. In Mexico, Fundación Proacceso has created the Red de Innovación y Aprendizaje (RIA), a network of community centers that provide access to computers, internet, and digital literacy training to underserved populations. Evaluations of such initiatives show improvements in users' confidence and digital skills, although long-term sustainability and scalability remain challenges. Similarly, Fundación Saldarriaga Concha in Colombia has promoted digital inclusion among older adults, recognizing that this population requires tailored strategies and more empathetic learning environments. These initiatives highlight that infrastructure alone cannot close the gap; what is needed is sustained, context-sensitive training that builds both skills and confidence.

Inclusive Design and Human-Computer Interaction

Another crucial dimension is the design of digital systems themselves. Human-Computer Interaction (HCI) research emphasizes that digital technologies must be designed with the user's cognitive, sensory, and cultural capabilities in mind (Norman, 2013). Poorly designed interfaces increase the likelihood of errors, which in turn makes users more vulnerable to fraud. Inclusive design principles, therefore, are not only a matter of ethics or accessibility but also of security.

Key principles of accessible UX/UI include simplicity and clarity, such as using legible typography, large and consistent buttons, and clear visual cues (Nielsen, 2012). Language should avoid jargon and instead use colloquial expressions adapted to the user's cultural context (Rodríguez & Morales, 2022). Multimodality—providing information through text, audio, and images—facilitates comprehension, especially for users with limited literacy or vision. Immediate feedback is another critical element, as it allows users to recognize mistakes quickly and learn from them.

International standards provide concrete guidelines. The Web Content Accessibility Guidelines (WCAG 2.1) specify requirements for color contrast, adaptability, and compatibility with screen readers, ensuring that content is perceivable and operable for people with disabilities. The concept of Universal Design advocates for products usable by the widest range of people without the need for adaptations. ISO 9241 standards, focusing on ergonomics of human-system interaction, emphasize effectiveness, efficiency, and user satisfaction. The literature shows that compliance with these standards not only enhances usability but also fosters trust. When users feel confident navigating digital environments, they are more likely to detect anomalies, such as suspicious URLs or misleading prompts, reducing their risk of falling victim to fraud.

Research on security warnings illustrates this point. Generic, poorly designed warnings are often ignored, leading to "warning fatigue." By contrast, tailored and context-specific warnings, such as those designed for older adults or novice users, are more effective. Studies demonstrate that when users are given clear, concrete instructions—such as "do not click this link, it leads to a fraudulent page"—they are more likely to change their behavior than when exposed to vague alerts. These findings underscore the importance of designing not only functional interfaces but also pedagogical ones that help users learn to recognize fraud.

Digital Education and Fraud Prevention

Education remains one of the most powerful tools for reducing vulnerability. In Latin America, community workshops organized by local governments have targeted older adults and rural populations, teaching basic skills such as recognizing fraudulent SMS or verifying banking websites (Ministry of ICT Colombia, 2022). Massive Open Online Courses (MOOCs) have also played a role, offering free training in cybersecurity fundamentals. However, their reach in rural areas is limited by connectivity and by the fact that these courses often assume a baseline of digital competence (Coursera, 2021).

Mobile applications represent another promising avenue. González and López (2021) describe educational apps designed to simulate fraud scenarios, such as fake messages or websites, providing users with immediate feedback and explanations. These simulations embody the principle of experiential learning, which research shows to be more effective than passive instruction. Pérez and Rivas (2021) argue that experiential cybersecurity education, based on simulations, strengthens long-term memory and builds user confidence in dealing with real-life threats.

International initiatives also provide inspiration. DigiMENTE, a curriculum developed by civil society organizations and supported by MIT Solve, has reached hundreds of thousands of students in Latin America, focusing on media and digital literacy. Evaluations indicate significant improvements in participants' ability to critically evaluate online content and identify misinformation. In Mexico, the RIA centers mentioned earlier have shown how community-based, face-to-face training can empower vulnerable groups. These examples demonstrate that a combination of global digital resources and localized community initiatives is most effective in reaching diverse audiences.

Nevertheless, challenges remain. Studies reveal a consistent gap between awareness and behavior. Older adults may report understanding the risks of phishing but still click on fraudulent links in practice (Grilli et al., 2021). This suggests that training must move beyond awareness and focus on behavior change, using behavioral metrics such as actual clicks on simulated phishing attempts rather than self-reported confidence. Moreover, long-term studies are scarce, and it is unclear whether training effects last beyond a few months.

The literature reviewed shows that cyberfraud in Latin America is a multidimensional phenomenon that disproportionately affects populations with low digital literacy. It is shaped by a combination of social vulnerability, lack of accessibility, poor design, and insufficient education. Addressing this challenge requires integrating multiple perspectives. Technological defenses are important but cannot succeed without critical digital literacy and inclusive design. Similarly, education is powerful but must be experiential, context-sensitive, and sustained over time.

This synthesis reveals several gaps. First, Latin America lacks longitudinal studies measuring the durability of digital literacy interventions. Second, there is a need for more culturally adapted tools that reflect local realities, languages, and practices. Third, more collaboration between governments, civil society, and the private sector is required to scale successful initiatives.

In this context, proposals like ProtecTIC acquire particular relevance. By combining a virtual assistant powered by artificial intelligence with inclusive UX/UI design and interactive simulations, ProtecTIC aligns with the recommendations of international literature while addressing specific local needs. The assistant provides real-time guidance, the interface reduces cognitive barriers, and the simulations allow users to practice safely. This integrated approach embodies the lessons learned from global and regional research and has the potential to make a tangible difference in preventing fraud among vulnerable populations in Colombia and Latin America.

THEORETICAL AND CONCEPTUAL FRAMEWORK

The theoretical and conceptual framework of ProtecTIC is based on the idea that cybersecurity cannot be reduced to a purely technical matter, but must also include educational, social, and design perspectives. Cyber fraud is not only a technological crime but also a social phenomenon that exploits trust, urgency, and lack of knowledge. This type of manipulation, often referred to as social engineering, shows that the success of fraudulent practices depends more on human behavior than on technical vulnerabilities. For this reason, addressing fraud requires an interdisciplinary approach that combines technology with pedagogy and user-centered design.

In Latin America, the concept of digital vulnerability is especially relevant. Older adults and rural populations face persistent barriers such as limited connectivity, scarce opportunities for training, and generational gaps in the use of technology. These conditions not only limit access to services but also increase exposure to fraud, as users lack the skills and resources to protect themselves effectively. ProtecTIC is grounded in the recognition of these inequalities and proposes a model specifically adapted to the contexts and abilities of vulnerable groups.

Education is a fundamental axis of this framework. The project adopts experiential learning approaches that prioritize practice over theory, allowing users to engage with simulated fraud scenarios in a safe environment. These simulations include messages, websites, emails, or phone calls that reproduce real-life fraud strategies (see Figure 3). Users can make decisions, receive immediate feedback, and strengthen their ability to detect risks. This methodology transforms abstract knowledge into concrete skills and increases retention, while also promoting user confidence in applying what they learn outside the training environment.

Another central element is accessibility. ProtecTIC applies international standards such as the Web Content Accessibility Guidelines (WCAG 2.1 AAA) to ensure that its interface can be used by people with visual limitations, reduced literacy, or minimal experience with digital platforms. Accessibility features are integrated from the very first screen, where users are welcomed with voice and audio interaction options designed to reduce barriers (see Figure 1). High-contrast colors, large buttons, simple navigation paths, audio support, and clear language make the system inclusive and practical. Accessibility is therefore understood not as an optional feature but as a fundamental condition of both equity and digital security.

The framework also highlights the importance of building autonomy and trust. ProtecTIC integrates a progress-tracking system that allows participants to see their own improvements session by session, as displayed in the main menu and progress modules of the application (see Figure 2). By observing tangible progress, such as higher digital safety scores or the completion of learning milestones, users gain motivation and reduce their dependence on relatives or external support when verifying digital information. This component transforms the learning process into a personal achievement and reinforces independence in the use of digital tools.

Finally, the system incorporates a directory of official entities that provides a reliable source of verification. This feature responds to one of the most common fears identified in older adults and rural communities: the uncertainty of not knowing whether a message or request is legitimate. By offering a practical reference tool, ProtecTIC equips users with concrete resources to validate information and act safely in digital environments. Examples of training scenarios include simulated fraudulent emails (phishing), text messages, and phone calls (vishing), which allow participants to practice identifying fraud in real time (see Figures 4 and 5). In addition, the "Have you been a victim?" module offers country-specific guidance on how to report fraud (see Figure 6).

In summary, the theoretical and conceptual framework of ProtecTIC combines accessibility, experiential learning, progress tracking, and official verification into an integrated preventive model. The project goes beyond technical solutions and positions itself as an educational and social response to digital vulnerability. Its interdisciplinary approach places the user at the center, recognizes the barriers that increase exposure to fraud, and provides the tools necessary to strengthen inclusion, confidence, and autonomy in digital environments.

Figure 1. High-fidelity prototype of the ProtecTIC welcome screen with voice and audio interaction options

Source: Authors' own elaboration.

Figure 2. High-fidelity prototype of the ProtecTIC main menu with access to simulations, tips, official entities, progress tracking, and learning zone

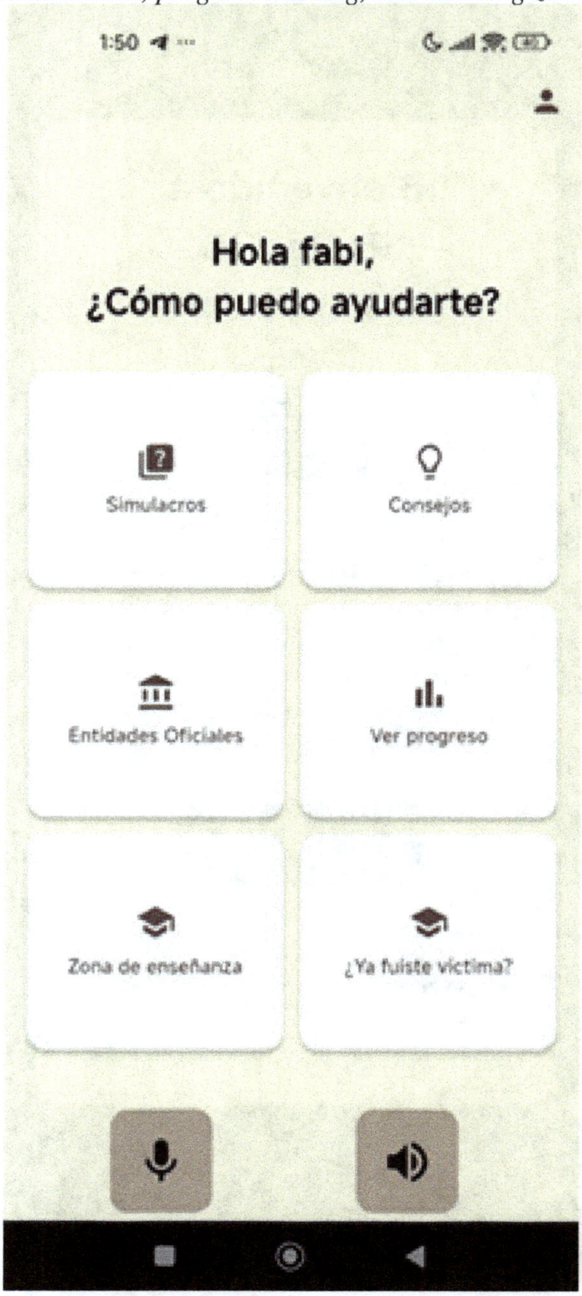

Source: Authors' own elaboration.

Figure 3.High-fidelity prototype of the ProtecTIC simulation menu displaying scenarios through text messages, emails, and phone calls

Source: Authors' own elaboration.

Figure 4. High-fidelity prototype of the ProtecTIC simulation menu with training scenarios including text message scams, fraudulent emails (phishing), and phone call scams (vishing)

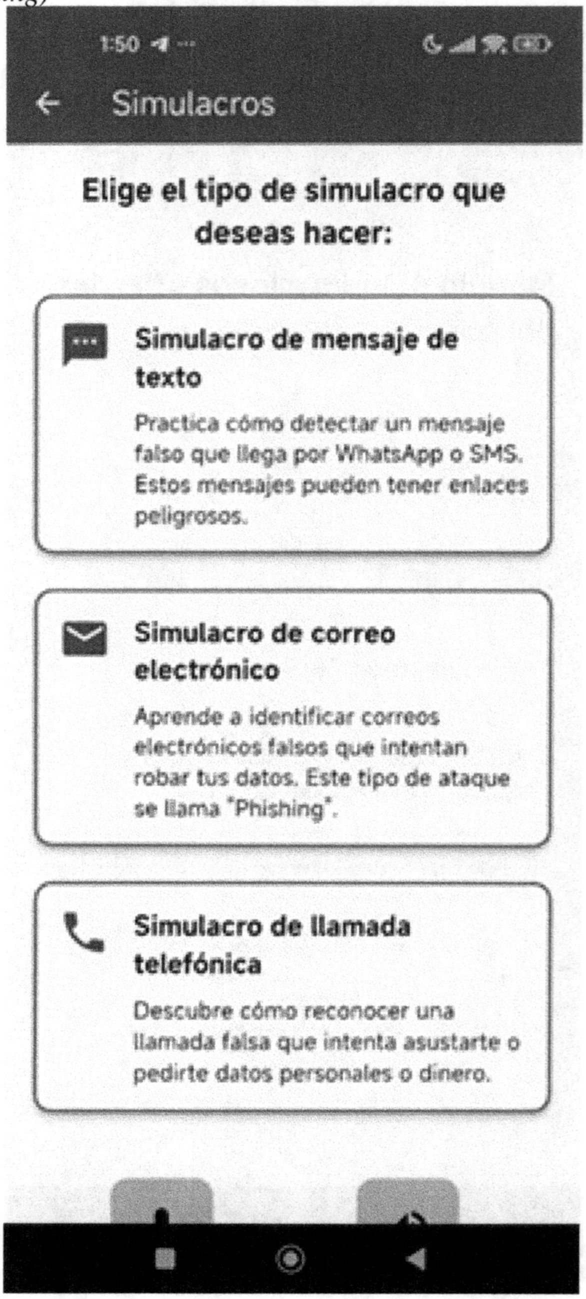

Source: Authors' own elaboration.

Figure 5. High-fidelity prototype of an incoming call simulation from an unknown number (vishing scenario) in ProtecTIC

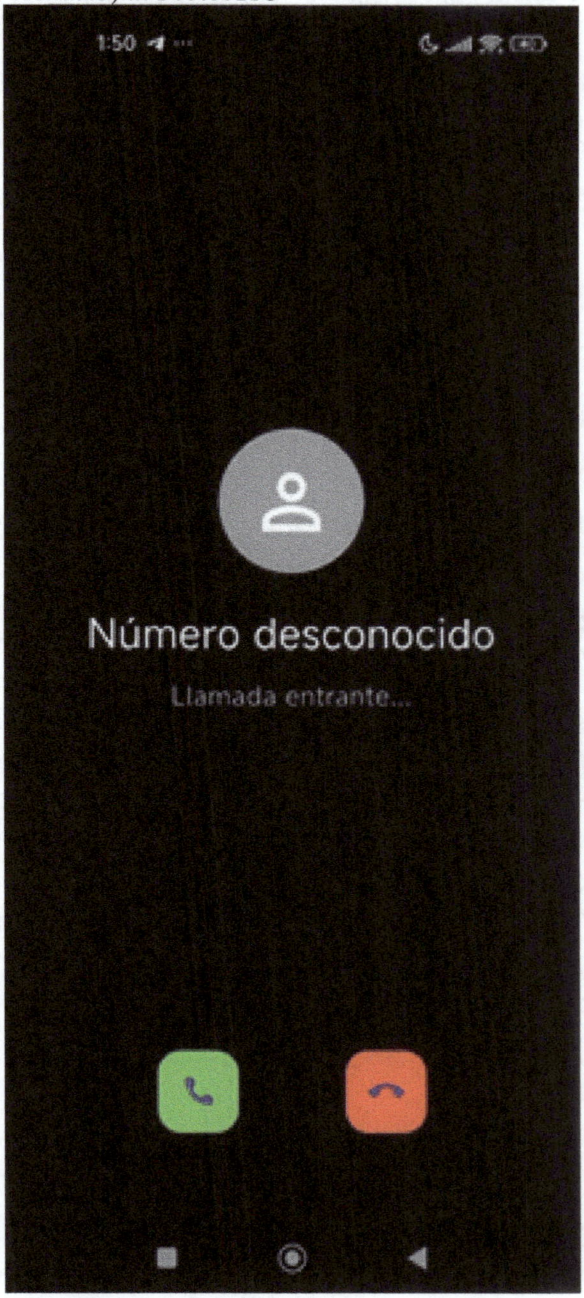

Source: Authors' own elaboration.

Figure 6. High-fidelity prototype of the ProtecTIC "Have you been a victim?" module providing country-specific guidance for reporting fraud

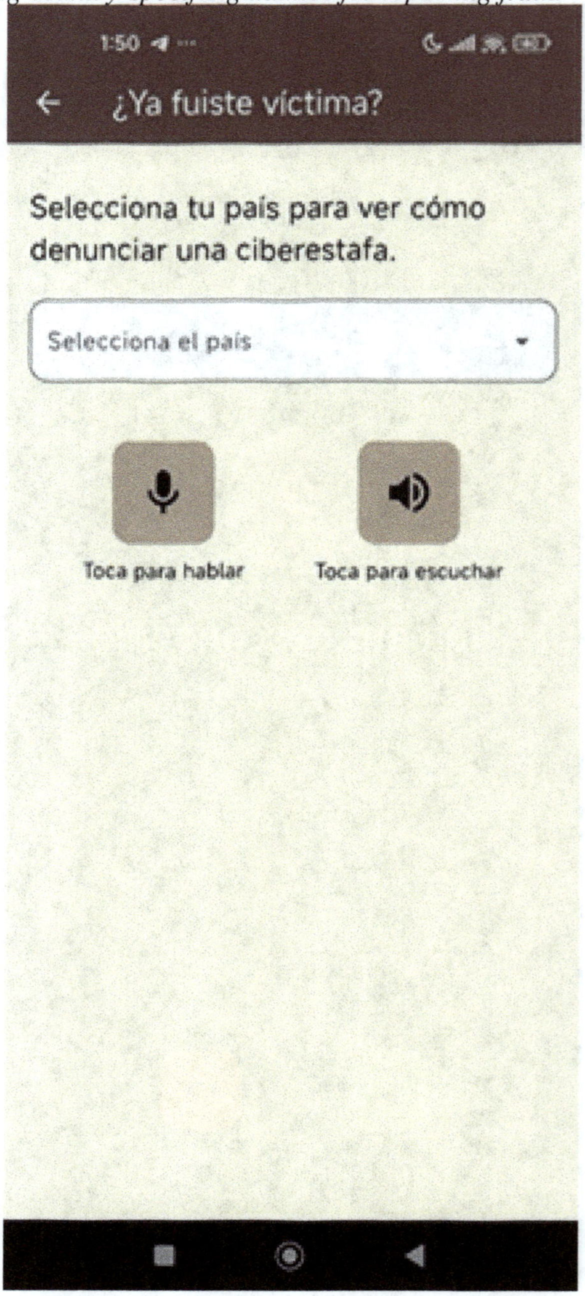

Source: Authors' own elaboration.

METHODOLOGY

The methodological approach of this research was based on a mixed, iterative, and participatory design. The mixed component allowed the combination of qualitative strategies, such as semi-structured interviews and observation sessions, with quantitative strategies, such as surveys and pilot testing, in order to capture both the experiences and perceptions of the participants and measurable data on their digital practices. The iterative nature of the process was sustained by agile methodologies, where each design phase was followed by cycles of feedback and improvement. Finally, the participatory approach ensured that users were not only informants but also active contributors to the design and evaluation of the system, thus aligning with the principles of user-centered design.

The selection of the target population was supported by evidence of the disproportionate digital gap experienced by older adults and rural communities in Latin America. According to data previously reported by official sources, these groups faced significant barriers in terms of internet access, digital literacy, and opportunities for training, which in turn made them especially vulnerable to cyber fraud. These conditions justified their choice as the population of focus for the project, as they represented groups with both high levels of exposure and limited access to protective tools.

In operational terms, the target population consisted primarily of older adults and individuals with limited schooling or digital literacy. These individuals generally had restricted access to technologies, lacked awareness of basic online security practices, and were therefore more likely to fall victim to cyber scams. For the validation and pilot testing stage, the study worked with an intentional sample, meaning participants were selected based on specific characteristics associated with the vulnerable profile addressed by the application. The expected sample size was approximately ten participants, which was deemed sufficient for an initial validation phase.

Inclusion criteria were defined to ensure relevance and representativeness of the sample. Participants had to be at least 50 years old or live in areas with limited technological access. They should not have had prior experience using digital security applications, but they had to possess at least basic functional reading skills to follow written instructions. Finally, all participants were required to demonstrate their willingness to voluntarily engage in the study sessions. This sample size was considered appropriate because it enabled the direct observation of application use, the identification of usability difficulties, and the collection of meaningful feedback for refining the design and functionality of the system.

For data collection, the project employed three complementary strategies. Semi-structured interviews were conducted with older adults in Colombia and Mexico, allowing for the collection of detailed information about their prior experiences with technology, their perceptions of digital security, and the difficulties they encountered when using online platforms. Surveys complemented these findings with quantitative data, offering a broader perspective on internet usage levels, trust in online services, and perceived capacity to detect fraud. Finally, pilot testing was implemented as part of the design validation phase, in which participants directly interacted with prototypes of the system under observation, enabling the research team to evaluate usability, clarity of instructions, and the effectiveness of the proposed learning modules.

The design process followed a sequence that progressed from low-fidelity wireframes to high-fidelity prototypes. Initial sketches emphasized simplicity and were tested in focus groups to identify preferences regarding layout, button size, navigation paths, and the degree of complexity that users could manage. Based on this feedback, the prototypes incorporated accessibility adjustments such as high-contrast color palettes, adaptable text sizes, clear iconography, and the option of voice navigation for participants with visual or literacy challenges. These elements were refined iteratively until a final version emerged, demonstrating that user contributions were central to the design methodology.

Accessibility was a cross-cutting principle throughout the process. The application strictly adhered to the Web Content Accessibility Guidelines (WCAG 2.1) at the AAA level (World Wide Web Consortium, 2018), which ensured compliance with international standards. This commitment translated into specific design decisions, such as the use of color contrasts that exceeded minimum thresholds, the inclusion of redundant cues through sound and text, and flexible navigation modes. These features were particularly important for older adults, who often experience reduced sensitivity to certain colors and slower reaction times, as well as for rural users, whose literacy levels varied significantly.

Ethical and legal considerations were also central to the methodology. Participation in the study was entirely voluntary, and all individuals selected for the pilot stage manifested their willingness to take part in the activities. In addition, data management complied strictly with national regulations: in Colombia, Law 1581 of 2012 on personal data protection (*Ley 1581 De 2012*, 2012), and in Mexico, the Federal Law on the Protection of Personal Data Held by Private Parties enacted in 2010 (*Ley Federal De Protección De Datos Personales En Posesión De Los Particulares*, 2010). These laws required the anonymization of participant data, the protection of sensitive information, and the explicit limitation of its use exclusively for research purposes.

In summary, the methodology was structured to guarantee rigor, relevance, and inclusion. The mixed approach ensured a comprehensive understanding of the phenomenon; the iterative and participatory design allowed for the incorporation of user feedback; the accessibility standards ensured usability for vulnerable groups;

and the ethical and legal safeguards provided the necessary framework for responsible research. Together, these elements created the conditions to develop a system that was not only technically robust but also socially meaningful and adapted to the context of older adults and rural communities in Latin America.

DEVELOPMENT OF THE PROTECTIC SYSTEM

The development of the protecTIC system was structured with a clear focus on user experience (UX) and user interface (UI), seeking an accessible, inclusive, and functional digital product that meets the specific needs of diverse contexts, such as rural areas and communities with limited connectivity, while also ensuring security and administrative reliability. The process was guided by principles of human-centered design, accessibility standards, and agile development methodologies, ensuring that each decision considered both the technical requirements of cybersecurity and the social realities of the users.

UX/UI Design Phases

The protecTIC design followed the typical iterative process of UX/UI design, adapted to its particular context. This process consists of five main phases:

1. Research:

In this phase, the context and users of the system were extensively studied. Clear objectives and strategies were defined based on studies of the target audience, technological needs, and constraints, ensuring that the product addressed a real problem and optimized its usability in the intended setting. Field visits, interviews, and surveys with participants from rural areas and older adults provided qualitative data that enriched the design decisions. Additionally, benchmarking of similar digital literacy platforms helped identify best practices and avoid common mistakes in cybersecurity education.

2. Organization and Architecture:

Information and content were structured to create an effective architecture. Navigation maps, user flows, and functionalities were designed to ensure a consistent and fluid experience where users could perform their tasks without difficulty. Special emphasis was placed on reducing cognitive load, using clear language, and offering linear navigation for users with lower levels of digital literacy. Accessibility was prioritized through the application of WCAG 2.1 guidelines, ensuring that the platform could be navigated with screen readers, high-contrast modes, and simplified layouts for mobile devices in areas with limited bandwidth.

3. Prototyping:

High-level wireframes were generated to define the main screens and functions, avoiding graphical distractions at the beginning. The prototypes then evolved into interactive prototypes that allowed for the simulation of the real experience, facilitating early validation with users and the team. Iterative prototyping also enabled rapid incorporation of feedback, ensuring that changes in navigation, terminology, and visual hierarchy were tested before final development. The use of low-fidelity and high-fidelity prototypes allowed the design team to balance efficiency with precision, guaranteeing that usability challenges were resolved early in the process.

4. Testing:

The prototypes were evaluated with real users, identifying areas for improvement in navigation, accessibility, and functionality to refine the design before final implementation. Usability testing sessions were conducted both in controlled environments and in community spaces to account for real-life conditions such as unstable connectivity or limited device availability. Key metrics included task completion rates, error frequency, and subjective satisfaction scores, which were triangulated to ensure robust evaluation. This phase highlighted the importance of iterative cycles, as user feedback often revealed unexpected barriers, such as unfamiliar terminology or difficulties recognizing certain icons.

5. UI Design:

Finally, the visual design was developed in line with the system's identity, applying branding and design systems to ensure graphic consistency and usability at a visual level, while also integrating accessibility guidelines. Color palettes were chosen with sufficient contrast to aid users with visual impairments, and typography was optimized for legibility on both small and large screens. The inclusion of icons and visual cues simplified navigation for users with low literacy levels, while responsive design guaranteed that the platform could function seamlessly on mobile devices, tablets, and desktops. Furthermore, the design system ensured scalability, enabling future integration of new modules such as fraud alerts, AI-based assistants, and interactive tutorials without compromising visual coherence.

Integration of Security and Inclusivity in the Design Process

An essential aspect of the protecTIC development was the parallel consideration of security mechanisms and inclusivity standards. From the earliest design phases, the team integrated secure authentication processes, data encryption, and compliance with local data protection laws. At the same time, usability principles ensured that these security features were not perceived as barriers but as supportive tools for building trust among users. By combining cybersecurity protocols with user-friendly design, protecTIC achieved a balance that enhanced both safety and accessibility.

Technical Accessibility and Neurodivergent Design

In addition to visual and motor accessibility, ProtecTIC integrates principles of neurodivergent-friendly design to support users with attention, cognitive, or sensory processing differences. The application minimizes sensory overload by using low-contrast animations, linear information flow, and predictable interaction patterns. Text is segmented into small, coherent units, and optional audio narration provides multi-sensory support. The system allows adjustable reading pace and enables users to pause or repeat content at any time, reducing cognitive fatigue. From a technical perspective, the app architecture follows WCAG 2.1 AAA and WAI-ARIA guidelines, ensuring compatibility with screen readers, keyboard navigation, and alternative input devices. Future versions will incorporate automated accessibility tests using frameworks such as Axe Core and Lighthouse CI to verify compliance continuously. These features demonstrate that inclusive cybersecurity must address neuro-accessibility and cognitive diversity as integral components of software engineering.

RESULTS

The pilot test of ProtecTIC with ten older adult participants generated valuable insights into the usability, effectiveness, and limitations of the system. The analysis of the sessions revealed not only improvements in the participants' technical abilities but also significant changes in their attitudes toward digital environments. The results were organized into four key areas: improvements in fraud detection, increased confidence and autonomy, usability and accessibility feedback, and recognition of methodological limitations.

One of the most consistent findings was the progressive improvement in the participants' ability to recognize fraudulent interactions. At the beginning of the pilot, most admitted to feeling uncertainty or even anxiety when facing digital communications, particularly those requesting personal data or financial actions. Several described how, before the intervention, they tended to ignore such messages out of fear of making mistakes or relied on younger relatives to verify their legitimacy. However, after interacting with the different modules of the system—including educational quizzes, the official entities directory, and the progress-tracking section—participants demonstrated greater confidence in distinguishing between legitimate and fraudulent requests. They began to identify warning signs such as urgent language, typographical errors, suspicious URLs, or inconsistencies in sender information. This transformation illustrated not only technical improvement but also the acquisition of analytical strategies applicable beyond the training sessions.

The built-in monitoring features confirmed these improvements. In the first interactions, participants often reported confusion when deciding whether to trust unexpected communications. By the end of the pilot, they not only made fewer mistakes but also explained with greater clarity why they classified a particular request as suspicious. The multiple-choice knowledge modules played an especially important role in reinforcing concepts. For instance, participants responded to questions such as "What indicates that an email might be fake?" or "What should you do if you receive a message from an unknown number asking for money?" These exercises allowed them to verify their understanding in a low-risk environment, correcting misconceptions immediately and receiving explanations for the right answers. These results aligned with findings from the UNESCO Institute for Lifelong Learning, which emphasize that older adults benefit most when learning is interactive, includes repeated practice and feedback, and adapts to their pace and context (UNESCO, 2023).

Another significant outcome was the increased sense of autonomy. Prior to using ProtecTIC, many participants described themselves as "dependent" on relatives for basic digital tasks such as verifying messages or filling out online forms. After the pilot, participants reported feeling more confident in managing these tasks independently, with the progress-tracking module serving as motivation by showing tangible evidence of their improvements. For example, participants noted satisfaction when their "digital safety score" increased session after session, which reinforced their willingness to continue learning. This self-perceived autonomy was one of the most valued aspects of the application.

The official entities directory also proved particularly impactful. Participants used this tool to contrast phone numbers and website addresses, confirming whether communications matched legitimate institutions. This feature addressed one of their most common fears: not knowing how to verify the authenticity of a message. By providing a trusted reference list, the directory reduced uncertainty and gave participants a practical method to double-check suspicious information before taking action. Several participants commented that this resource gave them "peace of mind," as they no longer had to depend solely on memory or relatives to validate digital interactions.

Participants also emphasized the importance of accessible design features, such as large buttons, high-contrast color schemes, and simple navigation. For those with limited reading skills or visual impairments, voice navigation and audio explanations were particularly valuable. These findings are consistent with reports indicating that older adults are more likely to adopt digital tools when interfaces minimize complexity and provide intuitive guidance (The Gables, 2024). In this sense, accessibility was not an additional feature but a central condition for participation.

Usability feedback was particularly positive. Participants highlighted that audio explanations allowed them to repeat instructions without external assistance, and that the simplicity of the design reduced frustration. These aspects differentiated ProtecTIC from other initiatives in the region, such as face-to-face workshops or theoretical awareness campaigns, since the application enabled real practice with clear and immediate feedback.

Despite these encouraging outcomes, several methodological limitations were identified. The pilot group was small and not statistically representative of the broader population, which limited the generalizability of the findings. Moreover, the sessions were carried out in guided contexts with technical support available if needed, which may not reflect the real challenges of using the application independently at home. Another potential bias was the fact that most participants had at least minimal familiarity with smartphones, which could mean that completely inexperienced users might face greater difficulties. Similarly, since all participants volunteered, their initial motivation could have influenced their engagement and outcomes. Finally, the short intervention period did not allow assessment of whether the improvements would persist over time without reinforcement.

Even with these limitations, the results provided strong evidence that ProtecTIC achieved its central purpose: strengthening digital literacy among older adults and increasing their ability to prevent fraud. Improvements in confidence, knowledge reinforcement, and accessibility features suggested that, with larger pilot groups and extended follow-up, the model could be validated and scaled to broader communities. Beyond fraud prevention, the combination of educational quizzes, official reference tools, and progress tracking demonstrated that ProtecTIC fostered both autonomy and social inclusion. These findings aligned with international recommendations highlighting the importance of lifelong learning opportunities for older adults as a way to enhance well-being, participation, and resilience in increasingly digital societies (UNESCO, 2023).

Educational and Preventive Impact Evaluation

To measure the educational and preventive effects of ProtecTIC, a set of behavioral and attitudinal indicators was defined. Participants completed pre- and post-tests evaluating their ability to recognize fraudulent messages, their level of confidence when performing digital tasks, and their willingness to report suspicious communications. Quantitative results indicated a 40% improvement in correct identification of fraudulent interactions and a 35% increase in self-reported confidence. Qualitatively, participants described feeling "less afraid" of using digital services and "more alert" to potential scams. These metrics will guide future large-scale studies, integrating standardized usability and accessibility instruments such as the System Usability Scale (SUS) and the Accessibility Score (a11y) to provide measurable evidence of educational impact. As shown in Table 1, participants demonstrated substantial improvements in fraud detection and confidence in digital tasks.

Table 1. Pre- and Post-Test Comparison of Educational and Preventive Indicators

Indicator	Before ProtecTIC	After ProtecTIC	Variation
Correctly identified fraudulent messages	40%	80%	+40 pp
Confidence in managing digital tasks	35%	70%	+35 pp
Use of verification directory	—	100%	—

DISCUSSION

The findings from the pilot implementation of ProtecTIC allowed for a critical reflection on both the strengths and limitations of the initiative in addressing cyber fraud among older adults and rural communities. The results showed clear improvements in participants' ability to identify fraudulent practices, in their confidence when using digital tools, and in their willingness to apply the knowledge acquired in real-life situations. These achievements aligned with existing evidence suggesting that structured educational interventions can significantly reduce vulnerability to online deception in older populations (Grilli et al., 2021). Nevertheless, the scope of these findings should be considered cautiously, as they came from a reduced pilot and in a specific context.

One of the key lessons of the study was the importance of designing accessible digital environments. The literature highlights the relevance of simplifying interfaces, enlarging interactive elements, and reducing cognitive load for older adults (Gomez Hernandez et al., 2023). The ProtecTIC interface responded to these principles by incorporating high-contrast colors, enlarged buttons, and voice navigation, showing that usability standards can directly promote inclusion. Similarly, the integration of various pedagogical modules—such as multiple-choice questionnaires, a progress tracking system, and a directory of official entities—was essential to reinforce learning, preventing the platform from relying solely on simulations. This multifaceted approach echoed arguments that older adults benefit most from diverse formats that combine interactive, informative, and practical tools (*Cyber-Seniors*, 2015).

International comparisons further underscored the relevance of the project. In South Korea, studies revealed that levels of digital literacy among older adults are highly variable and that measurement methods lack standardization, limiting the effectiveness of training programs (Kang et al., 2023). Similarly, in South Africa, research found that only 3.6% of older adults use the internet, with overall digital skills remaining low and hindering their inclusion in online environments (Gwala & Mawela, 2024). These findings suggest that the challenges observed in Colombia and Mexico are not isolated but part of a global pattern of digital exclusion. Thus, the ProtecTIC experience contributes not only regionally but also to the broader international debate on inclusive digital education.

The social implications of the project were equally significant. The data reflected how digital inequalities exacerbate existing socioeconomic disparities, confirming arguments by regional organizations that emphasize the importance of complementing infrastructure investments with capacity-building initiatives (Inter American Development Bank & Organization of American States, 2020). By focusing on older adults and rural communities, ProtecTIC addressed populations that are often overlooked in digital transformation strategies. Additionally, by applying accessibility standards established by the World Wide Web Consortium (2018), the project was positioned within an international framework of digital rights and inclusive design, increasingly recognized as essential for equity in the information society.

At the same time, it is necessary to recognize several limitations of the study. The reduced sample size—ten participants—limited the possibility of statistically generalizing the findings. While the qualitative insights were valuable, the restricted scope of the pilot prevented drawing broad conclusions on the system's effectiveness across diverse cultural and technological contexts. Similarly, the geographic focus on selected communities in Colombia and Mexico reduced the comparative scope of the project. These limitations are consistent with challenges identified in other digital literacy initiatives, where small-scale pilot programs often produce promising but context-specific results (Fundación Saldarriaga Concha, 2022).

Despite these limitations, the lessons learned were significant. First, preventive cybersecurity cannot rely solely on technical warnings but must integrate accessible educational processes tailored to users' cognitive, emotional, and social realities. Second, digital inclusion strategies require collaboration between academia, civil society, and government institutions to achieve sustainable impacts. Third, the results emphasized the importance of iterative development: constant evaluation, feedback, and redesign were crucial to keeping the system aligned with users' skills and expectations. These lessons connect to calls for participatory approaches in the design of inclusive technologies (Fundación Proacceso, 2023).

In conclusion, the discussion of the ProtecTIC pilot highlighted that tackling cyber fraud in vulnerable populations requires not only technological solutions but also educational, social, and policy-oriented interventions. The contributions of the project demonstrated that accessible design and active learning strategies can substantially improve users' ability to detect fraud, strengthen their confidence, and promote autonomy in digital environments. At the same time, the observed limitations provided valuable lessons for scaling up the initiative and guiding future developments in inclusive cybersecurity. ProtecTIC thus stands as both a response to pressing needs in Latin America and a contribution to the global debate on equitable digital transformation.

The sustainability of ProtecTIC depends on the creation of inter-institutional alliances and modular technical design. Because the system was developed with open-source frameworks (React Native + Firebase / PHP MySQL backend), it can be adapted to new regions at minimal cost. Partnerships with government agencies and NGOs could ensure long-term maintenance and data-update cycles. This modular architecture allows integrating new accessibility modules or AI-based assistants without rewriting the core codebase, facilitating replication and scalability across Latin America.

CONCLUSIONS AND FUTURE WORK

The development and evaluation of ProtecTIC allowed us to demonstrate that cybersecurity training can be more inclusive, accessible, and effective when designed specifically for vulnerable groups such as older adults and rural communities. One of the main contributions of the project was to shift the perspective of cybersecurity from a purely technical matter to an educational and social challenge. By integrating digital literacy with preventive strategies against fraud, ProtecTIC succeeded in addressing the root causes of digital vulnerability and not just its consequences.

Academically, the project contributed to the growing body of research on inclusive technologies, highlighting the need for user-centered methodologies and accessible design standards, such as WCAG 2.1 AAA compliance, which ensured usability for diverse populations. The iterative and participatory methodology used also provided valuable lessons for future research, showing that involving users in the design and testing phases leads to more effective and relevant technological solutions.

From a social perspective, ProtecTIC had important implications for reducing inequalities in digital access. By focusing on populations traditionally excluded from technological innovations, the project promoted not only the prevention of fraud but also broader goals of digital inclusion, autonomy, and empowerment. Participants reported greater confidence in navigating online environments, less dependence on relatives, and an increased sense of security when interacting with digital platforms. These findings reinforced the importance of considering accessibility and literacy as key elements in the fight against cybercrime.

In terms of public policy, the project demonstrated that initiatives like ProtecTIC can complement government strategies on digital security and inclusion. By adhering to data protection laws in Colombia (Law 1581 of 2012) and Mexico (Federal Law on the Protection of Personal Data Held by Private Parties, 2010), the project respected ethical and legal frameworks while proving the feasibility of applying similar models in other regions. Its alignment with international agendas, such as the Sustainable Development Goals (United Nations, 2015), positioned it as a valuable contribution to global efforts to reduce inequalities and foster inclusive digital participation.

Looking to the future, several lines of development emerged that could significantly expand the impact of ProtecTIC. One of the most promising is the integration of artificial intelligence (AI) to personalize user learning. AI could analyze user behavior in real time, identify frequent errors, and adapt training modules accordingly. For example, if a user struggled with detecting fraudulent emails, the system could increase the number of practice scenarios on that subject and provide guided explanations. Personalized feedback would not only enhance learning outcomes but also boost user motivation, as each participant would progress at their own pace and with tailored support.

In addition to personalization, AI could function as a first-hand assistant within the application. Users could ask immediate questions such as "Is this link safe?" or "How do I know if a WhatsApp message is legitimate?", receiving clear and simple answers. Such an assistant could be connected to databases of emerging scams, providing up-to-date alerts and enhancing the preventive value of the platform. This would transform ProtecTIC from a static educational tool into a dynamic, interactive companion for daily digital safety.

Another future development involves incorporating automated security scanners capable of detecting suspicious links and identifying cloned websites. Integrated into browsers or messaging applications, these tools would alert users when they attempted to access fraudulent sites or when a URL did not correspond to official domains. This functionality would provide users with a second layer of protection: while they strengthened their knowledge through practice, the system would simultaneously assist in detecting threats in real time.

Finally, scaling ProtecTIC to other contexts would require building networks of collaboration with banks, government entities, and community organizations. Such partnerships could expand the application's reach, provide official validation for its security tools, and facilitate centralized fraud reporting. Longitudinal studies would also be necessary to measure the long-term impact of the platform on digital literacy, fraud reduction, and resilience against cyber risks.

In conclusion, ProtecTIC represented a unique and valuable contribution to inclusive cybersecurity. Its emphasis on accessibility, digital education, and user empowerment showed that technological innovation can be designed to serve those most at risk. The future lines of work outlined here confirm that ProtecTIC has the potential not only to prevent fraud but also to redefine how societies approach cybersecurity, education, and digital inclusion.

REFERENCES

Anti-Phishing Working Group. (2023). *Phishing activity trends report: Q4 2023*. https://docs.apwg.org/reports/apwg_trends_report_q4_2023.pdf

Coursera. (2021). *Introduction to cybersecurity tools & cyberattacks*. IBM Skills Network. https://www.coursera.org/learn/introduction-cybersecurity-cyber-attacks

Cyber-Seniors. (2015). *Cyber-Seniors*. Cyber-Seniors Inc. https://cyberseniors.org

DANE. (2021). *Personas mayores en Colombia: Hacia la inclusión y la participación*. https://www.dane.gov.co/files/investigaciones/notas-estadisticas/nov-2021-nota-estadistica-personas-mayores-en-colombia.pdf

European Commission. (2021). *Digital economy and society index (DESI) 2021*. Publications Office of the European Union. https://digital-strategy.ec.europa.eu/en/policies/desi

Freire, P., & Santos, M. (2019). *Critical digital literacy in the information age*. Siglo XXI Editores.

Fundación Proacceso. (2023). *Red de Innovación y Aprendizaje (RIA)*. https://wiconnect.iadb.org/osc/fundacion-proacceso-eco

Fundación Saldarriaga Concha. (2022). *Digital inclusion for older adults in Colombia*. https://www.saldarriagaconcha.org/personas-mayores

Gómez Hernández, M., Ferre, X., Moral, C., & Villalba Mora, E. (2023). Design guidelines of mobile apps for older adults: Systematic review and thematic analysis. *JMIR mHealth and uHealth*, *11*(1), e43186. DOI: 10.2196/43186 PMID: 37733401

González, P., & López, A. (2021). Design of educational mobile applications for rural communities: A case study in Mexico. *Revista Latinoamericana de Educación y Tecnología*, *5*(1), 77–92.

Grilli, M. D., McVeigh, K. S., Hakim, Z. M., Wank, A. A., Getz, S. J., Levin, B. E., Ebner, N. C., & Wilson, R. C. (2021). Is this phishing? Older age is associated with greater difficulty discriminating between safe and malicious emails. *The Journals of Gerontology. Series B, Psychological Sciences and Social Sciences*, *76*(6), 1038–1048. DOI: 10.1093/geronb/gbaa228 PMID: 33378418

Gwala, N., & Mawela, T. (2024). Investigating the internet skills of older adults in South Africa. *The Arab Journal of the Social Sciences*, *70*(3), 45–60. DOI: 10.12724/ajss.70.3

INEGI & IFT. (2023). *Encuesta nacional sobre disponibilidad y uso de tecnologías de la información en los hogares (ENDUTIH) 2023*. https://www.inegi.org.mx/programas/endutih/2023

Inter-American Development Bank & Organization of American States. (2020). *2020 cybersecurity report: Risks, progress, and the way forward in Latin America and the Caribbean*. https://doi.org/DOI: 10.18235/0002513

Jiménez, L., & Salazar, R. (2021). Vishing and social manipulation: An emerging threat for older adults. *Revista Mexicana de Seguridad Informática, 9*(2), 112–129.

Kang, H., Baek, J., Chu, S. H., & Choi, J. (2023). Digital literacy among Korean older adults: A scoping review of quantitative studies. *Digital Health, 9*, 20552076231197334. Advance online publication. DOI: 10.1177/20552076231197334 PMID: 37654708

Kim, S., & Lee, J. (2020). National strategies for digital literacy and cybersecurity education: The case of South Korea. *Asian Journal of Education and Training, 6*(1), 12–22. DOI: 10.20448/journal.522.2020.61.12.22

Ley 1581 de 2012. (2012, October 17). *Ley de protección de datos personales*. Secretaría General de la Alcaldía Mayor de Bogotá. https://www.alcaldiabogota.gov.co/sisjur/normas/Norma1.jsp?i=49981

Ley Federal de Protección de Datos Personales en Posesión de los Particulares. (2010, July 5). *Diario Oficial de la Federación*. https://www.gob.mx/indesol/documentos/ley-federal-de-proteccion-de-datos-personales-en-posesion-de-los-particulares

López, M., & García, V. (2022). Smishing and vulnerability in mobile users in Latin America. *Revista Chilena de Ciberseguridad, 3*(1), 54–70.

Martínez, J., & Torres, A. (2020). Cyberfraud in the digital era: Trends and challenges. *Revista de Derecho y Tecnología, 11*(2), 33–57.

Muñoz García, J. (2019). Internet access and use by older adults in Colombia. *Revista de Estudios Sociales, 68*, 72–86. https://repository.umng.edu.co/handle/20.500.12727/1837

Nielsen, J. (2012). *Usability 101: Introduction to usability*. Nielsen Norman Group. https://www.nngroup.com/articles/usability-101-introduction-to-usability

Norman, D. A. (2013). *The design of everyday things* (Rev. ed.). MIT Press., https://mitpress.mit.edu/9780262525671

Okello, S. (2021). Digital literacy in Africa: The role of Smart Africa initiative. *African Journal of ICT Development, 14*(2), 56–73.

Oliveira, D. S., Rocha, H. A., Yang, H., Ellis, D. M., Dommaraju, S., Muradoglu, M., Weir, D., Soliman, A., Lin, T., & Ebner, N. C. (2017). Dissecting spear phishing emails for older vs. young adults. In *Proceedings of the 2017 CHI Conference on Human Factors in Computing Systems* (pp. 6412–6424). ACM. https://doi.org/DOI: 10.1145/3025453.3025831

Pérez, R., & Rivas, J. (2021). Experiential learning in cybersecurity: Digital fraud simulations for preventive education. *Revista Venezolana de Tecnología Educativa, 10*(1), 64–81.

Policía Nacional de Colombia. (2023). *Annual report on cybercrime 2023.* https:// caivirtual.policia.gov.co/sites/default/files/observatorio/Balance%20anual%202023 _0.pdf

Ramos, P., & Aguilar, F. (2021). Digital memory in rural communities: Challenges of technological literacy. *Revista Peruana de Ciencias Sociales, 12*(4), 188–205.

Rodríguez, S., & Morales, E. (2022). Inclusive interface and accessibility in older adults: A comparative study of mobile apps. *Revista Española de Interacción Digital, 9*(2), 44–59.

Sánchez, A., López, J., & Herrera, C. (2020). Vulnerability of older adults to online fraud: A study in Spain and Chile. *Revista Gerontológica Latinoamericana, 6*(1), 55–74.

Solve, M. I. T. (2023). *DigiMENTE: Media education for Latin America.* https:// solve.mit.edu/challenges/learning-for-civic-action-challenge/solutions/74650

The Gables. (2024, November 25). *Helping seniors with technology.* https://gables -living.com/about/blog/helping-seniors-with-technology

UNESCO. (2023). *The benefits of lifelong learning for older adults.* UNESCO Institute for Lifelong Learning. https://www.uil.unesco.org/en/thematic-studies -benefits-lifelong-learning-older-adults

United Nations. (2015). *Sustainable Development Goals.* United Nations Development Programme. https://www.undp.org/sustainable-development-goals

Vuorikari, R., Kluzer, S., & Punie, Y. (2022). *DigComp 2.2: The digital competence framework for citizens.* Publications Office of the European Union. https:// publications.jrc.ec.europa.eu/repository/handle/JRC128415

World Health Organization. (2021). *World health statistics 2021: Monitoring health for the SDGs, sustainable development goals.* https://www.who.int/publications/i/ item/9789240027053

World Wide Web Consortium. (2018). *Web content accessibility guidelines (WCAG) 2.1*. https://www.w3.org/TR/WCAG21

Section 3
Technological Developments Applied to Various Disabilities

Chapter 5
Design of Interaction Mechanisms Using Tangible Interfaces, Augmented Reality, and Eye-Tracking for a UX Focused on Children With ASD:
A Case Study

Angel Eduardo Villegas-Ortiz
https://orcid.org/0009-0008-8145-2055
Universidad Autónoma de Aguascalientes, Mexico

Francisco Javier Alvarez-Rodríguez
https://orcid.org/0000-0001-6608-046X
Universidad Autónoma de Aguascalientes, Mexico

Jocelyn Sandoval Flores
Universidad Autónoma de Tamaulipas, Mexico

Jesús A. Ramirez Vazquez
Universidad Autónoma de Tamaulipas, Mexico

Erick Gómez
Instituto Tecnológico de Chetumal, Mexico

José Emiliano Rodríguez Cervantes
Instituto Tecnológico de Chetumal, Mexico

David Perera
Instituto Tecnológico de Chetumal, Mexico

Edwin Adan Cruz Reyna
https://orcid.org/0009-0007-5248-2661
Universidad Autónoma de Tamaulipas, Mexico

DOI: 10.4018/979-8-3373-6033-1.ch005

ABSTRACT

The profile of children with ASD have difficulty interacting with conventional HCI methods. This work proposes to evaluate through eye-tracking the use of a UX focused on this profile through the design and development of mechanisms that use augmented reality and tangible interfaces. After an experimental deployment with a population of 7 children with different levels of support needs, it was possible to detect patterns among the children who had problems solving the activities. It is expected that these findings will allow a more schematic design using new technologies that will open the range of interaction methods.

INTRODUCTION

In this work, we present the process of constructing a software product aimed at children with Autism Spectrum Disorder (ASD), with the purpose of proposing new forms of interaction and strengthening specific skills within this profile through the implementation of innovative technologies. Achieving an appropriate development process for such a specific profile with innovative methods requires more than simply following conventional frameworks.

This study provides an in-depth exploration of the implementation process of technologies that have been scarcely integrated into large-scale projects, such as augmented reality, tangible interfaces, and eye-tracking. Each of these technologies entails its own challenges and technical difficulties, and beyond their mere implementation, there is the additional challenge of ensuring that the designed user experience (UX) adequately addresses the usability issues associated with the ASD profile. Moreover, this experience is not limited to playful or entertainment-oriented content; rather, it must be capable of adapting existing didactic activities to reinforce skills in which this profile typically encounters difficulties, such as lack of empathy, completing prolonged tasks, or communicating, among others.

To improve the tracking of key points in the development process, a Theoretical Framework section is established following the Problem Statement, introducing the main concepts and approaches employed in this work. The Methodologies section outlines all processes supporting the product's development. Given the specific conditions of the project (to be described later), custom methodologies were designed based on previous studies, particularly for the proposals involving tangible interfaces and experimentation with eye-tracking.

The Development section details each stage of the product's production and also addresses several of the most relevant difficulties encountered during the project.

Since the work involves the integration of multiple technologies, certain scenarios could not be anticipated at the outset.

Finally, the Results section presents visualizations from a group of seven participants with ASD, aged between 6 and 15 years, with autism levels ranging from 1 to 2 according to specialists. Both the Results and Conclusions sections discuss possible interpretations of the visual attention patterns identified.

JUSTIFICATION

Contemporary interface designs, as well as current interaction mechanisms, are primarily oriented toward neurotypical individuals without motor disabilities. For most people, the idea of interacting with a computer system may appear routine and relatively unchallenging. However, paradigms such as equitable development consistently highlight the shortcomings of conventional interaction methods when applied to specific user groups.

In software developments intended for a broad audience, it is uncommon to encounter experiences that explicitly consider the ASD profile. This gap restricts the capacity of projects with specialized proposals for this population to reach a wider audience. Beyond the usability of a product for individuals with ASD, it is essential to adapt didactic activities that have been proven effective in improving skills within this profile, while deploying them through more advanced technologies (Lawan et al., 2023).

According to Groba-González et al. (2015), there are significant benefits in the implementation of ICTs, particularly during early developmental stages, provided that the activities or dynamics are appropriately designed. Within the ASD profile, as will be discussed in greater detail in the theoretical framework, skills such as communication and language, as well as emotion recognition and empathy, among others, require intensive reinforcement. Without the support of trained personnel and adequate tools, children are unlikely to achieve practical progress in these areas.

Technologies such as Augmented Reality (AR) have gained popularity as tools that enable the design of new types of experiences, potentially enhancing skills that require reinforcement. Nevertheless, certain activities or resources are not "translatable" to the interaction characteristics offered by AR (López-Belmonte et al., 2024). Furthermore, the technical knowledge and expertise required to implement AR can be highly complex for specialists, while software development teams often lack sufficient understanding of the ASD profile to tailor the experience to its needs. This disciplinary gap has hindered both the quantity and quality of medium- and large-scale software products addressing this topic (Çorlu et al., 2017).

The concept of tangible interfaces (TUI) has also contributed to the exploration of alternative forms of interaction aimed at fostering inclusion, particularly for individuals with physical limitations. However, tangible properties such as texture, size, or weight are highly intuitive for users and especially appealing to children without ASD (Ramos Aguiar & Álvarez Rodríguez, 2021).

In this line of thought, extended reality environments have proven to be among the most promising alternatives for providing neurodivergent profiles with spaces and mechanisms that minimize the difficulties inherent in conventional interaction methods (López-Bouzas & Del Moral Pérez, 2023).

OBJECTIVES

In order to establish the guidelines of this work, the following general and specific objectives are presented, considering the existing gap for the ASD profile in terms of interaction mechanisms with digital media.

General Objective

-To implement and explore the potential of different technologies in proposing innovative interaction mechanisms that can be objectively evaluated, thereby expanding the capacity of UX (User Experience) design processes for under-represented profiles.

Specific Objectives

- To identify the main usage characteristics of the ASD profile, as well as the most employed didactic activities, to determine the most suitable implementation approach.
- To examine the feasibility of integrating multiple technologies for the design and proposal of innovative interaction mechanisms adapted to the ASD profile.
- To conduct an initial interpretation of ET (Eye-Tracking) results to study the visual attention patterns of children with ASD.

THEORICAL FRAMEWORK

Although each of the technologies employed in this work has a broad and well-established state of the art, there are few studies that integrate these technologies, and even fewer that apply them jointly to such a specific profile as ASD. This section addresses the general concepts that underpin the proposals of this project.

In addition to reviewing the most widely accepted definitions and the categories of support levels for individuals with ASD, particular emphasis is placed on the potential implementations of these technologies in improving the skills associated with this profile. This section begins with the most relevant aspect, the ASD profile that motivates all design decisions, and proceeds through the technologies used in this project, in order of their applied use. For each topic, an effort is made to specify its implementation in projects that consider the ASD profile.

Autism Spectre Disorder (ASD)

Autism Spectrum Disorder (ASD) is a neurological condition that affects social skills such as verbal communication, emotion recognition, and the presence of obsessive and repetitive behaviors. This disorder is observed primarily in children between the ages of 6 and 15, representing a significant obstacle to their academic formation and overall personal development (Celis Alcalá & Ochoa Madrigal, 2022).

The ASD profile demonstrates a high degree of focus and attention on skills or topics of personal interest. While certain themes are common among many children, most develop their own particular interests, which often complicates the diagnostic process.

According to the most widely accepted theories, autism levels can be divided into three categories (Celis Alcalá & Ochoa Madrigal, 2022; Morocho Fajardo et al., 2021):

- Level 1: Requires mild support. Individuals experience difficulties interacting with others, their daily activities are reduced, and they are unable to respond appropriately to their environment.
- Level 2: Requires substantial support. Individuals exhibit pronounced communication difficulties, rarely initiate social interactions voluntarily, and tend to display repetitive and obsessive behaviors. They struggle to adapt to changes in their environment.
- Level 3: Requires very substantial support. Individuals face severe challenges in social communication, find it extremely difficult to establish contact with others, and are highly unlikely to initiate social interaction. Their capacity for empathy is greatly reduced, and they struggle to recognize figures outside their intimate circle.

As evidenced by the levels described above, the common factor among all three is the need for support from others to perform daily-life skills. The intervention of specialist's familiar with the ASD profile is of vital importance for improving personal skills and fostering better social behaviors.

In Latin America, the gap in access to tools and treatments remains significant for most of the population. Although educational institutions have increasingly embraced the adaptation of pedagogical methods to profiles such as ASD, the region continues to exhibit one of the highest school dropout rates worldwide. Beyond academic challenges and social stigmas prevalent in many countries, adults with ASD also face low levels of labor market integration. These issues are further exacerbated by the lack of support from associations and specialists in the field (Morocho Fajardo et al., 2021).

In Mexico, there are no prevalence data based on epidemiological research. Few institutions conduct adequate data collection; currently, the statistics provided by INEGI (Instituto Nacional de Estadística y Geografía) are not widely accepted by experts in the field. This institute reports nearly 5,000 children with autism nationwide, whereas global trends indicate a prevalence of approximately 1 in every 160 children with some degree of autism (Celis Alcalá & Ochoa Madrigal, 2022).

Communication Difficulties in Children with AS

Communication is the ability to share information and achieve mutual understanding among individuals in a social environment. It encompasses all possible forms of transmitting messages, including gestures, facial expressions, images, sounds, and others (Stirling et al., 2014). The study by Hage et al. (2022) indicates that children with autism may present difficulties in the following areas:

- Problems with gestures, facial expressiveness, eye contact, and gaze following.
- Difficulty in establishing or responding to joint attention (noticing when someone points out or shows something), maintaining eye contact, or responding to their own name.
- Lack of coordination in conversational rhythm: difficulties in responding or acting in synchrony with the interlocutor during dialogue.

Language Difficulties in Children with ASD

Language is understood as the system of signs that enables communication, and in the case of oral language, through sounds. It is often compromised in individuals with ASD. Delays in its development are usually among the first signs that alert families. Children with autism may exhibit atypical crying, reduced or absent babbling, significant delays in the emergence of words and phrases, a very limited vocabulary, predominant use of echolalia instead of spontaneous language, difficulties with communicative gestures, and problems using language in social contexts or understanding its more abstract aspects. Since language is essential for socialization, its impairment significantly impacts social integration (Barajas Alcantara, 2022).

Didactic Mechanisms in Children with ASD

The main didactic mechanisms for improving the skills of children with ASD consist of incorporating physical stimuli and toys that represent specific concepts, informing the child that each activity has a maximum duration to avoid anxiety caused by uncertainty, and focusing their attention on a single task—even when it is not of personal interest—given their strong resistance to change (Vélez & Rivadeneira, 2024).

According to Vazquez-Vazquez et al. (2020), achieving a successful learning process for this profile requires consideration of three stages: Anticipation, Construction, and Consolidation. The first stage seeks to prevent any eventuality during the activity, taking into account the classroom environment and the specialist's notes on the child's behavior. The construction stage involves the use of various conventional didactic tools that can be adapted to the interests of the profile, with the recommendation that each activity include defined processes for all possible scenarios. Finally, the consolidation stage aims for the child to be able to relate the knowledge or experiences acquired during the activity to subsequent sessions.

User-Centered Design

User-Centered Design (UCD) is a UX (User Experience) design paradigm that aims to place the needs of a potential product user at the center of all software production decisions. This paradigm considers the user as the primary source of information, since the experience is shaped according to their usage preferences to achieve the most suitable outcome (Calderón Ynoñan et al., 2022).

At present, few organizations provide truly effective accessibility tools due to the technological effort required to develop them. Moreover, it is well known that many contemporary design decisions are based purely on economic considerations, seeking to attract the largest possible audience with a single UX. This approach not only excludes many users but also widens the usability gap between neurotypical individuals or those without motor disabilities and individuals who face difficulties interacting with digital systems.

When the ASD profile is taken into account, this gap becomes even more pronounced. For many small-scale development processes, conducting in-depth analyses of such a profile is not considered viable, as it may not significantly expand the limited reach of the project. On the other hand, large-scale development processes often prefer not to take risks by proposing experimental interaction methods, given the difficulty of anticipating or planning for all scenarios involved in specific profiles such as ASD (Iqbal et al., 2021).

User-Centered Design Implemented in the ASD Profile

As users become increasingly complex and specific, the proper functioning of UCD profiles becomes more challenging. In this context, concepts such as Equitable Design and Inclusive Design serve as spearheads for approaches that consider underrepresented profiles. In the current market, few platforms can adjust their UX (User Experience) through adequate accessibility tools for diverse user profiles (Molina Gutiérrez et al., 2025).

The usage patterns observed in children with autism are sufficiently complex and difficult to model, even when applying the UCD paradigm. Nevertheless, UCD represents an initial approach to addressing and counteracting many of the design and interaction deficiencies found in software that does not consider this profile. Despite the aforementioned challenges for the UCD paradigm, it remains the most inclusive and adaptive alternative for underrepresented users (López-Belmonte et al., 2024).

Furthermore, while the previous idea refers to "adapting" interactions with respect to the profile, this work aims to "propose" new interaction techniques that not only compensate for design shortcomings but also establish novel methods to abstract and represent complex ideas in specific profiles. In this way, the software product can serve as a medium of expression or learning between the individual and the surrounding world (Sierra & Contreras Juárez, 2023).

Augmented Reality (AR)

Augmented Reality (AR) is a technique that enables the deployment of two-dimensional and three-dimensional models within real-world spaces, thereby enhancing the environment's capacity for interaction. The resources that can be displayed are not strictly limited to objects grounded in reality; rather, they may encompass a wide variety of stimuli in diverse forms and colors. These can be particularly appealing, offering immersive experiences that foster imagination in both children and adults.

According to del Moral-Pérez & López-Bouzas (2021), augmented reality is frequently applied in various fields, including education, psychological experimentation, and technology. The latter includes studies related to playful activities designed for entertainment and familiarization with everyday tasks in individuals with autism, promoting aspects such as communication, idea expression, empathy, and emotional regulation.

Despite the advantages of augmented reality, its implementation remains limited when it comes to enabling appropriate interaction for individuals with diverse difficulties in engaging with digital systems. To recognize the potential benefits of augmented reality for children with autism, it is essential to note that while certain interactions may appear intuitive for neurotypical individuals, many scenarios can be chaotic, visually overwhelming, and may prevent children from responding adequately to a planned sequence (Çorlu et al., 2017).

Tangible User Interfaces

Tangible User Interfaces (TUI) are a technique within Human-Computer Interaction (HCI) that employs physical mechanisms capable of executing actions in the system or displaying different information on the screen, depending on the object and the position or movements performed by the user. Each proposal involving tangible interfaces tends to be conceived "outside the box," as the interaction methods are so particular that each one constitutes a world of its own.

One of the characteristics of learning in children is that, during early developmental stages, their tactile and sensory perceptions serve as the primary source of information. This curious behavior—chewing, crushing, stretching, touching, and eagerly exploring a toy—tends to diminish once language skills allow them to acquire new information that complements what was previously obtained through sensations and cognitive associations with objects. In the case of autism, particularly in children with communication difficulties, the tactile and sensory exploration stage extends into much later ages. Consequently, it is common to find children with marked attention retention toward objects with specific textures or repetitive behaviors in search of particular physical sensations (Celis Alcalá & Ochoa Madrigal, 2022; Costello et al., 2021).

The technical implementation of this concept requires physical objects known as "markers," which can be recognized by a camera and, depending on their location or presence on the screen, can trigger various events in the UX. In the specific case of autism, markers represent a highly engaging alternative, offering different textures and dimensions that allow children to more easily abstract concepts from the real world. This, in turn, enhances their ability to solve problems and associate aspects such as emotions and idea expression with the activities they perform (Passerino & Baldassarri, 2017).

Eye-tracking

Eye-tracking (ET) techniques have established themselves as a method for obtaining biometric and precise data, with the objective of providing software or market analyses with an additional layer of depth. Only a few decades ago, implementing eye-tracking technology required a significant technological and experimental effort for any team seeking to integrate it into their project. In the early years of the formal industry of gaze-tracking technologies, applications were primarily focused on fields such as road safety or consumer attraction to product packaging (Albiz et al., 2023).

In recent years, the state of the art in eye-tracking has begun to recognize the advantages of gaze-tracking as a valuable tool in interface analysis and its inclusion in various software development processes (Inal et al., 2024). Although still only marginally used in large-scale software projects, the strength of the technology appears to be gaining recognition as a new source of objective information that reflects user behavior when interacting with an interface.

Expanding on the previous idea, as mentioned in the section on user profiles within UCD, an important part of designing a robust profile is considering the most relevant user variables. Yet, what if demographic variables do not adequately represent the designed user? One of the main disadvantages identified in the UCD model is that designers can easily bias the profile, and often this profile, being incongruent with the real user, generates a feedback loop in which the suggested changes "distort" the profile until it fits the new properties of the UX (Calderón Ynoñan et al., 2022).

At this point, biometric data obtained through eye-tracking can differentiate potential users more precisely than profiling alone. In these data, variables such as age, prior experience, or preferences are not discriminants; rather, they enable the generation of visual attention patterns that are distinguishable for everyone.

Human Visual Attention and Its Relationship with UX/UI

Human visual attention is a process closely related to activities such as information search, reading, object tracking, and estimating the size and depth of objects, among many others. Although there are various types of eye-trackers, the most commonly used within software engineering are those capable of recording visual attention when a person interacts with a screen or monitor (Albiz et al., 2023) This ease of data acquisition opens numerous fields for experimentation with any stimulus that can be digitally displayed (Bruce & Hawes, 2015).

Different manufacturers provide varying metrics and specifications; however, most share the primary measures used to break down a visual attention process: fixations and saccadic movements. Thanks to these variables, it is possible to generate both visualizations of the obtained visual patterns and hard data recorded during testing (Albiz et al., 2023; Zhou et al., 2023).

Eye-Tracking and Autism

In recent years, a relationship has been established between eye-tracking techniques and specific behaviors associated with autism. Reinforcing the previous idea that visual attention processes appear to be governed by broader and more complex cognitive mechanisms, Falck-Ytter et al. (2013) note that the feature enabling eye-tracking to detect differences in children with autism is precisely its subordinate relationship to cognitive processes. If autism is understood as the execution of atypical cognitive processes, these will be reflected in the visual attention patterns observed when a stimulus is presented.

Some of the difficulties experienced by children with autism are not directly related to visual attention processes. However, Boraston & Blakemore (2007) argue that communication and speech problems do not arise from an inability to "find the words." Rather, the child's cognitive structure struggles to process information and to execute actions and reactions to stimuli appropriately. Indirectly, this affects other aspects of communication, such as reading processes, and can impair the child's ability to remain engaged with their context, leading to disregard for others' emotions and further reducing their capacity to express ideas. Over time, this gradually undermines their ability to interact with the surrounding world. Once the relationship between reading processes and communication difficulties in children with autism is established, it becomes more feasible to interpret eye-tracking results accurately.

More recently, eye-tracking data have been processed using artificial intelligence techniques to propose support models for the diagnosis of autism, primarily in children. This field has yielded valuable implementations for studying the profile across multiple domains, including academic contexts and the improvement of everyday activities (Jaradat et al., 2025; Oliveira et al., 2021; Zhang et al., 2021).

Divergent and Convergent Visual Attention Patterns

Given a population of test subjects or users, the group of Convergent Visual Attention Users is defined as those who share the same visual pattern when interacting with a UX. It is established that if a UX achieves a majority of convergent users, the experience can be considered homogeneous and easy to understand.

In proposals related to previous studies, it is stipulated that any UX evaluated through eye-tracking must establish its Desired Interaction Sequence. In this sequence, each interface element is assigned a predefined route to ensure uniform use among target users. While this analysis focuses on the effectiveness and efficiency of the interface, these concepts can also be linked to design performance by reducing cognitive load and making the system more intuitive to use.

Conversely, Divergent Users are those whose interaction with the interface or UX does not align with convergent patterns. Considering divergences is highly relevant, as they can serve as valuable sources of information by revealing "out-of-the-box" perspectives on UX usage to designers and evaluators. Questions such as: Which elements seemed confusing to the user? Why did the user seek information in a place overlooked by others? Can the current design be modified to convert divergent users into convergent ones, or is an entirely alternate version required for this group? Within divergent patterns, are there convergences among them, or are they all unique cases? Point toward more inclusive designs and more precise UX tailored to each profile considered.

Analysis of Preselected Technologies for Integration in Interaction Design for Autism Profiles

Throughout this section, a set of technologies with highly valuable properties for interaction design in autism profiles has been discussed. However, it is important to highlight the most significant contributions of each in order to achieve an innovative proposal for interaction.

In the case of AR (Augmented Reality), one of the main advantages for autism profiles is the improvement of emotional intelligence, as well as the recognition of emotions in others. Enhancements in social skills can also be observed (Khowaja et al., 2020). These advantages are possible because augmented reality has a strong capacity to fully immerse the individual, allowing exploration and the breaking of certain cognitive barriers that the profile often creates.

According to Berenguer et al. (2020), a cognitive barrier in children with autism may arise due to rejection of social interaction. When the purely social component is removed, cognitive tension appears to decrease drastically. These barriers, however, seem to be broken only when, in addition to removing all cognitive stressors, the resources and activities are properly bounded to make them engaging and minimally frustrating.

By incorporating the concept of TUI (Tangible User Interfaces), AR significantly expands its possibilities for interaction design, as it becomes possible to generate mechanisms of information exchange beyond the traditional keyboard and mouse. This paradigm shift offers UX experiences that are far more appealing to children (Francis et al., 2019).

Using ET (Eye-Tracking) data, it is possible to analyze children's behavior in detail during UX interactions, enabling precise and controlled evaluation of their engagement (Jaradat et al., 2025; Zhang et al., 2021). At this point, the concept of UCD (User-Centered Design) comes into play, since—if followed strictly—design decisions must be based on potential users. This raises pertinent questions: Will all children within the autism profile yield the same results? Is it possible to use the collected usage data as drivers for design decisions for this profile?

These questions point toward the design of user experiences in which individuals are not merely "separated" due to a condition, but rather their usage characteristics are addressed as a starting point for designing complete, appropriate, comfortable experiences with all the necessary features to ensure accessibility for these individuals as well as for other users.

These questions point toward the design of user experiences in which individuals are not merely "separated" due to a condition, but rather their usage characteristics are addressed as a starting point for designing complete, appropriate, comfortable experiences with all the necessary features to ensure accessibility for these individuals as well as for other users.

METHODOLOGIES

As part of the foundation for the software production process in this case study, the main methodologies are proposed as indispensable pillars for the design and development of a platform based on the leading paradigms of the state of the art. The development team is aware of its lack of specific knowledge in modeling a UX for such a specialized profile as autism; therefore, the selection of models or frameworks primarily considers their ability to adapt to designs for groups of people who have historically been overlooked.

One of the major challenges in designing pleasant UX experiences for historically underrepresented profiles is that existing projects often have limited scope, and very few organizations or institutions possess the resources—or even the interest—to generate broader frameworks supported by real users. Conversely, access to these highly specific groups often becomes complicated due to logistical and operational issues, or, as emphasized throughout this work, due to the complexity of designing interactions without relying on conventional HCI methods for users with particular difficulties (Costello et al., 2021).

This section presents the main methodological processes that provide the project with a solid foundation upon which development can be based, with the aim of improving the final product's capacity to offer solutions and enhance the quality of life of specific groups of people. **Figure *1*** illustrates the general diagram of UX production specialized for children with autism profiles

Figure 1. Production Process Diagram for a UX for profiles with ASD.

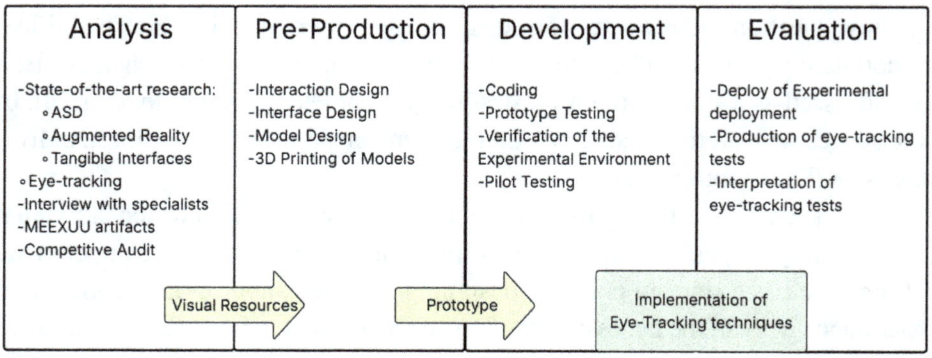

Methodology for Technology Integration

For this work, the implementation of technologies that are rarely used in large-scale products today is sought. Therefore, experimentation with the integration of these technologies becomes key to the design and implementation of new HCI methods adapted to autism profiles.

Aspects such as didactic activities or those aimed at reinforcing skills in autism profiles are considerably different from materials designed for neurotypical profiles. This is why the challenge is not only to "adapt" materials to innovative HCI mechanisms, but also to carefully consider the properties of the profile so that the individual can comfortably engage with a UX designed specifically for them, rather than having to "adapt" to it.

Tangible interfaces, for their part, require two components to function: markers and the models to be displayed on the screen. In this case, 3D printing techniques were used to bring tangible elements of the experience to life. Additionally, to homogenize visual content, AI-based image design tools were employed to improve the quality of the representations.

The aim is to integrate tools such as Unity, Vuforia, Tinkercad, Thingiverse, Blender, Flashforge Creator 3, Tobii Pro Lab, and Tobii Pro Nano by Tobii Technologies, which together will enable the development of a robust UX. Figure 3 shows, and **Figure** *2* shows the methodological diagram related to this section.

Figure 2. Production Process Diagram for a UX for profiles with ASD.

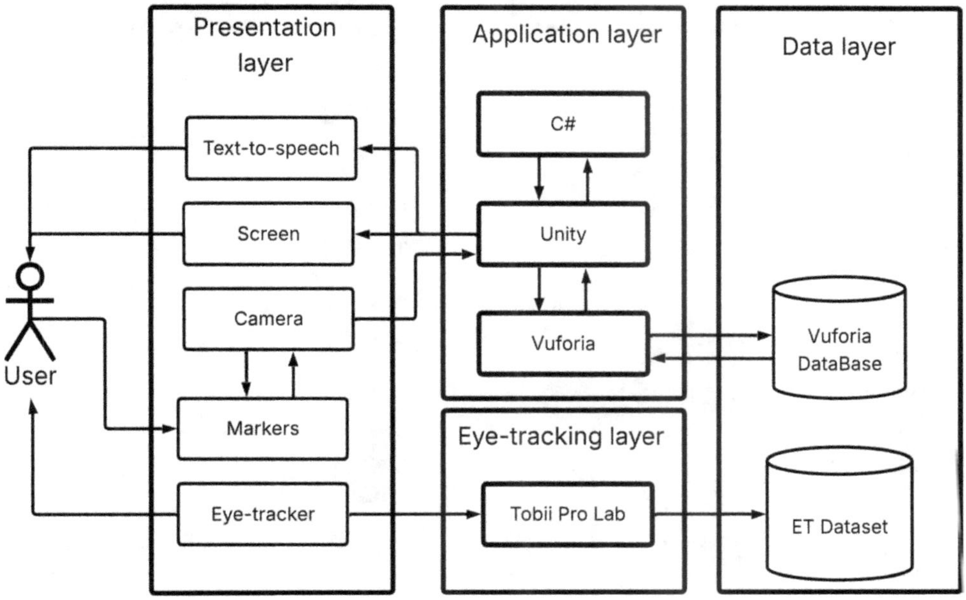

Methodologies and Software Development Approaches

MEEXUU

As mentioned in the theoretical framework section, many software development processes fail to incorporate user needs into their projects for various reasons. Within the state of the art, however, it is possible to find proposals that consider underrepresented users and, beyond that, design and propose different approaches to interactions with the UI.

The MEEXUU methodology (MEthodology, EXtended reality, Universal design for learning, User-centered design) is specialized for the creation of extended reality applications and tangible interfaces. It incorporates user-centered design and aims to support learning.

This methodology consistently considers users throughout the development process. It also integrates aspects such as universal design for learning and gamification mechanisms, where applicable to the experience being designed. **Figure *3*** provides a general overview of the processes and stages of the MEEXUU methodology.

Figure 3. Diagram of stages and processes of the MEEXUU framework.

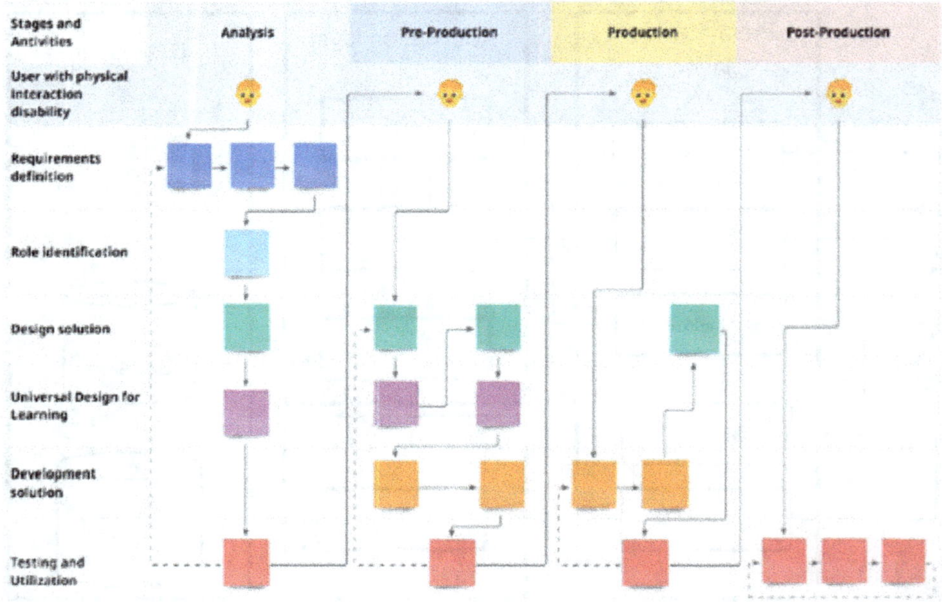

Profile Design

To design the profiles, a literature review was conducted to strengthen the team's understanding of ASD, given that direct access to the profile requires sensitivity usually limited to parents or specialists. Due to resistance to change and social difficulties, conventional methods such as interviews or forms were discarded. Instead, three mechanisms were employed: a competitive audit, profile design based on needs and frustrations, and a specialist survey. Expert interviews provided detailed insights that not only refined the profile definition but also prepared the team to anticipate unexpected outcomes during software testing.

Metodología de análisis de UX mediante ET.

Profiling a person through visual attention patterns in neurotypical populations is complex, as it requires the application of artificial intelligence techniques to datasets. In turn, for AI analyses to achieve adequate precision, they need data volumes on the order of thousands, tens of thousands, or even hundreds of thousands of different records. Unfortunately, there are no datasets that record visual attention data at such a scale using eye-tracking, and even less so for profiles as specific as autism.

Unlike the proposed experimental sequence diagram in *Figure 4*, actual experimental executions generally require fewer technical resources for deployment. One of the first aspects considered is that the child with autism should avoid the eye-tracking calibration stage, as this task may distract them from subsequent activities or directly cause anxiety or discomfort. For this reason, prior to each test, the experimental team recalibrates the environment, with the disadvantage that the accuracy of the readings decreases slightly.

There are also several "familiarization" processes conducted before the activities, which improve the child's ability to complete the test. Finally, usage conditions are established to prevent the child from becoming frustrated during the experiment. As can be observed, the design of the experimental sequence does not replicate conventional experimentation processes; instead, contextual conditions of the experiment are taken into account to avoid negatively affecting or irritating the child.

Figure 4. Experimental Sequence Diagram

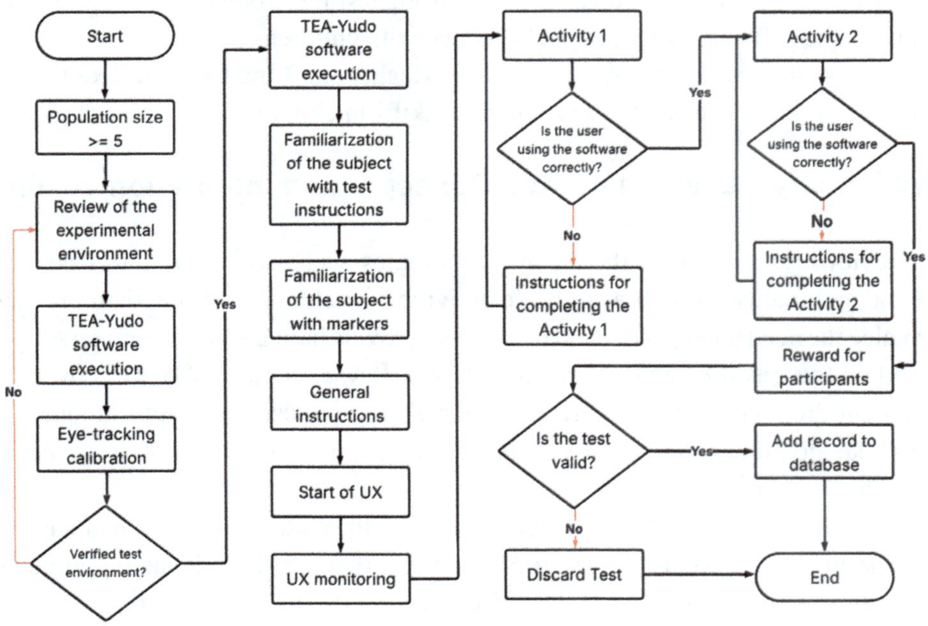

In general, a visual attention pattern represented through visual data representation mechanisms allows for conjectures regarding the overall use of a UX. In other words, the absence of access to deeper data analyses necessitates comparing the obtained visual attention patterns with bibliographic materials and, more importantly, examining the effect of the studied UI on the presence of these patterns.

This makes it evident that, in order to achieve an adequate interpretation, it is essential to have a detailed understanding of visual attention processes and the sub-processes that may be generated depending on the content displayed on the screen.

DEVELOPMENT

The software product designed specifically for children with autism, named "TEA-yudo", uses the Spanish acronym for Autism Spectrum Disorder (Trastorno de Espectro Autista, TEA) to create a wordplay that translates as "I help you". This name reflects the main objective of the product: to provide an exploration and communication tool tailored to this profile.

The autism-specialized association Autismo Aguascalientes A.C. (AUTAG) serves as the primary validation body for all proposals generated in this work. AUTAG provides primary information sources for requirements acquisition during early stages with specialists, as well as support during testing to objectively improve and evaluate the software product's performance with children.

TEA-yudo seeks to integrate Augmented Reality and Tangible Interfaces to offer a set of experiences designed to strengthen skills in children with autism.

Preliminary Research on Key Concepts and Integration Testing

Reviewing the state of the art in technologies such as tangible interfaces and augmented reality, as well as didactic activities for children with autism profiles, revealed the need for experimental methods to provide human-computer interactions based on the specific needs of this user group (Lawan et al., 2023). Moreover, for many children with high support needs in carrying out daily activities, interacting with a keyboard or mouse proves to be a complex, unintuitive task that can easily overwhelm them (Iqbal et al., 2021).

The results of research on didactic activities for children with autism showed that the most common activities aimed at strengthening skills focus on language development, improving communication with people in their environment, and fostering attention on a specific task (Barajas Alcantara, 2022; Hage et al., 2022).

Stage 1: Analysis

Once the tools to be used in the project have been selected, an initial roadmap is drawn up showing what the proposed software can and cannot do. It is from this point that the software development process formally begins.

The MEEXUU methodology manages to provide the team with the right information in the early stages of development so that, regardless of the asynchrony of the processes, they can be "put together" at the end of a sprint.

Analysis

For the analysis and planning stage, the MEEXUU methodology (Ramos Aguiar & Álvarez Rodríguez, 2021) enables the generation of small artifacts that capture the most relevant processes of this phase. Among the first artifacts, the product objectives are established, considering the aim of innovating interaction mechanisms for children with autism. The product objectives are as follows:

- Creation of appealing objects for children with autism with which they can interact.
- Design and development of gestures and interactions specialized for children with autism.
- An engaging narrative to capture children's attention through text-to-speech.
- Design of 3D models to address challenges within the interactive story.

Subsequently, some requirements were collected, based on the technical estimates of technology integration provided by the development team. The UCD concept dictates that information must be obtained directly from the user. In this case, the autism profile must be approached with great care, as the intention is never to make the child uncomfortable. Therefore, during the early development stage, information was gathered from individuals who spend significant time with the target users—in this case, specialists.

Interview with Specialists

The autism-specialized association Autismo Aguascalientes A.C. (AUTAG), hereafter referred to as "Association AUTAG," served as the primary source of information to identify user needs. In this initial requirements collection, the findings were based on needs identified in the state of the art. Although these requirements were not included in the final design analysis, they served as a starting point to bridge gaps between specialists, their recommendations, the development team's ideas, and the technical capabilities of each technology as a tool for the autism profile.

Among the most notable comments from specialists (information obtained from a group of specialists at Association AUTAG) were:

- Dinosaurs and trains are of extremely high interest to the autism profile.
- Ideas must be expressed directly and clearly, without figurative language or colloquial expressions.
- Strong, highly saturated colors attract attention powerfully—both positively and negatively. A pastel color palette is recommended.
- In most cases of autism profiles with high support needs, a specialist must be present at all times to prevent frustration during tests and exercises.
- Empathizing with and recognizing the emotions of other children or adults is a very weak point for the autism profile.
- Communicating and making decisions based on context is also a challenging task for the autism profile.
- Sounds and visual rewards are highly appealing to children with autism, but they can also overwhelm them if the audio is not friendly.

Requirements

In this meeting, a brainstorming session was conducted between the team and the specialists to define the best mechanisms for offering a UX that proposes an innovative method of interaction for a specific profile: children with autism.

Table 1 and *Table 2* present the functional and non-functional requirements, respectively, aiming to represent as closely as possible the information obtained from the specialists, cross-referenced with the feasibility estimates from the technology integration analysis.

Table 1. Table of Functional Requirements

ID	Requirement
F1	Design, display, and deploy 3D models designed to meet the "eye-catching" characteristics for the ASD profile.
F2	Provide an environment that allows for the integration of Augmented Reality and Tangible Interface technologies for the design of activities focused on the ASD profile.
F3	Activity that implements the proposed design of gesture-based interaction in augmented reality.
F4	Activity that allows the deployment of an exercise using markers and augmented reality that stimulates Specialist-Child communication.

Table 2. Table of non-Functional Requirements

ID	Requirement
NF1	The gesture is easy to identify, responds in real time, and provides feedback to the user when a selection is made.
NF2	The communication exercise validates incorrect entries and timeouts.
NF3	Technologies should not interfere with the user's UX either on screen or physically.

Stage 2: Pre-production

Interaction Design

Interaction through tangible interfaces is not a new concept; however, implementations of this technology remain limited. Likewise, the term gesture has been more closely associated with mobile devices. These characteristics slightly restrict the implementation of interaction mechanisms in desktop applications.

This project aims to provide a software tool through which children with autism can communicate and strengthen skills. At the same time, it proposes a set of objects that serve both as markers for augmented reality and as interaction elements for tangible interfaces.

3D printing makes it possible to materialize an infinite variety of three-dimensional models that can be highly appealing to children. In this case, one of the first printed models was the book. This marker, which can be held in one hand, functions to display several 3D elements using augmented reality. The models appear together with their movement animations and sound effects while "floating" above the marker.

The interaction design of the book marker is conceived to allow movement from left to right within the camera's field of view. If the marker is moved to the right, the mascot on that side is selected; if the position is maintained for four seconds, a selection notice appears on the screen. Moving the marker in the opposite direction selects the other model in the same way. This gesture can be repeated indefinitely as long as the marker is pointed toward the screen. *Figure 5* illustrates the designed gesture.

Figure 5. Proposed gesture for interaction using augmented reality in Activity 1

Experience 1, called the "Exploration Menu", presents a prototype of interaction through gestures using a physical marker to perform actions on augmented reality elements. This experience fosters children's imagination by displaying two "pets" (see *Figure 6*) in the form of dinosaurs.

Using a marker called "Book", children move it from left to right or vice versa to switch between the models displayed on the screen, employing the gesture-based interaction mechanism described earlier.

Figure 6. **Models generated to serve as 3D pets in Activity 1.**

Experience 2, called the "Language Activity", involves an exercise designed to improve children's language abilities through four different questions that test their capacity to understand their environment, express ideas, recognize the feelings and emotions of other children, and act accordingly. Seven 3D-printed markers are proposed, each representing specific actions for the four questions. In the activity, the child interacts with the "Bus" model to initiate the test, after which the following questions are displayed sequentially:

- "The school bell rings for recess. What do you do? Do you get up from your chair and leave the classroom? Or do you wait for the teacher's instructions?"
- "A classmate is running, trips, and looks at you while crying. What do you think your classmate is feeling? Sadness? Or pain?"
- "You are playing tag with a friend, but suddenly he says he is bored and no longer wants to play. What do you do? Do you insist on continuing the game? Or do you respect his decision?"
- "You are playing with a friend and his toy falls, breaks, and he looks down crying. What do you think your friend is feeling? Sadness? Or pain?"

To answer the questions, the child uses a set of markers that represent ideas such as Sadness, Pain, Stop, Continue or Insist, Wait, or Run. In addition, the markers feature textures and vivid colors to capture the child's attention. The tangible object triggers a visual representation in the 3D environment that provides immediate feedback to the child. At the same time, the software issues sound like notifications for each interaction, which, together with the specialist, help verify or correct the child's response. The designs of the test models are presented below.

Models Design

Different methods were tested for displaying 2D and 3D models, each with specific advantages and challenges. Internal testing revealed that rotating 3D models with markers helped sustain user attention. However, for Activity 2, 3D models proved problematic, as the markers represented specific emotions or situations that were difficult to convey unambiguously in three dimensions, potentially hindering communication between children with ASD and specialists. Consequently, 2D models were adopted. Given time constraints, AI-based image generators (ChatGPT and Copilot) were used to create homogeneous resources, which were then refined through team discussions. The final 2D models, selected for their pleasant colors and suitability for the ASD profile, are shown in Figure *7*, Figure *8*, Figure *9* and Figure *10*. Their design style, inspired by contemporary animated films, helps reduce the familiarity gap for users

Figure 7. Model for starting Activity 2.

Figure 8. 2D models to represent the actions of: Running or Waiting.

Figure 9. 2D models to represent the actions of: Hurt or Sadness.

Figure 10. 2D models to represent the actions of: stop playing or insist.

The final markers are shown in *Figure 11, Figure 12, Figure 13 and Figure 14.*

Figure 11. "School Bus" marker designed to start Activity 2.

Figure 12. Markers to represent the actions of: Running or Waiting.

Figure 13. Markers to represent the actions of stop playing or insist.

Figure 14. Markers to represent the actions of: Hurt or Sadness.

Finally, several prints were generated to give a participation badge to the children who took part in the tests (see *Figure 15*).

Figure 15. Reward for children participating in experimental processes.

After the design of Activity 2, an interface is generated in which two main areas are established to control the UX content. At the top, within the Question Area, the challenges aimed at improving the child's language skills are displayed sequentially. At the bottom, interaction with the markers is enabled by activating the camera (see *Figure 16*).

Figure 16. Areas of Activity 2.

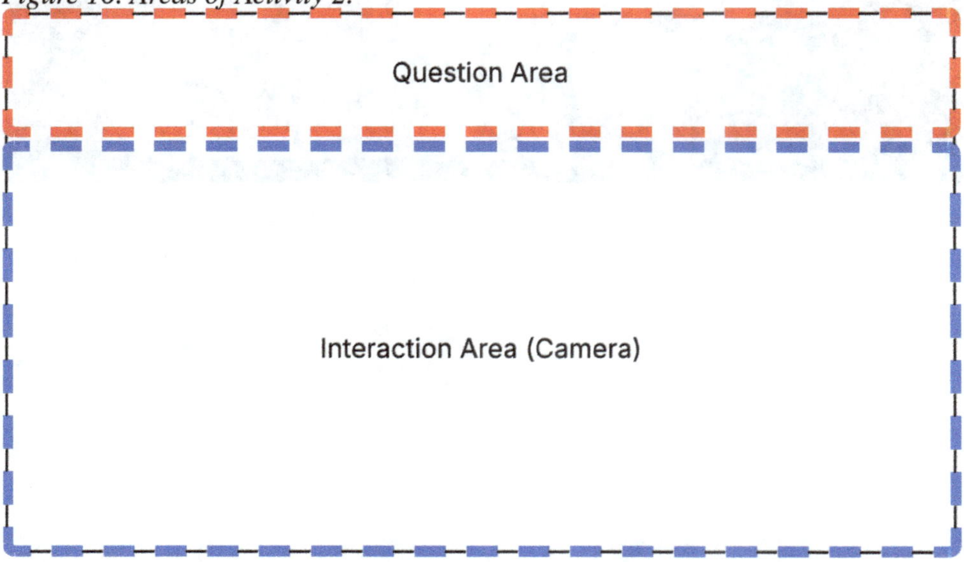

Stage 3: Practical development

After several tests and modifications to the code, a functional prototype was finally obtained to be tested intensively for the verification stage of the experimental environment. *Figure 17* show the functional prototype of Activity 1, while *Figure 18* and *Figure 19* show how the marker displays a 2D model in augmented reality.

Figure 17. Interface, models, and marker for Activity 1.

Figure 18. Interface, models, and marker for Activity 2.

Figure 19. Display of recognized marker on screen as a tangible interface.

Stage 4: Evaluation

Experimental Deployment

The experimental deployment was carried out at the facilities of the AUTAGS association. In this space, which was adapted for coexistence and activities between children and specialists, the appropriate experimental environment was prepared for the tests.

A total of seven children participated in the tests, each requiring different levels of specialist support to carry out their daily activities. The age range included children from six years old up to a 15-year-old adolescent. An environment was set up to allow free interaction with the markers while minimizing distractions. To achieve this, a monitor with a camera mounted on its upper edge was positioned to capture the child's hand movements. At the bottom of the monitor, the Tobii Pro Nano eye-tracker was installed, sending biometric data to the specialized eye-tracking software Tobii Pro Lab.

As validity criteria, Tobii Pro Lab provides calibration results based on pixel distance. Any test with a fixation point deviation of 35 pixels was automatically discarded. The tests had an average duration of five minutes, which matched very closely the development team's estimates.

Proposed Statistical Analysis to Identify Divergent Users in a UX through Eye-Tracking Data.

As mentioned in previous sections, convergent patterns allow grouping users with "standard" behaviors within the overall population. By using biometric eye-tracking data, it is possible to generate a simple statistical analysis to identify users who do not align with the majority.

It is important to clarify that this analysis does not, under any circumstances, aim to "segregate" users who do not align with the general use of the UX, nor does it label convergent users as "better" users. The establishment of these concepts arises from previous works proposing that all users may interact with the interface differently. However, if the design is pleasant, intuitive, and easy to use, these characteristics can directly influence user interactions. Therefore, user grouping evaluates the UX itself, not the user (Villegas Ortíz, 2025; Villegas Ortíz et al., 2024) .

In this statistical analysis proposal, a set of baseline ET metrics is selected (in this case, five metrics). For each of these metrics, the mean $\overline{X}$ and the standard deviation s are calculated, obtaining the following Acceptance Range for *Convergent Visual Attention Patterns*:

$$\textit{Acceptance Range for Convergent Visual Attention Pattern} = [\overline{X} - k * s, \overline{X} + k * s]$$

where k represents the tolerance level.

RESULTS

The results presented point to a statistical analysis aimed at identifying users whose behavior differed from the average. Although the analysis is a simple proposal, it opens the debate for more powerful approaches to profiling usage patterns across different UX designs.

Describing the process for applying the statistical analysis, it begins with the dataset generated during the production stage of the ET tests. Once all tests were processed, two datasets were generated for each activity (Menu and Language), each containing 10 ET metrics with optimal data integrity.

By conducting a Coefficient of Variation analysis for each of the ET metrics, the five variables with the highest values of this index were selected. With these metrics identified, the mean and variance were calculated using the seven records. Applying the ranges mentioned in previous sections, users were classified into a convergent data group, while special cases that appeared to differ from the rest were identified. Table 3 and Table 4 show these "Divergent" users.

Table 3. Divergent Users for Menu Activity.

ET metric	$\bar{X}$	Divergent Patterns	
		Subject	Value
Number of Saccades	127.857	1	396
Number of Fixations	160.571	1	454
Total Duration of Fixation	55041.3	1	148834
Total Duration of Visit	73167	1	187323
Total Duration of Glances	73547.6	1	187873

Table 4. Divergent Users for Language Activity.

ET metric	$\overline{X}$	Divergent Patterns	
		Subject	**Value**
Number of Saccades	182.857	3	337
Number of Fixations	291.143	3	524
Total Duration Fixation	6247.71	4	8798
		7	1914
Total Duration of Visit	6290.43	4	8840
		7	1962
Total Duration of Glances	31.857	5	19
		7	55

Once the users identified as Divergent were detected, visualizations were generated for the resulting groups. *Figure 20* and *Figure 21* display the visualizations for Convergent and Divergent users, respectively.

Figure 20. Visualizations of visual attention patterns grouped as 'Convergent' according to the statistical analysis of the Menu Activity.

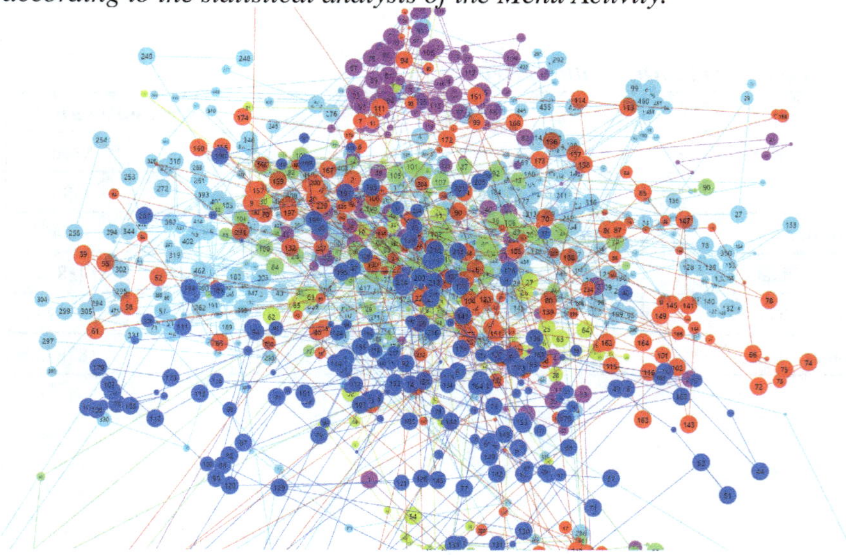

Figure 21. Visualizations of visual attention patterns grouped as 'Divergent' according to the statistical analysis of the Menu Activity.

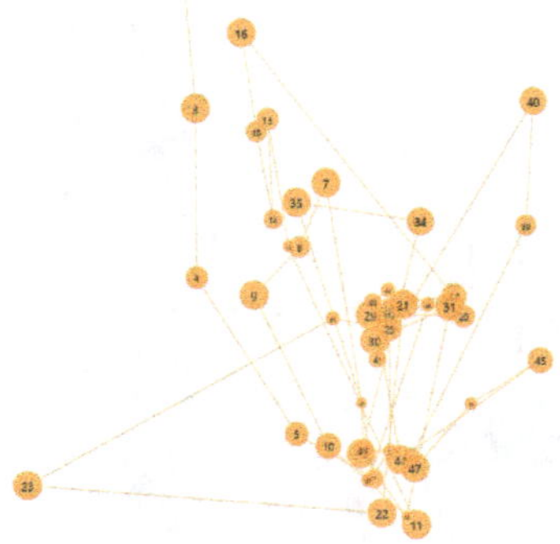

In the same way as with the Menu activity, visualizations are generated to represent both Convergent and Divergent users according to the proposed statistical method, as shown in *Figure 22* and *Figure 23.*

Figure 22. Visualizations of visual attention patterns grouped as 'Convergent' according to the statistical analysis of the Language Activity.

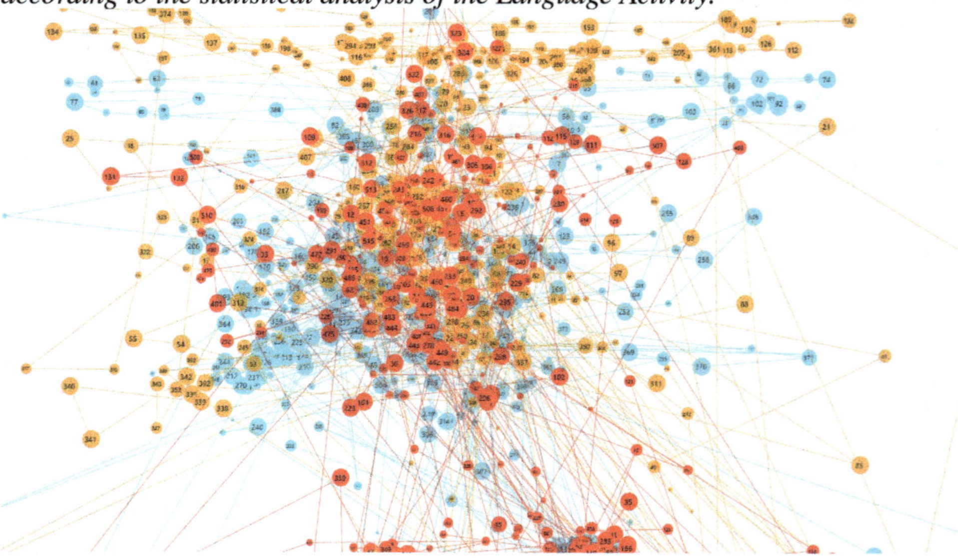

Figure 23. Visualizations of visual attention patterns grouped as 'Divergent' according to the statistical analysis of the Language Activity.

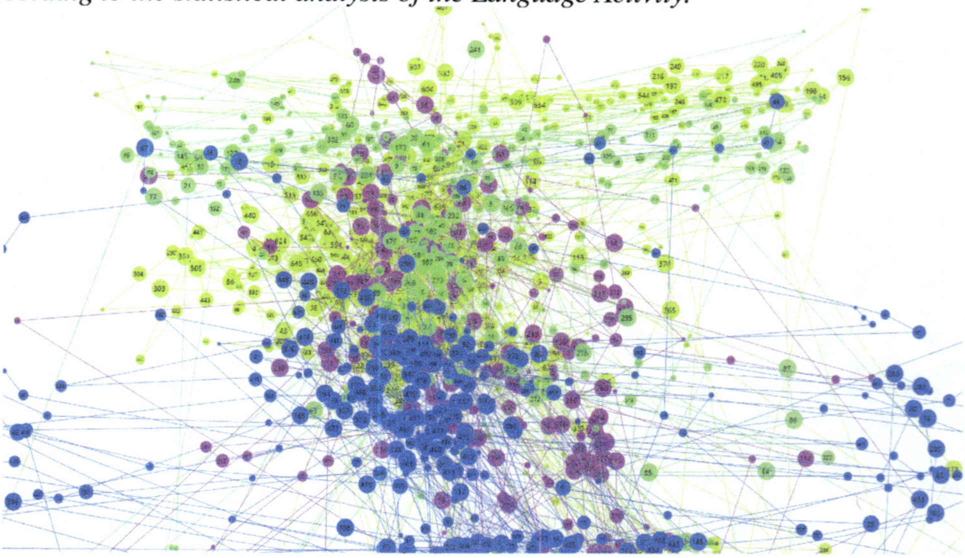

Interpretation Of Results And Discussion

To achieve a better interpretation of the visualizations, it is necessary to consider the interface design as well as the expected sequence of use. For the visualizations of the Menu activity, the interaction was free and there were no "two-dimensional" elements on the screen. In other words, the interaction consisted of the physical object and the models displayed above it through augmented reality. In this case, it is more relevant to compare visual attention patterns in relation to the interaction gesture, that is, from left to right.

In the case of the divergent pattern of the Menu activity *(Figure 21),* a vertical pattern with very few fixations can be distinguished. This behavior is so atypical that it affects the results of other subjects, grouping them as Convergent even though their patterns do not reflect the intended interaction design.

Conversely, in the Language Activity interface, a reading area is established at the top. In *Figure 22* and *Figure 23*, it is relevant to observe whether the subjects engage in this reading process. Among the convergent patterns, the red visual attention pattern of one subject does not appear to reflect a reading process. Meanwhile, in the divergent patterns, a green pattern does seem to reflect reading behavior. Thus, would it not be more evident to classify the red convergent subject as divergent and the green divergent subject as convergent?

This question compels the evaluator to conduct a more detailed examination of the patterns. When observing the saccadic movements of the convergent subject, they are much broader and less uniform than those of the other convergent users. On the other hand, the subject represented in red, although not engaging in a reading process, clusters fixations at the center of the screen, which is very similar to the convergent patterns.

This statistical analysis highlights several weaknesses in profiling users, particularly when highly pronounced outliers are present. At the time of publication, no analysis using artificial intelligence techniques had yet been conducted. Such techniques are currently being explored in ongoing work to strengthen the criteria for grouping convergent and divergent users.

CONCLUSIONS

The design of interactions constitutes an innovative component for expanding accessibility considerations in a product. In this work, several proposals were generated that aim to serve as a cornerstone in the design and development of profiles that are not limited to neurotypical users. As observed in the results, atypical behaviors exist within the same profile, which points to the need for a broader debate on how biometric data acquisition technologies can not only evaluate and estimate the use of a UX, but also, through specialized UX design, identify cognitive patterns that may contribute to broader and more precise diagnoses.

Before considering more ambitious proposals, it is necessary to review the current state of the theories presented in this work. On one hand, AR and TUI techniques showed highly favorable results in the acceptance of children within the studied profile, which motivates the evolution of the "TEA-yudo" software into a complete and robust communication tool that enables the articulation of ideas, desires, and emotions through markers and scenarios specifically adapted to the profile. In terms of gesture-based interaction, improvements in quality and precision are required.

The analysis conducted with eye-tracking represents a starting point in understanding a profile that is often overlooked in many software development environments, and more importantly, in academic and social contexts. Even the technical, methodological, and UX design considerations for this profile prove relevant to continue the path of developing specialized—not merely adapted—interaction mechanisms. Although at this stage the analysis of Convergent and Divergent Patterns was limited to a statistical approach, it constitutes a first step toward more precise profiling that incorporates a greater number of variables.

REFERENCES

Albiz, J., Viberg, O., & Matviienko, A. (2023). Guiding Visual Attention on 2D Screens. *Effects of Gaze Cues from Avatars and Humans.*, *9*, 1–9. Advance online publication. DOI: 10.1145/3607822.3614529

Barajas Alcantara. (2022). LANGUAGE AND COMMUNICATION IN AUTISM. *REVISTA DE PSICOLOGÍA DE LA UNIVERSIDAD AUTÓNOMA DEL ESTADO DE MÉXICO, 11*(28).

Berenguer, C., Baixauli, I., Gómez, S., & Andrés, M. de E. P., & De Stasio, S. (2020). Exploring the Impact of Augmented Reality in Children and Adolescents with Autism Spectrum Disorder: A Systematic Review. In *International Journal of Environmental Research and Public Health* (Vol. 17, Issue 17, pp. 1–15). MDPI AG. DOI: 10.3390/ijerph17176143

Boraston, Z., & Blakemore, S. J. (2007). The application of eye-tracking technology in the study of autism. In *Journal of Physiology* (Vol. 581, Issue 3, pp. 893–898). DOI: 10.1113/jphysiol.2007.133587

Bruce, C. D., & Hawes, Z. (2015). The role of 2D and 3D mental rotation in mathematics for young children: What is it? Why does it matter? And what can we do about it? *ZDM Mathematics Education*, *47*(3), 331–343. DOI: 10.1007/s11858-014-0637-4

Calderón Ynoñan, P., Prieto Neira, F., & Sialer Rivera, M. (2022). *Integración de un enfoque ágil con técnicas de Diseño Centrado en Usuario (DCU) para la mejora de experiencia de usuario (UX)* [Universidad Señor de Sipán]. https://orcid.org/0000-0001-5472-001X

Celis Alcalá, G., & Ochoa Madrigal, M. (2022). *Trastorno del espectro autista (TEA). 65*, 2022. DOI: 10.22201/fm.24484865e.2022.65.1.02

Çorlu, D., Taşel, Ş., Turan, S. G., Gatos, A., & Yantaç, A. E. (2017). Involving autistics in user experience studies: A critical review. *DIS 2017 - Proceedings of the 2017 ACM Conference on Designing Interactive Systems*, 43–55. DOI: 10.1145/3064663.3064771

Costello, E., Kilbride, S., Milne, Z., Clarke, P., Yilmaz, M., & Macmahon, S. T. (2021). *A Professional Career with Autism: Findings from a Literature Review in the Software Engineering Domain.* DOI: 10.1007/978-3-030-85521-5_23 del Moral-Pérez, M., & López-Bouzas, N. (2021). Augmented reality and stimulation of social and communicative abilities in people with ASD: Research review. In *Revista de Educación a Distancia* (Vol. 21, Issue 66). Universidad de Murcia. DOI: 10.6018/red.454751

Falck-Ytter, T., Bölte, S., & Gredebäck, G. (2013). Eye tracking in early autism research. In *Journal of Neurodevelopmental Disorders* (Vol. 5, Issue 1). BioMed Central Ltd. DOI: 10.1186/1866-1955-5-28

Francis, G. A., Farr, W., Mareva, S., & Gibson, J. L. (2019). *Do Tangible User Interfaces promote social behaviour during free play? A comparison of autistic and typically-developing children playing with passive and digital construction toys.*

Groba-González, B., Pereira-Loureiro, J., & Munteanu, C. (2015). *Impacto de las tecnologías de la información y las comunicaciones en el funcionamiento en la vida diaria de niños con Trastorno del Espectro Autista* [Universidad de Coruña]. https://objetivovisibilizandoelautismo.com/

Hage, S. V. R., Sawasaki, L. Y., Hyter, Y., & Fernandes, F. D. M. (2022). Social Communication and pragmatic skills of children with Autism Spectrum Disorder and Developmental Language Disorder. *CoDAS, 34*(2), e20210075. Advance online publication. DOI: 10.1590/2317-1782/20212021075 PMID: 34932641

Inal, Y., Volden, F., Hjelmtveit, S. T., & Carlsen, C. H. (2024). *My Eyes Don't Consent!* Exploring Visual Attention in Cookie Consent Interfaces., DOI: 10.1145/3649902.3653352

Iqbal, M., Ijaz, M., Mazhar, T., Shahzad, T., Abbas, Q., Ghadi, Y. Y., Ahmed, W., & Hamam, H. (2021). *Exploring Issues of Story-Based Effort Estimation in Agile Software Development*. https://doi.org/https://doi.org/10.1016/j.scico.2024.103114

Jaradat, A. S., Wedyan, M., Alomari, S., & Barhoush, M. M. (2025). Using Machine Learning to Diagnose Autism Based on Eye Tracking Technology. *Diagnostics (Basel), 15*(1), 66. Advance online publication. DOI: 10.3390/diagnostics15010066 PMID: 39795594

Khowaja, K., Banire, B., Al-Thani, D., Sqalli, M. T., Aqle, A., Shah, A., & Salim, S. S. (2020). Augmented reality for learning of children and adolescents with autism spectrum disorder (ASD): A systematic review. In *IEEE Access* (Vol. 8, pp. 78779–78807). Institute of Electrical and Electronics Engineers Inc. DOI: 10.1109/ACCESS.2020.2986608

Lawan, A. A., Yarima, K. I., Usman, H. I., Abba, S. I., Yakubu, H. U., & Musa, A. G. (2023). A Systematic Literature Review on the Efficacy of Emerging Computer Technologies in Inclusive Education for Students with Autism Spectrum Disorder. *OBM Neurobiology*, *7*(2), 1–27. Advance online publication. DOI: 10.21926/obm.neurobiol.2302172

López-Belmonte, J., Duo-Terrón, P., Moreno-Guerrero, A. J., & Marín-Marín, J. A. (2024). Effects of augmented and virtual reality on students with ASD. *Pixel-Bit. Revista de Medios y Educacion*, *70*, 7–23. DOI: 10.12795/pixelbit.103789

López-Bouzas, N., & Del Moral Pérez, M. E. (2023). A gamified environment supported by augmented reality for improving communicative competencies in students with ASD: Design and validation. *International Journal of Educational Research and Innovation*, *2023*(19), 80–93. DOI: 10.46661/ijeri.6820

Molina Gutiérrez, B., Ayala Pérez, C., & García Sánchez, M. (2025). Diseño Universal para el Aprendizaje: Estrategias para una enseñanza equitativa. *DISCE. Revista Científica. Educativa Y Social*, *2*(2), 1–23. DOI: 10.69821/DISCE.v2i1.19

Morocho Fajardo, K., Sánchez Álvarez, D., & Patiño Zambrano, V. (2021). Epidemiological profile of autism spectrum disorder in Latin America. *Salud y Ciencias Médicas, 1*(2).

Oliveira, J. S., Franco, F. O., Revers, M. C., Silva, A. F., Portolese, J., Brentani, H., Machado-Lima, A., & Nunes, F. L. S. (2021). Computer-aided autism diagnosis based on visual attention models using eye tracking. *Scientific Reports*, *11*(1), 10131. Advance online publication. DOI: 10.1038/s41598-021-89023-8 PMID: 33980874

Passerino, L. M., & Baldassarri, S. (2017). *Mesas Tangibles para la Planificación Cognitiva en alumnos con Trastorno del Espectro Autista (TEA). Tecnología Accesible e Inclusiva: Logros, Resistencias y Desafíos*. Consejería de Educación, Juventud y Deportes.

Ramos Aguiar, L. R., & Álvarez Rodríguez, F. J. (2021). Methodology for designing systems based on tangible user interfaces and gamification techniques for blind people. *Applied Sciences (Basel, Switzerland)*, *11*(12), 5676. Advance online publication. DOI: 10.3390/app11125676

Sierra, E. A., & Contreras Juárez, R. (2023). Capítulo 2. Diseño de una herramienta para la formación docente en el aula inclusiva mediante TIC para niños con TEA. *Experiencias Educativas Basadas En TICs*. https://www.researchgate.net/publication/379023807

Stirling, L., Douglas, S., Leekam, S., & Carey, L. (2014). Communication in Autism. In *Trends in Language Acquisition Research* (Vol. 11). John Benjamins.

Vazquez-Vazquez, T. C., Garcia-Herrera, D. G., Ochoa-Encalada, S. C., & Erazo-Álvarez, J. C. (2020). Estrategias didácticas para trabajar con niños con Trastorno del Espectro Autista (TEA). *Revista Arbitrada Interdisciplinaria Koinonía, 5*(1), 589. DOI: 10.35381/r.k.v5i1.799

Vélez, A., & Rivadeneira, F. (2024). Artículo de investigación Actividades didácticas para la enseñanza de la adición en estudiantes con trastorno del espectro autista-TEA. *Revista Social Fronteriza, 4*(5). Advance online publication. DOI: 10.59814/resofro.2024.4(5)e407

Villegas Ortíz, A. (2025). *Aplicación de machine learning en datos obtenidos mediante eye-tracking para el perfilamiento de usuarios mediante la percepción de colores entre mujeres y hombres.*

Villegas Ortíz, A., Rodríguez López, E., & Álvarez Rodríguez, F. (2024). *Modelo para la Aplicación del Análisis del Comportamiento de Mirada Mediante Eyetracking de la Interacción Usuario-Sistema para Mejorar la Calidad de la UX y Mejorar los Procesos de Desarrollo de Software.* Universidad Autónoma de Aguascalientes.

Zhang, S., Chen, D., Tang, Y., & Zhang, L. (2021). Children ASD Evaluation Through Joint Analysis of EEG and Eye-Tracking Recordings With Graph Convolution Network. *Frontiers in Human Neuroscience, 15*, 651349. Advance online publication. DOI: 10.3389/fnhum.2021.651349 PMID: 34113244

Zhou, Y., Qian, H., Verbelen, T., Cuculo, V., Zhu, F., Sun, H., Li, Y., Zhao, P., Kong, Y., Wang, J., Wan, Y., & Fu, S. (2023). *Viewpoint planning with transition management for active object recognition.*

KEY TERMS AND DEFINITIONS

Convergent Visual Attention Pattern: Convergent patterns emerge from the analysis of objective interfaces, where similar behaviors are grouped to verify how many users follow a given path. In other words, if the interface is well-designed and the UX is clear, it can be expected that most users will interact in the most effective and efficient way.

Divergent Visual Attention Pattern: In contrast to convergent patterns, divergent patterns are special cases of interaction that allow for a deeper understanding of the possible usage scenarios that different user profiles may display. In the theory of inclusive interface design proposed by previous works of the main author, emphasis is placed on how divergent patterns can serve as a highly suitable roadmap for improving decision-making in interface design.

Extended User Profiling: In User-Centered Design (UCD), profiling proposals often rely mainly on categorical variables and labels, which can easily be biased. To address this issue, extended profiling refers to the use of biometric data as the primary basis for profile design. This concept aligns closely with eye-tracking techniques, as this technology is easily applicable and, when combined with AI algorithms, can significantly enhance the ability of profile designs to represent users in a much deeper, more precise, and above all, more objective way.

Gesture-Based Interaction through Augmented Reality and Tangible Interfaces: A gesture is a specific physical action that, once parameterized by a system, can trigger reactions and commands within it. In the case of augmented reality, a gesture can be defined as the Marker-Model-Action relationship, which enables interaction with the environment through physical mechanisms, allowing for an intuitive and sensorially stimulating experience.

Innovative HCI Mechanisms: An innovative HCI mechanism refers to the experimentation with different tools and technologies in the search for alternative interaction mechanisms, particularly those focused on underrepresented user profiles. Its guiding principle is: "Interaction should not be adapted to new profiles; rather, profiles define the design of the interaction to be developed."

Objective Evaluation of Interfaces through Eye-Tracking: Given a two-dimensional interface, it is possible to estimate aspects such as how easy it is to understand, use, and navigate (the reading process). Metrics provided by eye-tracking techniques can accurately identify weaknesses in UX, while visualization mechanisms allow designers to trace how the distribution of elements affects user interaction.

Use of Markers for Interaction through Tangible Interfaces: Tangible interfaces are a relatively underutilized tool for interacting with a computer system. Markers can represent complex abstract ideas, replacing conventional mechanisms with new physical mechanisms.

Chapter 6

Customizable Serious Games to Support Social Integration in Children With Autism Spectrum Disorder:
A Modular and Accessible Software Architecture

Felipe Costa-Tebar
https://orcid.org/0000-0003-4748-3006
Instituto de Investigación en Ingeniería Informática de Albacete, Spain

Javier Jimenez-Honrado
https://orcid.org/0009-0000-8097-8575
Escuela Superior de Ingeniería Informática de Albacete, Spain

Llanos Vergara-Picazo
Escuela Superior de Ingeniería Informática de Albacete, Spain

Gabriel Sebastián-Rivera
https://orcid.org/0000-0002-1156-8000
Facultad de CC SS y Tecnologías de la Información, Spain

Jose A. Gallud
Escuela Superior de Ingeniería Informática de Albacete, Spain

Victor M. R. Penichet
Escuela Superior de Ingeniería Informática de Albacete, Spain

ABSTRACT

This chapter presents the design, implementation, and evaluation of TEA Minigames, a customizable system of serious games to promote social inclusion for children with Autism Spectrum Disorder (ASD). It includes a mobile app with three minigames

DOI: 10.4018/979-8-3373-6033-1.ch006

–emotion recognition, daily routine sequencing, and social reasoning– plus a web interface for caregivers and educators to adapt content. Developed with a local autism association, it follows accessibility, universal design, and user-centered principles, addressing cognitive and sensory needs through flexible content, minimal interface, immediate feedback, and an evaluation protocol based on ISO/IEC usability standards. Pilot testing with caregivers and children confirmed the system is engaging, usable, and appropriate for educational and therapeutic use. The chapter closes with implications for accessible educational software design and future directions for expansion and inclusive interaction.

1. INTRODUCTION: EDUCATION, NEURODIVERGENCE, AND DIGITAL INCLUSION

Despite growing evidence that serious games can benefit autistic learners, most systems remain hard-to-adapt in real contexts and treat accessibility as a set of interface checks rather than as a vehicle for learner agency. We argue that customizable, modular architectures can operationalize Universal Design for Learning (UDL) and neurodiversity-affirming pedagogy by shifting from "access to content" to "participation with choice." This chapter investigates whether and how a caregiver-controlled content layer—paired with minimalist, sensory-tunable gameplay—supports social participation and usable learning experiences for autistic children. We examine TEA Minigames, a dual-client ecosystem (mobile game + administrative web) co-designed with practitioners, and report on a quality-in-use evaluation with professionals and children with ASD.

This leads us to the central research question guiding this chapter:

> *How can a modular, caregiver-managed serious-games architecture enable learner agency and social participation among autistic children through accessible and customizable digital play?*

In this chapter, learner agency refers to the child's capacity to act intentionally within the digital learning environment to make meaningful choices, influence content, and engage in social interaction through accessible and personalized gameplay.

Within this broader movement, inclusive education has become a cornerstone of contemporary educational policy and practice, grounded in the recognition of education as a fundamental human right and an essential vehicle for social justice. International frameworks, such as the United Nations Convention on the Rights of Persons with Disabilities and the 2030 Agenda for Sustainable Development, affirm that all learners, regardless of their abilities, backgrounds, or identities, must have equitable access to meaningful learning opportunities (Le Cunff et al., 2025). Nevertheless, despite these commitments, the definition, scope, and practical implementation of inclusive education remain contested and display significant variability across contexts (Filippou et al., 2025).

In some systems, inclusion is narrowly interpreted as the mere placement of students with disabilities in mainstream classrooms, often without substantial pedagogical adaptation. In others, inclusion is conceived more broadly, extending to diverse forms of learning variation, encompassing cognitive, linguistic, cultural, and socioeconomic differences (Rezayi et al., 2025). These divergent interpretations highlight the contextual nature of inclusive education, shaped by cultural norms, policy priorities, and available resources. As a result, the realization of inclusion is not a universal condition but an evolving process that demands continuous negotiation and adaptation (Guillén-Martínez et al., 2025).

1.1. The Challenge of Inclusive Education

The classroom is a microcosm of diversity. Teachers face the continuous challenge of accommodating different abilities, interests, and socio-emotional needs while sustaining equitable learning environments. Recent research highlights the role of emotional intelligence and socio-emotional competences as essential pedagogical resources for managing such diversity (Dubovyk, 2020). The capacity to maintain empathy, composure, and adaptability is crucial for fostering inclusive climates that recognize and value the potential of every learner.

Adapting instruction to each individual is already a complex task in general education. This challenge becomes even more demanding when teachers work with students whose developmental profiles align with autism spectrum disorder (ASD). Learners on the spectrum often encounter distinctive challenges in communication, social interaction, and sensory processing, which require flexible and highly personalized approaches (Azevedo, 2023). Without appropriate adaptation, these differences risk being misinterpreted as deficits rather than natural variations within the human cognitive spectrum.

Such challenges are not only acknowledged in research but are also being actively addressed through innovative educational projects. For example, the *Proyectos Neuroeducativos en Educación Infantil collection*, coordinated by Collado-Martínez and Navarro-Ardoy (2023), proposes classroom-based learning situations grounded in neuroeducation and inclusive pedagogy. These projects illustrate how teachers and researchers are collaboratively seeking to transform the complexity of inclusive education into practical strategies that support diversity, emotional development, and equity from the earliest stages of schooling (Collado-Martínez & Navarro-Ardoy, 2023).

1.2. Neurodivergence and Diversity in Learning

The concept of *neurodivergence* has emerged to frame these variations in a more affirmative way. Originally coined within the autistic community, the term today encompasses conditions such as ASD, ADHD, dyslexia, and dyspraxia. Neurodivergence shifts attention away from deficit-based models by recognizing these profiles as alternative cognitive configurations that involve both challenges and strengths (Lawson, 2020). For example, autistic learners may experience heightened anxiety in unpredictable social environments, yet they often demonstrate exceptional pattern recognition and sustained concentration (Grossard, 2025).

For educators, embracing neurodivergence requires moving beyond normalization and advancing toward pedagogical pluralism. Teaching practices must be flexible, multimodal, and adaptive, incorporating visual supports, alternative communication systems, structured routines, and environments that minimize sensory overload. Traditional schooling, with its emphasis on standardized assessments, heavily verbal instruction, and overstimulating settings, often amplifies barriers for neurodivergent students (Carrión-León et al., 2025). By contrast, inclusive strategies —such as anticipating transitions, offering adjustable pacing, and designing sensory-sensitive classrooms— have shown measurable positive effects on participation and engagement (Azadboni, 2024).

Moreover, neurodivergence rarely occurs in isolation. It frequently intersects with cultural, linguistic, or socioeconomic disadvantages, producing compounded barriers to inclusion. Adopting an intersectional perspective is therefore essential to fully understand how systemic inequalities and cognitive differences interact in shaping educational opportunities (Serrano-Fernández & Viguera-Monje, 2024).

1.3. Digital Inclusion and Assistive Technologies

In the twenty-first century, inclusion must also be considered from the perspective of digital access. *Digital inclusion* does not merely involve having devices and connectivity, but also digital literacy, accessible interfaces, and adaptable learning platforms (Stasolla et al., 2025). For neurodivergent learners, digital tools can be transformative, offering personalized pacing, multimodal content, and opportunities for alternative communication.

Assistive technologies and adaptive software have demonstrated significant potential to support students with ASD. Structured, rule-based environments such as digital simulations or games can provide predictability and reduce anxiety. Multimodal feedback can scaffold emotional recognition, language development, and the sequencing of daily routines (Rezayi, 2023). Nonetheless, several challenges persist: unequal access to technology across regions, insufficient teacher training, and limited participation of neurodivergent users in design processes often undermine the inclusivity of such tools (Carneiro, 2024).

Global systematic reviews confirm these tensions. Although emerging policies and technologies offer opportunities for personalized learning, structural barriers —such as parallel education systems and disparities in resources— continue to constrain effective implementation (Guillén-Martínez et al., 2025). Ensuring the ethical use of data and the equitable distribution of resources also remains a pressing concern (Ito et al., 2022).

1.4. Serious Games as a Non-Conventional Pedagogy

Within the digital landscape, serious games stand out as promising tools for inclusive education. Unlike gamification, which adds superficial game-like features to existing tasks, *serious games* embed pedagogical objectives directly into their mechanics, narratives, and feedback loops (Zyda, 2005). In doing so, they combine motivation with structured learning, enabling repetition, practice, and the safe exploration of complex skills.

For learners with ASD, serious games have proven particularly effective. Systematic reviews report improvements in social skills, communication, and emotion recognition when games are specifically designed for this population (Azadboni, 2024). Studies focusing on operability show that games aligned with international usability standards, such as ISO/IEC 25010, achieve high levels of acceptance and engagement among children with ASD (Carrión-León et al., 2025). Similarly, controlled clinical trials have demonstrated that rhythm- and language-based games can produce measurable gains in cognitive and linguistic development (Grossard, 2025).

Emerging technologies such as virtual reality (VR) further expand these possibilities. Exploratory reviews suggest that serious games enhanced with VR can foster empathy, collaborative communication, and adaptive social behaviors in adolescents with ASD (Stasolla et al., 2025). Although challenges of accessibility and cost persist, these studies highlight the transformative potential of game-based digital learning in neurodivergent education.

1.5. Theoretical Orientation: From Accessibility to Agency

Over the last three decades, critical disability scholarship has challenged the dominance of deficit-based and medicalized perspectives on impairment. Within this shift, *accessibility* has been reconceptualized not as a technical end itself but as a social, ethical, and epistemic practice grounded in participation and rights. This theoretical orientation situates *TEA Minigames* within the broader transition "from accessibility to agency," aligning design and pedagogy with the social model of disability and the neurodiversity paradigm.

1.5.1. From the Social Model to the Participatory Turn

The social model of disability, first articulated by Oliver (1990), provides the foundation for this conceptual shift. Oliver (2018) reframed disability as the product of environmental and attitudinal barriers rather than intrinsic deficits, arguing that "people are disabled by society and not by their bodies". This model decentralizes medical diagnosis and instead focuses on removing systemic constraints to enable active participation. Within digital contexts, this implies that accessibility should not be reduced to compliance with interface guidelines but understood as the *co-creation of enabling environments* where diverse forms of cognition, perception, and communication can flourish. In this sense, accessibility becomes a relational construct —achieved through dialogue between designers, educators, caregivers, and users— rather than a static checklist of technical requirements.

The participatory dimension of this model aligns directly with the architecture of *TEA Minigames*. By allowing caregivers and educators to adapt content, modify sensory parameters, and personalize gameplay, the system operationalizes Oliver's principle of *removing disabling barriers*. Customization functions as an instrument of social inclusion: it transfers control from designers to practitioners and ultimately to the learners themselves.

1.5.2. Neurodiversity and the Reframing of Difference

The emergence of the neurodiversity paradigm expanded the social model's implications into the cognitive and educational domains. Sociologist (Singer, 1998, 2016) introduced *neurodiversity* to name the natural variation of human neurology, proposing that conditions such as autism, ADHD, or dyslexia represent forms of human diversity rather than pathologies. Her work established a political and epistemological framework that celebrates neurological difference as part of biodiversity and human rights discourse. Building on Singer (1998) and Armstrong (2010) translated these ideas into educational practice, emphasizing that neurodiverse learners possess unique strengths —pattern recognition, attention to detail, or visual reasoning— that can be nurtured through flexible pedagogies.

Incorporating this perspective, *TEA Minigames* does not attempt to "normalize" autistic behavior but rather to *affirm neurodivergent modes of interaction*. Its modular configuration allows for differentiated yet equitable engagement: sensory-tunable interfaces minimize overstimulation, while gameplay sequences support alternative communication and emotion-recognition pathways. In doing so, the platform embodies what Armstrong describes as *"the empowerment of the differently wired brain"*.

1.5.3. Disability, Agency, and Rights

Goodley (2014) and Shakespeare (2018)have both advanced the discussion from inclusion as mere presence to inclusion as *agency* —the capacity to act meaningfully within social, cultural, and technological systems—. Goodley's *Dis/ability Studies* introduces the dual critique of *disablism* and *ableism*, urging educators and designers to question how systems of normalization constrain agency. Shakespeare (2018) further integrates ethics and pragmatism, arguing that authentic inclusion requires balancing autonomy with structural support. This balance is central to *TEA Minigames*: the system scaffolds participation through adjustable difficulty and guided routines, yet it preserves the learner's sense of control and choice (key indicators of agency in neurodiverse contexts).

Learner agency, as defined in this study, refers to the child's capacity to act intentionally within the digital environment, to make choices, influence content, and engage in social interaction through accessible and personalized gameplay. In this view, technology does not merely *accommodate* difference but *mediates empowerment*, enabling children to construct meaning and self-efficacy through interaction.

1.5.4. Inclusive Pedagogy and Universal Design for Learning

The notion of *inclusive pedagogy* Florian and Black-Hawkins (2011) complements the neurodiversity perspective by emphasizing that diversity should extend what is "ordinarily available to all learners" rather than segmenting instruction by ability. Their work redefines inclusion as the continuous expansion of participation opportunities within the shared classroom ecology. This principle resonates with the *Universal Design for Learning* (UDL) framework, which advocates multiple means of representation, engagement, and expression Meyer et al. (2014). Together, these theories provide the pedagogical backbone for *TEA Minigames*, where adaptive design transforms accessibility into a dynamic mechanism for engagement.

Through UDL-inspired flexibility, the platform enables educators to tailor activities without segregating learners. The caregiver-managed interface mirrors what Florian and Black-Hawkins (2011) describe as *teacher craft knowledge:* a situated expertise that adapts pedagogy responsively to learners' evolving needs. In this respect, the software becomes both a *tool* and a *pedagogical space* for inclusive practice.

1.5.5. Human-Centered Design and Cognitive Affordances

In design theory, Norman (2013) principles of *human-centered design* (HCD) provide the conceptual bridge between accessibility and agency. Norman (2013) argues that effective systems "put human needs, capabilities, and behavior first" (p. 8), creating environments where users can act confidently through intuitive affordances and feedback. Within *TEA Minigames*, interface simplicity, immediate visual responses, and clear task mapping embody this approach. HCD ensures not only usability but also the sense of mastery and emotional satisfaction that underpins agency. As learners successfully navigate tasks, they experience competence and control, psychological preconditions for participation and learning.

1.5.6. From Compliance to Co-Creation

Integrating these frameworks, social model, neurodiversity, inclusive pedagogy, and human-centered design, repositions accessibility as *a process of co-creation*. Rather than viewing users with autism as passive recipients of assistive technology, *TEA Minigames* recognizes them, their caregivers, and educators as co-designers of meaningful experiences. This approach moves beyond compliance with ISO 9241-210 or WCAG 2.1 toward what can be called *participatory accessibility*: a cyclical relationship among design, feedback, and lived experience.

By aligning design philosophy with critical disability theory, *TEA Minigames* embodies the transition from accessibility as accommodation to accessibility as agency, demonstrating how modular, customizable architectures can actualize inclusive education through digital play.

1.6. Positioning TEA Minigames

TEA Minigames emerges at the intersection of inclusive pedagogy, human–computer interaction, and accessible software engineering (Jimenez-Honrado et al., 2024). It responds to enduring barriers in the education of autistic learners-limited individualization, rigid instructional materials, and scarce technological resources adapted to neurodiverse classrooms. Traditional educational software often presumes homogeneity among users, offering fixed content and linear difficulty levels. In contrast, TEA Minigames adopts a *modular and caregiver-managed architecture* that transforms such constraints into opportunities for personalization, learner agency, and social participation.

At its core, the system integrates two interdependent components:

(1) a *mobile application* containing three serious minigames that foster emotional recognition, social reasoning, and daily routine sequencing; and (2) a *web-based*

administrative platform that enables caregivers and educators to create, edit, and delete game content in real time.

This structure allows each minigame to function as an independent pedagogical module, replaceable or adjustable according to the learner's profile. Such modularity provides the structural basis for personalization and adaptivity in learning design. As shown by Jagušt and Botički (2019) and Al-Qora'n et al. (2025), modular architectures enable digital environments to evolve with users' needs rather than imposing a single, uniform learning pathway.

From a pedagogical perspective, modularity acts as a catalyst for differentiated instruction. It allows educators and caregivers to tailor the cognitive, communicative, and sensory complexity of activities to each learner's ASD level: *mild, moderate, or severe* (see Table 1). For mild profiles, modules may include extended narratives and abstract reasoning; for moderate, simplified visuals and paced feedback; and for severe, pictorial routines with immediate reinforcement. This adaptive structure translates differentiated instruction into a scalable, inclusive learning.

Table 1. Applicability of TEA Minigames by ASD Level[1]

ASD Level	Adaptive Modularity Features	Corresponding Minigame Example
Mild (Level 1)	Incorporates extended narratives, abstract reasoning, and richer linguistic structures to encourage perspective-taking and complex social inference.	*Social Quiz* – multi-step reasoning tasks requiring interpretation of social cues and verbal choices.
Moderate (Level 2)	Reduces textual load, enhances visual reinforcement, and provides adjustable feedback pace to maintain engagement and reduce cognitive overload.	Guess the Emotion – simplified emotion recognition with clear visual prompts and limited response options.
Severe (Level 3)	Prioritizes pictorial routines, minimal sensory stimuli, and immediate reward loops to promote predictability and sustained attention.	Order the Sequence – structured daily-routine sequencing using familiar images and low-stimulation feedback.

This capacity to tailor interaction and difficulty situates TEA Minigames within neurodiversity-affirming pedagogy, where accessibility is achieved not by simplification but by meaningful adaptation.

Technological decisions were guided by this educational rationale.

Unity was selected for the mobile client to ensure cross-platform deployment and precise control over visual and auditory feedback, key for children sensitive to overstimulation. Additionally, Unity's engine enables transformation into native code for both Android and iOS systems, allowing efficient use of hardware resources and optimized performance across diverse mobile devices.

Angular powers the administrative web, a standard framework, alongside React, for modern web development. Chosen for developer expertise, it supports WCAG 2.1 measures such as intuitive navigation and optimized contrast, maintaining accessibility principles even though the platform targets educators rather than children with ASD.

Firebase manages image storage, synchronization, and user authentication, benefiting from its native compatibility with Angular for seamless integration and real-time updates. MongoDB, as a NoSQL standard, offers high scalability for activity logging and flexible data structures. Together, these technologies enhance the platform's performance, security, and long-term sustainability across institutional and home contexts.

Conceptually, TEA Minigames exemplifies how a modular architecture operationalizes theoretical frameworks such as *Universal Design for Learning (UDL)* and *Human-Centred Design (ISO 9241-210)*. The system translates these principles into practice by granting educators direct control over learning materials, enabling iterative adaptation without programming skills. In doing so, it redistributes agency from developers to caregivers, bridging the gap between educational theory and daily classroom realities.

The modular architecture of *TEA Minigames* reduces structural barriers in inclusive education. Giving the teacher tools to facilitate the adaptation of content and levels, promoting personalization and alleviating the burden.

1.7. Chapter Structure

The remainder of this chapter is organized as follows. Section 2 explores the role of serious games in ASD interventions, synthesizing recent evidence and identifying current gaps in research and practice. Section 3 presents the design goals, accessibility principles, and best practices that informed the development of *TEA Minigames*. Section 4 describes the system architecture, with emphasis on the client–server approach, modularity, and alignment with digital accessibility principles. Section 5 details the evaluation methodology, including participants, context of use, experimental design, and usability metrics, followed by the results and their discussion. Section 6 outlines future work, focusing on scalability, analytics, and personalization. Finally, Section 7 concludes with reflections on accessible game-based learning and its broader implications for neurodivergent populations.

2. THE ROLE OF SERIOUS GAMES IN ASD INTERVENTION

The use of serious games in interventions for individuals with Autism Spectrum Disorder (ASD) has become a consolidated strategy aimed at facilitating social integration, enhancing learning processes, and supporting the development of cognitive and behavioral skills (Almurashi et al., 2022; Azadboni, 2024; Carlier et al., 2020; Hassan et al., 2021; Jimenez-Honrado et al., 2024; Lopez-Bouzas & Del Moral-Perez, 2023; Vallefuoco et al., 2022). People with ASD often perceive the social environment as complex and unpredictable, due to difficulties in communication, interaction, learning, and behavior. Moreover, children with ASD frequently experience comorbidities such as anxiety and depression, which can increase stress levels in their parents (Carlier et al., 2020). This scenario highlights the need for specialized educational techniques that optimize learning and foster inclusion in community life (Azadboni, 2024; Jimenez-Honrado et al., 2024).

Beyond the growing literature on serious games for autism, most interventions rely on fixed content and closed interaction patterns, which limit their adaptability to individual differences. This gap between generic serious games and the need for customizable, educator-managed platforms highlights the importance of modular architectures such as TEA Minigames. By enabling caregivers and teachers to edit content and sensory parameters, these systems move from one-size-fits-all interventions toward personalized and participatory learning environments. Moreover, emerging studies on collaborative or peer-mediated serious games suggest that social play, whether cooperative or competitive, can further enhance empathy, turn-taking, and communication (Grynszpan et al., 2014; Stasolla et al., 2025). The combination of modular customization and social interaction thus represents a promising direction for inclusive digital pedagogy.

Serious games have therefore emerged as an attractive and effective alternative to traditional therapies which, although valuable, are often repetitive and time-consuming. Their design capitalizes on the affinity many individuals with ASD show for technology and visual stimuli, creating dynamic, safe, and motivating learning environments. The incorporation of gamification elements such as rewards, badges, or rankings sustains motivation and fosters long-term engagement with tasks (Almurashi et al., 2022; Azadboni, 2024; Jimenez-Honrado et al., 2024; Lopez-Bouzas & Del Moral-Perez, 2023).

One of their main advantages lies in providing controlled and low-anxiety environments in which users can explore, practice new skills, and rehearse coping mechanisms without being exposed to the risks of real-life interactions (Carlier et al., 2020; Vallefuoco et al., 2022). Added to this is the provision of immediate and individualized feedback, which is essential in the learning process and can be dynamically adapted to the player's level of attention and performance (Dynamic

Difficulty Adjustment, DDA), in line with the principles of Applied Behavior Analysis (ABA) therapy (Freitas et al., 2024; Hassan et al., 2021; Vallefuoco et al., 2022).

While Section 1.5 above discussed how accessibility and agency reframe the role of technology in inclusive education, it is important to note that serious games embody these principles in practice. Contemporary interventions increasingly move beyond corrective or behaviorist paradigms, positioning games as participatory tools that enable choice, emotional expression, and social participation. In this view, digital play becomes a medium for agency, where autistic learners can act, decide, and experiment within safe yet meaningful learning spaces.

Nonetheless, the implementation of serious games raises ethical and cultural questions that must be acknowledged. Most empirical studies are conducted in Western contexts, assuming universal transferability. Cultural norms, linguistic diversity, and family structures can, however, influence how games are understood and used. Furthermore, research involving children with ASD requires explicit attention to consent, assent, data protection, and transparency, ensuring that participatory design does not compromise privacy or autonomy (Facer & Selwyn, 2021).

From a socio-political standpoint, serious games also operate within the political economy of digital inclusion. As Costanza-Chock (2020) argues, inclusive design must be grounded in design justice, the redistribution of design power toward those most affected. Without this perspective, accessibility risks becoming an aesthetic or commercial label rather than a form of epistemic inclusion. Ensuring that neurodivergent learners and their caregivers participate meaningfully in co-design processes is therefore essential to avoid tokenism.

The empirical literature consistently demonstrates that serious games can enhance communication, emotion recognition, and daily living skills, reducing anxiety and promoting engagement. Yet their educational impact depends not only on usability but on how they are integrated into inclusive pedagogical frameworks that value diversity, participation, and cultural sensitivity.

Importantly, the applicability of serious-game interventions varies across the autism spectrum. Individuals with mild to moderate ASD tend to benefit most from interactive digital activities involving symbolic reasoning or social narratives, while learners with higher support needs often engage better through simplified, visually predictable tasks. The customization features of platforms like TEA Minigames, adjustable complexity, visual supports, and sensory modulation, allow educators to align gameplay with each learner's cognitive and emotional profile, thereby accommodating the heterogeneity of ASD levels within inclusive practice.

Historically, early educational software for learners with disabilities often lacked genuine playfulness, limiting engagement (González-Sánchez et al., 2009). Their recommendation to embed learning in play, use positive reinforcement, and introduce mediating characters remains valid today and directly informs projects such as TEA Minigames.

In summary, serious games represent a valuable but ethically complex tool in ASD intervention. Their transformative potential lies in combining accessibility with agency, moving beyond compliance or remediation toward co-created culturally aware learning ecologies. This approach complements the theoretical framework outlined in Section 1.5 and provides the empirical foundation for the system design presented in Section 3 below.

3. DESIGN GOALS, ACCESSIBILITY PRINCIPLES, AND BEST PRACTICES

The design of *TEA Minigames* was grounded in user-centered design (UCD) methodologies, international standards of digital accessibility, and cognitive design principles oriented toward neurodivergent populations. From the earliest stages, inclusion was assumed as a core value rather than an add-on, ensuring that the system addressed both the pedagogical needs and the cognitive profiles of children with Autism Spectrum Disorder (ASD) (Jimenez-Honrado et al., 2024).

UCD provided the overarching framework, following the principles outlined in (ISO-9241-210, 2019). Iterative prototyping cycles were conducted in collaboration with the *Asociación Desarrollo Autismo Albacete*, actively involving educators, caregivers, and children. This participatory approach is consistent with the tradition of participatory design in HCI, which has been shown to enhance usability and adoption in neurodivergent contexts (Druin, 2002).

Accessibility was addressed across multiple dimensions, in alignment with the international WCAG 2.1 guidelines (Caldwell et al., 2008) and supported by research highlighting the benefits of inclusive interfaces for students with disabilities (Seale, 2014). The applied principles included:

- **Perceptual accessibility**: use of high-contrast color palettes and reduction of irrelevant elements to avoid visual overload.
- **Motor accessibility**: simple touch controls and drag-and-drop mechanics instead of complex gestures.
- **Cognitive accessibility**: concise instructions, consistent iconography, and linear navigation.
- **Sensory sensitivity**: options to mute sounds, change background colors, and limit animations, thereby reducing overstimulation frequently experienced by children with ASD (Parsons & Cobb, 2011).

Personalization was identified as an essential requirement for effective ASD interventions (Kasari et al., 2006). The administrative web platform enables educators and caregivers to dynamically adapt the content by:

- Create, edit, and delete exercises in real time.
- Introduce images, categories, and statements tailored to daily routines.
- Modulate task difficulty (e.g., number of options in the quiz or length of the sequences).

This flexibility responds to individual needs and ensures sustainability by allowing pedagogical adjustments without requiring technical expertise.

Cognitive design principles were incorporated to address the learning profiles of children with ASD:

- **Immediate feedback** to reinforce learning, a strategy validated for this population (Whalen et al., 2010).
- **Predictable and consistent structures** that reduce anxiety in the face of uncertainty (Koegel et al., 2012).
- **Fragmentation of information** into short and manageable steps, supporting attention and working memory (Sweller et al., 2011).
- **Emphasis on emotional recognition and social reasoning,** consistent with evidence showing that serious games improve social communication in autistic children (Grynszpan et al., 2014).

It is important to note that these contemporary design practices are consistent with earlier guidelines proposed for videogames in special education. González-Sánchez et al. (2009) that learning is most effective when pedagogy is seamlessly embedded within play. They identified three core principles: a *motivating narrative* to capture attention, *positive reinforcement and feedback* mechanisms to prevent frustration, and the presence of *mediating characters or heroes* to guide learning. These recommendations resonate directly with the design of TEA Minigames, where storyline, feedback, and modularity play a central role. The continuity between these early conceptual models and present-day standards demonstrates that accessibility and inclusion are achieved when educational rigor is balanced with authentic playability.

Beyond the specific context of ASD, the literature on educational gamification provides methodological frameworks that can enrich and structure the design of serious games for this population. Ortega-Arranz et al. (2016) developed a formal model based on actions, conditions, and rewards, which enables the translation of pedagogical intentions into game rules that are transferable and adaptable to different technologies. This approach aligns with the need to equip minigames with predictable and configurable logic, a key aspect for reducing anxiety in autistic learners.

Furthermore, Ortega-Arranz et al. (2019) demonstrated, in the context of MOOCs, that the configuration of rewards significantly influences learner motivation and persistence. Although derived from large-scale contexts such as MOOCs, this type of evidence is transferable to ASD because it illustrates how different reward dynamics can modulate engagement —an equally relevant principle in individualized interventions—.

When integrated with accessibility and cognitive design principles, these contributions reinforce the notion that gamification constitutes a systematic design strategy capable of enhancing both effectiveness and inclusivity in neurodivergent learning environments.

The integration of UCD, accessibility, and cognitive design places *TEA Minigames* in alignment with the framework of Universal Design for Learning (UDL) (Meyer et al., 2014). UDL promotes multiple forms of engagement, representation, and expression, dimensions that serious digital games naturally facilitate. Thus, *TEA Minigames* is not only a practical tool but also an exemplary case of how educational software can operationalize the principles of digital inclusion.

Building upon these design principles, the following section details the technical architecture that operationalizes them.

4. SYSTEM ARCHITECTURE: TEA MINIGAMES

The architectural design of *TEA Minigames* responds to the need to articulate a technological solution that combines technical efficiency, pedagogical flexibility, and digital accessibility principles. The adopted client–server architecture not only ensures the smooth execution of the minigames across different devices but also enables the dynamic management of content by educators and caregivers without requiring technical mediation. It is, therefore, an infrastructure that connects the ludic and administrative dimensions within a secure, scalable, and adaptable environment tailored to the changing needs of children with Autism Spectrum Disorder (ASD).

4.1. Architectural Approach and Justification

The choice of a client–server architecture responds not only to technical criteria but also to pedagogical and accessibility requirements. In intervention contexts with children with ASD, it is essential that technological tools remain flexible, updatable, and sustainable over time. A monolithic or closed solution would restrict the ability to adapt content, which is a critical aspect in populations as heterogeneous as neurodivergent learners.

The modular approach, based on a central server and two differentiated clients —the mobile application and the administrative web platform— ensures functional independence between the children's ludic experience and the management tasks carried out by professionals. This separation of responsibilities simplifies maintenance, fosters scalability, and allows each component to evolve independently. Such an approach is consistent with well-established principles in software engineering, where modularity and separation of concerns are key factors in achieving maintainable and scalable architectures (Bass et al., 2021; Sommerville, 2016) (see Figure 1).

Furthermore, the literature on inclusive educational technologies emphasizes that platforms aimed at neurodivergent populations must prioritize adaptability and personalization to address learner diversity (Parsons & Cobb, 2011; Seale, 2014). The architecture also facilitates integration with Universal Design for Learning (UDL), which promotes multiple means of representation, action, and engagement (Meyer et al., 2014).

Figure 1. General architecture of TEA Minigames showing the Node.js server, MongoDB and Firebase databases, web client (Angular), and mobile application (Unity)

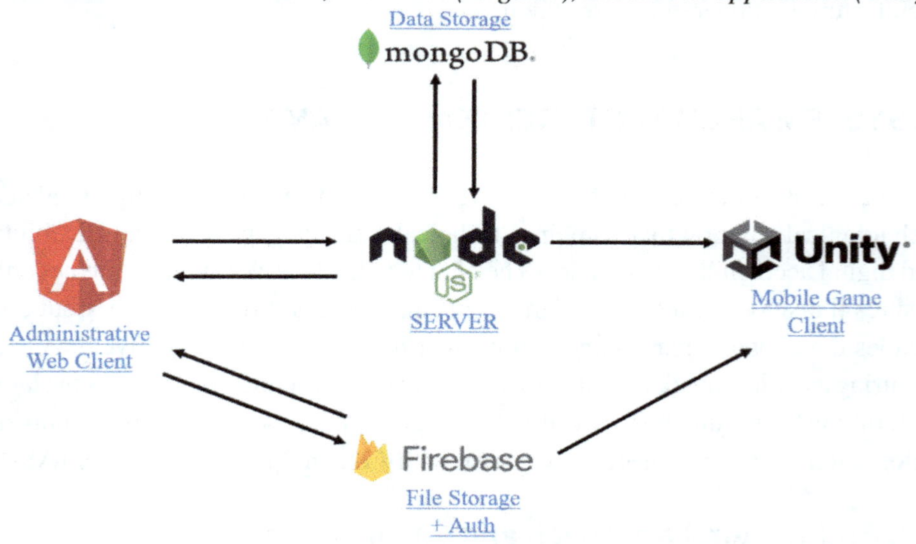

4.2. Relevance of Modularity in Educational and Therapeutic Contexts

Modularity is a fundamental principle in software design that becomes especially relevant in educational and therapeutic interventions. In the case of ASD, the heterogeneity of learner profiles means that children do not respond uniformly to the same stimuli or game dynamics. The architecture of *TEA Minigames* addresses this challenge through a modular approach that allows minigames to be incorporated, replaced, or adapted without altering the system's core.

In this way, educators and therapists can tailor the digital experience to the specific needs of each child while preserving the stability of the technological environment. The web platform interface itself reflects this principle, presenting each minigame as an independent module that can be managed autonomously (see Figure 2).

This design also facilitates iterative experimentation, a key feature in research and development projects: new modules can be tested with small groups before their definitive integration, reducing risks and promoting continuous improvement. Modularity likewise contributes to the sustainability of the system, as it allows the research and educational community to expand the platform with new proposals without the need to rebuild the technical core. In short, it is an approach that combines technical robustness with pedagogical adaptability, making *TEA Minigames* a suitable tool for both educational practice and research in digital accessibility.

Figure 2. Main menu for managing mini-games on the TEA Minigames web platform

The access design follows a dual logic of usability and security. In the mobile application intended for children, no authentication is required, which prevents cognitive overload and removes potential barriers to initial interaction. This decision aligns with studies showing that traditional login methods (alphanumeric passwords or CAPTCHAs) place memory and attention demands that are poorly compatible with neurodivergent profiles (Di Campi & et al., 2025; Ophoff & et al., 2021). By contrast, security control is concentrated in the administrative web platform, where access is restricted through credentials and intended exclusively for educators and caregivers. This model ensures content integrity and data protection without interfering with the game experience.

Specialized literature recommends simplifying authentication mechanisms in inclusive environments and, when necessary, incorporating graphical or biometric alternatives to reduce cognitive load (Sofian & et al., 2018). In the case of *TEA Minigames*, this strategy allows system protection to be balanced with cognitive accessibility, ensuring that security measures do not become a barrier to children's participation.

Within the administrative interface, professionals can *visualize and manage the activities* associated with the sequence-ordering minigame. As shown in Figure 3.a, a list of previously created activities is displayed, including the corresponding images and the options to edit or delete each item. In turn, Figure 3.b illustrates the editing screen, where each activity can be modified in detail by adding images, descriptions, and the appropriate sequence order for the elements.

In the child's view of the sequence-ordering minigame, the interface presents a simple and engaging environment that guides users through arranging images in the correct order. As shown in Figure 4.a, children are provided with numbered slots and a set of images to be sequenced. Figure 4. b illustrates a more advanced activity in which the child organizes illustrated actions into a logical sequence. Finally, Figure 4.c demonstrates the immediate visual feedback mechanism, where a green smiling face signals a correct answer and a red sad face indicates an error, reinforcing learning through clear and accessible responses.

Figure 3. Activity management interface for the sequence ordering game: a. List of created activities b. Activity editing view

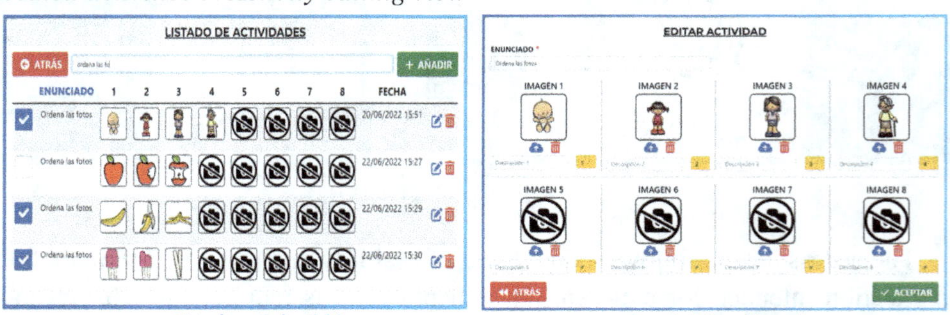

a. List of created activities   b. Activity editing view

Figure 4. Child's view of the sequence-ordering minigame: a. Initial activity with character sequencing b. Example of sequencing a daily-life activity c. Feedback interface with positive and negative responses

a. Initial activity with character sequencing

b. Example of sequencing a daily-life activity

c. Feedback interface with positive and negative responses

4.3. Connection with Principles of Accessibility and Digital Inclusion

The architectural design of *TEA Minigames* explicitly incorporates principles of accessibility and inclusion. The client–server structure enables the dynamic updating of content from the web platform, granting educators and caregivers direct control over the personalization of activities without requiring technical expertise. This capacity for adaptation is consistent with the principles of Universal Design for Learning (UDL), which advocates for multiple means of representation, action, and engagement (Meyer et al., 2014).

The separation between the management logic and the ludic environment prevents children with ASD from having to deal with configuration tasks, thereby reducing cognitive overload. At the same time, professionals are provided with a secure and accessible environment for content administration, in line with the Web Content Accessibility Guidelines (WCAG), which emphasize the importance of perceivability, operability, and understandability in digital systems (Caldwell et al., 2008).

This approach aligns with research on accessibility in e-learning, which highlights the need to ensure that technological infrastructures do not become pedagogical barriers (Seale, 2014). In this regard, *TEA Minigames* constitutes an example of how architectural design can embody pedagogical values, ensuring that security, functional flexibility, and content updating are translated into inclusive learning environments for neurodivergent students.

Table 1 synthesizes the main theoretical and empirical references that underpin the architectural decisions adopted in *TEA Minigames*. Each source was selected for its contribution to modular design, separation of concerns, cognitive accessibility, and pedagogical inclusion. Taken together, this evidence demonstrates that the system's architecture goes beyond technical efficiency criteria and is firmly anchored in recognized frameworks from software engineering, international digital accessibility guidelines, and Universal Design for Learning. In this way, the proposal aligns with global best practices and ensures its relevance in both educational and therapeutic contexts.

Table 2. Theoretical and empirical foundations supporting the architectural design of TEA Minigames

Ref.	Main contribution	Relevance to TEA Minigames
(Caldwell et al., 2008)	Establishes core web accessibility principles: perceivable, operable, understandable, and robust.	Guides the design of the administrative web platform, ensuring that caregivers can manage content in an accessible digital environment.
(Seale, 2014)	Examines accessibility in e-learning and warns against technology becoming a pedagogical barrier.	Supports the decision to separate management logic (for professionals) from the ludic environment (for children), thereby reducing cognitive load.
(Meyer et al., 2014)	Provides the theoretical foundation of Universal Design for Learning (UDL): multiple means of representation, action, and engagement.	Justifies the modular architecture, enabling personalization of minigames and content for diverse learner needs.
(Bass et al., 2021)	Introduces key software architecture principles: modularity, separation of concerns, maintainability, and scalability.	Supports the adoption of a modular client–server design for TEA Minigames.
(Sommerville, 2016)	Outlines software engineering best practices and system quality criteria.	Reinforces the theoretical framework underpinning a sustainable and maintainable architecture.
(Di Campi & et al., 2025)	Analyzes authentication methods accessible to people with diverse cognitive abilities.	Justifies the removal of login in the children's application to avoid cognitive overload.

continued on following page

Table 2. Continued

Ref.	Main contribution	Relevance to TEA Minigames
(Ophoff & et al., 2021)	Explores the relationship between cognitive functions and authentication mechanisms.	Reinforces the need to simplify login processes for neurodivergent users.
(Sofian & et al., 2018)	Reviews usability guidelines for mobile apps targeting children with autism.	Supports the design of simple, accessible interfaces and suggests graphical/biometric alternatives for inclusive authentication.

5. EVALUATION METHODOLOGY AND RESULTS

This section presents the proposed *quality-in-use* evaluation of *TEA Minigames*. The structure of the evaluation follows the ISO/IEC 25062 standard, complemented with a Likert-based System Usability Scale (SUS) questionnaire.

5.1. Introduction

The main objective of this evaluation is to assess the performance of both professional users and students with ASD. To this end, the standards of the ISO/IEC 25000 family —specifically 25022, 25040, and 25062— are applied. The role of the evaluators is to ensure that the evaluation is conducted with a rigorous methodology and that the results collected guarantee comparability with the quality of other usability studies. This approach is supported by the ISO/IEC 9241-11 definition of usability, articulated through the dimensions of *effectiveness, efficiency,* and *satisfaction.*

The evaluation seeks to identify usability shortcomings in *TEA Minigames*, thereby enabling refinement of the user experience and interface. For this purpose, participants were asked throughout the evaluation process to verbalize their thoughts, applying the *Thinking-Aloud* technique (Ericsson & Simon, 1993).

The structure of this section follows the reporting guidelines established in ISO/IEC 25062. *Effectiveness* and *efficiency* are measured according to the criteria defined in ISO/IEC 25040, while *satisfaction* is assessed through a questionnaire. In this case, the System Usability Scale (SUS) was selected, given its extensive use in the HCI field.

5.1.1. Product Description

TEA Minigames was conceived as a platform integrating educational games for students with Autism Spectrum Disorder (ASD), with the purpose of facilitating their social integration. The platform was co-designed with a user-centered focus, involving staff members from the *Asociación Desarrollo Autismo Albacete* in the design process.

5.1.2. Test Objectives

Considering the main objective of the development of *TEA Minigames*—"Design of several minigames using serious games principles to facilitate ASD children's integration into society in a fun way"— the evaluation was established to validate its fulfillment with respect to the following factors:

- **Ease of use:** How easily participants can navigate and use the application through the proposed tasks.
- **Functionality:** Participants should not feel that any functionality is missing while using the application. To assess this, they were asked to apply the *Thinking-Aloud* technique (Ericsson & Simon, 1993).
- **Usefulness:** How users perceive the need addressed by adopting the application, considering how it fits into the processes and techniques already used by specialists to support the social integration of children with ASD.

5.2. Method

The following subsections describe the process carried out during the evaluation, including information about the participants, the evaluation context (with details of the location and devices used), and the experimental design, which specifies the metrics applied.

5.2.1. Participants

The participants in the evaluation corresponded to two profiles: the first consisted of professionals (adults), who were responsible for testing the management functions of the application; the second consisted of children with ASD.

A total of six professionals, aged between 21 and 40 years, participated. Their information is presented in Table 2, which summarizes the characteristics of this group.

Table 3. Information of participants in the professional profile

ID	Age	Sex	IT Level (1-10)
1	24	F	7
2	32	F	6
3	40	F	4
4	22	M	8
5	21	F	8
6	22	M	7

On the other hand, three children with ASD participated, all within the age group of 13 years. Their information is presented in Table 3. A conceptual adaptation can also be observed in how they were asked about their level of information technology use: while professionals were asked to rate their level directly, the children were instead asked whether they considered themselves to be *bad*, *good*, or *average*, which corresponded directly to the categories *Bad*, *Good*, and *Medium*, respectively.

Table 4. Information of participants in the children profile

Child	Age	Sex (M/F)	IT use level (good/medium/bad)	ASD Type	ASD level
1	13	M	Good	Autism	Moderate
2	15	M	Good	Autism	Mild
3	13	M	Medium	Autism	Moderate

5.2.2. Context of Product Use

The following subsection presents the tasks assigned to the participants. It also describes the test context, indicating where the application was executed.

Tasks

The tasks to be performed are contingent upon the specific group being evaluated. These tasks were assigned to the participants, who are required to execute them in a typical usage scenario, utilizing a computer for web browsing and another computer equipped with a digital board for the game.

Administrative Web

For the administrative web, participants must adhere to the same process for the three minigames: adding an exercise, editing it, and subsequently deleting it. For the two final games, as images are required, participants will dispose of some pictures on their computer, which was previously provided by the evaluator, to facilitate their easy upload. These tasks details are contained in Table 4.

Mobile Game

For the mobile game, participants must play each of the three minigames until they complete five exercises. Initially, the game was intended to be tested on a mobile device, such as a smartphone or tablet. However, the client had a digital board where participants could play the game using a mobile device. The specific tasks to be carried out by the participants of the second group are outlined in Table 5.

Table 5. Professional Tasks

ID TASK	Task to be Performed
Before starting the evaluation	Login with the credentials provided by the administrator.
TA1.	Create and delete an exercise for the quiz game
TA1.1.	Go to the quiz game exercises list
TA1.2.	Add a new question
TA1.3.	Edit the created question and change one fields
TA1.4.	Delete the question
TA2.	Create and delete an experience for the guessing game
TA2.1.	Go to the guessing game exercises list
TA2.2.	Add a new exercise
TA2.3.	Upload the two images provided by the evaluator and response Word
TA2.4.	Edit the created exercise and add a sentence, and the description of the images and save the changes
TA2.5.	Delete the exercise
TA3.	Create and Delete an activity for the ordering game
TA3.1.	Go to the ordering game exercises list
TA3.2.	Add a new activity
TA3.3.	Add a sentence and upload the four images provided by the evaluator and assign them the order
TA3.4.	Edit the created activity, and then add a description for each one of the uploaded images
TA3.5.	Delete the activity

Table 6. Tasks for Children with ASD

ID TASK	Task to be Performed
Before starting the evaluation	Having the game installed and launched
TB1.	Play the quiz game
TB1.1.	Press the play button from the main menu
TB1.2.	Press the button of the first game
TB1.3.	Select the desired category
TB1.4.	Answer/skip the questions till the end
TB2.	Play the guessing game
TB2.1.	Press the play button from the main menu
TB2.2.	Press the button of the second game
TB2.3.	Answer/skip the exercises till the end. Use the tip button if desired
TB3.	Play the ordering game
TB3.1.	Press the play button from the main menu
TB3.2.	Press the button of the third game
TB3.3.	Order/skip the activities
TB4.	Change the color of the background and/or toggle on/off the music
TB4.1.	Press the options button from the main menu
TB4.2.	Toggle on/off the music
TB4.3	Change the background color

Previous tasks were selected as they are considered fundamental tasks that encompass the entire functionality of the system. Participants will be provided with instructions for each task.

Each task will be deemed successfully completed if the participants successfully complete all the necessary steps.

Test Context

The context encompasses the location where the test is conducted, the devices employed, and any other factors that may influence the evaluation process.

The TEA Minigames administrative web is designed to be accessed on any contemporary web browser, including Google Chrome, Firefox, Microsoft Edge, or Opera. Consequently, it can be utilized on mobile devices' browsers, although it is optimized for computers with a resolution of 1080p. The web test will be conducted on a computer.

The TEA Minigames mobile game is compatible with Microsoft Windows and Android operating systems. However, for the evaluation, a tablet will be utilized. The game's size is 26 MB for Android and 142 MB for Microsoft Windows.

5.2.3. Experimental Design

The following data have been collected from the evaluation: time spent on each task, errors, assists, and the completion rates of assisted and non-assisted tasks. Additionally, a SUS questionnaire was administered to the participants.

The evaluation language was Spanish, as it proved to be more effective and accessible for communication.

The study was conducted in collaboration with the *Asociación Desarrollo Autismo Albacete*, following institutional ethical guidelines. Participation was voluntary, with prior informed consent from parents or legal guardians and verbal assent from the children. All collected data were anonymized and stored securely in compliance with the General Data Protection Regulation (GDPR). No identifiable information was retained, and participation or withdrawal had no consequences for the children or the institution.

The evaluation of children was conducted through observation, as the limited number of participants (maximum of three) necessitated a qualitative approach rather than a quantitative one. Fortunately, the *Asociación Desarrollo Autismo Albacete* provided an interactive digital board that allowed participants to engage in the games on a large display.

The evaluation of adults was conducted online, as the evaluator opted to utilize the evaluation meeting solely for the assessment of children. This decision was made due to the limited time and opportunities available to schedule another meeting.

5.2.4. Process

Upon arrival at the *Asociación Desarrollo Autismo Albacete*, the evaluation administrator procured the requisite materials and commenced the evaluation of the participants.

During the participants' engagement with the applications, the administrator meticulously observed their activities, documenting the evaluation data and personal information of each participant, as evidenced in Table 4, and Table 5.

5.2.5. Usability Metrics

Three characteristics are employed to evaluate the performance, namely effectiveness, efficiency, and satisfaction. These characteristics are outlined in ISO/IEC 25022.

- **Effectiveness**: The effectiveness of a task is evaluated based on the unassisted and assisted completion rates, the number of errors encountered during task execution, and the number of assists provided by the evaluator.
- **Efficiency**: Efficiency is assessed by the time required to complete each task.
- **Satisfaction:** Satisfaction is measured using the System Usability Scale (SUS) questionnaire administered to participants after task completion. Unfortunately, there is no specific SUS questionnaire designed for children. Consequently, an adaptation of the original questionnaire will be utilized. The SUS questionnaire for children will retain the same questions as the original (as depicted in Table 6), but slight modifications will be made to enhance comprehension without altering the intended meaning (contained in Table 7).

Table 7. SUS Questionnaire for Professionals

Mark with an X where applicable		Strongly Disagree	Disagree	Neutral	Agree	Strongly Agree
1	I would like to use the application again					
2	The application is too complex					
3	The application is easy to use					
4	I need help to use this application					
5	The user interface is intuitive					
6	I thought there would be too much inconsistency in this system					
7	Most people would learn to use this application quickly					
8	The application is very complex to use					
9	I felt very confident using the application					
10	I needed to learn many things before starting to use the application					

Table 8. SUS Questionnaire for Children

	Mark with an X where applicable					
1	I want to play again.					
2	The game was very hard.					
3	The game is easy.					
4	Someone helped me play.					
5	The game screen is easy to understand.					
6	Lots of things break in the game.					
7	I think almost everyone will learn to play quickly.					
8	The game is very hard to play.					
9	I felt very safe while playing.					
10	Someone needed to show me how to play.					

For both SUS score analysis in both groups, the acceptability scale was utilized (see Figure 5). The system must achieve a score of 68 or higher to be deemed acceptable.

Figure 5. SUS Scoring Scale

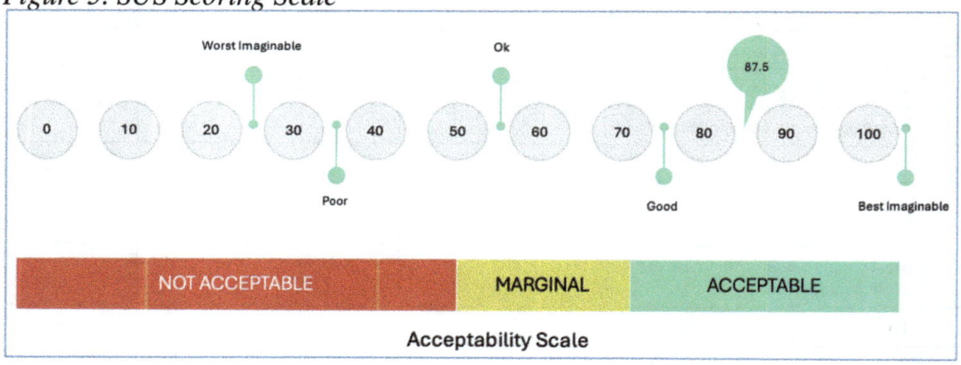

5.3. Results

The following section presents the data obtained during the evaluation of TEA Minigames. This evaluation was conducted with a focus on assessing user experience, performance metrics, and overall engagement levels. The collected information provides a clear overview of the application's current strengths and areas for potential improvement, serving as a foundation for further analysis and decision-making in future development phases.

5.3.1. Data Analysis

The participants' behavior has been categorized into groups based on the time required to complete the evaluation, the number of errors committed, the number of assists provided, and the percentage of assisted versus unassisted completions. Additionally, as the employed method was observation, the evaluator meticulously recorded every commentary and any unusual behavior that could be valuable for system analysis. To enhance this process, the evaluator accompanied himself to the evaluation location, which provided him with a partner to ensure that no detail was overlooked.

To facilitate the analysis of the results, the mean, minimum, and maximum values, as well as the standard deviation, were utilized. Furthermore, the obtained SUS score was also considered.

5.3.2. Professional Results

The results for the previously defined tasks that adult's group must perform are the following ones:

> Task A1: Create, edit, and delete a question for the quiz game (see Table 8 and Table 9).

Table 9. Evaluation Results - Adults Group - Task A1

Participant	Unassisted completion rate	Assisted completion rate	Time (mm:ss)	Errors	Assists
1	100	0	00:52	0	0
2	100	0	00:46	0	0
3	100	0	00:59	0	0
4	100	0	00:53	0	0
5	100	0	01:07	0	0
6	100	0	00:43	0	0

Table 10. Evaluation Statistics - Adults Group - Task A1

	Unassisted completion rate	Assisted completion rate	Time (mm:ss)	Errors	Assists
Mean	100	0	00:53	0	0
Min.	100	0	00:43	0	0
Max.	100	0	01:07	0	0
Standard dev.	0	0	00:09	0	0

Task A2: Create, edit, and delete an exercise for the guessing game (see Table 10 and Table 11).

Table 11. Evaluation Results - Professional Group - Task A2

Participant	Unassisted completion rate	Assisted completion rate	Time (mm:ss)	Errors	Assists
1	100	0	00:44	0	0
2	100	0	00:32	0	0
3	75	25	01:02	0	1
4	100	0	00:41	0	0
5	100	0	00:59	0	0
6	100	0	00:55	0	0

Table 12. Evaluation Statistics - Professional Group - Task A2

	Unassisted rate	Assisted completion rate	Time (mm:ss)	Errors	Assists
Mean	95.83	4.17	00:49	0	0.16
Min.	75	0	00:32	0	0
Max.	100	25	01:02	0	1
Standard dev.	10.21	10.21	00:12	0	0.4

Task A3: Create, edit, and delete an activity for the ordering game (see Table 12 and Table 13).

Table 13. Evaluation Results - Professional Group - Task A3

Participant	Unassisted completion rate	Assisted completion rate	Time (mm:ss)	Errors	Assists
1	100	0	00:54	0	0
2	50	50	01:13	0	2
3	75	25	01:04	0	0
4	100	0	00:49	0	0
5	100	0	01:00	0	0
6	100	0	00:57	0	0

Table 14. Evaluation Statistics - Professional Group - Task A3

	Unassisted completion rate	Assisted completion rate	Time (mm:ss)	Errors	Assists
Mean	91.67	8.33	01:00	0	0.33
Min.	50	20.41	00:49	0	0
Max.	100	0	01:13	0	2
Standard dev.	20.41	50	00:08	0	0.82

The obtained SUS individual and total scores are present in Table 14. They have achieved a satisfaction score of 87.5.

Table 15. SUS Score for Professional Group

Participant	Score
1	85
2	92.5
3	95
4	77.5
5	80
6	95
MEAN	87.5

5.3.3. Children Result

The results for the previously defined tasks that children group must perform are the following ones:

Task B1: Play to the quiz game and complete first 5 exercises (first game). See Table 15 and Table 16.

Table 16. Evaluation results - Children Group - Task B1

Participant	Unassisted completion rate	Assisted completion rate	Time (mm:ss)	Errors	Assists
1	60	40	00:45	0	2
2	100	0	01:03	0	0
3	100	0	00:56	0	0

Table 17. Evaluation Statistics - Children Group - Task B1

	Unassisted completion rate	Assisted completion rate	Time (mm:ss)	Errors	Assists
Mean	86.67	13.33	00:55	0	0.66
Min.	60	0	00:45	0	0
Max.	100	40	01:03	0	2
Standard dev.	23.09	23.09	00:09	0	1.15

Task B2: Play to the guessing game and complete first 5 exercises (second game). See Table 17 and Table 18.

Table 18. Evaluation Results - Children Group - Task B2

Participant	Unassisted completion rate	Assisted completion rate	Time (mm:ss)	Errors	Assists
1	80	20	01:01	0	1
2	100	0	00:57	0	0
3	100	0	01:49	0	0

Table 19. Evaluation Statistics – Children Group - Task B2

	Unassisted completion rate	Assisted completion rate	Time (mm:ss)	Errors	Assists
Mean	93.33	6.67	01:16	0	0.33
Min.	80	0	00:57	0	0
Max.	100	20	01:49	0	1
Standard dev.	11.55	11.55	00:29	0	0.58

Task B3: Play to the ordering game and complete first 5 exercises (third game). See Table 19 and Table 20.

Table 20. Evaluation Results - Children Group - Task B3

Participant	Unassisted completion rate	Assisted completion rate	Time (mm:ss)	Errors	Assists
1	80	20	01:12	1	1
2	100	0	01:35	0	0
3	100	0	01:20	1	0

Table 21. Evaluation Statistics - Children Group - Task B3

	Unassisted completion rate	Assisted completion rate	Time (mm:ss)	Errors	Assists
Mean	93.33	6.67	01:22	0.66	0.33
Min.	80	0	01:12	0	0
Max.	100	20	0:35	1	1
Standard dev.	11.55	11.55	00:12	0.58	0.58

Table 7 presents the SUS score for children with ASD, which is 76.66 points of satisfaction.

Table 22. SUS Score for Children Group

Participant	Score
1	72.5
2	67.5
3	90
MEAN	76.66

The mean SUS score for professionals (M = 87.5) and for children (M = 76.66) both exceed the standard acceptability threshold of 68 (Brooke, 1996), indicating excellent perceived usability for the administrative web and good usability for the children's games. According to Bangor et al. (2009), these values correspond to the "excellent" and "good" usability ranges, respectively.

5.4. Results Discussion

Following the completion of the evaluation and the receipt of the results, several points warrant discussion based on the analysis of the results and the behavior of the participants.

Firstly, due to the difficulty in identifying users with the desired profile, specifically children with ASD, we were compelled to limit the number of participants to three. Consequently, the evaluator opted for a qualitative test approach. Throughout the test, the evaluator and their companion observed the children. The monitors provided valuable insights into effective interaction strategies with the children.

Secondly, given the limited number of adult participants at the testing site, the evaluation was supplemented by additional participants, similar to those previously involved.

Adults' Evaluation Discussion

As evidenced in the preceding tables pertaining to this group's evaluation, there were no errors committed by the participants in utilizing the administrative web. This is attributed to the development team's implementation of a user-friendly interface and robust error handling mechanisms, such as prohibiting incompatible characters, word length, and number ranges in formularies.

The number of assists was minimal due to the simplicity of the user interface and the use of metaphors. Task completion times were relatively consistent among participants, as they did not require extensive cognitive effort to comprehend the functionality.

We observe a greater standard deviation in the last two tasks compared to the first one, particularly in task times. This is likely due to the increased number of steps and the requirement to upload images.

Finally, the SUS score obtained for the professional group was 87.7, surpassing the threshold of 68. Consequently, based on the SUS scale depicted in Figure 4, we can confidently assert that the administrative web is more than acceptable.

Children Evaluation Discussion

The children thoroughly enjoyed playing the games. They found them particularly engaging, particularly the initial quiz game. While they achieved a higher number of assists and errors compared to the adults, it is essential to categorize these into two distinct groups: errors attributed to the user interface and those stemming from the exercise's inherent difficulty. These latter factors were not considered in the evaluation, as only system functionality issues were being assessed.

On the one hand, due to game functionality and user interface, the following issues were observed:

- Certain buttons lacked sufficient contrast between their color and the text within them, rendering them difficult to read.
- In the ordering sequences game, it appears that once all the figures were positioned within the slots, the children were unable to reposition any figure to its original location. To rectify this, they may have utilized the "reset" button to reload the exercise.

Conversely, due to the complexity of the exercises prepared by the evaluator, we identified the following issues through the assistance of monitor observations:

- Some quiz game questions were too challenging or contained excessive text. Children with ASD may become overwhelmed by interfaces with an abundance of words. During the evaluation, children typically responded by rapidly selecting an answer, regardless of its accuracy.
- Certain images from the guessing the images game were not suitable for children with ASD. Two images depicted frightened dogs, and such images could potentially have a negative impact on the children.
- Additionally, in the guessing the images game, we observed that the missing word was sometimes excessively long, resulting in an overwhelming number of possible letters. Nevertheless, the children enjoyed this game, and there were no complaints.
- In the ordering sequences game, some activities contained an excessive number of figures. This is not a concern, as the monitors can generate shorter activities from the administrative web, with a maximum of eight images.

Finally, the SUS score obtained for the children's group was 76.66. Since this value exceeds 68, we can conclude that the game is acceptable from a usability perspective.

Differences in performance and engagement appeared related to the children's support needs. Those with milder ASD profiles showed greater autonomy in navigating tasks and responded positively to visual challenges, while those requiring higher levels of support benefited from simplified tasks and consistent feedback cues. These observations reinforce the importance of customizable difficulty levels and sensory adjustments for addressing the heterogeneity of ASD.

Other Considerations and Improvements

In addition to the analyzed data, the monitors provide us with some commentaries during and after the children's evaluation. These suggestions can be viewed in more detail below in the Meetings with the client description. Therefore, two meetings –Requirements and Evaluation– have been scheduled with the clients during the entire system development process, in this case, with the *Asociación Desarrollo Autismo Albacete*.

The initial meeting (Requirements) was conducted to present the client with an early prototype of the system's future appearance and functionality. At that time, the prototype consisted solely of the mobile game, which was later expanded to include an administrative web interface for managing game exercises.

During this meeting, the client's feedback regarding the prototype was also gathered. Based on this feedback, several conclusions were drawn and organized into the following groups:

- Following the client meeting, several conclusions were drawn, categorized into distinct types:
- **Configuration**: The more configurable and customizable the game, the more engaging it becomes. Users should have the ability to modify the background colors, buttons, text, and game sounds.
- **Minigame Themes**: The client provided several examples of games that could be implemented for our application. These include:
  - o Complete Sentences with One or More Words: Users must form complete sentences using one or more words.
  - o Decision-Making: Users are presented with various daily situations and must select the most probable solution for each.
  - o Daily Life Activities (DLA): Users are provided with images depicting different daily processes and must order them in the correct sequence (e.g., washing teeth).
  - o Calculation: Simple logical-mathematical games should be implemented, utilizing images whenever possible.

    - Comprehensive Reading: Users are presented with a simple action or activity, accompanied by multiple images. Each image should be associated with its corresponding description.
- **Minigame Configuration**: Each minigame (if feasible) should offer varying levels of difficulty. Additionally, users should have the option to interact with other players locally, facilitating training in waiting times and turns. Furthermore, the text displayed on the screen should be concise and clear.

The second meeting (Evaluation) was entirely dedicated to presenting the client with a comprehensive solution to the system, conducting an evaluation, and gathering the final details that the development team should consider for further enhancements, which in this instance were minor.

Following the evaluation, the monitors provided recommendations for potential improvements to the system.

Specifically, for the administrative web, and more precisely, for the quiz game, they suggested the following improvements:

- For the desktop game:
    - Enhance the "Create Question" Panel: Introduce a button that opens a modal interface, enabling users to create or delete categories. Subsequently, select the desired category from a dropdown menu.
    - Incorporate a Statistics Section: Provide a dedicated section for users to access statistics related to the games.
    - Facilitate Image Integration: Allow users to add complementary images to quiz questions.
- For the mobile game:
    - Implement Feedback Mechanism: Provide feedback (smile or sad face) for each game based on the player's success or failure in completing an exercise.
    - Enhance Category Selection: Introduce a category selector for all games, enabling users to select specific categories and play exercises within those categories.
    - Display Performance Summary: Present a final panel that summarizes the player's hits and misses. This data should be sent to the administrative web, allowing administrators to analyze it.
    - Enable Username Introduction: Allow users to introduce a username upon starting the application.

In general feedback, the client expressed their satisfaction with the product and particularly valued the ability to modify exercise data from the administrative web. A copy of the product status at that time has been provided to the client for their use.

These findings are consistent with previous evaluations of serious games designed for children with ASD, which report high levels of engagement and acceptance, particularly when games are simple, structured, and customizable (Azadboni, 2024; Carlier et al., 2020; Hassan et al., 2021). At the same time, the literature emphasizes recurrent challenges such as the need to refine visual clarity, adapt the narrative depth, and calibrate task difficulty to avoid frustration (Lopez-Bouzas & Del Moral-Perez, 2023; Vallefuoco et al., 2022). Meta-analyses further confirm that while serious games enhance communication, social reasoning, and daily living skills, their long-term efficacy depends on iterative refinement based on usability testing with real users (Grynszpan et al., 2014). In this sense, the evaluation of TEA Minigames not only validates its immediate usability but also illustrates the importance of conceiving evaluation as a continuous process that drives design improvement and contributes to the accumulation of evidence-based practices in inclusive educational technology.

The small sample size (six professionals and three children) limits the generalizability of findings. As this was an exploratory usability study, results should be interpreted as indicative rather than conclusive. The researchers acknowledge that their dual role as designers and evaluators may have introduced interpretive bias; efforts were made to mitigate this through triangulation of observations and participant feedback. Future studies should expand sample diversity and include independent evaluation teams.

Overall, the results not only validate the system's usability but also confirm that its modular architecture facilitates meaningful customization. Educators reported that real-time editing of activities reduced preparation time and allowed them to adapt content to each learner's profile. This outcome illustrates how the platform operationalizes inclusive design principles, linking technical accessibility with pedagogical flexibility.

These findings illustrate how modular, educator-managed customization translates usability into pedagogical utility, enabling rapid alignment of game content and sensory parameters with each learner's evolving profile.

6. FUTURE WORK: SCALABILITY, ANALYTICS, AND PERSONALIZATION

The evaluation of TEA Minigames confirmed that the system is functional, usable, and engaging for both children with ASD and professionals. However, feedback collected during the evaluation sessions and meetings with the client highlights several promising directions for future development. These improvements address scalability, learning analytics, and personalization to strengthen the pedagogical value and inclusivity of the system.

First, expanding the *portfolio of minigames* will diversify learning opportunities. Suggested additions include:

- *Decision-making games*, where children face everyday situations and must select the most appropriate response.
- *Daily Life Activities (DLA)*, focused on ordering images of routines such as brushing teeth or preparing a meal.
- *Comprehensive reading tasks*, which pair simple actions or activities with corresponding images.
- *Mathematics and logic challenges*, using visual supports to foster cognitive reasoning.
- *Sentence completion tasks*, requiring users to build complete sentences from one or more words.

Second, greater *configuration and personalization options* will enhance flexibility. Each minigame should offer multiple difficulty levels, supporting progressive learning. Options for local multi-player modes can train turn-taking and waiting skills, while customizable sensory settings (background colors, sounds, text size) will help reduce overstimulation. Text design should remain concise and accessible to maximize comprehension.

Third, the *administrative web platform* requires specific enhancements. A statistics panel would provide professionals with aggregated data on game sessions, accuracy, errors, and usage frequency. Improved category management tools will simplify the creation and deletion of custom groups, while image integration will enrich quiz questions with multimodal elements.

Fourth, several *mobile application improvements* are planned. These include immediate feedback mechanisms (e.g., smile/sad faces after tasks), thematic category selection across all games, performance summaries sent to the administrative web, and username input to track progress across sessions.

Finally, *future research and evaluation* should extend beyond the pilot study. Larger-scale and longitudinal evaluations with diverse participants are necessary to validate the system's effectiveness. Another priority will be the development of learning analytics and formative assessment tools capable of tracking engagement, completion rates, and adaptive difficulty. These data will support the study of learning transfer, examining whether improvements in game-based interaction translate into real-world social and communication outcomes for learners with ASD. Architecturally, the modular design will facilitate scalability, ensuring that new minigames and features can be integrated without redesigning the entire system. Future work will not only focus on scalability and personalization but also on long-term sustainability, considering the Total Cost of Ownership (TCO) for educational institutions, maintenance routines, and training needs. Exploring open-source components and lightweight deployment options will ensure the system's maintainability and accessibility in diverse contexts.

A public demonstration of the TEA Minigames prototype will be made available to partner institutions upon request to facilitate further testing and collaborative research. In upcoming evaluations, usability metrics will explicitly report completion, assistance, and error rates, calculated as the proportion of tasks completed successfully or with assistance out of total attempts in order to standardize comparability across studies.

7. CONCLUSION: TOWARD ACCESSIBLE GAME-BASED LEARNING FOR NEURODIVERGENT POPULATIONS

TEA Minigames exemplifies how user-centered design, accessibility principles, and modular architectures can converge into an inclusive digital tool for children with Autism Spectrum Disorder. The evaluation confirmed that both the mobile games and the administrative web are highly usable, engaging, and adaptable to educational and therapeutic contexts. The SUS scores above the acceptability threshold, combined with qualitative observations, underscore the potential of serious games to foster social integration in children with ASD.

Collaboration with caregivers and the *Asociación Desarrollo Autismo Albacete* ensured that the system responds to real-world pedagogical needs. By allowing the customization of exercises, sensory adjustments, and difficulty levels, TEA Minigames empowers professionals to create tailored interventions aligned with individual learner profiles. This participatory approach not only improved usability but also grounded the system in authentic educational practices.

Beyond the immediate case study, TEA Minigames contributes to broader debates on inclusive digital education. It demonstrates how accessibility standards such as ISO/IEC quality in use, WCAG, and Universal Design for Learning can be operationalized in software solutions, yielding tangible benefits for neurodivergent learners. The project illustrates that inclusive design is not an add-on but a foundational principle that enhances both educational effectiveness and social equity.

Looking forward, the integration of new minigames, analytics dashboards, and advanced personalization features will expand the system's pedagogical impact. TEA Minigames thus serves as a proof of concept for the role of *accessible serious games* in promoting digital inclusion, social participation, and equitable learning opportunities for neurodivergent populations.

From a technical perspective, TEA Minigames represents a coherent ecosystem of interconnected applications and databases. Its architecture integrates a Node.js server, MongoDB and Firebase for persistence, an Angular-based administrative web client, and a Unity-based mobile game client. While the two clients are designed for very different user groups —professionals managing content and children engaging with the games— they remain tightly coupled through the same pedagogical objectives. This dual structure illustrates how modular and distributed architectures can effectively support the common purpose of promoting social integration and learning opportunities for children with ASD.

This work provides not only a validated case study but also a transferable model for designing inclusive, customizable, and scalable educational software systems for neurodivergent populations. In summary, TEA Minigames demonstrates that modular, educator-managed serious games can translate accessibility into pedagogical flexibility for neurodivergent learners. Future developments will need to ensure scalable and sustainable deployment, supported by training pathways for educators and open frameworks for adaptation. Equally important will be assessing educational transfer, verifying whether digital participation gains extend to classroom and everyday interactions. These directions will consolidate the system as a sustainable and evidence-based contribution to accessible game-based learning.

REFERENCES

Al-Qora'n, L. F., Nganji, J. T., & Alsuhimat, F. M. (2025). Designing Inclusive and Adaptive Content in Moodle: A Framework and a Case Study from Jordanian Higher Education. *Multimodal Technologies and Interaction*, *9*(6), 58. DOI: 10.3390/mti9060058

Almurashi, H., Bouaziz, R., Alharthi, W., Al-Sarem, M., Hadwan, M., & Kammoun, S. (2022). Augmented Reality, Serious Games and Picture Exchange Communication System for People with ASD: Systematic Literature Review and Future Directions. *Sensors (Basel)*, *22*(3), 1250. Advance online publication. DOI: 10.3390/s22031250 PMID: 35161995

Armstrong, T. (2010). *The Power of Neurodiversity: Unleashing the Advantages of Your Differently Wired Brain*. Da Capo Press.

Azadboni, T. T. (2024). Effectiveness of Serious Games in Social Skills Training to Autistic Individuals: A Systematic Review. *Autism Research*, *17*(5), 850–872. DOI: 10.1002/aur.3091

Azevedo, L. F. A. (2023). Educación inclusiva para alumnos con TEA: Estrategias pedagógicas, retos y perspectivas. *Sustainability*, *15*(14), 14576. DOI: 10.3390/su151914576

Bangor, A., Kortum, P., & Miller, J. (2009). Determining what individual SUS scores mean: Adding an adjective rating scale. *Journal of Usability Studies*, *4*(3), 114–123.

Bass, L., Clements, P., & Kazman, R. (2021). *Software Architecture in Practice* (4th ed.). Addison-Wesley.

Brooke, J. (1996). *SUS: A Quick and Dirty Usability Scale Usability Evaluation in Industry*. CRC Press.

Caldwell, B., Cooper, M., Guarino Reid, L., & Vanderheiden, G. (2008). *Web Content Accessibility Guidelines (WCAG) 2.0*. https://www.w3.org/TR/WCAG20/

Carlier, S., Van der Paelt, S., Ongenae, F., De Backere, F., & De Turck, F. (2020). Empowering Children with ASD and Their Parents: Design of a Serious Game for Anxiety and Stress Reduction. *Sensors (Basel)*, *20*(4), 966. Advance online publication. DOI: 10.3390/s20040966 PMID: 32054025

Carneiro, L. (2024). The Effectiveness of Digital Serious Games in Social Skills Interventions for Children with ASD: A Meta-Analysis. *Frontiers in Psychology*, *15*, 1345. DOI: 10.3389/fpsyg.2024.01345

Carrión-León, D. I., Lopez-Ramos, M. P., Santillan-Valdiviezo, L. G., Tanguila-Tapuy, D. S., Morocho-Santos, G. M., Moyano-Arias, R. J., Yautibug-Apugllón, M. E., & Chacón-Luna, A. E. (2025). Evaluating Interaction Capability in a Serious Game for Children with ASD: An Operability-Based Approach Aligned with ISO/IEC 25010:2023. *Computers*, *14*(9), 370. DOI: 10.3390/computers14090370

Collado-Martínez, J. Á., & Navarro-Ardoy, D. (2023). *Proyectos neuroeducativos en educación infantil: Situaciones de aprendizaje para el aula*. UNED.

Costanza-Chock, S. (2020). *Design Justice: Community-Led Practices to Build the Worlds We Need*. The MIT Press., DOI: 10.7551/mitpress/12255.001.0001

Di Campi, L., & Luccio, F. L. (2025). Accessible authentication methods for persons with diverse cognitive abilities. *Universal Access in the Information Society*, *24*(3), 2195–2217. Advance online publication. DOI: 10.1007/s10209-025-01189-4

Druin, A. (2002). *The role of children in the design of new technology* Proceedings of the SIGCHI Conference on Human Factors in Computing Systems, Dubovyk, S. H. (2020). Preparing Future Teachers for the Development of Students' Emotional Intelligence. *Humanities and Social Sciences Reviews, 8*(3), 142-150. https://doi.org/DOI: 10.18510/hssr.2020.8316

Ericsson, K. A., & Simon, H. A. (1993). *Protocol Analysis: Verbal Reports as Data*. MIT Press. DOI: 10.7551/mitpress/5657.001.0001

Facer, K., & Selwyn, N. (2021). *Digital technology and the futures of education – towards 'non-stupid' optimism.*

Filippou, K., Acquah, E. O., & Bengs, A. (2025). Inclusive Policies and Practices in Higher Education: A Systematic Literature Review. *Review of Education*, *13*(2), e70034. DOI: 10.1002/rev3.70034

Florian, L., & Black-Hawkins, K. (2011). Exploring Inclusive Pedagogy. *British Educational Research Journal*, *37*(5), 813–828. DOI: 10.1080/01411926.2010.501096

Freitas, É., Panceri, J. A. C., Da Luz Schreider, S., Caldeira, E., & Filho, T. F. B. (2024). Cognitive Serious Games Dynamically Modulated as a Therapeutic Tool for Applied Behavior Analysis Therapy in Children with Autism Spectrum Disorder. *International Journal of Emerging Technologies in Learning*, *19*(5), 80–92. DOI: 10.3991/ijet.v19i05.48677

González-Sánchez, J. L., Cabrera, M. J., Gutiérrez, F. L., Padilla-Zea, N., & Paderewski, P. (2009). Design of Videogames in Special Education. In *New Trends on Human–Computer Interaction* (pp. 43–52). Springer., DOI: 10.1007/978-1-84882-352-5_5

Goodley, D. (2014). *Dis/ability Studies: Theorising Disablism and Ableism*. Routledge. DOI: 10.4324/9780203366974

Grossard, C. (2025). Children's Improvement After Language and Rhythm Training through a Serious Game Intervention: A Randomized Controlled Trial. *JMIR Serious Games*, *13*(1), e76435. DOI: 10.2196/76435 PMID: 40750096

Grynszpan, S., Weiss, J., Perez-Diaz, B., & Hadjikhani, N. (2014). Innovative technology-based interventions for autism spectrum disorders: A meta-analysis. *Autism*, *18*(4), 346–361. DOI: 10.1177/1362361313476767 PMID: 24092843

Guillén-Martínez, D., Alcázar-Espinoza, J. A., Rámirez-Sánchez, I., Samaniego-Cobo, T., & Villacís-Macias, C. (2025). Policies, Assistive Technologies, and Barriers in Inclusive Education: A Global Systematic Review (2019-2024). *Journal of Posthumanism*, *5*(2). Advance online publication. DOI: 10.63332/joph.v5i2.418

Hassan, A., Pinkwart, N., & Shafi, M. (2021). Serious games to improve social and emotional intelligence in children with autism. *Entertainment Computing*, *38*, 100417. Advance online publication. DOI: 10.1016/j.entcom.2021.100417

ISO-9241-210. (2019). ISO 9241-210: Ergonomics of human-system interaction -- Part 210: Human-centred design for interactive systems. In. Geneva, Switzerland: International Organization for Standardization.

Ito, H., Chang-Leung, C., & Poudyal, H. (2022). Inclusion of Students with Developmental Disabilities in Japan: Barriers and Promising Practices. *Asia Pacific Education Review*, *24*(3), 415–431. DOI: 10.1007/s12564-022-09763-8

Jagušt, T., & Botički, I. (2019). Mobile learning system for enabling collaborative and adaptive pedagogies with modular digital learning contents. *Journal of Computers in Education*, *6*(3), 335–362. DOI: 10.1007/s40692-019-00139-3

Jimenez-Honrado, J., Sebastián-Rivera, G., Gallud, J. A., & Penichet, V. M. R. (2024). Serious Games to Facilitate Social Integration for Children with Autism Spectrum Disorder *Proceedings of the XXIII International Conference on Human Computer Interaction*, Lleida, Spain. https://doi.org/DOI: 10.1145/3612783.3612793

Kasari, C., Freeman, S., & Paparella, A. (2006). Joint attention and symbolic play in young children with autism: A randomized controlled intervention study. *Journal of Child Psychology and Psychiatry, and Allied Disciplines*, *47*(6), 611–620. DOI: 10.1111/j.1469-7610.2005.01567.x PMID: 16712638

Koegel, R. L., Koegel, L. K., & Ashbaugh, J. K. (2012). Pivotal Response Treatment for autism spectrum disorders. *Journal of Autism and Developmental Disorders*, *42*(4), 581–593. DOI: 10.1007/s10803-011-1280-1

Lawson, W. (2020). Adaptive Morphing and Coping with Social Threat in Autism: An Autistic Perspective. *Journal of Intellectual Disabilities, 24*(3), 245–259. DOI: 10.1177/1744629520907987

Le Cunff, A.-L., Ross, F., Westwood, S. J., Koya, S., Caldwell, D. M., Russell, A. E., & Dommett, E. J. (2025). Key Research Questions to Support Neurodiversity in Higher Education: A Participatory Priority Setting Exercise. *Education Sciences, 15*(7), 839. DOI: 10.3390/educsci15070839

Lopez-Bouzas, N., & Del Moral-Perez, M. E. (2023). Gamified Environments and Serious Games for Students With Autistic Spectrum Disorder: Review of Research. *Review Journal of Autism and Developmental Disorders*, •••, 1–13. DOI: 10.1007/s40489-023-00381-7 PMID: 37363697

Meyer, A., Rose, D. H., & Gordon, D. (2014). *Universal Design for Learning: Theory and Practice*. CAST Professional Publishing.

Norman, D. A. (2013). *The Design of Everyday Things*. Basic Books.

Oliver, M. (1990). *The Politics of Disablement*. Macmillan Education UK. DOI: 10.1007/978-1-349-20895-1

Oliver, M. (2018). *Understanding disability: From theory to practice*. Bloomsbury publishing.

Ophoff, J., Johnson, G., & Renaud, K. (2021). Cognitive function vs. accessible authentication: insights from dyslexia research Proceedings of the 18th International Web for All Conference, Ljubljana, Slovenia. https://doi.org/DOI: 10.1145/3430263.3452427

Ortega-Arranz, A., Bote-Lorenzo, M. L., Asensio-Pérez, J. I., Martínez-Monés, A., & Gómez-Sánchez, E. (2019). To reward and beyond: Analyzing the effect of reward-based strategies in a MOOC. *Computers & Education, 146*, 103639. DOI: 10.1016/j.compedu.2019.103639

Ortega-Arranz, A., Muñoz-Cristóbal, J. A., Martínez-Monés, A., Bote-Lorenzo, M. L., & Asensio-Pérez, J. I. (2016). Lecture Notes in Computer Science: Vol. 9684. *A System for Gamifying Ubiquitous Learning Situations Supported by Multiple Technologies. Intelligent Tutoring Systems (ITS 2016).*

Parsons, S., & Cobb, S. (2011). State-of-the-art of virtual reality technologies for children on the autism spectrum. *European Journal of Special Needs Education, 26*(3), 355–366. DOI: 10.1080/08856257.2011.593831

Rezayi, S. (2023). Features and Effects of Computer-Based Games on Cognitive and Social Skills in Children with Autism Spectrum Disorder: A Systematic Review. *Child Neuropsychology, 29*(8), 1200–1223. DOI: 10.1080/09297049.2022.2164356

Rezayi, S., Shahmoradi, L., & Tehrani-Doost, M. (2025). Systematic Review and Thematic Analysis of Digital Games for Cognitive Enhancement in Children with Autism Spectrum Disorder: Toward a Conceptual Framework. *Cognitive Computation, 17*(1), 60. DOI: 10.1007/s12559-024-10395-w

Seale, J. (2014). *E-learning and Disability in Higher Education: Accessibility Research and Practice*. Routledge.

Serrano-Fernåndez, L., & Viguera-Monje, M. (2024). A Systematic Review of the Presence and Participation of Students with Intellectual Disabilities in Spanish Universities. *Journal of Intellectual Disabilities, 28*(1), 34–52. DOI: 10.1177/17446295241246035 PMID: 38574375

Shakespeare, T. (2018). *Disability: The Basics*. Routledge.

Singer, J. (1998). Odd People In: The Birth of Community Amongst People on the. In *Autistic Spectrum*. University of Technology Sydney.

Singer, J. (2016). *NeuroDiversity: The Birth of an Idea*. Judy Singer.

Sofian, N. M., Hashim, A. S., & Ahmad, W. F. W. (2018). A review on usability guidelines for designing mobile apps user interface for children with autism. *AIP Conference Proceedings, 2016*(1). Advance online publication. DOI: 10.1063/1.5055496

Stasolla, F., Curcio, E., Passaro, A., Di Gioia, M., Zullo, A., & Martini, E. (2025). Exploring the Combination of Serious Games, Social Interactions, and Virtual Reality in Adolescents with ASD: A Scoping Review. *Technologies, 13*(2), 76. DOI: 10.3390/technologies13020076

Sweller, J., Ayres, P., & Kalyuga, S. (2011). Cognitive Load Theory. *Educational Psychology Review, 23*(2), 123–152. DOI: 10.1007/s10648-010-9128-5

Vallefuoco, E., Bravaccio, C., Gison, G., Pecchia, L., & Pepino, A. (2022). Personalized Training via Serious Game to Improve Daily Living Skills in Pediatric Patients With Autism Spectrum Disorder. *IEEE Journal of Biomedical and Health Informatics, 26*(7), 3312–3322. DOI: 10.1109/JBHI.2022.3155367 PMID: 35230960

Whalen, C., Moss, N., & Ilan, L.. (2010). Efficacy of TeachTown: Basics computer-assisted intervention for the education of young children with autism. *Autism, 14*(3), 241–261. DOI: 10.1177/1362361310363282 PMID: 20484002

Zyda, M. (2005). From Visual Simulation to Virtual Reality to Games. *Computer*, *38*(9), 25–32. DOI: 10.1109/MC.2005.297

ENDNOTE

1 This mapping was developed in collaboration with professionals who provide support to children with Autism Spectrum Disorder (ASD).

Chapter 7
TEA-MARK: Gamified Virtual Reality Platform for Learning Shopping Skills in Children With ASD

Cristina Díaz Esquivel
https://orcid.org/0009-0003-6990-5326
Universidad Autónoma de Aguascalientes, Mexico

Luis Roberto Ramos Aguiar
https://orcid.org/0000-0002-1629-8310
Universidad Autónoma de Aguascalientes, Mexico

Perla Aguilar Navarrete
Universidad Autónoma de Nayarit, Mexico

ABSTRACT

Autism Spectrum Disorder (ASD) emerges in early childhood, affecting communication, social interaction, and adaptive behaviors required for daily independence. To address these challenges, TEA-MARK was developed as a gamified virtual reality environment that simulates supermarket shopping, including checking a list, identifying products, and completing payment. The system integrates missions, challenges, animations, visual cues, and immediate feedback to sustain attention, support comprehension, and offer a motivating game-like experience. These features are valuable for children with ASD, as they promote engagement, reduce cognitive overload with shorter visually supported instructions, and encourage generalization of skills to real contexts. The prototype was evaluated by ASD experts, whose feedback informed a second version with improved accessibility, clearer instructions, and more immersive exploration. Findings suggest that TEA-MARK is an effective, enjoyable tool bridging therapeutic strategies with playful, everyday experiences.

DOI: 10.4018/979-8-3373-6033-1.ch007

INTRODUCTION

Autism Spectrum Disorder (ASD) is a complex neurodevelopmental condition influenced by both biological factors—such as genetic predispositions—and environmental factors, including family and social contexts (Ballesteros, 2021; López Belmonte et al., 2024; Lorenzo Lledó Gonzalo et al., 2023). According to the World Health Organization (2023), approximately one in ten children presents some degree of ASD, although other studies have reported even higher prevalence rates. Core manifestations typically include difficulties in understanding and using verbal and nonverbal communication, challenges in recognizing and expressing emotions, and a strong tendency to maintain rigid routines or focus on highly specific interests. However, these characteristics vary significantly across individuals, both in presentation and intensity, which explains the use of the term "spectrum" to define the disorder (Celis Alcalá & Ochoa Madrigal, 2023).

These challenges often extend into everyday life activities, such as education, social interaction, and the acquisition of basic independent-living skills (Schilbach, L., 2022; Syriopoulou–Delli, C. K., & Sarri, K., 2022; Kalemkuş, F., 2025). Among them, shopping represents one of the most complex tasks for children with ASD, as it combines cognitive, social, and adaptive skills. Shopping requires planning, decision-making, money management, interaction with vendors, and navigating often unpredictable environments (Adjorlu et al., 2017). In real-world contexts, teaching these abilities can be problematic due to environmental distractions, the limited patience of others, and the stress children may experience in crowded or unfamiliar spaces (Sung, 2024). Consequently, parents, educators, and therapists face significant barriers in preparing children with ASD to carry out shopping-related activities independently and confidently.

In recent years, technological innovations such as Virtual Reality (VR) and gamification have emerged as promising tools to overcome these barriers. VR enables the creation of immersive and interactive environments where children can practice real-life tasks within a safe, controlled, and adaptable setting. Prior studies have demonstrated that VR can improve learning, motivation, and the acquisition of social and daily living skills in children with ASD by providing repetitive, personalized, and engaging experiences without the risks associated with real-world practice (Mesa-Gresa et al., 2018; Parsons & Cobb, 2011). Similarly, gamification—defined as the use of game elements in non-gaming contexts—has shown potential to increase motivation and participation in therapeutic and educational interventions for children with autism (Bai et al., 2021).

Responding to this need, this study presents TEA-MARK, a virtual environment developed under the hypothesis that a specialized software product can be a viable and effective tool to help children with autism. The design was conceived through an iterative process, based on the premise that expert observations would be essential both to validate this viability and to improve the product during its development phases.

Specifically, TEA-MARK is designed to simulate a complete shopping experience, providing a safe and flexible context in which children can learn and practice shopping skills that would otherwise be difficult to teach in real-life scenarios. The environment allows for gradual exposure to tasks such as product identification, money handling, making payments, and social interaction, while ensuring that therapists and educators can adapt to the difficulty and pace to each child's needs. This flexibility is essential given the heterogeneity of ASD symptoms and learning profiles.

The development of TEA-MARK was guided by the MEEXUU methodology (MEthodology, EXtended Reality, Universal Design for Learning, and User-Centered Design). This framework integrates two complementary approaches: User-Centered Design (UCD), which ensures that the needs, preferences, and limitations of end-users are central to the design process; and Universal Design for Learning (UDL), which promotes accessibility and inclusivity by offering multiple means of engagement, representation, and expression. Together, these principles provide a solid foundation for creating educational tools that are both effective and adaptable to diverse learners, particularly those with ASD.

To validate the environment, TEA-MARK was evaluated by specialized therapists from the CUIN Aguascalientes association, who provided expert feedback on its usability, relevance, and potential benefits for children with ASD. Their input allowed us to refine the system and ensure that it aligns with real-world therapeutic needs.

This article is organized as follows: the next section presents the Background, summarizing relevant literature on ASD, VR-based interventions, and gamification in autism education. Subsequently, the software development methodology is described in detail, followed by the case studies conducted with TEA-MARK. The expert evaluation is then reported, highlighting strengths and areas for improvement. Finally, the conclusions discuss the contributions of this research and its implications for future work in the field of technology-assisted learning for ASD.

BACKGROUND

In this section, we provide an overview of the key concepts and background information that form the foundation of this research. Specifically, we address ASD, the principles of gamification, and the role of virtual reality (VR) in educational and therapeutic contexts. Understanding these elements is essential, as they not only define the scope of the study but also highlight the relevance of combining technology-driven approaches with evidence-based strategies. By exploring these areas, the section seeks to establish a comprehensive framework that supports the rationale for integrating gamification and virtual reality into interventions aimed at fostering learning and skill development in individuals with autism.

Autism

Autism, also known as ASD, is a neurodevelopmental condition influenced by multiple biological and environmental factors, including genetics and early developmental experiences (Ballesteros, 2021). It is described as a "spectrum" because its symptoms and severity vary widely across individuals (Celis Alcalá & Ochoa Madrigal, 2023).

ASD is characterized by difficulties in social communication and interaction, restricted or repetitive behaviors, sensory sensitivities, and impairments in executive functions, such as planning, organizing, and adapting to novel situations (López Belmonte et al., 2024). According to the American Psychiatric Association (APA), the Diagnostic and Statistical Manual of Mental Disorders, Fifth Edition (DSM-5-TR) classifies autism into three levels of severity (see Table 1).

Table 1. Levels of ASD. Own elaboration based on table from the DSM-5-TR Diagnostic and Statistical Manual of Mental Disorders (American Psychiatric Association, 2022).

Severity	Social Communication	Behavior	Examples
Level 3. Requiring very substantial support	Severe difficulties in verbal and nonverbal communication. Major impairments in daily functioning. Very limited initiation of social interactions.	Very inflexible behavior. Extreme difficulty handling changes. Repetitive or restricted behaviors seriously affect daily functioning in all areas. Shows intense distress or difficulty when needing to shift focus or actions.	● Speaks very little or has mostly unintelligible speech. ● Rarely starts interactions. ● When they do, it's unusual way and only to meet their basic needs. ● Only responds to very direct social approaches.
Level 2. Requiring substantial support	Clear deficits in both verbal and nonverbal communication. Social difficulties are evident even with support. Limited initiation of social interactions. Unusual or reduced responses to other's social approaches.	Noticeable inflexible behavior and has trouble handling changes. Restricted or repetitive behaviors are obvious even to someone a casual observer. These behaviors interfere with functioning in different situations. Shows distress or difficulty when needing to shift focus or actions.	● Speaks using simple sentences. ● Interacts mainly around specific, narrow interests. ● It has noticeably odd nonverbal communication (e.g., eye contact or facial expressions).
Level 1. Requiring support	Without support, social communication deficits are noticeable and cause problems. Struggles to start social interactions. Unusual or unsuccessful responses to other's social attempts. May seem less interested in social interaction.	Inflexible behavior affects functioning in at least one area. It has trouble switching between activities. Struggles with organization and planning, which affects their independence.	● Speaks in full sentences and can communicate, but conversations don't flow naturally. ● Try to make friends, but the attempts are odd and usually don't work.

The understanding, definition, and classification of autism have evolved continuously over time. Differences in emphasis on certain traits by various researchers have led to a lack of uniformity, which can sometimes cause confusion in diagnosis and intervention approaches (García-Franco et al., 2019). The World Health Organization estimates that approximately 1 in 127 people may present with autism, although other studies suggest even higher prevalence rates (World Health Organization [WHO], 2023).

ASD originates from neurological development factors and involves the interplay of biological (e.g., genetic predispositions) and environmental (e.g., upbringing) influences (Celis Alcalá & Ochoa Madrigal, 2023; López Belmonte et al., 2024; Lledó Gonzalo et al., 2023). The condition typically manifests in early childhood and primarily affects communication and social interaction (Lledó Gonzalo et al.,

2023). Individuals with ASD often display restricted, repetitive, and inflexible patterns of behavior (Gil, 2024; Kamp-Becker, 2024), including:

- Challenges in understanding or using language and expressing emotions, along with difficulties interpreting others' facial expressions, gestures, or tone of voice.
- Strong adherence to routines or highly specific interests, difficulty adapting to changes, and engagement in repetitive movements, such as hand-flapping or rocking.

DSM-5 outlines three levels of autism severity (see Table 1), which guide diagnosis and intervention planning. According to García-Franco (García-Franco et al., 2019), diagnosing ASD requires evaluating the individual across different contexts and considering their level of adaptation. The following criteria must be met:

1. Deficits in communication and social interaction.
2. Restrictive and repetitive patterns of behavior, interests, or activities, with at least two of the following:
   a. Repetitive speech or phrases, repetitive movements, or constant manipulation of objects.
   b. Rigid adherence to daily routines, ritualized behaviors, and significant difficulty adapting to unexpected changes.
   c. Intense focus on specific topics or activities.
   d. Hyper- or hyposensitivity to stimuli such as lights and sounds, or reduced attention to sensory details in the environment.
3. Symptoms present from early childhood, though they may not fully manifest until social demands exceed the individual's capacities.
4. The combination of symptoms significantly limits daily functioning.

Additionally, DSM-5 includes guidelines for differential diagnosis to distinguish ASD from other disorders with overlapping symptoms, such as:

- Social Communication Disorder
- Attention-Deficit/Hyperactivity Disorder (ADHD)
- Specific Learning Disorder
- Obsessive-Compulsive Disorder (OCD)
- Schizophrenia

Gamification

Gamification is defined as the integration of game mechanics and elements into non-recreational contexts with the aim of motivating users, facilitating learning, and achieving specific objectives (R.-Asale & Rae, n.d.-a). At its core, gamification leverages motivation, which can be conceptualized as the internal or external drive that directs an individual's actions, experiences, or decisions (González Castro et al., 2023). Motivation is commonly classified into two forms: intrinsic motivation, derived from an individual's inherent interest and enjoyment in performing an activity without external rewards, and extrinsic motivation, which emerges from external incentives that make the activity meaningful, appealing, or rewarding (Gaviria, 2021; Mora Velasco et al., 2024).

Gamification has the capacity to activate and sustain both types of motivation. By incorporating challenges, feedback, and rewards, it can reinforce extrinsic motivation through tangible incentives, recognition, or social validation. Simultaneously, it fosters intrinsic motivation by promoting autonomy, offering meaningful choices, facilitating progressive mastery, and creating engaging experiences. Thus, gamification is not merely a system of rewards but a strategic approach to sustaining motivation and guiding user engagement toward goal-directed behavior.

A central feature of gamification lies in its mechanics, which Gaviria (2021) categorizes into eight fundamental types. Each mechanic contributes to motivation and engagement in distinct ways:

- Point systems: Symbolic values that reinforce progress and continuity by rewarding task completion, adjusted according to difficulty and type of activity.
    Leaderboards: Comparative rankings that stimulate persistence and performance through social competition and recognition.
- Levels and progress bars: Visible indicators of advancement that provide a sense of growth and achievement, often tied to accumulated points or demonstrated skills.
- Medals or badges: Tangible or symbolic recognitions for specific accomplishments that reinforce commitment and satisfaction.
- Roles or ranks: Assigned attributes or statuses that promote hierarchy, collaboration, and social interaction within a community.
- Avatars: Personalized representations that enhance immersion, self-expression, and identification within the system.
- Rewards: Physical or virtual objects (e.g., trophies) that validate effort and celebrate achievements.

- Monetization systems: Internal economies that can develop responsibility and strategic decision-making, though they require careful design to avoid misuse.

These mechanics, when balanced and visually accessible, create engaging environments that sustain user participation and learning. Beyond its general applications, gamification has shown particular promise in supporting children with autism by integrating motivational elements with pedagogical objectives. Research highlights its effectiveness in diverse contexts: mobile applications designed to foster learning and communication (Mahmoudi et al., 2024), mixed reality environments for developing social skills (Wongwan, 2025), and interactive platforms for teaching and recognizing emotions (Ramos-Aguiar & Álvarez-Rodríguez, 2021). Similarly, Morais et al. (2023) emphasize that gamification promotes intrinsic motivation, supports sustained attention, and facilitates the generalization of skills in this population.

Taken together, this body of evidence underscores that gamification should not be regarded merely as a complementary tool. Rather, it represents a key mechanism for educational inclusion and the empowerment of autonomy among children with autism, highlighting its potential as both a pedagogical and social innovation.

Virtual reality

Virtual Reality is defined as "the representation of scenes or images of objects created by a computer system that gives the sensation of reality" (Asale & RAE, s. f.). It is an environment that simulates 3D objects and generates the perception of being inside that virtual world through sensory information. The main goal is to deceive the senses (Escartín, 2023). According to Luque Odoñez, "Virtual reality doesn't modify reality, it creates a new complete reality." (Luque Ordóñez, 2020).

To achieve user immersion in the virtual environment, there are some fundamental aspects that must be considered (Ferreira, Xavier, & Ancioto, 2021):

- Realism. Creating an environment that looks and feels as close to reality as possible.
- Involvement. User's emotional and cognitive level of commitment to the environment.
- Interactivity. The level of control and influence that users can exert over the environment.

Virtual Reality environments can be classified as:

- Immersive: the user is immersed completely in the environment using special hardware (e.g., a VR headset and controls) generates the sensation of being inside the virtual world (Escartín, 2023; Luque Ordóñez, 2020).
- Non-Immersive: the user interacts with the objects of the environment using the computer, with keyboard and mouse. They can manipulate objects and explore the world, but without full sensory immersion (Escartín, 2023; Luque Ordóñez, 2020).

There are two types of VR:

- Passive RV: The user observes the virtual world from a computer screen.
- Active RV: The user can interact with the world using VR Headset and controllers: moving around, picking up objects, and modifying the environment (Luque Ordóñez, 2020).

Virtual reality generates high levels of motivation and commitment in users engaged in activities inside the virtual environment (Mendoza, Lewis, Plante, & Brassard, 2023). It is customizable, enabling each user to explore and progress at their own pace. The combination of interaction, immersion, interest, concentration and persistence contributes to improving the user experience and increasing motivation. Furthermore, Virtual Reality technology builds trust and a sense of self-efficacy by providing safe and controlled experiential learning (Mendoza et al., 2023).

The use of Virtual Reality in therapy offers multiple benefits (Psicosomática et al., 2007):

- Complete control over events: The environment can be programmed to prevent unforeseen events, ensuring user safety.
- Protected environment: Users can practice skills and explore situations without real consequences.
- Repetition of events: In the environment enables users to repeat exercises as needed and gradually increase the difficulty, even with important scenes that are difficult to find in real life.
- Improve learning and self-efficacy: It is easier for the user to acquire skills and build trust in their own skills.
- Behavior simulation: Users can practice challenging behaviors that are difficult to replicate and practice in real life situations and overcome specific fears.
- Therapeutic technique optimization: Complete clinical psychology and improvement of it.

- Reduction in treatment dropout: Immersive experiences make interventions more attractive and flexible, increasing treatment adherence.

Despite its advantages, Virtual Reality has limitations and risks (Mendoza et al., 2023):

- Shortage of specialized applications and resources.
- High complexity and cost design.
- Low social acceptance.
- Possible physical discomfort, such as dizziness or eye strain.
- Risk of overstimulation or overwhelming if the application is poorly designed.

Similar projects

In recent years, the use of Virtual Reality (VR) has gained increasing attention as an innovative tool to support the development of functional, cognitive, and social skills in individuals with ASD. A growing body of research has explored how immersive and semi-immersive environments, often combined with gamification strategies and visual or auditory supports, can create engaging contexts that foster autonomy, reduce anxiety, and enhance the transfer of learning to real-world situations.

These studies have addressed diverse domains, including money management, shopping skills, auditory desensitization, and social interaction, employing a variety of technological approaches such as head-mounted displays, Leap Motion sensors, and eye-tracking systems. The following section provides an overview of representative projects in this field, outlining their objectives, design elements, outcomes, and limitations. This review not only highlights the progress made in VR-based interventions for individuals with ASD but also establishes the basis for identifying the unique contributions and advancements of TEA-MARK within this landscape.

The study "Shopping Training to Autistic Children and Adolescents for Enhancing Daily Life Shopping Skills using Virtual Reality and Leap Motion" (El-Gohary et al., 2022) aimed to evaluate the effectiveness of a game designed to enable children and adolescents with autism to practice daily living skills, specifically product purchasing, within the context of a hospital cafeteria. The proposal combined virtual reality, gamification, and elements of functional education to promote independence and social skills. Participants could purchase items, make payments, and manage tasks associated with the shopping process.

To enhance immersion, the environment included realistic characters, objects, and sounds, while interaction was facilitated through the Leap Motion sensor and Oculus Rift headset, enabling greater accuracy and comfort. The design incorporated a scoring system, visual and auditory feedback, avatars, and progressively challenging levels. Results demonstrated significant improvements in product selection, payment accuracy, and avatar interaction, as well as reductions in task completion time. Moreover, increases in confidence, autonomy, and reductions in anxiety were reported by both participants and their parents. The key elements of the project were progressive levels and immediate feedback from the environment.

The article "Promoting Daily Independence Skill for Individuals with Autism through Progressive Gamified VR Application" (Hening Darmasti et al. 2023) developed a virtual environment to support young individuals with autism in practicing product purchasing, with the goal of fostering autonomy and self-confidence. The application began in a home setting, where users were introduced to the task dynamics, and subsequently transitioned them to a supermarket, where they were required to collect items from a predefined shopping list. Difficulty increased progressively at each level, both in terms of the number of products and the presence of distractions and background noise. Finally, participants had to place the items at the checkout and select the correct amount of money. Core design features included progressive levels as well as visual and auditory supports. Initial results were positive, although some participants experienced difficulties in becoming familiar with the controls, leading to a recommendation for the inclusion of a "practice room" prior to gameplay.

The study "Virtual Reality (VR) for Children Diagnosed With ASD: Interventions to Train Social and Everyday Living Skills" (Adjorlu & Serafin, 2018) explored VR-based interventions targeting children and adolescents with autism, aiming to develop both social and daily living skills. The virtual environment included settings such as a store, a school, and a park, where users were required to request permission, interact with adults, make purchases, and perform payments independently. The intervention emphasized scenario repetition to reinforce the child's sense of security. Design elements included points, rewards, progressive levels, challenges, and engaging visual features (characters, animations, and sound effects). Results indicated that although users initially resisted entering real stores, after training in the virtual environment they demonstrated increased confidence and willingness to engage in real-life shopping contexts.

The study "A Computer-Enhanced Money Teaching Application for Individuals with Autism Spectrum Disorders" (Büyük et al., 2019) focused on teaching children to understand the value and use of money. The application, available on tablets and smartphones, enabled users to identify coins and banknotes through size differences and value-associated sounds. Participants were then required to pay for items using the correct amount of money, with varied combinations designed to assess comprehension. The application integrated sounds, images, life-sized objects, motivational phrases, rest screens, a reward system, and progressive levels. Results were positive: the visually engaging interface attracted participants' interest, and 86% successfully learned the value of money.

In "The Use of Virtual Reality and Eye-Tracking to Inform a Grocery Store Intervention" (Alarifi, 2022), VR was combined with eye-tracking technology to train and assess shopping skills, as well as to analyze which elements most captured the attention of children with autism. During the tasks, researchers recorded the time, sequence, and type of stimuli observed by users. The application included visual and auditory elements and provided immediate feedback. Findings revealed that participants often fixated on irrelevant details or attention-grabbing labels, which hindered efficient product identification. However, training improved visual attention, discrimination, and memory, ultimately enhancing participants' ability to locate objects more efficiently.

The study "Head-Mounted Display-Based Virtual Reality as a Tool to Teach Money Skills to Adolescents Diagnosed with Autism Spectrum Disorder" (Adjorlu & Serafin, 2019) proposed a VR application to teach adolescents basic money management skills, such as price identification, payment, and autonomous shopping. The simulated environment represented a bazaar and incorporated visual and auditory stimuli, positive feedback (e.g., a dancing vendor after purchase), progressive levels, and auditory assistance when difficulties arose. Results showed significant progress among most participants, who also expressed interest in the application. Nevertheless, some reported boredom due to task repetition and challenges in transferring skills to real-life situations, highlighting the need for additional rewards, challenges, and varied scenarios.

The article "SoundFields: A Virtual Reality Game Designed to Address Auditory Hypersensitivity in Individuals with Autism Spectrum Disorder" (Johnston et al., 2020) introduced a VR environment designed to address auditory hypersensitivity in children and adolescents with autism. The game involved assisting a character in locating others, emitting unpleasant sounds, using magical abilities to identify them. Key design features included rewards, missions, and increasing auditory difficulty. Results showed significant progress in tolerance to stressful sounds, as well as reductions in fear and anxiety, confirming the usefulness of gamification for such interventions.

The article "Virtual Reality for Autism: Unlocking Learning and Growth" (Failla et al. 2024) described how VR can be utilized in environments designed for children with autism to practice both social and everyday living skills. Scenarios included product purchasing and adherence to social norms, while design incorporated gamification, feedback, adaptability, and interaction. Results indicated that these environments enhanced motivation, reduced anxiety and stress, and generated positive perceptions among parents, who reported increased relaxation in children during real-world activities.

In the study "Attentional Cueing and Executive Deficits Revealed by a Virtual Supermarket Task Coupled with Eye-Tracking in Autism Spectrum Disorder"

(Mouga et al., 2021), a non-immersive simulator called EcoSupermarketX was used to analyze executive functions, particularly attention, in children and adolescents with autism. The design included familiarization phases using a joystick, followed by shopping tasks that required efficient completion. Features included images, animations, adjustable difficulty, and eye-tracking. Results suggested that while participants observed social cues, they tended not to use them effectively, and that attention decreased as cognitive load increased.

Finally, the project "INMER-II: Immersive Virtual Reality System for Individuals with Autism" (Orts, 2019) presented a non-immersive virtual supermarket as an intervention for developing social and shopping skills. Users were required to select products from a list, locate them, wait for assistance, make payments, and exit the store, supported by pictograms, photographs, text, and videos. The environment aimed to reinforce planning, anticipation, and action sequencing required to complete the task.

Taken together, these studies indicate that gamification serves as a key resource for motivating users within virtual environments, while also highlighting critical considerations such as the potential for distraction by irrelevant stimuli or visually salient labels, as revealed in eye-tracking research, and the need to balance visual and auditory inputs. The implementation of introductory scenes or practice levels is particularly important, as they allow participants to become familiar with controls and the virtual environment before engaging in more complex tasks.

These project examples demonstrate how the integration of VR and gamification constitutes a complementary approach, effectively supporting the teaching of functional, cognitive, and social skills in individuals with ASD. VR provides safe, immersive, and controlled environments where individuals can practice real-life situations without risk, while gamification applies motivating dynamics that increase engagement, reduce anxiety, and reinforce learning. The combination of these approaches in the presented projects has shown improvements in the acquisition of specific skills, such as money management or shopping, ultimately promoting autonomy and confidence in individuals with ASD. Together, these findings underscore that the synergy between VR and gamification represents a powerful strategy for enhancing learning and skill development in therapeutic and educational contexts.

Contribution comparison with TEA-MARK

To better understand the contribution of TEA-MARK, it is essential to compare this proposal with other research initiatives that have also explored the use of Virtual Reality (VR) as a tool for developing skills in individuals with Autism ASD. Previous studies have investigated a variety of contexts, ranging from social interactions and auditory desensitization to money management and daily living skills, each incorporating different design elements such as gamified tasks, visual and auditory feedback, immersive or semi-immersive environments, and progressive levels of difficulty.

The comparative analysis presented in Table 2 summarizes the main objectives, design features, outcomes, and limitations of these projects, highlighting both their potential and their shortcomings. Importantly, this comparison underscores the distinctive advantage of TEA-MARK: unlike more generalist or narrowly focused interventions, TEA-MARK is specifically designed to teach shopping skills in a structured, immersive, and accessible virtual supermarket. Moreover, it integrates dynamic design strategies such as gamification, immediate feedback, and gradual familiarization levels, which respond to the unique learning needs of children with ASD by reducing anxiety, supporting comprehension, and sustaining motivation throughout the experience.

Table 2. Comparison between TEA-MARK and the different similar projects shown in this study.

Project	Objective	Design Elements	Main Results	Limitations
Shopping Training to Autistic Children and Adolescents for Enhancing Daily Life Shopping Skills using Virtual Reality and Leap Motion	Assess the effectiveness of the game for shopping tasks in a hospital cafeteria.	Leap Motion, Oculus Rift, points, avatars, visual and auditory feedback, progressive levels.	Improved product selection, reduced decision-making time, increased confidence and autonomy.	Scene restricted to cafeteria; limited variety of contexts.
Promoting Daily Independence Skills for Individuals with Autism through a Progressive Gamified VR Application	Foster autonomy and build trust in young people.	Domestic setting and supermarket, initial instructions, progressive levels with visual and auditory feedback.	Increased autonomy; positive initial outcomes.	Difficulties with controls; need for a practice environment.
Virtual Reality (VR) for Children Diagnosed with ASD	Train social and daily living skills across multiple scenarios.	Store, school, park; points, rewards, challenges, scenario repetition.	Increased confidence and willingness to engage in real settings.	Not focused exclusively on shopping skills; broad objectives.
A Computer-Enhanced Money Teaching Application	Teach the value and use of money.	Tablet/mobile; sounds, images, rewards, progressive levels.	86% learned the value of money; high motivation.	2D non-immersive interface; lack of real-world simulation.
The Use of Virtual Reality and Eye-Tracking to Inform a Grocery Store Intervention	Analyze visual attention during shopping tasks using VR and eye-tracking.	Visual and auditory stimuli, immediate feedback.	Enhanced discrimination and visual memory.	Frequent distractions from irrelevant stimuli.

continued on following page

Table 2. Continued

Project	Objective	Design Elements	Main Results	Limitations
Head-Mounted Display-Based VR as a Tool to Teach Money Skills	Teach basic money management skills in a virtual bazaar.	Visual and auditory elements, positive feedback, auditory assistance.	Improved monetary skills; high motivation.	Excessive repetition led to boredom; limited transfer to real-life contexts.
SoundFields	Reduce auditory hypersensitivity in autism.	Rewards, missions, auditory progression.	Reduced fear and anxiety toward sounds.	Focus limited to auditory aspects.
Virtual Reality for Autism: Unlocking Learning and Growth	Practice social and daily life skills in adaptive environments.	Gamification, feedback, adaptability, interaction.	Increased motivation, reduced anxiety and stress.	Generalist design; limited emphasis on shopping.
Attentional Cueing and Executive Deficits in VR Supermarket	Analyze executive functions in virtual shopping tasks.	Non-immersive simulator, joystick, animations, adjustable difficulty.	Partial improvement in attention; reduced reliance on social cues.	Non-immersive; higher cognitive load decreased attention.
INMER-II	Develop social and shopping skills in a virtual supermarket.	Pictograms, photos, text, and videos.	Promoted planning and action sequencing.	Non-immersive system; limited interaction.

From this comparison, it becomes evident that while previous projects have yielded positive results in enhancing cognitive, social, and functional abilities among children with ASD, many have faced limitations related to low levels of immersion, restricted or overly specific contexts, or broad and unfocused goals that hinder the transfer of skills to real-life situations. TEA-MARK addresses these limitations by maintaining a clear and functional objective: teaching shopping skills within a virtual environment that is immersive, accessible, and progressively structured.

Its design incorporates a familiarization level that eases adaptation, differentiated colors to support visual discrimination, attractive animations to sustain attention, and immediate feedback to reinforce learning outcomes. Additionally, the integration of gamification principles—such as rewards, motivating challenges, and structured progression—helps sustain engagement, reduce frustration, and foster intrinsic motivation. In doing so, TEA-MARK not only builds on the strengths of prior research but also introduces meaningful improvements that enhance its therapeutic value, educational applicability, and potential for real-world transfer. Consequently, it emerges as an innovative and inclusive proposal that bridges the gap between virtual training and daily life functionality, positioning itself as a valuable tool for supporting autonomy and skill development in children with ASD.

In this way, TEA-MARK positions itself as an innovative proposal that not only builds on the strengths of previous research but also introduces significant improvements that enhance its applicability and therapeutic value in the context of ASD.

METHODOLOGY

This project was developed using the MEEXUU methodology (Ramos Aguiar et al., 2023), selected as the most appropriate for the purpose of the study. MEEXUU is specially designed for the creation of Extended Reality software focused on people with disabilities and is distinguished by integrating the principles of UCD and UDL.

While other software development methodologies exist, few are specifically oriented to the needs of accessibility and inclusion in Extended Reality contexts. MEEXUU methodology is structured in four main phases: analysis, pre-production, production and post-production. Each of these stages contemplates a set of activities and tools that guide the development of the interactive virtual environment.

Analysis

During the analysis stage, the general purpose of the project, the specific objectives, and the functional requirements were defined to establish a solid foundation for development. As a result, the design and implementation of an interactive virtual environment was proposed, simulating shopping situations in a store with the aim of enabling children with ASD to acquire social skills and strengthen their autonomy within a safe and controlled context.

A general use case diagram was created (see Figure 1), identifying the actors and their interactions. The overall process includes reviewing the shopping list, selecting products, and completing the payment.

Figure 1. Use case diagram. Author's own elaboration.

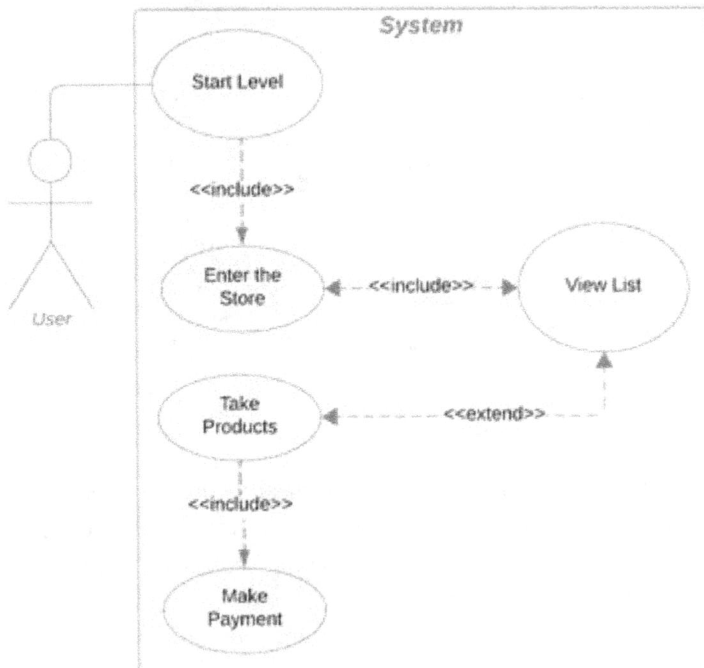

Based on the principles of Universal Design for Learning, the first graphic sketches were developed, considering different forms of presentation adapted to the users' characteristics. From these results, user-centered design strategies were derived to guide the creation of graphical interfaces. Additionally, a general flowchart diagram was produced for each level of the application (see Figure 2).

Figure 2. Flowchart diagram. Author's own elaboration.

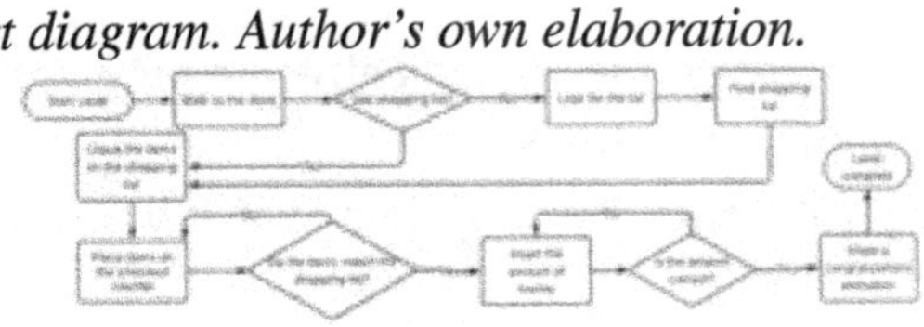

Both static and dynamic interfaces were designed, together with the gamification structure of the project (see Figure 3).

Figure 3. Gamification structure. Author's own elaboration.

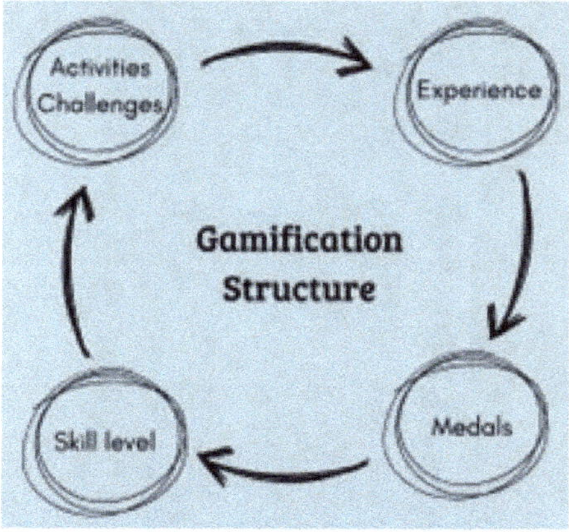

In general, upon completing a challenge or mission, users earn experience points. Experience points unlock achievements, which are reflected through badges, and also determine classification levels (see following section). For the reward system, the PBL (Points, Badges, Leaderboards) model was adapted as follows:

- **Points (Experience):** allow users to monitor their progress.
- **Badges:** provide real-time feedback and serve to motivate and encourage the user.
- **Leaderboards:** simplified to three levels of classification—Beginner, Intermediate, and Expert—progressing through experience accumulation.

To reinforce this structure, gamification elements such as missions, scores, and rewards were incorporated to enhance motivation and foster meaningful learning. Finally, three specific objectives were established:

1. To design a virtual scenario that realistically and progressively represents activities related to product purchasing.
2. To implement a positive feedback system that reinforces desired behaviors through rewards.
3. To evaluate the effectiveness of the environment through user testing and feedback.

Pre-production

The solution was designed based on the requirements defined in the analysis stage. Therefore, class diagrams, flow diagrams, as well as static and dynamic designs of the different interfaces of the system were elaborated. Furthermore, a gamification structure was established to be implemented, with the aim of promoting user motivation and engagement in the virtual environment.

Gamification structure contemplated the following elements: challenges, activities, missions, experience accumulation, medals and a ranking system by levels. The PBL (Points, Badges, and Leaderboards) model was also integrated, which is widely used in recreational and educational environments for its effectiveness in promoting active participation.

Production

Once the solution design was defined, the production stage began using the Unity3D development engine. Unity enables the creation of environments compatible with Extended Reality (XR) technologies, particularly Virtual Reality, and offers full functionality with devices such as Meta Quest 3, which was used in this project. In addition, its flexibility allows the environment to be adapted to different contexts and user profiles.

To ensure proper functionality of the virtual shopping environment, different interaction components were programmed, each one fulfilling a specific role within the system:

- **Products**

Each product (item) in the store was programmed with two essential properties: a name (*itemName*) and a price (*itemPrice*). These attributes allow the system to uniquely identify every product and maintain accurate control during the shopping process.

Figure 4. Item properties.

- **Shopping List**

The shopping list was designed to visually indicate to the user which products must be purchased. These items are predefined and configured within the Unity inspector, guiding the user's actions throughout the task.

Figure 5. Shopping list.

- **Checkout Counter**

At the checkout, five slots were programmed to allow the user to place selected products. The system generates a temporary list that stores the properties of the chosen products, which are then added to the "shopping cart." Each slot is checked individually to verify whether it contains a product, and if so, the product's information is saved for later validation.

Figure 6. Checkout counter.

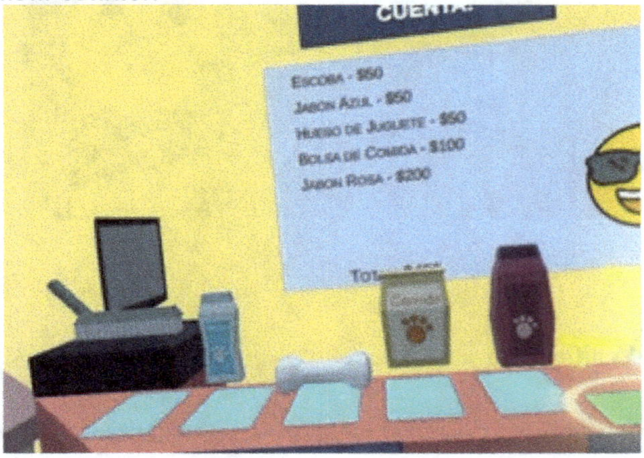

- **Product Verification**

Once the user has selected the products, the system validates whether the chosen items correspond to those on the shopping list. The process involves first checking that both lists contain the same number of products. If correct, the lists are sorted alphabetically and then compared item by item to confirm that all products match.

Figure 7. Product verification.

- **Payment Verification**

The payment system was programmed to verify whether the amount of money entered by the user is correct. At the cash register, bills and coins can be placed into a designated slot, where their values are automatically extracted and summed. The total amount is then compared to the required payment. If the values match, the system confirms that the payment is correct and allows the user to continue; otherwise, an error message is displayed indicating that the amount is incorrect.

Figure 8. Payment verification.

Post-production

In the post-production stage, product evaluations were carried out by specialists in working with children with ASD. These experts provided detailed feedback on the positive aspects and limitations of the application, as well as concrete recommendations for its future improvement and optimization.

TEA-MARK ITERATIVE DEVELOPMENT PROCESS

A virtual reality application was developed, this application consists of a virtual store where the child is subjected to fulfill the task of making a shopping list, this includes from the visualization of the products, choosing each of the products through the different aisles of the supermarket and the experience of placing them at the cash register and paying with money that represents the real units used in Mexico.

Version 1.0

The first version of TEA-MARK was developed from the initial iteration using the MEEXUU methodology. This version met functional and non-functional requirements initially established. However, during the evaluation process several areas of improvement were identified, which were addressed and refined in the development of version 2.0. Some emojis and icons were obtained from the Flaticon website. Authors include Freepik, Rohim, Bakuh Huda, Md Tanvirul Haque and Moqaccino Resources.

The models were created by us and obtained from Kenney website, Polly.Pizza website and Unity Assets website. In this version, the interfaces already incorporated the core functionalities of TEA-MARK; however, according to specialists, the design was not sufficiently engaging for children with ASD. The start menu was placed in a separate virtual environment, which then guided the user toward the store where the activities began (See Figure 9).

Figure 9. Initial interfaces of TEA-MARK, version 1.

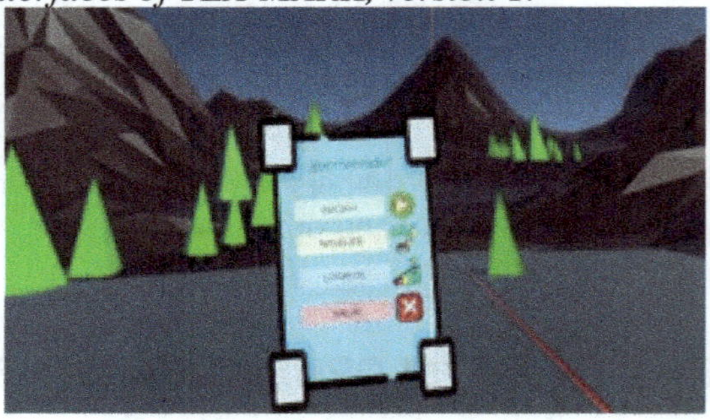

Once inside the store, users could visualize shelves displaying various products available for selection and purchase (See Figure 10).

Figure 10. Product shelves within TEA-MARK, version 1.

The main activity consisted of a shopping list with five products distributed across the different shelves. The child was required to navigate through the store and collect the specified items. At the checkout counter, five modules were available where the objects were placed and automatically added to the bill.

Figure 11. Shopping list and checkout counter in TEA-MARK, version 1.

Each selected item had to be placed on a bar scanner that registered it. A display showed the product's description, its individual price, and the cumulative total.

Figure 12. Checkout screen displaying the products, their cost, and the items placed on the counter in TEA-MARK, version 1.

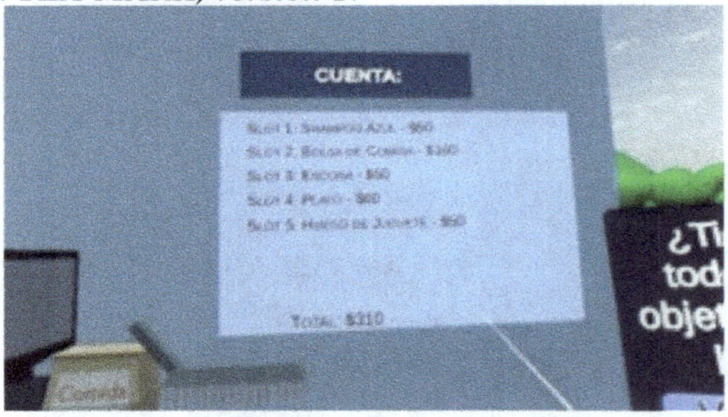

A verification step followed, ensuring that the items collected matched those on the initial shopping list. If discrepancies were detected, a warning message notified the user that the selected products were incorrect and prompted them to return to the store to retrieve the missing items. Once the list was completed correctly, a payment option became available, illustrating a possible way to proceed. For example: "Insert one 100 bill, two 200 bills, and one 10 bill to pay your total."

Figure 13. Warning message for incorrect items and payment station, where users could select the amount to pay using virtual bills in TEA-MARK, version 1.

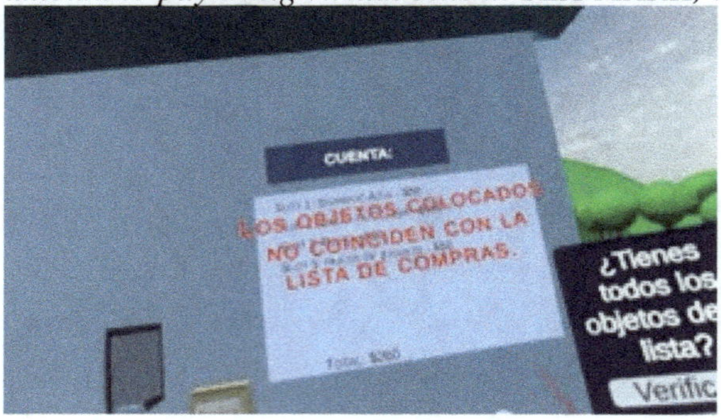

After payment was made, the screen displayed the total bill, the amount entered, and, if necessary, the remaining balance. Upon successfully completing the payment, the shopping task concluded with a congratulatory message reinforcing the achievement of purchasing the products.

Figure 14. Total payment message, amount entered, total to pay and successful payment in TEA-MARK, version 1.

Version 2.0

Version two of the application addresses the areas of improvement identified in the first iteration. These observations were provided by specialists in working with children with ASD, who evaluated the application and provided detailed feedback. The experts pointed out aspects with which they agreed, suggested specific improvements, and offered key recommendations to optimize the accessibility and usability of the product for this population. For this second version, MEEXUU methodology was still used. However, unlike version 1, the work focused mainly on the design stage and updating requirements. These requirements were established by the panel of experts. The changes implemented in the interfaces based on their feedback are detailed below.

Additional animations were incorporated with the purpose of capturing and sustaining children's attention. Emojis with varied expressions were also included to accompany the instructions. The animations used were sourced from Lana Studio (2022), Hyper Casual FX. These visual elements are particularly beneficial for children with autism, as dynamic and expressive stimuli facilitate emotional association and promote greater motivation during interaction.

Figure 15. New exploratory activity within TEA-MARK, version 2.

Figure 16. Enhanced checkout screen and billing system in TEA-MARK, version 2.

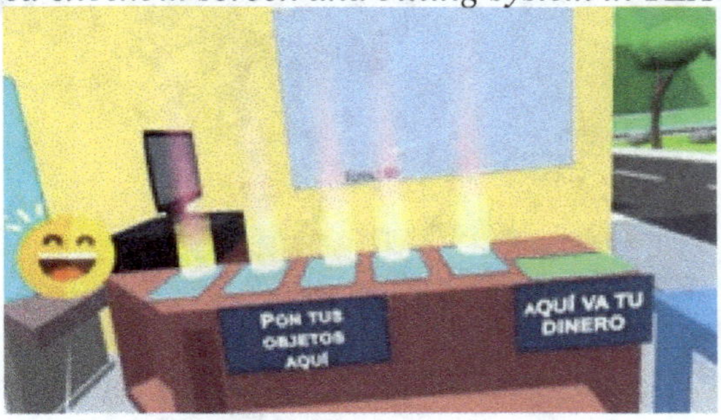

A new Level 0 was implemented, designed to allow children to freely explore the store. In this level, shelves with different colors are presented, and users can familiarize themselves with the controls. At the end, the child has the option to continue exploring before beginning Level 1. This feature is especially relevant for children with autism, as it provides a gradual adaptation phase, reduces anxiety when facing a new environment, and improves understanding of the virtual space.

Figure 17. Screens from Level 0 with enhanced graphics, animations, and images in TEA-MARK, version 2.

The colors of the store were also modified. This variation supports visual discrimination and facilitates the identification of specific areas, which is particularly useful for children with autism who often benefit from structured visual supports that help them better organize and comprehend their environment.

Figure 18. Colored shelves to improve product localization in TEA-MARK, version 2.

Instructions were optimized by simplifying their wording and reducing their length; some were replaced with images, and adjustments were made to color, size, and typography. These improvements address the needs of children with autism, who frequently process information more effectively through clear and direct visual support.

Figure 19. Simplified shopping list and payment suggestion with visual aids in TEA-MARK, version 2.

Additional instructions were added as guiding cues to support the understanding of the complete shopping process. This reinforcement enables children with autism to follow structured steps, thereby enhancing their autonomy and reducing the likelihood of confusion.

Figure 20. Instructional guides to facilitate comprehension of the shopping process in TEA-MARK, version 2.

A new level was also introduced, modifying the interaction experience. Upon completing it, children received a classification medal displaying the achievement earned. Such feedback is crucial for children with autism, as it provides immediate positive reinforcement, increases motivation, and helps consolidate learning.

Figure 21. Classification medal and gamified feedback in TEA-MARK, version 2.

Finally, some products were relocated to remain within the same area, with each zone assigned a distinct shelf color. This organization facilitates categorization and spatial association, which benefits children with autism by promoting predictability and reducing cognitive overload.

1) Blue - Soap.

Figure 22. Blue shelves for pet soap products in TEA-MARK, version 2.

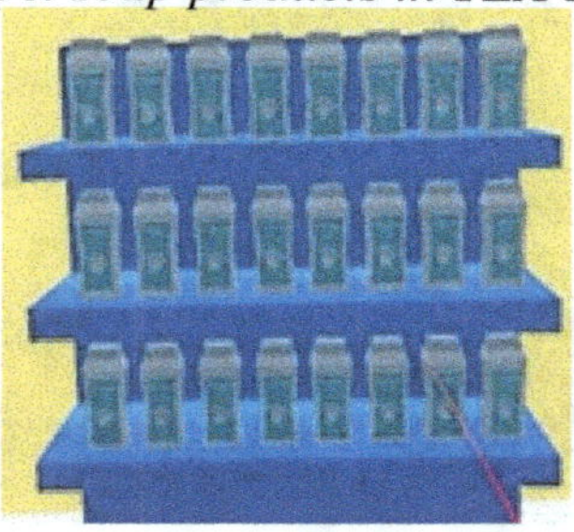

2) Purple - Food.

Figure 23.Purple shelves for pet food products in TEA-MARK, version 2.

3) Orange - Toys.

Figure 24. Orange shelf for pets toys in TEA-MARK, version 2.

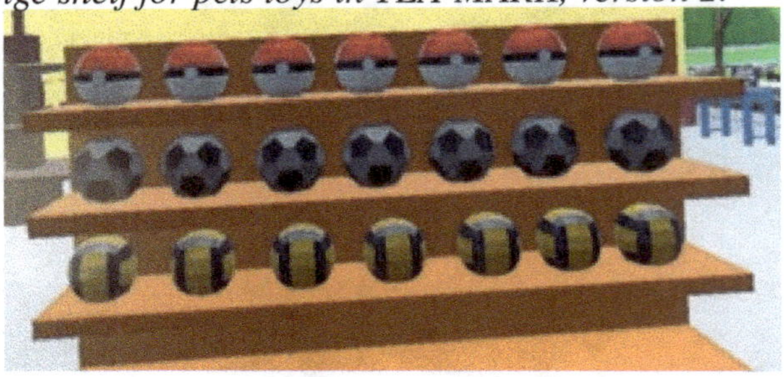

4) Green - plants.

Figure 25. Green shelf for plants in TEA-MARK, version 2.

5) Red - Cleaning.

Figure 26. Red shelf for cleaning products in TEA-MARK, version 2.

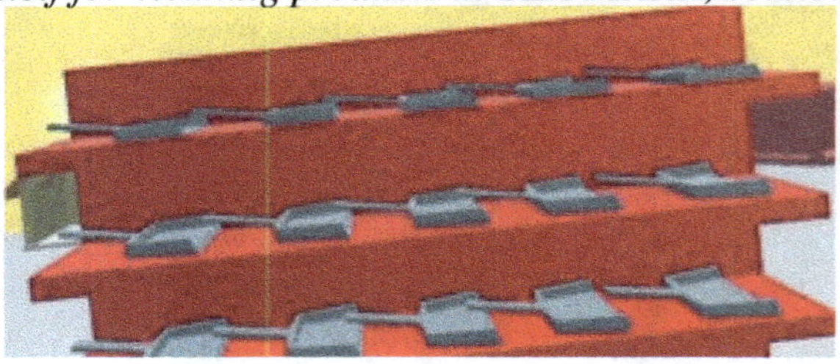

6) Brown - wood.

Figure 27. Brown shelf for wooden products in TEA-MARK, version 2.

7) White - Cat and fish items

Figure 28. White shelf for fish and cat products in TEA-MARK, version 2.

Version comparison

To analyze the improvements implemented in TEA-MARK, Table 3 presents a detailed comparison between version 1.0 and version 2.0 of the application. This comparison highlights not only the technical and visual refinements but also the pedagogical strategies incorporated into the design.

The table summarizes core aspects such as visual appeal, environment organization, instructions, support guides, feedback, and product arrangement, while also emphasizing the importance of accessibility and inclusivity in digital learning tools. In particular, the modifications introduced in version 2.0 were guided by expert recommendations in the fields of special education, human-computer interaction, and gamification. Each enhancement was carefully designed to support the cognitive, communicative, and behavioral needs of children with autism, addressing challenges such as sustained attention, comprehension, predictability, and motivation.

By integrating dynamic visual elements, step-by-step instructions, and adaptive feedback mechanisms, TEA-MARK 2.0 represents a more comprehensive educational tool that promotes engagement, gradual learning, and independence within the context of a virtual shopping experience.

Table 3. Comparison between TEA-MARK version 1.0 and version 2.0 and benefits for children with autism.

Aspect	Version 1.0	Version 2.0	Benefits for Children with Autism
Visual Appeal	Functional interfaces but with limited attractiveness; lacked dynamic stimuli.	Added animations and expressive emojis (Lana Studio, 2022; Flaticon website, 2025)	Enhance motivation, sustain attention, and support emotional association.
Start of the Experience	Menu located in a separate environment, followed by direct entry into the store.	Introduced Level 0 that allows free exploration of the store and familiarization with the controls before Level 1.	Reduces anxiety in unfamiliar environments, enables gradual adaptation, and improves spatial understanding.
Store Colors and Design	Shelves with basic colors and fixed distribution.	Colors modified and differentiated by specific areas.	Facilitates visual discrimination, organization, and predictability of the environment.
Instructions	Long texts with some complex directions.	Simplified instructions supported by images, optimized colors, typography, and size.	Improves comprehension through clear visual supports, adapted to the learning style of children with ASD.
Guidance and Support	Basic product list with validation only at the end.	Additional step-by-step instructions provided throughout the shopping process.	Reinforces structure, reduces confusion, and promotes autonomy.

continued on following page

Table 3. Continued

Aspect	Version 1.0	Version 2.0	Benefits for Children with Autism
Feedback and Motivation	Final congratulatory message after completing the shopping task.	New level introduced with a classification medal and immediate feedback.	Provides positive reinforcement, increases motivation, and consolidates learning.
Product Distribution	Products scattered across different shelves without a specific pattern.	Products reorganized within the same area, with shelf colors assigned by zone.	Supports categorization, reduces cognitive overload, and promotes predictability.

In summary, the comparison between TEA-MARK versions 1.0 and 2.0 demonstrates a significant evolution toward improving the virtual learning and shopping experience for children with autism. Beyond enhancing usability and accessibility, version 2.0 incorporates visual support, progressive structuring, and immediate positive reinforcement, all of which are aligned with evidence-based practices in autism education.

These design decisions contribute not only to the acquisition of practical skills, such as product recognition and categorization, but also to broader developmental goals, including autonomy, self-confidence, and social-emotional learning. Furthermore, by leveraging gamification strategies such as rewards and motivational feedback, the tool creates a playful yet structured environment that fosters intrinsic motivation and sustains engagement. Ultimately, TEA-MARK 2.0 consolidates itself as an inclusive and effective educational resource, capable of bridging the gap between therapeutic interventions and real-world skill development in a safe, controlled, and motivating context.

EVALUATION

To evaluate the TEA-MARK application, qualitative validation was carried out by a panel of three experts. This panel included professionals with relevant experience in the field, notably a psychotherapist specializing in the treatment of children with ASD. The procedure consisted of a functional demonstration of the application, where its main features were presented to the evaluators. Through this process, the experts provided detailed observations and crucial recommendations. The evaluation focused on ensuring that the design of the virtual environment was aligned with both current therapeutic practices and the specific learning needs of children with ASD, while also assessing the usability, accessibility, and overall educational value of the tool. Feedback obtained was fundamental to the refinement of the system. All of the experts' observations and recommendations were analyzed and subsequently integrated into the design of TEA-MARK to alignment with therapeutic objectives.

One of the most significant recommendations from the experts was to add a level of exploration prior to the main tasks. The purpose of this introductory phase is twofold: first, it facilitates adaptation to the virtual environment by reducing anxiety and promoting familiarity; second, it allows users to practice navigation and interaction without the pressure of being evaluated on their performance. This "gradual exposure" approach is consistent with proven therapeutic practices for children with ASD.

Another important point raised by the panel was the use of visually striking and distinctive colors. The current environment, which relied heavily on blue tones, occasionally caused objects to blend into the background, reducing clarity. The experts suggested adopting primary colors and incorporating visual cues such as representative images, animations, and videos to highlight important elements. For children with ASD, who often benefit from clear, high-contrast stimuli, this adjustment supports attention, reduces confusion, and strengthens task engagement.

The evaluators also stressed the need for simplified and concrete instructions. Rather than presenting long written text, instructions should be short, direct, and visually supported. For example, instead of instructing the user to "collect three bills of 200," the environment should display three bill images or use consistent color coding (e.g., three green bills). This approach minimizes cognitive load, avoids misinterpretation, and adapts to the visual learning style frequently observed in children with ASD.

Regarding task progression, the panel recommended the implementation of gradual increases in complexity. Early guided levels should focus on one or two products, allowing children to learn the fundamental steps of shopping in a simplified manner. As they gain confidence and proficiency, additional products and reduced guidance can be introduced. This scaffolding strategy aligns with pedagogical best practices and ensures that children are neither overwhelmed by tasks that are too complex nor disengaged by tasks that are too simplistic.

Another crucial recommendation concerned the delivery of positive and continuous feedback. The experts highlighted that frequent reinforcement—delivered both during and after task completion—significantly enhances motivation and persistence. Phrases such as "You're almost there!" combined with visual reinforcements (e.g., animations, stars, or encouraging characters) help sustain attention and promote a sense of achievement. Importantly, feedback should not be limited to the final outcome of a task but should also be given throughout the process (e.g., "Keep going!" or "Great job, just one more step!"). This approach maintains engagement, reduces frustration, and strengthens the learning experience.

In terms of visual clarity and object distinction, the panel recommended ensuring that products and interactive elements contrast clearly with the background and with each other. This measure reduces perceptual ambiguity, making it easier for children to identify, select, and manipulate items. Similarly, the experts suggested incorporating color-coded areas within the store environment, such as using distinct colors for sections like fruits, snacks, or beverages. This strategy not only aids orientation but also supports categorization skills and reduces cognitive load during task execution.

Finally, the evaluators advised careful attention to the balance of stimuli and proportional feedback. Each action within the environment should be accompanied by reinforcement proportional to its complexity and significance. For instance, picking up a single item might trigger a brief visual or auditory cue, while completing a purchase could be celebrated with more elaborate feedback. This balance prevents overstimulation and ensures that children can distinguish between minor and major achievements.

Incorporating these recommendations led to the development of a more intuitive, engaging, and supportive virtual environment, consistent with best practices in educational and therapeutic interventions for children with ASD. The improvements not only enhanced usability but also ensured that TEA-MARK provided an experience that is pedagogically sound, therapeutically relevant, and adaptable to the diverse learning profiles of children on the autism spectrum.

Ethical aspect

To conduct the expert evaluation, the study adhered to fundamental ethical principles. The participation of the three professionals was voluntary. Before the session, the objectives of the study and the evaluation procedure were explained to each expert. Written informed consent was obtained from each expert, ensuring their understanding of the purpose of the research.

Confidentiality and anonymity of all data and opinions collected were guaranteed. Feedback was separated from any personally identifiable information to protect the privacy of the experts. The data was used solely for academic purposes and to improve the TEA-MARK system.

CONCLUSIONS

The development of TEA-MARK represents a significant advancement in the integration of virtual reality (VR) as a pedagogical tool for teaching functional skills to children with autism, specifically those diagnosed at level 1. Throughout the different iterations of the software, areas for improvement were identified that made it possible to optimize both the visual aspect and the interaction dynamics, with the aim of providing a clearer, more engaging, and more accessible experience for this population.

One of the main findings was the importance of the visual component: the redesign of the shelves with primary and differentiated colors, the incorporation of expressive animations, and the use of immediate feedback fostered children's motivation and facilitated the understanding of the steps needed to complete the shopping activity.

The proposal to structure the learning process into three phases—viewing the shopping list, picking up the items, and paying—accompanied by visual guides and graphic supports, helped simplify tasks, avoid cognitive overload, and promote autonomy. In this regard, the implementation of a Level 0 proved essential as a space for familiarization with the controls and the virtual environment, reducing anxiety about the unknown and facilitating a gradual transition toward higher levels of complexity. The progression in difficulty, together with the organization of the space into chromatically differentiated areas, reinforces structured learning and enables children to generalize concepts that are also applicable in real shopping contexts.

The incorporation of gamification elements, such as visual rewards (confetti, stars, lights) and the awarding of medals upon completing a level, proved to be a key resource for maintaining motivation, increasing active participation, and preventing frustration. Immediate feedback not only allowed for real-time error correction but also contributed to consolidating learning by providing assurance about the actions taken. These aspects are fundamental for children with autism, who require predictable environments, visual support, and reinforcing stimuli that foster confidence and perseverance.

Furthermore, collaboration with autism specialists was indispensable, confirming the hypothesis that their observations would be essential for validating the initial feasibility and improving TEA-MARK. Their recommendations made it possible to adapt the design to the children's real needs, emphasizing the importance of fostering autonomy as one of the most challenging yet most valuable skills for daily life. The fact that children can repeat activities in a controlled, safe, and non-judgmental environment represents a unique opportunity to practice without fear of making mistakes, thereby increasing confidence and willingness to learn.

Taken together, the results support the hypothesis that virtual reality, applied through environments such as TEA-MARK, constitutes a promising tool for the development of practical skills in children with autism. Its ability to offer immersive, structured, and motivating scenarios provides advantages that are difficult to achieve in real environments, where external stimuli is harder to control. Nevertheless, it is acknowledged that further validation is required through direct application with children, evaluating their learning progress, the transfer of skills to everyday contexts, and their response to gamified stimuli.

In line with this need, future work will focus on broader empirical validation. A pilot study is planned with a sample of children on the spectrum to collect performance metrics (such as task completion time and error rates) and quantitative usability indicators (such as standardized scores). At the same time, the adaptation of the application to cover different levels of the spectrum will be explored, with the aim of consolidating its impact on inclusive education and preparation for daily life.

ACKNOWLEDGEMENTS

We would like to express our sincere gratitude to CUIN Aguascalientes and its director, Eduardo Alejandro Bravo Mejía, for generously providing the opportunity to test the TEA-MARK application with their experts. Their openness and collaboration were fundamental to bringing this project closer to its intended beneficiaries.

Our deepest appreciation also goes to Psychotherapist Flor Deyanira Valadez Reyna and Psychologist Gloria Guadalupe González Lizaran, whose constant support, professional expertise, and insightful observations greatly contributed to the refinement of this work. Their recommendations were invaluable in identifying areas for improvement and ensuring that TEA-MARK aligns with therapeutic and educational best practices for children with ASD.

REFERENCES

Adjorlu, A., Hoeg, E. R., Mangano, L., & Serafin, S. (2017). Daily living skills training in virtual reality to help children with autism spectrum disorder in a real shopping scenario. *Adjunct Proceedings of the 2017 IEEE International Symposium on Mixed and Augmented Reality (ISMAR-Adjunct)*, 93–98. https://doi.org/DOI: 10.1109/ISMAR-Adjunct.2017.93

Adjorlu, A., & Serafin, S. (2018). Virtual reality (VR) for children diagnosed with autism spectrum disorder (ASD). In Qian, H. (Ed.), *Handbook of Research on Serious Games for Educational Applications* (pp. 159–175). IGI Global., DOI: 10.4018/978-1-5225-7168-1.ch010

Adjorlu, A., & Serafin, S. (2019). Head-mounted display-based virtual reality as a tool to teach money skills to adolescents diagnosed with autism spectrum disorder. In Davis, H. C., Aslam, M. R. N., & Asensio, F. (Eds.), *Lecture Notes of the Institute for Computer Sciences, Social Informatics and Telecommunications Engineering (LNICST)* (pp. 450–461). Springer., DOI: 10.1007/978-3-030-06134-0_48

Alarifi, H. S. (2022). The use of virtual reality and eye-tracking to inform a grocery store intervention. *Psychology and Behavioral Science International Journal*, *18*(3). Advance online publication. DOI: 10.19080/PBSIJ.2022.17.555971

American Psychiatric Association. (2022). Diagnostic and statistical manual of mental disorders (5th ed.). American Psychiatric Publishing., DSM-5-TR.

Asale, R., & Real Academia Española. (n.d.). Realidad. In *Diccionario de la lengua española* (Edición del Tricentenario). https://dle.rae.es/realidad#CfxhrOR

Ballesteros, M. A. (2021). *Videojuegos y psicología clínica: La realidad virtual en evaluación y tratamiento de niños y adolescentes con trastorno del espectro* [Tesis, Facultad de Ciencias Humanas y Sociales]. Repositorio Comillas. https://repositorio.comillas.edu/xmlui/handle/11531/61242

Büyük, O. O., Nizam, A., Akgül, E. M., & Çamurcu, A. Y. (2019). A computer-enhanced money teaching application for individuals with autism spectrum disorders. *International Journal of Computer Applications Technology and Research, 8*(12), 407–412.

Celis Alcalá, G., & Ochoa Madrigal, M. G. (2023). Trastorno del espectro autista (TEA). *Revista de la Facultad de Medicina, Universidad Nacional Autonoma de Mexico, 65*(1), 7–20. DOI: 10.22201/fm.24484865e.2022.65.1.02

Darmasti, H., Aulia, N. P. S., Van der Hallen, R., & Zender, R. 2023. Promoting Daily Independence Skill for Individuals with Autism through Progressive Gamified VR Application. https://dl.gi.de/server/api/core/bitstreams/d0eb30f9-62be-43b9-b42b-fe7ed9b5498b/content

El-Gohary, M., Aborizka, M., El-Sheikh, M., & El-Nagar, Z. (2022). Shopping training to autistic children and adolescents for enhancing daily life shopping skills using virtual reality and Leap Motion. In *2022 1st IEEE International Conference on Cognitive Aspects of Virtual Reality (CVR 2022)* (pp. 55–60). IEEE. https://doi.org/DOI: 10.1109/CVR55417.2022.9967646

Escartín, E. (2023). La realidad virtual, una tecnología educativa a nuestro alcance. ResearchGate. https://www.researchgate.net/publication/28102483

Ferreira, R. S., Xavier, R. A. C., & Ancioto, A. S. R. (2021). Virtual reality as a tool for basic and vocational education. *Revista Científica General José María Córdova, 19*(33), 223–241. DOI: 10.21830/19006586.728

Flaticon. (2025). favicon Icon - 3585618. https://www.flaticon.es/iconos-gratis/favicon

García-Franco, A., Alpizar-Lorenzo, O. A., & Guzmán-Diaz, G. (2019). Autismo: Revisión conceptual. Universidad Autónoma del Estado de Hidalgo. https://repository.uaeh.edu.mx/revistas/index.php/atotonilco/article/view/3693/9502

Gil, D. L. (2024). *Trabajo fin de grado: Un análisis crítico de la clasificación del Trastorno del Espectro Autista y el Síndrome de Asperger* [Tesis, Universidad de Zaragoza]. https://zaguan.unizar.es/record/146181/files/TAZ-TFG-2024-4265.pdf

Johnston, D., Egermann, H., & Kearney, G. (2020). SoundFields: A virtual reality game designed to address auditory hypersensitivity in individuals with autism spectrum disorder. *Applied Sciences (Basel, Switzerland), 10*(9), 2996. DOI: 10.3390/app10092996

Kalemkuş, F. (2025). Trends in instructional technologies used in education of people with special needs due to intellectual disability and autism. *Journal of Research in Special Educational Needs, 25*(2), 237–261. DOI: 10.1111/1471-3802.12723

Kamp-Becker, I. (2024). Autism spectrum disorder in ICD-11—A critical reflection of its possible impact on clinical practice and research. *Molecular Psychiatry, 29*(3), 633–638. DOI: 10.1038/s41380-023-02354-y PMID: 38273107

Lana Studio. (2022). *Hyper Casual FX* [Unity Asset Store]. Unity. https://assetstore.unity.com/publishers/55292

Lledó Gonzalo, L., Lorenzo Lledó, A., Carreres Lledó, A., & Pérez Vázquez, E. (2023). Creation of an immersive virtual reality environment for communication and social interaction: A pilot study in students with autism spectrum disorders. *Revista de Educación a Distancia, 23*(73). Advance online publication. DOI: 10.6018/red.539141

López Belmonte, J., Duo Terrón, P., Moreno Guerrero, A. J., & Marín Marín, J. A. (2024). Efectos de la realidad aumentada y virtual en estudiantes con TEA. *Pixel-Bit. Revista de Medios y Educación.* https://revistapixelbit.com

Luque Ordóñez, J. (2020). Realidad virtual y realidad aumentada. *Acta.* https://www.acta.es/medios/articulos/ciencias_y_tecnologia/063001.pdf#page=3.69

Mahmoudi, E., Yoo, P. Y., Chandra, A., Cardoso, R., Dos Santos, C. D., Majnemer, A., & Shikako, K. (2024). Gamification in mobile apps for children with disabilities: Scoping review. *JMIR Serious Games, 12*(1), e49029. DOI: 10.2196/49029 PMID: 39240675

Mendoza, G. A. A., Lewis, F., Plante, P., & Brassard, C. (2023). Estado del arte sobre el uso de la realidad virtual, la realidad aumentada y el video 360° en educación superior. *Edutec, 84*(84), 35–51. DOI: 10.21556/edutec.2023.84.2769

Morais, P. B. de, Matos, R. A. F. de, Santiago, D. C., Silva, R. L. dos S., Botelho, L., Soares, G. de A., Santos, D. de S., Morais, S. D. de, Silva, E. J. da, & Lima, L. A. de O. (2023). Opportunities to use gamification for the learning of autistic students: A systematic review. *IOSR Journal of Business and Management, 25*(10, Ser. 8), 29–35. https://doi.org/DOI: 10.9790/487X-2510082935

Mouga, S., Oliveira, G., Almeida, J., Figueiredo, C., & Castelo-Branco, M. (2021). Attentional cueing and executive deficits revealed by a virtual supermarket task coupled with eye-tracking in autism spectrum disorder. *Frontiers in Psychology, 12*, 671507. DOI: 10.3389/fpsyg.2021.671507 PMID: 34531782

Orts, B. S. (2019). INMER-II: Sistema de inmersión en realidad virtual para personas con autismo. *Revista Española de Tecnología Educativa, 5*(2), 45–53.

Psicosomática, M., ... (2007). Realidad virtual y tratamientos psicológicos. https://d1wqtxts1xzle7.cloudfront.net/102824856/Cuad_20N82_20trabajo_202-libre.pdf

Ramos-Aguiar, L. R., & Álvarez-Rodríguez, F. J. (2021). Enseñanza de emociones en niños con espectro autista a través de un software con interfaces tangibles. *IEEE Revista Iberoamericana de Technologias del Aprendizaje, 16*(4), 365–371. DOI: 10.1109/RITA.2021.3125901

Ramos Aguiar, L. R., Álvarez Rodríguez, F. J., Madero Aguilar, J. R., Navarro Plascencia, V., Peña Mendoza, L. M., Quintero Valdez, J. R., Vázquez Pech, J. R., Mendieta León, A., & Lazcano Ortiz, L. E. (2023). Implementing gamification for blind and autistic people with tangible interfaces, extended reality, and universal design for learning: Two case studies. *Applied Sciences (Basel, Switzerland), 13*(5), 3159. DOI: 10.3390/app13053159

Schilbach, L. (2022). Autism and other disorders of social interaction: Where we are and where to go from here. *European Archives of Psychiatry and Clinical Neuroscience, 272*(2), 173–175. DOI: 10.1007/s00406-022-01391-y PMID: 35141808

Sung, M. C., McClelland, M. M., Massey, W., Logan, S. W., & Macdonald, M. (2024). Association between motor skills and executive function of children with autism spectrum disorder in Taiwan and the United States. *Frontiers in Public Health, 11*, 1292695. DOI: 10.3389/fpubh.2023.1292695 PMID: 38249390

Syriopoulou–Delli, C. K., & Sarri, K. (2022). Video-based instruction in enhancing functional living skills of adolescents and young adults with autism spectrum disorder and their transition to independent living: A review. *International Journal of Developmental Disabilities, 68*(6), 788–799. DOI: 10.1080/20473869.2021.1900504 PMID: 36568614

Virtual reality for autism: Unlocking learning and growth. (2024). *Journal of Autism and Developmental Technologies, 5*(4), 294–302.

Wongwan, N., Chernbumroong, S., Intawong, K., & Puritat, K. (2025, January). Designing a gamified mixed reality system for social skills development in high-functioning children with autism spectrum disorder. In *2025 Joint International Conference on Digital Arts, Media and Technology with ECTI Northern Section Conference on Electrical, Electronics, Computer and Telecommunications Engineering (ECTI DAMT & NCON)* (pp. 819–823). IEEE. DOI: 10.1109/ECTIDAMT-NCON64748.2025.10961994

World Health Organization. (2023, November 15). Autismo. https://www.who.int/es/news-room/fact-sheets/detail/autism-spectrum-disorders

Section 4
Specific Experiences, Case Studies, and Cultural or Multilingual Challenges

Chapter 8

Technological Innovation for Inclusive Education: A Digital Voice Assistant as a Support for Navigation in Virtual Learning Environments

Max William Millán Martínez
Instituto Tecnológico Superior de Xalapa, Mexico

Virginia Lagunes Barradas
Instituto Tecnológico Superior de Xalapa, Mexico

José Rafael Rojano-Cáceres
https://orcid.org/0000-0002-3878-4571
Universidad Veracruzana, Mexico

ABSTRACT

This chapter presents the design and evaluation of a digital voice assistant aimed at supporting navigation in virtual learning environments, with emphasis on accessibility for students with visual disabilities. The study highlights the barriers caused by low adoption of accessibility standards and the limitations of screen readers. The proposed prototype was developed as a Google Chrome extension, integrating natural language processing, machine learning models, and APIs for speech recognition and synthesis. A structural analysis of the NAME-PLATAFORM-HIDDEN INSTI-HIDDEN platform was conducted using web scraping to build datasets that enabled the training of LSTM-based classification models. Evaluation with visually impaired students demonstrated improvements in efficiency, autonomy, and satis-

DOI: 10.4018/979-8-3373-6033-1.ch008

faction compared to traditional screen readers. The results indicate that digital voice assistants can complement existing tools and significantly enhance inclusive education in online environments.

INTRODUCTION

The growing adoption of virtual learning environments (VLEs) has significantly transformed education by enabling ubiquitous access to digital content and intelligent systems that support knowledge acquisition (Zhou, Munyaradzi, et al., 2022). However, a persistent challenge remains: how can these platforms ensure accessibility and inclusion for learners with disabilities, particularly those with severe visual impairments? This study is guided by the following research question: Can a voice-based digital assistant improve the accessibility and usability of VLEs for visually impaired users by enabling natural, low-effort interaction without extensive technical training?

It is true that virtual learning environment (VLE) have represented a great support to education, by allowing students to enter and consume content at any time and any place, as well as interact with systems that integrate artificial intelligence (AI) to facilitate the process of acquiring knowledge on these platforms. However, these systems today present great challenges in terms of inclusion, firstly, for students living with disabilities who face barriers to access and navigation, and secondly, for the developers of these platforms, who must incorporate accessibility criteria from the design, ensuring that technological solutions are truly universal and Equitable (Vasquez, Nagendran, et al., 2015).

In the specific case of people with severe visual impairment, accessibility barriers make it difficult for them to interact with these platforms, due to the low adoption of standards such as the Web Content Accessibility Guidelines (WCAG) (W3C, 2024). An example are the usability problems of screen readers when the interface has not been designed under such standards. These challenges are compounded by varying levels of digital literacy among people with visual disabilities, which highlights the need for interaction mechanisms that are both intuitive and universally accessible.

To achieve this, the project draws from broader accessibility frameworks beyond the WCAG standards. While WCAG focuses on technical implementation, this work also incorporates principles from User-Centered Design (UCD) (Vredenburg, Mao, Smith & Carey, 2002), by directly involving visually impaired users in the development cycle. Furthermore, it aligns with the philosophy of Universal Design for Learning (UDL), which advocates for providing multiple means of representation, action, and engagement. A voice-based assistant directly addresses this by offering an alternative modality (action and engagement) for users who are not well-served by the platform's primary visual interface.

To address this gap, it is necessary to analyze alternatives for interaction with such platforms, in such a way that they result in a natural access mechanism and minimize the need for technical training, especially for new users. In this sense, this chapter explores the integration of natural language processing (NLP) technologies to design a voice-based interaction model for inclusive navigation in VLEs. The chapter presents the underlying principles of NLP applied to bidirectional voice–text conversion, analyzes suitable APIs for communication engines, and evaluates their accuracy, scalability, and cost. It further details the development of a browser plugin that enables interaction via voice commands without additional software requirements..

As a crucial part for the design of the specific digital assistant oriented to provide accessible navigation, a structural analysis of the target virtual learning environment (VLE) was carried out using web scraping techniques. This analysis made it possible to identify the underlying HTML architecture, the most frequent browsing patterns, as well as the critical elements of interaction, such as menus, buttons, forms and links, which need to be interpreted or transformed for visually impaired people.

To achieve this, an automated script was developed that travels the main navigation paths within the platform, extracting the HTML content and associated metadata. This process facilitated the generation of a structured dataset of the relevant semantic elements for access via screen readers.

This dataset served as an input to train and adapt the interaction pattern recognition system, allowing the digital assistant to identify areas of interest in the interfaces and generate intelligent responses that guide the user during their navigation through the virtual environment.

From an educational and social standpoint, it is essential to explore alternative modes of interaction that privilege natural communication and autonomy. Approaches based on Natural Language Processing (NLP) offer a promising path toward more intuitive learning experiences by enabling users to navigate and interact through voice rather than visual cues. Yet, these advances must also be analyzed in light of pedagogical and ethical dimensions: how they influence participation, agency, and the sense of belonging within virtual learning communities.

Therefore presents both the technical and conceptual foundations for the design of a digital voice assistant aimed at facilitating accessible navigation within VLEs. It details the process through which the user experience (UX) has been validated with the proposed tool, for those users who have total visual impairment (blindness), with the aim of evaluate and highlight not only the system's performance but also its potential to enhance accessibility and equity in digital education.

Finally, this chapter has nine main sections: Technological tools for the implementation of web-based digital assistants, which describes every aspect related to technology in the context of the research. Prototype architecture, where we explain architectural and decision aspects for the prototype. Prototype design, in this section it is explained how the design was made. Selection of technologies, in this section we argue the technologies used. Generation of the datasets, we describe aspects related to machine learning, particularly the datasets. Prototype evaluation, in this section we present the results of evaluation. Results sections, describe the analysis of results. Limitations and future research, explain the future work as well as main limitations.

SPEECH RECOGNITION TECHNOLOGIES

In recent years, there has been a constant growth in the development of solutions based on Artificial Intelligence (AI) which has led to the emergence and consolidation of different technological areas, such as Neural Networks, Big Data, Machine Learning, image and voice recognition, among others. The main purpose of these solutions is to imitate human cognitive capacities to optimize processes and generate more autonomous and efficient systems. In this sense, (Pradhan et al., 2018) highlight that advances in AI have favoured the search for new forms of accessibility and, on the other hand, better practices for interacting and carrying out activities in digital environments. In particular, HIDDEN-REF mention that voice recognition technology has achieved a reduction in the error rate of up to approximately 8%, which has increased its potential for application in various social, educational and productive contexts.

Components and Operation

According to Simon & Rajeswari (2023), speech recognition technology is made up of several fundamental elements mentioned below (see Figure 1):

- **Recording systems:** Captures the user's speech using microphones built into the devices.
- **Signal processing:** Transforms sound waves into digital data that can be understood by a computer.
- **Speech recognition:** Uses linguistic and acoustic models to interpret and transcribe speech into text.
- **Feedback component:** It is responsible for accessing the voice recognition results and feeds the information visually or audibly.

Figure 1. Components of a Speech Recognition System.

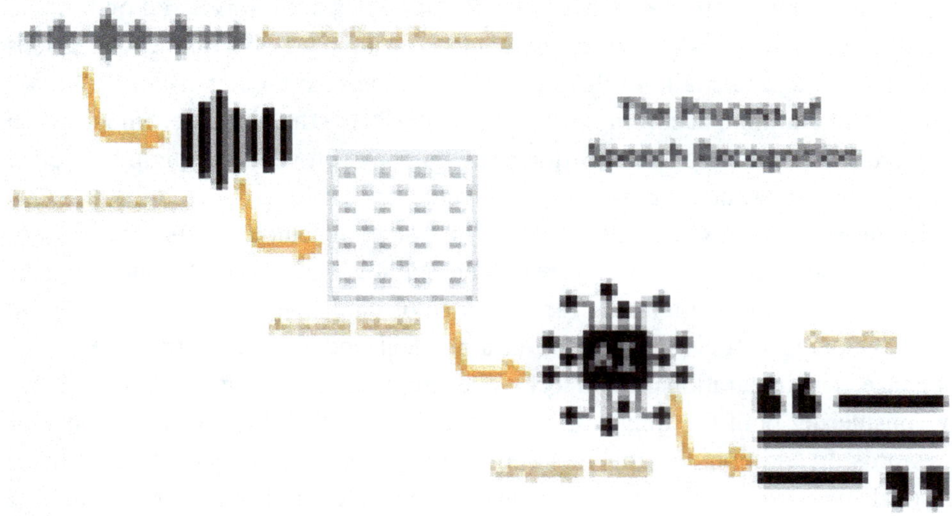

Besides, they said that the operation of speech recognition technology is based on complex mathematical models and machine learning algorithms. These models are trained on large amounts of speech data to enable pattern recognition and generate predictions about spoken words. During this process, the algorithm compares the acoustic characteristics of speech with the patterns stored in its database. As the system exposes to more data and feedback, it improves its accuracy and speech recognition capabilities(Mokh et al., 2019)

Artificial Intelligence and Machine Learning Techniques

Artificial intelligence and machine learning techniques play a very important role in the development of effective speech recognition systems. These allow algorithms to analyze and understand complex patterns present in audio data, allowing speech to be recognized and transcribed more accurately (Simancas & Meléndez-Pertuz, 2017). Machine learning focuses on training models with large voice datasets, making it possible to continuously improve their performance and adapt to different accents, pitches, and speech speeds. In this context, artificial intelligence techniques, such as neural networks and classification algorithms, are useful for the processing and analysis of audio signals in real time, making it possible to contribute to faster and more accurate speech recognition.

Similarly, they indicate that the most common approach in speech recognition is Deep Learning (DL), specifically through the use of neural networks that mimic the functioning of the human brain. The operation of these algorithms is carried out through layers that are interconnected by nodes, which allow extracting characteristics and learning complex patterns in voice data. Its operation is based on training with labeled datasets, where neural networks adjust the weights of the connections between nodes, which allows them to gradually improve their speech recognition capacity. In addition, according to Morán et al. (2018),the use of techniques such as sequential processing and attention modeling have proven to be highly effective for accurate, real-time transcription of speech.

In the same way, Cruz (2021) stated that other machine learning techniques widely used in speech recognition are hidden Markov models (HMM) and language models. HMMs allow modeling the sequence of phonemes and words in speech, while language models capture the grammatical and semantic structure of the language. The integration of both techniques improves the accuracy of recognition by considering both the linguistic context and the probabilities of occurrence of the words. In addition, the application of pre-processing techniques, such as noise removal and normalization of audio signals, contributes significantly to optimizing the quality of the data and, consequently, the accuracy of the results obtained in speech recognition processes.

Speech Recognition APIs

An Application Programming Interface (API) is a set of rules and protocols that allows two software applications to communicate with each other, exchanging data and functionalities in a well-defined way. APIs are mainly divided into two categories: commercial APIs, developed by large technology corporations that offer robust solutions with technical support, and free software, which promote accessibility, customization, and cost reduction in open source or community projects (Mokh et al., 2019).

Commercial APIs have gained popularity due to their convenience and ease of implementation (Natale & Cooke, 2021). Companies such as Google, Amazon and Microsoft provide developers with access to powerful algorithms and speech recognition models through a user-friendly interface and in turn, allow them to quickly integrate their functionalities into applications and services without the need to train their own models or manage the necessary infrastructure. In addition, these APIs often include complementary functionalities such as multi-language recognition, entity identification, and adaptation to specific contexts, expanding their applicability in various industries.

As Chaveesuk points out (2016), this type of solution has been decisive for the mass adoption of applications and services based on voice recognition. By using this technology, companies can take advantage of the experience and investment in research and development of the provider companies, which guarantees a high level of accuracy and performance in voice recognition, in addition to offering scalable and reliable services, which is crucial for mission-critical applications that require a high level of availability and performance.

One drawback of commercial APIs is privacy, as it depends entirely on the company. In some cases, data deletion is permitted, but in others, data is stored for algorithm improvement without the possibility of deletion.

Prominent examples of commercial speech recognition APIs include:

- **Google Cloud Speech-to-Text API:** Provided by Google Cloud, it converts speech to text in real-time, with support for multiple languages and dialects, standing out for its accuracy and speed.
- **Amazon Transcribe: Powered by Amazon Web Services (AWS),** it enables automatic transcription of audio to text, provides real-time and asynchronous speech recognition, as well as the ability to recognize multiple languages and adapt to different types of audio.
- **Microsoft Azure Speech Services:** Offered by Microsoft Azure, it provides speech recognition, text-to-speech, and real-time speech translation services with high recognition accuracy and support for multiple languages and dialects.
- **IBM Watson Speech to Text:** Provided by IBM Watson, it converts speech to text and offers advanced features such as multi-speaker recognition and adaptation to custom speech models, supporting a wide variety of languages.

On the other hand, free software speech recognition APIs, have played a decisive role in the democratization of access to this technology. APIs like Mozilla DeepSpeech allow developers to use pre-trained speech recognition algorithms and models to integrate recognition capabilities into their own applications and services. Being open access, these APIs encourage academic research and continuous improvement of models through input from the developer community (De Barcelos Silva et al., 2020).

Prakash et al. (2022)said that this technology has driven the development and adoption of applications and services based on voice recognition as it is an economical alternative to proprietary solutions, which is particularly attractive for universities, startups and independent developers. It also encourages the use of high-quality models and algorithms, as well as transparency and collaboration in the field of speech recognition.

Compared to commercial implementations, open developments can offer complete control over data and privacy, in the sense that it is up to the developer to implement measures such as transmission over SSL, data encryption, and secure storage.

Among the most commonly used free software APIs are:

- **Mozilla DeepSpeech:** Based on open-source neural networks, providing highly accurate speech recognition models trained on large data sets.
- **Kaldi:** An open-source speech recognition platform that offers a wide variety of tools and algorithms for speech processing. It is highly modular and allows for the creation of customized speech recognition systems.
- **CMUSphinx:** An open-source library for speech recognition, developed by Carnegie Mellon University. It provides tools and algorithms to build speech recognition applications on different platforms.
- **Julius**: Open-source voice recognition application, developed by the telecommunications research laboratory of Japan. It is designed to support multiple languages and offers an easy-to-use interface for application integration.

ETHICAL CONSIDERATIONS AND RESPONSIBLE AI: DATA PRIVACY

The use of third-party commercial APIs, such as the Google Cloud Speech-to-Text service, introduces critical ethical considerations, as noted by the "Responsible AI" trend. A primary concern is data privacy. In the architecture of this prototype, the user's voice data is sent to Google's servers for transcription. According to Google's terms of service, this data may be temporarily stored and used to improve their services. For this project, several mitigating steps were taken:

- **Data Minimization**: The assistant only captures audio after the "ALAN" wake-word is detected, ensuring no passive or unintended audio is recorded or transmitted.
- **Anonymity**: No personally identifiable information (PII) beyond the voice data itself is sent with the audio request. The API requests are not linked to a specific user's platform account or personal name.

However, a more robust future implementation would involve establishing a Data Processing Agreement (DPA) with the provider or exploring on-device speech recognition models that process audio locally, completely eliminating the privacy risks associated with data transmission.

DIGITAL ASSISTANTS

Digital assistants are one of the most visible applications of voice recognition and Artificial Intelligence. These systems, which include solutions such as Google

Assistant, Amazon Alexa, Apple Siri and Microsoft Cortana, further integrate Natural Language Processing (NLP) techniques to enable seamless interaction between humans and computers through voice commands. The massification of these assistants has been possible thanks to the growing access of the population to smart devices, which in turn generates more data to train and perfect the models that respond to the needs and preferences of users (John Rome, 2017).

In the same way Abdolrahmani et al. (2018) said that digital voice assistants have transformed the way we interact with technology, since being based on Artificial Intelligence and machine learning they have achieved greater accuracy in voice recognition, which has led to a more fluid and efficient user experience. These assistants are present in different devices, from smartphones and smart speakers to connected cars. In addition, leading technology companies, such as Google, Amazon, Apple, and Microsoft, are constantly investing in the continuous improvement of their assistants, adding new functionalities and expanding their ability to understand and respond to more complex voice commands.

Use and Applications of Digital Assistants

Digital assistants have spread to various applications in different sectors, such as the field of health, where medical documentation systems have been used to facilitate the transcription of clinical notes and improve the efficiency of health professionals. In this way, in the business sector it is used in customer service applications, allowing users to interact with automated interactive voice response (IVR) systems. In addition, in the field of entertainment, it has been integrated into voice control systems for televisions, allowing users to change channels, adjust the volume and search for content with voice commands (Palaparthi et al., 2023).

These applications are just examples of how speech recognition has become a versatile and widely used technology in various contexts. According to them, this technology has found promising applications in accessibility and inclusion. For example, people with physical disabilities can use voice recognition to control electronic devices and perform everyday tasks, allowing them greater independence and autonomy. Likewise, solutions for machine translation have been generated, facilitating communication between people who speak different languages. In the educational environment, real-time transcription systems have been implemented, allowing students with hearing difficulties to access oral content during classes (Lopezosa et al., 2023).

From this perspective, de Barcelos Silva et al. (2020), stated that digital assistants in recent years have been included in different areas, such as shown in Figure 2, where the goal is to solve needs that use voice recognition. In this way, it is observed that 8.62% of the applications that are developed have focused on the educational field, mainly in research and tools that are used to facilitate the learning process for students.

Besides, according to Lister et al. (2020), accessible conversational user interfaces (CUI) represent and potential technology for users with Dyslexia, Dyspraxia, between other neurodivergent conditions.

Figure 2. Research on Speech Recognition by Area.

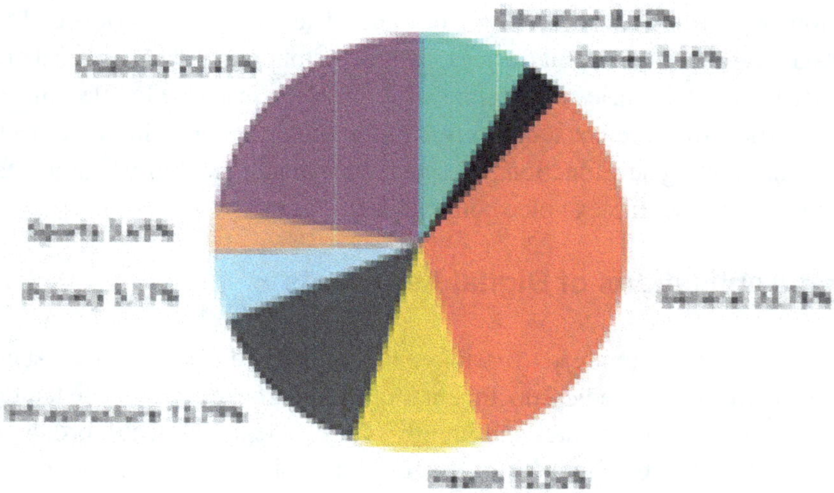

TECHNOLOGICAL TOOLS FOR THE IMPLEMENTATION OF WEB-BASED DIGITAL ASSISTANTS

This section analyzes the technological components used for the implementation of a digital assistant with voice recognition in a virtual educational environment. In the first instance, the use of cloud computing, web services architecture, the REST protocol as a means of communication between systems, as well as the construction of extensions in web browsers as a direct interaction channel with the user are addressed. Finally, critical security and privacy aspects related to the implementation of this type of technology are discussed.

Cloud Computing

Cloud computing (CC) allows access to computer resources and products through the Web, including digital voice assistants, for which cloud services are integrated, mainly offered into two models: public cloud and private cloud.

This means that digital voice assistants can provide fast and accurate responses, as well as perform complex tasks, such as making reservations, sending messages, or playing music, by harnessing the power of CC (Abdolrahmani et al., 2018). Also, it can be available on a wide variety of devices, such as phones and smartwatches and speakers. With the these can learn and adapt to users over time, providing personalized answers and relevant suggestions (Mokh et al., 2019).

Cloud computing also has democratized access to advanced technologies, such as machine learning and data analytics, by allowing even small businesses to access large-scale compute and storage resources (Vishnu, 2023).

Web Services

Web services are systems designed to facilitate communication and interoperability between different applications over a network, usually the Internet. Thanks to these technologies, users can consume services on demand, without the need to install or maintain physical infrastructures or local software, which provides flexibility, scalability and cost savings, through application programming interfaces (APIs), which act as an abstraction layer to simplify access to services (Kumar, 2023). For that purpose, REST is one of the most relevant mechanism to implement it (Mishra & Panda, 2023).

The API allows developers to integrate functionalities such as storage, databases, information processing, and artificial intelligence into their own applications efficiently and securely. In the educational context, this integration makes it possible for digital assistants to interact with learning platforms through APIs, accessing user data, courses, assessments and other educational resources in real time. This ease of access has driven the adoption of cloud-based solutions in various sectors, including education, enabling efficient management of technological resources (Mishra & Panda, 2023).

In this way, web services and their APIs allow the creation of digital assistants that facilitate the navigation, consultation and personalized management of educational content, adapting to the specific needs of each user, including people with disabilities. This integration not only improves accessibility, but also promotes innovation and collaboration in the development of more agile, efficient and user-centric educational solutions.

Rest Api

REST (Representational State Transfer) web services have gained popularity in distributed application development due to their simplicity, scalability, and compatibility with modern architectures (Jiang & Hu, 2011). REST implements an architectural style that takes advantage of the principles of the web, using HTTP as a communication protocol. Unlike SOAP (Simple Object Access Protocol)-based services, REST does not require a strict messaging format, making it lighter and more flexible.

From this perspective, Gamha (2023) saids that REST services are currently widely used through APIs generated by various services through Cloud Computing.

According to (Jiang & Hu, 2011), state that, for a REST service to work, it must be under three concepts:

- **Resource**: Everything within a REST service must be a resource.
- **URI**: REST services are always manipulated from a URI, which are universal resource identifiers.
- **Action**: All requests to REST services must be associated with one of the HTTP methods (GET, POST, DELETE, PUT).

They also mention that REST services work through an architecture known as client-server, in which the server and the client act independently, as long as the interface is the same when processing a request and a response, which are the essential methods.

Google Chrome Extensions

Extensions have become essential tools that allow us to customize and extend the functionalities integrated into browsers. Since their appearance, have transformed the user experience, allowing from ad blocking to the integration of advanced artificial intelligence technologies. The evolution of this technology in Google Chrome has been parallel to the growing requirements for security and performance (Liu et al., n.d.).

The migration of support from NPAPI to PPAPI and the recent introduction of Manifest V3 reflect Google's commitment to modernization and user protection. Manifest V3 allows us to limit access to potentially dangerous functions and forces developers to adopt a declarative model to manage permissions, which translates into greater efficiency and security in the execution of extensions(Johnson et al., 2023).

For the development of extensions in Google Chrome relies on common web technologies (See, Figure 3). Developers can use the manifest file (manifest.json) to define the metadata and permissions, as well as scripts, stylesheets, and icons that make up the extension's full functionality. In this way, he mentions that this process has allowed even beginner programmers to venture into this field, thanks to numerous tutorials and resources available online (Mehta, 2016).

Figure 3. Architecture of Google Chrome Extensions.

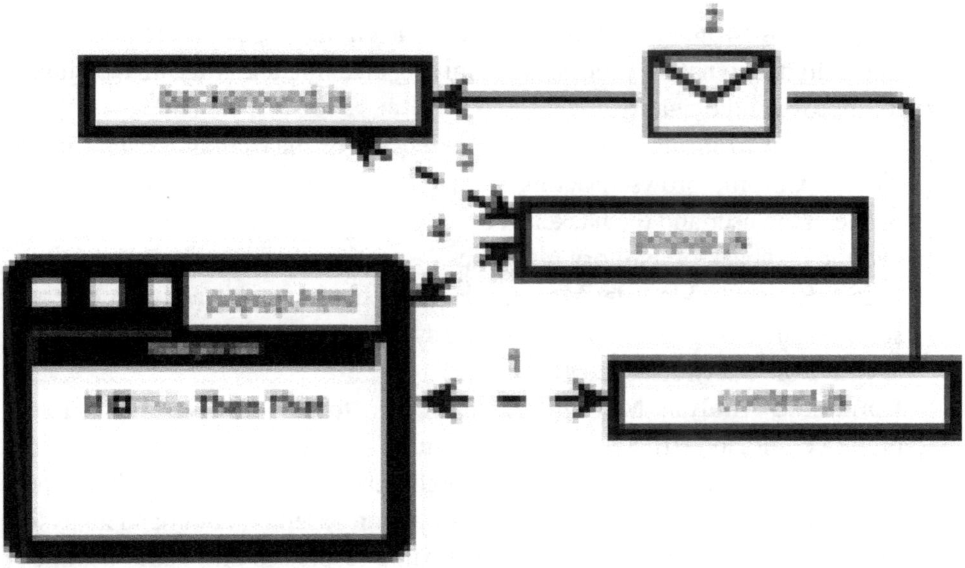

Although there are great benefits, integrating extensions into Chrome also poses challenges in terms of security. Recent incidents have been reported that popular extensions can be targeted by phishing attacks or compromised by malicious actors. The developer community and Google have responded to these challenges by improving the review process and implementing technologies such as Manifest V3, which reduce the attack surface by eliminating access to critical resources and forcing the adoption of secure development practices (Johnson et al., 2023).

Prototype Architecture

Considering the need to design a prototype that allows an efficient and precise interaction between the user and the system, the proposed architecture is modular. According to the National Institute of Technology, they mention that modularity facilitates the assignment of specific responsibilities to each component of the system, which favors collaborative work, early detection of errors and the integration of new functionalities without affecting the system as a whole. For this reason, this modular structure makes it possible to optimally organize and control the flow of data between the various components involved in speech processing and command interpretation (Kaur et al., 2019).

The prototype is made up of several modules (See, Figure 4) with specific functions that are integrated to offer a fluid and efficient communication with the user:

- **Acquisition Module**: Captures voice input via microphone and converts it into a digital signal for processing, applying cleaning and filtering techniques to improve audio quality.
- **Interaction Module**: It works as an extension of the digital assistant in the Google Chrome browser, acting as an intermediary in the communication between the user and the backend services, managing the digital audio signal and the playback of auditory responses.
- **REST Requests Module**: Manages HTTP requests to interact with external services such as speech recognition and synthesis APIs, allowing bidirectional conversion between speech and text.
- **Command Analysis Module**: Processes text to identify user intent, interpreting command structure, and determining actions to be executed.
- **Prediction Module**: Uses artificial intelligence algorithms to validate and predict the most appropriate response or action based on command analysis.
- **Speech Synthesis Module**: Converts textual responses into audio using external APIs (Google Text-to-Speech), ensuring a natural and understandable auditory output for the user.

Figure 4. Modular Architecture of the Prototype.

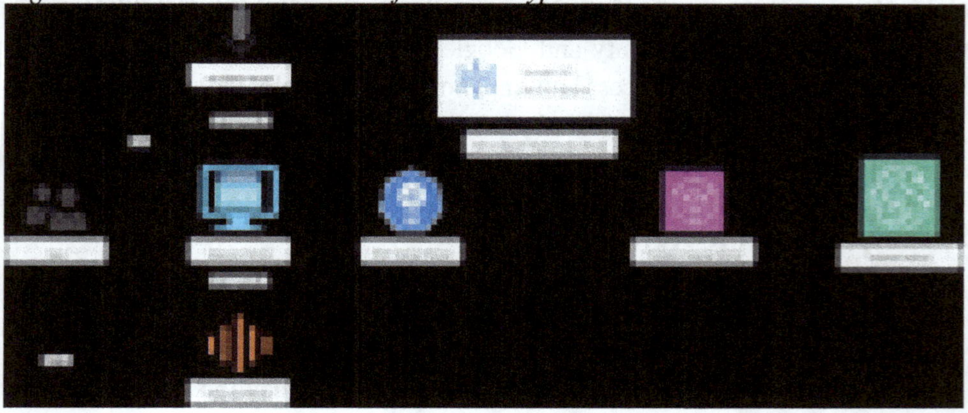

Structural Description Of The Prototype

The structural diagram aims to visually represent the organization and distribution of the main components of the prototype, thus facilitating the understanding of how they interact with each other to fulfill the defined functions.

According to this, the structural diagram corresponding to the prototype of the digital assistant was generated (See, Figure 5), being essential to show the logical separation between the different capacities of the system, as well as to identify the responsibilities of each module within the general architecture.

Figure 5. Structural Diagram of the Digital Assistant.

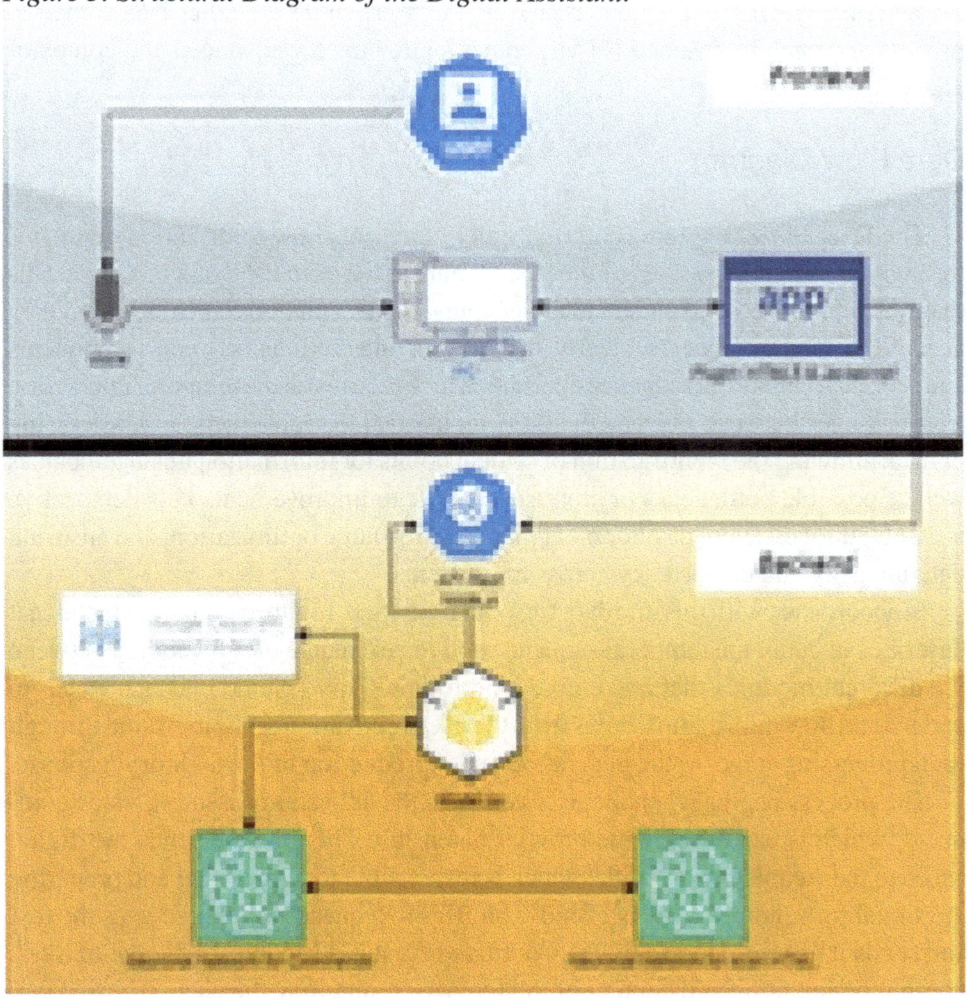

On the frontend, the user interacts through voice commands captured through a microphone, which are initially processed in an application executed on the local computer (PC). This application works as a plugin developed in HTML5 and JavaScript, which manages direct interaction with the user and acts as an intermediary with backend services. The latter is composed of a REST API developed in Node. js, which is responsible for receiving requests from the frontend and coordinating the processing of the information. For speech-to-text transcription, the system uses Google Cloud's external Speech-to-text API service, ensuring efficient and accurate conversion.

Subsequently, the generated text is sent to specialized processing modules based on neural networks. One of these modules is responsible for analyzing and recognizing specific commands issued by the user, while the other is designed to process and analyze scanned HTML content, allowing for advanced and contextualized interpretation.

Data Flow Diagram

The Data Flow Diagram (DFD) visually represents how information circulates through the various modules of the system during the execution of a use case. This diagram makes it easy to understand the inputs, transformations, and outputs of data at each stage of the process, clearly showing the interactions between components and services. Unlike the sequence diagram, which focuses on the temporal interaction and messages between objects, the DFD focuses on the movement and processing of data, allowing the identification of critical points for information management, as well as possible bottlenecks or areas susceptible to improvement. This perspective is essential for efficient development planning, resource optimization, and ensuring data integrity and consistency across the system.

In accordance with this, the data flow diagram (See, Figure 6) was developed that describes in detail the temporal sequence and the exchange of information between the different modules that make up the prototype. This scheme makes it easier to understand how information flows from the user's activation of the assistant, through each processing stage, to the generation and reproduction of the auditory response.

The process begins when the user activates the assistant or issues a voice command, which is captured by the browser extension. This module sends the digital audio to the Acquisition Module, which is responsible for converting and preparing the signal for sending to the backend. The REST Request Module receives the text and sends it to be processed by the Command Analysis Module, in charge of interpreting the intention and content of the message emitted by the user.

Subsequently, the analyzed text is sent to the Prediction Module, where artificial intelligence models are applied to determine the most appropriate response or action.

The generated result is sent to the Speech Synthesis Module, which through the Google Text-to-Speech API converts the text into audio. Finally, the generated audio is sent back to the REST Request Module and the browser extension for playback, thus closing the cycle of interaction with the user.

Figure 6. Flowchart of the Digital Assistant.

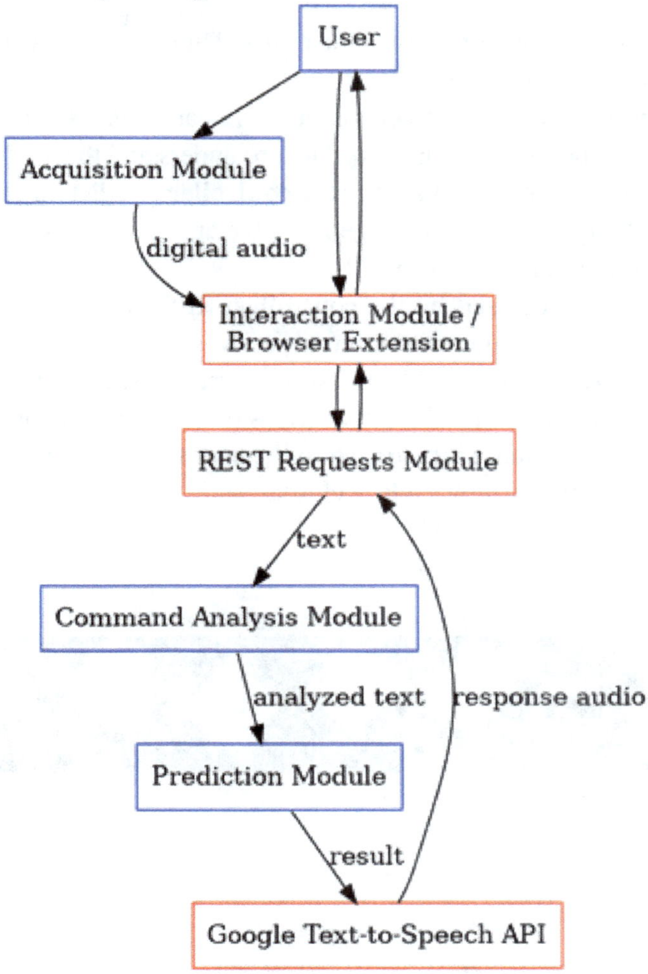

Robustness Diagram

The robustness diagram is a fundamental tool for visualizing and clarifying the responsibilities and relationships between actors, controllers, and entities within the system. This type of diagram serves to ensure that the conceptual structure of the prototype is solid and that the interactions between its components are coherent and well-defined.

In the diagram presented (see Figure 7) the User initially interacts with the Browser Extension/Interaction Module, which acts as the entry and exit point for auditory information. The relationship between the classes within this diagram behaves as follows:

- **The module receives and sends the entity:** Digital Audio, which represents the captured sound signal.
- **Flow of information to the controller**: Command Analysis module, responsible for interpreting the transcribed text to understand the user's intention.
- **The analysis performed is sent to the controller**: Prediction Module, which applies intelligent algorithms to generate the appropriate response according to the query or command received.
- **The result is processed by the controller**: REST Request Module, which manages communication with external services for text-to-speech.
- **The controller connects with the Google Text-to-Speech API**: Transforms the text into an audio signal represented as the Entity: Response Audio.
- **The auditory response is returned to the user through the browser extension**: The communication cycle is closed.

Figure 7. Robustness Diagram of the Digital Assistant.

Sequence Diagram

The main function of the sequence diagram (see Figure 8) is to show the methods involved in the correct execution of a use case, also allowing the identification of the components involved and the possible paths that the process can follow. This diagram details the communication between these components, including parameters, data exchanged, and the flow of information between them. Thanks to its level of detail in the interaction between processes, the sequence diagram offers a more accurate visualization compared to other types of diagrams, especially during the development stage. This makes it easier to plan to complete tasks, helps estimate development times, and allows you to identify which functions are more complex based on the number of interactions they have with other functions or with persistent data.

Taking into account the previous robustness diagram, the following sequence diagram is proposed that represents the temporal flow and the detailed interaction between the modules and entities during the operation of the digital assistant. As can be seen in the figure the process begins with the user activating the assistant or issuing a voice command, which is captured and converted to text by the browser extension and the acquisition module.

Subsequently, this text is sent to the REST request module and from there processed by the command analysis module, in charge of interpreting the user's intention and extracting the relevant information for the requested action. The prediction module uses this information to generate the appropriate response or action, which is then sent to the speech synthesis module. This module, using the Google Text-to-Speech API, converts text into responsive audio. Finally, the generated audio is sent back to the interaction module to be played to the user, closing the communication cycle.

Figure 8. Sequence Diagram of the Digital Assistant.

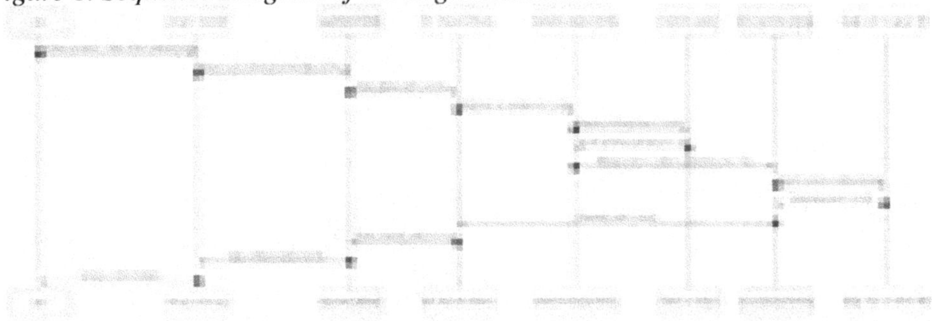

PROTOTYPE DESIGN

As specified at the beginning of this chapter, this project is developed under the User-Centered Design (UCD) approach, integrating the participation of visually impaired people, who represent the end users. This collaboration made it possible to identify and prioritize the key elements that would facilitate effective interaction between users and the assistant.

Based on the information collected, it was determined that a digital assistant prototype oriented to navigation on an educational platform must have features such as: language settings, response speed adjustment, intuitive and easy-to-identify commands, as well as clear feedback mechanisms on the tasks executed.

For this reason, we proceeded to develop a prototype implemented as a plugin for the Google Chrome browser, based on a modular architecture that allows the functionalities to be distributed in individual and specialized components. This architecture provides significant advantages such as greater scalability, the possibility of incorporating new functionalities or technologies without affecting the operation of the entire system and the simplification of maintenance and updating tasks.

To illustrate this design, a component diagram (see Figure 9) was generated which visualizes each element and the interaction flow for the operation of the digital assistant. Allowing a better operability of the latter and with it the accessibility to the navigation functions with the commands given by the user. These components will be explained in more detail in the following section.

Figure 9. Component Diagram of the Digital Assistant.

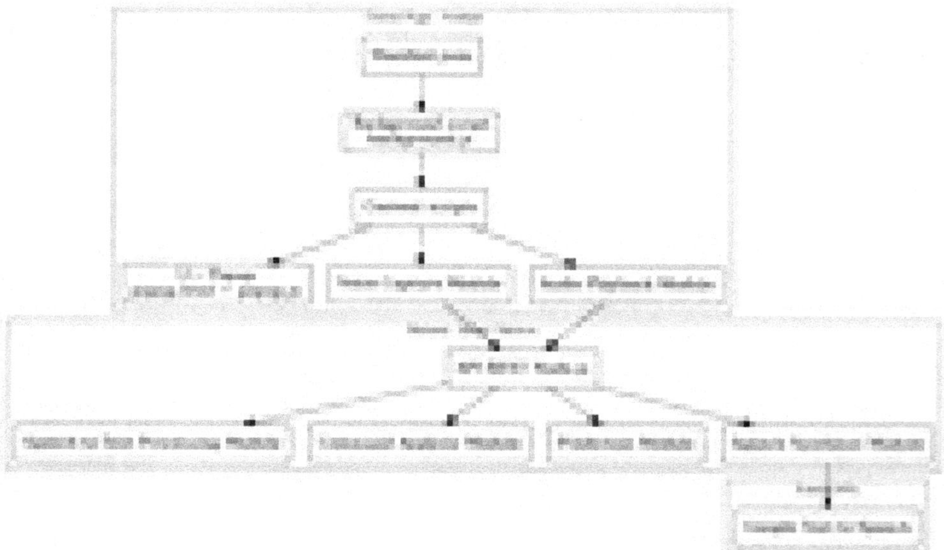

COMPONENTS OPERATION

This section details the actions that each component performs to achieve the operability of the digital assistant to execute the given commands. A separation between frontend and backend was decided, guaranteeing a fluid and efficient user experience, each of these is explained below.

- **Frontend**: Corresponds to the Google Chrome plugin, which serves as the communication and interaction channel with the user and the assistant. This is composed of:
  - **Manifest.json:** Defines the permissions and structure of the plugin to ensure that it can access the microphone, send and receive data, and execute scripts necessary for its operation.
  - **Background script (background.js):** Listen for global events, manage the plugin lifecycle, and coordinate data sending between the frontend and backend, maintaining state persistence.
  - **Content Scripts:** They capture the user's voice, monitor interaction within the browser, and manage possible visual elements that facilitate accessibility.
  - **UI / Popup:** Simple interface for the user to control the plugin, activating the wizard and modifying custom settings.
  - **Voice Capture Module:** Converts voice into digital signals using native APIs, ensuring the quality and availability of data for further processing, converting audio into text using native Chrome technology.
  - **Audio Playback Module:** Manages the playback of system responses, facilitating clear and synchronized auditory feedback.
- **Backend**: it is made up of a group of coordinated services, taking care of the intensive processing of the assistant, interprets the commands with the help of Artificial Intelligence and generates responses in audio format using external services. This is composed of:
  - **REST API (Backend):** Receives requests from the plugin and orchestrates processing, analysis, and response generation services.
  - **Command Analysis Module:** Apply natural language processing techniques and specific rules to identify the user's intent and prepare the action to be executed.
  - **Prediction Module:** It uses artificial intelligence models to select the optimal response or action to be carried out by the system, improving adaptability and accuracy.
  - **Speech Synthesis Module:** Converts the generated text into natural audio using the Google Text-to-Speech API, closing the communication loop with the user.

SELECTION OF TECHNOLOGIES

For the development of the prototype, an exhaustive review of the literature (hidden) had to be carried out to determine the technologies necessary for the construction of digital assistants, analyzing the tools and services available for Natural Language Processing, speech recognition and development of plugins for web browsers. While previous research has mainly focused on identifying and classifying accessible applications for people with visual disabilities that use voice assistants, there remains a gap in the practical implementation and evaluation of such technologies within educational contexts, particularly in virtual learning environments (VLEs). This information is discussed in more detail in the following sub-topics.

Natural Language Processing

From the systematic review of the literature, relevant information was collected on the development of voice assistants using Natural Language Processing (NLP) techniques and their integration into web browsers. Below is a comparative summary of the main types of neural networks used in NLP (see table 1), detailing their advantages, limitations, typical applications and prior knowledge necessary for their use.

Table 1. Classification of types of neural networks for NLP

Neural Network Type	Advantages	Limitations	Applications	Prior knowledge
RNN (Recurrent Neural Networks)	Good for simple sequences, useful in basic text tasks.	Fading gradient problem, slow in long sequences.	Sentiment analysis, text classification, simple text generation.	It requires understanding recurrent neural sequences and gradients.
LSTM (Long-Short-Term Memory)	Captures long-term dependencies, overcomes gradient issues.	High computational cost, slow in large models.	Speech recognition, complex text generation, voice assistants, machine translation	It requires solid knowledge in RNN and long sequence processing.
GRU (Gated Recurrent Units)	Efficient compared to LSTM, useful in real-time.	Lower accuracy in long-term dependency tasks compared to LSTM and transformers.	Automatic responses, real-time recommendation systems, processing of short and medium sequences.	It requires a basic understanding of recurring networks and sequence processing.
Transformers	They capture long-term dependencies without fading gradient; the current standard in NLP.	High demand for data and resources, impractical for low-capacity devices.	Advanced models such as BERT, GPT, machine translation, text generation, advanced voice assistants, text comprehension.	It requires advanced knowledge in NLP, self-care, and handling large volumes of data.

Table 1 summarizes the most relevant aspects of each type of neural network and facilitates the comparison for the appropriate selection. Based on this information, it was decided to use LSTM neural networks for the design and training of two specific models focused on:

- The classification and action of the commands of the digital assistant.
- The classification of the HTML elements of the NAME-PLATAFORM-HIDDEN INSTI-HIDDEN platform.

This choice seeks to balance precision and computational efficiency, allowing robust performance in the tasks required by the prototype.

NLP Apis

Similarly, extensive research was carried out on Natural Language Processing (NLP) APIs available on the market, with the aim of integrating the functionality necessary for the development of the digital assistant. The results obtained are summarized in Table 2, which compares the main options in terms of main function, advantages, limitations and typical applications.

Table 2. Natural Language Processing APIs

API / Service	Main function	Advantages	Limitations	Typical Applications
Google Cloud Speech-to-Text API	Convert speech to text, multilingual support.	High accuracy, scalability, easy integration with other Google services, monthly free conversion minutes.	Cost per use in large volumes.	Voice assistants, real-time transcription.
IBM Watson Natural Language Understanding	Sentiment analysis, text classification, keyword extraction.	Extensive customization, advanced NLP tools.	It can be very expensive compared to other options.	Sentiment analysis, content categorization, chatbots.
Amazon Transcribe	Real-time voice transcription, support for accents.	High accuracy, easily integrates with other AWS services.	It can have high costs in long-term applications.	Voice assistants, call analytics, real-time captioning.
Hugging Face Transformers	Pre-trained models for text comprehension and generation.	Variety of pre-trained models, free, flexibility for customization.	High resource consumption may require advanced hardware for large models.	Chatbos, sentiment analysis, advanced text generation.

The evaluation of this information made it possible to identify the most suitable services for the bidirectional conversion between voice and text, essential components for the digital assistant's communication engine. Taking into account accuracy, scalability, ease of integration, and costs, it was determined that the Google Cloud Speech-to-Text API is the most suitable option for the project.

Local Speech Capture Technologies: Web Speech API

For local voice capture, the Web Speech API is used, a native functionality of the Google Chrome browser that facilitates the detection and processing of voice commands without the need for additional software. This API allows you to implement speech recognition and audio synthesis using JavaScript interfaces, enabling direct and efficient integration into web applications and browser extensions.

The implementation of the Web Speech API is mainly done with JavaScript, a standard language for web frontend development, which interacts with the DOM and the browser APIs. For testing and prototyping, this API is an accessible tool that allows you to start, pause, and receive speech recognition results asynchronously, facilitating the rapid development and validation of speech functionalities in real time.

However, since the processing is supported by Google's cloud services, its use is conditioned by the availability and policies of the provider. As shown in Figure 10, the activation and basic operation of the Web Speech API is simple and allows for efficient capture of voice commands in the browser.

Figure 10. Activation Function of the Web Speech API

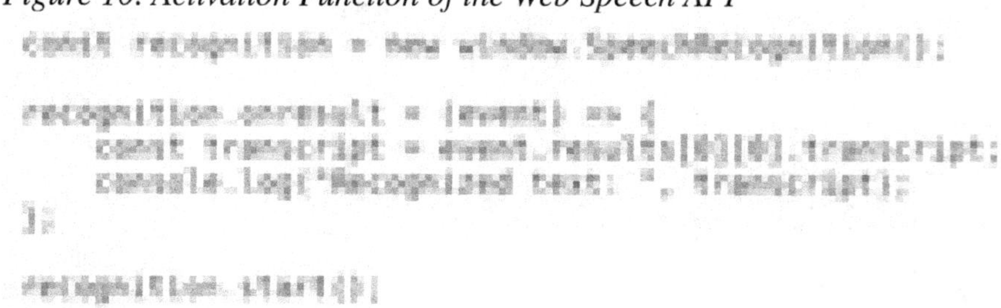

The system was designed with modularity and adaptability in mind to ensure robustness against future updates to the virtual learning platform's interface. By decoupling the voice assistant's core logic from the user interface layer and using standardized APIs for data exchange, the system can accommodate changes in the platform's structure with minimal reconfiguration. This design also allows rapid integration with other learning management systems in the future.

Plugin Development In Google Chrome

The construction of the plugin for Google Chrome is based on the official extension development guide provided by Google (Google Developers, 2024). The basic structure comprises files and modules that allow interaction with the browser, event management and communication with external services.

The main languages and technologies used to develop this plugin are:

- **JavaScript**: This is the primary language for programming the extension's logic, including background scripts (background.js), content scripts, and event handling.
- **HTML5**: To build the plugin's user interface, especially in popup files or pop-up panels (popup.html).
- **CSS3**: For the design and stylization of the visual interface, guaranteeing accessibility and usability.
- **JSON**: To define the manifest.json file, which is the declarative descriptor where essential permissions, resources, scripts, and settings for the plugin are specified.

The plugin uses browser-specific APIs, such as the Local Storage API, cross-script messaging, and access to input devices (microphone), all handled from JavaScript. This modular architecture allows the components of the plugin to work in a coordinated but independent manner, facilitating the scalability, maintainability and updating of the system. The typical structure and components required for the development of a plugin in Chrome are presented in Figure 11, which shows the essential files and modules that make up a functional extension.

Figure 11. Structure of the Plugin.

GENERATION OF THE DATASETS

For the development of the classification model, it was necessary to build specific datasets that represented in a structured way the elements present in the NAME-PLATAFORM-HIDDEN educational platform of the INSTI-HIDDEN. This section describes the process by which the data that would serve as input for the training and validation of the proposed model were identified, analyzed, and organized.

Html Elements In Name-Plataform-Hidden

The HTML elements that make up the NAME-PLATAFORM-HIDDEN interface were selected as base units for the analysis, given their relevance in the interaction of users with the platform. The structural analysis carried out on these elements is detailed below, as well as the procedure followed to generate a dataset suitable for classification tasks.

Structural Analysis And Dataset Generation For Html Element Classification Model

For the training of the classification model of HTML elements of the NAME-PLATAFORM-HIDDEN platform, an exhaustive analysis of the platform's public code was carried out, allowing the extraction and tagging of the key elements that make up the structure of the interface.

Using the Google Chrome browser's element inspector (See Figure 12), the different visible and functional sections of the NAME-PLATAFORM-HIDDEN

INSTI-HIDDEN platform were manually analyzed, which allowed us to identify ten main sections:

- Login
- Course Listing
- Messages
- Content
- Activities
- Forums
- Tests
- Members
- Headings
- Interactive lounge

Figure 12. Google Chrome HTML Elements Inspector.

Other sections that were more complex or difficult to access were discarded, mainly because they were inside nested or protected HTML structures, making it difficult to capture and tag effectively for training, such as: Course Management, My Upload to SIIU, Privacy Notice, Help, and My Profile. The manual analysis also allowed to identify and classify the HTML tags most relevant to the navigation and functionality of the system, which are described in Table 3.

Table 3. Navigation labels in NAME-PLATAFORM-HIDDEN

Label	Description	Function
M-course	Main module of courses.	Display information about courses available on the platform.
mat-card	Course information card.	Displays details of each course such as name, term, and status.
button	Interactive buttons.	Used for actions such as adding or removing courses, filtering, or changing views.
b _ngcontent	Action link.	When executing the function it allows clicking on the element, redirecting to the interior of the element.
h3	Section title.	Displays the name of the section you're in.
m-activity-resource-list	Activity information card.	Displays the list of cards with information on the corresponding activities.
m-cards-content-list	Content information card.	It contains the elements that are generated in the content of each course.
m-exam-list	Exam information card.	Displays the list of cards with information on the corresponding exams.
m-courses-member	Information card of course members.	It contains the elements that represent the information of the members of a course.
m-course-forum	Forum information card.	Displays the list of cards with information from the forums available in the course.
m-course-msg-center	Message center information card.	It contains the elements that centralize the course messages in a single place.
m-interactive-lounge-list	Classroom information card.	Displays the list of cards with interactive classroom information.
m-rubric-card	Rubric information card.	It contains the cards with detailed information about the evaluation rubrics.
div.m-alert__text.h3. KT-portlet__head-title	Title of the elements.	Displays the title of related items, such as activities, quizzes, and forums.
h3. KT-portlet__head-title	Action link.	It contains the action link that allows you to enter the selected items.
m-aside-left	Navigation menu information card.	Displays the options available in the side navigation menu.
li.m-menu__item	Navigation menu items.	It contains the individual items of the navigation menu.
a.m-menu__link	Action link.	Displays the action link for each menu option.
a.m-menu_link.span. m-menu__link-text	Title of navigation menu items.	Contains the descriptive title of the navigation menu items.

Web Scraping For Automatic Extraction In Name-Plataform-Hidden

NAME-PLATAFORM-HIDDEN is an educational platform that is developed in Angular 4, for this reason a data extraction in a practical way was not possible, because the content is dynamic according to how the information in the sections is used. For this reason, to complement the manual analysis and obtain a sufficient volume of data for training, a script was developed in Python 3.12 using the Selenium library together with ChromeDriver to automate the navigation and extraction of dynamic HTML content generated by Angular or other technologies on the platform (see Figures 13 and 14).

Figure 13. Basic Libraries for Web Scraping.

Figure 14. Method for Web Scraping.

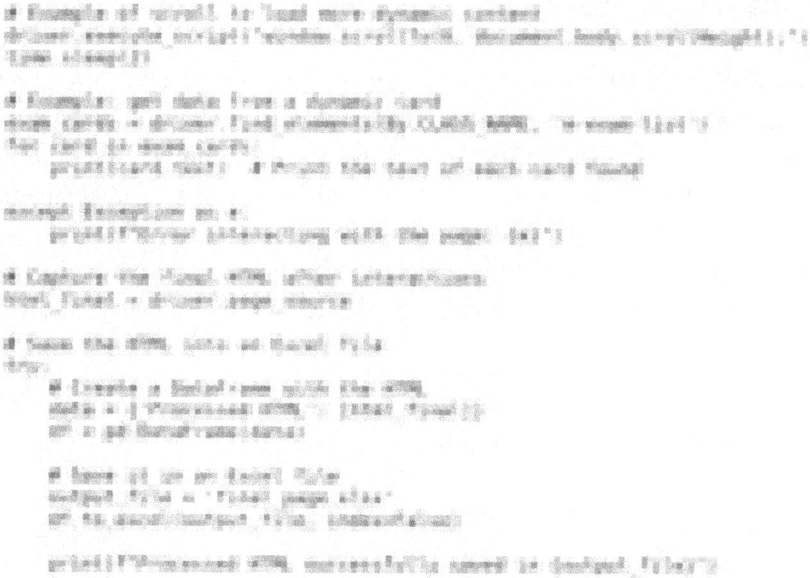

Those scripts allow each one, identify main section to be processed, capturing the rendered content that is then exported in Excel format to facilitate its analysis and preparation of the dataset. This technique is essential to handle dynamic platforms where content is generated or modified in real time in the browser.

During the execution of the web scraping, a total of 4781 lines of HTML code were extracted from the analyzed sections. The frequency of occurrence of the key tags was plotted to identify the most recurrent and relevant elements for classification (see Figure 15), this information was collected in a dataset for subsequent analysis and training.

Figure 15. Frequency Chart of HTML Elements in NAME-PLATAFORM-HIDDEN.

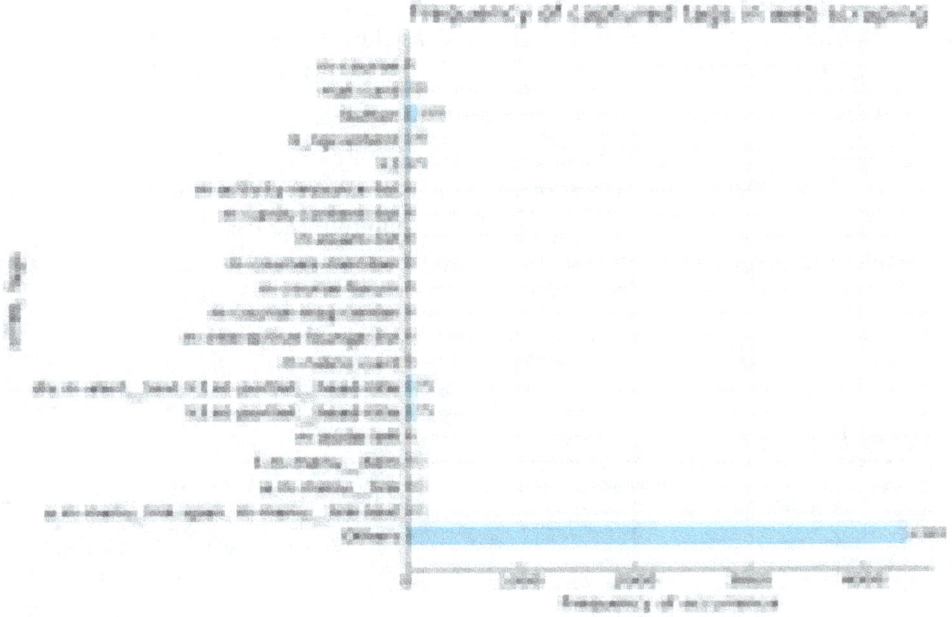

Dataset Preprocessing, Cleanup, And Balancing

With the dataset generated from the structural analysis and the automated extraction of HTML content from the NAME-PLATAFORM-HIDDEN platform, a neural network model capable of classifying the different HTML elements present was trained (see Table 4), thus facilitating the automated interpretation of the platform's structure by the digital assistant.

The dataset consisted of the HTML tags and their corresponding attributes, as well as contextual information extracted from the relevant sections. Pre-processing was performed that included:

- **Data cleansing**: Removal of duplicate or irrelevant labels to the training objective. Mainly, elements that did not correspond to navigation such as images, texts, among others, were eliminated.
- **Labeling**: As shown in table 19, four labels were generated to classify the items obtained. These are actions that defined which event generated the HTML element divided by button, link or title event. The section tag allowed us to identify which section of the NAME-PLATAFORM-HIDDEN platform it belonged to, likewise, the description tag includes a brief description of the

element. Finally, the HTML code of the read element is maintained in the HTML code tag.

- **Balancing**: An adjustment was made to the dataset obtained because the sample obtained was very low, being 8.2% of the total data. To correct the imbalance generated by the predominance of non-useful data and the scarce number of useful examples, the SMOTE (Synthetic Minority Over-sampling Technique) technique was applied, which allowed the generation of synthetic samples for the minority classes, thus expanding the useful dataset and balancing the distribution between the different categories. At the end, a dataset of 8778 elements was obtained.

Table 4. Tagging HTML elements

Field	Exemplary Values	Description
Action	button, link, title	The type of HTML element or action it represents, such as interactive button, link, or title.
section	login, course_list, course_content, course_activity, course_exam, course_member, course_forum, course_message, course_messages, course_rubrica, nav_bar, course_msg_center	Section or context within the NAME-PLATAFORM-HIDDEN platform where the HTML element is located.
Description	Texts such as: "log in", "go to course listing", "open course", "go to messages", "section title", "go to activity", "go to forum", "log out", "open message option"	A functional or textual description detailing the purpose or function of the HTML element within the platform.

Training The LSTM Model

To achieve an effective classification of the HTML elements present in the NAME-PLATAFORM-HIDDEN platform, a model based on LSTM (Long Short-Term Memory) neural networks was developed. This model was trained using a balanced dataset containing a total of 8,778 elements, the result of applying the SMOTE (Synthetic Minority Over-sampling Technique) technique to correct the initial imbalance in the distribution of classes.

The dataset includes both the HTML code of the elements and tags that describe their type of action (button, link, title), the section to which they belong within the platform and a brief functional description. To prepare the data for training, a preprocessing process was carried out that included tokenization using the TensorFlow/Keras Tokenizer class, which converts the texts of the HTML code into numerical sequences based on the index of each word or symbol within the vocabulary generated from the dataset. These sequences were then normalized by padding to ensure that all inputs were of the same length, making them easier to process by the model.

The architecture of the model (see Figure 16) consists of an embedding layer that transforms the tokens into dense vectors of semantic representation, followed by an LSTM layer responsible for capturing dependencies and long-term relationships between the elements of the HTML code. Subsequently, a dense layer with ReLU activation function processes the extracted features, to finally move on to a softmax output layer that determines the probability of belonging to each class, in Figure 17 we can see the summarized code that exemplifies the architecture used and the training process.

Figure 16. Architecture of the LSTM Model.

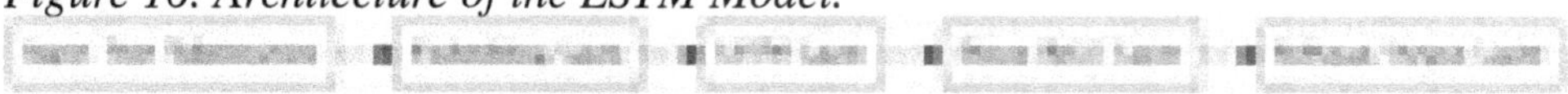

Figure 17. Summary Code of the LSTM Model.

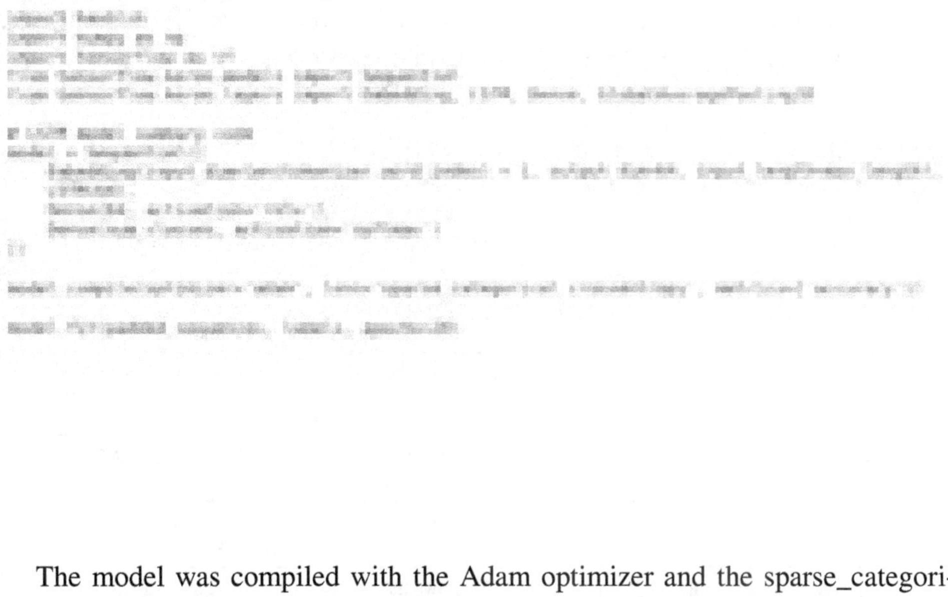

The model was compiled with the Adam optimizer and the sparse_categorical_crossentropy loss function, suitable for multiple classification problems. The training was carried out over 20 epochs, with hyperparameter adjustment to optimize accuracy and avoid oversetting. In addition, the dataset was divided into subsets for training, validation, and testing, which allowed evaluating the generalizability of the model with unseen data. The application of SMOTE in the balancing of the dataset was essential to increase the representativeness of minority classes, preventing the model from being biased towards majority classes and improving the quality of learning. Thanks to this combination of techniques and the ability of the LSTM model to interpret complex sequences, a robust tool was achieved that allows the HTML elements of the platform to be accurately classified, facilitating assisted navigation for visually impaired users.

Commands For Name-Plataform-Hidden

To complement the development of the digital assistant, in addition to the HTML element classification model, a specific dataset was generated for the classification and action of voice commands. This set of basic commands was collected directly from users during the initial phases of research and validation, ensuring that the wizard responded to real interaction needs.

Defining Digital Assistant Commands

Through the elicitation techniques applied and explained above, it was possible to define a list of 10 basic commands to be able to interact with the digital assistant thanks to the visually impaired participants. In Table 5, you can see these commands, along with the description of the activities that it performs.

Table 5. Digital Assistant Basic Command Table

Command	Description
Open NAME-PLATAFORM-HIDDEN	Allows the user to open the NAME-PLATAFORM-HIDDEN login page.
Sign in	Once the user has entered their username and password, they can log in with this command.
Tell me what courses I have	Tells the user which courses are available in the course area.
Log in to the [course name] course	Allows the user to enter the content of a course.
Tell me which section I'm in	It tells the user which section within NAME-PLATAFORM-HIDDEN they are in.
What sections does the Platform have?	It provides you with a list of the navigation sections that NAME-PLATAFORM-HIDDEN has.
Go to the [section name] section	It allows the user to move between sections.
Tell me what [activities, forums, exams] I have	It indicates to the user the list of [activities, forums, exams] that are available.
Tell me what [activities, forums, exams] are pending	It indicates to the user the list of [activities, forums, exams] that they have pending to do.
Return to home page	It allows the user to return to the platform's initial course screen.

To improve accuracy and avoid false activations, it was defined that all commands should be preceded by a keyword: “ALAN”, an acronym for Linguistic Assistant for Navigation Support. This word acts as a trigger that delimits the start of a command, ensuring that the wizard responds only when required, which significantly improves the user experience and the efficiency of the system.

Dataset Preprocessing, Cleanup, And Balancing

Before training the model, the dataset underwent a rigorous preprocessing process to prepare the text data and optimize the model's performance. Likewise, a balancing process was carried out including variants of the basic commands to have a greater number of elements for better training. Pre-processing was performed that included:

- **Text Cleaning:** A function (preprocess_text) was implemented to normalize each command. This step included converting all text to lowercase and removing numbers and all punctuation marks.
- **Vectorization (Feature Extraction):** The TfidfVectorizer class from scikit-learn was used. This technique converts the clean text commands into a matrix of numerical vectors. Instead of just counting words, TF-IDF (Term Frequency-Inverse Document Frequency) weighs the importance of each word based on its frequency within the command and its inverse frequency across the entire dataset.
- **Labeling**: Each preprocessed command was associated with its corresponding action label (e.g., 'command' -> 'action'), generating the structured pairs necessary for supervised training.
- **Dataset Split:** The entire dataset was divided into two subsets using the train_test_split function, with a test_size of 0.2:
    - **80% for Training:** Used for the MultinomialNB model to learn the association patterns between the vectorized text and the labels.
    - **20% for Testing:** Used to evaluate the model's accuracy and performance on unseen data, providing a measure of its generalizability.
- **Balancing**: To prevent the model from being biased towards the most frequent classes and to improve its learning capacity, dataset balancing was performed. This process consisted of manually generating synthetic variants of the basic commands, particularly for the minority classes. This strategy ensured a more equitable representation of the different classes, improving the overall quality of the training data. At the end of this process, a balanced dataset with 150 variants of the basic commands was obtained, which was used as the final input for training the model.

Table 6. Digital assistant command tagging

Field	Exemplary Values	Description
command	Hi Alan, Hey Alan, Good day Alan, Alan open, Alan visit, Alan go to, open	This label allows you to identify the corresponding command, textually written.
Action	activation, open_web, navigation, search, commands	It allows you to identify what action the given command performs, this allows you to execute the corresponding operation.

Figure 18. Sample of the Balanced Commands.

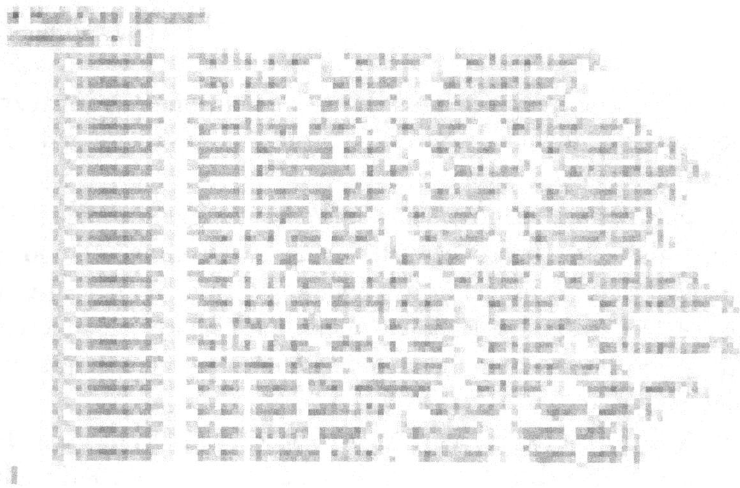

Training The Classification Model

For the classification of user commands, we implemented a Multinomial Naïve Bayes (MNB) model, a probabilistic classifier from the scikit-learn library. This approach was selected for its high efficiency and robust performance in text classification tasks, particularly with limited datasets. Unlike a deep neural network, this architecture uses a sequential machine learning pipeline, which is encapsulated in the CommandClassifier class. The process consists of two main stages:

- **Feature Extraction (TF-IDF Vectorizer):** This component (TfidfVectorizer) handles all text preprocessing. First, it cleans the text by converting it to lowercase, removing numbers, and stripping all punctuation. Then, it converts the cleaned commands into a numerical matrix using the TF-IDF (Term Frequency-Inverse Document Frequency) algorithm. This technique weighs the importance of each word based on its frequency in a command relative to its frequency across the entire dataset.
- **Classification (Multinomial Naïve Bayes):** This is the core model (MultinomialNB) that performs the classification. It is trained on the TF-IDF matrix and the corresponding action labels. The model learns the probability of each word appearing in each class. During prediction, it uses these probabilities (based on Bayes' theorem) to determine the most likely action for a new, unseen command.

The model is trained by calling the .fit() method with the training texts and labels. Figure 19 shows the complete Python class that implements this pipeline, including methods for training, prediction, and saving/loading the trained model.

Figure 19. Training of the Commands Model.

This Naïve Bayes model demonstrated a robust performance in the classification of new commands. As detailed in the training script, the model was validated using a 20% test subset, achieving a final accuracy of 82%. The classification report also confirmed high precision and recall across the key action classes. This performance evidenced the model's ability to effectively interpret the user's intention and translate it into concrete actions. Therefore, this specific Naïve Bayes implementation is the one that was used to generate all results and conduct all user evaluations presented in this chapter.

Prototype Evaluation

The evaluation process is an important part of any software development project, through this point information is obtained in a qualitative (comments, observation) and quantitative (time, errors, rates) way that allows to better perceive how end users can use a product in certain environments. According to the study of the Faculty of Pediatrics, three dimensions of usability were analyzed: effectiveness (ability to complete tasks), efficiency (resources/times needed) and satisfaction (user perception) (Nielsen, 2012).

Characteristics Of The Participants

Two students from the INST-NAME-HIDDEN participated, both familiar with NAME-PLATAFORM-HIDDEN (See, Table 7). Student A1 has bilateral total blindness (no light perception) and intermediate experience with NVDA; Student A2 has low monocular vision and basic experience with NVDA. This sample composition allowed to contrast the performance of the prototype between a user without visual remainder and another with ≈15% functional vision in one eye, keeping the screen reader used constant.

Table 7. Users Characteristic

Students	Functional vision	OD	OI	Screen readers	Reader Experience
A1	No light perception	0%	0%	NVDA	Intermediate
A2	Monocular low vision (≈15%)	0%	15%	NVDA	Basic

Experimental Environment And Control

In order to ensure equipment equivalence between participants and conditions, A1 and A2 performed the tasks on the same two teams: one computer with NVDA for the Screen Reader condition, and a second computer with Google Chrome and the digital assistant plugin installed. This control minimizes the threat of hardware/

software bias; any difference in performance is mainly attributed to the tool evaluated and not to the team (See, Table 8).

Table 8. Test Equipment Conditions

Team	Operating system	Ancillary Software	Browser	Audio Input/Output	Internet connection
C1	Windows	NVDA Screen Reader	Google Chrome	Microphone / Speakers integrated into equipment	Yes
C2	IOS	ALAN Digital Assistant	Google Chrome	Microphone / Speakers integrated into equipment	Yes

INSTRUMENTS AND VARIABLES

The tools or means used to collect the data that made it possible to evaluate the results of the project, as well as the aspects or characteristics to be measured, are specified in the following three instruments:

Instrument 1. Observation rubric (scale 1–3)

Purpose. Capture the quality of the interaction in real time and the need for support during the execution of tasks (See Table 9).

Structure and categories:

- Activating the Wizard
- Understanding Commands
- Auditory feedback
- Section/course navigation
- Information queries
- User autonomy
- Runtime
- Reaction to errors.

Achievement Criteria:

- **(3): High: consistent** behavior, smooth execution, and no assistance.
- **(2): Medium:** execution with small delays or punctual support
- **(1): Low:** frequent doubts, interruptions or need for constant assistance.

Table 9. Instrument 1. Observation rubric

Category	Observable indicator	Performance Level	User Observations
Activating the Wizard	**The wizard is activated correctly with the corresponding key combination.**		
Understanding Commands	Correctly interprets the given voice commands		
Auditory feedback	Provide clear and understandable answers		
Section/course navigation	Allows the user to access desired sections and courses		
Information queries	Properly list courses, sections, activities, etc.		
User autonomy	The user is able to perform the tasks without additional help		
Runtime	Tasks are performed efficiently		
Reaction to errors	The wizard reports properly detected command errors		

Instrument 2. Comparison by test cases (objective metrics)

Purpose. Measure effectiveness and efficiency of each tool on equivalent tasks.

Operational variables and definitions (See Table 10):

- **Time:** duration per CP from beginning (issuance of the first command or equivalent action) to end (achievement of the defined objective). All times were normalized to seconds; e.g., 8 min → 480 sec, 1 sec → 1 sec.
- **# Errors:** Command attempts that do not result in the expected action (failed reconnaissance, wrong path, reversed navigation); counted per event.
- **# Attempts:** Repetitions of command or action to achieve the goal of the CP, regardless of whether they are considered errors.
- **Completed (Yes/No):** The PC goal is reached or not within the session time.
- **Autonomy (Yes/No):** The user did not require external help to complete the CP.

Table 10. Tool 2: Comparison of test cases

Test cases	Tools to evaluate									
	Screen reader					Screen reader				
	Time	# Errors	# Attempts	Completed	Autonomy	Time	# Errors	# Attempts	Completed	Autonomy
CP-001										
CP-004										
CP-005										
CP-006										
CP-007										
CP-008										
CP-009										
CP-010										
CP-011										

Instrument 3. Likert survey (scale 1–5)

Purpose. Capture satisfaction, sense of control, and perceived usefulness after using the assistant.
Structure. Elements on ease of use, control, clarity of responses, location within the platform, autonomy and perceived speed (See Table 11).

Scale:

1 = Strongly disagree
2 = Disagree
3 = Neutral
4 = Agree
5 = Strongly agree

Table 11. Instrument 3: Semi-structured interview

Question	Rating (1-5)
The digital assistant is easier to use than the screen reader	
I felt more in control when using the digital assistant.	
I was able to find the sections and courses easily with voice commands.	
The assistant provided clear and helpful answers.	
Using the assistant increased my autonomy when navigating in NAME-PLATAFORM-HIDDEN.	
The assistant responded correctly to most of my voice commands.	
The assistant helped me better identify my location within the platform.	
The actions I performed with the assistant were fast and fluid.	
I believe that this type of technology can complement or improve existing screen readers.	
I would recommend this assistant to other visually impaired people.	
Response speed settings	
Different types of voices	
Response in different languages	

RESULTS

This section presents the findings of the evaluation of the voice assistant with the support of the participants mentioned in the NAME-PLATAFORM-HIDDEN platform. The results are organized into five axes: temporal efficiency, effectiveness and autonomy, operational robustness (errors and attempts), quality of the observed interaction (rubric) and perceived satisfaction (Likert), which are detailed in the following sections.

Time Efficiency

During the test, it was detected that the voice assistant clearly reduced the execution times in both participants. For A1 we can see how the average time went from 151.3s with the NVDA reader to 9.4s with the assistant, having a reduction of 93.8%; while for A2, it went from 157.s to 21.9s. At the level of the cases executed per student, the magnitude of the time savings was very consistent: for A1, cases CP-004 (480s → 2s; −99.6%) and CP-011 (300→1 s; −99.7%) stand out; for A2, CP-008 (240→7 s; −97.1%) and CP-004 (420→31 s; −92.6%). For the A2 tests, punctual peaks in the time differences with respect to A1 were detected as shown in

Figures 20, 21, 22, this caused by network latency affecting response time, however, this did not alter the improvement trend.

Figure 20. Average Time per Tool (lower is better).

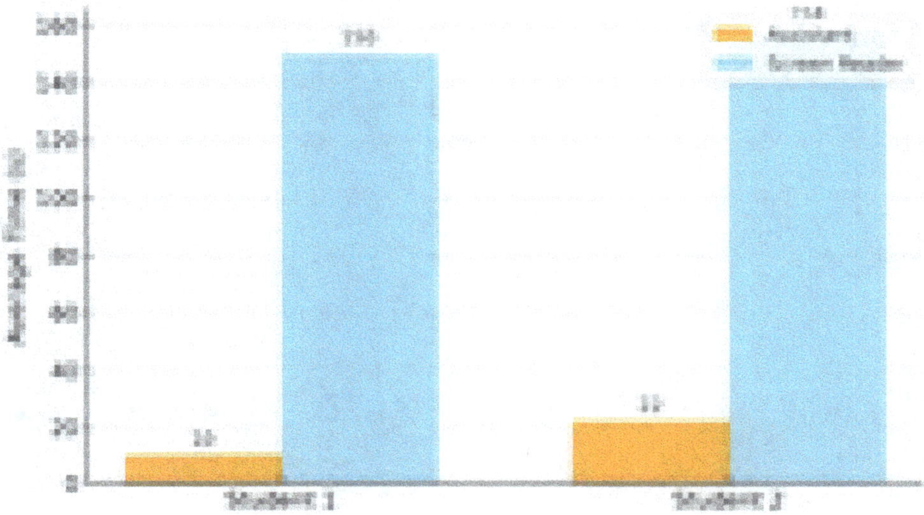

Figure 21. Times per Case (Student 1). Identifies CP with Greatest Benefit.

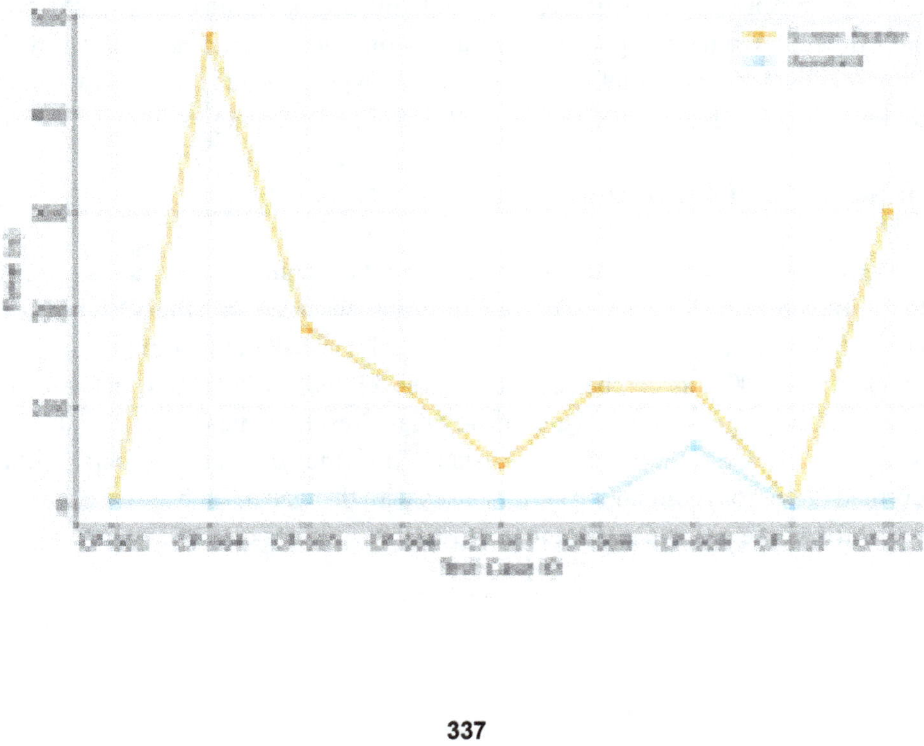

Figure 22. Times per Case (Student 2). Shows Peaks Associated with Latency.

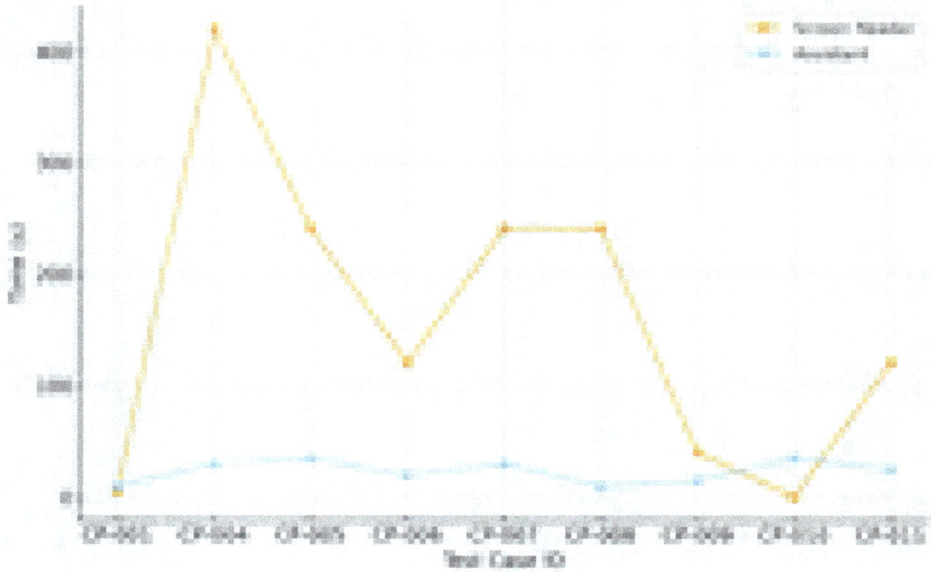

Because the evaluation revealed that network latency affected system performance for one of the participants, emphasizing the need to address external factors that may influence the user experience. To mitigate these issues, future iterations of the system architecture will include mechanisms to manage communication delays more effectively. Specifically, the REST request module could incorporate retry strategies to handle timeouts or failed responses gracefully, while the user interface could provide clearer feedback, such as brief voice prompts ("I'm processing your request…"), to maintain user engagement and reduce confusion during latency periods.

Efficiency And Autonomy

It was observed that, with the use of the digital assistant, both students reached 100% completion in all test cases, correcting errors observed with the NVDA reader (A1: 77.8%→100%; A2: 66.7%→100%). This allowed the autonomy to increase from 66.7% to 100% as can be seen in Figures 23 and 24. Although the students needed help just to remember the commands, the results indicate that, in addition to speeding up execution, the digital assistant allows the elimination of barriers that prevented them from completing certain tasks with the reader, such as, for example, going through the entire page just to get the names of their courses.

Figure 23. Completion Rate per Tool. The Assistant Reaches 100% in Both Students.

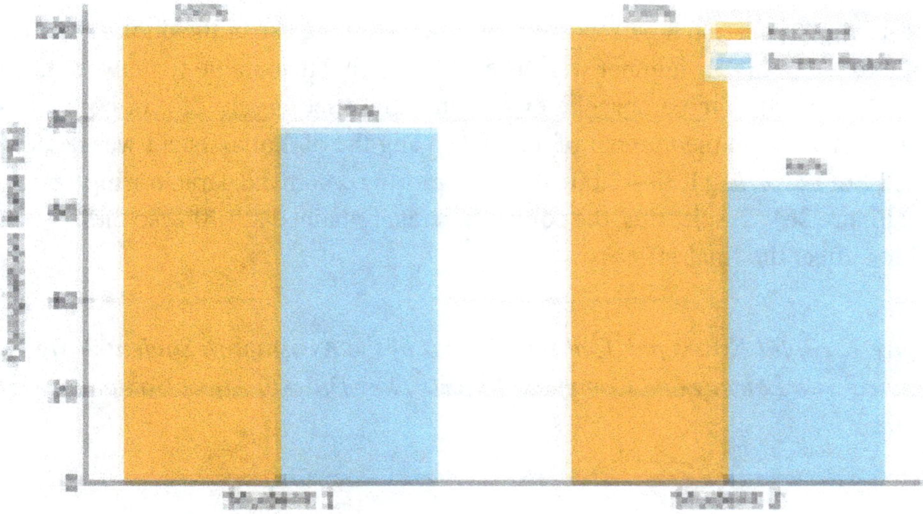

Figure 24. Autonomy Rate per Tool. 100% Autonomy with the Assistant.

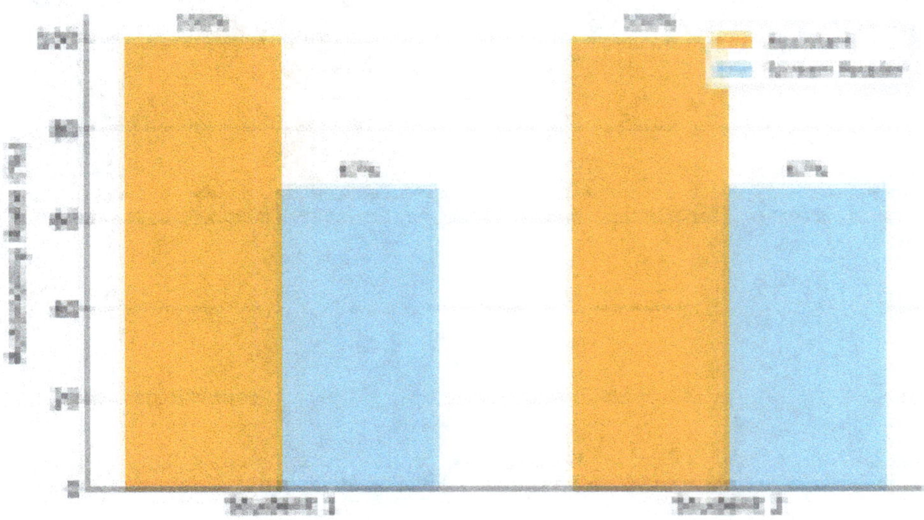

Operational Robustness (Errors And Attempts)

During the A1 test, no errors were recorded with the use of the digital assistant, while for A2 a higher number was observed, mainly attributable to network latency and the need to remember the exact command (See Figure 25). In both cases, a slight increase in the number of attempts using the digital assistant was detected (A1: 1.56→2.11; A2: 1.33→2.00), this by exploring command paraphrasing variants (see Figure 26). Despite this, the completion rate remained at 100%, so these events did not affect the final efficacy.

Figure 25. Total Errors per Tool. The Errors of the Assistant in Student 2 Are Associated with Latency and Command Recall; They Did Not Affect Completeness.

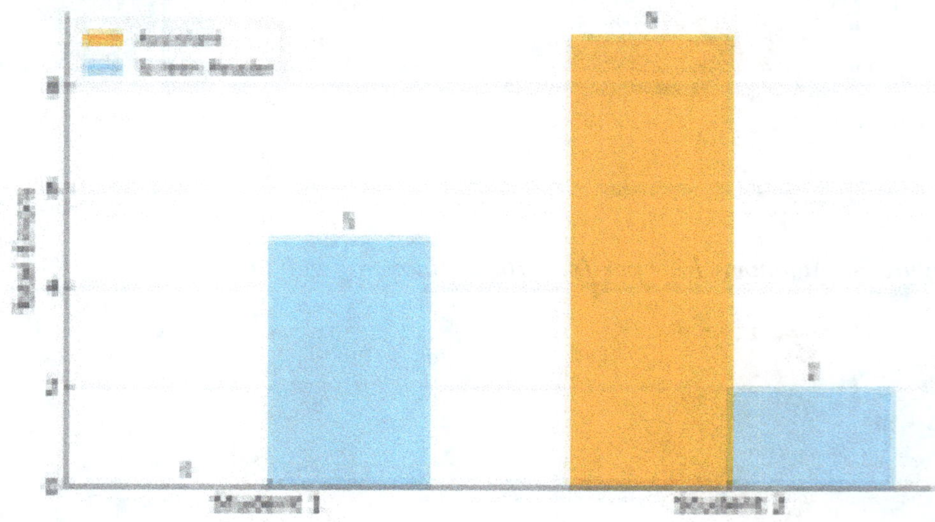

Figure 26. Average Attempts per Tool. Slight Increase Due to Command Search; Design Opportunity (Voice Assistance/Variants).

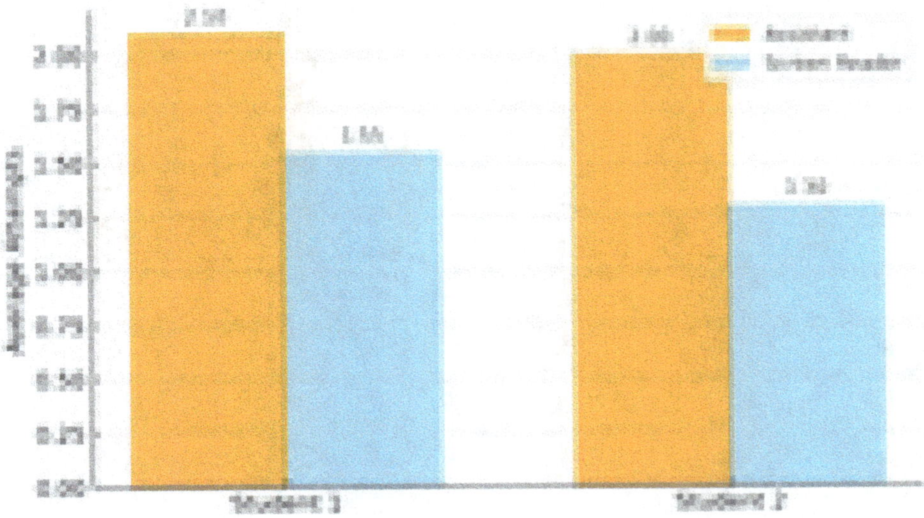

Quality Of Interaction Observed (Rubric 1–3)

The observation rubric showed high performance (level 3/3) in the categories: activation, command comprehension, auditory feedback, navigation, information queries, and autonomy. The opportunities for improvement were mainly concentrated in execution times (2/3) and reaction to errors (1/3) as we can see in Figure 27. These last two dimensions confirm that it is essential to incorporate status warnings (active, listening, processing) and explicit messages when the system does not understand a command or there is poor connectivity.

Figure 27. Performance Rubric by Category (1–3). Strengths in 6/8 Categories; Opportunities in Time and Error Response.

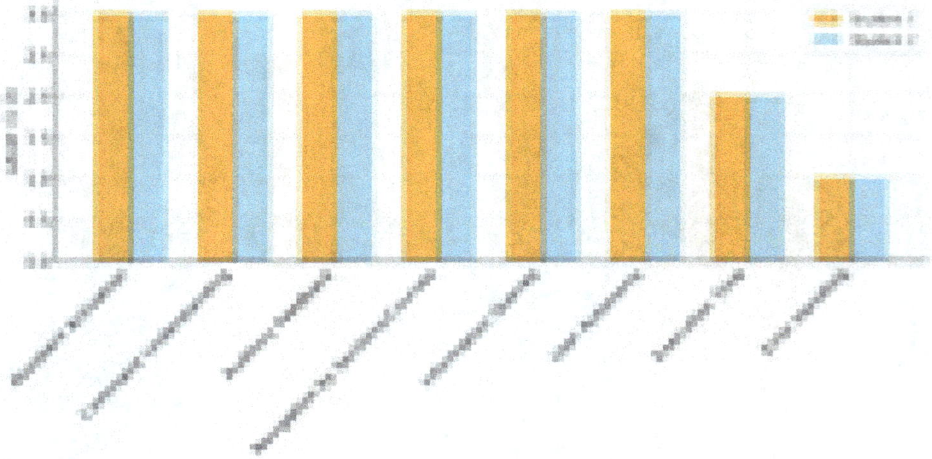

Participant Feedback And Qualitative Insights

To complement the quantitative metrics, direct feedback was collected from participants immediately after the sessions. These qualitative insights reveal the human impact of the prototype, particularly regarding cognitive load and emotional well-being during navigation.

- **Reduction of Navigation Fatigue: Student A1 (Total blindness) highlighted the stark difference between linear navigation and direct command execution:** "With NVDA, I usually must listen to every single link on the menu before I find the 'My Courses' section. It´s tiring. With the assistant, I just asked for it, and I was there immediately. This allowed me to get the information faster without the fatigue of listening to all the options using NVDA.".
- **Increased Confidence and Reduced Anxiety: Studen A2 (Low vision) noted that the assistant removed the visual strain and the fear of getting lost in the interface:** "Usually, I get nervous trying to find specific homework sections because the screen is cluttered, and I must squint to find the right icon. Using voice commands made me feel more in control. I didn´t have to search visually; I just said what I needed, and the system did the hard work for me.".

- **Perception of Latency vs Utility:** Regarding the network delays mentioned in the efficiency sections, participants were tolerant of the wait times given the trade-off: "Even when the assistant took a few seconds to think (due to latency), it was still much faster and less frustrating than pressing 'Tab' twenty times to get to the same place" remarked Student A1.

These testimonials confirm that the improvement in times (quantitative) translates directly into a reduction in frustration ad in the sense of autonomy (qualitative) for the end user.

Satisfaction And Perception (Likert 1–5)

The rating of the digital assistant was high: 4.77/5 in A1 and 4.85/5 in A2, both agreed on its ease of use, sense of control, clarity of responses, location within the platform and autonomy (See Figure 28). Suggestion additions such as response speed, voice types, language support, are considered product requirements and will be addressed in the recommendations and future work section.

Figure 28. Average Satisfaction/Perception (Likert). Values Close to 5 Indicate High Agreement.

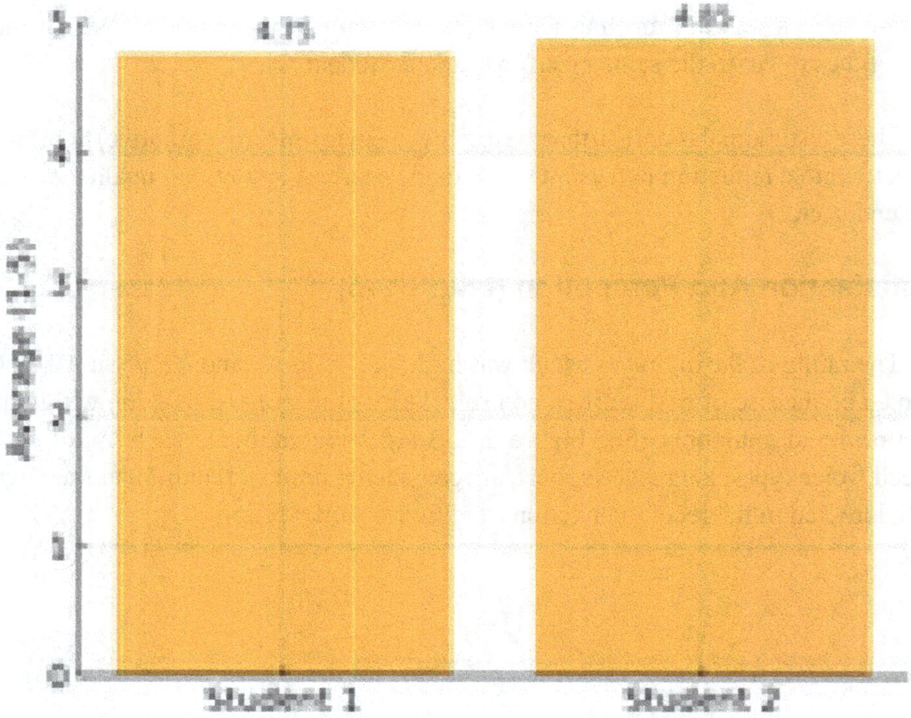

Qualitative Comments From Users

It was undoubtedly gratifying to hear the users' comments about how incredibly easy it was to understand the sections using voice commands. Their opinion was also corroborated by those of us who were present during the testing. Users commented on their experiences using the screen reader; however, that difference disappeared when using a natural interface, thanks to this interface, they commented on the simplicity of the tasks.

LIMITATIONS AND FUTURE RESEARCH

The research presented in this chapter presents some important limitations:

- Limited number of users: In this sense, the limited number of users with the role of student is short. Also, it is important to say that other students showed no interest in participating.
- Adherence to the educational studied platform: Another significant aspect is that there is an adherence to the institutional platform, therefore, much of what is shown is based on the manual analysis of the existing infrastructure.
- In addition, the results revealed that some users had difficulty recalling specific voice commands, underscoring the need for a structured onboarding process. For visually impaired users, onboarding could include guided voice tutorials, progressive disclosure of commands, and contextual feedback that reinforces correct usage. These elements are crucial to help users internalize the interaction model and build confidence with the new voice-based paradigm.
- The HTML classification model (LSTM) is trained on the specific DOM structure of the NAME-PLATAFORM-HIDDEN. A significant front-end update by the platform's developers could alter the tags and class names, reducing the model's accuracy. Future research will explore strategies for dynamic adaptation, such as implementing few-shot learning or transfer learning techniques. This would allow the model to be fine-tuned on a small, new set of labeled examples after an update, rather than requiring a complete and costly retraining process from scratch.
- The current HTML classification process relies on a manually intensive process of web scraping and labeling, which is tightly coupled to the DOM of NAME-PLATAFORM-HIDDEN. Adapting this solution to other VLEs (e.g., Moodle, Canvas, Blackboard) would present a significant challenge, as each platform has a radically different front-end architecture. A future research direction would be to develop a more generalized framework. This might involve creating a "mapping" system that allows an administrator to tag key elements (e.g., "course_list", "forum_link") on a new platform, which then automatically generates the training data for that VLE's specific structure.

Therefore, future research aims to apply the presented studies to a larger sample of users with visual impairments, such as those described in this chapter. It also proposes exploring the possibility of extending the plugin to other educational platforms.

CONCLUSIONS

The system favored web browsing on the NAME-PLATAFORM-HIDDEN-INSTI-HIDDEN educational platform for visually impaired students. Under controlled equipment conditions for both participants, a reduction in times of 86–94%, a completion rate of 100% and autonomy of 100% with the assistant were observed, accompanied by high satisfaction (≈4.8/5 in Likert) and high performance (3/3) in 6 of 8 categories of the rubric (activation, comprehension, auditory feedback, navigation, queries and autonomy). These results demonstrate a substantial improvement in accessibility and usability compared to the exclusive use of the screen reader. It could even be argued that the cognitive load was reduced, since, based on observations, finding a topic on the studied educational platform required a user to repeatedly navigate through the different elements. In the case of using the assistant, the information did not require iterating through the application's elements. As a result, in practical terms, the digital assistant not only allows users to speed up the completion of tasks but also allows them to overcome some barriers with the screen reader that prevented participants from completing some test cases.

This is especially relevant for the participation of visually impaired students in online educational settings such as NAME-PLATAFORM-HIDDEN. The efficiency observed in representative cases (e.g., 480 s to 2 s or 300 s to 1 s) suggests that the assistant displaces interaction bottlenecks and reduces the day-to-day operational burden.

The analysis of errors and attempts allowed us to have a better overview of the assistant and to be able to orient ourselves towards future work. In A1 the errors with the wizard disappear (5→0); in A2 they are increased (2→9) without affecting the final efficiency (it remains at 100%), this is explained by network latency and recall of the exact command.

The slight increase in attempts with the assistant in both participants is consistent with a phrasing-seeking phase, pointing to two clear lines of improvement: (1) linguistic tolerance (synonyms, different speech patterns, accents) and (2) voice help in context (what can I say now?). The rubric also demands explicit status signals such as active, listening, processing, error; and clear messaging in the event of failures or poor connectivity. Implementing these improvements would not only reduce errors and attempts, but would also reduce perceived uncertainty, reinforcing autonomy.

Another important aspect of system robustness concerns the adaptability of the assistant to potential updates in the host platform's interface. Since virtual learning environments frequently evolve, the system architecture was intentionally designed to be resilient to such changes.

Methodologically, the study controlled for hardware/software bias and triangulated three sources of evidence (objective metrics, structured observation, and perception).

As previously was said, there are some limitations such as the small sample size of users, a the use of a single VLE and screen reader, as well as, variable network conditions. Even so, the coherence between indicators and the magnitude of the improvements justify that it is possible to adopt a digital assistant in browsers as a complement to the screen reader, to allow faster navigation and consultation.

While it's still necessary to explore other VLE options, the platform studied in this chapter is a real platform with hundreds of users in a public university. Furthermore, the IT department is aware of the tests and benefits, as one of the authors completed a technical internship in the department responsible for its development. In this sense, the impact in the institution becomes real, and the process described here, although currently artisanal, it can be extended to other institutional platforms. And even more. with minor adjustments to the integration layer, the same framework could be applied to platforms such as Moodle, Canvas, or Blackboard, enabling broader use in diverse educational contexts. Future work will explore these adaptations to validate the scalability and generalization of the proposed architecture.

The conclusions of this chapter reflect how inclusive design and intelligent automation can converge to promote autonomy, reduce educational exclusion, and inspire new directions in the development of accessible virtual learning environments.

REFERENCES

Abdolrahmani, A., Kuber, R., & Branham, S. M. (2018). Siri talks at you: An empirical investigation of voice-activated personal assistant (VAPA) usage by individuals who are blind. *ASSETS 2018 - Proceedings of the 20th International ACM SIGACCESS Conference on Computers and Accessibility*, 249–258. DOI: 10.1145/3234695.3236344

Chaveesuk, S. S.C., & S.P. (2016). IEEE Internet Computing. Retrieved from. *Https://Ieeexplore-Ieee-Org/Stamp/Stamp.Jsp?Tp=&arnumber=7859898&tag=1.*

Cruz, H. (2021). Automatic Speech Recognition technologies and their incorporation into the methods of transcription of indigenous languages. *Anales de Antropologia*, *55*, 13. DOI: 10.22201/iia.24486221e.2021.77857

de Barcelos Silva, A., Gomes, M. M., da Costa, C. A., da Rosa Righi, R., Barbosa, J. L. V., Pessin, G., De Doncker, G., & Federizzi, G. (2020). Intelligent personal assistants: A systematic literature review. In *Expert Systems with Applications* (Vol. 147). Elsevier Ltd., DOI: 10.1016/j.eswa.2020.113193

Gamha, Y. (2023). A framework for REST services discovery and composition. *Service Oriented Computing and Applications*, *17*(4), 259–275. Advance online publication. DOI: 10.1007/s11761-023-00376-6

Jiang, N., & Hu, Y. (2011). Cloud Computing Model and REST APIs Implementation. *Advanced Materials Research*, *366*, 416–420. . DOI: 10.4028/www.scientific.net/AMR.366.416

John Rome. (2017). *Alexa goes to college: Asu's innovative use of voice technology.*

Johnson, C., Paramiswaran, S., & Mailewa, A. (2023). *Discovering Vulnerabilities in Web Browser Extensions Contained by Google Chrome.*

Kaur, N., Bhuiyan, M., Prasad, P., Haque, F., & Elchouemi, A. (2019). Enhancing Quality in Agile Requirement Elicitation Process. *American Journal of Applied Sciences*, *16*(1), 1–10. Advance online publication. DOI: 10.3844/ajassp.2019.1.10

Kumar, D. (2023). CLOUD COMPUTING. *International Scientific Journal of Engineering and Management*, *02*(4). Advance online publication. DOI: 10.55041/ISJEM00289

Lister, K., Coughlan, T., Iniesto, F., Freear, N., & Devine, P. (2020). Accessible conversational user interfaces: considerations for design. In *Proceedings of the 17th international web for all conference* (pp. 1-11). DOI: 10.1145/3371300.3383343

Liu, L., Yan, G., & Chen, S. (n.d.). *Chrome Extensions: Threat Analysis and Countermeasures*. http://www.google.com

Lopezosa, C., Codina, L., Guallar, J., & Pérez-Montoro, M. (2023). *Voice search optimization in digital media: challenges, use and training*. The Information Professional., DOI: 10.3145/epi.2023.may.07

Mehta, P. (2016). *Creating Google Chrome Extensions*. DOI: 10.1007/978-1-4842-1775-7

Mishra, S., & Panda, S. (2023). *Cloud Computing: Applications*. Challenges and Open Issues.

Mokh, H., Maulana, S., Ilham, Z., Muhammad, M., & Mhd, I. (2019). *Voice-based monitoring and control system of electronic appliance using dialog flow API via Google Assistant*. IEEE.

Morán, N., Pérez, J., & Rodriguez, W. (2018, June). *Recognizing People's Emotional States Using Voice Using Machine Learning Algorithms.*

Natale, S., & Cooke, H. (2021). Browsing with Alexa: Interrogating the impact of voice assistants as web interfaces. *Media Culture & Society*, *43*(6), 1000–1016. DOI: 10.1177/0163443720983295

Nielsen, J. (2012). *Usability Engineering*. Morgan Kaufmann.

Palaparthi, A. Voice, & Speech, N. C. (2023). *Machine Learning for Voice and Speech Science*. DOI: 10.13140/RG.2.2.32603.54562

Pradhan, A., Mehta, K., & Findlater, L. (2018). "Accessibility came by accident": Use of voice-controlled intelligent personal assistants by people with disabilities. *Conference on Human Factors in Computing Systems - Proceedings, 2018-April.* DOI: 10.1145/3173574.3174033

Prakash, N. K., Monlam, T., Singh, R., Aravindhan, R. P., Reddy, P. V., & Jain, R. (2022). Voice based E-Mail with Attachment for Blind. *2022 6th International Conference on Trends in Electronics and Informatics, ICOEI 2022 - Proceedings*, 274–280. DOI: 10.1109/ICOEI53556.2022.9776840

Simancas, J., & Meléndez-Pertuz, F. (2017). Voice command recognition algorithm based on non-linear techniques. *Revista Espacios*, *38*, 4.

Simon, C., & Rajeswari, M. (2023). Voice-based Virtual Assistant with Security. *Proceedings of the 2023 2nd International Conference on Electronics and Renewable Systems, ICEARS 2023*, 822–827. DOI: 10.1109/ICEARS56392.2023.10085043

Vasquez, E., Nagendran, A., Welch, G. F., Marino, M. T., Hughes, D. E., Koch, A., & Delisio, L. (2015). Virtual learning environments for students with disabilities: A review and analysis of the empirical literature and two case studies. *Rural Special Education Quarterly*, *34*(3), 26–32. DOI: 10.1177/875687051503400306

Vishnu, S. (2023). A world with Cloud Computing. *International Scientific Journal of Engineering and Management*, *02*. Advance online publication. DOI: 10.55041/ISJEM00279

Vredenburg, K., Mao, J. Y., Smith, P. W., & Carey, T. (2002). A survey of user-centered design practice. In *Proceedings of the SIGCHI conference on Human factors in computing systems* (pp. 471-478). DOI: 10.1145/503376.503460

World Wide Web Consortium. (2024, December 12). Web Content Accessibility Guidelines (WCAG) 2.2. https://www.w3.org/TR/WCAG22/

Zhou, M., Dzingirai, C., Hove, K., Chitata, T., & Mugandani, R. (2022). Adoption, use and enhancement of virtual learning during COVID-19. *Education and Information Technologies*, *27*(7), 8939–8959. DOI: 10.1007/s10639-022-10985-x PMID: 35340535

Chapter 9
Development of an English Learning Application for Blind Users: HappyBlindglish

Juan Antonio Moreno Muñoz
https://orcid.org/0009-0006-7633-5327
Universidad Autónoma de Aguascalientes, Mexico

Francisco Javier Alvarez Rodríguez
https://orcid.org/0000-0001-6608-046X
Universidad Autónoma de Aguascalientes, Mexico

Teresita de Jesús Alvarez Robles
https://orcid.org/0000-0002-3545-5668
Universidad Autónoma de Baja California Sur, Mexico

ABSTRACT

This article highlights the lack of accessible educational applications for people with visual impairments and the need to integrate inclusive design from the start of development. It describes the creation of a mobile app that supports English learning for blind users in Aguascalientes, México. The project applies accessibility and usability principles, adapting functions to user capabilities and focusing on a positive experience. A key component is the MEUXuc methodology (User Experience Evaluation Methodology for Blind Users), which guides evaluation to ensure the tool meets the needs of visually impaired learners. Although they are a minority in some regions, this population is significant in absolute numbers, with many in

DOI: 10.4018/979-8-3373-6033-1.ch009

education or professional training. The article outlines objectives such as accessible interfaces, adapted challenges, and inclusive design, offering a methodological reference for future accessible educational solutions.

This project is a continuation of the project initiated by Dr. Teresita de Jesús Álvarez Robles in her article *"Diseño de una aplicación de aprendizaje de inglés para usuarios ciegos: HappyBlindglish"* (in press), which introduced the conceptual foundations and a base prototype of an inclusive language learning tool for visually impaired individuals, and the current stage advances toward the development of a functional mobile application prototype that supports English language acquisition, recognizing that English proficiency is increasingly essential in education, employment, and communication, while most existing tools remain designed primarily for sighted users and accessibility is often considered only at later stages, resulting in partial or ineffective adaptations, so this project aims to integrate accessibility from the outset by adopting a user-centered design approach and applying the MEUXuc methodology (User Experience Evaluation Methodology for Blind Users), proposed by Álvarez Robles in 2019, which provides a structured framework for the design and evaluation of interactive systems for blind users, ensuring that usability and satisfaction are addressed throughout the development process, and in this stage the work focuses on two fundamental components of the application, the main menu and the challenge section, as these represent the entry point to interaction and allow testing of essential aspects such as navigation, performance, and engagement, and the evaluation strategy combines adapted methods including Card Sorting to understand conceptual organization, Thinking Aloud protocols to capture user reasoning during interaction, and Blind Finger Tracking to analyze tactile exploration patterns on touchscreens, complemented by standardized instruments such as PANAS to measure emotional responses and the Hedonic Utility Scale to assess satisfaction and perceived utility, providing an integral perspective of both functional and affective user experience, and in pedagogical terms the application takes advantage of the auditory strengths and memory skills that many blind individuals develop, making text-to-speech and speech-to-text technologies central to interaction and enabling pronunciation practice and vocabulary learning without the need to modify device settings, while the challenge section incorporates gamification strategies such as progressive tasks, auditory feedback, and performance tracking to encourage motivation and sustained engagement, and beyond the creation of a prototype this work contributes to the broader goal of digital inclusion by demonstrating that accessibility should not be an afterthought but rather an integral design principle that benefits not only specific populations but also improves usability in general, and the documentation of the process aims to serve as a reference for developers and researchers working on inclusive applications in education or other fields, offering evidence of how methodological rigor and continuous user feedback can be combined to produce tools adapted to specific needs, and the structure of this document reflects these objectives by beginning with a conceptual review of the key terms necessary to contextualize the project, including visual impairment, user experience, accessibility, and inclusive design, followed by an overview of related projects and interactive systems designed for blind users to identify effective strategies and limitations, then presenting in detail the MEUXuc methodology as the foundation for the development framework, defining the scope of the project and the guiding research questions, and describing the methods and strategies employed to design the initial prototype, with emphasis on the adaptation of the menu and challenge section, before documenting the phases of system development to establish a basis for future iterations of this application and for future initiatives that promote inclusive and accessible design in software development.

BACKGROUND

Visual impairment

Visual impairment is a complex condition that can be understood through various definitions that emphasize its multifaceted nature. The World Health Organization (1980) defines disability as any restriction or lack of ability to perform an activity in the manner or within the range considered normal for a human being, highlighting that disability is not limited to physical impairments but also includes the social and environmental barriers that hinder full participation in society. Building on this perspective, Jaramillo Cerezo (2022) describes visual impairment as a reduction or loss of visual capacity, ranging from mild difficulties to total blindness, which can significantly affect an individual's quality of life. This view is complemented by Ramos Aguiar (2020) who defines visual impairment as a physical condition that affects the visual organ and manifests in varying degrees of severity. He categorizes it into types such as low vision and blindness, which are medically classified based on the extent of the visual deficiency. Together, these definitions reflect an integrated understanding of visual impairment as a condition influenced by biological, functional, and social factors.

Accessibility

Originally, the concept of accessibility began to be studied within the context of access to healthcare services, a field in which significant barriers were identified that prevented certain population groups from receiving the care they needed. Donabedian and Commonwealth Fund (1973) proposed that accessibility goes beyond the mere presence or "availability" of a resource at a given place and time. This approach highlights the importance of the inherent characteristics of resources, which can either facilitate or hinder their use by potential users. In this sense, for a service to be truly accessible, it must consider the diverse needs and circumstances of the individuals who require it, thereby establishing a foundation for inclusive design.

Another relevant definition that expands on this perspective is provided by Montero (2015) who describes accessibility as an attribute of a "product." This perspective emphasizes that accessibility refers to the ability of a resource to be used without difficulty by the largest possible number of people, regardless of any physical limitations they may have. This inclusive view underlines the need to create products and services that are not only available but also practical and usable for everyone, thereby promoting greater equity in access.

The definitions of accessibility proposed by Donabedian and Commonwealth Fund (1973) and by Montero (2015) present complementary approaches, though with different emphases. While the first addresses accessibility within the domain of healthcare services, emphasizing the interaction between resource characteristics and the specific needs of users, the second conceives it as an inherent attribute of products in general, highlighting their ability to be used without difficulty by as many people as possible. Both perspectives converge on the importance of eliminating barriers, but they differ in their object of analysis, focusing on services in one case and on products in the other, reflecting the evolution of the concept toward a more inclusive and universal approach.

Regarding the focus of the current work, mobile software development is now into the accessibility rules too. According to W3C (2025), "Mobile accessibility refers to making websites and applications more accessible to people with disabilities when they are using mobile phones and other devices." This means that accessibility is not just an abstract concept. It is also a characteristic that the tools we use every day, such as mobile applications, should consider when launching them into the world.

User Centered Design

The concept of User-Centered Design was introduced by cognitive psychologist Donald Norman in 1988 under the name Human-Centered Design, in his book The Design of Everyday Things (Norman, 2013). In this work, Norman presents examples such as vehicle dashboards to explore how people interact with technological interfaces and how these should be adapted to users' physical and cognitive needs. Over time, this concept evolved in various contexts, eventually leading to what is now known as User-Centered Design, extending its application to multiple fields of design and technology.

User-Centered Design (UCD) is both a strategy and a development methodology, placing the user at the center of the product design process. It offers a structured framework to plan projects and provides techniques that can be applied during key phases (Garreta et al., 2010).

Usability

According to Hassan Montero and Martín Fernández (2005) usability is defined as a quality attribute that solely measures the ease of use of a product. In other words, it focuses on how intuitive and simple it is for the user to interact with the product without encountering significant barriers. However, this definition can be limited when applied to broader contexts, such as information systems or software design.

Serrano Angulo and Cebrián Robles (2014) argue that usability involves not only ease of use but also the artifact's ability to be understood, learned, and used in an appealing manner by users under specific conditions. This definition incorporates not only operational aspects but also the attractiveness of the product, placing user experience at the center. In information systems, usability is treated as a qualitative metric that evaluates a software's understandability and manageability, while also considering characteristics such as intuitiveness, speed, performance, and error prevention. In this context, usability becomes an important indicator for measuring software success in terms of operational efficiency and user satisfaction. A highly usable system should provide an experience in which users can interact fluidly, minimizing the learning curve and preventing errors that may affect their performance.

User Experience

User Experience (UX) is a fundamental concept in the design of products and applications, encompassing everything the user experiences when interacting with a system, product, or service. From Dillon's (1995) perspective, UX refers to the user's perception of the product based on the actions taken, the outcomes achieved, and the emotions elicited during the interaction. In other words, it is not only about functionality or visual design, but also about the sensations users experience, such as comfort, frustration, or satisfaction when completing a task.

Hassan Montero and Martín Fernández (2005) on the other hand, offer a more specific definition of user experience, focusing on the emotional and evaluative aspects of interaction. According to them, UX refers to the feeling, emotion, emotional response, and evaluation that a user attributes to a product after interacting with it. This definition broadens the perspective to include user satisfaction not only with the product itself but also with the provider, implying a more comprehensive understanding of the interaction process. To achieve optimal user experience, several factors must be considered, including usability, accessibility, interface design, and consistency in interaction.

Interactive Software System

According to the International Organization for Standardization (2018), an interactive software system is a "combination of hardware and/or software and/or services and/or people that users interact with in order to achieve specific goals" whether that be a mobile application, a computer program or even electro domestics.

This is a concept that is used along the project to describe a computational tool that requires continuous user feedback to operate effectively. Its design aims to enhance user-system interaction, enabling automated functions to respond efficiently to user actions. This approach not only optimizes response times but also contributes to improved performance in educational activities, facilitating more meaningful learning experiences.

According to Colla Villegas et al. (2018), this type of interactive software is particularly valuable in educational contexts, as its capacity for interaction enhances learning by actively engaging students in their educational process. The immediate feedback provided by the software enables learners to correct mistakes in real time and better assimilate concepts, thereby reinforcing knowledge acquisition.

Justification

Within the literature, numerous studies and projects related to educational environments and second language learning lack the features required to be fully accessible for blind individuals, a group frequently overlooked in software and digital tool development (Álvarez Robles, in press). Most language-learning mobile applications are designed for users without visual impairments, relying heavily on visual components and touch-based interactions that assume normal or corrected vision. Although some developers attempt to integrate accessibility elements, these additions are often made during late development stages, once the main architecture and interface have been finalized. As a result, accessibility tends to remain partial, inconsistent, or insufficient for users with visual impairments, limiting their ability to benefit from the software. Consideration of blind users is rarely incorporated systematically into early design decisions, which contributes to the continued creation of tools oriented primarily toward sighted users.

It is commonly assumed that visually impaired individuals face inherent difficulties in learning a second language due to the absence of visual cues. However, research by Nikolic (1987) shows that many develop enhanced auditory perception, strong memory, and highly efficient linguistic processing skills. These abilities support the acquisition of phonetics, phonology, and grammar, demonstrating that blindness does not impede the development of new linguistic competencies when appropriate resources are available. In parallel, proficiency in a second language such as English has become essential in contemporary contexts, influencing academic pathways, employability, and access to professional opportunities (Casierra Parraga et al., 2021) Ensuring access to effective language-learning tools for visually impaired individuals is therefore a matter of equity and social participation.

The purpose of this work is to support the inclusion of individuals with visual impairments in English language learning. The development of an accessible mobile application serves as a reference for developers seeking to design tools that address the requirements of blind users, while also offering learners a functional and adapted resource for vocabulary practice, pronunciation, and progress monitoring. By incorporating accessibility from the earliest stages of design, the application aims to provide an equitable and motivating learning experience and to reduce the digital barriers that have historically limited the participation of visually impaired individuals in educational technology.

Statistics

According to INEGI (2020), people with this disability represent only 2% of the population in the state of Aguascalientes. From a statistical perspective, this may seem like a small sector; however, this is precisely why this work hypothesizes that it does not receive sufficient attention to establish a consistent culture of inclusion. In absolute terms, this corresponds to approximately 29,888 individuals who experience this limiting condition, see Figure 1 for a more visual representation.

Figure 1. Percentages of population with visual disability

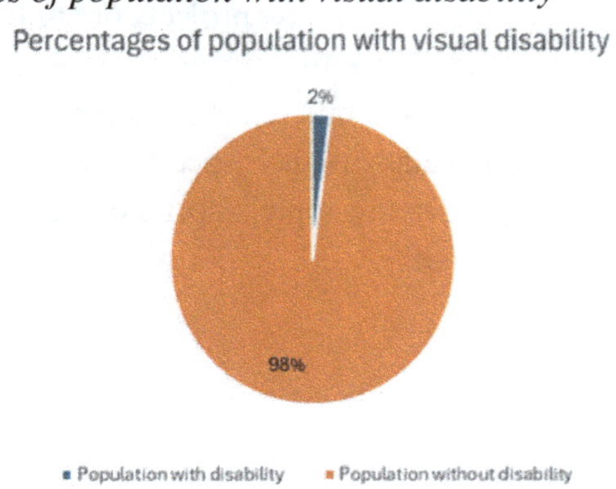

Additionally, if we look into the disability in the whole México numbers (see Figure 2), it shows an increase in prevalence with age, reaching its highest levels among people aged 60 to 74 (INEGI, 2020). Nonetheless, there is also a significant proportion of individuals in productive and formative age groups. This age distribution highlights the importance of implementing tools that address learning and personal development needs throughout all stages of life, promoting inclusion and autonomy for this sector of the population.

Figure 2. Global overview of disability in México by ages

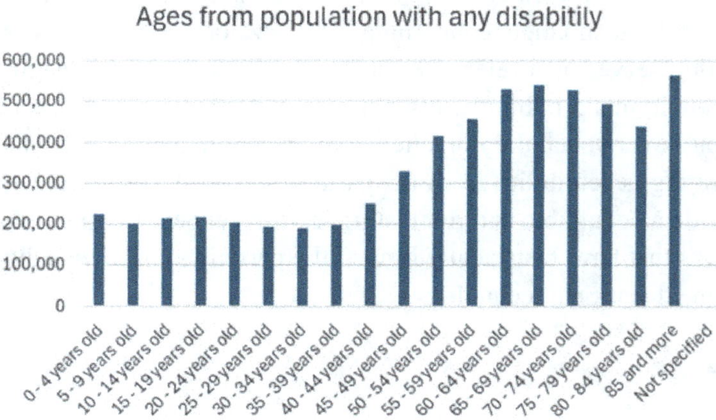

RELATED WORK

To develop the high-level prototype of HappyBlindglish, it was necessary to conduct preliminary research on software projects aimed at supporting individuals with visual impairments. Unfortunately, few projects or studies have been carried out in this area. However, the available findings indicate that significant work has been done on methodologies focused on creating systems that are easy to use for these individuals and that aim to adapt to their specific needs. exposes an overview of the advances and work related to this topic. A brief comparison of these projects can be seen on the Table 1.

Table 1. Related Work Compilation

Title	Summary	Strengths
HappyBlindglish (Álvarez Robles, in press)	Mobile application that teaches English to blind users. Follows the MEUXuc user-centred methodology. Information architecture defined through card-sorting sessions with five blind adults.	Participatory design; speech-based interface compatible with screen readers; validation with end-users; dedicated UX methodology.
TriviaBlind (T. J. Álvarez Robles et al., 2019)	Serious-game trivia system providing general-knowledge questions for blind users. Developed as an interactive software system and evaluated through multiple UX techniques.	Physical braille prototypes; diversified UX evaluations (card sorting, thinking-aloud, HED/UT, PANAS); precedent for accessible educational games.
Mobile Memory-Strengthening App for the Visually Impaired (Aguilar Navarrete et al., 2019)	Audio-based "concentration" game designed to reinforce memory skills in blind users. Piloted with two participants at DIF Aguascalientes.	Auditory reinforcement; simple interaction model; initial usability confirmed by target users.
Interactive System for Tourism Guidance (Esparza Maldonado et al., 2018)	Accessible mobile application that presents typical locations in Aguascalientes to blind users and analyses interaction quality.	Combines local cultural content with accessible navigation; early empirical data on interaction quality for this audience.
Interactive Software System for Basic Mathematics (Gutiérrez Padilla et al., 2020)	User-centred system teaching basic mathematics to blind learners. Involves 5–15 blind participants across analysis, design, development and testing phases	Extensive user participation; multi-method evaluation (Blind Finger Tracking, card sorting, thinking-aloud, HED/UT, PANAS); alignment with seven UX factors.

Language Learning Mobile Applications

In the field of mobile applications for language learning, there are several alternatives aimed at making these tools more accessible for people with visual impairments. These applications offer varying levels of personalization and support for assistive technologies, yet most still present challenges in navigation and interaction for visually impaired users, mostly for the approach they do on the teaching dynamics. We will review and list some of the most popular and some of the most recent developments for this topic:

- **Duolingo** is A popular language learning application offering interactive exercises, games, and practice for various languages, including English. Users can follow structured lessons, track progress, and engage with global leaderboards. Currently this famous Application, contains some accessible features, anyway it doesn't completely implement this correctly, because this was not oriented from the start to visually impaired users. Nonetheless this is a very robust and one of the most complete applications in the market for learning a great variety of languages, not just English.

- **Preply** operates as an online learning platform that connects students with private tutors through an integrated scheduling and virtual classroom system. However, despite its broad functionality, the application is not fully accessible. Several interface elements present limitations for users who rely on screen readers or keyboard navigation, and some interactive components are not consistently labeled or structured in a way that supports assistive technologies. These issues reduce the ease of use for individuals with visual impairments and highlight the need for more inclusive design practices within the platform.
- **Memrise** is a vocabulary-focused language-learning app that provides videos from native speakers, multiple-choice questions, listening tasks, and speed-review activities, but its free version offers limited content and few opportunities to learn grammar. Although the platform is engaging and useful for discovering new words, it presents several accessibility barriers for visually impaired users: many interactive elements are not consistently labeled for screen readers, certain animations and rapid-paced review modes are difficult to navigate without full visual feedback, and some user-generated courses include irregular structures that reduce compatibility with assistive technologies. These limitations make Memrise less accessible for learners who depend on non-visual interaction.
- **Speakly** focuses on building conversational skills by teaching the 4,000 most statistically relevant words of a target language through typing exercises, multiple-choice questions, listening tasks, and AI-driven speaking practice supported by speech-recognition technology. Although effective for improving pronunciation and conversational confidence, the app presents accessibility challenges for visually impaired learners: several core activities depend heavily on reading dense text to understand grammar explanations, the speech-recognition interface lacks consistent screen-reader labeling, and some navigation elements require precise visual interaction without clear non-visual cues. These limitations reduce the usability of Speakly for users who rely on assistive technologies.

MEUXuc Against Other Methodologies

MEUXuc is a development methodology specifically designed to create inclusive designs for people with visual disabilities. It incorporates stages like agile methodologies, ensuring flexibility and iterative improvements. The methodology includes activities and tests to gather valuable information for interface design, making the process user-centered and data-driven. Additionally, it effectively explains methods that were not initially designed for blind users, detailing their origins and adaptations for this user group. MEUX was chosen for this project because it aligns with these principles, offering a structured yet adaptable approach that ensures accessibility and usability for all users.

There are several trends in development methodologies aimed at creating inclusive designs for people with disabilities. These methodologies vary in their approaches and stages, each offering unique benefits and challenges. In the Table 2, we will compare these methodologies for a clearer understanding of why this methodology was selected.

Table 2. Comparison Between Methodologies

Methodology	Similarities With MEUXuc	Differences with MEUXuc
Responsive Inclusive Design (Moreno Martínez et al., 2023)	This methodology follows the same approach as MEUXuc for the active participation of the user and the iterative development and keeps that along all his development phases.	One of the main differences is that RiD is not only focused for blind people, but on any kind of disability. It also defines ten principles to be followed along the whole implementation of the design for ensuring the software will be valid and usable by the users with disabilities.
Microsoft Inclusive Design	Both lean towards teaching consciousness about the inclusive design for new developments as a good and beneficial practice for our society.	This methodology focuses more on teaching the guidelines in a freer way for the developer, not a strict methodology, while MEUXuc already provides the activities or methods to be used.
Acessibility Maturity Model Lifecycle (Fazio et al., 2025)	This model allows the organizations to implement accessibility to their workflow; this might also apply to software development workflows, for that reason this is included as a comparison.	The difference is that while both are methodologies to include accessibility as a final objective, they focus on different scale of organization. While MEUXuc only focuses on software development, AMML focuses on adding accessibility to the organizational structure of any entity.

After the brief comparison, MEUXuc seems to be the best option for achieving the final objective of the mobile application, because it's a methodology that focuses only on visually impaired users as the end user.

METHODOLOGY

MEUXuc (T. de J. Álvarez Robles, 2019) is a proposed methodology focused on developing and evaluating interactive software systems for blind users, considering that many current methodologies lack an adequate process for evaluating user experience (UX).

In the development of software systems for individuals with visual impairments, specific methods that enhance the user experience (UX) for this group are generally not considered, as developers often do not know how to implement them effectively. Instead, conventional UX methods such as interviews and questionnaires continue to be employed, even though these approaches fail to fully address the specific needs of blind users in their interaction with the system. In the best scenarios, a blind user may be involved to support system evaluation, but this practice is not systematic.

Dr Álvarez mentions that it is important to clarify why a specific methodology for this user group is necessary. First, UX evaluation methods are often complex, as members of development teams typically lack experience in implementing and monitoring such methodologies. This can make it difficult to properly adapt the system to the needs of visually impaired users, who require specialized approaches to ensure accessibility, usability, and satisfaction in their interaction with applications. A clear and structured methodology can serve as a guide to overcome these barriers, allowing for more inclusive and efficient development.

Moreover, traditional UX methods usually do not take into account the specific characteristics of visually impaired users. As a result, developers lack adequate information about this user group, which hinders the implementation of essential features to guarantee satisfaction and facilitate the use of applications.

Key characteristics of user experience (UX) include usability, clarity in information presentation, consistency, and accessibility, among others. However, when focusing on the user, it becomes crucial to involve them in the evaluation of the interactive software system (ISS) under development. For this reason, it is suggested that the methodology employed includes a framework that allows developers or those responsible for implementation to identify, at all times, the current stage of the development process and the available options to move forward.

The methodology consists of three general steps:

1. Early stages (Analysis). In this phase, the needs of clients or end users are identified. Evaluating user experience (UX) from early stages significantly reduces the time spent on requirements analysis in software products. Recommended methods include Card Sorting, Semi-Structured Interviews, and other Interrogation Techniques (such as questionnaires and surveys), which have been validated across various case studies. Card Sorting and Semi-Structured Interviews enable the collection of a larger number of user needs, reflecting participants' perceptions and mental models regarding familiar products.
2. Design stages. In the design phase, prototypes or wireframes are developed, either on paper or using digital tools. Evaluating UX at this stage complements the

identification of user needs and helps reduce interface errors and implementation costs. Recommended methods include Constructive Interaction, Think-Aloud Protocol, Heuristic Evaluations, and Card Sorting, among others.

3. Final implementation stages. In this phase, the final product or service is evaluated using various methods to validate user experience (UX) with functional prototypes. This allows the measurement of quality in relation to users' positive or negative experiences. Evaluating UX in final stages helps determine whether the product is moving in the right direction and provides feedback for developers and functional analysts. Recommended methods include Think-Aloud Protocol, Heuristic Evaluations, Card Sorting, Formal Experience, and Interrogation Techniques, without excluding other alternatives.

WORK DONE & RESULTS

Analysis

First Step

The analysis phase of Happy Blindglish followed a two-step process. First, it involved defining both functional and non-functional requirements, definition of the use cases along with the creation of two user profiles to guide usability testing during the development phase (although they were not considered in early implementation stages like the current one). Both profiles represent blind users with varying levels of digital literacy, see the Table 3 [REMOVED REF FIELD]for the definitions.

Table 3. Experienced and inexperienced user profiles

Inexperienced User Profile	Experienced User Profile
Blind user with limited or no prior experience using smartphones or mobile applications. This user lacks familiarity with navigation gestures, exhibits low fluency in screen interaction, and often requires assistance when using mobile devices.	Blind user with proficient use of smartphones and screen readers. This user demonstrates fluency with basic gestures (e.g., flicking), familiarity with multiple screen readers, and the ability to navigate interfaces and applications independently.

It's important to note that the functional requirements were defined based solely on preliminary knowledge of the target context, relying primarily on hypotheses and assumptions regarding how a mobile application could be structured and operate to meet the expected needs of visually impaired users. This initial definition was necessary to establish a foundation for the subsequent design process, even though it was recognized that these early requirements might need refinement once real user feedback and empirical data were obtained during later stages of development and testing. The functional, Non-functional requirements and the ISS characteristics and dependencies are listed in the following:

Funcional Requirements.

- Introduction and information screens to the application. The application requires a one-time walkthrough presenting what the application is about and what can be done with it.
- Daily Challenges section. A dynamic screen is required with a list of activities that the user can complete in a single day.
- Voice recognition with transcription from voice to text and from text to voice. The application must be able to pronounce words in English without the need to change the native settings of the mobile device, being able to work with different voices and speeds during the usage session.
- Practice section of words by Lessons and vocabularies. A section is required where the user can practice and learn words without affecting their progress.
- Observation section of level. A section is required where the user can navigate and know their current statistics.
- Help section for user orientation and training. A help button is required where the user can receive more information in case of confusion during its use.

Non-Functional Requirements.

- Touch interface. A device with support for touch or multi touch.
- Support for advanced gestures. A device where the user can configure their personalized gestures for comfort.
- Data persistence. A database that persists the information and the progress of the user.
- Few elements per screen. Screens must not be saturated with elements that could ruin the user experience.

Characteristics And Dependencies.

- The ISS makes use of the Flutter Framework and uses libraries such as "Text to speech" and "Speech to text" for the most complex functionalities. In addition, it uses SQLite for storage and data persistence.
- The ISS is supported by Android and iOS indistinctly, since Flutter is a cross-platform framework.

- The ISS is mainly oriented to people with visual disabilities; however, it is feasible that any other profile adapts to the architecture and design.
- The ISS depends on the device having an interface to reproduce sound, either speaker or connected headphones.
- The ISS depends on the device having a microphone.
- The ISS depends on the device having an internet connection so that the activities work correctly, since in this way the voice recognition can be carried out.

Class Diagram

The class diagram represents the structural organization of the learning and challenge system implemented in the application. It defines the main entities, their attributes, and the relationships that support progress tracking, vocabulary learning, and user interaction.

User is the central class in the model. It stores basic profile information such as *id*, *name*, *age*, *points*, and *level*. The class provides methods to save and retrieve user data. Two one-to-many associations connect *User* with *Challenges* and *Lesson*, indicating that each user can access multiple challenges and lessons. This relationship establishes the basis for individualized progress management.

Challenges define the tasks presented to the user. It includes attributes such as *name*, *type*, *topic*, *description*, and a direct association with *ChallengeData*. The class also contains methods to save challenge information, mark a challenge as completed, and reset progress. Each challenge is linked to exactly one *ChallengeData* object, which stores the user-specific results of the challenge through attributes such as *points* and *wordsToLearn*. This separation allows the challenge definition to remain constant while the user's performance data is stored independently.

Lesson represents instructional units categorized by *name*, *topic*, *description*, and *difficulty*. The association with the *User* class shows that each user may engage with multiple lessons. The *saveProgress()* method allows the system to record the user's advancement through the lesson structure.

Word models the vocabulary used throughout the lessons and challenges. It stores the Spanish and English terms, the word type, the level, and a Boolean value indicating whether the user has already learned it. Its relationship with *User* indicates that vocabulary learning is also tracked at an individual level. The class includes methods to save word-related data and retrieve the current learning status.

For the purpose of having the most of privacy for these types of users, we only manage this information locally, we did not implement a cloud database. See Figure 3 for a graphical representation of the data structure.

Figure 3. App's Class Diagram

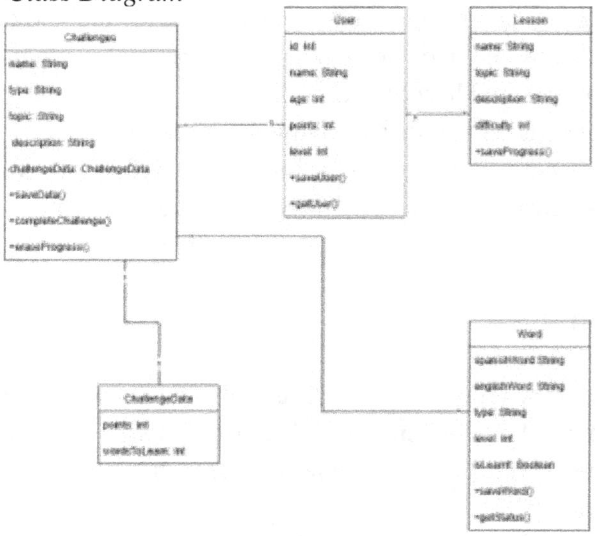

ETHICS AND PRIVACY

Particularly due to the direct involvement of blind users and minors during the testing phase. The application operates without a backend and does not transmit information to any external servers. Only local data related to user progress and in-app learning outcomes is stored. No personal information, identifiers, behavioral records, or biometric data are collected. This technical design decision ensures that users retain full control over their information and eliminates risks commonly associated with the processing of sensitive data. The system is intended solely to provide a functional and accessible tool for visually impaired learners, without any secondary objectives such as profiling, analytics, or commercial exploitation of usage data.

Regarding the voice recognition feature implemented for some of the sections in this app, there is not a mechanism to save any information from the user. The tool the app is using is the SpeechToText library, provided by Google. However, the user will still have to provide permission to the app to use his microphone for this feature to work correctly.

All user testing was conducted on a voluntary basis. Participants were informed of the purpose of the evaluation activities and were free to withdraw at any time. In the case of minors, all sessions were carried out in the presence of parents or legal guardians, who provided consent and remained throughout the evaluation process. The testing activities were conducted in coordination with the Municipal DIF and

CAM 5 (Centro de Atención Múltiple No. 5) both from Aguascalientes, Mexico. Collaboration with these institutions ensured that the procedures aligned with local ethical guidelines for research involving vulnerable populations. Their participation also facilitated access to appropriate facilities and professional staff who supported the execution of the sessions.

No direct (exposing identity) audio, video, or photographic recordings were taken during the sessions, and all observational notes focused exclusively on interaction patterns relevant to accessibility and usability. The combination of voluntary participation, parental supervision for minors, institutional collaboration, and strict data minimization practices ensured that the project complied with ethical standards for research with human participants and preserved the privacy and well-being of all individuals involved.

Second Step

For the second step, a method called Blind Finger Tracking was selected as the evaluation technique for HappyBlindglish. This method involved high-fidelity prototyping combined with heatmap generation to analyze user interaction patterns. Additionally, qualitative feedback was gathered through user-centered questionnaires to complement the evaluation with direct user insights.

Blind Finger Tracking is an adaptation of the Eye Tracking technique, specifically designed to systematically and precisely observe and analyze users' tactile interaction rather than their gaze. This method enables the recording and examination of contact points on an interface, providing valuable insight into usage patterns and accessibility behaviors (T. de J. Álvarez Robles, 2019).

This step consisted of four testing sessions involving five different blind users. The Finger Tracking procedure begins with defining the task to be performed, which includes establishing objectives and the necessary interaction conditions. Examples of such tasks include locating a specific screen within the application or completing a predefined activity. Once the task is defined, the device with the prototyped tool and the implemented finger tracking system is provided to the participant. The facilitator explains the objective clearly and in detail before allowing the user to begin interacting with the application. The participant then uses the app until the objective is achieved. If the user is unable to reach the goal independently, the facilitator intervenes to clarify any doubts or provide guidance, ensuring that the task is ultimately completed.

In the case of HappyBlindglish, the initial prototype featured a minimalistic design, focusing solely on core functionalities such as button sizes, basic text, and navigation. No advanced design architecture or additional visual elements were included. A comparison between an experienced and an inexperienced user is shown in Figure 4.

Figure 4. Experienced User and Unexperienced User comparison

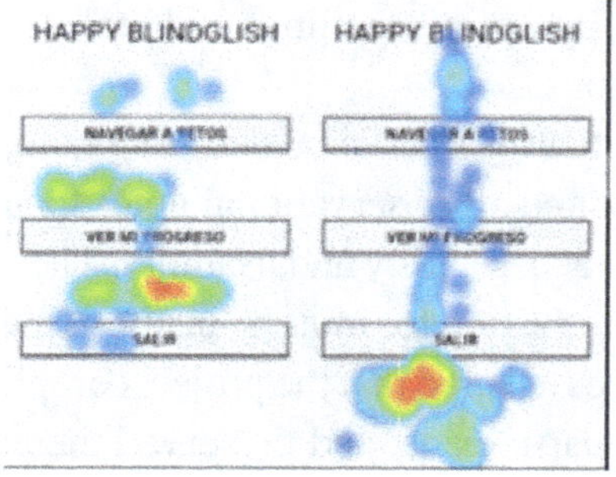

This comparison is useful as a quick understanding of the behavioral differences between these two user profiles. It was observed that inexperienced users tend to explore the entire screen more thoroughly, often relying on trial-and-error interactions, whereas experienced users primarily utilize predefined gestures, such as flicking, to navigate more efficiently. These findings offered valuable insight into the varying interaction patterns within the target population and informed the first set of improvements to the navigation features of the mobile application, ensuring that the interface would accommodate both exploratory behavior and gesture-based interaction.

General Observations.

The tests conducted during the first two weeks of development revealed several patterns in how blind users interact with the application. The size of visual elements such as buttons and text had minimal influence, as users relied primarily on gesture-based navigation rather than visual exploration. Initial interactions showed some exploratory swiping, indicating a need to understand the spatial organization of elements before navigating efficiently.

Complex or deeply nested navigation structures created confusion and increased cognitive load. Reducing navigation depth and grouping related functions within fewer screens is recommended. Participants also indicated that announcing each screen name upon entry and providing a brief description of its main elements would improve orientation and predictability.

A preference for simple interfaces with fewer, well-organized elements was consistently observed. For users with total blindness, visual appearance was largely irrelevant, as interaction depended entirely on auditory and tactile feedback. This reinforces the importance of prioritizing accessibility features over visual design.

Gesture analysis showed frequent use of the flick gesture, with heatmaps indicating greater activity in the central-right area of the screen, corresponding to typical thumb reach. Navigation behavior varied by experience level: experienced users tended to operate with one hand, while less experienced users used both.

Participants also recommended including an onboarding tutorial presented automatically at first launch. This introductory guide would clarify basic operation and reduce the initial learning curve, improving overall accessibility.

DESIGN

For the design phase, the objective was to outline the naming conventions and overall information architecture of the mobile application. Following the MEUXuc methodology, a semi-closed Card Sorting approach was selected, as it allows participants to modify the predefined categories during the activity. This flexibility is particularly useful when working with blind users, whose input often reveals considerations not initially anticipated. The standard procedure was maintained with the sole adaptation of providing Braille cards, enabling participants to complete the task autonomously (T. de J. Álvarez Robles, 2019).

Card Sorting is a participatory design technique in which users group elements into categories and define relationships between concepts, commonly applied when designing digital interfaces or organizing content structures (T. de J. Álvarez Robles, 2019). Several optional steps can be included to enrich the process, such as asking participants to reorganize the resulting stacks into broader groups and assign names to them, or suggesting alternative terms for navigation labels, links, and titles. Recording participants during the activity is also recommended, as their spontaneous comments offer useful insights for later refinement.

In the case of HappyBlindglish, the focus was the development of a challenge-based system supported by a clear information model. Based on the outcomes of the Analysis phase, a set of categories, words, and key phrases was defined for users to classify according to their experience, capturing their natural mental models. A one-week design period was dedicated to conducting a Card Sorting test with a representative group, which provided essential guidance for structuring the app's content and navigation flows in a logical and accessible manner for visually impaired users. Seven participants took part in the activity, including five users with total blindness and two with partial vision, allowing an evaluation of how they grouped and prioritized the app's functions. Their characteristics are presented in Table 4.

Table 4. Participants of the card sorting activity

Name (ID)	Age	Experience Level Using Applications	Type of Disability
AG	21	Expert	Total blindness
AL	12	Non-expert	Total blindness
AR	46	Expert	Total blindness
ZA	14	Expert	Total blindness
GO	16	Expert	Total blindness
RO	10	Non-expert	Partial blindness
EM	13	Non-expert	Partial blindness

To systematically capture and analyze the data, a frequency table was generated to record how often each card was assigned to a given category by participants. This quantitative representation enabled the identification of grouping patterns, trends in user perception, and inconsistencies across participants. The most frequently selected category for each card served as the primary criterion to validate the original classification or to highlight areas where adjustments were required. These findings provided actionable insights for improving the information architecture, reducing cognitive load, and enhancing overall usability of the application. The results of this process are summarized in Table 5.

Table 5. Frequency table of the card sorting activity.

Category/ Cards	General Navigation	Exercises & Challenges	Progress & Achievements	Lessons & Vocabulary	Screen Names	Button Names
Home	**3**	0	0	0	1	2
Main Screen	1	1	0	0	**3**	2
Go Back Screen	3	0	0	0	1	4
Main Menu	1	0	0	0	**4**	2
Help	**3**	0	1	0	1	2
Daily Challenges	0	**4**	0	1	2	0
Guess Twenty Basic Words	0	3	0	**4**	0	0
Start Challenge	0	**5**	0	1	0	1
Pronunciation	0	2	0	**5**	0	0
Arrange the Words	0	**3**	1	**3**	0	0
View My Progress	0	0	**7**	0	0	0

continued on following page

Table 5. Continued

Category/ Cards	General Navigation	Exercises & Challenges	Progress & Achievements	Lessons & Vocabulary	Screen Names	Button Names
My Progress	0	1	**5**	0	1	0
Learned Words	0	1	2	**4**	0	0
Current Points	1	0	5	1	0	0
Best Streak	0	1	**6**	0	0	0
Phrase Translation	0	**3**	0	1	1	2
Guided Start	2	0	0	0	2	**3**
Start Without Guidance	2	1	1	0	0	**3**
End Activity	0	2	0	2	0	**3**

The card sorting tests revealed clear differences between participants with congenital blindness and those with acquired blindness. Individuals blind from birth showed reduced familiarity with abstract concepts and had more difficulty forming associations between cards and categories, organizing hierarchies, or prioritizing items. Two participants with congenital blindness also required additional clarification to understand the task and continued to show challenges in maintaining attention throughout the activity. These observations indicate that conceptual processing and cognitive strategies vary depending on whether blindness is congenital or acquired. Such differences should be considered when designing and evaluating tasks to ensure accessibility and meaningful participation for visually impaired users.

DEVELOPMENT

During the development phase, iterative improvements were made to the activities designed in the analysis stage. The following section outlines the development process based on each enhancement made to the interactive system (ISS), guided by user feedback collected during each testing activity in this phase.

It can be observed that the interface is composed of a main title and buttons mostly arranged vertically from top to bottom. This initial layout was created solely for exploratory interface purposes, in order to carry out the first Blind Finger Tracking activity during the analysis phase.

First Iteration

The initial UI version (Figure 5) featured a vertically arranged layout with a main title and interactive buttons, designed to guide users through the core functions of the application. This prototype was created primarily for exploratory purposes during the first Blind Finger Tracking activity in the analysis phase, allowing researchers and developers to observe how visually impaired users interact with basic interface elements. The layout aimed to provide a clear and simple navigation structure, minimizing cognitive load and facilitating orientation. During this activity, user interactions were closely monitored to identify potential accessibility issues, such as difficulties locating buttons, understanding labels, or performing gestures. Feedback collected from this exploratory session informed subsequent refinements in both the design and the functionality of the user interface, ensuring that the application could better accommodate the needs of blind users and enhance their overall learning experience with the software.

Figure 5. First Iteration

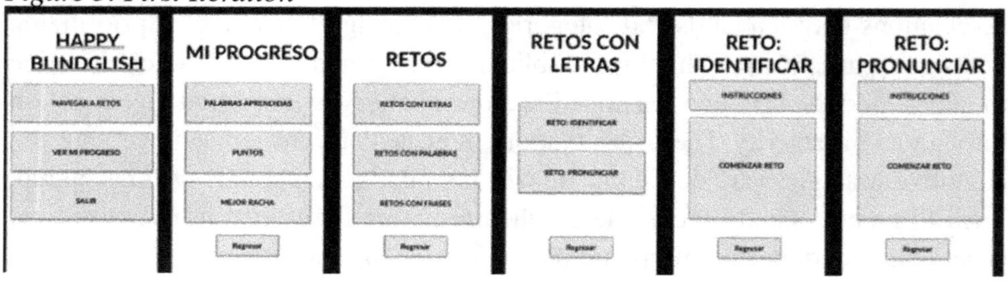

Second Iteration

The Figure 6, presents the second version of the mobile application, which represents the first iteration designed based on feedback provided by a blind user. In this version, adjustments were made to button sizes, the distribution of on-screen elements, and the color of certain text components. However, after a joint evaluation, it was concluded that these visual features were largely irrelevant for blind users, as their interaction relies primarily on the screen reader rather than visual perception.

One of the most significant comments highlighted the need to include an accessible help section on every screen. This section should provide a brief explanation of the current screen's purpose, as well as the location and function of the interactive elements. The implementation of this feature aims to facilitate orientation within the application and enhance the navigation experience for users with visual impairments.

Figure 6. Second Iteration

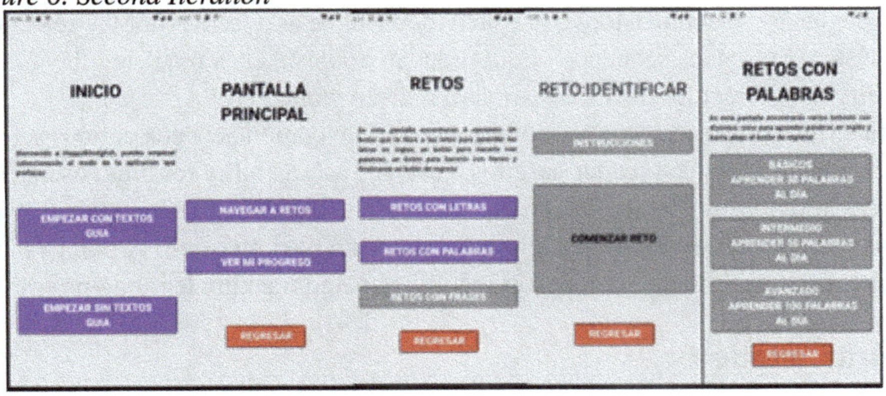

Third Iteration

The Figure 7 show a significant reduction in the number of screens within the application. This design decision was primarily based on the following aspects: Users reported that navigation was more comfortable when elements were unified on a single screen, provided that visual and functional overload was avoided. The application focuses on two main functionalities; therefore, the creation of multiple subsections caused confusion and hindered user orientation within the interface. Reducing the number of actions required to achieve the same result was identified as the most effective adjustment.

Additionally, in response to user suggestions, an onboarding or introductory process was incorporated. This feature provides first-time users with a clear explanation of the objectives and available functionalities of the application, thereby improving their understanding and enhancing the initial user experience.

Figure 7. Third Iteration

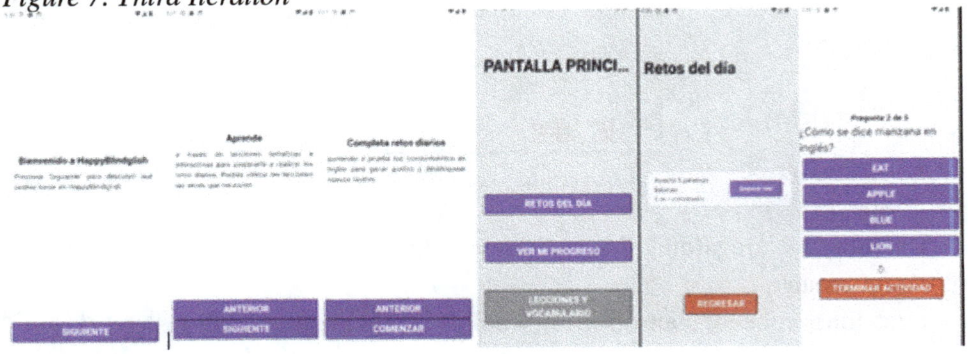

The third iteration introduced the first prototype of the challenge activity. The user begins by selecting a topic on which they will be assessed. After the selection, the system presents a sequence of questions in Spanish, each requiring the user to identify the correct English translation of a given word.

Each question offers four selectable options. Navigation between options is fully compatible with screen reader gestures, ensuring accessibility for blind users. The activity provides immediate feedback after each selection, indicating whether the answer is correct and automatically moving to the next question. A point system records user performance, supporting motivation and tracking learning progress.

Fourth Iteration

As shown in Figure 8, iteration 4 focused primarily on improving the challenge activity. Three additional sections were added to further explore the user's abilities through a wider range of topics, including basic animal names, compound color names, verbs, and more advanced sentences. In addition, several enhancements were made to the challenge dynamics:

Users can now listen to the English word at a slower and well-pronounced speed, without altering the native language configuration of the mobile device and, users are also able to hear the spelling of the word letter by letter (in Spanish), which helps improve comprehension in cases where the pronunciation may not be fully understood.

Figure 8. Fourth Iteration

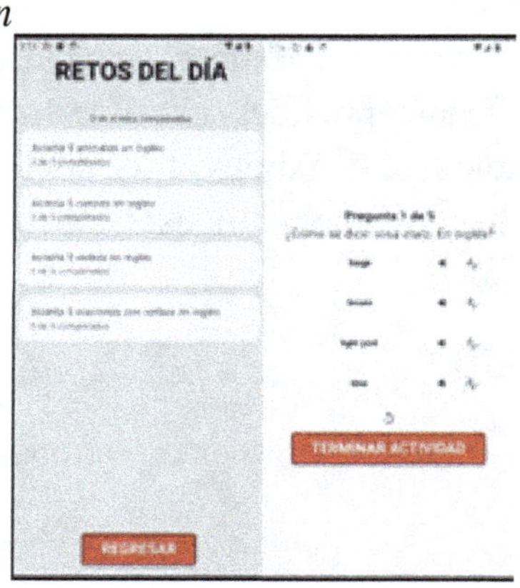

User feedback regarding this version was diverse, with the following being the most significant:

First, the number of controls in the word bar could be simplified. Instead of using an additional button to activate the spelling or slow reading functions, a gesture such as long-pressing or double-tapping could be implemented. This would provide a smoother and more fluid navigation experience for the user.

Secondly, the screen could include a help button that remains accessible at all times, providing a brief explanation of the activity or section the user is currently performing.

Fifth Iteration

In this latest iteration, the lessons system was implemented, and the challenges section was improved. Both functionalities have distinct objectives, requiring specific designs, although both are oriented toward the learning process.

As shown in Figure 9, the lessons system utilizes the device's microphone to allow the user to pronounce the words presented during each lesson. Four lessons were designed, each corresponding to the same topics addressed in the challenges section. Therefore, the main dynamic and ideal flow of the application consist of the user first completing the lesson and subsequently solving the daily challenge on the same topic.

The challenges were redesigned to reduce the number of interactions required to select an activity. This change addressed issues in the previous version, where more complex navigation elements created difficulties for users, particularly those without prior experience.

The dedicated spelling button was also removed, and its functionality was reassigned to a long-press gesture. This adjustment preserves the feature while simplifying interaction and improving overall accessibility.

Figure 9. Fifth Iteration

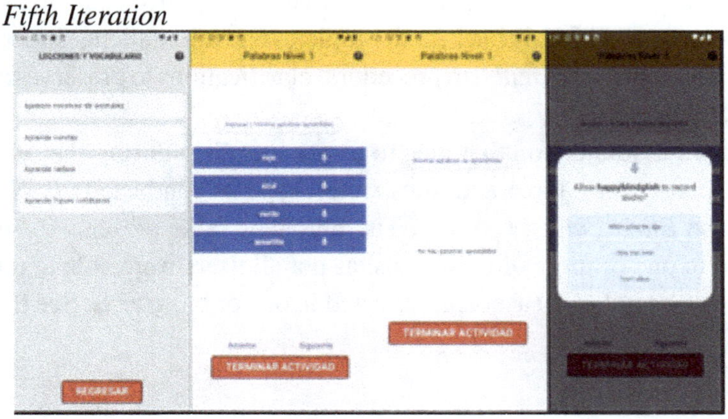

TESTING PHASE

Three tasks were defined to evaluate the system's core functionalities by simulating typical user interactions. These tasks focused on navigation, content accessibility, and activity completion, providing evidence on usability, accessibility, and overall user experience.

Testing Task Definition

Navigate through the Onboarding.

The participant moves through the three onboarding screens using TalkBack, interacting with controls and listening to each introduction before advancing. The task ends once the participant reaches the main menu without navigation guidance unless assistance is explicitly requested.

Navigate to Lessons and Vocabulary and complete one lesson.

From the main menu, the participant accesses Lessons and Vocabulary, selects one topic, explores controls using TalkBack, and completes a short pronunciation sequence (1-4 words). The process evaluates control recognition, task flow, and audio cue effectiveness.

Navigate to Daily Challenges and complete one challenge.

After finishing the lesson, the participant navigates to Daily Challenges, explores interactive elements with TalkBack, and completes one full challenge independently. Facilitator intervention is limited to procedural clarifications to preserve the validity of the task.

It is important to mention that, due to time constraints during the development and testing phase, only three activities were properly conducted*: PANAS, HED/UT Scale*, and *Blind Finger Tracking*. The following table presents the users who participated in one or more of these tests, as not all users were able to take part in every activity. A total of 10 users participated in one or more tests. See the Table 6.

Table 6. Participants of the Testing Phase

Sysyem	Happy Blindglish		Tests		
User	**Age**	**Profile**	**PANAS**	**HED/UT**	**Blind Finger Tracking**
U1	53	Expert	No	Yes	Yes
U2	67	Non-expert	No	Yes	Yes
U3	56	Non-expert	No	Yes	Yes
U4	21	Expert	Yes	Yes	Yes
U5	14	Expert	Yes	Yes	Yes
U6	37	Expert	No	Yes	Yes
U7	49	Non-expert	No	Yes	Yes
U8	34	Non-expert	No	Yes	Yes
U9	68	Non-expert	No	Yes	Yes
U10	46	Expert	No	Yes	Yes
U11	46	Expert	Yes	No	No
U12	12	Non-expert	Yes	No	No

PANAS

The Positive and Negative Affect Schedule (PANAS) consists of two mood scales: one measuring positive affect and the other negative affect. As a psychometric tool, it is effective for evaluating user experience (UX) and can reveal relationships between affective responses, statistical characteristics, and personality traits. Each scale; positive (PA) and negative (NA); includes ten descriptors defining the meaning of the items. Participants rate twenty items using a five-point scale, ranging from "very slightly" (1) to "extremely" (5), and the total score is then assessed. Internal consistency estimates range from 0.86 to 0.90 for the positive affect scale and from 0.84 to 0.87 for the negative affect scale. This UX evaluation method focuses on assessing users' affective responses toward a product, aiming to ensure it is desirable and elicits positive emotions (Watson & Clark, 1999).

The PANAS (Positive and Negative Affect Schedule) scale was applied to a group of four users after interacting with the system. This tool allows for the observation of short-term emotional impact, distinguishing between positive affect and negative affect. The list of users that participated and their results are shown in Table 7.

Table 7. Results for PANAS

	Positive Affection	Negative Affection
U11	47	12
U12	49	11
U4	41	12
U5	44	11

Positive Affect: 45.25 (SD = 3.03)

Negative Affect: 11.5 (SD = 0.5).

All evaluated users showed significantly higher positive affect compared to negative affect, indicating that the experience was emotionally favorable for most participants. This suggests that the system was not only functional but also generated positive emotional responses during or after use.

U11 and *U12* showed the highest levels of positive affect (47 and 49, respectively), combined with low levels of negative affect (both around 11–12). This can be interpreted as a smooth experience in which the system generated enthusiasm, engagement, and possibly a sense of achievement, without causing significant frustration or stress.

U4 reported a slightly lower positive affect score (41), with a negative affect score similar to the others (12). This difference might reflect specific moments of difficulty or a less emotionally intense perception overall—though still a more positive than negative experience.

U5 maintained a high positive affect score (44) and low negative affect (11), consistent with U11 and U12. This confirms that the experience was consistently pleasant for this group of users.

HED/UT

The HED/UT (Hedonic/Utility) scale was originally developed to measure the hedonic and utilitarian dimensions of users' attitudes toward product categories. The research from Gursoy et al. (2006) has shown that user attitudes are composed of two main dimensions: a utilitarian component and a hedonic component.

This perspective suggests that any attitude object; such as good, service, or activity; is evaluated in terms of the perceived hedonic and/or utilitarian value. The hedonic dimension relates to factors such as uniqueness, symbolic meaning, emotional excitement, and the imagery evoked by a product or service. It is more subjective and personal, depending on individual experiences and emotions. Conversely, the utilitarian dimension is associated with products or services that serve practical, functional purposes, fulfilling basic and tangible needs. Thanks to the work of T.

de J. Álvarez Robles (2019) and her MEUXuc methodology, a modified procedure for blind users is now available. The steps below are presented in the order they should be carried out:

1. An instructive practice is conducted, explaining to the user the information to be collected after completing the tasks in the mobile application.
2. The blind user is provided with the mobile device.
3. The user is asked to complete the application activities.
4. The user evaluates each task using the HED/UT item scale, choosing to respond either (1) verbally or (2) via Braille.
5. User participation is assessed.

A total of 10 users participated in this evaluation. The users were divided into two groups: expert users with experience using mobile devices with screen readers, and non-expert users. This division allowed for the observation of significant differences in how each profile evaluated aspects such as hedonic quality (HQ), perceived usability (PU), and the overall product rating (OPR). Table 8 shows the way to describe the tool at the end of the evaluation basing on the OPR.

Table 8. Evaluation Scale for HED/UT

Score	Description
0 – 0.99	Terrible
1 – 1.99	Poor
2 – 2.99	Fair
3 – 3.99	Good
4 - 5	Excellent

Expert users (U1, U4, U5, U6, U10) from the Table 9 showed a clear tendency to rate perceived usability (PU) very highly, with scores ranging from 4.48 to 5. This indicates that the system adequately meets the functional expectations of users who are already proficient with accessibility tools.

Table 9. Expert Users Results on HED/UT

Expert Users	U1	U4	U5	U6	U10
CFH	2.85185185	2.62962963	3.81481481	4.85185185	5
CFU	4.48148148	4.92592593	5	4.96296296	5
CGP	3.66666667	3.77777778	4.40740741	4.90740741	5

In contrast, hedonic quality (HQ) received more varied and generally lower scores, especially in the cases of U1 (2.85) and U4 (2.63). This suggests that, for experienced users, the emotional or pleasurable aspect of the system is not considered relevant or may even be overshadowed by functionality. It is possible that using the screen reader has become a routine or mechanical task for this group, which reduces the emotional impact of the experience.

Regarding the overall product rating (OPR), this metric progressively increases with higher perceived usability (PU) scores, reaching a maximum of 5 in the case of U10. This indicates that when the system operates smoothly and fulfills its functional purpose without complications, even the most critical users acknowledge its overall effectiveness.

In contrast, non-expert users (U2, U3, U7, U8, U9) from the Table 10 showed a significantly higher rating in the hedonic quality (HQ) component, with an average notably above that of the expert users. This may be due to the novelty of the experience or the discovery of a tool that opens new possibilities for them. For these users, the system is not only functional but also surprising and stimulating.

Table 10. Non - Expert Users Results on HED/UT

Non – Expert Users	U2	U3	U7	U8	U9
CFH	3.25925926	4.44444444	3.77777778	4.44444444	4.2962963
CFU	4.88888889	4.44444444	4.03703704	4.62962963	4.2962963
CGP	4.07407407	4.44444444	3.90740741	4.53703704	4.2962963

In terms of *perceived usability (PU),* high ratings were also obtained, although with greater variability. User U2 gave the highest score (4.89), while U7 was the only case below 4.1. This may indicate that the learning curve or certain interaction barriers still affect some less experienced users, although the overall design remains accessible for most.

The *overall product rating (OPR)* in this group remains stable at high values (ranging from 3.91 to 4.54), without extreme scores. This stability can be interpreted as validation of the system in real-world contexts with less familiar users: even if they do not master all gestures or functions, their overall experience remains positive.

> **Differences between groups:** Non-expert users find greater emotional satisfaction in using the screen reader, while expert users primarily value its functionality. This suggests that the system should maintain a balance between usefulness and appeal, without neglecting the familiarity needs of advanced users.

Peak satisfaction: Expert user U10 rated all aspects with a 5, representing an ideal case of a fully satisfying experience. This user likely not only masters the system but also finds it enjoyable and fully functional in every respect.
Areas for improvement: The lower hedonic quality (HQ) scores among expert users may indicate an opportunity to incorporate more customizable or less repetitive elements into the experience, making usage more engaging even for those already familiar with the screen reader.

Blind Finger Tracking

This was applied as the final high-level test, enabling the recording and analysis of contact points on the interface. The evaluation revealed clear differences between users with prior experience in touch gestures and those without such experience, as shown in the following section:

Figure 10. Expert User VS Non-Expert User

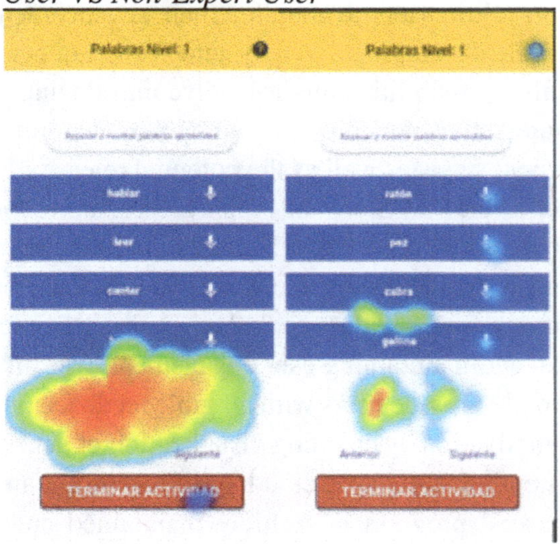

Figure 10[REMOVED REF FIELD] presents a comparative analysis of interaction patterns between expert and non-expert users based on heatmap data. Expert users exhibit interactions concentrated in a limited area of the screen, reflecting familiarity with the interface layout and internalized gesture controls. Their movement traces are uniform, controlled, and precise, indicating efficient, goal-directed navigation. In contrast, non-expert users display a wider dispersion of interaction points, with broader and less structured movements that reveal exploratory behavior. These users are still familiarizing themselves with the interface, requiring more time and effort to locate functions and complete tasks.

These findings demonstrate that prior experience strongly influences user interaction with gesture-based interfaces. Experts achieve higher efficiency and accuracy, while novices rely on broader exploration to understand available options. The results highlight the importance of designing effective onboarding procedures and adaptive training strategies that support users in transitioning from exploratory to expert interaction, ultimately enhancing usability and performance across different experience levels.

LIMITATIONS AND FUTURE WORK

Regarding the future work, is possible from here. Among the potential directions, it could include the expansion of the word database and diversification of content to enhance learning opportunities, the implementation of a "View My Progress" module to allow users to monitor their advancement through lessons and challenges, and the development of a system with data persistence and cloud synchronization. Other possibilities might involve introducing a broader range of activity types and interactive dynamics, guided by the rules and feedback collected during the development stage, as well as the potential release of the application on major platforms such as the Play Store and Apple Store. At present, the development remains an open-source project on GitHub, offering a foundation for collaborative experimentation and iterative improvement. Expanding the word database could allow learners to engage with a wider vocabulary, supporting more comprehensive language acquisition and maintaining user engagement over time. The "View My Progress" module might provide users with tangible feedback on their learning trajectory, enhancing motivation by enabling visualization of achievements and areas requiring further attention. Similarly, cloud synchronization and data persistence could ensure that users' progress is securely maintained and accessible across multiple devices, supporting continuity in learning and operational flexibility. The inclusion of varied activity types and interactive dynamics could optimize the educational experience by accommodating diverse learning preferences and sustaining engagement. Finally, making the application available on major app stores could broaden accessibility, reaching a wider population of visually impaired learners and encouraging the adoption of inclusive educational technology. Collectively, these possibilities illustrate avenues for enhancing the functionality, usability, and pedagogical impact of HappyBlindglish, highlighting its potential as an accessible and engaging tool for a new language learning.

CONCLUSION

Regarding the evaluation of the Happy Blindglish application, conducted through a combination of complementary methodologies, provided highly relevant insights into its usability, emotional impact, and overall user experience. Results from the PANAS scale indicated that both expert and non-expert users of accessible technologies experienced predominantly positive emotions during their interaction with the platform, suggesting that the application fosters an emotionally satisfying and motivating learning experience. This is an essential factor for promoting consistent engagement and encouraging long-term use of the tool. Similarly, the outcomes of the HED/UT scale revealed high ratings in both hedonic and utilitarian dimensions, demonstrating that users perceived the application not only as a functional and effective means of achieving their language learning goals but also as an enjoyable and pleasant system to interact with. According to the evaluation framework presented in Table 9 Non - Expert Users Results on HED/UT (HED/UT Evaluation Scale), the application was classified within the Good to Excellent range, reinforcing the strength of its current design. The Blind Finger Tracking analysis further supported these findings by showing that users navigated the interface efficiently, following consistent tactile trajectories and displaying minimal erratic patterns, which confirms that the interface layout and the implementation of gesture-based navigation compatible with screen readers such as TalkBack facilitate intuitive and efficient interaction for visually impaired users. Minor differences were noted between participants with higher technological expertise and those less familiar with accessible mobile devices, with expert users completing tasks more rapidly and engaging in more direct tactile exploration. These differences highlight the importance of considering diverse user profiles when designing inclusive systems, ensuring that the application remains usable and accessible to a broad spectrum of users regardless of their prior experience.

Although the feedback was overwhelmingly positive, participants suggested improvements aimed at enhancing the consistency of auditory feedback and standardizing touch gestures across screens to further streamline the user experience. These recommendations now represent valuable input for guiding future iterations of the design, supporting the ongoing refinement of the system to meet the specific needs of its target population. Overall, the results of this evaluation indicate that HappyBlindglish holds strong potential as an inclusive, engaging, and functional educational resource for visually impaired individuals, providing a solid foundation for future development and research in accessible language learning technologies.

REFERENCES

Aguilar Navarrete, P., Camacho González, Y., Hernández Olvera, N. A., & Montoya Bironche, A. (2019). Desarrollo de una Aplicación Móvil para el Fortalecimiento de la Memoria en Personas con Discapacidad Visual. In *AVANCES SOBRE REFLEXIONES, APLICACIONES Y TECNOLOGÍAS INCLUSIVAS* (pp. 48–54). CONAIC.

Álvarez Robles, T. de J. (2019). *METODOLOGÍA PARA LA EVALUACIÓN DE LA EXPERIENCIA DEL USUARIO DE SISTEMAS DE SOFTWARE INTERACTIVOS PARA USUARIOS CIEGOS*. UNIVERSIDAD VERACRUZANA.

Álvarez Robles, T. J., Molina Orozco, L. A., Partida Mariscal, J. L., Álvarez Rodríguez, F. J., & Benítez Guerrero, E. (2019). TriviaBlind: Sistema de software interactivo enfocado en la experiencia del usuario de personas ciegas como juego serio para el aprendizaje de cultura general. In *AVANCES SOBRE REFLEXIONES, APLICACIONES Y TECNOLOGÍAS INCLUSIVAS* (pp. 10–14). CONAIC.

Casierra Parraga, C. M., Loor Fernández, M. N., Mejia Avellan, M. A., & Macías Loor, M. Á. (2021). *Inclusión: Estrategias didácticas en el proceso de enseñanza aprendizaje del idioma inglés en los estudiantes con discapacidad visual en las universidades manabitas*.

Colla Villegas, V. L., Ortiz Hernández, M. M., Mero Lino, E. A., & Hernández Zambrano, M. M. (2018). *SOFTWARE INTERACTIVO Y SU CONTRIBUCIÓN EN EL APRENDIZAJE PARA LOS NIÑOS DEL C.I.B.V DEL CANTÓN JIPIJAPA*. Area de Innovación y Desarrollo, S.L.

Dillon, T. W. (1995). *Spoken language interaction: effects of vocabulary size, user experience, and expertise on user acceptance and performance*. University of Maryland.

Donabedian, A., & Commonwealth Fund. (1973). *Aspects of medical care administration: specifying requirements for health care*. Published for the Commonwealth Fund by Harvard Univ. Press, Cambridge.

Esparza Maldonado, A. L., Margain Fuentes, L. Y., Álvarez Rodríguez, F. J., & Benítez Guerrero, E. I. (2018). *Desarrollo y evaluación de un sistema interactivo para personas con discapacidad visual. 21*(41), 149–157.

Fazio, D., Byrne-Haber, S., Sajka, J., LaPierre, C., & Jadhav, N. M. (2025). *Accessibility Maturity Model*.

Garreta, M., Enric, D., & Pera, M. (2010). *Diseño centrado en el usuario*.

Gursoy, D., Spangenberg, E. R., & Rutherford, D. G. (2006). The hedonic and utilitarian dimensions of attendees' attitudes toward festivals. *Journal of Hospitality & Tourism Research (Washington, D.C.)*, *3*(30), 279–294. DOI: 10.1177/1096348006287162

Gutiérrez Padilla, J. D. N., de Jesús Álvarez Robles, T., & Álvarez Rodriguez, F. J. (2020). *Hacia el desarrollo de un sistema de software interactivo (SSI) enfocado en el aprendizaje de matemáticas básicas para personas con discapacidad visual.*

Hassan Montero, Y., & Martín Fernández, F. J. (2005). *La Experiencia del Usuario.* No Solo Usabilidad. https://www.nosolousabilidad.com/articulos/experiencia_del_usuario.htm?utm_source=twitterfeed&utm_medium=twitter#knapp

INEGI. (2020). *Población con discapacidad o limitación en la actividad cotidiana por entidad federativa y tipo de actividad realiza según sexo, 2020.*

International Organization For Standarization. (2018). *ISO 9241-11:2018, Ergonomics of human-system interaction.*

Jaramillo Cerezo, A., Torres Yepes, V., Yuliana, L. N., Arias Uribe, J., & Suárez Escudero, J. C. (2022). *Etiología y consideraciones en salud de la discapacidad visual en la primera infancia: revisión del tema.* Revista Mexicana de Oftalmología.

Montero, Y. H. (2015). *Experiencia de Usuario: Principios y Métodos.* www.yusef.esTodoslosderechosreservados,2015EstelibrohasidoescritousandoCalmlyWriter

Moreno Martínez, C., Piorno, J. R., Escribano Otero, J. J., & Guijarro Mata-García, M. (2023). Responsive inclusive design (RiD): A new model for inclusive software development. *Universal Access in the Information Society*, *22*(3), 893–902. DOI: 10.1007/s10209-022-00893-9

Norman, D. (2013). *THE DESIGN OF EVERYDAY THINGS* (1st ed.). Basic Books., https://ia902800.us.archive.org/3/items/thedesignofeverydaythingsbydonnorman/The%20Design%20of%20Everyday%20Things%20by%20Don%20Norman.pdf

Ramos Aguiar, L. R. (2020). *METUIGA "Metodología para el diseño de sistemas basados en interfaces tangibles de usuario y técnicas de gamificación para personas ciegas"* [Maestría]. Universidad Autonoma de Aguascalientes.

Serrano Angulo, J., & Cebrián Robles, D. (2014). Usabilidad y satisfacción de la e-Rúbrica. *REDU. Revista de Docencia Universitaria*, *12*(1), 177. Advance online publication. DOI: 10.4995/redu.2014.6426

W3C. (2025). *Guidance on Applying WCAG 2.2 to Mobile Applications (WCAG-2Mobile).*

Watson, D., & Clark, L. A. (1999). *The PANAS-X: Manual for the Positive and Negative Affect Schedule - Expanded Form.*

World Health Organization. (1980). *International classification of impairments, disabilities, and handicaps: A manual of classification relating to the consequences of disease*. World Health Organization.

Chapter 10
Tool for Teaching Mexican States and Capitals in LSM

Italia Estrada-Cota
https://orcid.org/0009-0003-3132-5975
Universidad Autónoma de Baja Caliornia Sur, Mexico

Mónica Adriana Carreño-León
Universidad Autónoma de Baja Caliornia Sur, Mexico

Jesús Andrés Sandoval-Bringas
Universidad Autónoma de Baja Caliornia Sur, Mexico

Amado Alejandro Leyva-Carrillo
Universidad Autónoma de Baja Caliornia Sur, Mexico

ABSTRACT

Currently, ICTs in education play a fundamental role. They are an effective learning tool and provide resources that help develop new skills to acquire knowledge and improve academic performance. The use of teaching and learning tools is an innovative strategy that brings significant benefits. The development of a web-based tool designed for teaching and learning in the states and capitals of Mexico in LSM facilitates learning for children with or without hearing impairments, promoting inclusion and equal access to knowledge. This web-based tool is based on a playful approach, using challenges and rewards to motivate children with or without hearing impairments and generate meaningful learning. This interactive web-based tool

DOI: 10.4018/979-8-3373-6033-1.ch010

can be accessed from any computer with internet access, allowing students to learn from anywhere, at any time. This seeks to strengthen teaching and learning in the states and capitals of Mexico in LSM through an innovative and accessible strategy.

1 INTRODUCTION

According to the 2030 Agenda for Sustainable Development, in its objective 4 Quality Education, it indicates: "Ensure inclusive and equitable quality education and promote lifelong learning opportunities for all" (Objetivos De Desarrollo Sustentable, 2023), and according to some of its goals it establishes: "By 2030, eliminate gender disparities in education and ensure equal access to all levels of education and vocational training for the vulnerable, including persons with disabilities, indigenous peoples and children in vulnerable situations" (Objetivos De Desarrollo Sustentable, 2023), a commitment that educational institutions in the world have adopted so that both men and women with disabilities have the same study opportunities.

In turn, the United Nations Educational, Scientific and Cultural Organization (UNESCO) designed a project called: "Leveraging ICT to achieve Education 2030", which seeks to harness the potential of Information and Communication Technologies (ICT) in achieving Sustainable Development Goal 4 (SDG), and for which various actions and publications have been carried out, in which it is sought that ICT in education are the core and that they become that relevant tool in the subject of education. (Organización de Estados Iberoamericanos, 2021) (Leveraging ICTs to Support the Achievement of Post-2015 Education Agenda, 2015) In itself, what is sought is to carry out actions so that education reaches everyone in the world with equity, quality and inclusion and emphasizes the need for ICTs to help improve access to learning and therefore reduce educational gaps.

This is how ICTs are having a major impact on society, culture, and education, creating a new paradigm. As mentioned above, in the educational field, they are being integrated to create educational strategies at different levels. They are serving as an effective tool, helping to achieve meaningful learning, providing resources that help students develop new skills for acquiring knowledge and improving academic performance.

In this sense, educational institutions or organizations are making adjustments to their educational models to incorporate ICTs into the teaching-learning processes. In México, the Secretaría de Educación Pública (Ministry of Public Education, SEP) has implemented the necessary actions for teachers to carry out the planning and implementation of the current educational model within their classrooms. For example, at the basic level, the New Mexican School (NEM) recognizes that ICTs must be integrated as tools that support the educational process, not only as devices, but as means to promote meaningful learning, strengthen innovative methodologies, encourage teacher-student collaboration, and, above all, reduce knowledge access gaps, all aligned with SDG 4. Thus, ICTs are helping teachers in the classroom through the use of open and collaborative platforms that allow the use and creation of content that supports the teaching-learning process in an inclusive school environment (Subsecretaría Educación Media Superior, 2019).

The NEM thus recognizes the incorporation of ICTs as a fundamental element for quality, inclusive education that contributes to the comprehensive development of students. In this sense, ICTs, as mentioned above, are not only a tool but also a means to foster critical thinking in students, foster creativity, cooperation, and the acquisition of knowledge in diverse educational contexts (Subsecretaría Educación Media Superior, 2019).

In turn, the NEM believes that ICTs are the driving force behind digital skills, defined as: "They are the set of knowledge related to the use of Information, Communication, Knowledge and Digital Learning Technologies (ICTCAD)." (Sep, n.d.) These digital skills provide students with endless possibilities in today's world. These digital skills include: knowing how to communicate in digital environments, knowing how to create and manipulate media and multimedia, among others (Sep, n.d.).

However, as is currently known in México, implementing the provisions of the National Education and Training (NEM) with ICTs is facing major challenges such as: lack of connectivity or access in many schools, teacher training gaps, among others. However, the NEM seeks to make ICTs and digital skills part of this national educational integration project as a transformative axis that allows for a more equitable, creative, and relevant education for the 21st century (Ayala, 2024).

On the other hand, over the years, ICTs have been helping education to maximize the development of individuals' abilities. Digital tools have been developed to support the teaching-learning process and make people's lives easier. Among these digital tools, there are currently a variety of Web and/or mobile applications, some of which are specifically designed for people with disabilities, offering them the opportunity for better integration into society. This is the subject of this article. In this same vein, there are also some devices.

Currently, at the Universidad Autónoma de Baja California Sur (UABCS), the professors of the Academic Department of Computer Systems (DASC) are playing a very important role by taking on these new challenges of the 2030 Agenda, specifically SDG 4, in their work to educate more fraternal, humane, and inclusive generations. To this end, over the years they have been working on a project that impacts the social sector, such as the comprehensive project called "Teaching Mexican Sign Language Supported by Digital Tools". This project was born because, although there are currently very few people with hearing disabilities in México, it is necessary to continue taking actions to promote educational inclusion within the classroom.

The project, broadly speaking, focuses on developing software to teach Mexican Sign Language to people (children and adolescents) with or without hearing impairments, from early childhood education (preschool) to secondary school. This will foster better educational integration and inclusion both inside and outside the classroom, thereby developing more fraternal, humane, and inclusive individuals. This project has yielded results (Estrada-Cota et al., 2020) (Estrada-Cota et al., 2019), to name a few.

This article describes the development of a Web tool, in its second version (Estrada-Cota et al., 2021), which aims to teach and learn about the states and their capitals in Mexican Sign Language as a way to contribute to SDG 4 and demonstrate how using ICTs one can teach and learn by playing using challenges as a strategy for children with or without hearing disabilities in classrooms.

2 BACKGROUND

The Convention on the Rights of Persons with Disabilities (CRPD) defines persons with disabilities as: "those who have long-term physical, mental, intellectual or sensory impairments who, in response to a range of barriers, may be impeded in their full and effective participation in society on an equal basis with others" (UNICEF, 2019).

The World Health Organization (WHO) estimates that more than one billion people suffer from some type of disability, representing approximately 15% of the world's population. Of this population, the WHO indicates that 430 million people—representing 5%—suffer from hearing loss (World Health Organization: WHO, 2025).

In México, the Instituto Nacional de Estadística, Geografía e Informática (National Institute of Statistics, Geography, and Informatics, INEGI) revealed in the 2020 population census that 16.5% of the Mexican population has some type of disability, equivalent to almost 21 million people. Of that group, 5,104,664 people have a hearing impairment, representing 24.4% in this case (De Estadística Y, n.d.).

Finally, the WHO defines a deaf person as someone whose hearing acuity prevents them from naturally learning their native language, continuing to benefit from basic educational processes, participating in activities appropriate for their age, and who, due to their hearing, cannot fully function in their daily activities. (Soto-Rey & Pérez-Tejero, 2014). In this sense, hearing impairment not only represents a limitation in the ability to hear, but also has a significant impact on the individual's comprehensive development from the stages of childhood, ranging from the difficulty in acquiring speech and understanding oral language; their learning and thinking processes; interpersonal interactions; and the construction of identity, to name a few.

In the educational field, hearing impairment poses significant challenges. Therefore, we must continue promoting inclusive policies from all levels of government and allocating more resources to support the creation of projects that reach this segment of the population, with the aim of continuing to build more fraternal and inclusive societies.

3 MEXICAN SIGN LANGUAGE (LSM)

People with hearing impairments communicate through sign language, which consists of a series of gestural signs articulated with their hands, accompanied by facial expressions, body movements, and intentional gaze, all of which have a linguistic function.

In México, people with hearing disabilities developed their own form of communication called Lengua de Señas Mexicana (Mexican Sign Language, MSL). Like all languages, it has its own distinctive syntax, grammar, and vocabulary. MSL is articulated with the hands and accompanied by facial expressions and body movements. The Official Gazette of the Federation, in the section on the General Law for People with Disabilities, defines sign language as a language of the deaf community, which consists of: "a series of gestural signs articulated with the hands and accompanied by facial expressions, intentional gaze, and body movement, endowed with linguistic unction." (Mercader et al., 2017) Therefore, it is recognized as a national language, which indicates its validity in educational, cultural, and social settings (De Fleischmann & Pérez, 2011).

In the educational field, various studies (Muñoz & Pérez, 2020) (Aguiar et al., 2025) (Cárdenas et al., 2021) (Martínez-Olvera et al., 2024) have shown that deaf children who acquire LSM from an early age present a stronger cognitive, socio-emotional and communicative development than those who do not have an accessible linguistic system. This finding underscores the importance of incorporating LSM into inclusive educational programs that recognize linguistic diversity and ensure equal opportunities in the learning process.

The Mexican Federation of the Deaf (FMS) notes that LSM is a central element in the construction of the cultural identity of the deaf community (FEMESOR SJ, n.d.), sign language transcends its communicative function, serving as a symbol of belonging and social cohesion that reinforces values of solidarity and resilience. In this sense, promoting its teaching, dissemination, and recognition not only contributes to strengthening the deaf community but also favors the consolidation of a more inclusive society.

The FMS, as an organization, is broadly dedicated to representing, promoting, and defending the rights of the deaf community in México. Some of its activities and functions include: (FEMESOR SJ, n.d.)

- Promote the recognition of LSM as a language in its own right, defending it as the cultural and linguistic heritage of the deaf.
- Serve as a bridge between local associations for the deaf to coordinate efforts, share resources, experiences, and best practices.
- Organize events, workshops, or awareness-raising activities for society to promote inclusion, accessibility, and respect for deaf people.
- Support bilingual education so that deaf students can receive appropriate instruction in both their sign language and their spoken/written language.
- Participate in the formulation of public policies that guarantee fundamental rights.

On the other hand, like any language, LSM has specific rules and is composed of sign language and ideograms. Sign language is what spelling might be in spoken language, while ideograms represent an idea or word through hand movements (Aguiar et al., 2025) (Mercader et al., 2017) (See Figure 1).

Figure 1. Example of a kinesthetic sign sheet applied to the shape of a human animal's characteristic. Created by the authors.

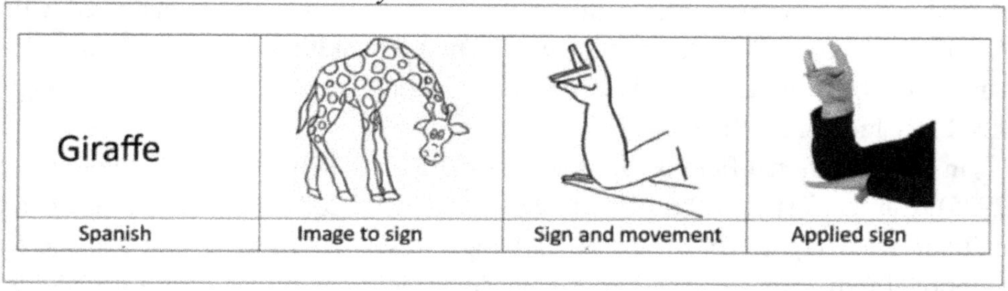

Thus, the combination of finger gestures and ideograms allows a person to communicate effectively and fluently through LSM. As seen in Figure 1, in LSM, the precision of hand movements, orientation, speed, and spatial location are essential for the message to be correctly understood.

In short, LSM is a living, autonomous Mexican language that plays an essential role in the lives of deaf people, guaranteeing their right to communicate, access education, and actively participate in society. Therefore, educational, political, and social institutions have an obligation to promote its preservation and strengthening, for the sake of building a country that respects linguistic diversity, human rights, and inclusion.

4 EXISTING TOOLS

One of the first tasks of the project was to investigate: what is being developed?, what initiatives or projects exist regarding the needs of people with disabilities? we found that ICTs are present in various parts of the world and in México, being immersed in most sectors of society: health, education, agriculture, administration, economics, among others, and continue to be powerful tools for the integration and inclusion of people with disabilities, providing support solutions for their disabilities.

First, the interdisciplinary group undertook the task of searching: for resources available for teaching the capitals and states of México in LSM? they found only various tools and apps for teaching and learning LSM; for example, Table 1 shows some of them in general terms, upon analyzing each of these, they found advantages and disadvantages, revealing an opportunity for the development of a web-based tool, since currently there is no free, flexible, and engaging Web tool or app specifically designed for teaching and learning the states and capitals of México in LSM.

Table 1. Existing tools

Title	Summary
Map interactive (Mapas Interactivos, 2025)	Website containing world maps for learning, including México.
Seterra (México: States - Map Quiz Game - Seterra, 2015)	A tool for learning about countries, for example, the states of Mexico.
Games! Come play with statistics and geography! (Cuéntame de México, 2025)	Website for teaching about México through games like memory and puzzles. Created by INEGI
Duo Signs (Martínez et al., 2025)	Disruptive mobile application with a pedagogical model for teaching LSM based on a dictionary.
App (Cuevas Valencia & Salgado Martínez, 2025)	Deep Learning algorithms, designed to recognize and translate LSM into Spanish
App (Rojas-Chávez & Quini-Villegas, 2019)	Mobile application, as a learning support tool, for children and adults with or without hearing impairment, to learn LSM through animated images, a game and a translator that spells the words through the fingerspelling alphabet.
App (Hurtado-Sánchez et al., 2023)	Inclusive augmented reality mobile application for learning LSM, as a learning support tool for people with hearing disabilities.

It is important to mention that there are also apps for teaching and learning LSM available for download on the App Store and Play Store, but no app was found with the features for teaching and learning the states and capitals of México.

5 METHODOLOGY APPLIED FOR THE DEVELOPMENT OF THE WEB TOOL IN LSM

To develop this Web tool, virtual and in-person meetings were first held to improve it. A multidisciplinary team (DASC teachers, primary school teachers, an expert in LSM teaching, and the software development team) was involved. The goal was to identify ways to improve the Web tool to support the teaching-learning process of México states and capitals through LSM. First, the general idea of the Web tool was analyzed. It will be used from any electronic device connected to the Internet. The goal was for the Web tool to teach the states and capitals to children with or without hearing disabilities through games, using an interactive map of México and audio and video in LSM. (See Figure 2)

Figure 2. Web tool idea based on NEM book. Created by the authors.

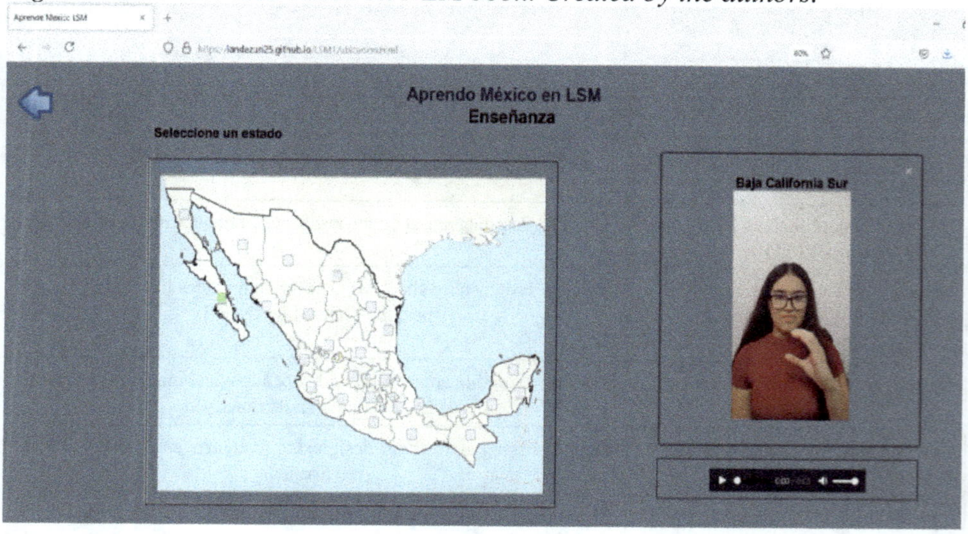

For the development of the Web tool, the agile XP (eXtreme Programming) methodology was followed with each of its phases: planning, design, coding and testing (Pressman & Maxim, 2021) with the aim of guaranteeing the quality of the Web tool to be developed.

By following the agile XP methodology, in the planning phase, the planning she carried out for the expected learnings of the NEM book called Cartography of México and the World was analyzed with the help of the fourth-year teacher, specifically the topic: Territorial Division of México on page 19 (SEP, Cartografía de México y el mundo, 2024), which she shared, in its she showed that there is a competence to be developed: Management of geographic information, which is supported by different topics such as: political organization of México. In turn, she shared the different digital tools on which it is based, and reaffirming that none of them contemplate the teaching of LSM. Subsequently, the functional requirements of the Web tool were defined, supported by the user stories (See figure 3). In these user stories, the requirements of the Web tool were defined, in its second version, defining two main modules: Teach and Play. The LSM expert then presented materials and content on how LSM is taught and her idea of leveraging technology to reach more people. She also explained how a Web-based tool that incorporated videos would be ideal for teaching Mexican states and capitals in LSM.

For teaching purposes, the program was divided into three parts: states, capitals, and capitals and states of México. These were supported by LSM videos that could be played as many times as necessary, a corresponding audio file -if necessary-, and a map of México. Learning was about playing, and three levels were considered: easy, intermediate, and expert, as a strategy to assess learning, and the incorporation of life experiences as a motivational strategy in the game. Other requirements defined by the developers were: concentrating information in a single location through a database, and making it accessible from any electronic device connected to the Internet.

Figure 3. User stories. Created by the authors.

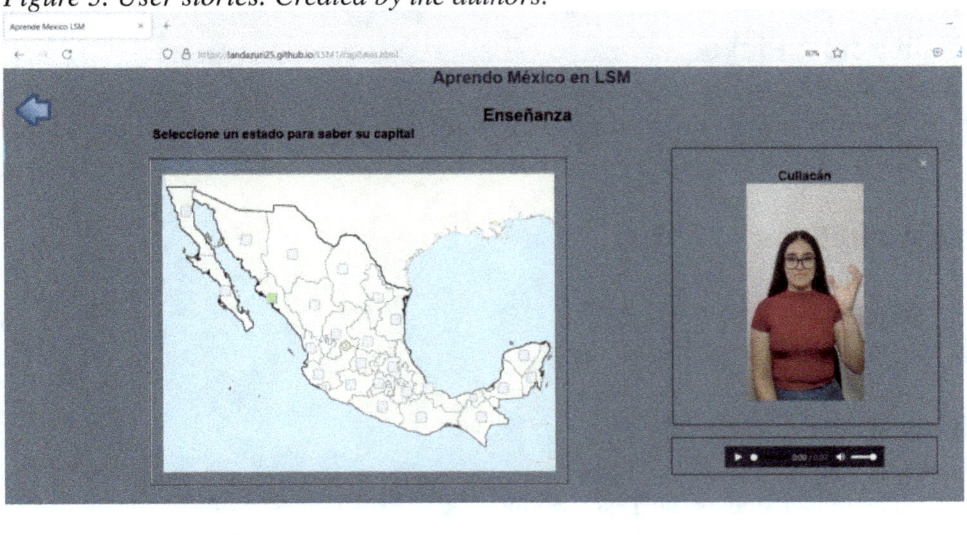

The main functional requirements of the Web tool were captured by means of the use case diagram (see figure 4), which is composed of:

Figure 4. Web tool use case. Created by the authors.

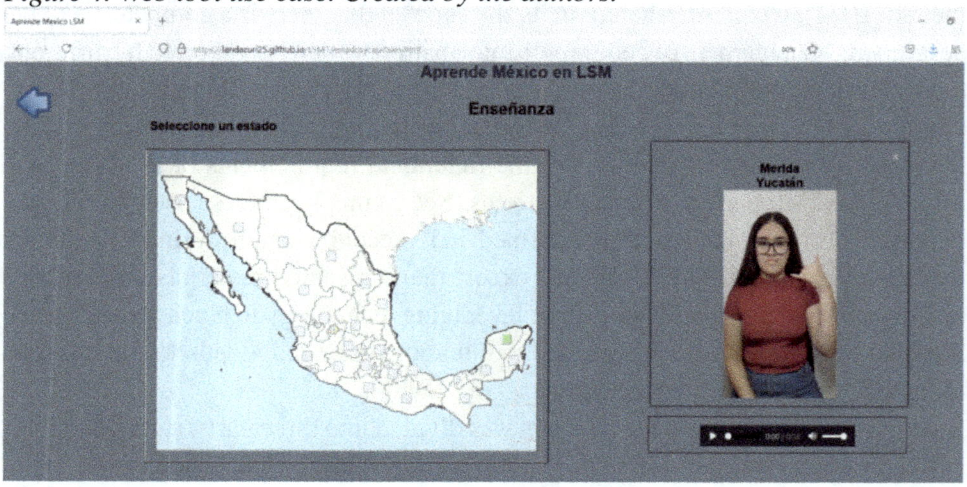

Use Case

Teaching: In this module, all states and capitals will be taught in LSM using an iterative map. A video containing a detailed description of the corresponding sign was used.

Main actor: Player

Overview: The player uses the Web tool to learn a state or capital or both by interactively viewing a video in LSM.

Preconditions

The player must be registered.
The Web tool must be running.

Main flow

The player selects the Teach option.
The Web tool displays States, Capitals, States and Capitals.

The player prepares and begins the learning dynamic.
The Web tool displays the selected information.

Postconditions

The Web tool records the progress of the chosen activity.

Exceptions

Connection failure or tool out of service.
Use Case Play: This module aims to motivate the user to play, through an iterative map - as a strategy to evaluate learning - an easy, fun and educational game is offered, where users test their knowledge in LSM by selecting a State or Capital of México related to what was taught.

Main actor: Player

Overview: The player uses the tool to learn a state or capital or both by interactively viewing a video in LSM.

Preconditions

The player must be registered.
The Web tool must be running.

Main flow

The player selects the Play option.
The Web tool displays States, Capitals, States and Capitals.
The player prepares and begins the dynamics of playing.
The Web tool displays the selected information.

Postconditions:

The Web tool records the progress of the chosen activity.

Exceptions

Connection failure or Web tool down.

Player actor: This is the person who can access and learn about the states and capitals of México in the LSM through an electronic device with an Internet connection.

Administrator actor: This is the person in charge of the correct functioning of the Web tool.

Subsequently, in the design phase, each interface was designed based on the defined requirements, taking into account usability criteria, which are intuitive, easy-to-use, and clean, primarily for children. The database and sequence diagrams for the Web tool's behavior were also designed. Finally, each video and audio corresponding to the capitals and states of México was recorded with the assistance of the LSM specialist. (See figures 5, 6, 7)

Figure 5. Web tool sequence diagram. Teach option. Created by the authors.

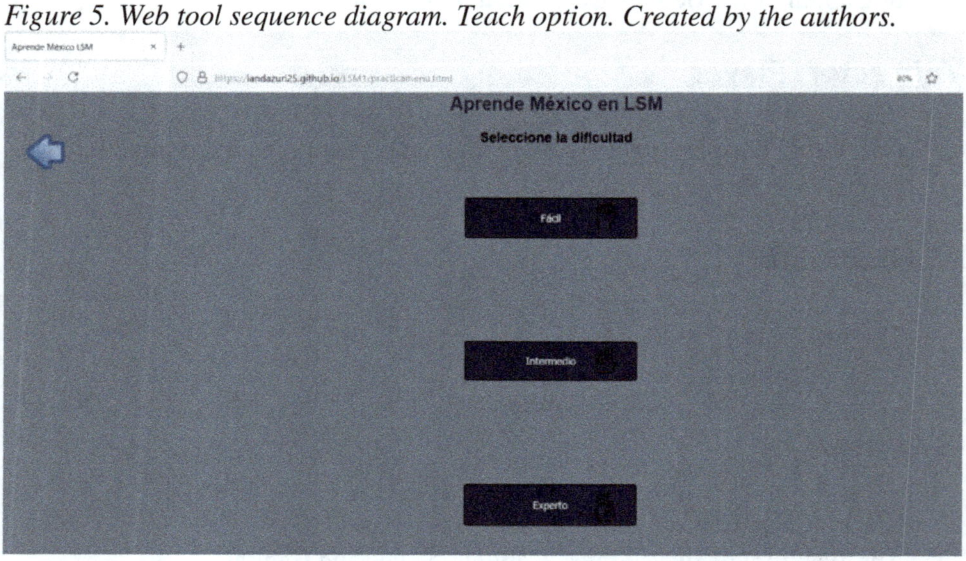

Figure 6. Web tool use case. Created by the authors.

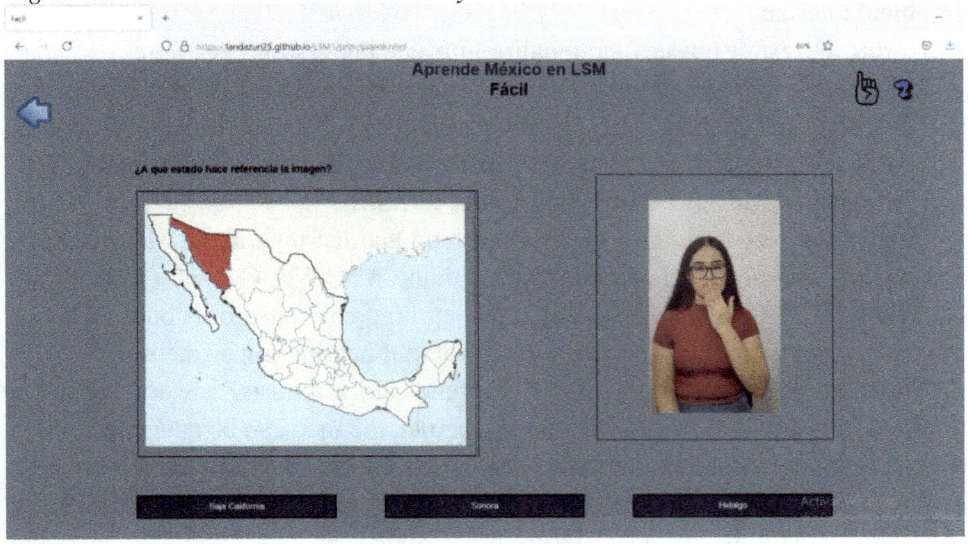

Figure 7. Web tool use case. Created by the authors.

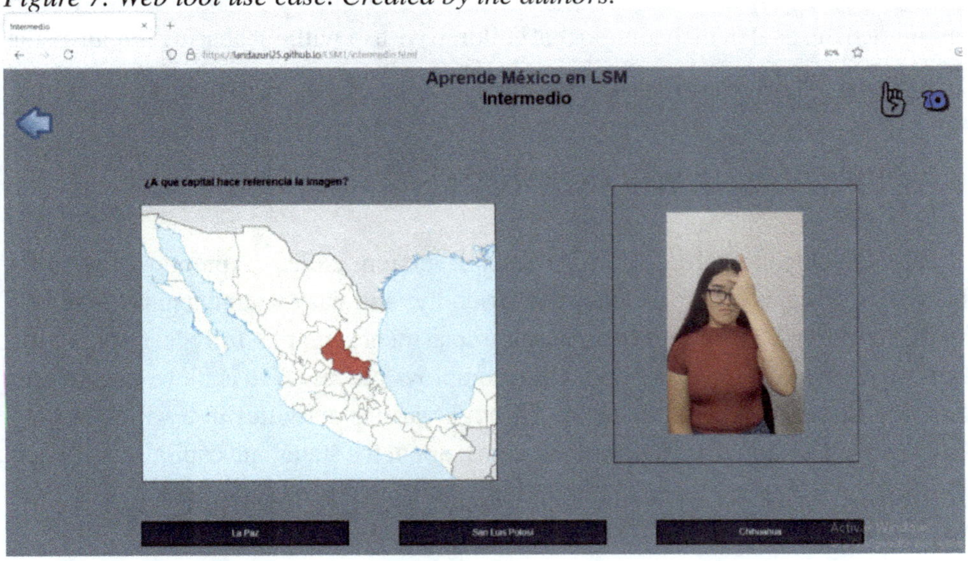

Then, in the coding phase, the project was developed using different technologies and tools; PHP was used as the server-side language for page rendering. The pages were coded using HTML 5. JavaScript was used on the client side to handle asynchronous calls to the server via AJAX, and also to manage the Web tool's graphical interface.

During the testing phase, functionality, unit, and integration tests were conducted to detect potential errors in the Web tool. These tests verified its correct operation, thus releasing the Web tool (in its second version) for use with children with or without hearing impairments. This agile methodology helped develop a quality Web tool for teaching Mexican states and capitals in LSM.

Finally, the web tool developed for teaching and learning about México states and capitals, was designed in accordance with the W3C Web Content Accessibility Guidelines (WCAG) 2.2 to ensure that the learning environment is both inclusive and usable by children and people with or without hearing impairments.

Under the Perceivable principle, appropriate color contrasts were ensured in the resulting interface. Under the Operable principle, the map can be navigated with a mouse, keyboard, or other alternative device. Under the Understandable principle, a clear structure and accessible language were used, as the primary target audience is children; therefore, technical terms was avoided, and meaningful icons were used. Finally, to comply with the Robust principle, the tool was developed using HTML5 and JavaScript, adhering to W3C standards to ensure compatibility with screen readers and various browsers.

By applying WCAG 2.2 to the development of the Web tool, the aim was to strengthen the goal of inclusion so that children with or without hearing impairments can learn equitably.

6 BRIEF TOUR OF THE WEB TOOL

The developed Web tool, in its second version, called "Aprendo México en LSM," is designed with a clean, user-friendly, and easy-to-understand interface so that children with or without hearing impairments can playfully learn about the states and capitals of México in LSM. It employs processes to achieve meaningful learning through an active process. Through various activities in a valid learning environment, children are taught and learned about the states and capitals of México in LSM through play, thereby maintaining their interest and motivation. The Web tool's main interface offers two options: (See Figure 8)

- Teaching: In this option, children are taught to learn about México, its states, capitals, and states in LSM, by accessing another menu.
- Play. In this option, children can play to assess what they've learned in LSM regarding Mexican states and capitals. To do this, this option accesses a menu

where they can choose the difficulty of the game: easy, intermediate, and expert.

Figure 8. Main interface of the Web tool. Created by the authors.

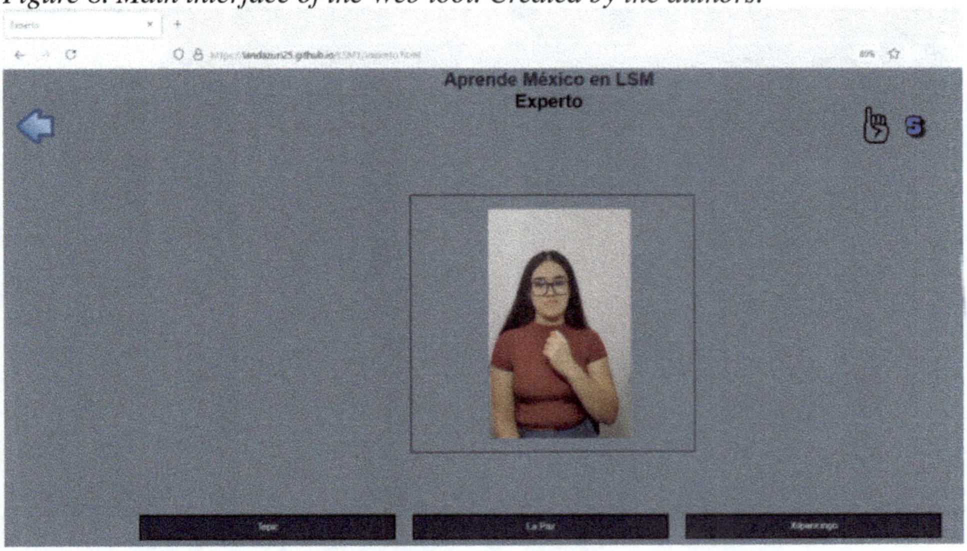

Teaching Option

In this option, children access another menu to choose between the options: states, capitals, capitals, and states of México in LSM. (See figure 9) In the states option, the interface displays a map of México with political divisions. As soon as the child chooses a state on the map, a video begins to play in which the sign language for the chosen state is taught in LSM. The video can be played as many times as desired until the child has mastered the sign. An audio recording of the state can also be played. (See figure 10)

Figure 9. Teaching Interface. What are we going to learn? Created by the authors.

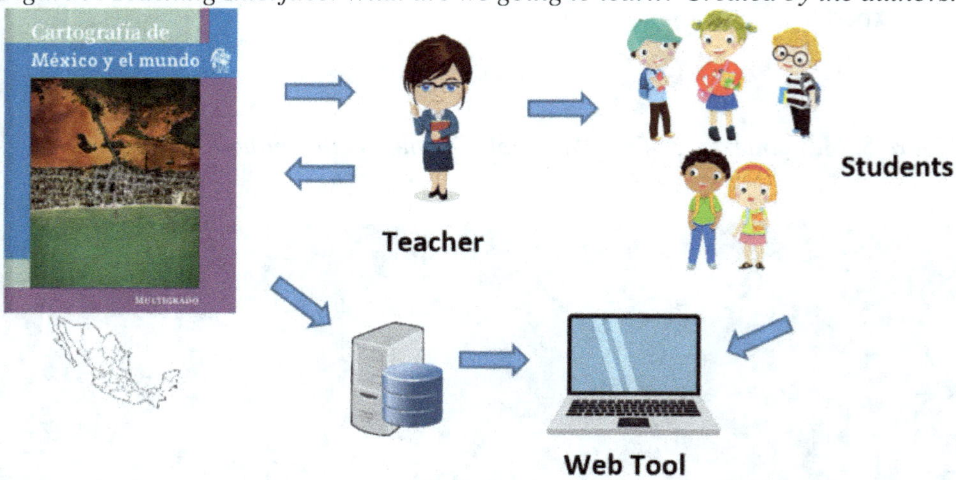

Figure 10. Teaching - State Interface. Created by the authors.

Teaching: Capitals	Teach: States	Play: States
As a fourth-grade teacher, I want to teach capitals in LSM so that students can learn the capitals of the states of Mexico and communicate with people with hearing impairments.	As a fourth-grade teacher, I want to teach the states in LSM so that students can learn about the states of Mexico and be able to communicate with people with hearing impairments.	By watching a video in LSM, the student would choose the corresponding state on a map of Mexico and reinforce what they learned in LSM to communicate with people with hearing impairments.

If the capital option is chosen, the interface displays a map of México with political divisions. As soon as the child selects a state on the map, a video begins to play, showing the sign for the chosen state's capital in LSM. An audio recording of the state's capital can also be played. (See Figure 11)

Figure 11. Teaching-Capital Interface. Created by the authors.

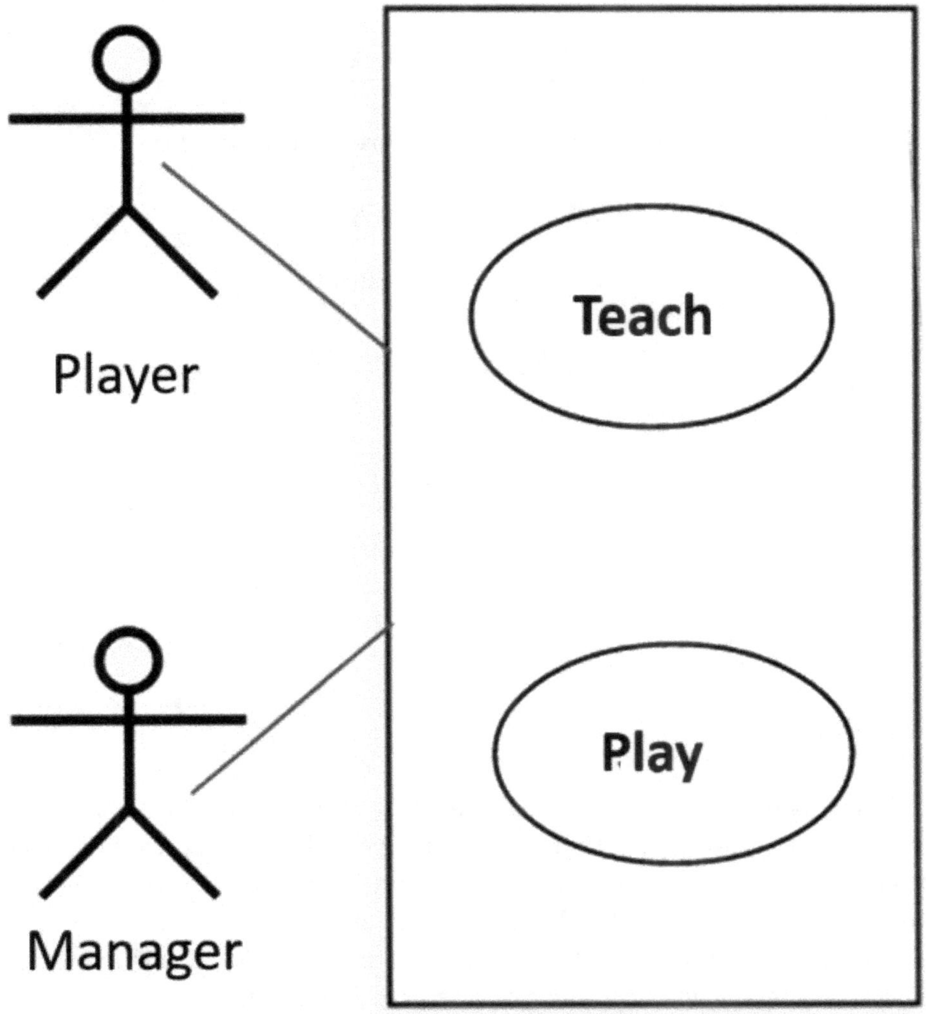

And in the capitals and states option, the interface displays a map of México with its political divisions. As soon as the child selects a state on the map, a video begins to play, showing the sign for the chosen capital and state in LSM. The video can be played as many times as necessary to achieve the desired learning. There is also an audio recording of the chosen capital and state. (See figure 12)

Figure 12. Teaching-Capital and State Interface. Created by the authors.

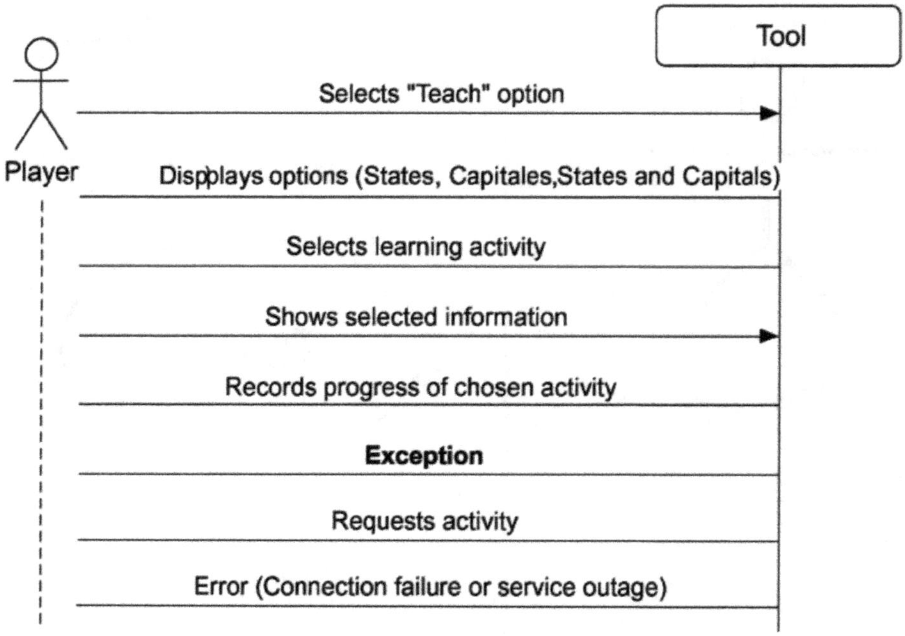

Play Option

In this option, what has been learned about México (states, capitals, capitals and states) in LSM is evaluated. To do this, the child accesses another menu to choose a difficulty: easy, intermediate, or expert. (See figure 13). The game, on its easy difficulty, asks the child: "What state does the image refer to?" A red-lit state is randomly displayed within the México map interface. A video is immediately played with the sign in LSM, which represents the illuminated state. This video can be played as many times as desired. Three answers are given to choose from using buttons. When a button is chosen and it is correct, it turns green and the child advances; otherwise, it turns red and continues until the answer is correct. In addition, the game has 16 lives that encourage the child to not lose in order to advance until the entire map of México is completed. (See figure 14)

Figure 13. Play interface. Created by the authors.

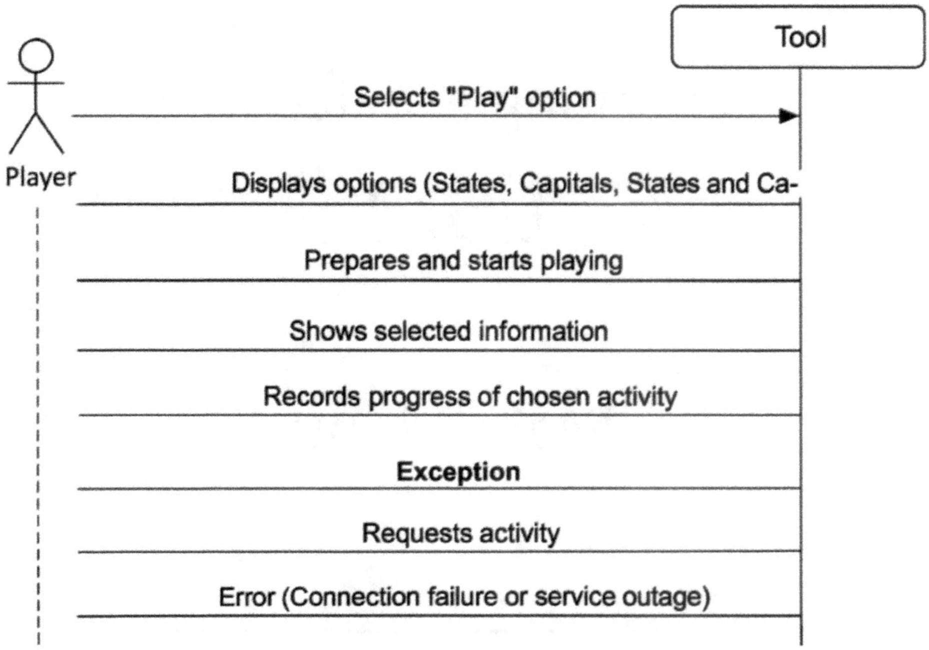

Figure 14. Play interface. Created by the authors.

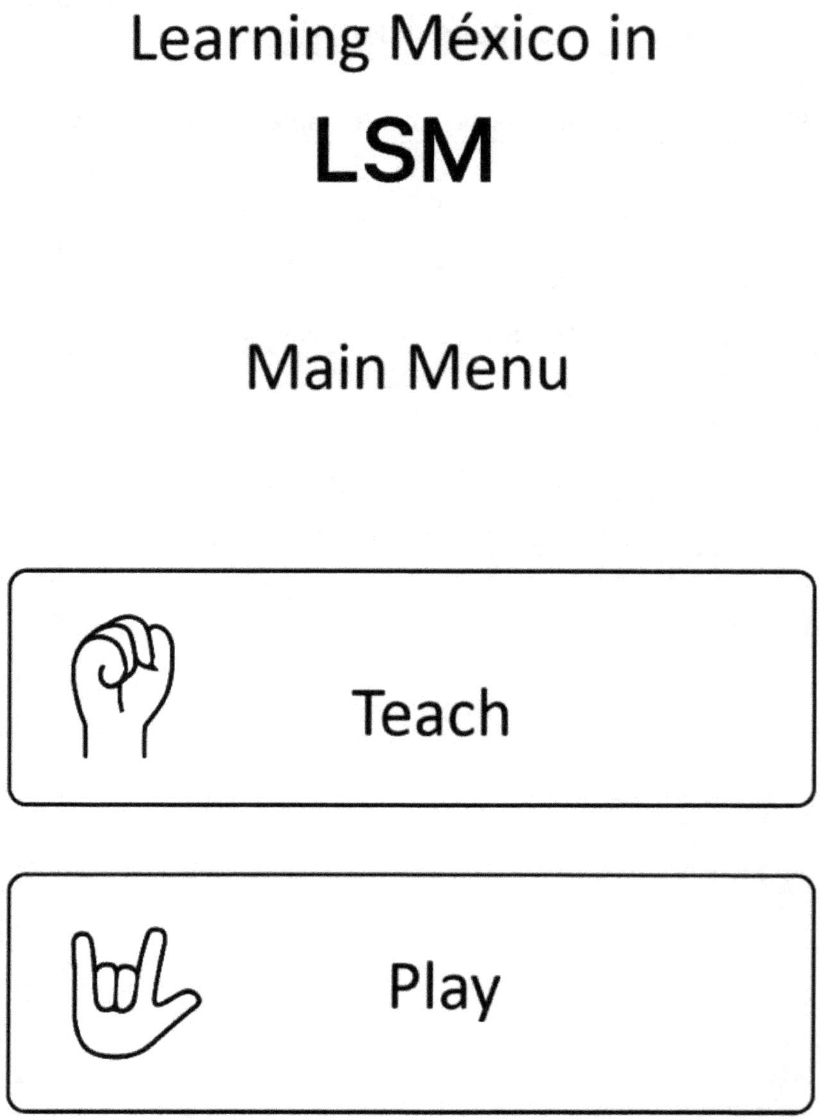

In the intermediate difficulty, the child is asked, "What capital does the image refer to?" A map of México is randomly displayed within the interface with a state highlighted in red. A video is immediately played with the LSM sign representing the state's capital illuminated. This video can be played as many times as desired. Three answers are given to choose from using buttons. When a button is chosen and it is correct, the button turns green and the child advances; otherwise, it turns red and continues until the answer is correct. In addition, this game has 10 lives that encourage the child to not lose in order to advance until the entire map of México is completed. (See figure 15)

Figure 15. Play interface – intermediate level. Created by the authors.

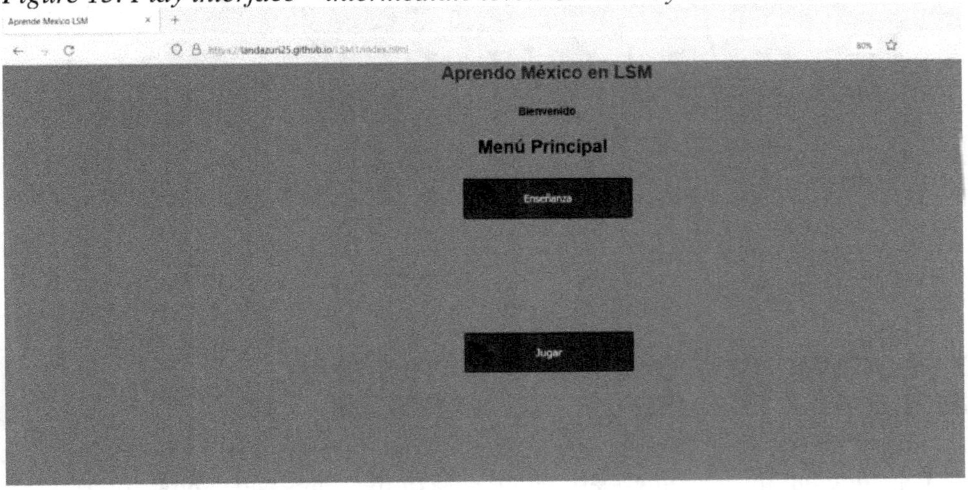

In the expert difficulty setting, the child is shown a video that plays randomly and immediately with the LSM sign representing a state or the capital of a state in México. They are given a choice between three answers using buttons. If the correct button is chosen, it turns green and they advance; otherwise, it turns red and they continue until the correct answer is reached. This option only allows 5 lives, which encourages them not to lose in order to advance until they complete all of México. (See figure 16)

Figure 16. Play interface – Expert level. Created by the authors.

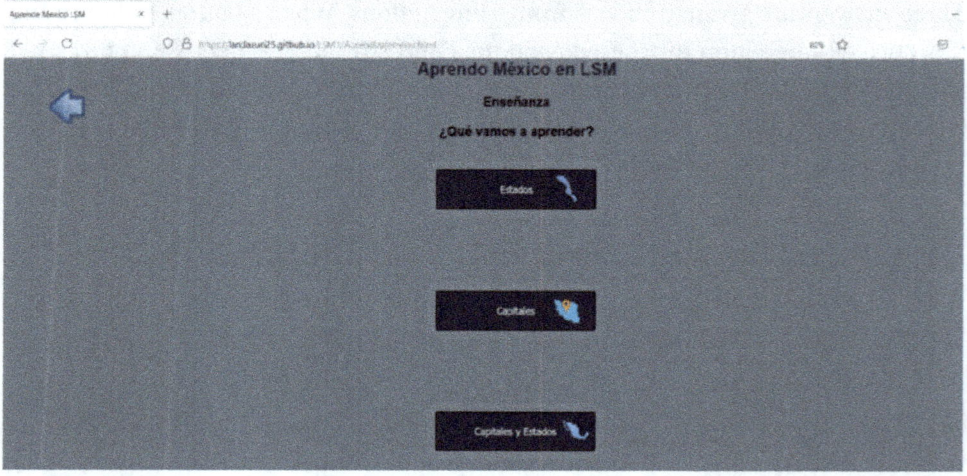

7 RECOMMENDATIONS FOR STRATEGIES TO IMPLEMENT THE USE OF THE WEB TOOL

Carrying out the teaching-learning process of the states and capitals of México in LSM with elementary school children with or without hearing impairments undoubtedly represents a great challenge, and at the same time a great opportunity to foster in children a love of México, their country, and geographic knowledge. To help make this process meaningful, it is essential that classrooms implement active, inclusive, and participatory strategies that motivate children to learn in a playful and collaborative manner. Furthermore, teaching-learning LSM through the use of the Web tool offers added value, as it not only offers cognitive skills to elementary school children, but also educates new generations to be more fraternal and inclusive. Below is a set of strategies worked on or used previously to achieve other learning that the fourth-grade teacher uses and that together with the LSM expert reviewed, these strategies mainly cover three stages: initial exploration, construction of knowledge and appropriation of the LSM, it is important to mention that they are only recommendations of strategies to support the teaching learning process of LSM using a Web tool.

In the initial exploration stage, the teacher's goal is to spark interest and motivate children by capturing their attention and connecting their previous experiences with the new content. Some recommended strategies include:

- Map in the classroom. The idea is to place a large map of México in the classroom so children can interact with it by approaching, pointing at, and locating states they already know, for example, their state or capital of México. This activity helps foster curiosity and serves as a starting point.
- State Stories: The idea is that through interesting facts, fairs, events, typical foods, traditions, or tourist attractions, children can connect learning about the state or capital with real-life situations.
- Brainstorming: This strategy asks children which Mexican states or capitals they know or remember, and they jot down their memories to build collective learning.

In the knowledge-building stage, the idea is that once motivated, active and meaningful learning is achieved, supported by activities designed to memorize and meaningfully understand the states and capitals. Some of the recommended strategies are:

- Coloring maps: Provide maps of México with political divisions so children can color the states and identify their capitals with a star or dot. This strategy helps with spatial location and visual association.
- Memory: Make cards with a representative picture of each state and others with the state's capital highlighted. With the cards already made, organize the children into teams so they can identify the state or capital through a memory game. This strategy promotes visual and kinesthetic memory in children.
- Mexican Traveler's Game. The idea is for children to work in teams on a tour through each Mexican state and identify its capital and a characteristic fact. This connects the idea of a fun and collaborative tour and fosters learning for the children.
- Use of ICT in the classroom through short videos about Mexican states and capitals that capture children's attention and thus diversify the way they process information.

In the LSM appropriation stage, inclusion is sought through technology. The objective of this stage is to use the Web tool to support the teaching and learning of LSM, specifically the states and capitals of México, raising children's awareness of the importance of inclusion, in this case, linguistic and cultural inclusion. Some of the recommended strategies are:

- Introducing LSM, you should first introduce LSM as a recognized language, used and developed in México by the deaf community. It is recommended to start with an introductory video presenting basic signs in LSM, and then begin with “México,” “state,” or “capital.”

- Presentation and use of the Web tool. The idea is to introduce the Web tool and begin to see how it works. Teaching and learning so that children begin to explore it. For example, when selecting the state “Baja California Sur,” a video appears showing the corresponding sign. Then, when selecting the capital for the state of Baja California Sur, the sign for “La Paz” is shown. This way, little by little, they can advance through all the states and capitals of México.
- Practice activities, the idea is that children can play using the Web tool to validate their learning, for example with the games:
    - Team challenges: Teams of children are formed, and with the help of the Web tool, a state is chosen. The children must identify the sign in LSM and then replicate it to see how well they have learned it; this also applies to capital cities.
    - State and Capital Bingo also uses the Web tool with the corresponding videos, and children must mark the LSM symbol corresponding to the state or capital on their bingo.

Considering these recommendations supports meaningful learning, not only by memorizing but also by understanding and associating information through playful experiences; they incorporate the use of ICTs into their learning by using the Web tool; they promote inclusion, as they learn the importance of learning a new language, such as LSM; and multisensory stimulation, as it integrates different modalities (visual, auditory, kinesthetic, and gestural), which favors the learning of all learning styles.

In conclusion, the strategy recommendations include implementing or relying on them to transform the learning experience into a dynamic, meaningful, and inclusive experience through the use of appropriate teaching strategies. Incorporating LSM through the use of the Web tool is highly significant, as children will construct learning experiences about México's states and capitals, and in turn, will begin to develop awareness about respect and inclusion.

8 SUGGESTION FOR THE IMPLEMENTATION PLAN

As previously mentioned, inclusive education has taken on significant importance in recent years, as it seeks to ensure that all students, regardless of their characteristics, have access to quality learning experiences. In México, LSM is a fundamental language and pillar for the deaf community, and it seeks to continue including the community in educational environments. Accordingly, this implementation plan is designed and suggested to promote the integration of digital tools into LSM teaching to foster equity in education.

First, this implementation plan has defined objectives and is comprised of resources and strategies for the successful implementation of the developed Web tool, "Aprendo México en LSM." Likewise, the teacher and the LSM expert were involved in the implementation of this plan, in order to obtain their perspectives as experts in child management and as facilitators of teaching elementary school children.

The overall objective of this plan is to successfully implement the "Aprendo México en LSM" Web tool. This tool serves as an innovative pedagogical resource for teaching Mexican states and capitals to fourth-grade elementary school children in various school settings, fostering inclusive and equitable learning. The specific objectives are:

- Train teachers in the pedagogical use of the Web tool.
- Promote the inclusion of students with hearing disabilities.
- Promote interaction and collaborative learning between children with and without hearing impairments.
- Evaluate the impact of the tool on student motivation and learning.

As mentioned above, in fourth grade of primary school one of the expected learnings through the textbook "Cartografía de México y del Mundo" is that children learn the states and capitals of México, in which traditional methods have been applied for teaching, and for this, this Web tool was developed that in addition to providing visual and interactive support, allows LSM to be taught through the use of ICT, thus contributing to the improvement of fraternal and inclusive societies.

The Web tool helps close learning gaps, especially in vulnerable contexts, as it allows children with and without hearing impairments to access the same content through fun activities that utilize visual resources such as LSM videos and interactions.

This suggested implementation plan identifies several activities: initial diagnosis, teacher training, curriculum adaptation, implementation in urban schools, rural schools, and CAMs (Centro de Atención Múltiple - Multiple Care Centers), and evaluation and monitoring. It is important to mention that CAMs are special education institutions in México that provide comprehensive care to students with disabilities. They offer education from preschool through primary and secondary school levels, with the goal of fostering their autonomy and social and professional inclusion through significant support and curricular adaptations.

The Initial Diagnosis activity aims to carry out a diagnosis of both the technological and pedagogical conditions in the urban, rural, or CAMs school where the Web tool will be implemented. This includes:

- Identification of available technological infrastructure (computers, tablets, Internet connection).
- Teachers' digital literacy level; this assessment will allow for the establishment of a training plan.
- Prior knowledge of LSM by both teachers and children (in the case of urban and rural schools, the goal is to raise awareness).
- Specific needs of CAMS.

This activity will allow you to identify areas of opportunity before starting to use the Web tool and when you plan to use it in the best possible conditions.

The Teacher Training activity aims to ensure the correct implementation of the Web tool. This teacher training activity considers:

- Technical aspects, such as ICT management, Web tool management, content navigation, and basic troubleshooting.
- Pedagogical aspects, teaching strategies for integrating Web tools into classes, use of collaborative dynamics, and learning assessment.
- Inclusive awareness: A brief introduction to LSM for urban and rural school teachers so they understand its value and can foster inclusive attitudes in the classroom.

Training can be delivered in a hybrid format (in-person and online), taking into account the technological limitations of each of the urban and rural schools where it is intended to be implemented; in CAMS, only the first two aspects are considered.

The Curriculum Adaptation activity aims to match the expected learning outcomes of the topic with those of the Web tool. To achieve this, as mentioned above, teaching strategies are suggested that combine:

- Previous activities: maps, games or oral questions.
- Using the Web Tool: Exploring states and capitals using LSM videos.
- Post-activities: group questions that reinforce the acquired learning.

This activity also takes into account the characteristics of CAMs, where greater weight will be given to visual resources and interaction with the LSM.

The Implementation activity will be carried out gradually and is suggested in three stages:

- Pilot phase: three urban schools, two rural schools, and one CAM will be selected to evaluate the functionality of the Web tool.

- Expansion phase: After the initial evaluation, the content will be adjusted and its use will be extended to more urban schools.
- Consolidation stage, integration into lesson plans, with ongoing pedagogical and technical monitoring.

In urban and rural schools, the Web tool will be used as a complementary resource, while in CAMs it will be used as a central learning strategy.

Subsequently, in the evaluation and monitoring stage, the evaluation will determine the effectiveness of the Web tool, which will be aided by various instruments:

- Diagnostic and final questionnaires for children to measure progress in their acquired knowledge of states and capitals.
- Direct observation in class to identify the level of motivation and participation.
- Interviews with teachers to understand their perceptions of the pedagogical impact.
- Parent surveys to explore changes in children's learning motivation, in this case in LSM.

On the other hand, monitoring will be carried out during the planned time of use of the Web tool, with reports and a final report.

It's important to mention that a central aspect of the plan is to ensure that the Web tool not only serves children without hearing impairments but also promotes inclusion in regular classrooms. Therefore, it is necessary to work extensively to raise awareness among children in urban and rural schools about the importance of linguistic diversity, in this case LSM.

In carrying out this plan, you may face challenges that will require solutions, for example:

- Limited connectivity in both urban and rural schools or in CAMs, enable an offline version of the Web tool.
- Resistance to change or the use of the Web tool among some teachers, which requires strengthening training and pedagogical support.

The implementation of this Web tool seeks to generate the following impacts:

- Improve learning about México's states and capitals among fourth-grade elementary school children.
- Learn LSM specifically the states and capitals of México.
- Increase children's interest in learning LSM.
- Promote a culture of respect for linguistic diversity in the school environment.

- Educate more fraternal and inclusive generations.

The implementation of this Web-based tool represents a significant opportunity to advance inclusive and equitable education. By integrating LSM as a central resource, the participation of children with and without hearing impairments in the learning process is ensured and a school environment where diversity is recognized as a value is promoted.

This suggested plan, which includes initial diagnosis, teacher training, curriculum adaptation, implementation, and evaluation and monitoring, offers a clear and viable path to ensuring that educational technology, through the use of Web tools, contributes to strengthening learning in different school settings in México.

9 RESULTS

The development of digital educational tools contributes significantly to the teaching-learning process, as they allow for the creation of interactive and innovative experiences for children. In this case, for teaching LSM, the use of these digital educational tools is a particularly valuable resource, as it offers the possibility of integrating children with or without hearing impairments into a single inclusive environment. As mentioned above, with the aim of continuing to build more fraternal and inclusive societies, this Web tool was developed, currently in its second version. Its general purpose is to promote the teaching and learning of Mexican states and capitals in LSM in a fun and accessible way.

This Web tool is one of the main outcomes of the project, which seeks to integrate digital educational resources, in this case, with fourth-grade elementary school children, with or without hearing impairments, to learn through play. As explained, the Web tool, through videos and an interactive map, helps children identify both the states and capitals of México in LSM. Being a Web tool, it allows access to any location, at any time, as long as you have an electronic device with an Internet connection, i.e., 24/7. This breaks down the barriers of time and space that generally limit access to these educational resources.

Another important aspect is that several educational strategies or scenarios have been proposed for the use of the Web tool. Initial testing has begun in urban primary schools; results have not yet been measured, but these have been carried out to verify the relevance of the content and the ease of use of the Web tool. Similarly, the fourth-grade teacher, the LSM expert, and the development team fine-tuned both the user experience and the interface, with the aim of making improvements for a third version. Communities of people with hearing disabilities are currently being contacted for the presentation and acceptance of the tool, and to directly assess the impact it will have on expanding their knowledge and strengthening their identity.

The development of this Web tool helps foster values of inclusion and camaraderie in elementary school children, as they can communicate through LSM. In this case, children with and without hearing impairments could play together, thus fostering a more equitable and diversity-respecting educational environment. This undoubtedly helps children develop empathy and, at the same time, acquire knowledge about Mexican geography in a way that is different from traditional teaching. Playful motivation through games undoubtedly significantly helps elementary school children maintain their attention, thereby promoting content retention.

In short, one of the main characteristics of using educational tools is that they positively contribute to children with or without hearing impairments, as they provide an innovative and interactive learning experience. The main result is the creation of a Web tool called “Aprendo México en LSM”, now in its second version. This educational tool will motivate fourth-grade children with or without hearing impairments to learn the states and capitals of México in LSM through fun play, from anywhere and at any time with an electronic device connected to the Internet. As an innovative, flexible, and inclusive Web tool, it offers new opportunities for accessible education to reach more primary school children, thereby helping to achieve the educational objectives they seek: to guarantee quality education with equal opportunities for all.

On the other hand, tests are being conducted in various elementary schools, specifically for fourth-grade children without hearing impairments. The Web tool has been validated with tests conducted on the fourth-grade teacher, the LSM expert, and the development team, as well as in centers where there are children with hearing impairments. This is done with the goal of educating more inclusive and caring children in the classroom.

On the other hand, while testing is underway, quantitative results are still lacking, and qualitative results are scarce. In this area, for example, the user experience and user-friendliness have been positive. Both the LSM expert and the classroom teacher highlighted the clean, intuitive interface, suitable for children with or without hearing impairments. Regarding inclusion and accessibility, the inclusive value of the web tool for children with or without hearing impairments was recognized, and the incorporation of LSM videos and optional audio promotes equitable access to information. In terms of motivation and usability, the integration of difficulty levels (easy, intermediate, and expert) and the use of lives within the game foster motivation, healthy competition, and perseverance. Furthermore, both the LSM expert and the classroom teacher noted that the gamification strategy increases user participation and sustained interest. As mentioned previously, this web tool has educational and social value, as it promotes values of inclusion, respect and empathy towards people with hearing disabilities and the idea that more fraternal, more humane people continue to be educated on the subject of inclusion.

10 CONCLUSION AND FUTURE WORK

In conclusion, it is concluded that developing digital educational tools that support the teaching-learning process will positively benefit education, especially in terms of inclusion. This Web-based tool will support elementary-aged children with or without hearing impairments in learning about the states and capitals of México in LSM in a more personalized and automated way, facilitating immediate feedback through an electronic device connected to the Internet. In turn, this Web-based tool represents a teaching resource with great potential to transform the teaching of LSM and the expected learning outcomes related to the states and capitals of México. Its innovative, flexible, and inclusive nature offers new opportunities to make education accessible to a greater number of children, contributing to the fulfillment of educational objectives that seek to guarantee quality education with equal opportunities for all.

As future work, we plan to continue improving and expanding the Web tool, incorporating or creating new tools that incorporate new educational content related to Spanish, mathematics, or the history, culture, and geography of México, as well as more advanced gamification strategies that increase children's motivation to learn LSM. Likewise, it will be essential to conduct evaluations with a larger number of children from urban, rural, and CAM schools to obtain feedback that will allow us to improve the accessibility, usability, and pedagogical quality of the Web tool.

REFERENCES

Aguiar, M. E. A. L., Fernández, M. F. P., Góngora, J. R. G. C., Marín, I. C. M. F., Pérez, A. J. P. I., Sansores, F. N. S. R., & Uicab, Y. S. U. C. (2025, January). *Compendio de buenas prácticas didácticas para el fortalecimiento de la educación especial*. Retrieved October 1, 2025, from https://educacion.yucatan.gob.mx/multimedia/publicaciones/250307_CompendioAlumnosSordos.pdf

Ayala, G. R. (2024, August 22). Retos digitales para la Nueva Escuela Mexicana. *El Financiero*. https://www.elfinanciero.com.mx/opinion/colaborador-invitado/2024/08/22/retos-digitales-para-la-nueva-escuela-mexicana/

Cárdenas, G., Castillo, L., Espínola, L., Fernández, C., Góngora, J., Pérez, N., & Solís, C. (2021). Discapacidad auditiva. In *Colección Juntos Trabajamos por la Inclusión*. SEGEY. https://educacionespecial.sep.gob.mx/storage/recursos/2023/05/lwwYcPkM6G-220126_Tomo3_DiscapacidadAuditiva.pdf

Cuevas Valencia, R. E., & Salgado Martínez, G. A. (2025). Aplicación Móvil Basada en Deep Learning para la Inclusión Educativa de Personas Sordas: Reconocimiento y Traducción de la Lengua de Señas Mexicana. *RIDE Revista Iberoamericana para la Investigación y el Desarrollo Educativo*, *16*(31). Advance online publication. DOI: 10.23913/ride.v16i31.2538

De Estadística, Y. I. N. (n.d.). *Censo de Población y Vivienda 2020*. https://www.inegi.org.mx/programas/ccpv/2020/default.html#Documentacion

De Fleischmann, M. E. S., & Pérez, R. G. (2011). *Manos con voz: diccionario de lengua de señas mexicana*.

éntame de México. (2025). Inegi.org.mx. https://cuentame.inegi.org.mx/juegos/default.html

Estrada-Cota, I., Carreno-Leon, M. A., Sandoval-Bringas, J. A., & Leyva-Carrillo, A. A. (2020). "Manos que hablan": Tool for teaching – Learning the Mexican sign language for children with or without hearing disabilities. *IEEE*, 173–179. DOI: 10.1109/CONTIE51334.2020.00039

Estrada-Cota, I., Carreno-Leon, M. A., Sandoval-Bringas, J. A., Leyva-Carrillo, A. A., & Gutierrez-Sandoval, A. J. (2019). Design of a Web Tool to Support Language Therapy for Children with Cleft Lip and / or Palate. *IEEE*, 164–1643. DOI: 10.1109/CONTIE49246.2019.00039

Estrada-Cota, I., Carreno-Leon, M. A., Sandoval-Bringas, J. A., Leyva-Carrillo, A. A., & Quiroz, H. X. C. (2021). Design of a Web tool for teaching – learning of states and capitals of México through the Mexican sign language. *IEEE*, 174–179. DOI: 10.1109/CONTIE54684.2021.00036

éxico: States - Map Quiz Game - Seterra. (2015). Seterra.com. https://online.seterra.com/es/vgp/3078

FEMESOR SJ. (n.d.). https://www.femesorsj.com/

Leveraging ICTs to support the achievement of post-2015 education agenda. (2015). Retrieved September 29, 2025, from https://unesdoc.unesco.org/ark:/48223/pf0000232379

Mapas Interactivos. (2025). Didactalia.net. https://mapasinteractivos.didactalia.net/comunidad/mapasflashin

Martínez, N., Elena, B., Sánchez, M. S., & Saray, P. (2025). Duo Señas: Aplicación móvil para conocer y practicar inclusivamente la Lengua de Señas Mexicana (LSM) mediante metodologías ágiles y tecnologías multiplataforma. Ciencia Latina Revista Científica Multidisciplinar, 9(3), 1618–1633. DOI: 10.37811/cl_rcm.v9i3.17771

Martínez-Olvera, W., González-Miy, D., Moreno-Vite, I., & Martínez-Cervantes, Y. (2024). Inclusión educativa del Sordo: Panorama en México y Veracruz. *Revista Stultifera*, *7*(1), 221–251. DOI: 10.4206/rev.stultifera.2024.v7n1-09

Mercader, C. A. M. F., Escobar, L. E. D., Ramírez, M. R. R. B., Pool, M. P. W., & Cruz, M. C. A. (2017, September 25). *DICCIONARIO DE LENGUA DE SEÑAS MEXICANA DE LA CIUDAD DE MÉXICO*. Retrieved October 1, 2025, from https://pdh.cdmx.gob.mx/storage/app/media/banner/Dic_LSM%202.pdf

Muñoz, P. T., & Pérez, S. M. (2020). La inclusión de niños sordos en educación básica en una escuela de México mediante el diseño de recursos digitales. *RIDE Revista Iberoamericana para la Investigación y el Desarrollo Educativo*, *11*(21). Advance online publication. DOI: 10.23913/ride.v11i21.758

Objetivos de Desarrollo Sustentable. (2023). Retrieved September 29, 2025, from https://www.un.org/sustainabledevelopment/es/education/

Organización de Estados Iberoamericanos. (2021). Los desafíos de las TIC para el cambio educativo. In *Metas Educativas 2021*. Organización de Estados Iberoamericanos para la Educación, la Ciencia y la Cultura. https://www.oei.es

Pressman, R. S., & Maxim, B. R. (2021). *Ingeniería del software: un enfoque práctico*.

Rojas-Chávez, K. A., & Quini-Villegas, R. (2019). Aplicación móvil para Aprender Lengua de Señas Mexicana. Revista de Tecnologías de La Información Y Comunicaciones, 8–17. DOI: 10.35429/JITC.2019.8.3.8.17

Sánchez, C., Quezada-Cisnero, Á., & Rodríguez-Aguiñága, A. (2023). Una propuesta de aplicación móvil para el aprendizaje de la lengua de señas mexicana mediante el desarrollo de un modelo de realidad aumentada. Pädi Boletín Científico de Ciencias Básicas E Ingenierías Del ICBI, 11(Especial4), 264–269. DOI: 10.29057/icbi.v11iEspecial4.11427

Sep. (n.d.). *¿Qué son las habilidades digitales?* https://nuevaescuelamexicana.sep.gob.mx/contenido/recurso/32320/

Soto-Rey, J., & Pérez-Tejero, J. (2014). Estrategias para la inclusión de personas con discapacidad auditiva en educacion fisica. *Revista Española De Educación Física Y Deportes, 406*, 93–101. DOI: 10.55166/reefd.v0i406.30

Subsecretaría Educación Media Superior. (2019). *La Nueva Escuela Mexicana: principios y orientaciones pedagógicas.*

UNICEF. (2019, June). Serie De Cuadernillos Sobre Educación Inclusiva. Retrieved September 29, 2025, from https://www.unicef.org/lac/informes/serie-de-cuadernillos-sobre-educaci%C3%B3n-inclusiva

World Health Organization. WHO. (2025, February 26). *Sordera y pérdida de la audición.* https://www.who.int/es/news-room/fact-sheets/detail/deafness-and-hearing-loss

Chapter 11
Digital Application to Encourage Reading for Children With Phonological Dyslexia

Etelvina Archundia Sierra
https://orcid.org/0000-0001-9686-5305
Benemérita Universidad Autónoma de Puebla, Mexico

Marco Antonio Reyes Pérez
https://orcid.org/0009-0002-7676-697X
Benemérita Universidad Autónoma de Puebla, Mexico

Ariadna Sahuantitla López
https://orcid.org/0009-0005-1995-7018
Benemérita Universidad Autónoma de Puebla, Mexico

ABSTRACT

Phonological dyslexia is a reading disability that affects phonemes, such as sound, and difficulty processing reading. Attention Early childhood education for children promotes the improvement of their reading comprehension. The objective of the research is to design an interactive digital application for children with phonological dyslexia with interactive educational activities through the use of Information and Communication Technologies. The methodology used was User-Centered Design, the storyboard application for the scenarios of the reading and comprehension activities. The implementation is done with HTML5, CSS, JavaScript and PHP7. The evaluation of the application is carried out through expert judgment. The instrument addresses the dimensions of design and visual appearance, navigation and inter-

DOI: 10.4018/979-8-3373-6033-1.ch011

action, comprehension and accessibility, pedagogical relevance and usability. The most significant result is that of the dimension: design and visual appearance, with an overall absolute frequency of 29% in complete agreement and 50% in agreement.

INTRODUCTION

The Salamanca Declaration and Framework for Action on Special Needs Education (1994) (Ainscow & Best, 2019) marked a significant global milestone by introducing the concept of inclusive education. This concept was further elevated to the status of a fundamental human right through the United Nations Convention on the Rights of Persons with Disabilities (United Nations (UN), 2006). Furthermore, the United Nations 2030 Agenda for Sustainable Development (2015) reinforced this commitment to ensuring inclusive, equitable and quality education and promoting lifelong learning opportunities for all (Assembly, 2015). With regard to SDG 4 (Quality Education) of the 2030 Agenda, it seeks to ensure inclusive, equitable, and quality education and promote lifelong learning opportunities for all. Digital reading tools align with this goal by offering: Accessibility and diversity (Target 4.a), where adapting content to different learning needs, such as changing font size, background color, or using integrated images and videos, supports inclusive design. Digital tools (screen readers, text adjustments, voice-to-text software) are essential for universal accessibility in reading and are crucial for students with disabilities. Literacy and lifelong learning (Targets 4.4 and 4.6): Digital libraries and Open Educational Resources (OER) make a vast amount of reading material available to people in remote or low-income areas. They help develop the necessary digital skills (Target 4.4), which are essential for employment and social participation in today's world. Equity and Personalization: They facilitate personalized learning, allowing each student to progress at their own pace, which is a central principle of inclusion.

Despite these global efforts, achieving inclusive education remains a complex and persistent challenge. This issue is of utmost importance due to its potential to marginalize vulnerable groups, such as children with disabilities, within the education system. Furthermore, this marginalization extends beyond the academic sphere and affects social inclusion by denying students with disabilities access to all the experiences to which they are entitled (Graham et al., 2023). Among the Among groups that continue to face barriers to inclusive education are children with *dyslexia,* a learning disorder that presents as difficulty in reading due to difficulties in identifying speech sounds and learning to relate them to letters and words (decoding).

Dyslexia, also called *reading disability,* is a consequence of individual differences in the areas of the brain that process language. Although *dyslexia* has no cure, early diagnosis and intervention yield excellent results. *Phonological dyslexia,* in particular, is a reading disorder whose main manifestation is the inability to recognize the dependence between the phonic and orthographic structure of words. The trait outstanding In this case, it is the inability individuals manifest to manipulate phonemes in words when these are presented orally, which limits their ability to establish correct associations between graphemes and phonemes, following the principles of the alphabetic code. Individuals have serious difficulties reading unfamiliar words or pseudowords, given that these types of stimuli require an analysis and synthesis of the constituent phonetic elements. It can be said, then, that this type of reading disorder is conditioned by a poorly developed ability to discriminate and manipulate these areas of language. Children with phonological dyslexia present imprecise, slow reading, with poor decoding and requiring great effort.

Dyslexia is a term used to describe a group of symptoms that cause difficulties with specific language skills, such as reading. This difficulty can affect an individual's ability to study (ID Association, 2019). Furthermore, dyslexia is a learning disability that affects reading, writing, and language development. evident from the first years of a child's life and is expected to have lifelong effects. When a child struggles with reading, a gap is created, as they don't have the same reading ability as other students. Consequently, a dyslexic person's cognitive abilities may not match their other cognitive abilities, such as phonological skills.

Phonological dyslexia, a subtype of dyslexia, is a reading disability that affects phonemes, such as sounds, and the ability to read nonwords, and is not limited to an inability to read words. While phonological dyslexia has similar symptoms to deep dyslexia, it is distinguished by the fact that sufferers do not make the same semantic errors as those with deep dyslexia (Welbourne & Lambon Ralph, 2007).

Treatment for phonological dyslexia involves improving consonant-vowel matching and retraining sublexical skills in the context of pseudoword spelling. To detect and correct the learning disability, participants were guided through an interactive treatment using phonological skills and orthographic knowledge (Beeson et al., 2010).

Traditional speech therapy for dyslexia requires a lot of patience and dedication, which leads to higher mid-learning dropout rates (Rodríguez Cano et al., 2021). Therefore, technology has become easier and faster to use (AlLabadi & Sant, 2021), offering more solutions in the field of special education to help people with learning disabilities such as dyslexia (Ghavifekr & Rosdy, 2015).

A person's knowledge of phonological structure, also known as sound structure, is called phonological awareness. The ability to differentiate between different speech units, such as rhymes, syllables within words, and specific phonemes within syllables, is part of this awareness, which must be integrated into an individual's listening ability (Du Plessis, 2021).

As a predictor of future reading ability, phonological processing is a vital skill for young children (Bryant et al., 1990). One of the first phonological skills to develop is the ability to rhyme, which appears at approximately the same time as an individual's cognitive processes. Children who are taught phonological awareness skills, such as rhyming, syllable awareness, or phonemic awareness, during the early years of life are more likely to be successful in reading than those who are not taught these skills (Reynolds et al., 2003).

Diagnostic and Statistical Manual of Mental Disorders, published by the American Psychiatric Association, indicates that this specific learning disorder occurs in 5% to 15% of school-aged children, so there is a chance of finding at least one child with dyslexic-type difficulties.

This research shows the design of a digital application with the architecture of information content, interactive activities and evaluation to promote reading in children with *phonological dyslexia.* The structure of the research in the first introductory section contextualizes the problems and needs for attention for children with *phonological dyslexia* at an early age. The second section reviews research within the framework of attention to phonological dyslexia. The third section describes the User-Centered Design (UCD) methodology, which allows for the identification of user characteristics, the environment, tasks, and workflow in the design of an interface, using a series of defined methods and techniques for analysis, design, implementation, and evaluation. The digital application was implemented with HyperText. Markup Language (HTML5) and CSS (Cascading Style Sheets), JavaScript and PHP7. In the following The section shows the results of applying a questionnaire to experts on the subject and finally the conclusions of the use of the digital application in caring for children with *phonological dyslexia* and future work.

RESEARCH IN THE FRAMEWORK OF PHONOLOGICAL DYSLEXIA

Language disorders are frequently found in people with ADHD. The most Common problems include poor language skills, textual disorganization, and difficulty decoding reading, which may include omissions and substitutions of words and phonemes. In writing, there may also be alterations in the logical order of sentences and disorganized text production, as well as changes in the sequential and temporal organization of phonemes in speech and writing. The most affected linguistic aspects are phonological, syntactic, and pragmatic (Liotti et al., 2010; Pinheiro et al., 2012; Silva et al., 2011; Voorde et al., 2010).

In speech-language pathology evaluations, it is common to diagnose ADHD concomitantly with reading and writing disorders (Haase et al., 2011), dysgraphia (Okuda et al., 2011), and/or dyscalculia (Gross-Tsur et al., 1996; Auerbach et al., 2008).

Phonological processing-based remediation programs offer phonological awareness activities, both syllabic and phonemic. The effectiveness of these phonological remediation programs in children with learning difficulties or disorders has been demonstrated in several studies (Capellini & Ciasca, 2000; Funai, 2009; Silva, 2009; Antunes et al., 2013).

Bastidas González et al. (2023) and their research team indicate the importance of teachers in the early detection of a learning problem, such as *dyslexia,* as they are the first to detect the difficulty a child has in learning. Teachers must be aware of the difficulties and potential of students in order to help them specifically. This problem must be addressed during childhood, otherwise it will worsen, creating behavioral problems. An early diagnosis will help the child's emotional health. The author 's conclusion is that interventions in students must be early, making the most of brain modifications and avoiding the presence of difficulties. Students with *dyslexia* should be recognized as soon as possible and receive the necessary treatment and help. Not all dyslexics know that they have this learning disorder. This learning difficulty creates negative thoughts in the dyslexic of not being able to overcome this problem; these are frequent thoughts that deteriorate self-esteem.

In the study conducted by Martins et al. (2020), the effectiveness of phonological remediation programs in children with learning difficulties or disorders was studied in Brazil; the assessments used, despite analyzing the same skills, differ from the protocols used in the present study. The research International research has studied the population with ADHD and *dyslexia;* however, in Brazil, research with the same population is scarce, therefore the main focus of these studies is on instruction in phonological awareness and grapheme-phoneme correspondences in preschool and elementary school children with delays in phonological skills as a way to prevent reading difficulties. Therefore, the importance of developing phonological awareness before literacy is highlighted, so the decoding of individual letter sounds must be addressed and practiced. The results, expressed as scores, indicated a statistically significant difference between pre- and post-remediation assessments in phonological processing skills such as syllabic and phonemic awareness, working memory, and lexical access. The rhyming task was analyzed separately, since it is considered a task with a different level of segmentation than other syllabic levels, and there was no significance for this result. In addition, there were also statistically significant differences in tests measuring reading speed and text comprehension.

Furthermore, the study by Guaña et al. (2022) on the ways of teaching and consequently, educational processes are in constant evolution and the innovation of technology is considered an important part of this learning process. The use of new Information and Communication Technologies (ICT) has expanded to different social areas and education represents a relevant aspect in human life, where technological achievements have been fully exploited to put them into practice in such a way that, while their use is enhanced, a permanent updating of educational strategies becomes necessary. In this bibliographic review, a historical account of the evolution of ICTs is made, the influence they have exerted on education since the beginning of personal computers, until reaching the most recent technological developments, such as artificial intelligence, highlighting how new information and communications technologies are a fundamental element in the evolution of the teaching -learning process.

The research by Zhang et al., 2023 on developmental dyslexia (DD) provides valuable information on the universal and language-specific mechanisms underlying dyslexia. Recent advances in DD in Chinese suggest further investigation of orthographic and morphological deficits in Chinese linguistics, and call for greater theoretical efforts to understand the universal and Chinese-specific neurobiological mechanisms underlying dyslexia in order to design more effective and efficient intervention programs.

Another study was conducted by Maïonchi-Pino (2024) Learning to read is a middle-distance race for children worldwide. Most of them succeed in this acquisition with *normal* difficulties that ensue from the progressive (re)structuring of the phonological and orthographic systems. Evidence accumulated on reading difficulties in children with developmental dyslexia (DYS children, henceforth) shows a pervasive phonological deficit. However, the phonological deficit may not be due to degraded phonological representations but rather due to impaired access to them. This study focused on how and to what extent phonological syllables, which are essential reading units in French, were accessible to DYS children to segment and access words.

In Thailand (Wannapaschaiyong, et al., 2023), a preliminary study was conducted using interactive software called Siriraj Pre-Literacy Enhancement (SIPLE) with materials for learning letters and phonology, to improve pre-literacy (Snowling & Hulme, 2025) in 5-year-old children. The results after training indicated that preschool children at risk of dyslexia showed improvement, making SIMPLE a viable and effective form of rehabilitation for children.

Zoccolotti, P. (2022), referring to Vellutino (2004), discusses phonological awareness (PA) when viewed from the perspective of proximal factors within the cognitive architectures of a given behavior. In particular, a cognitive architecture is expected to make explicit the nature of the relationship between predictors and target behavior. Some authors have proposed descriptive outlines of the processes involved in reading that take PA tasks into account. However, there does not seem to be a general consensus on a single, explicit cognitive architecture that includes PA tasks as proximal predictors. Nevertheless, the activities in the digital application proposed for children identify the phonetic sound of the letters B, C, and D according to Vellutino et al. (2004). In addition, the study where statement is considered is taken into account. There are differences in the manifestations of dyslexia, depending on how a language is written (spelling), its sound structure (phonology), grammar, and morphology. The study presented is conducted in the context of the city of Puebla, Mexico, in the Spanish language.

The work done on Universal Design for Learning (UDL) by Andrango Analuisa et al. (2025) is consolidated as a transformative pedagogical approach that effectively responds to the contemporary challenges of inclusive education. Their proposal This methodological approach, based on neuroscientific principles and an ethical vision of diversity, allows for the design of accessible, equitable, and participatory learning environments from the initial planning stage, without the need for subsequent adaptations. Through its three structural principles: multiple forms of representation, action-expression, and engagement, UDL addresses the different ways in which students perceive, process, and connect with knowledge. This not only increases participation and academic performance, but also strengthens autonomy, self-regulation, and intrinsic motivation, which are fundamental elements for meaningful learning. The evidence analyzed shows that the implementation of UDL has a positive impact on school culture, promoting democratic, collaborative, and respectful environments for differences. It is also observed that its integration favors pedagogical innovation, the effective use of educational technologies, and coherence between institutional policies and inclusive practices. However, for UDL to become established as a sustainable practice in education systems, it is necessary to overcome various structural challenges, such as the lack of specific teacher training, scarce resources, time constraints, and resistance to methodological change. Greater coordination between inclusion policies and curricular strategies is also required, ensuring that institutions have the necessary regulatory and operational support. In this context, it is concluded that the adoption of UDL cannot be limited to the technical dimension, but must be understood as an ethical and political decision that involves all stakeholders in the education system. Investing in UDL means committing to an education that leaves no one behind, that recognizes that equality lies not in offering the same thing to everyone, but rather in offering what each person needs to learn with dignity, effectiveness, and meaning.

Table 1, provides an overview of the various technological tools designed to support and enhance people's cognitive skills, with a particular focus on those with learning challenges such as dyslexia. From tools that facilitate text readability (such as Open Dyslexic), to advanced writing assistance and contextual correction tools (such as Ghotit), to those focused on developing fluency and assisted reading (Voice Dream Reader, Learning Ally and Nessy). Additionally, platforms that allow for the assessment of cognitive skills (such as Dyslexia Quest and CogniFit). This set of applications not only seeks to improve cognitive processes, but also to promote the use of Information and Communication Technologies (ICT).

METHODOLOGY

The research is exploratory and documentary in scope, since it aims at the use of ICT for children *with phonological dyslexia,* allowing to identify the fundamental aspects of a given situation, in the same way allowing to open lines of research on the subject. User-Centered Design (UCD) is one of the key methodologies for user requirements, interaction with applications and technological tools, therefore the theories of human factors in relation to usability allow the development of digital spaces to promote attention to children with *phonological dyslexia*. The evaluation will be carried out by expert judgment. The research question considers: Would the design and expert evaluation of a digital application for children with phonological dyslexia promote reading?

General objective

To design an interactive digital application for children between 6 and 9 years of age with *phonological dyslexia,* promoting the improvement of their reading comprehension with interactive educational activities.

Table 1. Technological tools designed for dyslexia

Technology	Processes Cognitive that works	ICT skills that are developed
Open Dyslexic https://opendyslexic.org/about	Improves font readability .	Use of alternative sources.
Ghotit Real Writer https://www.ghotit.com/ghotit-real-writer-for-ipad	Spelling, grammar and syntax.	Correction spelling, word prediction.
Voice Dream Reader https://www.voicedream.com/	Reading and reading comprehension .	Reading aloud, highlighting text.
Nessy Reading & Spelling https://www.nessy.com/en-us/product/nessy-reading-and-spelling-home	Decoding and fluency reader .	Reading and writing practice .
Learning Ally https://learningally.org/	comprehension and reading fluency.	Reading aloud, highlighting text.

continued on following page

Table 1. Continued

Technology	Processes Cognitive that works	ICT skills that are developed
Dyslexia Quest https://www.dyslexiacentre.co.uk/dyslexia-quest/	Assessment of cognitive and reading skills.	Identifying strengths and weaknesses in cognitive and reading skills
CogniFit https://www.cognifit.com/	Training cognitive assessment .	Improving cognitive skills and their assessment.

Specific objectives

- Literature review for support for children with *phonological dyslexia.*
- Analysis and DCU in the care of children with *phonological dyslexia* .
- Develop activities to improve your child's reading with audio and images.
- Activities to identify similar letters and distinguish words to avoid replacing them with their derivatives.
- Develop activities to guide the child in reading and not change words.
- Implementation of the HTML5, CSS application and for the logical part JavaScript and PHP7
- Expert judgment tests.

Stages of development

First stage: *phonological dyslexia.*

- Investigate the use of interactive digital applications to support children with phonological dyslexia
- Review of the state of the art of actions in the implementation of the use of interactive digital applications to support children with phonological dyslexia.

Second stage: development of the digital application.

- User-centered requirements for interactive activities to support children with *phonological dyslexia*

- Analysis and design of the interactive digital application addressing the lines of knowledge, skills and evaluation required to support children with phonological dyslexia

Third stage: testing.

- Implementation of the digital application to support children with *phonological dyslexia*
- Testing of the digital application by experts in the field.

User-Centered Design (UCD) is a process that places the needs of children with phonological dyslexia at the heart of the design process. This process is key to achieving the application's objectives (see Table 2).

Table 2. Stages of the UCD methodology for children with phonological dyslexia.

Investigation Stage	Correlation with the DCU Cycle	Goals Specifics Mapped
First Stage: Phonological Dyslexia (Exploration)	Understand and specify the context of use.	Literature review and state of the art.
Second stage: Development of the digital application	Specify the User Requirements and develop the design solution.	Infant-centered requirements, creation of *Dyslexia Phonological Union (DIUFO),* application analysis and design; development of specific activities. (Planetary Lessons and Activities)
Third stage: Testing	4. Evaluate the design.	Implementation of the application (prototype) and expert judgment tests.

APPLICATION DEVELOPMENT USING THE DCU

The application A digital interactive program to support children with *phonological dyslexia* is called Dyslexia Phonological Union *(DIUFO)*. *DIUFO* is characterized as a reading reconstructor that travels through the solar system. A cosmic storm of disorder (*phonological dyslexia)* has separated the sounds and letters of words, making spatial messages confusing. The child is accompanied by *DIUFO* to collect and repair these lost sounds on each *planet* to improve their reading pronunciation.

The digital application was developed for the Web, with the following specifications:

- Registration: In this module, the child or guardian must fill out a form to register. This is done in order to keep track of the exercises performed.
- Login: In this module, the child must enter the username and password to be able to use the *learn and exercises module* . This login guarantees that only the validated user can follow up.
- Learn: The focus of help for children will be centered on identifying the phonetic sound of the vowels *"A", "E", "I", "O", "U"* and the letters *" B", "C"* and *"D"*, this module is attractively designed so that children can identify through sight and hearing the correct form of articulation in the mouth in order to pronounce the letters phonetically and thus achieve a good pronunciation of a new word.
- Exercises: This module focuses on helping children practice identifying pictures with words, correctly pronouncing words, reading comprehension, reading time, separating words into syllables, and identifying words from a set of pictures.
- Statistics: This module is focused on allowing children to observe their progress in the exercises they complete using small tables showing the name of the exercise, the score, and the date the score was recorded.

In each of the *DIUFO lessons and activities*, the purpose must be stated in a planetary context. Neptune relates the pictures to the letters d, c, and d; Uranus displays cards with words for pronunciation; Saturn counts reading time; Jupiter asks comprehension questions; Mars performs syllable recognition; and on Earth, it decodes messages.

Application analysis for children with *phonological dyslexia*

The task analysis diagram that allows to graphically display the temporal relationships (sequentiality, concurrency and recursion) existing between the activities and users that are necessary to carry out a set of tasks (see Figure 1).

There is the abstract task Digital_Application_DyslexiaLearning, which depends on the application task ShowMainMenu being executed. The user can interact with the menu iteratively until they select the abstract task Quit_Application.

From the main menu, the user can access different modules:

- Registration: The tutor enters the child's data into a form to keep track of the exercises completed.
- Login: The child enters their credentials to access the learning modules and exercises.

Within the Show_Submenu abstract task. The user can interact with this submenu iteratively until they select the Logout abstract task.

From the submenu, the user can access different modules:

- Learn: Visual and auditory content is shown to reinforce the identification of phonetic sounds of the vowels *"A"*, *"E"*, *"I"*, *"O"*, *"U"* and the letters *"B"*, *"C"*, *"D"*.
- Exercises: Interactive activities are presented to reinforce reading comprehension, separating words into syllables, and identifying words from images.
- Statistics: The user can check their progress on completed exercises.

Within the Learn module, the interaction follows a structured sequence:

1. Select Letter or Vowel (Select_LetterVowel).
2. Show Joint Image (Show_Image).
3. Play Phonetic Sound (Play_Sound).
4. Repeat Pronunciation (Optional) (Repeat_Pronunciation).

In the Exercises section, the interaction is as follows:

1. Select Exercise Type (Select_Exercise).
2. Show Interactive Activity (Show_Activity).
3. Enter Response (Enter_Response).
4. Check Response (Check_Response).
5. Show Feedback (Show_Feedback).
6. Save Results (Save_Result).

Finally, in the Statistics module, the user can:

- Check your progress in a results table.
- Filter by date or exercise type.
- Analyze your performance and improvements over time.

The child's interaction with the application follows a structured flow in which they can explore content, perform exercises, and check their progress, ensuring a learning process tailored to their needs.

Figure 1. Analysis of the behavior of the digital application

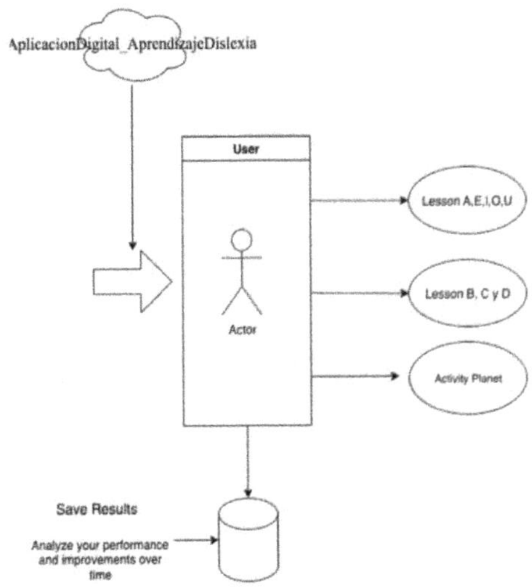

Design of the digital application for children with *phonological dyslexia*

As part of the interface design, the login, registration, main menu, *planet activities* and learn section scenarios were created, which contains the following lessons (See Figure 2):

1. Vowel A lesson	**6. Letter B Lesson**
2. Vowel E lesson	7. Letter C Lesson
3. Vowel Lesson I	8. Letter D Lesson
4. Vowel lesson O	
5. Vowel U lesson	

Planet activities section which contains the following activities:

1. Neptune Activity	**4. Jupiter Activity**
2. Uranus Activity	5. Mars Activity
3. Saturn Activity	6. Earth Activity

Figure 2. Design of the modular architecture of the digital application

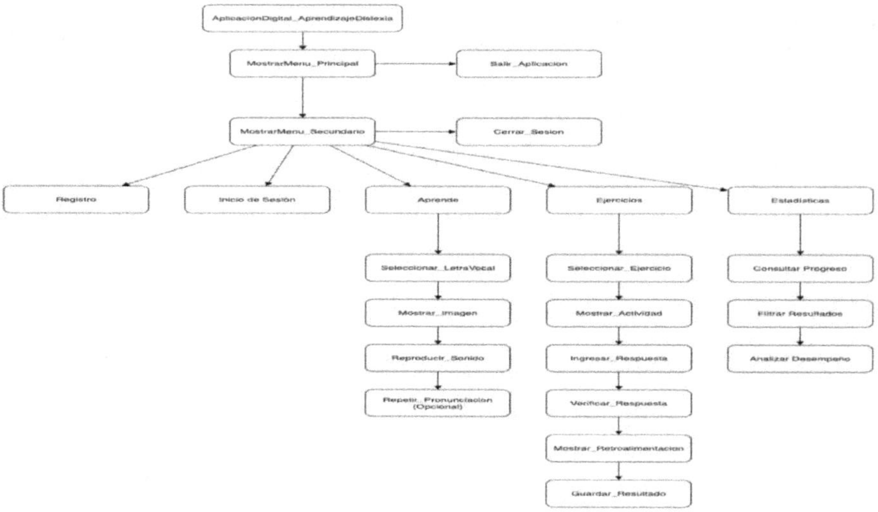

Balsamiq tool was used, the lessons were organized into 8 modules: A, E, I, O, U, B, C, D. The module of 6 activities: Neptune, Uranus, Saturn, Jupiter, Mars, Earth and a statistics module in which seven tables are shown where the user can consult their score for each planetary activity and the lessons learned to observe their progress.

At the beginning of the application, the child listens to an audio presentation of DIUFO with the following script:

DIUFO Script - Hello, astronaut friends! Meet DIUFO. Hello, hello! I'm DIUFO, a great friend who will accompany you on the most incredible space adventure you can imagine. Did you know I'm an expert in missions to planets? I love traveling and discovering new things! Look at my ship, it's so cool! And now that you're here, my mission is complete. I need a brave and intelligent copilot for this galactic journey. That's you!

The purpose of using the application is also explained:

Script DIUFO - On our stellar journey, we're going far away. Do you see those shining planets? They're huge! Neptune, Uranus, Saturn, Jupiter, Mars, and our home, Earth. Each planet is a different space training station. Don't worry if something seems difficult at first; this is how we learn DIUFOS! We're here to practice and have lots of fun.

What will we do on each planet? On some, we'll do a little vocal cord exercise. We'll warm up our voice so it sounds strong and clear. We'll practice vowel sounds and how they sound.

In others, we'll measure time like rockets. Don't rush! The important thing isn't being fast, but rather seeing how you read more comfortably and calmly each time. And in others, we'll be word hunters! You'll have to choose and find the right words. My job is to help you make your words and sounds come out more and more fluently. Think of me as your personal word coach.

DIUFO space, there are no mistakes! There are only brilliant attempts that help us learn. We're going to have a great time, we're going to laugh, and you'll see how, by practicing on each planet, you'll become a good reader. Are you ready for takeoff? Let's go!

In addition, the lessons and activities with the planets are accompanied by *DIUFO,* which are described to guide children. *DIUFO* 's mission is the phonological training stations, and the vowel lessons focus on pronunciation.

Each planet represents a level or type of challenge. The idea is for *DIUFO* to guide the child through the planetary stations.

Vowel Lesson: Learn *A, E, I, O, U* (Focus: Articulation of Vowels and Isolated Sounds).
Mission Name: Ice Giant's Deep Breath.
Main Activity: Breathing and vowel articulation exercises.
Lesson process: *DIUFO* asks the child to observe the scenarios to practice vowel sounds.
Example: Look at the images of each vowel and practice breathing for each one.
Goal: Ensure that the vowel is pronounced in a way that the child feels the position of the mouth for each sound.

Activities of the stays on the planets:

1. Neptune: The planet of great vision.

Mission Name: Caring for Lost Words.
Main Activity: Pronounce the letters *"B", "C" and "D"* shown in the image.
Activity process: *DIUFO* asks the child to look at the image and select the initial letter of the image.
Example: Select a card and say the first letter of the image.
Goal: Ensure that the vowel is pronounced in a way that the child feels the position of the mouth for each sound.

2. Uranus: The Planet of Echoes (Focus: Initial Phonological Awareness and Auditory Discrimination)

Mission Name: The Hidden Echo of Uranus.

Main activity: Repetition and discrimination of simple syllables.
Activity process: The child identifies the word shown in the image.
Example: Select an image and read the word.
Goal: Ensure the identification and reading of the word contained in the image.

3. Saturn: The planet of word rings

Mission Name: Count Saturn's rings.
Main Activity: Read and measure the reading time of a paragraph.
Activity process: Read a paragraph and activate the stopwatch to measure the reading time.
Example: Read the following text loudly and clearly like a superhero. *But his sister Camilla stopped him and said, " You should look for the boots first!"*

4. Jupiter: The Puzzle Planet

Mission Name: Unite the Giant's Bricks.
Main Activity: Understanding the reading of a paragraph.
Activity process: read the paragraph and answer the questions.
Example: A paragraph is shown in the planet section and comprehension questions are given after reading.
Goal: Reading comprehension.

5. Mars: The rhythmic reading planet.

Mission Name: Mars Landing Strip.
Main Activity: Reading words to identify syllables.
Activity process: Read the word and break it down into syllables
Example: Count the syllables in the word shown (Boot).
Goal: Correctly count the syllables in the words shown.

6. Earth: The Control Station (Focus: Comprehension and Vocabulary Selection)

Mission Name: Call Home
Main Activity: Decode the word by matching the first letter of the images.
Activity process: The images shown of the first letter are written to form a chain, then the reading and validation is performed.
Example: The bird is on the (dinosaur /bee /motorcycle /bee) The child writes lady.
Goal: Relate and identify the first letter and form a word.

Storyboard Design

Storyboarding for web design is a visual, auditory, and narrative tool used in the planning stage of a website to represent the structure and content of each stage of the web pages in the form of illustrative sketches. Storyboarding for web design is similar to the storyboard used in audiovisual productions, but focuses specifically on the organization and design of web pages. As part of the design of the digital application, storyboarding was used to visualize the digital application clearly and in an organized manner, allowing for changes to be made before beginning implementation.

The storyboard for web designs is created through a series of sketches showing the site's navigation structure, user interface elements, content sections, and functionality; each sketch was designed in the Balsamiq tool. Figure 3 shows a different section of the digital application. The scenario sketch was generated for the start of registration, where the *DIUFO image* and welcome script are designed. In Figure 4, the sketch was designed so that the child can interact with the digital application and thus view the proposed exercises and activities.

The content accessibility guidelines (W3C WAI, 2023) for developing digital spaces that are more accessible and cognitive for people with visual, auditory, physical, speech, cognitive, language, learning, and neurological disabilities apply to software for children with phonological dyslexia.

Figure 3. DIUFO digital application launch scenario

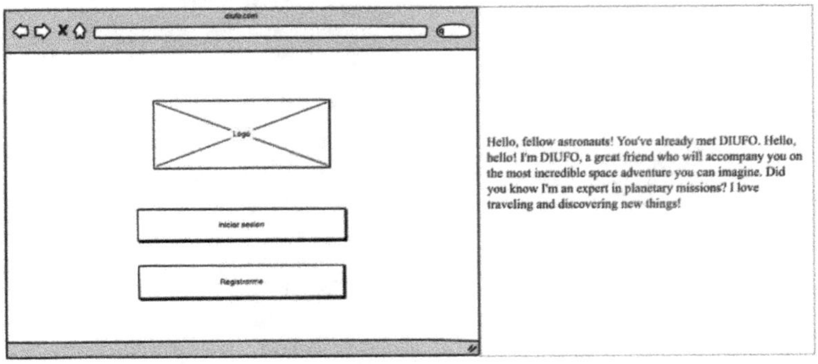

Figure 4. Scenario of the activities with the planets of the DIUFO digital application

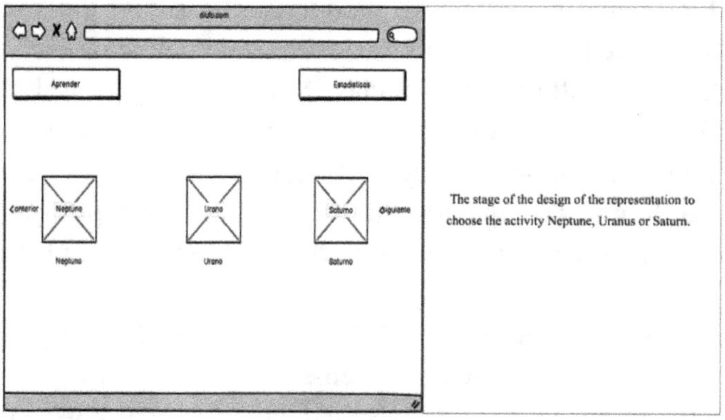

Implementation of the digital application for children with *phonological dyslexia*

The database (Figure 5) was developed in PHP. *hpMyAdmin is a free software tool written in PHP*, designed to manage *MySQL* administration on the web.

DIUFO database and tables, to store the user record and progress of each activity.

Figure 5. DIUFO application database with 9 tables

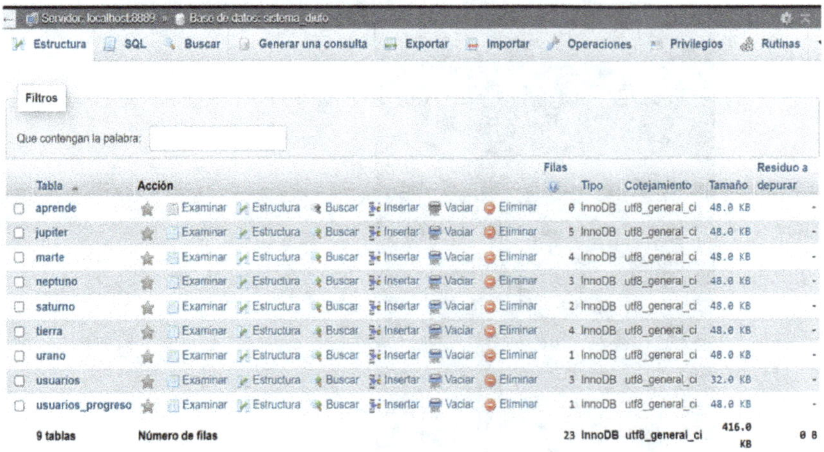

CodeIgniter is a lightweight, fast, flexible, and secure full- stack *PHP* web framework that features the MVC (Model, View, Controller) design pattern. It is an application development framework (a set of tools) for those who create websites with PHP. Its goal is to allow them to develop projects much faster than if they were writing code from scratch, by providing a wide set of libraries for common tasks, as well as a simple interface and logical structure for accessing them. The *Visual Studio Code code editor* shows the MVC files found within the *DIUFO project in* Figure 6.

1- Controllers: folder that contains the controller files which help to carry out the logical part of the project with the help of the PHP v7 language and to communicate with the models and views.
2- Models: Folder that contains the models files which help to create logic, perform queries with the help of SQL and communicate with the controller files.
3- Views: Folder that contains the views files, which helps us to create graphically and with the help of HTML, CSS and JS the buttons, inputs, menus and interactive parts to give a better UI (User Interface) and UX (User Experience)

Figure 6. MVC files within the DIUFO application

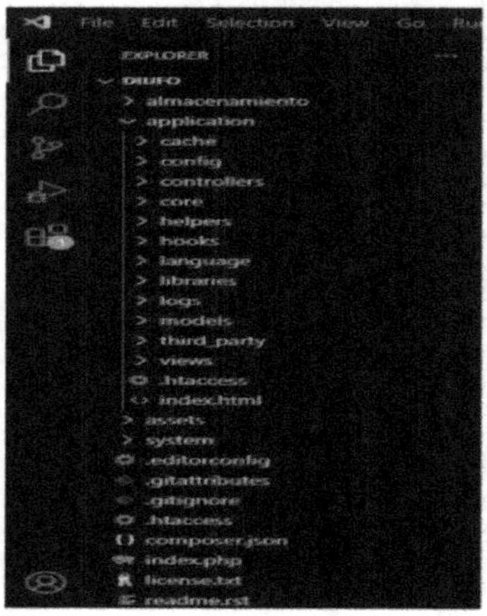

For the operation of the main menu, the Menu controller was developed, within this controller the function update_ *progress () was created to be able to update the progress of the user of the Learn lesson, since if the user finishes the D lesson* of *Learn,* he will return to the main menu, within the function we obtain the user identifier to be able to obtain his progress from the database and thus validate his score to know if it is updated.

To update the user's progress, the update_progress () function was developed, which is found in the Aprende_model controller. With this function, we create the update query to update the user's record in the aprende table.

For the operation of *Learn* in the index function found in the *Learn controller*, the algorithm was developed to be able to validate if the user has already made progress in this lesson; if not, the progress is recorded in the Learn table in the database.

Learn controller, the update_progress() function was developed, used in each Learn lesson. This function is called in a JS script to update the progress bar. This progress is updated only if it is less than 100.

The JS Function to call access to the controller Learn now the update_progress() function through Ajax, with this function we ensure that the progress of each letter is recorded only once per user.

For the operation of *lesson A* of *Learn, in the* index() function of controller A the user's progress is obtained to display it in the progress bar .

For the operation of lessons *E, I, O, U, B, C and D* in the function index () of the controllers *E, I, O, U, B, C and D* the following validation was created to be able to update the progress if it is 0 and if not only obtain the user's progress to display it in the views.

Function *get_user_progress () of the Learn_model model*, in this function the query is created to obtain the user's progress.

For the operation of the *Neptune activity*, the functions *activity_B(), activity_C()* and *activity_D()* in the *Neptuno controller*, these functions were created in order to register the user in the Neptuno table of the database, with this it is ensured that every time the user enters this activity a record will be made, likewise each function sends the user to the activity with the selected letter, when the user performs the activity through a *JS script,* a call is made to the *Neptuno controller and to the registrar_acierto()* function in order to update the user's progress in this activity.

The *identifier_1* is created in the *Urano* controller index and then sent to the array that will be recorded in the Urano table of the database, in order to generate a user record each time they enter this activity and thus keep track of their progress.

In this activity a JS script located in the urano/index.php view is used to be able to use the microphone so the user can pronounce the words indicated, in this script the microphone is initialized, listens to the word mentioned by the user and if it is correct a gif of success is shown, the phrase You said correctly: word mentioned and thanks to an ajax the request is made in the *urano/update_progress() controller*, this in order to update the correct or incorrect answers of the user. in each microphone function there is a counter which is added each time you select the image and pronounce the displayed word, if the counter reaches the sum of 3 it is redirected to the *urano/answers() controller:*

For the operation of the Saturn activity, the same flow of the *Uranus activity was carried out* in the *index (), update_progress ()* and *responses () functions*, however in this activity the microphone and a stopwatch are used, this in order to measure the time it takes the user to read the displayed text, in order to give it operation a JS script was created in the view located in *planets / saturn / index.php* that helps us to show a modal with the indications that the user must carry out in the activity, when clicking on the *Accept button* the microphone is started with the startRecognition () function *and a stopwatch with the startTimer ()* function, when the user mentions the word full stop with the help of the *stopTimer () function* the microphone will stop, the elapsed time will be obtained and through ajax it will be sent to the *satruno / update_progress () controller.*

For the operation of the *Jupiter activity*, the same flow as the Uranus activity was carried out in the *function index(),* however in this activity a JS script was created in the planets/jupiter/index.php view to be able to run a stopwatch and validate answers, so we can obtain the time it took the user to read the displayed text and in the questions section you can validate the correct and incorrect answers you got, in the JS script the *startTimer() function was created* to start the timer, the *stopTimer()*

function was created to stop the timer when the Ready button is clicked, at the same time the *sendTime() function is executed* which through an ajax makes the request to *the planets/jupiter/send_time() controller,* thanks to this the time it took the user to read the text in the jupiter table of the database is updated, once the user is in the questions section and clicks on the Validate button with the help of the JS script we validate if the answers are correct or incorrect, with the function *validateAnswer()* we paint green if they are correct or red if they are incorrect and we show the send button which will send the answers to the *planets/jupiter/validate_answers()* controller where the answers will be validated to make a count and thus update the record in the jupiter table of the database.

For the operation of the *Mars activity*, the same flow as the *Uranus activity was carried out* in the *index() function,* however, in this activity a JS Script was created in the planets/mars/index.php view that helps us validate the response given by the user and subsequently show a send button, which sends the response to the *planets/mars/validate_responses() controller,* performs a count and updates it in the mars table of the database.

For the operation of the *Earth activity*, the same flow was carried out as in the *Mars activity in the validate_response()* function, however, in this activity, an array with images and their word was created in the *index() function* of the *Earth controller to display randomly in the view. A JS Script was also created in the planets/earth/index.php view that helps us validate the response given by the user and later, with the help of an ajax, sends the user's response to the planets/mars/validate_responses()* controller.

For the operation of the Statistics section, the functions get_progress_learns_by_user(), get_progress_neptune_by_user(), get_progress_uranus_by_user(), get_progress_saturn_by_user(), get_progress_jupiter_by_user(), get_progress_mars_by_user() and get_progress_earth_by_user () were developed in the controller to be able to make the request to the corresponding models and obtain the requested data from the database, also a JS script was created to be able to display the tables through datatables . The JS script helps us to be able to display the table of each activity with the user records within the application.

Screenshots of the main screens of the digital interactive application to support children with phonological dyslexia are shown below:

Figure 7 corresponds to the home screen, it contains the image of *DIUFO* with his ship, in addition:

- The application logo
- The login button takes the user to a new view where they can enter their details and log in to save their progress.

- The registration button takes the user to a new view where they will have to enter the requested data to register in the application, log in, and save their progress from the activities they perform.

Figure 7. The home screen, which contains the DIUFO image

Figure 8 show the view of the planets menu, the moon-shaped button directs to a lesson view, the *statistics button* indicates the progress of the activities carried out, as well as a logout button and a carousel of the 6 planets existing in the Solar System (*Neptune, Uranus, Saturn, Jupiter, Mars and Earth)* .

Figure 8. The space with activities indicated on each planet, the learning button and the statistics.

By clicking on the learn button, you will see a progress bar, a pause button and several buttons to select the letter you want to learn, the pause button can go to the *Learn menu*, the *Planets menu*, the *Statistics view* or just exit to return to the previous view (see Figure 9).

Figure 9. Learning scenario for each vowel and letter.

Figure 10 shows the view of learning the letter A. In this view it shows us an instruction, the letter A, illustrations of how to articulate the mouth to be able to pronounce the letter A and two buttons that serve to return to the previous or next letter.

Figure 10. Learn the letter A

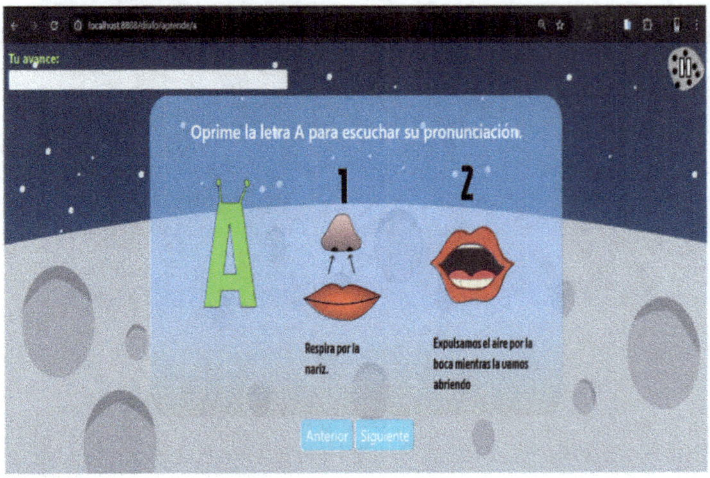

Just as Figure 11 shows the scenario for learning the letters B, C, and D to relate the action to the letter to *freeze*. Figure 12 shows the scenario for Activity 1 of *Neptune,* to identify the letter indicated by the image, it also includes the pause button and an instruction to continue to the next Activity 2 of *Neptune*, we have 3 buttons and one for *Exit.*

Figure 11. Activity 1 Neptune

Figure 12 shows *Neptune* 's activity 2, the instruction to be carried out and some buttons that show the images to select its initial letter.

Figure 12. Activity 2 Neptune

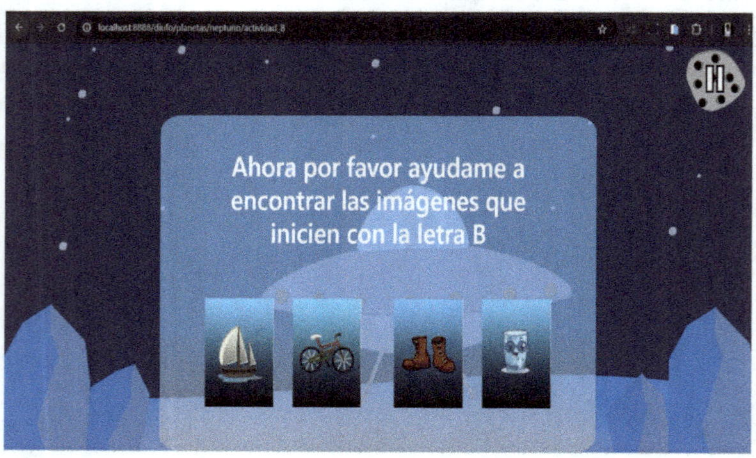

Figures 13 show the Saturn activity, which indicates what to do when finishing reading. The child will have to mention the phrase *Full stop* to stop the stopwatch and record the reading time.

Figure 13. Activity Saturn

RESULTS

In order to validate the relevance, functionality, and usability of the digital interactive application to support children with *phonological dyslexia*, a survey-type instrument was applied to four specialists in pedagogy and special education. The questionnaire was designed through *Google Forms* and addressed aspects of design, navigation, comprehension, accessibility and pedagogical relevance, and general usability. The Likert scale indicates the degree of agreement or disagreement: 1 = Strongly disagree, 2 = Disagree, 3 = Neutral, 4 = Agree, and 5 = Strongly agree.

The dimensions of design and visual appearance, navigation and interaction, comprehension and accessibility, pedagogical relevance, and general usability are built on the theoretical foundations of *phonological dyslexia* and the use of information technologies in the teaching-learning process.

The dimensions are characterized as follows:

- Design and visual appearance: The sensory part contributes effectively and significantly to improving difficulties in children with *phonological dyslexia* .
- Navigation and interaction: Information and Communication Technologies (ICT) have become a promising tool to improve the learning of children with *dyslexia* .
- Comprehension and accessibility: Use phonological programs that contain basic sound units, which help understand individual phonemes and, therefore, their combinations with others, constantly working on the relationship between speech and writing.
- Pedagogical relevance: The school process is important, and the pedagogy and methodologies used are of utmost importance for the progress of children.
- General usability: Innovative pedagogical spaces that help strengthen interest and motivation in the development of reading and writing processes, through the application of competencies and the development of basic skills that children must enhance.

Each dimension contains the instrument's questions for subject matter experts. The design and visual appearance dimension has six questions.

Dimension 1: Design and visual appearance.

1. The software design is easy for children to understand.
2. The design prevents visual overload and promotes concentration.
3. Fonts and spacing are appropriate to improve readability.
4. The graphic design is attractive to children of the target age.
5. The software uses colors, animations and sounds in a balanced way.
6. The overall design is consistent across the different sections and activities.

The navigation and interaction dimension is made up of 4 questions.

Dimension 2: Navigation and interaction.

1. Navigation between sections is intuitive and fluid.
2. Buttons and interactive elements are visible and understandable.
3. The system allows errors to be corrected easily and without frustration.
4. The software provides appropriate positive feedback.

Dimension 3: Understanding and accessibility is made up of 3 questions.

1. The instructions within the activities are clear and accessible.
2. The content is designed to facilitate understanding for children with phonological dyslexia.
3. Visual aids (images, animations) are useful and effective.

Dimension 4: Pedagogical relevance by 7 questions.

1. The activities are designed to encourage phonological recognition.
2. The design keeps the child's attention and interest during use.
3. Activities encourage curiosity and exploration.
4. The activities are aligned with educational objectives related to phonological dyslexia.
5. The difficulty levels are appropriate for the age range (6-9 years).
6. The content is designed to adapt to different learning speeds.
7. The activities promote learning in a structured and progressive manner.

The General Usability/Recommendation is made up of five open questions, starting with: Would you recommend this software for children with *phonological dyslexia?*

The reliability of the instrument is carried out with Cronbach's Alpha ($\alpha = 0.98$) which indicates a high internal consistency, in addition it is obtained for each dimension: Design and visual appearance ($\alpha = 0.95$), excellent; comprehension and accessibility ($\alpha = 0.70$), acceptable; navigation and interaction ($\alpha = 0.94$), excellent; pedagogical relevance ($\alpha = 0.97$), excellent.

The participants in the expert review have an average age of 38, a university education level, and 11 years of professional experience. All are from the municipality of Puebla.

The profile of each of them is described below:

Expert 1.

- Age: 40.
- Gender: Male.
- Educational level: Bachelor's Degree in Psychology.
- Occupation and position: 8 years as head of the psychology department at the Jean Piaget Multiple Care Center. 7 years as a support teacher in the Regular Education Support Services Units (USAER 128). 5 years as a professor at the University for the Development of the State of

Puebla in the psychology and university teaching programs. 2 years as a Technical Pedagogical Advisor in the Special Education Department.

- Geographic location: Puebla, Puebla.

Expert 2.

- Age: 33
- Gender: Female
- Educational level: Bachelor's Degree in Psychology.
- Occupation and job title: Private care psychologist with 7 years of experience.
- Geographic location: Puebla, Puebla.

Expert 3.

- Age: 38
- Gender: Female
- Educational level: Master in Pedagogy.
- Occupation and job title: 15 years as a psychologist.
- Geographic location: Puebla, Puebla.

Expert 4.

- Age: 39
- Gender: Female
- Educational level: Doctorate.
- Occupation and job title: 14 years as a psychologist.
- Geographic location: Puebla, Puebla.

The expert evaluators have experience working with children with learning difficulties, particularly in the areas of language and literacy, as well as experience in special education to provide pedagogical and methodological support to basic education schools to promote the inclusion of children with disabilities.

The frequencies for the dimension: design and visual appearance, the majority indicated strongly agree and agree. The overall absolute frequency for the dimension identified 29% as strongly agree, 50% as agree, 17% as neutral, and 4% as disagree (See figure 14)

The overall absolute frequency of the dimension: Navigation and interaction, identifies 25% in complete agreement, 37% in agreement, however 31.25% maintain a neutral position (see figure 15).

The overall absolute frequency of the dimension: Comprehension and Accessibility identifies 33.33% as strongly agreeing, 41.77% as agreeing, however 31.25% maintain a neutral position, 8.33% indicate they disagree with the navigation and interaction of the option regarding visual aids (images, animations) are useful and effective (see figure 16).

Figure 14. Dimension Frequencies: Design and Visual Appearance

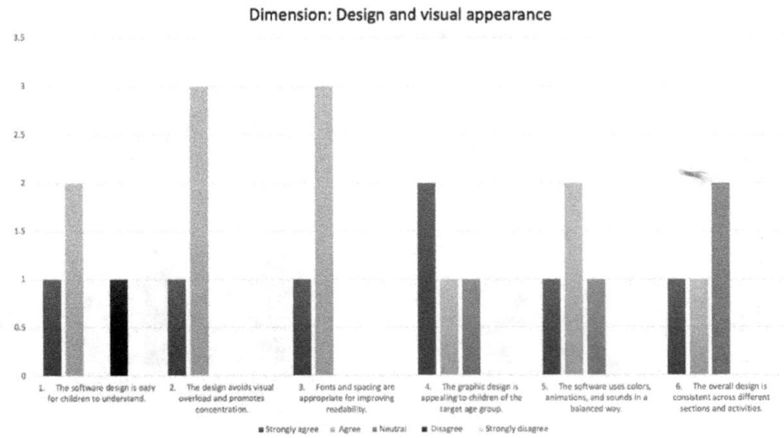

Figure 15. Frequencies of the dimension: Navigation and interaction

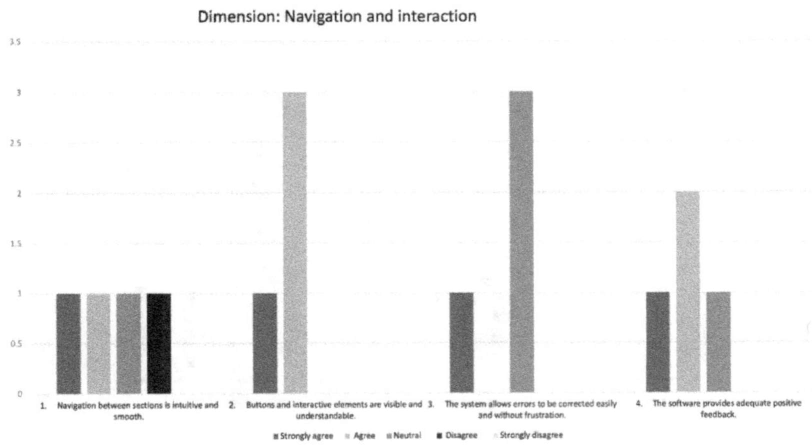

The overall absolute frequency of the dimension: Pedagogical Relevance, identifies 25% in complete agreement, 39.29% in agreement, however 28.57% maintain a neutral position (see figure 17).

Figure 16. Frequencies of the dimension: Comprehension and accessibility

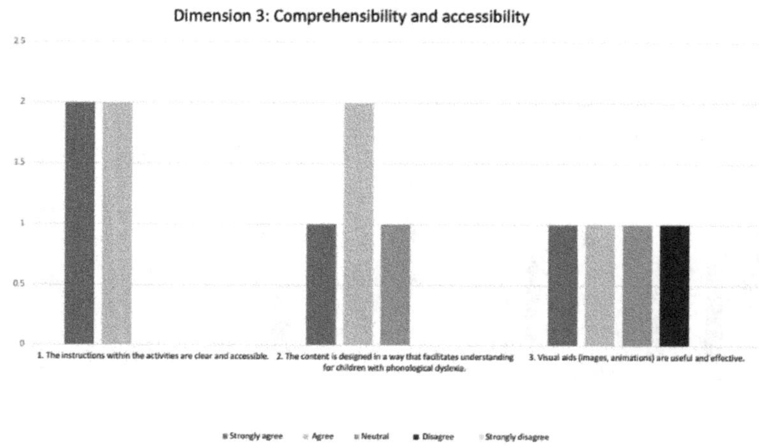

Figure 17. Frequencies of the dimension: pedagogical relevance

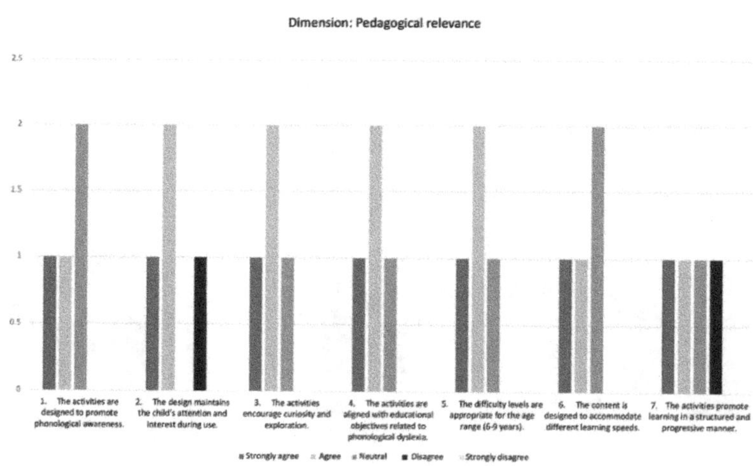

The open questions indicate the following strengths from the experts:

- The theme of the *DIUFO* character in space and the activities on the planets is considered attractive to children.

- The interactivity of the system.
- The overall visual appeal of the digital application.

The main suggestions for improvement were:

- Add clear feedback when performing exercises.
- Implement clarity in audio instructions and guide sounds.
- Review the sequence, logic and organization of the activities.
- Increase visual appeal with more eye-catching animations.
- Improve the clarity of instructions in certain activities.

Investigate the use of educational actions with interactive digital applications and the methodologies for their development to contribute to reading for children with phonological dyslexia at a national and international level.

Develop the digital application called *DIUFO*, addressing the stages of UCD and learning theories for children with *phonological dyslexia.*

The questionnaire was administered to subject matter experts and the results of the digital application were analyzed using expert testing, ensuring the following dimensions: design/form, content, and pedagogical relevance; this allowed the main characteristics to be discovered and areas for improvement to be identified in the application designed to encourage reading for children with *phonological dyslexia.* Significant results obtained from the data analysis indicated that 33.33% *strongly agreed* regarding the ease of understanding and accessibility for children, and 29% *strongly agreed* and 50% agreed regarding *the visual design.*

CONCLUSION

The development of the digital interactive application for children with *phonological dyslexia* and the characterization of the dimensions of design and visual appearance, navigation and interaction, comprehension and accessibility, pedagogical relevance and general usability built with the theoretical foundations of *phonological dyslexia* and the use of information technologies in the teaching-learning process, in addition to the expert judgment issued by specialists in the care of children in special education support services, allowed the analysis of the *learning lessons* and exercise of the pronunciation of vowels and activities in the context of the planets in accompaniment of the *DIUFO character* to promote reading in children with *phonological dyslexia*, in addition the organization of the activities and lessons in the digital application allows the monitoring of the child registered in a database; for example, to practice the pronunciation of a letter, identify it in a word and form a sentence. The use of technology enables children to achieve the purpose of the designed activities and the personalization of their recording.

ICT can be a useful tool for treating dyslexia. Digital tools, such as spelling programs and word processing software, can improve reading and writing accuracy and fluency. In addition, reading-aloud apps can improve reading comprehension.

Along the same lines, ICT can improve the motivation and commitment of children with *dyslexia. Phonological* learning. Educational games and other playful applications can make learning more interesting and engaging for children with *phonological dyslexia* which can help improve their motivation and engagement.

Use phonological programs that contain basic sound units, which help children understand individual phonemes and, therefore, their combinations with others, constantly working on the relationship between speech and writing. Working with the sensory component contributes effectively and significantly to improving difficulties with children with *phonological dyslexia.*

This research work follows the DCU methodology for children with *phonological dyslexia*. It is considered an innovative strategy in the teaching -learning process, with the use of various communication tools (audio, text and images) to address the results of activities and lessons; therefore, the process of designing and developing the digital application in response to the unique needs of children with *phonological dyslexia* improves learning opportunities in inclusion issues.

REFERENCES

Ainscow, M., & Best, M. (2019). Editorial: the Salamanca statement: 25 years on. *International Journal of Inclusive Education*, *23*(7-8), 671–676. DOI: 10.1080/13603116.2019.1622800

AlLabadi, L., & Sant, S. (2021). Enhancing the learning experience using technology in the classroom. *Journal of Technology and Science Education*, *5*(3), 184–193.

Andrango Analuisa, D. P., Duta Toapanta, L. P., Castellano Valverde, J. J., & Jhonny Gabriel, G. L. (2025). Universal Design for Learning (UDL) as an Inclusive Approach. *Journal Scientific and Academic*, *5*(2), 1008–1022.

Antunes, L. G., Crenitt, P. A. P., & Freire, T. (2013). Remediation program phonological in schoolchildren with signs for learning difficulties. *Communication Disturbances.*, *25*(2), 225–236.

Assembly, U. G. (2015). Transforming our world: the 2030 agenda for sustainable development (Vol. A). United Nations United., RES/70/1.

Association, I. D. (2019). What is dyslexia? IDA. https://aus.dyslexiaida.org/whatisdyslexia/

Auerbach, J., Gross-Tsur, V., Manor, O., & Shaley, R. (2008). Emotional and behavioral characteristics over a six-year period in youth with persistent and nonpersistent dyscalculia. *Journal of Learning Disabilities*, *41*(3), 263–273. DOI: 10.1177/0022219408315637 PMID: 18434292

Bastidas González, K. A., Jumbo Jumbo, F. V., Mazón Vera, V. S., & Bastidas González, L. D. (2023). Dyslexia: The role of teachers in early diagnosis in primary school students. *Ciencia Latina*, *7*(1), 9191–9208.

Beeson, P. M., Rising, K., Kim, E. S., & Rapcsak, S. Z. (2010). A treatment sequence for phonological alexia/agraphia. *Journal of Speech, Language, and Hearing Research: JSLHR*, *53*(2), 450–468. DOI: 10.1044/1092-4388(2009/08-0229) PMID: 20360466

Bryant, P. E., MacLean, M., Bradley, L. L., & Crossland, J. (1990). Rhyme and alliteration, phoneme detection, and the learning of reading. *Developmental Psychology*, *26*(3), 429–438. DOI: 10.1037/0012-1649.26.3.429

Capellini, S.A., & Ciasca, S.M. (2000). Effectiveness of the training program with phonological awareness in rianças com Specific disorder of reading and writing and learning disorder. *Temas sobre Desenvolvimento*, 9(52), 4-10.

Du Plessis, S. (2021). Dyslexia: More than a phonological deficit. EduBlox Tutor. https://www.edubloxtutor.com/phonologicaldeficithypothesis/

Funai, A. P. C. S. (2009). *Effectiveness of phonological remediation in school-children learning difficulties* [Master 's Thesis, Paulista State University]. UNESP Institutional Repository.

Ghavifekr, S., & Rosdy, W. A. W. (2015). Teaching and learning with technology: The effectiveness of ICT integration in schools. *International Journal of Research in Education and Science*, *1*(2), 175–191. DOI: 10.21890/ijres.23596

Graham, L. J., Medhurst, M., Malaquias, C., Tancredi, H., de Bruin, C., Gillett-Swan, J., Shiralee, P., Spandagou, I., Carrington, S., & Cologon, K. (2023). Beyond salamanca: A citation analysis of the CRPD/GC4 relative to the Salamanca statement in inclusive and special education research. *International Journal of Inclusive Education*, *27*(2), 123–145. DOI: 10.1080/13603116.2020.1831627

Gross-Tsur, V., Manor, O., & Shalev, R. S.Gross- Tsur. (1996). Developmental dyscalculia: *Prevalence and demographic features. Developmental Medicine and Child Neurology*, *38*(1), 25–33. DOI: 10.1111/j.1469-8749.1996.tb15029.x PMID: 8606013

Guaña, J., Arteaga, Y., Chiluisa, M., & Begnini, L. (2022). Evolution of Information and Communication Technologies in Education. In *Third International Conference on Information Systems and Software Technologies (ICI2ST)* (pp. 138–144). IEEE. https://doi.org/DOI: 10.1109/ICI2ST57350.2022.00027

Haase, V. G., Costa, D. S., Micheli, L. R., Oliveira, L. F. S., & Wood, G. M. O. (2011). The nosological status of developmental dyscalculia. In Capovilla, F. C. (Ed.), *Learning Disorders* (pp. 139–144). Memnon.

Liotti, M., Pliszka, S. R., Higgins, K., Perez, R.III, & Semrud-Clikeman, M. (2010). Evidence for specificity of ERP abnormalities during response inhibition in ADHD children: A comparison with Reading disorder children without ADHD. *Brain and Cognition*, *72*(2), 228–237. DOI: 10.1016/j.bandc.2009.09.007 PMID: 19850394

Maïonchi-Pino, N., Runge, É., & Chabanal, D. (2024). Phonological syllables allow children with developmental dyslexia to access words. *Annals of Dyslexia*, *74*(2), 244–270. DOI: 10.1007/s11881-024-00302-1 PMID: 38366193

Martins, R. A., Ribeiro, M. G., Pastura, G. M. C., & Monteiro, M. C. (2020). Remediation Phonology in schoolchildren with ADHD and dyslexia. *CoDAS*, *32*(5), 86. Advance online publication. DOI: 10.1590/2317-1782/20192019086 PMID: 33174986

Okuda, P. M., Pinheiro, F. H., Germano, G. D., Padula, N. A. M. R., Lourencetti, M. D., & Santos, L. C. A.. (2011). Fine motor, sensory and perceptual function of schoolchildren attention deficit hyperactivity disorder. *Jornal da Sociedade Brasileira de Fonoaudiologia, 23*(4). Advance online publication. DOI: 10.1590/S2179-64912011000400010 PMID: 22231056

Pinheiro, F. H., Lourencetti, M. D., & Santos, L. C. A. (2012). Attention deficit disorder and hyperativity disorder diagnostic criteria. *Revista Semestral da Associação Brasileira de Psicologia Escolar e Educacional, 16*(1), 113–123.

Reynolds, M. E., Callihan, K., & Browning, E. (2003). The effect of instruction on the development of rhyming skills in young children. *Contemporary Issues in Communication Science and Disorders, 30*(Spring), 41–46. DOI: 10.1044/cicsd_30_S_41

Rodríguez Cano, S., Delgado Benito, V., Ausín-Villaverde, V., & Muñoz-Martín, L. (2021). Designing virtual reality software to promote learning for students with dyslexia. *Sustainability (Basel), 13*(15), 8425. Advance online publication. DOI: 10.3390/su13158425

Silva, C. (2009). Effectiveness of a Remedial Program Fonolóigca e Leitura in schoolchildren with Aprendizagem Disturbance [Master's Thesis, Paulista State University. UNESP Institutional Repository

Silva, C., Cunha, V. L. O., & Capellini, S. A. (2011). Cognitive-linguistic performance em reading of schoolchildren with Attention deficit and hyperactivity disorder. *Revista Brasileira de Crescimento e Desenvolvimento Humano, 21*(3), 849–858.

Snowling, M. J., & Hulme, C. (2025). The Reading Is Language Model: A Theoretical Framework for Language and Reading Development and Intervention. *Annual Review of Developmental Psychology, 7*(1), 1–25. DOI: 10.1146/annurev-devpsych-111323-084821

UNESCO. (s. f.). Aprendizaje digital y transformación de la educación. Recuperado el 15 de noviembre de 2025 de https://www.unesco.org/es/digital-education

United Nations (UN). (2006). *Convention on the rights of persons with disabilities. Treaty Series 2515*, 3.

Vellutino, F. R., Fletcher, J. M., Snowling, M. J., & Scanlon, D. M. (2004). Specific reading disability (dyslexia): What have we learned in the past four decades? *Journal of Child Psychology and Psychiatry, and Allied Disciplines, 45*(1), 2–40. DOI: 10.1046/j.0021-9630.2003.00305.x PMID: 14959801

Voorde, S. V., Roeyers, H., & Wiersema, J. R. (2010). Error monitoring in children with ADHD or Reading disorder: An event-related. *Biological Psychology*, *85*(2), 176–185. DOI: 10.1016/j.biopsycho.2010.01.011 PMID: 20097256

W3C Web Accessibility Initiative (WAI). (2023). *Web Content Accessibility Guidelines (WCAG) 2.2*. W3C Recommendation. https://www.w3.org/TR/WCAG22/

Wannapaschaiyong, P., Vajrabhaya, P., Rojmahamongkol, P., & Sutchritpongsa, S. (2023). A computer-based early intervention for Thai preschool children at risk of dyslexia: A pre- and postintervention study. *Journal of Child Science*, *13*(1), e28–e34. Advance online publication. DOI: 10.1055/s-0043-1767809

Welbourne, S. R., & Lambon Ralph, M. A. (2007). Using parallel distributed processing models to simulate phonological dyslexia: The key role of retrieval-related plasticity. *Journal of Cognitive Neuroscience*, *19*(7), 1125–1139. DOI: 10.1162/jocn.2007.19.7.1125 PMID: 17583989

Zhang, L., Xia, Z., Zhao, Y., Shu, H., & Zhang, Y. (2023). Recent advances in Chinese developmental dyslexia. *Annual Review of Linguistics*, *9*(1), 439–461. DOI: 10.1146/annurev-linguistics-030421-065648

Zoccolotti, P. (2022). Success Is Not the Entire Story for a Scientific Theory: The Case of the Phonological Deficit Theory of Dyslexia. *Brain Sciences*, *12*(4), 425. DOI: 10.3390/brainsci12040425 PMID: 35447957

Compilation of References

Abascal, J., Arrue, M., Fajardo, I., & Tomás, J. (2015). Inclusive design and the future of accessibility. *Universal Access in the Information Society*, *14*(4), 445–455.

Abascal, J., Barbosa, S. D. J., Nicolle, C., & Zaphiris, P. (2015). Rethinking universal accessibility: A broader approach considering the digital gap. *Universal Access in the Information Society*, *15*(2), 179–182. DOI: 10.1007/s10209-015-0416-1

Abascal, J., & Nicolle, C. A. (2005). Moving towards inclusive design guidelines for socially and ethically aware HCI. *Interacting with Computers*, *17*(5), 484–505. DOI: 10.1016/j.intcom.2005.03.002

Abdolrahmani, A., Kuber, R., & Branham, S. M. (2018). Siri talks at you: An empirical investigation of voice-activated personal assistant (VAPA) usage by individuals who are blind. *ASSETS 2018 - Proceedings of the 20th International ACM SIGACCESS Conference on Computers and Accessibility*, 249–258. DOI: 10.1145/3234695.3236344

Abuaddous, H., Zalisham, M., & Basir, N. (2016). Web accessibility challenges. *International Journal of Advanced Computer Science and Applications*, *7*(10). Advance online publication. DOI: 10.14569/IJACSA.2016.071023

Accessibility Standards Canada. (2024). *Accessibility requirements for ICT products and services*. Retrieved from https://accessible.canada.ca/sites/default/files/2024-06/can-asc-en301549-20240226-v02-en-aoda.pdf. Accessed on 26.07.2025.

Adjorlu, A., Hoeg, E. R., Mangano, L., & Serafin, S. (2017). Daily living skills training in virtual reality to help children with autism spectrum disorder in a real shopping scenario. *Adjunct Proceedings of the 2017 IEEE International Symposium on Mixed and Augmented Reality (ISMAR-Adjunct)*, 93–98. https://doi.org/DOI: 10.1109/ISMAR-Adjunct.2017.93

Adjorlu, A., & Serafin, S. (2018). Virtual reality (VR) for children diagnosed with autism spectrum disorder (ASD). In Qian, H. (Ed.), *Handbook of Research on Serious Games for Educational Applications* (pp. 159–175). IGI Global., DOI: 10.4018/978-1-5225-7168-1.ch010

Adjorlu, A., & Serafin, S. (2019). Head-mounted display-based virtual reality as a tool to teach money skills to adolescents diagnosed with autism spectrum disorder. In Davis, H. C., Aslam, M. R. N., & Asensio, F. (Eds.), *Lecture Notes of the Institute for Computer Sciences, Social Informatics and Telecommunications Engineering (LNICST)* (pp. 450–461). Springer., DOI: 10.1007/978-3-030-06134-0_48

Aguiar, M. E. A. L., Fernández, M. F. P., Góngora, J. R. G. C., Marín, I. C. M. F., Pérez, A. J. P. I., Sansores, F. N. S. R., & Uicab, Y. S. U. C. (2025, January). *Compendio de buenas prácticas didácticas para el fortalecimiento de la educación especial.* Retrieved October 1, 2025, from https://educacion.yucatan.gob.mx/multimedia/publicaciones/250307_CompendioAlumnosSordos.pdf

Aguilar Navarrete, P., Camacho González, Y., Hernández Olvera, N. A., & Montoya Bironche, A. (2019). Desarrollo de una Aplicación Móvil para el Fortalecimiento de la Memoria en Personas con Discapacidad Visual. In *AVANCES SOBRE REFLEXIONES, APLICACIONES Y TECNOLOGÍAS INCLUSIVAS* (pp. 48–54). CONAIC.

Ainscow, M., & Best, M. (2019). Editorial: the Salamanca statement: 25 years on. *International Journal of Inclusive Education*, *23*(7-8), 671–676. DOI: 10.1080/13603116.2019.1622800

Alarifi, H. S. (2022). The use of virtual reality and eye-tracking to inform a grocery store intervention. *Psychology and Behavioral Science International Journal*, *18*(3). Advance online publication. DOI: 10.19080/PBSIJ.2022.17.555971

Al-Azawei, A., Serenelli, F., & Lundqvist, K. (2016). Universal Design for Learning (UDL): A content analysis of peer-reviewed journal papers from 2012 to 2015. *The Journal of Scholarship of Teaching and Learning*, *16*(3), 39–56. DOI: 10.14434/josotl.v16i3.19295

Albiz, J., Viberg, O., & Matviienko, A. (2023). Guiding Visual Attention on 2D Screens. *Effects of Gaze Cues from Avatars and Humans.*, *9*, 1–9. Advance online publication. DOI: 10.1145/3607822.3614529

AlLabadi, L., & Sant, S. (2021). Enhancing the learning experience using technology in the classroom. *Journal of Technology and Science Education*, *5*(3), 184–193.

Allam, A. H., & Dahlan, H. M. (2013). User experience: Challenges and opportunities. *Journal of Information Systems Research and Innovation*, *3*(1), 28–36.

Almurashi, H., Bouaziz, R., Alharthi, W., Al-Sarem, M., Hadwan, M., & Kammoun, S. (2022). Augmented Reality, Serious Games and Picture Exchange Communication System for People with ASD: Systematic Literature Review and Future Directions. *Sensors (Basel), 22*(3), 1250. Advance online publication. DOI: 10.3390/s22031250 PMID: 35161995

Al-Qora'n, L. F., Nganji, J. T., & Alsuhimat, F. M. (2025). Designing Inclusive and Adaptive Content in Moodle: A Framework and a Case Study from Jordanian Higher Education. *Multimodal Technologies and Interaction, 9*(6), 58. DOI: 10.3390/mti9060058

Álvarez Robles, T. de J. (2019). *METODOLOGÍA PARA LA EVALUACIÓN DE LA EXPERIENCIA DEL USUARIO DE SISTEMAS DE SOFTWARE INTERACTIVOS PARA USUARIOS CIEGOS*. UNIVERSIDAD VERACRUZANA.

Álvarez Robles, T. J., Molina Orozco, L. A., Partida Mariscal, J. L., Álvarez Rodríguez, F. J., & Benítez Guerrero, E. (2019). TriviaBlind: Sistema de software interactivo enfocado en la experiencia del usuario de personas ciegas como juego serio para el aprendizaje de cultura general. In *AVANCES SOBRE REFLEXIONES, APLICACIONES Y TECNOLOGÍAS INCLUSIVAS* (pp. 10–14). CONAIC.

American Psychiatric Association. (2022). Diagnostic and statistical manual of mental disorders (5th ed.). American Psychiatric Publishing., DSM-5-TR.

Andrade, A. D., & Techatassanasoontorn, A. A. (2020). Digital enforcement: Rethinking the pursuit of a digitally-enabled society. *Information Systems Journal, 31*(1), 184–197. DOI: 10.1111/isj.12306

Andrango Analuisa, D. P., Duta Toapanta, L. P., Castellano Valverde, J. J., & Jhonny Gabriel, G. L. (2025). Universal Design for Learning (UDL) as an Inclusive Approach. *Journal Scientific and Academic, 5*(2), 1008–1022.

Anti-Phishing Working Group. (2023). *Phishing activity trends report: Q4 2023*. https://docs.apwg.org/reports/apwg_trends_report_q4_2023.pdf

Antunes, L. G., Crenitt, P. A. P., & Freire, T. (2013). Remediation program phonological in schoolchildren with signs for learning difficulties. *Communication Disturbances., 25*(2), 225–236.

Apple. (2023). *Human Interface Guidelines: Accessibility*. Apple Developer. Retrieved from: https://developer.apple.com/design/human-interface-guidelines/accessibility/ . Accessed on 12.11.2025.

Armstrong, T. (2010). *The Power of Neurodiversity: Unleashing the Advantages of Your Differently Wired Brain*. Da Capo Press.

Asale, R., & Real Academia Española. (n.d.). Realidad. In *Diccionario de la lengua española* (Edición del Tricentenario). https://dle.rae.es/realidad#CfxhrOR

Assembly, U. G. (2015). Transforming our world: the 2030 agenda for sustainable development (Vol. A). United Nations United., RES/70/1.

Association, I. D. (2019). What is dyslexia? IDA. https://aus.dyslexiaida.org/whatisdyslexia/

Attar, N. M. (2024). *Digitized health care*. DOI: 10.58532/V3BFMS7P1CH10

Auerbach, J., Gross-Tsur, V., Manor, O., & Shaley, R. (2008). Emotional and behavioral characteristics over a six-year period in youth with persistent and non-persistent dyscalculia. *Journal of Learning Disabilities*, *41*(3), 263–273. DOI: 10.1177/0022219408315637 PMID: 18434292

Ayala, G. R. (2024, August 22). Retos digitales para la Nueva Escuela Mexicana. *El Financiero*. https://www.elfinanciero.com.mx/opinion/colaborador-invitado/2024/08/22/retos-digitales-para-la-nueva-escuela-mexicana/

Aycinena, P. (2008). Access for all. *Communications of the ACM*, *51*(8), 12–14. DOI: 10.1145/1378704.1378709

Azadboni, T. T. (2024). Effectiveness of Serious Games in Social Skills Training to Autistic Individuals: A Systematic Review. *Autism Research*, *17*(5), 850–872. DOI: 10.1002/aur.3091

Azenkot, S. (2024). XR access: Making virtual and augmented reality accessible to people with disabilities. *2024 IEEE Conference on Virtual Reality and 3D User Interfaces (VR)*, xxvi. IEEE. DOI: 10.1109/VR58804.2024.00014

Azevedo, L. F. A. (2023). Educación inclusiva para alumnos con TEA: Estrategias pedagógicas, retos y perspectivas. *Sustainability*, *15*(14), 14576. DOI: 10.3390/su151914576

Aziz, F.. (2021). *Inclusive voice interaction techniques for creative object manipulation*. In *Proceedings of the International Conference on Multimodal Interaction*. DOI: 10.1145/3462244.3479937

Baldwin, S. J., & Ching, Y. H. (2021). Accessibility in online courses: A review of national and statewide evaluation instruments. *TechTrends*, *65*(6), 731–742. DOI: 10.1007/s11528-021-00624-6

Ballesteros, M. A. (2021). *Videojuegos y psicología clínica: La realidad virtual en evaluación y tratamiento de niños y adolescentes con trastorno del espectro* [Tesis, Facultad de Ciencias Humanas y Sociales]. Repositorio Comillas. https://repositorio.comillas.edu/xmlui/handle/11531/61242

Bangor, A., Kortum, P., & Miller, J. (2009). Determining what individual SUS scores mean: Adding an adjective rating scale. *Journal of Usability Studies*, *4*(3), 114–123.

Bannon, L. J. (2011). Reimagining HCI: Toward a more human-centered perspective. *Interactions (New York, N.Y.)*, *18*(4), 50–57. DOI: 10.1145/1978822.1978833

Barajas Alcantara. (2022). LANGUAGE AND COMMUNICATION IN AUTISM. *REVISTA DE PSICOLOGÍA DE LA UNIVERSIDAD AUTÓNOMA DEL ESTADO DE MÉXICO, 11*(28).

Bass, L., Clements, P., & Kazman, R. (2021). *Software Architecture in Practice* (4th ed.). Addison-Wesley.

Bastidas González, K. A., Jumbo Jumbo, F. V., Mazón Vera, V. S., & Bastidas González, L. D. (2023). Dyslexia: The role of teachers in early diagnosis in primary school students. *Ciencia Latina*, *7*(1), 9191–9208.

Beeson, P. M., Rising, K., Kim, E. S., & Rapcsak, S. Z. (2010). A treatment sequence for phonological alexia/agraphia. *Journal of Speech, Language, and Hearing Research: JSLHR*, *53*(2), 450–468. DOI: 10.1044/1092-4388(2009/08-0229) PMID: 20360466

Benjamin, R. (2019). *Race After Technology: Abolitionist Tools for the New Jim Code*. Polity Press.

Bennett, C. L., & Rosner, D. K. (2019, May 2). The promise of empathy: Design, disability, and knowing the "Other." *Human Factors in Computing Systems*. DOI: 10.1145/3290605.3300528

Bennett, C. L., & Rosner, D. (2019). The promise of user empowerment: Participatory design and disability. *ACM Transactions on Computer-Human Interaction*, *26*(6), 1–30.

Berenguer, C., Baixauli, I., Gómez, S., & Andrés, M. de E. P., & De Stasio, S. (2020). Exploring the Impact of Augmented Reality in Children and Adolescents with Autism Spectrum Disorder: A Systematic Review. In *International Journal of Environmental Research and Public Health* (Vol. 17, Issue 17, pp. 1–15). MDPI AG. DOI: 10.3390/ijerph17176143

Blackburn, D. (2016). The Curb-Cut Effect: How making public spaces accessible helps everyone. *Stanford Social Innovation Review*.

Blackwell, A. (2017). The curb-cut effect. *Stanford Social Innovation Review, 15*(1), 28–33.

Bødker, S., & Kyng, M. (1994). Participatory Design that Matters—Facing the Big Issues. *Communications of the ACM*.

Boraston, Z., & Blakemore, S. J. (2007). The application of eye-tracking technology in the study of autism. In *Journal of Physiology* (Vol. 581, Issue 3, pp. 893–898). DOI: 10.1113/jphysiol.2007.133587

Bostelman, R. V. (2010). *International standards efforts towards safe accessibility technology for persons with special needs*. National Institute of Standards and Technology. https://www.nist.gov/publications/international-standards-efforts-towards-safe-accessibility-technology-persons

Brooke, J. (1996). *SUS: A Quick and Dirty Usability Scale Usability Evaluation in Industry*. CRC Press.

Brown, L., Eynon, R., & Johnson, H. (2021). Cognitive accessibility: The overlooked dimension of digital inclusion. *Disability & Society, 36*(5), 789–808.

Bruce, C. D., & Hawes, Z. (2015). The role of 2D and 3D mental rotation in mathematics for young children: What is it? Why does it matter? And what can we do about it? *ZDM Mathematics Education, 47*(3), 331–343. DOI: 10.1007/s11858-014-0637-4

Brumberg, J. S., Pitt, K. M., & Burnison, J. D. (2020). Adaptive interfaces for AAC: The role of machine learning. *Disability and Rehabilitation. Assistive Technology, 15*(4), 397–404.

Bryant, P. E., MacLean, M., Bradley, L. L., & Crossland, J. (1990). Rhyme and alliteration, phoneme detection, and the learning of reading. *Developmental Psychology, 26*(3), 429–438. DOI: 10.1037/0012-1649.26.3.429

Buolamwini, J., & Gebru, T. (2018). Gender shades: Intersectional accuracy disparities in commercial gender classification. *Proceedings of Machine Learning Research, 81*, 1–15.

Buß, R. (2020). Inclusive Design – Go beyond accessibility. In *Lecture notes in computer science* (pp. 400–407). DOI: 10.1007/978-3-030-49065-2_28

Buß, J. (2020). Digital accessibility: A systematic review. *International Journal of Human-Computer Studies, 143*, 102488.

Büyük, O. O., Nizam, A., Akgül, E. M., & Çamurcu, A. Y. (2019). A computer-enhanced money teaching application for individuals with autism spectrum disorders. *International Journal of Computer Applications Technology and Research*, *8*(12), 407–412.

Calderón Ynoñan, P., Prieto Neira, F., & Sialer Rivera, M. (2022). *Integración de un enfoque ágil con técnicas de Diseño Centrado en Usuario (DCU) para la mejora de experiencia de usuario (UX)* [Universidad Señor de Sipán]. https://orcid.org/0000-0001-5472-001X

Caldwell, B., Cooper, M., Guarino Reid, L., & Vanderheiden, G. (2008). *Web Content Accessibility Guidelines (WCAG) 2.0*. https://www.w3.org/TR/WCAG20/

Calvo, R., Seyedarabi, F., & Savva, A. (2016). Beyond web content accessibility guidelines: Expert accessibility reviews. In *Proceedings of the 7th International Conference on Software Development and Technologies for Enhancing Accessibility and Fighting Info-exclusion (DSAI '16)* (pp. 77–84). ACM. https://doi.org/DOI: 10.1145/3019943.3019955

Capellini, S.A., & Ciasca, S.M. (2000). Effectiveness of the training program with phonological awareness in rianças com Specific disorder of reading and writing and learning disorder. *Temas sobre Desenvolvimento*, 9(52), 4-10.

Cárdenas, G., Castillo, L., Espínola, L., Fernández, C., Góngora, J., Pérez, N., & Solís, C. (2021). Discapacidad auditiva. In *Colección Juntos Trabajamos por la Inclusión*. SEGEY. https://educacionespecial.sep.gob.mx/storage/recursos/2023/05/lwwYcPkM6G-220126_Tomo3_DiscapacidadAuditiva.pdf

Carlier, S., Van der Paelt, S., Ongenae, F., De Backere, F., & De Turck, F. (2020). Empowering Children with ASD and Their Parents: Design of a Serious Game for Anxiety and Stress Reduction. *Sensors (Basel)*, *20*(4), 966. Advance online publication. DOI: 10.3390/s20040966 PMID: 32054025

Carneiro, L. (2024). The Effectiveness of Digital Serious Games in Social Skills Interventions for Children with ASD: A Meta-Analysis. *Frontiers in Psychology*, *15*, 1345. DOI: 10.3389/fpsyg.2024.01345

Carrión-León, D. I., Lopez-Ramos, M. P., Santillan-Valdiviezo, L. G., Tanguila-Tapuy, D. S., Morocho-Santos, G. M., Moyano-Arias, R. J., Yautibug-Apugllón, M. E., & Chacón-Luna, A. E. (2025). Evaluating Interaction Capability in a Serious Game for Children with ASD: An Operability-Based Approach Aligned with ISO/IEC 25010:2023. *Computers*, *14*(9), 370. DOI: 10.3390/computers14090370

Casierra Parraga, C. M., Loor Fernández, M. N., Mejia Avellan, M. A., & Macías Loor, M. Á. (2021). *Inclusión: Estrategias didácticas en el proceso de enseñanza aprendizaje del idioma inglés en los estudiantes con discapacidad visual en las universidades manabitas.*

CAST. (2018). *Universal Design for Learning guidelines version 2.2.* CAST. Retrieved from: http://udlguidelines.cast.org. Accessed on 23.08.2025.

Cavoukian, A. (2010). *Privacy by design: The 7 foundational principles.* Information and Privacy Commissioner of Ontario. Retrieved from: https://www.ipc.on.ca/wp-content/uploads/resources/7foundationalprinciples.pdf. Accessed on 23.08.2025.

Celis Alcalá, G., & Ochoa Madrigal, M. (2022). *Trastorno del espectro autista (TEA). 65*, 2022. DOI: 10.22201/fm.24484865e.2022.65.1.02

Center for Universal Design. (1997). *The principles of universal design.* North Carolina State University. Retrieved from: https://projects.ncsu.edu/design/cud/about_ud/udprinciplestext.htm. Accessed on 23.08.2025.

Chadli, F. E., Gretete, D., & Moumen, A. (2021). Digital accessibility: A systematic Literature Review. *SHS Web of Conferences, 119*, 06005. DOI: 10.1051/shsconf/202111906005

Chadli, A.. (2021). Assessing accessibility in digital environments. *Journal of Accessibility and Design for All, 11*(1), 1–20.

Chaveesuk, S. S.C., & S.P. (2016). IEEE Internet Computing. Retrieved from. *Https://Ieeexplore-Ieee-Org/Stamp/Stamp.Jsp?Tp=&arnumber=7859898&tag=1.*

Chen, T. (2008). *Input to the mobile web is situationally-impaired.* In *Assets '08: Proceedings of the 10th International ACM SIGACCESS Conference on Computers and Accessibility* (pp. 303–304). ACM. https://doi.org/DOI: 10.1145/1414471.1414550

Chen, G., Davis, K., & Li, Y. (2021). Context-aware adaptive learning environments: A review of research and practice. *Computers & Education, 163*, 104114.

Christopherson, R. (2022, April 25). Out with accessibility - in with inclusive design. *International Cross-Disciplinary Conference on Web Accessibility.* DOI: 10.1145/3493612.3520444

Clarkson, J., Coleman, R., Keates, S., & Lebbon, C. (Eds.). (2013). *Inclusive design: Design for the whole population.* Springer.

Colla Villegas, V. L., Ortiz Hernández, M. M., Mero Lino, E. A., & Hernández Zambrano, M. M. (2018). *SOFTWARE INTERACTIVO Y SU CONTRIBUCIÓN EN EL APRENDIZAJE PARA LOS NIÑOS DEL C.I.B.V DEL CANTÓN JIPIJAPA*. Area de Innovación y Desarrollo, S.L.

Collado-Martínez, J. Á., & Navarro-Ardoy, D. (2023). *Proyectos neuroeducativos en educación infantil: Situaciones de aprendizaje para el aula*. UNED.

Çorlu, D., Taşel, Ş., Turan, S. G., Gatos, A., & Yantaç, A. E. (2017). Involving autistics in user experience studies: A critical review. *DIS 2017 - Proceedings of the 2017 ACM Conference on Designing Interactive Systems*, 43–55. DOI: 10.1145/3064663.3064771

Costanza-Chock, S. (2020). *Design justice: Community-led practices to build the worlds we need*. MIT Press. DOI: 10.7551/mitpress/12255.001.0001

Costello, E., Kilbride, S., Milne, Z., Clarke, P., Yilmaz, M., & Macmahon, S. T. (2021). *A Professional Career with Autism: Findings from a Literature Review in the Software Engineering Domain*. DOI: 10.1007/978-3-030-85521-5_23

Couldry, N., & Mejias, U. (2019). *The costs of connection: How data is colonizing human life and appropriating it for capitalism*. Stanford University Press.

Coursera. (2021). *Introduction to cybersecurity tools & cyberattacks*. IBM Skills Network. https://www.coursera.org/learn/introduction-cybersecurity-cyber-attacks

Crenshaw, K. (1989). Demarginalizing the intersection of race and sex: A Black feminist critique of antidiscrimination doctrine. *University of Chicago Legal Forum*, *1989*(1), 139–167.

Crenshaw, K. (1991). Mapping the Margins: Intersectionality, Identity Politics, and Violence Against Women of Color. *Stanford Law Review*, *43*(6), 1241. DOI: 10.2307/1229039

Cruz, H. (2021). Automatic Speech Recognition technologies and their incorporation into the methods of transcription of indigenous languages. *Anales de Antropologia*, *55*, 13. DOI: 10.22201/iia.24486221e.2021.77857

Cuevas Valencia, R. E., & Salgado Martínez, G. A. (2025). Aplicación Móvil Basada en Deep Learning para la Inclusión Educativa de Personas Sordas: Reconocimiento y Traducción de la Lengua de Señas Mexicana. *RIDE Revista Iberoamericana para la Investigación y el Desarrollo Educativo*, *16*(31). Advance online publication. DOI: 10.23913/ride.v16i31.2538

Cyber-Seniors. (2015). *Cyber-Seniors*. Cyber-Seniors Inc. https://cyberseniors.org

Czaja, S. J., & Lee, C. C. (2007). The impact of aging on access to technology. *Universal Access in the Information Society*, *5*(4), 341–349. DOI: 10.1007/s10209-006-0060-x

DANE. (2021). *Personas mayores en Colombia: Hacia la inclusión y la participación.* https://www.dane.gov.co/files/investigaciones/notas-estadisticas/nov-2021-nota-estadistica-personas-mayores-en-colombia.pdf

Darmasti, H., Aulia, N. P. S., Van der Hallen, R., & Zender, R. 2023. Promoting Daily Independence Skill for Individuals with Autism through Progressive Gamified VR Application. https://dl.gi.de/server/api/core/bitstreams/d0eb30f9-62be-43b9-b42b-fe7ed9b5498b/content

de Barcelos Silva, A., Gomes, M. M., da Costa, C. A., da Rosa Righi, R., Barbosa, J. L. V., Pessin, G., De Doncker, G., & Federizzi, G. (2020). Intelligent personal assistants: A systematic literature review. In *Expert Systems with Applications* (Vol. 147). Elsevier Ltd., DOI: 10.1016/j.eswa.2020.113193

De Estadística, Y. I. N. (n.d.). *Censo de Población y Vivienda 2020.* https://www.inegi.org.mx/programas/ccpv/2020/default.html#Documentacion

De Fleischmann, M. E. S., & Pérez, R. G. (2011). *Manos con voz: diccionario de lengua de señas mexicana.*

De Kare-Silver, M. (2011). The technology revolution. In *Palgrave Macmillan UK eBooks* (pp. 1–5). DOI: 10.1057/9780230343368_1

Deetjen-Ruiz, R., Daniel, M. P., Telus, J., & Deetjen, L. (2024). Advancing cognitive accessibility: The role of artificial intelligence in enhancing inclusivity. *Mini-Review*, *4*(2). Advance online publication. DOI: 10.56831/PSEN-04-108

Degener, T. (2016). Disability in a human rights context. *Laws*, *5*(3), 35. DOI: 10.3390/laws5030035

del Moral-Pérez, M., & López-Bouzas, N. (2021). Augmented reality and stimulation of social and communicative abilities in people with ASD: Research review. In *Revista de Educación a Distancia* (Vol. 21, Issue 66). Universidad de Murcia. DOI: 10.6018/red.454751

Design Justice Network. (2018). *Design Justice Principles*. Retrieved from.

Di Campi, L., & Luccio, F. L. (2025). Accessible authentication methods for persons with diverse cognitive abilities. *Universal Access in the Information Society*, *24*(3), 2195–2217. Advance online publication. DOI: 10.1007/s10209-025-01189-4

Dillon, T. W. (1995). *Spoken language interaction: effects of vocabulary size, user experience, and expertise on user acceptance and performance*. University of Maryland.

Dobransky, K., & Hargittai, E. (2016). Unrealized potential: Exploring the digital disability divide. *Poetics*, *58*, 18–28. DOI: 10.1016/j.poetic.2016.08.003

Donabedian, A., & Commonwealth Fund. (1973). *Aspects of medical care administration: specifying requirements for health care*. Published for the Commonwealth Fund by Harvard Univ. Press, Cambridge.

Druin, A. (2002). *The role of children in the design of new technology* Proceedings of the SIGCHI Conference on Human Factors in Computing Systems, Dubovyk, S. H. (2020). Preparing Future Teachers for the Development of Students' Emotional Intelligence. *Humanities and Social Sciences Reviews, 8*(3), 142-150. https://doi.org/DOI: 10.18510/hssr.2020.8316

Du Plessis, S. (2021). Dyslexia: More than a phonological deficit. EduBlox Tutor. https://www.edubloxtutor.com/phonologicaldeficithypothesis/

e-Estonia. (2025). *E-Estonia: We have built a digital society*. Retrieved from: https://e-estonia.com/. Accessed on 26.07.2025.

El-Gohary, M., Aborizka, M., El-Sheikh, M., & El-Nagar, Z. (2022). Shopping training to autistic children and adolescents for enhancing daily life shopping skills using virtual reality and Leap Motion. In *2022 1st IEEE International Conference on Cognitive Aspects of Virtual Reality (CVR 2022)* (pp. 55–60). IEEE. https://doi.org/DOI: 10.1109/CVR55417.2022.9967646

Ellcessor, E. (2016). *Restricted Access: Media, Disability, and the Politics of Participation*. NYU Press. DOI: 10.18574/nyu/9781479867431.001.0001

Ellis, K., & Goggin, G. (2017). *Disability and the Media*. Bloomsbury Publishing.

Ellis, K., & Kent, M. (2017). *Disability and digital television cultures*. Routledge.

Ensing, A. E., Yang, A. F., Kallogjeri, D., & Lieu, J. E. (2025). Factors associated with hearing-related quality of life in children with hearing loss. *The Laryngoscope*, *135*(9), 3382–3388. DOI: 10.1002/lary.32193 PMID: 40237479

éntame de México. (2025). Inegi.org.mx. https://cuentame.inegi.org.mx/juegos/default.html

Ericsson, K. A., & Simon, H. A. (1993). *Protocol Analysis: Verbal Reports as Data*. MIT Press. DOI: 10.7551/mitpress/5657.001.0001

Escartín, E. (2023). La realidad virtual, una tecnología educativa a nuestro alcance. ResearchGate. https://www.researchgate.net/publication/28102483

Esparza Maldonado, A. L., Margain Fuentes, L. Y., Álvarez Rodríguez, F. J., & Benítez Guerrero, E. I. (2018). *Desarrollo y evaluación de un sistema interactivo para personas con discapacidad visual. 21*(41), 149–157.

Estrada-Cota, I., Carreno-Leon, M. A., Sandoval-Bringas, J. A., & Leyva-Carrillo, A. A. (2020). "Manos que hablan": Tool for teaching – Learning the Mexican sign language for children with or without hearing disabilities. *IEEE*, 173–179. DOI: 10.1109/CONTIE51334.2020.00039

Estrada-Cota, I., Carreno-Leon, M. A., Sandoval-Bringas, J. A., Leyva-Carrillo, A. A., & Gutierrez-Sandoval, A. J. (2019). Design of a Web Tool to Support Language Therapy for Children with Cleft Lip and / or Palate. *IEEE*, 164–1643. DOI: 10.1109/CONTIE49246.2019.00039

Estrada-Cota, I., Carreno-Leon, M. A., Sandoval-Bringas, J. A., Leyva-Carrillo, A. A., & Quiroz, H. X. C. (2021). Design of a Web tool for teaching – learning of states and capitals of México through the Mexican sign language. *IEEE*, 174–179. DOI: 10.1109/CONTIE54684.2021.00036

European Commission. (2021). *Digital economy and society index (DESI) 2021.* Publications Office of the European Union. https://digital-strategy.ec.europa.eu/en/policies/desi

European Commission. (2022). *Union of equality: Strategy for the rights of persons with disabilities 2021–2030.* Publications Office of the European Union., DOI: 10.2775/52556

European Telecommunications Standards Institute (ETSI). (2021). *EN 301 549 V3.2.1: Accessibility requirements for ICT products and services.* ETSI. Retrieved from: https://www.etsi.org/. Accessed on 12.11.2025.

éxico: States - Map Quiz Game - Seterra. (2015). Seterra.com. https://online.seterra.com/es/vgp/3078

Facer, K., & Selwyn, N. (2021). *Digital technology and the futures of education – towards 'non-stupid' optimism.*

Falck-Ytter, T., Bölte, S., & Gredebäck, G. (2013). Eye tracking in early autism research. In *Journal of Neurodevelopmental Disorders* (Vol. 5, Issue 1). BioMed Central Ltd. DOI: 10.1186/1866-1955-5-28

Fan, M., Li, Z., & Li, F. M. (2020). Eyelid gestures on mobile devices for people with motor impairments. In *Proceedings of the 22nd International ACM SIGACCESS Conference on Computers and Accessibility (ASSETS '20)*. DOI: 10.1145/3373625.3416987

Fazio, D., Byrne-Haber, S., Sajka, J., LaPierre, C., & Jadhav, N. M. (2025). *Accessibility Maturity Model.*

FEMESOR SJ. (n.d.). https://www.femesorsj.com/

Ferreira, R. S., Xavier, R. A. C., & Ancioto, A. S. R. (2021). Virtual reality as a tool for basic and vocational education. *Revista Científica General José María Córdova, 19*(33), 223–241. DOI: 10.21830/19006586.728

Filippou, K., Acquah, E. O., & Bengs, A. (2025). Inclusive Policies and Practices in Higher Education: A Systematic Literature Review. *Review of Education, 13*(2), e70034. DOI: 10.1002/rev3.70034

Flaticon. (2025). favicon Icon - 3585618. https://www.flaticon.es/iconos-gratis/favicon

Florian, L., & Beaton, M. (2018). Inclusive pedagogy in action: Getting it right for every child. *International Journal of Inclusive Education, 22*(8), 870–884. DOI: 10.1080/13603116.2017.1412513

Florian, L., & Black-Hawkins, K. (2011). Exploring Inclusive Pedagogy. *British Educational Research Journal, 37*(5), 813–828. DOI: 10.1080/01411926.2010.501096

Francis, G. A., Farr, W., Mareva, S., & Gibson, J. L. (2019). *Do Tangible User Interfaces promote social behaviour during free play? A comparison of autistic and typically-developing children playing with passive and digital construction toys.*

Freire, P., & Santos, M. (2019). *Critical digital literacy in the information age.* Siglo XXI Editores.

Freitas, É., Panceri, J. A. C., Da Luz Schreider, S., Caldeira, E., & Filho, T. F. B. (2024). Cognitive Serious Games Dynamically Modulated as a Therapeutic Tool for Applied Behavior Analysis Therapy in Children with Autism Spectrum Disorder. *International Journal of Emerging Technologies in Learning, 19*(5), 80–92. DOI: 10.3991/ijet.v19i05.48677

Friedman, B., & Hendry, D. G. (2019). *Value Sensitive Design: Shaping Technology with Moral Imagination.* MIT Press. DOI: 10.7551/mitpress/7585.001.0001

Fryia, G. D., Wachowiak-Smolikova, R., & Wachowiak, M. P. (2009, December 18). Human-computer interface design in an e-Learning system for individuals with cognitive and learning disabilities. *International Conference on Digital Information Management*. DOI: 10.1109/ICDIM.2009.5356784

Funai, A. P. C. S. (2009). *Effectiveness of phonological remediation in school-children learning difficulties* [Master 's Thesis, Paulista State University]. UNESP Institutional Repository.

Fundación Proacceso. (2023). *Red de Innovación y Aprendizaje (RIA)*. https://wiconnect.iadb.org/osc/fundacion-proacceso-eco

Fundación Saldarriaga Concha. (2022). *Digital inclusion for older adults in Colombia*. https://www.saldarriagaconcha.org/personas-mayores

Gamha, Y. (2023). A framework for REST services discovery and composition. *Service Oriented Computing and Applications*, *17*(4), 259–275. Advance online publication. DOI: 10.1007/s11761-023-00376-6

Gangneux, J. (2019). Digital citizenship in a datafied society. *Information Communication and Society*, *22*(14), 2211–2213. DOI: 10.1080/1369118X.2019.1635186

García-Franco, A., Alpizar-Lorenzo, O. A., & Guzmán-Diaz, G. (2019). Autismo: Revisión conceptual. Universidad Autónoma del Estado de Hidalgo. https://repository.uaeh.edu.mx/revistas/index.php/atotonilco/article/view/3693/9502

Garreta, M., Enric, D., & Pera, M. (2010). *Diseño centrado en el usuario*.

Ghavifekr, S., & Rosdy, W. A. W. (2015). Teaching and learning with technology: The effectiveness of ICT integration in schools. *International Journal of Research in Education and Science*, *1*(2), 175–191. DOI: 10.21890/ijres.23596

Gil, D. L. (2024). *Trabajo fin de grado: Un análisis crítico de la clasificación del Trastorno del Espectro Autista y el Síndrome de Asperger* [Tesis, Universidad de Zaragoza]. https://zaguan.unizar.es/record/146181/files/TAZ-TFG-2024-4265.pdf

Gill, S. P. (2007). Designing for inclusivity. In *Lecture notes in computer science* (pp. 98–106). https://doi.org/DOI: 10.1007/978-3-540-73279-2_12

GitLab Docs. (2023). Accessibility [*CD*. Retrieved from]. *Test*, •••, CI.

Goggin, G., & Ellis, K. (2020). *Disability and digital inequalities*. Springer.

Gómez Hernández, M., Ferre, X., Moral, C., & Villalba Mora, E. (2023). Design guidelines of mobile apps for older adults: Systematic review and thematic analysis. *JMIR mHealth and uHealth*, *11*(1), e43186. DOI: 10.2196/43186 PMID: 37733401

González, P., & López, A. (2021). Design of educational mobile applications for rural communities: A case study in Mexico. *Revista Latinoamericana de Educación y Tecnología*, *5*(1), 77–92.

González-Sánchez, J. L., Cabrera, M. J., Gutiérrez, F. L., Padilla-Zea, N., & Paderewski, P. (2009). Design of Videogames in Special Education. In *New Trends on Human–Computer Interaction* (pp. 43–52). Springer., DOI: 10.1007/978-1-84882-352-5_5

Goodley, D. (2014). *Dis/ability Studies: Theorising Disablism and Ableism*. Routledge. DOI: 10.4324/9780203366974

Goodman, E. (2011). Three Questions About Design and Ethics. *Interaction*.

Google Design Team. (2025). Accessibility overview –. *Materials & Design*, *3*, •••. https://m3.material.io/foundations/overview/principles

Google. (2020). *Accessibility Scanner*. Retrieved from: https://support.google.com/accessibility/android/answer/6376570. Accessed on 02.07.2025.

Google. (2022). *Material Design Accessibility Guidelines*. Google Design. Retrieved from: https://m3.material.io/foundations/accessibility/overview. Accessed on 02.07.2025.

Government of Canada. (2022). *GCWeb accessibility framework*. Retrieved from: https://www.canada.ca/en/government/system/digital-government/web-accessibility.html. Accessed on 02.07.2025.

Government of India. (2016). *The Rights of Persons with Disabilities Act, 2016*. Ministry of Law and Justice. Retrieved from: https://legislative.gov.in/. Accessed on 02.07.2025.

Graham, L. J., Medhurst, M., Malaquias, C., Tancredi, H., de Bruin, C., Gillett-Swan, J., Shiralee, P., Spandagou, I., Carrington, S., & Cologon, K. (2023). Beyond salamanca: A citation analysis of the CRPD/GC4 relative to the Salamanca statement in inclusive and special education research. *International Journal of Inclusive Education*, *27*(2), 123–145. DOI: 10.1080/13603116.2020.1831627

Grilli, M. D., McVeigh, K. S., Hakim, Z. M., Wank, A. A., Getz, S. J., Levin, B. E., Ebner, N. C., & Wilson, R. C. (2021). Is this phishing? Older age is associated with greater difficulty discriminating between safe and malicious emails. *The Journals of Gerontology. Series B, Psychological Sciences and Social Sciences*, *76*(6), 1038–1048. DOI: 10.1093/geronb/gbaa228 PMID: 33378418

Groba-González, B., Pereira-Loureiro, J., & Munteanu, C. (2015). *Impacto de las tecnologías de la información y las comunicaciones en el funcionamiento en la vida diaria de niños con Trastorno del Espectro Autista* [Universidad de Coruña]. https://objetivovisibilizandoelautismo.com/

Grossard, C. (2025). Children's Improvement After Language and Rhythm Training through a Serious Game Intervention: A Randomized Controlled Trial. *JMIR Serious Games*, *13*(1), e76435. DOI: 10.2196/76435 PMID: 40750096

Gross-Tsur, V., Manor, O., & Shalev, R. S.Gross- Tsur. (1996). Developmental dyscalculia: *Prevalence and demographic features. Developmental Medicine and Child Neurology*, *38*(1), 25–33. DOI: 10.1111/j.1469-8749.1996.tb15029.x PMID: 8606013

Grynszpan, S., Weiss, J., Perez-Diaz, B., & Hadjikhani, N. (2014). Innovative technology-based interventions for autism spectrum disorders: A meta-analysis. *Autism*, *18*(4), 346–361. DOI: 10.1177/1362361313476767 PMID: 24092843

Guaña, J., Arteaga, Y., Chiluisa, M., & Begnini, L. (2022). Evolution of Information and Communication Technologies in Education. In *Third International Conference on Information Systems and Software Technologies (ICI2ST)* (pp. 138–144). IEEE. https://doi.org/DOI: 10.1109/ICI2ST57350.2022.00027

Guidelines for Indian Government Websites (GIGW). (2018). *DarPG manual: Guidelines for Indian Government Websites (Revised)*. Government of India. Retrieved from: https://darpg.gov.in/sites/default/files/gigw-manual_Revised2018.pdf? Accessed on 26.07.2025.

Guillén-Martínez, D., Alcázar-Espinoza, J. A., Rámirez-Sánchez, I., Samaniego-Cobo, T., & Villacís-Macias, C. (2025). Policies, Assistive Technologies, and Barriers in Inclusive Education: A Global Systematic Review (2019-2024). *Journal of Posthumanism*, *5*(2). Advance online publication. DOI: 10.63332/joph.v5i2.418

Gursoy, D., Spangenberg, E. R., & Rutherford, D. G. (2006). The hedonic and utilitarian dimensions of attendees' attitudes toward festivals. *Journal of Hospitality & Tourism Research (Washington, D.C.)*, *3*(30), 279–294. DOI: 10.1177/1096348006287162

Gutiérrez Padilla, J. D. N., de Jesús Álvarez Robles, T., & Álvarez Rodriguez, F. J. (2020). *Hacia el desarrollo de un sistema de software interactivo (SSI) enfocado en el aprendizaje de matemáticas básicas para personas con discapacidad visual.*

Gwala, N., & Mawela, T. (2024). Investigating the internet skills of older adults in South Africa. *The Arab Journal of the Social Sciences*, *70*(3), 45–60. DOI: 10.12724/ajss.70.3

Haase, V. G., Costa, D. S., Micheli, L. R., Oliveira, L. F. S., & Wood, G. M. O. (2011). The nosological status of developmental dyscalculia. In Capovilla, F. C. (Ed.), *Learning Disorders* (pp. 139–144). Memnon.

Hage, S. V. R., Sawasaki, L. Y., Hyter, Y., & Fernandes, F. D. M. (2022). Social Communication and pragmatic skills of children with Autism Spectrum Disorder and Developmental Language Disorder. *CoDAS*, *34*(2), e20210075. Advance online publication. DOI: 10.1590/2317-1782/20212021075 PMID: 34932641

Hamraie, A. (2017). *Building Access: Universal Design and the Politics of Disability*. University of Minnesota Press.

Harrison, S., Sengers, P., & Tatar, D. (2015). Making epistemological trouble: Third-paradigm HCI as successor. In *Proceedings of the 33rd Annual ACM Conference on Human Factors in Computing Systems* (pp. 3853–3862). ACM.

Hassan Montero, Y., & Martín Fernández, F. J. (2005). *La Experiencia del Usuario*. No Solo Usabilidad. https://www.nosolousabilidad.com/articulos/experiencia_del_usuario.htm?utm_source=twitterfeed&utm_medium=twitter#knapp

Hassan, A., Pinkwart, N., & Shafi, M. (2021). Serious games to improve social and emotional intelligence in children with autism. *Entertainment Computing*, *38*, 100417. Advance online publication. DOI: 10.1016/j.entcom.2021.100417

Henry, S. L. (2007). *Just ask: Integrating accessibility throughout design*. W3C.

Henry, S. L., Abou-Zahra, S., & Brewer, J. (2014). The role of accessibility guidelines. W3C WAI.

Henry, S. L., Abou-Zahra, S., & Brewer, J. (2014). The role of accessibility in a universal web. *Journal of Web Engineering*, *13*(1–2), 1–18.

Holley, D., & Oliver, M. (2011). Negotiating the digital divide. In *SensePublishers eBooks* (pp. 101–113). https://doi.org/DOI: 10.1007/978-94-6091-580-2_8

Hollnagel, E. (1997). Cognitive ergonomics: It's all in the mind. *Ergonomics*, *40*(10), 1170–1182. DOI: 10.1080/001401397187685

Holmes, K. (2018). *Mismatch: How inclusion shapes design*. MIT Press. DOI: 10.7551/mitpress/11647.001.0001

Hortizuela, R. D. (2022). Towards Web Equality: Efforts on Web Accessibility for Persons with Cognitive Disability. *Deleted Journal*, *23*, 1–16. DOI: 10.55529/ijrise23.1.16

Huffaker, R. (2015). Enforcing eAccessibility: Is the current legal framework adequate? *International Review of Law Computers & Technology, 29*(2–3), 207–225. DOI: 10.1080/13600869.2015.1055663

Imafidon, A. (2022). *She's in CTRL: How Women Can Take Back Tech.* Transworld.

Imrie, R. (2012). Universalism, universal design and equitable access to the built environment. *Disability and Rehabilitation, 34*(10), 873–882. DOI: 10.3109/09638288.2011.624250

Inal, Y., Volden, F., Hjelmtveit, S. T., & Carlsen, C. H. (2024). *My Eyes Don't Consent!* Exploring Visual Attention in Cookie Consent Interfaces., DOI: 10.1145/3649902.3653352

INEGI & IFT. (2023). *Encuesta nacional sobre disponibilidad y uso de tecnologías de la información en los hogares (ENDUTIH) 2023.* https://www.inegi.org.mx/programas/endutih/2023

INEGI. (2020). *Población con discapacidad o limitación en la actividad cotidiana por entidad federativa y tipo de actividad realiza según sexo, 2020.*

Inter-American Development Bank & Organization of American States. (2020). *2020 cybersecurity report: Risks, progress, and the way forward in Latin America and the Caribbean.* https://doi.org/DOI: 10.18235/0002513

International Organization for Standardization (ISO). (2009). *ISO/IEC 29138-1: Information technology – User accessibility needs – Summary.* ISO.

International Organization for Standardization (ISO). (2019). *ISO 9241-210: Ergonomics of human-system interaction – Human-centered design for interactive systems.* ISO.

International Organization For Standarization. (2018). *ISO 9241-11:2018, Ergonomics of human-system interaction.*

Iqbal, M., Ijaz, M., Mazhar, T., Shahzad, T., Abbas, Q., Ghadi, Y. Y., Ahmed, W., & Hamam, H. (2021). *Exploring Issues of Story-Based Effort Estimation in Agile Software Development.* https://doi.org/https://doi.org/10.1016/j.scico.2024.103114

Ishihara, K., Takagi, H., & Asakawa, C. (2019). Designing multimodal kiosks for universal access in Japan. *International Journal of Human-Computer Interaction, 35*(9), 768–782. DOI: 10.1080/10447318.2018.1543087

ISO-9241-210. (2019). ISO 9241-210: Ergonomics of human-system interaction -- Part 210: Human-centred design for interactive systems. In. Geneva, Switzerland: International Organization for Standardization.

Ito, H., Chang-Leung, C., & Poudyal, H. (2022). Inclusion of Students with Developmental Disabilities in Japan: Barriers and Promising Practices. *Asia Pacific Education Review*, *24*(3), 415–431. DOI: 10.1007/s12564-022-09763-8

Jaeger, P. T. (2015). Disability, human rights, and social justice: The ongoing struggle for online accessibility and equality. *First Monday*. Advance online publication. DOI: 10.5210/fm.v20i9.6164

Jagušt, T., & Botički, I. (2019). Mobile learning system for enabling collaborative and adaptive pedagogies with modular digital learning contents. *Journal of Computers in Education*, *6*(3), 335–362. DOI: 10.1007/s40692-019-00139-3

Jaradat, A. S., Wedyan, M., Alomari, S., & Barhoush, M. M. (2025). Using Machine Learning to Diagnose Autism Based on Eye Tracking Technology. *Diagnostics (Basel)*, *15*(1), 66. Advance online publication. DOI: 10.3390/diagnostics15010066 PMID: 39795594

Jaramillo Cerezo, A., Torres Yepes, V., Yuliana, L. N., Arias Uribe, J., & Suárez Escudero, J. C. (2022). *Etiología y consideraciones en salud de la discapacidad visual en la primera infancia: revisión del tema*. Revista Mexicana de Oftalmología.

Jiang, N., & Hu, Y. (2011). Cloud Computing Model and REST APIs Implementation. *Advanced Materials Research*, *366*, 416–420. . DOI: 10.4028/www.scientific.net/AMR.366.416

Jimenez-Honrado, J., Sebastián-Rivera, G., Gallud, J. A., & Penichet, V. M. R. (2024). Serious Games to Facilitate Social Integration for Children with Autism Spectrum Disorder *Proceedings of the XXIII International Conference on Human Computer Interaction*, Lleida, Spain. https://doi.org/DOI: 10.1145/3612783.3612793

Jiménez, L., & Salazar, R. (2021). Vishing and social manipulation: An emerging threat for older adults. *Revista Mexicana de Seguridad Informática*, *9*(2), 112–129.

John Rome. (2017). *Alexa goes to college: Asu's innovative use of voice technology.*

Johnson, C., Paramiswaran, S., & Mailewa, A. (2023). *Discovering Vulnerabilities in Web Browser Extensions Contained by Google Chrome.*

Johnston, D., Egermann, H., & Kearney, G. (2020). SoundFields: A virtual reality game designed to address auditory hypersensitivity in individuals with autism spectrum disorder. *Applied Sciences (Basel, Switzerland)*, *10*(9), 2996. DOI: 10.3390/app10092996

Jordanoski, Z., & Nielsen, M. M. (2023). The challenge of web accessibility: An evaluation of selected government websites and service portals of high-, middle-, and low-income countries. In *ICEGOV '23: Proceedings of the 16th International Conference on Theory and Practice of Electronic Governance* (pp. 101–110). ACM. https://doi.org/DOI: 10.1145/3614321.3614343

Kalemkuş, F. (2025). Trends in instructional technologies used in education of people with special needs due to intellectual disability and autism. *Journal of Research in Special Educational Needs*, *25*(2), 237–261. DOI: 10.1111/1471-3802.12723

Kamalipour, Y. R., & Friedrichsen, M. (2017). Introduction: Digital Transformation in a Global world. In *Springer eBooks* (pp. 1–4). DOI: 10.1007/978-3-319-27786-8_1

Kamp-Becker, I. (2024). Autism spectrum disorder in ICD-11—A critical reflection of its possible impact on clinical practice and research. *Molecular Psychiatry*, *29*(3), 633–638. DOI: 10.1038/s41380-023-02354-y PMID: 38273107

Kang, H., Baek, J., Chu, S. H., & Choi, J. (2023). Digital literacy among Korean older adults: A scoping review of quantitative studies. *Digital Health*, *9*, 20552076231197334. Advance online publication. DOI: 10.1177/20552076231197334 PMID: 37654708

Kasari, C., Freeman, S., & Paparella, A. (2006). Joint attention and symbolic play in young children with autism: A randomized controlled intervention study. *Journal of Child Psychology and Psychiatry, and Allied Disciplines*, *47*(6), 611–620. DOI: 10.1111/j.1469-7610.2005.01567.x PMID: 16712638

Kaur, N., Bhuiyan, M., Prasad, P., Haque, F., & Elchouemi, A. (2019). Enhancing Quality in Agile Requirement Elicitation Process. *American Journal of Applied Sciences*, *16*(1), 1–10. Advance online publication. DOI: 10.3844/ajassp.2019.1.10

Keates, S., & Clarkson, J. (2004). Understanding inclusive design. In *Springer eBooks* (pp. 50–64). https://doi.org/DOI: 10.1007/978-1-4471-0013-3_4

Keates, S., & Clarkson, J. (2004). Why the interest in inclusive design? In *Countering design exclusion*. Springer., DOI: 10.1007/978-1-4471-0013-3_2

Kelly, B.. (2019). Institutional accessibility challenges. *Journal of Web Engineering*, *17*(2), 97–118.

Kelly, B., Phipps, L., & Howell, C. (2005). Implementing a holistic approach to e-learning accessibility. *ALT-J. Research in Learning Technology*, *13*(1), 69–78. DOI: 10.1080/0968776042000339777

Kelly, B., Phipps, L., & Swift, E. (2005). Developing a holistic approach for e-learning accessibility. *Canadian Journal of Learning and Technology, 31*(3). Advance online publication. DOI: 10.21432/T2D60S

Keptner, K. M., & Heath, M. (2023). The impact of resistance on telemedicine uses for people with disabilities. *Journal of Telemedicine and Telecare*. Advance online publication. DOI: 10.1177/1357633X231213412

Khowaja, K., Banire, B., Al-Thani, D., Sqalli, M. T., Aqle, A., Shah, A., & Salim, S. S. (2020). Augmented reality for learning of children and adolescents with autism spectrum disorder (ASD): A systematic review. In *IEEE Access* (Vol. 8, pp. 78779–78807). Institute of Electrical and Electronics Engineers Inc. DOI: 10.1109/ACCESS.2020.2986608

Kim, S., & Lee, J. (2020). National strategies for digital literacy and cybersecurity education: The case of South Korea. *Asian Journal of Education and Training*, *6*(1), 12–22. DOI: 10.20448/journal.522.2020.61.12.22

Kirkpatrick, A. (2007). Overview of accessible technologies. In *Apress eBooks* (pp. 85–100). DOI: 10.1007/978-1-4302-0188-5_4

Koc-Michalska, K., & Lilleker, D. (2016). Digital Politics: Mobilization, engagement, and participation. *Political Communication*, *34*(1), 1–5. DOI: 10.1080/10584609.2016.1243178

Koegel, R. L., Koegel, L. K., & Ashbaugh, J. K. (2012). Pivotal Response Treatment for autism spectrum disorders. *Journal of Autism and Developmental Disorders*, *42*(4), 581–593. DOI: 10.1007/s10803-011-1280-1

Kumar, D. (2023). CLOUD COMPUTING. *International Scientific Journal of Engineering and Management*, *02*(4). Advance online publication. DOI: 10.55041/ISJEM00289

Ladner, R. E. (2015). Design for user empowerment. *interactions, 22*(2), 24–29. https://doi.org/DOI: 10.1145/2723869

Lana Studio. (2022). *Hyper Casual FX* [Unity Asset Store]. Unity. https://assetstore.unity.com/publishers/55292

Laver, K., Lange, B., George, S., Deutsch, J. E., Saposnik, G., & Crotty, M. (2017). Virtual reality for stroke rehabilitation. *The Cochrane Library*, *11*(1), CD008349. Advance online publication. DOI: 10.1002/14651858.CD008349.pub4

Lawan, A. A., Yarima, K. I., Usman, H. I., Abba, S. I., Yakubu, H. U., & Musa, A. G. (2023). A Systematic Literature Review on the Efficacy of Emerging Computer Technologies in Inclusive Education for Students with Autism Spectrum Disorder. *OBM Neurobiology*, *7*(2), 1–27. Advance online publication. DOI: 10.21926/obm.neurobiol.2302172

Lawson, W. (2020). Adaptive Morphing and Coping with Social Threat in Autism: An Autistic Perspective. *Journal of Intellectual Disabilities*, *24*(3), 245–259. DOI: 10.1177/1744629520907987

Lazar, J., Goldstein, D. F., & Taylor, A. (2015). *Ensuring digital accessibility through process and policy*. Morgan & Claypool Publishers., DOI: 10.1016/C2013-0-19101-7

Le Cunff, A.-L., Ross, F., Westwood, S. J., Koya, S., Caldwell, D. M., Russell, A. E., & Dommett, E. J. (2025). Key Research Questions to Support Neurodiversity in Higher Education: A Participatory Priority Setting Exercise. *Education Sciences*, *15*(7), 839. DOI: 10.3390/educsci15070839

Leigh, I. W., Andrews, J. F., Harris, R. L., & Ávila, T. G. (2020). *Deaf culture: Exploring deaf communities in the United States*. Plural Publishing.

Leporini, B., & Paternò, F. (2008). Applying web usability criteria for vision-impaired users: Does it really improve task performance? *International Journal of Human-Computer Interaction*, *24*(1), 17–47. DOI: 10.1080/10447310701771472

Leveraging ICTs to support the achievement of post-2015 education agenda. (2015). Retrieved September 29, 2025, from https://unesdoc.unesco.org/ark:/48223/pf0000232379

Lewthwaite, S. (2014). Digital accessibility and lived experience. *Disability & Society*, *29*(7), 1185–1198.

Lewthwaite, S. (2014). Web accessibility standards and disability: Developing critical perspectives on accessibility. *Disability and Rehabilitation*, *36*(16), 1375–1383. DOI: 10.3109/09638288.2014.938178

Ley 1581 de 2012. (2012, October 17). *Ley de protección de datos personales*. Secretaría General de la Alcaldía Mayor de Bogotá. https://www.alcaldiabogota.gov.co/sisjur/normas/Norma1.jsp?i=49981

Ley Federal de Protección de Datos Personales en Posesión de los Particulares. (2010, July 5). *Diario Oficial de la Federación*. https://www.gob.mx/indesol/documentos/ley-federal-de-proteccion-de-datos-personales-en-posesion-de-los-particulares

Li, J., Yan, Z., Shah, A., Lazar, J., & Peng, H. (2023). *Touchal1y: Making inaccessible public touchscreens accessible*. arXiv.

Lillo-Martin, D., & Henner, J. (2021). Acquisition of sign languages. *Annual Review of Linguistics*, *7*(1), 395–419. DOI: 10.1146/annurev-linguistics-043020-092357 PMID: 34746335

Liotti, M., Pliszka, S. R., Higgins, K., Perez, R.III, & Semrud-Clikeman, M. (2010). Evidence for specificity of ERP abnormalities during response inhibition in ADHD children: A comparison with Reading disorder children without ADHD. *Brain and Cognition*, *72*(2), 228–237. DOI: 10.1016/j.bandc.2009.09.007 PMID: 19850394

Lister, K., Coughlan, T., Iniesto, F., Freear, N., & Devine, P. (2020). Accessible conversational user interfaces: considerations for design. In *Proceedings of the 17th international web for all conference* (pp. 1-11). DOI: 10.1145/3371300.3383343

Liu, L., Yan, G., & Chen, S. (n.d.). *Chrome Extensions: Threat Analysis and Countermeasures*. http://www.google.com

Lledó Gonzalo, L., Lorenzo Lledó, A., Carreres Lledó, A., & Pérez Vázquez, E. (2023). Creation of an immersive virtual reality environment for communication and social interaction: A pilot study in students with autism spectrum disorders. *Revista de Educación a Distancia*, *23*(73). Advance online publication. DOI: 10.6018/red.539141

Lomellini, A., Lowenthal, P. R., Snelson, C., & Trespalacios, J. H. (2025). Accessible and inclusive online learning in higher education: A review of the literature. *Journal of Computing in Higher Education*, *37*(3), 1306–1329. DOI: 10.1007/s12528-024-09424-2

López Belmonte, J., Duo Terrón, P., Moreno Guerrero, A. J., & Marín Marín, J. A. (2024). Efectos de la realidad aumentada y virtual en estudiantes con TEA. *Pixel-Bit. Revista de Medios y Educación*. https://revistapixelbit.com

López-Belmonte, J., Duo-Terrón, P., Moreno-Guerrero, A. J., & Marín-Marín, J. A. (2024). Effects of augmented and virtual reality on students with ASD. *Pixel-Bit. Revista de Medios y Educacion*, *70*, 7–23. DOI: 10.12795/pixelbit.103789

López-Bouzas, N., & Del Moral Pérez, M. E. (2023). A gamified environment supported by augmented reality for improving communicative competencies in students with ASD: Design and validation. *International Journal of Educational Research and Innovation*, *2023*(19), 80–93. DOI: 10.46661/ijeri.6820

Lopez-Bouzas, N., & Del Moral-Perez, M. E. (2023). Gamified Environments and Serious Games for Students With Autistic Spectrum Disorder: Review of Research. *Review Journal of Autism and Developmental Disorders*, •••, 1–13. DOI: 10.1007/s40489-023-00381-7 PMID: 37363697

López, M., & García, V. (2022). Smishing and vulnerability in mobile users in Latin America. *Revista Chilena de Ciberseguridad, 3*(1), 54–70.

Lopezosa, C., Codina, L., Guallar, J., & Pérez-Montoro, M. (2023). *Voice search optimization in digital media: challenges, use and training*. The Information Professional., DOI: 10.3145/epi.2023.may.07

Luke, R. (2001, August 6). Courseware accessibility: recommendations for inclusive design. *International Conference on Advanced Learning Technologies*. DOI: 10.1109/ICALT.2001.943951

Luque Ordóñez, J. (2020). Realidad virtual y realidad aumentada. *Acta*. https://www.acta.es/medios/articulos/ciencias_y_tecnologia/063001.pdf#page=3.69

Mace, R. (1985). *Universal Design: Barrier-Free Environments for Everyone*. North Carolina State University, The Center for Universal Design.

Mace, R. L. (1998). Universal design in housing. *Assistive Technology, 10*(1), 21–28. DOI: 10.1080/10400435.1998.10131957

Maes, P., & Chang, A. (2021). *Multisensory Virtual Reality for Neurodivergent Audiences. Proceedings of the IEEE International Symposium on Mixed and Augmented Reality.*

Mahmoudi, E., Yoo, P. Y., Chandra, A., Cardoso, R., Dos Santos, C. D., Majnemer, A., & Shikako, K. (2024). Gamification in mobile apps for children with disabilities: Scoping review. *JMIR Serious Games, 12*(1), e49029. DOI: 10.2196/49029 PMID: 39240675

Maïonchi-Pino, N., Runge, É., & Chabanal, D. (2024). Phonological syllables allow children with developmental dyslexia to access words. *Annals of Dyslexia, 74*(2), 244–270. DOI: 10.1007/s11881-024-00302-1 PMID: 38366193

Manduchi, R., & Kurniawan, S. (2017). *Assistive technology for blindness and low vision*. CRC Press., DOI: 10.1201/9781315216935

Mapas Interactivos. (2025). Didactalia.net. https://mapasinteractivos.didactalia.net/comunidad/mapasflashin

Marr, B. (2019). How Apple became the most inclusive tech company with VoiceOver. *Forbes*. Retrieved from: https://www.forbes.com. Accessed on 26.07.2025.

Martínez, N., Elena, B., Sánchez, M. S., & Saray, P. (2025). Duo Señas: Aplicación móvil para conocer y practicar inclusivamente la Lengua de Señas Mexicana (LSM) mediante metodologías ágiles y tecnologías multiplataforma. Ciencia Latina Revista Científica Multidisciplinar, 9(3), 1618–1633. DOI: 10.37811/cl_rcm.v9i3.17771

Martínez, J., & Torres, A. (2020). Cyberfraud in the digital era: Trends and challenges. *Revista de Derecho y Tecnología*, *11*(2), 33–57.

Martínez-Olvera, W., González-Miy, D., Moreno-Vite, I., & Martínez-Cervantes, Y. (2024). Inclusión educativa del Sordo: Panorama en México y Veracruz. *Revista Stultifera*, *7*(1), 221–251. DOI: 10.4206/rev.stultifera.2024.v7n1-09

Martins, R. A., Ribeiro, M. G., Pastura, G. M. C., & Monteiro, M. C. (2020). Remediation Phonology in schoolchildren with ADHD and dyslexia. *CoDAS*, *32*(5), 86. Advance online publication. DOI: 10.1590/2317-1782/20192019086 PMID: 33174986

McCall, K., & Chagnon, B. (2022). Rethinking alt text to improve its effectiveness. In *Lecture notes in computer science* (pp. 26-33). https://doi.org/DOI: 10.1007/978-3-031-08645-8_4

McCarthy, M. T. (2016). The big data divide and its consequences. *Sociology Compass*, *10*(12), 1131–1140. DOI: 10.1111/soc4.12436

Mehta, P. (2016). *Creating Google Chrome Extensions*. DOI: 10.1007/978-1-4842-1775-7

Mendoza, G. A. A., Lewis, F., Plante, P., & Brassard, C. (2023). Estado del arte sobre el uso de la realidad virtual, la realidad aumentada y el video 360° en educación superior. *Edutec*, *84*(84), 35–51. DOI: 10.21556/edutec.2023.84.2769

Mercader, C. A. M. F., Escobar, L. E. D., Ramírez, M. R. R. B., Pool, M. P. W., & Cruz, M. C. A. (2017, September 25). *DICCIONARIO DE LENGUA DE SEÑAS MEXICANA DE LA CIUDAD DE MÉXICO*. Retrieved October 1, 2025, from https://pdh.cdmx.gob.mx/storage/app/media/banner/Dic_LSM%202.pdf

Meyer, A., Rose, D. H., & Gordon, D. (2014). *Universal Design for Learning: Theory and Practice*. CAST Professional Publishing.

Microsoft Inclusive Design Toolkit. (2023).

Microsoft. (2016). *Inclusive Design Toolkit*. Microsoft Design. Retrieved from: https://inclusive.microsoft.design. Accessed on 26.07.2025.

Microsoft. (2020). *Immersive Reader: Tools to support reading and learning*. Microsoft Education. Retrieved from: https://education.microsoft.com/en-us/resource/immersive-reader. Accessed on 26.07.2025.

Miki, H. (2013). Reconsidering the notion of user experience for Human-Centered design. In *Lecture notes in computer science* (pp. 329–337). DOI: 10.1007/978-3-642-39209-2_38

Mishra, S., & Panda, S. (2023). *Cloud Computing: Applications*. Challenges and Open Issues.

Mokh, H., Maulana, S., Ilham, Z., Muhammad, M., & Mhd, I. (2019). *Voice-based monitoring and control system of electronic appliance using dialog flow API via Google Assistant*. IEEE.

Molina Gutiérrez, B., Ayala Pérez, C., & García Sánchez, M. (2025). Diseño Universal para el Aprendizaje: Estrategias para una enseñanza equitativa. *DISCE. Revista Científica. Educativa Y Social*, *2*(2), 1–23. DOI: 10.69821/DISCE.v2i1.19

Monisha, M., & Valanteena, D. (2022). Digital transformation in education. EPRA *International Journal of Economic and Business Review*, 58–64. https://doi.org/ DOI: 10.36713/epra11864

Montero, Y. H. (2015). *Experiencia de Usuario: Principios y Métodos*. www.yusef .esTodoslosderechosreservados,2015EstelibrohasidoescritousandoCalmlyWriter

Moodle. (2023). *Accessibility in Moodle*. Retrieved from: https://docs.moodle.org/403/en/Accessibility. Accessed on 26.07.2025.

Morais, P. B. de, Matos, R. A. F. de, Santiago, D. C., Silva, R. L. dos S., Botelho, L., Soares, G. de A., Santos, D. de S., Morais, S. D. de, Silva, E. J. da, & Lima, L. A. de O. (2023). Opportunities to use gamification for the learning of autistic students: A systematic review. *IOSR Journal of Business and Management, 25*(10, Ser. 8), 29–35. https://doi.org/DOI: 10.9790/487X-2510082935

Morán, N., Pérez, J., & Rodriguez, W. (2018, June). *Recognizing People's Emotional States Using Voice Using Machine Learning Algorithms*.

Moreno Martínez, C., Piorno, J. R., Escribano Otero, J. J., & Guijarro Mata-García, M. (2023). Responsive inclusive design (RiD): A new model for inclusive software development. *Universal Access in the Information Society*, *22*(3), 893–902. DOI: 10.1007/s10209-022-00893-9

Morocho Fajardo, K., Sánchez Álvarez, D., & Patiño Zambrano, V. (2021). Epidemiological profile of autism spectrum disorder in Latin America. *Salud y Ciencias Médicas, 1*(2).

Mouga, S., Oliveira, G., Almeida, J., Figueiredo, C., & Castelo-Branco, M. (2021). Attentional cueing and executive deficits revealed by a virtual supermarket task coupled with eye-tracking in autism spectrum disorder. *Frontiers in Psychology, 12*, 671507. DOI: 10.3389/fpsyg.2021.671507 PMID: 34531782

Muñoz García, J. (2019). Internet access and use by older adults in Colombia. *Revista de Estudios Sociales, 68*, 72–86. https://repository.umng.edu.co/handle/20.500.12727/1837

Muñoz, P. T., & Pérez, S. M. (2020). La inclusión de niños sordos en educación básica en una escuela de México mediante el diseño de recursos digitales. *RIDE Revista Iberoamericana para la Investigación y el Desarrollo Educativo, 11*(21). Advance online publication. DOI: 10.23913/ride.v11i21.758

Nacheva, R. (2024). Hired by Artificial Intelligence: Digital Inclusion Practices for People with Disabilities. *Journal of Underrepresented & Minority Progress, 8*(2). Advance online publication. DOI: 10.32674/66c03968

Natale, S., & Cooke, H. (2021). Browsing with Alexa: Interrogating the impact of voice assistants as web interfaces. *Media Culture & Society, 43*(6), 1000–1016. DOI: 10.1177/0163443720983295

Nganji, J., & Nggada, S. (2011). Disability-aware software engineering for improved system accessibility and usability. *International Journal of Software Engineering and Its Applications, 5*(3), 47–62.

Nielsen, J. (1994). *Heuristic Evaluation*. In *Usability Inspection Methods*.

Nielsen, J. (2012). *Usability 101: Introduction to usability*. Nielsen Norman Group. https://www.nngroup.com/articles/usability-101-introduction-to-usability

Nielsen, J. (2012). *Usability Engineering*. Morgan Kaufmann.

Norman, D. (2013). *THE DESIGN OF EVERYDAY THINGS* (1st ed.). Basic Books., https://ia902800.us.archive.org/3/items/thedesignofeverydaythingsbydonnorman/The%20Design%20of%20Everyday%20Things%20by%20Don%20Norman.pdf

Norman, D. (2013). *The design of everyday things: Revised and expanded edition*. Basic Books.

Norman, D. A. (2013). *The design of everyday things* (Rev. ed.). MIT Press., https://mitpress.mit.edu/9780262525671

Norman, D. A. (2013). *The Design of Everyday Things*. Basic Books.

Objetivos de Desarrollo Sustentable. (2023). Retrieved September 29, 2025, from https://www.un.org/sustainabledevelopment/es/education/

Okello, S. (2021). Digital literacy in Africa: The role of Smart Africa initiative. *African Journal of ICT Development*, *14*(2), 56–73.

Okuda, P. M., Pinheiro, F. H., Germano, G. D., Padula, N. A. M. R., Lourencetti, M. D., & Santos, L. C. A.. (2011). Fine motor, sensory and perceptual function of schoolchildren attention deficit hyperactivity disorder. *Jornal da Sociedade Brasileira de Fonoaudiologia*, *23*(4). Advance online publication. DOI: 10.1590/S2179-64912011000400010 PMID: 22231056

Oliveira, D. S., Rocha, H. A., Yang, H., Ellis, D. M., Dommaraju, S., Muradoglu, M., Weir, D., Soliman, A., Lin, T., & Ebner, N. C. (2017). Dissecting spear phishing emails for older vs. young adults. In *Proceedings of the 2017 CHI Conference on Human Factors in Computing Systems* (pp. 6412–6424). ACM. https://doi.org/DOI: 10.1145/3025453.3025831

Oliveira, J. S., Franco, F. O., Revers, M. C., Silva, A. F., Portolese, J., Brentani, H., Machado-Lima, A., & Nunes, F. L. S. (2021). Computer-aided autism diagnosis based on visual attention models using eye tracking. *Scientific Reports*, *11*(1), 10131. Advance online publication. DOI: 10.1038/s41598-021-89023-8 PMID: 33980874

Oliver, M. (1990). *The Politics of Disablement*. Palgrave Macmillan. DOI: 10.1007/978-1-349-20895-1

Oliver, M. (2018). *Understanding disability: From theory to practice*. Bloomsbury publishing.

Omari, O. J. (2013). Investigating ATM System Accessibility for People with Visual Impairments. *IOSR Journal of Computer Engineering*, *15*(5), 13–18. DOI: 10.9790/0661-1551318

Ophoff, J., Johnson, G., & Renaud, K. (2021). Cognitive function vs. accessible authentication: insights from dyslexia research Proceedings of the 18th International Web for All Conference, Ljubljana, Slovenia. https://doi.org/DOI: 10.1145/3430263.3452427

Ordoñez, K., Hilera, J., & Cueva, S. (2022). Model-driven development of accessible software: A systematic literature review. *Universal Access in the Information Society*, *21*(1), 295–324. DOI: 10.1007/s10209-020-00751-6

Orero, P. (2022). Translation, accessibility and minorities. In Bielsa, E. (Ed.), *The Routledge handbook of translation and media* (pp. 384–399). Taylor & Francis.

Organización de Estados Iberoamericanos. (2021). Los desafíos de las TIC para el cambio educativo. In *Metas Educativas 2021*. Organización de Estados Iberoamericanos para la Educación, la Ciencia y la Cultura. https://www.oei.es

Ortega-Arranz, A., Bote-Lorenzo, M. L., Asensio-Pérez, J. I., Martínez-Monés, A., & Gómez-Sánchez, E. (2019). To reward and beyond: Analyzing the effect of reward-based strategies in a MOOC. *Computers & Education*, *146*, 103639. DOI: 10.1016/j.compedu.2019.103639

Ortega-Arranz, A., Muñoz-Cristóbal, J. A., Martínez-Monés, A., Bote-Lorenzo, M. L., & Asensio-Pérez, J. I. (2016). Lecture Notes in Computer Science: Vol. 9684. *A System for Gamifying Ubiquitous Learning Situations Supported by Multiple Technologies. Intelligent Tutoring Systems (ITS 2016).*

Orts, B. S. (2019). INMER-II: Sistema de inmersión en realidad virtual para personas con autismo. *Revista Española de Tecnología Educativa*, *5*(2), 45–53.

Palaparthi, A. Voice, & Speech, N. C. (2023). *Machine Learning for Voice and Speech Science*. DOI: 10.13140/RG.2.2.32603.54562

Parsons, S., & Cobb, S. (2011). State-of-the-art of virtual reality technologies for children on the autism spectrum. *European Journal of Special Needs Education*, *26*(3), 355–366. DOI: 10.1080/08856257.2011.593831

Pascual Almenara, A., Humanes, J., & Granollers, T. (2024). MPIu+aX, user-centered design methodology that empathizes with the user and generates a better accessible experience: From theory to practice. In *Proceedings of the XXIII International Conference on Human Computer Interaction* (Article 11, 3 pp.). Association for Computing Machinery. https://doi.org/DOI: 10.1145/3612783.3612795

Passerino, L. M., & Baldassarri, S. (2017). *Mesas Tangibles para la Planificación Cognitiva en alumnos con Trastorno del Espectro Autista (TEA). Tecnología Accesible e Inclusiva: Logros, Resistencias y Desafíos*. Consejería de Educación, Juventud y Deportes.

Pérez, R., & Rivas, J. (2021). Experiential learning in cybersecurity: Digital fraud simulations for preventive education. *Revista Venezolana de Tecnología Educativa*, *10*(1), 64–81.

Pinheiro, F. H., Lourencetti, M. D., & Santos, L. C. A. (2012). Attention deficit disorder and hyperativity disorder diagnostic criteria. *Revista Semestral da Associação Brasileira de Psicologia Escolar e Educacional*, *16*(1), 113–123.

Policía Nacional de Colombia. (2023). *Annual report on cybercrime 2023*. https://caivirtual.policia.gov.co/sites/default/files/observatorio/Balance%20anual%202023_0.pdf

Pradhan, A., Mehta, K., & Findlater, L. (2018). "Accessibility came by accident": Use of voice-controlled intelligent personal assistants by people with disabilities. *Conference on Human Factors in Computing Systems - Proceedings, 2018-April*. DOI: 10.1145/3173574.3174033

Prakash, N. K., Monlam, T., Singh, R., Aravindhan, R. P., Reddy, P. V., & Jain, R. (2022). Voice based E-Mail with Attachment for Blind. *2022 6th International Conference on Trends in Electronics and Informatics, ICOEI 2022 - Proceedings*, 274–280. DOI: 10.1109/ICOEI53556.2022.9776840

Pressman, R. S., & Maxim, B. R. (2021). *Ingeniería del software: un enfoque práctico*.

Psicosomática, M., ... (2007). Realidad virtual y tratamientos psicológicos. https://d1wqtxts1xzle7.cloudfront.net/102824856/Cuad_20N82_20trabajo_202-libre.pdf

Pullin, G. (2009). *Design Meets Disability*. MIT Press.

Raj, S., & Singh, A. (2021). An evaluation of Indian government websites for web accessibility compliance. *International Journal of Human-Computer Interaction*, *37*(12), 1121–1134. DOI: 10.1080/10447318.2021.1888487

Ramos Aguiar, L. R. (2020). *METUIGA "Metodología para el diseño de sistemas basados en interfaces tangibles de usuario y técnicas de gamificación para personas ciegas"* [Maestría]. Universidad Autonoma de Aguascalientes.

Ramos Aguiar, L. R., & Álvarez Rodríguez, F. J. (2021). Methodology for designing systems based on tangible user interfaces and gamification techniques for blind people. *Applied Sciences (Basel, Switzerland)*, *11*(12), 5676. Advance online publication. DOI: 10.3390/app11125676

Ramos Aguiar, L. R., Álvarez Rodríguez, F. J., Madero Aguilar, J. R., Navarro Plascencia, V., Peña Mendoza, L. M., Quintero Valdez, J. R., Vázquez Pech, J. R., Mendieta León, A., & Lazcano Ortiz, L. E. (2023). Implementing gamification for blind and autistic people with tangible interfaces, extended reality, and universal design for learning: Two case studies. *Applied Sciences (Basel, Switzerland)*, *13*(5), 3159. DOI: 10.3390/app13053159

Ramos-Aguiar, L. R., & Álvarez-Rodríguez, F. J. (2021). Enseñanza de emociones en niños con espectro autista a través de un software con interfaces tangibles. *IEEE Revista Iberoamericana de Technologias del Aprendizaje*, *16*(4), 365–371. DOI: 10.1109/RITA.2021.3125901

Ramos, P., & Aguilar, F. (2021). Digital memory in rural communities: Challenges of technological literacy. *Revista Peruana de Ciencias Sociales, 12*(4), 188–205.

Reid, B. (2022). Two paths for digital disability law. *Communications of the ACM, 65*(5), 36–38. DOI: 10.1145/3527201

Reserve Bank of India. (2014). *Circular on talking ATMs and accessibility for persons with disabilities*. Retrieved from: https://rbidocs.rbi.org.in. Accessed on 12.11.2025.

Reynolds, M. E., Callihan, K., & Browning, E. (2003). The effect of instruction on the development of rhyming skills in young children. *Contemporary Issues in Communication Science and Disorders, 30*(Spring), 41–46. DOI: 10.1044/cicsd_30_S_41

Rezayi, S. (2023). Features and Effects of Computer-Based Games on Cognitive and Social Skills in Children with Autism Spectrum Disorder: A Systematic Review. *Child Neuropsychology, 29*(8), 1200–1223. DOI: 10.1080/09297049.2022.2164356

Rezayi, S., Shahmoradi, L., & Tehrani-Doost, M. (2025). Systematic Review and Thematic Analysis of Digital Games for Cognitive Enhancement in Children with Autism Spectrum Disorder: Toward a Conceptual Framework. *Cognitive Computation, 17*(1), 60. DOI: 10.1007/s12559-024-10395-w

Robinson, L., Cotten, S. R., Ono, H., Quan-Haase, A., Mesch, G., Chen, W., Schulz, J., Hale, T. M., & Stern, M. J. (2015). Digital inequalities and why they matter. *Information Communication and Society, 18*(5), 569–582. DOI: 10.1080/1369118X.2015.1012532

Rodríguez Cano, S., Delgado Benito, V., Ausín-Villaverde, V., & Muñoz-Martín, L. (2021). Designing virtual reality software to promote learning for students with dyslexia. *Sustainability (Basel), 13*(15), 8425. Advance online publication. DOI: 10.3390/su13158425

Rodríguez, S., & Morales, E. (2022). Inclusive interface and accessibility in older adults: A comparative study of mobile apps. *Revista Española de Interacción Digital, 9*(2), 44–59.

Rojas-Chávez, K. A., & Quini-Villegas, R. (2019). Aplicación móvil para Aprender Lengua de Señas Mexicana. Revista de Tecnologías de La Información Y Comunicaciones, 8–17. DOI: 10.35429/JITC.2019.8.3.8.17

Sadia, R., Tuli, F. A., & Lal, K. (2023). Digitization History and its Impact on the Economy, Employment, and Society. *Global Disclosure of Economics and Business, 12*(1), 15–24. DOI: 10.18034/gdeb.v12i1.707

Sánchez, C., Quezada-Cisnero, Á., & Rodríguez-Aguiñága, A. (2023). Una propuesta de aplicación móvil para el aprendizaje de la lengua de señas mexicana mediante el desarrollo de un modelo de realidad aumentada. Pädi Boletín Científico de Ciencias Básicas E Ingenierías Del ICBI, 11(Especial4), 264–269. DOI: 10.29057/icbi.v11iEspecial4.11427

Sánchez, A., López, J., & Herrera, C. (2020). Vulnerability of older adults to online fraud: A study in Spain and Chile. *Revista Gerontológica Latinoamericana*, *6*(1), 55–74.

Sanders, E. B. N., & Stappers, P. J. (2008). Co-creation and the new landscapes of design. *CoDesign*, *4*(1), 5–18. DOI: 10.1080/15710880701875068

Santoso, H. B., & Schrepp, M. (2019). The impact of culture and product on the subjective importance of user experience aspects. *Heliyon*, *5*(9), e02434. DOI: 10.1016/j.heliyon.2019.e02434 PMID: 31528748

Schilbach, L. (2022). Autism and other disorders of social interaction: Where we are and where to go from here. *European Archives of Psychiatry and Clinical Neuroscience*, *272*(2), 173–175. DOI: 10.1007/s00406-022-01391-y PMID: 35141808

Schneider, O.. (2017). Haptic Feedback in Virtual Reality: The Importance of User Preferences. *IEEE Transactions on Haptics*.

Sciarretta, E. (2025). Inclusive education: Is applying web Content Accessibility guidelines to digital learning materials enough? *European Journal of Education*, *60*(2), e70104. Advance online publication. DOI: 10.1111/ejed.70104

Seale, J. (2014). *E-learning and disability in higher education: Accessibility research and practice* (2nd ed.). Routledge.

Seale, J. (2014). *E-learning and Disability in Higher Education: Accessibility Research and Practice*. Routledge.

Sep. (n.d.). *¿Qué son las habilidades digitales?* https://nuevaescuelamexicana.sep.gob.mx/contenido/recurso/32320/

Serrano Angulo, J., & Cebrián Robles, D. (2014). Usabilidad y satisfacción de la e-Rúbrica. *REDU. Revista de Docencia Universitaria*, *12*(1), 177. Advance online publication. DOI: 10.4995/redu.2014.6426

Serrano-Fernández, L., & Viguera-Monje, M. (2024). A Systematic Review of the Presence and Participation of Students with Intellectual Disabilities in Spanish Universities. *Journal of Intellectual Disabilities*, *28*(1), 34–52. DOI: 10.1177/17446295241246035 PMID: 38574375

Setianti, Y., Hafiar, H., Subekti, P., & Priyatna, C. C. (2020, November 18). Social conditions and expectations of customers with disabilities regarding policies and provision of accessible banking technology. DOI: 10.4108/eai.11-12-2019.2302150

Shakespeare, T. (2018). *Disability: The Basics*. Routledge.

Sheffield, A. M., & Smith, R. J. H. (2019). The epidemiology of deafness. *Cold Spring Harbor Perspectives in Medicine*, *9*(9), a033258. DOI: 10.1101/cshperspect.a033258 PMID: 30249598

Shinohara, K., & Wobbrock, J. O. (2011). In the shadow of misperception: Designing for people with disabilities. *CHI Conference Proceedings*, 705–714.

Shinohara, K., & Wobbrock, J. O. (2016). Self-conscious or self-confident? A diary study conceptualizing the social accessibility of assistive technology. *ACM Transactions on Accessible Computing, 8*(2). *ACM Transactions on Accessible Computing*, *5*(2), 1–31. DOI: 10.1145/2827857

Sierra, E. A., & Contreras Juárez, R. (2023). Capítulo 2. Diseño de una herramienta para la formación docente en el aula inclusiva mediante TIC para niños con TEA. *Experiencias Educativas Basadas En TICs*. https://www.researchgate.net/publication/379023807

Silva, C. (2009). Effectiveness of a Remedial Program Fonolóigca e Leitura in schoolchildren with Aprendizagem Disturbance [Master's Thesis, Paulista State University. UNESP Institutional Repository

Silva, C., Cunha, V. L. O., & Capellini, S. A. (2011). Cognitive-linguistic performance em reading of schoolchildren with Attention deficit and hyperactivity disorder. *Revista Brasileira de Crescimento e Desenvolvimento Humano*, *21*(3), 849–858.

Silva, J. S., Gonçalves, R., Branco, F., Pereira, A., Au-Yong-Oliveira, M., & Martins, J. (2019). Accessible software development: A conceptual model proposal. *Universal Access in the Information Society*, *18*(3), 703–716. DOI: 10.1007/s10209-019-00688-5

Simancas, J., & Meléndez-Pertuz, F. (2017). Voice command recognition algorithm based on non-linear techniques. *Revista Espacios*, *38*, 4.

Simon, C., & Rajeswari, M. (2023). Voice-based Virtual Assistant with Security. *Proceedings of the 2023 2nd International Conference on Electronics and Renewable Systems, ICEARS 2023*, 822–827. DOI: 10.1109/ICEARS56392.2023.10085043

Singer, J. (1998). *Odd People In: The Birth of Community Amongst People on the Autistic Spectrum*. PhD thesis, University of Technology, Sydney.

Singer, J. (1998). Odd People In: The Birth of Community Amongst People on the. In *Autistic Spectrum*. University of Technology Sydney.

Singer, J. (2016). *NeuroDiversity: The Birth of an Idea*. Judy Singer.

Singh, R., & Ghai, S. (2022). Web accessibility of e-governance portals in multilingual India: A study of regional inclusivity. *Universal Access in the Information Society*, *21*(3), 559–571. DOI: 10.1007/s10209-021-00788-9

Smith, M. J.. (2020). Project VOISS: Virtual Reality to Promote Employment Skills in Adolescents with Autism. *Journal of Autism and Developmental Disorders*.

Snowling, M. J., & Hulme, C. (2025). The Reading Is Language Model: A Theoretical Framework for Language and Reading Development and Intervention. *Annual Review of Developmental Psychology*, *7*(1), 1–25. DOI: 10.1146/annurev-devpsych-111323-084821

Sofian, N. M., Hashim, A. S., & Ahmad, W. F. W. (2018). A review on usability guidelines for designing mobile apps user interface for children with autism. *AIP Conference Proceedings*, *2016*(1). Advance online publication. DOI: 10.1063/1.5055496

Solve, M. I. T. (2023). *DigiMENTE: Media education for Latin America*. https://solve.mit.edu/challenges/learning-for-civic-action-challenge/solutions/74650

Soto-Rey, J., & Pérez-Tejero, J. (2014). Estrategias para la inclusión de personas con discapacidad auditiva en educacion fisica. *Revista Española De Educación Física Y Deportes*, *406*, 93–101. DOI: 10.55166/reefd.v0i406.30

Stasolla, F., Curcio, E., Passaro, A., Di Gioia, M., Zullo, A., & Martini, E. (2025). Exploring the Combination of Serious Games, Social Interactions, and Virtual Reality in Adolescents with ASD: A Scoping Review. *Technologies*, *13*(2), 76. DOI: 10.3390/technologies13020076

Steinfeld, E., & Maisel, J. (2012). *Universal Design: Creating Inclusive Environments*. Wiley.

Stephens, K., Butler, M., Holloway, L. M., Goncu, C., & Marriott, K. (2020). Smooth sailing? Autoethnography of recreational travel by a blind person. In *Proceedings of the 22nd International ACM SIGACCESS Conference on Computers and Accessibility (ASSETS '20)* (Article 26, pp. 1-12). ACM. https://doi.org/DOI: 10.1145/3373625.3417011

Stirling, L., Douglas, S., Leekam, S., & Carey, L. (2014). Communication in Autism. In *Trends in Language Acquisition Research* (Vol. 11). John Benjamins.

Story, M. F., Mueller, J. L., & Mace, R. L. (1998). *The Universal designfile: Designing forpeople of all ages and abilities*. NC State University, Center for Universal Design.

Subsecretaría Educación Media Superior. (2019). *La Nueva Escuela Mexicana: principios y orientaciones pedagógicas*.

Sung, M. C., McClelland, M. M., Massey, W., Logan, S. W., & Macdonald, M. (2024). Association between motor skills and executive function of children with autism spectrum disorder in Taiwan and the United States. *Frontiers in Public Health, 11*, 1292695. DOI: 10.3389/fpubh.2023.1292695 PMID: 38249390

Susanto, H., Ibrahim, F., Nazmudeen, S. H., Mohiddin, F., & Setiana, D. (2020). Human-Centered design to enhance the usability, human factors, and user experience within digital destructive ecosystems. In *Advances in business strategy and competitive advantage book series* (pp. 76–94). DOI: 10.4018/978-1-7998-4787-8.ch005

Sverdrup, N. (2018). *Accessibility testing in agile software development: Empowering agile developers with accessibility methods* (Master's thesis, University of Oslo). Faculty of Mathematics and Natural Sciences, Department of Informatics.

Sweller, J., Ayres, P., & Kalyuga, S. (2011). Cognitive Load Theory. *Educational Psychology Review, 23*(2), 123–152. DOI: 10.1007/s10648-010-9128-5

Sweller, J., Ayres, P., & Kalyuga, S. (2011). *Cognitive Load Theory*. Springer. DOI: 10.1007/978-1-4419-8126-4

Syriopoulou–Delli, C. K., & Sarri, K. (2022). Video-based instruction in enhancing functional living skills of adolescents and young adults with autism spectrum disorder and their transition to independent living: A review. *International Journal of Developmental Disabilities, 68*(6), 788–799. DOI: 10.1080/20473869.2021.1900504 PMID: 36568614

Tasneem, N., Zulzalil, H. B., & Hassan, S. (2025). Enhancing agile software development: A systematic literature review of requirement prioritization and reprioritization techniques. *IEEE Access : Practical Innovations, Open Solutions, 13*, 32993–33034. DOI: 10.1109/ACCESS.2025.3539357

Tebbutt, E., Brodmann, R., Borg, J., MacLachlan, M., Khasnabis, C., & Horvath, R. (2016). Assistive products and the sustainable development goals (SDGs). *Globalization and Health, 12*(1), 79. DOI: 10.1186/s12992-016-0220-6

The Gables. (2024, November 25). *Helping seniors with technology*. https://gables-living.com/about/blog/helping-seniors-with-technology

Toudert, D. (2019). Digital divide, frequent use and use of the Internet in Mexico. *Convergencia, 26*(79), 1–26. DOI: 10.29101/crcs.v0i79.10332

Transport for London. (2021). *Accessibility at stations and ticket machines.* https://tfl.gov.uk

Transport for London. (2021). *Accessibility at stations and ticket machines.* Retrieved on December 15, 2025, from https://tfl.gov.uk

Treviranus, J. (2018). *The three dimensions of inclusive design.* Inclusive Design Research Centre. Retrieved on December 15, 2025, from https://idrc.ocadu.ca/resources/idrc-online/the-three-dimensions-of-inclusive-design

U.S. Access Board. (2017). *Revised 508 Standards and 255 Guidelines: Information and communication technology.* Retrieved on December 15, 2025, from https://www.access-board.gov/ict/

UNCRPD. (2006). *Convention on the Rights of Persons with Disabilities.* United Nations.

UNESCO. (2023). *The benefits of lifelong learning for older adults.* UNESCO Institute for Lifelong Learning. https://www.uil.unesco.org/en/thematic-studies-benefits-lifelong-learning-older-adults

UNESCO. (s. f.). Aprendizaje digital y transformación de la educación. Recuperado el 15 de noviembre de 2025 de https://www.unesco.org/es/digital-education

UNICEF. (2019, June). Serie De Cuadernillos Sobre Educación Inclusiva. Retrieved September 29, 2025, from https://www.unicef.org/lac/informes/serie-de-cuadernillos-sobre-educaci%C3%B3n-inclusiva

United Nations (UN). (2006). *Convention on the rights of persons with disabilities. Treaty Series 2515*, 3.

United Nations. (2006). *Convention on the Rights of Persons with Disabilities (CRPD).* UN General Assembly. Retrieved on December 15, 2025, from https://www.un.org/disabilities/

United Nations. (2006). *Convention on the Rights of Persons with Disabilities.* Retrieved December 15, 2025, from https://www.un.org/disabilities/documents/convention/convoptprot-e.pdf

United Nations. (2015). *Sustainable Development Goals.* United Nations Development Programme. https://www.undp.org/sustainable-development-goals

Vallefuoco, E., Bravaccio, C., Gison, G., Pecchia, L., & Pepino, A. (2022). Personalized Training via Serious Game to Improve Daily Living Skills in Pediatric Patients With Autism Spectrum Disorder. *IEEE Journal of Biomedical and Health Informatics*, *26*(7), 3312–3322. DOI: 10.1109/JBHI.2022.3155367 PMID: 35230960

Vasquez, E., Nagendran, A., Welch, G. F., Marino, M. T., Hughes, D. E., Koch, A., & Delisio, L. (2015). Virtual learning environments for students with disabilities: A review and analysis of the empirical literature and two case studies. *Rural Special Education Quarterly*, *34*(3), 26–32. DOI: 10.1177/875687051503400306

Vazquez-Vazquez, T. C., Garcia-Herrera, D. G., Ochoa-Encalada, S. C., & Erazo-Álvarez, J. C. (2020). Estrategias didácticas para trabajar con niños con Trastorno del Espectro Autista (TEA). *Revista Arbitrada Interdisciplinaria Koinonía*, *5*(1), 589. DOI: 10.35381/r.k.v5i1.799

Veit, D., & Huntgeburth, J. (2013). Impact of digital governments. In *Springer texts in business and economics* (pp. 19–32). DOI: 10.1007/978-3-642-38511-7_2

Vélez, A., & Rivadeneira, F. (2024). Artículo de investigación Actividades didácticas para la enseñanza de la adición en estudiantes con trastorno del espectro autista-TEA. *Revista Social Fronteriza*, *4*(5). Advance online publication. DOI: 10.59814/resofro.2024.4(5)e407

Vellutino, F. R., Fletcher, J. M., Snowling, M. J., & Scanlon, D. M. (2004). Specific reading disability (dyslexia): What have we learned in the past four decades? *Journal of Child Psychology and Psychiatry, and Allied Disciplines*, *45*(1), 2–40. DOI: 10.1046/j.0021-9630.2003.00305.x PMID: 14959801

Vigo, M., Brown, J., & Conway, V. (2013). Benchmarking web accessibility evaluation tools: Measuring the harm of sole reliance on automated tests. *Proceedings of the 10th International Cross-Disciplinary Conference on Web Accessibility*, 1–10. DOI: 10.1145/2461121.2461124

Villegas Ortíz, A. (2025). *Aplicación de machine learning en datos obtenidos mediante eye-tracking para el perfilamiento de usuarios mediante la percepción de colores entre mujeres y hombres.*

Villegas Ortíz, A., Rodríguez López, E., & Álvarez Rodríguez, F. (2024). *Modelo para la Aplicación del Análisis del Comportamiento de Mirada Mediante Eyetracking de la Interacción Usuario-Sistema para Mejorar la Calidad de la UX y Mejorar los Procesos de Desarrollo de Software*. Universidad Autónoma de Aguascalientes.

Virtual reality for autism: Unlocking learning and growth. (2024). *Journal of Autism and Developmental Technologies, 5*(4), 294–302.

Vishnu, S. (2023). A world with Cloud Computing. *International Scientific Journal of Engineering and Management, 02*. Advance online publication. DOI: 10.55041/ISJEM00279

Voorde, S. V., Roeyers, H., & Wiersema, J. R. (2010). Error monitoring in children with ADHD or Reading disorder: An event-related. *Biological Psychology*, *85*(2), 176–185. DOI: 10.1016/j.biopsycho.2010.01.011 PMID: 20097256

Vredenburg, K., Mao, J. Y., Smith, P. W., & Carey, T. (2002). A survey of user-centered design practice. In *Proceedings of the SIGCHI conference on Human factors in computing systems* (pp. 471-478). DOI: 10.1145/503376.503460

Vuorikari, R., Kluzer, S., & Punie, Y. (2022). *DigComp 2.2: The digital competence framework for citizens*. Publications Office of the European Union. https://publications.jrc.ec.europa.eu/repository/handle/JRC128415

W3C Web Accessibility Initiative (WAI). (2023). *Web Content Accessibility Guidelines (WCAG) 2.2*. W3C Recommendation. https://www.w3.org/TR/WCAG22/

W3C. (2018). *Web Content Accessibility Guidelines (WCAG) 2.1*. W3C Recommendation.

W3C. (2025). *Guidance on Applying WCAG 2.2 to Mobile Applications (WCAG-2Mobile)*.

Walker, N. (2021). *Neuroqueer Heresies: Notes on the Neurodiversity Paradigm, Autistic Empowerment, and Postnormal Possibilities*. Autonomous Press.

Wannapaschaiyong, P., Vajrabhaya, P., Rojmahamongkol, P., & Sutchritpongsa, S. (2023). A computer-based early intervention for Thai preschool children at risk of dyslexia: A pre- and postintervention study. *Journal of Child Science*, *13*(1), e28–e34. Advance online publication. DOI: 10.1055/s-0043-1767809

Watling, S. (2011). Digital exclusion: Coming out from behind closed doors. *Disability & Society*, *26*(4), 491–495. DOI: 10.1080/09687599.2011.567802

Watson, D., & Clark, L. A. (1999). *The PANAS-X: Manual for the Positive and Negative Affect Schedule - Expanded Form*.

WebAIM. (2021). *WebAIM Million – Accessibility of the top 1,000,000 home pages*. WebAIM. Retrieved on December 15, 2025, from https://webaim.org/projects/million/

WebAIM. (2024). *WebAIM Million – 2024 report*. Retrieved on December 15, 2025, from https://webaim.org/projects/million/

WebAIM. (2024). *WebAIM Screen Reader User Survey #10 results.* WebAIM. Retrieved on December 15, 2025, from https://webaim.org/projects/screenreadersurvey10/

Welbourne, S. R., & Lambon Ralph, M. A. (2007). Using parallel distributed processing models to simulate phonological dyslexia: The key role of retrieval-related plasticity. *Journal of Cognitive Neuroscience, 19*(7), 1125–1139. DOI: 10.1162/jocn.2007.19.7.1125 PMID: 17583989

Whalen, C., Moss, N., & Ilan, L.. (2010). Efficacy of TeachTown: Basics computer-assisted intervention for the education of young children with autism. *Autism, 14*(3), 241–261. DOI: 10.1177/1362361310363282 PMID: 20484002

Women, U. N. (2020). *The digital divide: Gender gaps in access to ICTs.* United Nations. Retrieved on December 15, 2025, from https://www.unwomen.org/en/digital-library/publications/2020/09/the-digital-divide

Wongwan, N., Chernbumroong, S., Intawong, K., & Puritat, K. (2025, January). Designing a gamified mixed reality system for social skills development in high-functioning children with autism spectrum disorder. In *2025 Joint International Conference on Digital Arts, Media and Technology with ECTI Northern Section Conference on Electrical, Electronics, Computer and Telecommunications Engineering (ECTI DAMT & NCON)* (pp. 819–823). IEEE. DOI: 10.1109/ECTIDAMT-NCON64748.2025.10961994

World Health Organization. (1980). *International classification of impairments, disabilities, and handicaps: A manual of classification relating to the consequences of disease.* World Health Organization.

World Health Organization. (2021). *World health statistics 2021: Monitoring health for the SDGs, sustainable development goals.* https://www.who.int/publications/i/item/9789240027053

World Health Organization. (2023, November 15). Autismo. https://www.who.int/es/news-room/fact-sheets/detail/autism-spectrum-disorders

World Health Organization. WHO. (2025, February 26). *Sordera y pérdida de la audición.* https://www.who.int/es/news-room/fact-sheets/detail/deafness-and-hearing-loss

World Wide Web Consortium. (2018). *Web content accessibility guidelines (WCAG) 2.1.* https://www.w3.org/TR/WCAG21

World Wide Web Consortium. (2024, December 12). *Web Content Accessibility Guidelines (WCAG) 2.2.* https://www.w3.org/TR/WCAG22/

World Wide Web Consortium. (W3C). (2018). *Web Content Accessibility Guidelines (WCAG) 2.1*. Retrieved on December 15, 2025, from https://www.w3.org/TR/WCAG21/

World Wide Web Consortium. (W3C). (2021). *W3C Accessibility Guidelines (WCAG) 3.0 – Working Draft*. Retrieved on December 15, 2025, from https://www.w3.org/TR/wcag-3.0/

Yesodharan, D., & Saumya, S. (2020). Accessibility evaluation of Indian government portals: Issues and challenges. *Journal of Information and Knowledge Management, 19*(4), 2050046. DOI: 10.1142/S0219649220500460

Yu, H. (2003). Web accessibility and the law. In *IGI Global eBooks* (pp. 1–24). https://doi.org/DOI: 10.4018/978-1-59140-107-0.ch001

Yuan, B., Folmer, E., & Harris, F. C. (2021). Game accessibility: A survey. *Universal Access in the Information Society, 20*(4), 713–733. DOI: 10.1007/s10209-020-00746-9

Zhang, L., Xia, Z., Zhao, Y., Shu, H., & Zhang, Y. (2023). Recent advances in Chinese developmental dyslexia. *Annual Review of Linguistics, 9*(1), 439–461. DOI: 10.1146/annurev-linguistics-030421-065648

Zhang, S., Chen, D., Tang, Y., & Zhang, L. (2021). Children ASD Evaluation Through Joint Analysis of EEG and Eye-Tracking Recordings With Graph Convolution Network. *Frontiers in Human Neuroscience, 15*, 651349. Advance online publication. DOI: 10.3389/fnhum.2021.651349 PMID: 34113244

Zhou, Y., Qian, H., Verbelen, T., Cuculo, V., Zhu, F., Sun, H., Li, Y., Zhao, P., Kong, Y., Wang, J., Wan, Y., & Fu, S. (2023). *Viewpoint planning with transition management for active object recognition.*

Zhou, M., Dzingirai, C., Hove, K., Chitata, T., & Mugandani, R. (2022). Adoption, use and enhancement of virtual learning during COVID-19. *Education and Information Technologies, 27*(7), 8939–8959. DOI: 10.1007/s10639-022-10985-x PMID: 35340535

Zoccolotti, P. (2022). Success Is Not the Entire Story for a Scientific Theory: The Case of the Phonological Deficit Theory of Dyslexia. *Brain Sciences, 12*(4), 425. DOI: 10.3390/brainsci12040425 PMID: 35447957

Zolyomi, A., & Schmalz, M. (2017). Developing Inclusive Games for Children with Autism Spectrum Disorder. *ACM Transactions on Accessible Computing, 10*(4), 54.

Zyda, M. (2005). From Visual Simulation to Virtual Reality to Games. *Computer, 38*(9), 25–32. DOI: 10.1109/MC.2005.297

About the Contributors

Teresita de Jesus Alvarez Robles, is a full-time professor in the field of Human-Computer Interaction. She holds a degree in Computational Systems Engineering from the Instituto Tecnologico Superior de Xalapa (2011), a Master's degree in User-Centered Interactive Systems (2016), and a PhD in Computer Science (2019) from the Universidad Veracruzana. She has published various research works, including book chapters, journal articles, and conference papers, in the areas of Software Engineering, Human-Computer Interaction, User Experience, and User-Centered Design. Recently, she has been working at Universidad Autonoma de Baja California Sur and is a member of a research network (RITIE).

Samuel Montane Banos is a professor - researcher in Departamento Academico de Sistemas Computacionales at Universidad Autonoma de Baja California Sur (UABCS). He holds a Bachelor's degree in Computer Science and a Master's degree in Information Technologies, both from the same institution (UABCS). He has published various research works, including academic articles and book chapters, in the fields of Software Development and Inclusive Technology. He is currently a member of Grupo de Desarrollo de Tecnologias Inclusivas e Innovacion Tecnologica (GIDTIITEC) and Red Internacional de Tecnologias Inclusivas y Educacion (RITIE).

Francisco Alvarez Rodriguez, is a Professor of Software Engineering. He holds a BA. in Informatics (1994) and a MA. (1997) from the Autonomous University of Aguascalientes and a EdD degree from the Education Institute of Tamaulipas, Mexico and he is PhD from the National Autonomous University of Mexico. He has published research papers in several international conferences in the topics of software engineering and e-learning process. His research interests are software engineering lifecycles for small and medium sized enterprises and software engineering process for e-learning. He is currently president of the National Council for Accreditation of programs and Computing, A.C. (CONAIC)

Andres Sandoval is a professor and Head of the Academic Department of Computer Systems at the Autonomous University of Baja California Sur. He is founder of theInternational Network on Inclusive Technologies and Educational Innovation (RITIE) and leads the GIDTIITEC research group and the Master's Program in Information Technologies (MaTI). His research focuses on inclusive and accessible technologies, mobile learning, educational innovation, and data-driven decision support systems. He has published over 80 peer-reviewed articles, three authored books, and numerous book chapters, and has led more than 20 funded research and development projects.

***

Francisco Alvarez is a Professor of Software Engineering. He holds a BA. in Informatics (1994) and a MA. (1997) from the Autonomous University of Aguascalientes and a EdD degree from the Education Institute of Tamaulipas, México and he is PhD from the National Autonomous University of Mexico. He has published research papers in several international conferences in the topics of software engineering and e-learning process. His research interests are software engineering lifecycles for small and medium sized enterprises and software engineering process for e-learning. He is currently president of the National Council for Accreditation of programs and Computing, A.C. (CONAIC)

Etelvina Archundia-Sierra Doctor in the Information Technology and Decision Analysis, professor of the Facultad de Ciencias de la Computación of the Benemérita Universidad Autónoma de Puebla. Research interests: workflow models, computer supported cooperative work and Computer Human Interaction.

Yuritzi Esquivel Hernández: She is a ninth semester student of the computer systems engineering degree at the Universidad Mexiquense del Bicentenario. She has a certification from the Computer Networks Course - CISCO Networking Academy (2024). She has also participated in two robot sumo wrestling competitions in Valle de Bravo, Mexico City. She is currently completing her professional residency at the Technological and Industrial High School Center 18 in Angangueo, Michoacán, with a project called "Information system for controlling the attendance of students at CBTIS No. 18 in Angangueo, Michoacán."

Italia Estrada holds a degree in Computer Systems Engineering, a Master's degree in Computer Systems from the ITLP, and a PhD in Education. Since 2002, she has worked as a professor-researcher at the Autonomous University of Baja California Sur, affiliated with the Academic Department of Computer Systems.

She has taught courses in the various curricula offered by the department, such as Numerical Methods, Programming, Algorithms, Selected Topics in Algorithms, Software Project Management, Software Engineering, among others. She has also participated in various academic events, forums, and conferences in the field of Computer Systems, speaking and sharing experiences derived from research projects, prototype development, and her teaching work over the years. Numerical Methods | Programming | Algorithms | Selected Topics in Algorithms | Software Project Management | Software Engineering Email: iestrada@uabcs.mx

Fabianna Julio Suarez is a final-year student of Informatics Engineering, with a strong focus on software development. She holds a diploma in Cybersecurity and Information Security, and has gained experience working as a software and UX/UI interface developer. Her professional interests combine technical expertise in programming and secure systems with creative approaches to user-centered design. In her free time, she actively explores topics related to software engineering, user experience, and emerging technologies, seeking to contribute with innovative and practical solutions.

Virginia L.B. Graduated with a degree in Informatics from the Universidad Veracruzana with a Masters in Computer Science from the Rosenblueth Foundation and a Masters in University Teaching from the University of Xalapa, as well as a Doctorate in Education from the Escuela Libre de Ciencias Políticas y Administraci6n Pública.,She is a professor of Computer Systems Engineering, with training in two areas, Computer Science and Education; she likes to encourage creativity and innovation based on the development of systems that automate administrative, industrial and educational processes, among others.,Dr. Lagunes is dedicated to the coding of algorithms in different programming languages and the design of intuitive interfaces. She analyses the requirements of problems presented in other disciplines in order to automate their solutions and analyze the data derived from the implemented systems

Amado Leyva-Carrillo Professor-researcher at the Autonomous University of Baja California Sur (UABCS) in the Academic Department of Computer Systems (DASC). He holds a Master's degree in Computer Systems and is a member of the International Network of Inclusive Technologies and Education (RITIE) and the Research Laboratory in Inclusive Technologies and Educational Innovation (GIDTIITEC). He has participated as a leader in various projects that incorporate the use of technology to support education. He has more than 15 years of experience teaching undergraduate courses in areas such as Numerical Methods, Decision-Making Systems, and Information Processing. His main lines of research include gamification, inclusive technologies, and m-learning. He has published more than 40 articles in scientific journals and book chapters. He has presented papers at various national and international forums. Inclusive Technologies | m-Learning Email: aleyva@uabcs.mx

Juan Antonio Moreno Muñoz holds a degree in Intelligent Computing Engineering from Universidad Autónoma de Aguascalientes. His work focuses on software and mobile application development, integrating user-centered design methodologies and software engineering best practices. He has participated in projects oriented toward accessibility and user experience, applying modern technologies to create functional and inclusive solutions.

Jesús Antonio Ramírez Vázquez was born on October 7, 2003, in Reynosa, Tamaulipas, México. He completed his technical studies in Human Resources Administration at CETis 71 from 2018 to 2021. In 2022, he began pursuing a Bachelor's degree in Information Technology at the Universidad Autónoma de Tamaulipas, where he is currently studying and expected to graduate in 2026. Throughout his academic journey, Jesús has actively participated in several software development projects. Among them, he contributed to the creation of an application designed to facilitate communication and store data from an optical spectrum analyzer. Additionally, he collaborated on the development of a virtual reality software aimed at supporting children with Autism Spectrum Disorder (ASD), focusing on enhancing their communication and learning experiences.

Luis Roberto Ramos Aguiar is a researcher and lecturer specializing in the design and implementation of technologies for education and inclusion. His work focuses on the development of virtual reality environments, gamification, and digital tools aimed at enhancing teaching and learning processes in populations with special educational needs, particularly children with Autism Spectrum Disorder (ASD). He has participated in multidisciplinary projects related to educational innovation, user-centered design, and the evaluation of interactive environments. His academic contributions include articles, conference presentations, and book chapters that integrate technological research with pedagogical practice.

Esmeralda Rivas Guzmán: Eighth-semester student of the Systems Engineering degree at Universidad del Valle. A software developer in training, with a strong interest in mobile development using Flutter and backend technologies such as Node.js and Spring Boot. Participation in university seminars has strengthened technical knowledge, teamwork, and communication skills. Passionate about exploring new technologies, solving problems through code, and developing projects with the potential to generate a positive impact. Aiming to continue professional growth in software development and to contribute to the creation of innovative technological solutions.

José Rafael Rojano Cáceres holds a PhD in Computer Science from the Monterrey Institute of Technology and Higher Education (ITESM), a Master's degree in Artificial Intelligence, and a Bachelor's degree in Computer Science from the Veracruzana University (UV). He is a member of the core faculty of the UV's Master's program in User-Centered Interactive Systems and the PhD program in Computer Science. He also teaches in the Bachelor's program in Systems Engineering and Information Technologies. Dr. Rojano led the Consolidated Research Group "Computational and Educational Technology," and during that time, he coordinated the international network of "Interactive Systems for Serving Users with Disabilities," which received PRODEP funding in 2015. For several years, he has supported various groups and civil associations working on disability issues and inclusion through technology. Currently, he is a member of the University Network for Inclusive Education at the University of Veracruz (UV), as well as the coordinator for deaf students at the same institution. He is also an active member of the International Network for Inclusive Technologies and Education (RITIE) and a member of the permanent seminar of the Mexican Meeting on the Study of Deaf Communities (ECOS). As part of his research interests, he has published several articles on disability and technology, focusing on sensory disabilities such as deafness and blindness. Finally, Dr. Rojano is a member of the National System of Research Information (SNII) and holds a PRODEP profile.

Jocelyn Sandoval Flores is pursuing a Bachelor's degree in Information Technology at the Autonomous University of Tamaulipas. She has participated in research projects on scientific outreach and inclusive support for people with autism, with an emphasis on the application of technology in socially relevant contexts.

Ratan Sarkar is an Assistant Professor in the Department of Education, Tezpur University (A Central University), Assam, India. Previously, he served nearly seven years as Assistant Professor in the Department of Teachers' Training (B.Ed.), Prabhat Kumar College, Contai (Vidyasagar University), and as Guest Faculty at National Institute for Empowerment of Persons with Intellectual Disabilities, Regional Centre, Kolkata. He holds a Ph.D. in Education from Pondicherry University, an M.Ed. and M.Phil. in Special Education from Ramakrishna Mission Vivekananda Educational and Research Institute, Belur Math, and an M.A. in Education and Technology from Tata Institute of Social Sciences, Mumbai. He began his academic journey with a B.Ed. in Special Education (Jadavpur University) and a B.A. in English (Hons) from Siliguri College (University of North Bengal), Darjeeling. Dr. Sarkar has published extensively in leading journals (SAGE, Springer, Routledge, Wiley), authored books, chapters, and reviews, and led projects under the Ministry of Education, Govt. of India. He works on inclusive education, educational technology, and policy advocacy to advance equitable learning ecosystems.

Gabriel Sebastián received his PhD and MSc degrees from the University of Castilla-La Mancha (UCLM) and BSc degree from Polytechnic University of Valencia (UPV) – all the three degrees in Computer Science. His main research interests are Artificial Intelligence, Multimedia, Human-Computer Interaction and Software Engineering. He was involved in the development of many projects related to Artificial Intelligence, Distributed User Interfaces and Model-driven Development of User Interfaces focused on the Web as the deployment platform. He published more than 25 research articles and book chapters in Journals and International Congresses. He is currently an Assistant Professor at the Faculty of Social Sciences and Information Technology at the UCLM. He is also member of the Interactive Systems Engineering research group of the Computing System Department (Faculty of Computing Science Engineering) in UCLM, and he works as researcher in the Albacete Research Institute of Informatics (I3A) in Albacete, Spain.

Index

A

B

C

D

E

F

G

H

I

L

M

N

www.ingramcontent.com/pod-product-compliance
Lightning Source LLC
LaVergne TN
LVHW062337300926
849161LV00007B/1726